Organizational Behaviour

David A.
Buchanan

Cranfield University School of Management

Andrzej A.
Huczynski

*Formerly University of Glasgow, Adam Smith
Business School*

Organizational
Behaviour

Ninth edition

PEARSON

Harlow, England • London • New York • Boston • San Francisco • Toronto • Sydney • Auckland • Singapore • Hong Kong
Tokyo • Seoul • Taipei • New Delhi • Cape Town • São Paulo • Mexico City • Madrid • Amsterdam • Munich • Paris • Milan

Pearson Education Limited
Edinburgh Gate
Harlow CM20 2JE
United Kingdom
Tel: +44 (0)1279 623623
Web: www.pearson.com/uk

First published by Prentice Hall International (UK) Ltd 1985 (print)
Second edition published by Prentice Hall International (UK) Ltd 1991 (print)
Third edition published by Prentice Hall Europe 1997 (print)
Fourth edition published by Pearson Education Ltd 2001 (print)
Fifth edition 2004 (print)
Sixth edition 2007 (print)
Seventh edition 2010 (print)
Eighth edition 2013 (print and electronic)
Ninth edition published 2017 (print and electronic)

Contains public sector information licensed under the Open Government Licence (OGL) v3.0. http://www.nationalarchives.gov.uk/doc/open-government-licence/version/3/.

Contains Parliamentary information licensed under the Open Parliament Licence (OPL) v3.0. http://www.parliament.uk/site-information/copyright/open-parliament-licence/

The screenshots in this book are reprinted by permission of Microsoft Corporation.

Pearson Education is not responsible for the content of third-party internet sites.

The Financial Times. With a worldwide network of highly respected journalists, The Financial Times provides global business news, insightful opinion and expert analysis of business, finance and politics. With over 500 journalists reporting from 50 countries worldwide, our in-depth coverage of international news is objectively reported and analysed from an independent, global perspective. To find out more, visit www.ft.com/pearsonoffer.

ISBN: 978–1–292–09288–1 (print)
      978–1–292–11749–2 (PDF)
      978-1-292-16296-6 (ePub)

British Library Cataloguing-in-Publication Data
A catalogue record for the print edition is available from the British Library

Library of Congress Cataloging-in-Publication Data
A catalog record for the print edition is available from the Library of Congress

10 9 8 7 6 5 4 3 2 1
20 19 18 17 16

Cover photo: 'Bunch of banners' © Lesley F. Buchanan

Print edition typeset in 9/12pt Slimbach Std by Lumina Datamatics, Inc.
Print edition printed and bound by L.E.G.O. S.p.A., Italy

NOTE THAT ANY PAGE CROSS REFERENCES REFER TO THE PRINT EDITION

From David

To Lesley, Andrew, Mairi, Rachel, Séan, Charlie, Cíara and Archie

From Andrzej

To Janet, Sophie, Gregory, Tom, Magnus, Freya and Rosa

Outline contents

Full contents

Acknowledgements

A large number of friends, colleagues and students have contributed their ideas, criticisms and advice to the development of this new edition of this text. Our special thanks in this regard is therefore extended to Lesley Buchanan, Tom Hill, Janet Huczynska, Mary Lince, Joan Dale Lace David Hemsley and Doreen Magowan.

Publisher's acknowledgements

We are grateful to the following for permission to reproduce copyright material:

Cartoons

Cartoon on p. 27 from Cartoon Bank, www.cartoonbank.com; Cartoon on p. 48 from Cartoon stock (search ID forn 672), www.cartoonstock.com, CartoonStock.com; Cartoon on p. 53 from www.negotiationlawblog.com/conflict-resolution/know-your-negotiating-partner-boom-gen-x-gen-y/, Neek#7, 2006Aug-13, goonmail@netspace.net.au; Cartoon on p. 78 from Cartoon Stock (Search ID mban1493), www.cartoonstock.com, CartoonStock.com; Cartoon on p. 81 from Mark O'Collin collinstoons.com; Cartoon on p. 92 from joyoftech. com © 2007 Geek Culture; Cartoon on p. 152 from United Syndicate Features, PEANUTS © 1989 Peanuts Worldwide LLC, dist. by Universal Uclick, reprinted with permission. All rights reserved; Cartoon on p.153 from Craig Swanson, www.perspicuity.com; Cartoon on p. 202 from Mark Weinstein, http://prometheuscomic.wordpress.com/tag/personality-test/ © 2008 Mark Weinstein; Cartoon on p. 189 from Jantoo (search ID 01436546), Jantoo cartoons, www.jantoo.com; Cartoon on p. 228 from Mike Seddon, Cartoon on p. 228 copyright Mike Seddon www.seddoncartoons.co.uk; Cartoon on p. 235 from Jantoo (Search ID 03131257); Cartoon 8.2 from Cartoon Bank/New Yorker, ID 52971, © Barbara Smaller/ The New Yorker Collection/www.cartoonbank.com; Cartoon on p. 291 from Search ID: hsc0695, www.cartoonstock.com, CartoonStock.com; Cartoon on p. 599 from Cartoonstock ID forn2724, CartoonStock.com; Cartoon on p. 608 from Roger Beale, previously appeared in: *Why Women Mean Business*, Wiley (Wittenberg-Cox, A. and Maitland, A., 2009) © Roger Beale; Cartoon on p. 609 (Cartoon 18.3) from Eric and Bill Tietelbaum, Tribune Content Agency, © 2006 Tribune Media Services Inc. All rights reserved; Cartoon on p. 613 from Joseph Mirachi; Cartoons on pp. 184 and 644 from Drew Fairweather; Cartoon on p. 737 (Cartoon 22.1) from *The New Yorker*, cartoonbank.com, © 3/4/1967, www.cartoonbank. com; Cartoon on p. 759 from joyoftech.com © 2002 Geek Culture; Cartoon on p. xviii from Cartoon code/description: 2003 06 16 173 SGR.HG Think, Cartoon Bank, www.cartoonbank. com © Sam Gross/Condé Nast Publications/www.cartoonbank.com, © Sam Gross/The New Yorker Collection/www.cartoonbank.com.

Figures

Figure 1.4 adapted from *Understanding the People and Performance Link: Unlocking the Black Box*, London: Chartered Institute of Personnel and Development (Purcell, J., Kinnie, N., Hutchinson, S., Rayton, B. and Stuart, J. 2003) p. 7, reprinted by permission of the Chartered Institute of Personnel and Development; Figure 2.7 adapted from Organizational statesmanship and dirty politics: ethical guidelines for the organizational politician, *Organizational Dynamics, Autumn*, vol. 12, no. 2, p. 72, Figure 1: Ethical models (Velasquez, M., Moberg, D.J.

and Cavanagh, G.F., 1983), reprinted from Organizational Dynamics, vol. 12, no. 2, Velasquez, M., Moberg, D.J. and Cavanagh, G.F., Organizational statesmanship and dirty politics: ethical guidelines for the organizational politician, p. 72, Copyright 1983, with permission from Elsevier; Figure 2.8 after *Exploring Corporate Strategy: Text and Cases*, 8th edn, Financial Times Prentice Hall (Johnson, G., Scholes, K. and Whittington, K. 2008) p. 189, Exhibit 4.7, *Exploring Corporate Strategy: Text and Cases*, Johnson, G., Scholes, K. and Whittington, K. Pearson Education Limited, © Pearson Education Limited 2008; Figure 4.1 adapted from *Organizational Behaviour and Analysis: An Integrated Approach*, 4th edn, Financial Times Prentice Hall (Rollinson, D. 2008) p. 592, *Organizational Behaviour and Analysis: An Integrated Approach*, Rollinson, D. Pearson Education Limited, © Pearson Education Limited 2008; Figure 4.2 from *Organizational Behaviour*, 15th edn, Pearson Education, Harlow, Essex (Robbins, S.P. and Judge, T.A. 2013) p. 523, Exhibit 16.4, Robbins, Stephen P.; Judge, Timothy A., *Organizational Behavior*, 15th edn, © 2013, printed and electronically reproduced by permission of Pearson Education, Inc., Upper Saddle River, New Jersey.; Figure 4.3 from Organizational socialization: its content and consequences, *Journal of Applied Psychology*, 79(5), pp. 730–43 (Chao, G.T., O'Leary-Kelly, A.M., Wolf, S., Klein, H.J. and Gardner, P.D., 1994), Chao, G.T., O'Leary-Kelly, A.M., Wolf, S., Klein, H.J. & Gardner, P.D. Organizational socialization: Its content and consequences. *Journal of Applied Psychology*, Vol. 79 No. 5, pp. 730–743, 1994, American Psychological Association (APA), reprinted with permission; Figure 4.4 from The paradox of organization culture: reconciling ourselves to socialization, *California Management Review*, 27(2), pp. 26–41 (Pascale, R.T., 1985), © 1985, by The Regents of the University of California, reprinted from the *California Management Review*, Vol. 27, No. 2, by permission of The Regents; Figure 4.5 from Corporate culture; the last frontier of control? *Journal of Management Studies*, 23(3), pp. 287–97 (Ray, C.A. 1986), Corporate culture; the last frontier of control? *Journal of Management Studies*, 23(3), pp. 287–97 (Ray, C.A. 1986) © Blackwell Publishing Ltd and Society for the Advancement of Management Studies 1986; Figure 4.7 from *Organizational Behaviour: Individuals, Groups and Organization*, 2nd edn, Financial Times Prentice Hall (Brooks, I. 2003) p. 266, *Organizational Behaviour: Individuals, Groups and Organization*, Brooks, I. Pearson Education Limited © Pearson Education Limited 2003; Figure 4.8 from *International Business: A Managerial Perspective*, Pearson Prentice Hall (Griffin, R. and Putsay, M.W. 2007,) Fig. 4.3, p. 102, ISBN: 0131995340 / 9780131995345, Griffin, Ricky W.; Pustay, Michael W., *International Business*, 5th edn, © 2007, p. 102, reprinted and electronically reproduced by permission of Pearson Education, Inc., Upper Saddle River, New Jersey; Figure 4.9 from Navigating the cultural minefield, *Harvard Business Review*, 92 (5), 119–23 (Meyer, E 2014); Figure on page 154 from www.behaviormodel.org, Dr B.J. Fogg, © 2007 BJ Fogg; www.behaviormodel.org. For permissions contact BJ Fogg; Figure 5.4 from http://selfleadership.com/blog/topic/leadership/reflecting-and-leaning-2009-to-2010/; Figure on p. 229 from Toyota chief bows to pressure over pedal defect, *The Times*, 06/02/2010, p. 13 (Lewis, L. and Lea, R.,), © Lewis and Lea, News International Trading Ltd, 6 February 2010; Figure on p. 224 from *Gesture in Naples and Gesture in Classical Antiquity*, Indiana University Press (de Jourio, A., trans by Adam Kenton, 2001) Cambridge University Press, reprinted by the permission of the Syndics of Cambridge University Library; Figure 7.3 from *Making the Connections: Using Internal Communication to Turn Strategy into Action*, Gower Publishing (Quirke, B., 2008) p. 236, © *Making the Connections: Using Internal Communication to Turn Strategy into Action*, Quirke, B., 2008, Gower Publishing; Figure on p. 257 from W.H. Hill (cartoonist), 1915, artwork supplied by The Broadbent Partnership, London; Figure on p. 286 from http//lunchbreath.com/cartoons/thoughts-on-maslows-hierarchy-2; Figure 10.2 adapted from *Groups: Interaction and Performance*, Prentice Hall (McGrath, J.E.) p. 61, Figure 5.1, ISBN: 0133657000, McGrath, J. E.groups: *Interaction and Performance*, 1st edn, © 1984, p. 61. reprinted and electronically reproduced by permission of Pearson Education, Inc., Upper Saddle River, New Jersey. From Donelson R. Forsyth, Group Dynamics, Thomson Wadsworth, London, 2006, p. 14. Modified from Joseph E. McGrath, Groups: Interaction and Performance, Prentice-Hall, Upper Saddle River, NJ, 1984, p. 61.; Figure 10.4 adapted from *Behaviour in Organizations*, Pearson/Prentice Hall (Greenberg, J. and Baron, R.A., 1997)

6th edn, 0135217253, based on data from Roethlisberger and Dickson (1939). From Greenberg, Jerald; Baron, Robert A., Behavior in Organizations, 6th edn © 1997, reprinted and electronically reproduced by permission of Pearson Education, Inc. Upper Saddle River, New Jersey; Figure 10.6 after New Patterns of Management, 1961, McGraw-Hill (Likert, R.) p. 105, 0070378509, © The McGraw Hill Companies, Inc.; Figure 11.3 from *Group Processes*, Elsevier (Berkowitz, L. (ed.), 1978) pp. 351–61; Figure 11.4 from *Behaviour in Organizations*, 6th edn, Pearson/Prentice Hall (Greenberg, J. and Baron, R.A., 1997) p. 306, 0135217253, from Greenberg, Jerald; Baron, Robert A., *Behavior In Organizations*, 6th edn © 1997, reprinted and electronically reproduced by permission of Pearson Education, Inc., Upper Saddle River, New Jersey; Figure 11.6 from Fluid teams: Solutions to the problems of unstable team membership, *Organizational Dynamics*, 40(3), pp.181–188 (p. 183, Figure 2 (Bushe, G.R. and Chu, A. 2011), reprinted from *Organizational Dynamics*, 40(3), Bushe, G.R. and Chu, A., *Fluid teams: Solutions to the problems of unstable team membership*, pp. 181–188 (p. 183, Figure 2 Problems and solutions for Fluid Teams) © 2011, with permission from Elsevier; Figure 11.7 from Leading global virtual teams to success, *Organizational Dynamics*, 42 (3), 228–37. (Zander, L., Zetting, P. and Mäkelä, K. 2013), Elsevier; Figure 12.2 from *Interactive Behaviour at Work*, Financial Times Prentice Hall (Guirdham, M., 2002) p. 119, *Interactive Behaviour at Work*, Guirdham, M. Pearson Education Limited, © Pearson Education LImited 2002; Figure on p. 404 from *Asch, S.E., Effects of group pressure upon the modification and distortion of judgements in, Groups, Leadership and Men,* pp. 177–90 (Guetzkow, H. (ed.), 1951), reprinted with the permission of Scribner, a Division of Simon & Schuster, Inc. from *Groups, Leadership and Men* edited by Harold Guetzkow © 1951 Carnegie Press; © 1979 Harold Guetzkow (Russell & Russell, NY, 1963); Figure 12.3 adapted from *Essential Psychology: A Concise Introduction*, London: Sage (Banyard, P. E., Davies, M.N.O., Norman, C. and Winder, B. 2010) p. 200, Figure 10.1, reproduced by permission of SAGE Publications, London, Los Angeles, New Delhi and Singapore, from Banyard, P E., Davies, M.N.O., Norman, C. and Winder, B., *Essential Psychology: A Concise Introduction*, © Sage Publications, 2010; Figure 12.5 from *Managing Behaviour in Organizations*, 2nd ed., Prentice Hall (Greenberg, J. 1999) p. 158, Greenberg, Jerald, *Managing Behavior in Organizations*, 2nd edn, © 1999, p. 158, reprinted and electronically reproduced by permission of Pearson Education, Inc., Upper Saddle River, New Jersey; Figure 12.6 from *Interactive Behaviour at Work*, Financial Times Prentice Hall (Guirdham, M., 2002) p. 465, *Interactive Behaviour at Work*, Guirdham, M., Pearson Education Limited, © Pearson Education LImited 2002; Figure 12.8 after Moreland, R.L. and Levine, J.M., Socialization in small groups: temporal changes in individual-group relations, in, *Advances in Experimental and Social Psychology*, Volume 15, pp. 137–92 (L. Berkowicz (ed.), 1982), Academic Press; Figure 12.8 from *Social Psychology*, 5th edn, Pearson Education Limited (Hogg, M.A. and Vaughan, G.M., 2008) p. 290, reproduced with permission from Hogg & Vaughan, *Social Psychology* © 2011 Pearson Australia, pp. 55, 290 & 424; Figure 12.9 from *Social Psychology*, 5th edn, Pearson Education Limited (Hogg, M.A. and Vaughan, G.M. 2008) p. 424, reproduced with permission from Hogg & Vaughan, Social Psychology © 2011 Pearson Australia, pp. 55, 290 & 424; Figure 13.1 from *Organizational Behaviour*, International Thomson Publishing (Daft, R.L. and Noe, R.A., 2001) p. 218, From Daft. Organizational Behavior, 1E. © 2001 South-Western, a part of Cengage Learning, Inc., reproduced by permission. www.cengage.com/permissions; Figure 13.2 from Work teams: applications and effectiveness, *American Psychologist*, 45(2), pp. 120–33 (Sundstrom, E., De Meuse, K.P. and Futrell, D., 1990), Sundstrom, E., De Meuse, K.P. and Futrell, D., Work teams: applications and effectiveness, *American Psychologist*, 45(2), pp. 120–33 (Figure on p. 122) 1990 American Psychological Society, reprinted with permission; Figure 14.2 from *The Realities of Work*, 3rd edn, Palgrave (Noon, M. and Blyton, P., 2007) p. 173, Mike Noon and Paul Blyton, *The Realities of Work*, published 1997, Palgrave, reproduced with permission of Palgrave Macmillan; Figure 15.4 from *Organizational Behaviour*, 15th edn, Pearson Education (Robbins, S. P. and Judge, T.A., 2013) p. 486, Exhibit 15.3, ISBN-10: 0132834871/ISBN-13: 9780132834872; Figure 15.6 from *Management: An Introduction*, 5th edn, Financial Times Prentice Hall (Boddy, D., 2011) p. 296, *Management: An Introduction*, Boddy, D. Pearson Education Limited, © Pearson Education Limited 2011;

Figure 15.7 from http://www.royalnavalmuseum.org/info_sheets_nav_rankings.htm, Trustees of the Royal Naval Museum; Figure 15.11 from Organizational Analysis, Supplement to the, *British Journal of Administrative Management*, No. 18, March/April (Lysons, K., 1997); Figure 16.2 adapted from Manu Cornet (Cartoonist), http://www.bonkersworld.net/ organizational-charts/, Robbins, Stephen P.; Coulter, Mary, *Management*, 10th edn, © 2009, p. 45, reprinted and electronically adapted by permission of Pearson Education, Inc., Upper Saddle River, New Jersey; Figure 16.3 from *Creative Organization Theory*, Sage Publications, Inc. (Morgan, G. 1989) p. 66; Figure 16.4 from *Managing*, Financial Times Prentice Hall (Mintzberg, H., 2009) p. 48; Figure 16.5 from *Management and Technology*, HMSO (Woodward, J.,) p. 11, contains public sector information licensed under the Open Government Licence (OGL) v3.0.http://www.nationalarchives.gov.uk/doc/open-government-licence; Figure 16.7 from *Organizational Analysis: A Sociological View*, 1st ed., Wadsworth (Perrow, C. 1970) p. 78; Figure on p. 564 from Boeing 787 Dreamliner Engineering Chief Describes Partners Organization, *Design News* (2007), http://www.designnews.com/ article/2659-Boeing_787_Dreamliner_Engineering_Chief_Describes_Partners_Organization. php, Copyrighted 2013. UBM Electronics. 98714:313BC; Figure 17.8 adapted from *Human Resource Management: A Strategic Introduction*, 2nd edn, Blackwell (Mabey, C., Salaman, G. and Storey, J., 1998) p. 235; Figure 17.15 from The contribution revolution: Letting volunteers build your business, *Harvard Business Review*, 86(10), pp. 60–9 (Cook, S.), R0810C-HCB-ENG, reprinted by permission of *Harvard Business Review*. From 'The contribution revolution: Letting volunteers build your business' by Cook, S., 86(10) 2008 © 2008 by the Harvard Business School Publishing Corporation, all rights reserved; Figure 17.16 from Which kind of collaboration is right for you?, *Harvard Business Review*, 86(12), pp. 78–86 (Pisano, G. and Verganti, R. 2008), R0812F-HCB-ENG, reprinted by permission of *Harvard Business Review*. From 'Which kind of collaboration is right for you?' by Pisano, G. and Verganti, R., 86(12) 2008 © 2008 by the Harvard Business School Publishing Corporation; all rights reserved; Figure 18.2 from How to choose a leadership pattern, *Harvard Business Review*, Vol. 37, March–April (Tannenbaum, R. and Schmidt, W.H., 1958), reprinted in May–June, 1973; 73311-HCB-ENG, reprinted by permission of *Harvard Business Review*, From 'How to choose a leadership pattern' by Tannenbaum, R. and Schmidt, W.H., Vol. 37, March–April, 1958 reprinted in May–June, 1973. © 1958 by the Harvard Business School Publishing Corporation; all rights reserved; Figure 19.1 from Be a model leader of change, *Management Review*, 87(3), pp, 41–5 (Figure (Schneider, D. M. and Goldwasser, C. 1998), Republished with permission of American Management Association from Management Review, 'Be a model leader of change', Schneider, D.M. and Goldwasser, C., 87(3), 1998; permission conveyed through Copyright Clearance Center, Inc.; Figure 20.2 adapted from Leadership and the decision making process, *Organizational Dynamics*, 28(4), pp. 82–94 (Vroom, V.H. 2000), reprinted from Organizational Dynamics, 28(4), Vroom, V.H., Leadership and the decision making process, pp. 82–94, © 2000, with permission from Elsevier; Figure 20.5 from Is decision-based evidence making necessarily bad?, *Sloan Management Review*, 51(4), pp. 71–76 (Tingling, P. and Brydon, M. 2010), © 2010 from MIT Sloan Management Review/Massachusetts Institute of Technology, All rights reserved, distributed by Tribune Content Agency; Figure 21.4 from Support for a two-dimensional model of conflict behaviour, *Organizational Behaviour and Human Performance*, Vol. 16 No. 1, pp. 143–55 (Ruble, T.H. and Thomas, K., 1976), reprinted from *Organizational Behaviour and Human Performance*, Vol. 16 No. 1, T.H. Ruble and K. Thomas, *Support for a two-dimensional model of conflict behaviour*, p. 145, copyright 1976, with permission from Elsevier.

Tables

Table 2.1 from *The Portable Conference on Change Management*, HRSD Press Inc. (Alexander Watson Hiam (ed.) 1997) pp. 67–83, I. Ansoff, 'Measuring and managing for environmental tubulence: the Ansoff Associates approach', in Alexander Watson Haim (ed.), The Portable Conference on Change; Table 4.3 from *Cultures in Organizations: Three Perspectives*, Oxford University Press (Martin, J. 1992) p. 13, reproduced with permission of Oxford University Press, from *Cultures in Organizations: Three Perspectives* (Martin, J. 1992) p. 13 (© 1992 Oxford University Press Inc. www.oup.com. Adapted from Pondy et al (1988), Martin and Meyerson (1987) and Martin and Frost ed. (1991)); permission conveyed through Copyright Clearance Centre, Inc.; Table 6.6 adapted from A survey of UK selection practices across different organization sizes and industry sectors, *Journal of Occupational and Organizational Psychology*, 83(2), pp. 499–511 (Zibarras, L.D. and Woods, S.A.,) © The British Psychologcial Society, A survey of UK selection practices across different organization sizes and industry sectors, *Journal of Occupational and Organizational Psychology*, 83(2), pp. 499–511 (Table 3 on p. 506) (Zibarras, L.D. and Woods, S.A. 2010) © The British Psychologcial Society; Table 11.1 adapted from The knowledge, skill and ability requirements for teamwork: Implications for human resource management, *Journal of Management*, vol. 20, no. 2, pp, 503–530 (Stevens, M.J. and Campion, M.A., 1994), Stevens, M.J. and Campion, M.A., Journal of Management, vol. 20, no. 2, pp, 503–530,The knowledge, skill and ability requirements for teamwork: Implications for human resource management, © 1994, Southern Management Association. Reprinted by permission of SAGE Publications; Table 11.4 from *A Primer on Organizational Behaviour*, 5th edn, John Wiley & Sons, Inc. (Bowditch, J.L. and Buono, A.F. 2001) p. 170, 9780471384533, *A Primer on Organizational Behaviour*, 5th edn, (Bowditch, J.L. and Buono, A.F. 2001) p. 170, © 2001 John Wiley & Sons, Inc., reproduced with the permission of John Wiley & Sons, Inc.; Table 11.5 from Nature of virtual teams: A summary of their advantages and disadvantages, *Management Research News*, 31(2), pp. 99–110 (Bergiel, B.J., Bergiel, E.B.and Balsmeier, P.W. 2008), Nature of virtual teams: A summary of their advantages and disadvantages, *Management Research News*, 31(2), pp. 99–110, p. 107 Table 1: The advantages of using virtual teams (Bergiel, B.J., Bergiel, E.B.and Balsmeier, P.W. 2008) © Emerald Group Publishing Limited all rights reserved; Table 12.4 from *A Diagnostic Approach to Organizational Behaviour*, Allyn & Bacon (Gordon, J. 1993) p. 184, ISBN: 0205145205; Table 13.1 from Work teams: applications and effectiveness, *American Psychologist*, 45(2), pp. 120–33 (Sundstrom, E., De Meuse, K.P. and Futrell, D., 1990), Sundstrom, E., De Meuse, K.P. and Futrell, D., Work teams: applications and effectiveness, *American Psychologist*, 45(2), pp. 120–33 (Table on p. 125) 1990 American Psychological Society, reprinted with permission; Table 13.3 from 1996 Industry Report – 'What self-managing teams manage', *Training*, vol. 33, no. 10, p. 69 (1996), *Training Magazine*, www.Trainingmagazine.com; Table 13.5 from *Managing and Organizations*, 3rd edn, London: Sage Publications (Clegg, S. R., Kornberger, M., and Pitsis, T., 2011) p. 269, Table 7.2, reproduced by permission of Sage Publications, London, Los Angeles, New Delhi and Singapore, from Clegg, S. R., Kornberger, M. and Pitsis, T., Managing and Organizations, Copyright Sage Publications 2011; Table 13.6 from The art of building a car: the Swedish experience re-examined, *New Technology, Work and Employment,* 6(2), pp. 85–90 Table (Hammarstrom, O. and Lansbury, R.D. 1991), The art of building a car: the Swedish experience re-examined, *New Technology, Work and Employment*, 6(2), pp. 85–90 (Table on p. 89) (Hammarstrom, O. and Lansbury, R.D. 1991) © Blackwell Publishing Ltd 1991; Table 15.3 after *Organizational Behavior: Concepts and Applications*, 3rd ed., Pearson Education, Inc (Gray, J.L. and Starke, F.A. 1984) p. 412 (Table 10.1), 0675200989, Gray,J.L/Starke, F.A., *Organizational Behavior Concepts and Application*, 3rd edn, (c)1984, p.412, reprinted and electronically adapted by permission of Pearson Education, Inc., Upper Saddle River, New Jersey; Table 15.5 adapted from *Organization: Contemporary Principles and Practice*, 2nd edn, Chichester: Wiley (2015) Wiley, reproduced with permission of Blackwell Scientific in the format Republish in a book via Copyright Clearance Center; Table 16.3 from *Organization: Contemporary Principles and Practice*, 2nd edn, Chichester: Wiley. (Child, J.) p. 32, reproduced with permission of Blackwell Scientific in the format republish in a book via Copyright Clearance Center; Table 16.5 after *The Analysis of Organization*, John Wiley, Inc. (Litterer, J.A., 1973) p. 339, reproduced by permission of the estate of Joseph A. Litterer; Table 18.1 after *Managing*, Financial Times Prentice Hall (Mintzberg, H., 2009) Table 3.1 Roles of; Table 18.4 adapted from *Woman Matter 2012: Making the Breakthrough*, McKinsey & Company (Devillard, S., Graven, W., Lawson, E., Paradise, R. and

Sancier-Sultan, S., 2012) p. 9, Exhibit 4; Table 19.9 adapted from Strategies for learning from failure, *Harvard Business Review*, 89(4), pp. 48–55 (Edmondson, A.C., 2011), R1104B-HCB-ENG, reprinted by permission of *Harvard Business Review*, From "Strategies for learning from failure" by Edmondson, A.C., 89(4) 2011 © 2011 the Harvard Business School Publishing Corporation; all rights reserved; Table 20.11 from *A Diagnostic Approach to Organizational Behaviour*, 4th edn, Prentice-Hall, Inc. (Gordon, J.R. 1993) p. 253; Table 21.1 adapted from Can marketing and manufacturing coexist?, *Harvard Business Review*, 55(5), September–October, pp. 104–14 (Shapiro, B.S., 1977), 77511-HCB-ENG, reprinted by permission of Harvard Business Review, adapted from 'Can marketing and manufacturing coexist?' by Shapiro, B.S., 55 (September–October) 1977 © 1977 by the Harvard Business School Publishing Corporation; all rights reserved; Table 21.3 adapted from *Developing Management Skills for Europe*, 2nd edn, Financial Times/Prentice Hall (Whetton, D., Cameron, K. and Woods, M., 2000) p. 345, Table 6.2, Developing Management Skills for Europe, Whetton, D., Cameron, K. and Woods, M. Pearson Education Ltd © Pearson Education Ltd 2000, p. 345; Table 21.4 after *Joining Together: Group Theory and Group Skills*, Allyn and Bacon (Johnson, D.W. and Johnson, F.P., 1975) pp. 182–3, ISBN: 0135103703, Johnson & Johnson, *Joining Together: Group Theory & Group Skills*, 1st edn, (c)1975, pp. 182–183. Reprinted and Electronically adapted by permission of Pearson Education, Inc., Upper Saddle River, New Jersey; Table 21.6 from *The Psychology of People in Organizations*, Pearson Education (Ashleigh, M. and Mansi, A., 2012) p. 258 Table 9.2 Adapted from Ackroyd and Thompson (1999), *The Psychology of People in Organizations*, Ashleigh, M. and Mansi, A. Pearson Education Limited © Pearson Education Limited 2012; Table 21.6 adapted from *Organizational Misbehaviour*, Sage Publications (Ackroyd, S. and Thompson, P. 1999), reproduced by permission of Sage Publications, London, Los Angeles, New Delhi and Singapore, from Ackroyd, S. and Thompson, P., Organizational Misbehaviour, © Sage Publications, 1999; Table 22.2 from *Power, Politics, and Organizational Change: Winning the Turf Game,* 2nd ed., Sage Publications (Buchanan, D.A. and Badham, R.J., 2008) p. 296, Table 9.1, From Buchanan, D.A. and Badham, R.J., Power, Politics, and Organizational Change: Winning the Turf Game, Copyright (© Sage Publications 2008); Table 22.7 adapted from *Power, Politics, and Organizational Change: Winning the Turf Game*, 2nd edn, Sage Publications ("Turf Buchanan, D.A. and Badham, R.J., 2008) p. 16, Table 1.4, from Buchanan, D.A. and Badham, R.J., *Power, Politics, and Organizational Change: Winning the Turf Game,* (© Sage Publications 2008); Table 22.8 adapted from *Power, Politics, and Organizational Change: Winning the Turf Game*, 2nd edn, Sage Publications (Buchanan, D.A. and Badham, R.J., 2008) p. 159, Table 5.1, from Buchanan, D.A. and Badham, R.J., *Power, Politics, and Organizational Change: Winning the Turf Game*, (© Sage Publications 2008).

Text

Extract on p. 53 from *Management 2020: Leadership to Unlock Long-Term Growth*, Chartered Management Institute (2014) p. 20, acknowledge link with the report http://www.managers.org.uk/management-2020; Box on p. 90 from Chui, M., Manyika, J., Bughin, J., Brown, B., Roberts, R., Danielson, J. and Gupta, S. New York: McKinsey & Company/McKinsey Global Institute, 2013; Box 3.1 from Workspaces: the new word for workplace?, *The Times, Raconteur on IT Supplement*, 06/10/2011, p. 17 (Twentyman, J.), © Twentyman, News International Trading Ltd, 6 October 2011; Box 3.1 from *Organizational Behavior: Experiences and Cases*, 4th edn, St Paul, MN: West Publishing (Marcic, D., 1995) pp. 285–6, from MARCIC. *Organizational Behavior*, 4th edn © 1995 South-Western, a part of Cengage Learning, Inc., reproduced by permission. www.cengage.com/permissions; Box on page 111 from Professor Phillip Beaumont, University of Glasgow, Thanks to Professor Phil Beaumont for his assistance in helping to develop this exercise; Boxes on pp. 121 & 402 from Schumpeter: Down with fun, *The Economist*, 18/09/2010, p. 84, © The Economist Newspaper Limited, London (18/09/2010); Box on p. 167 adapted from *Is yours a learning organization*, Harvard Business School Publishing (Garvin, D.A., Edmondson, A. and Gino, F., 2008) 86(3); Extract on p. 180 from The early bird really does catch the worm, *Harvard Business Review*, 88(7/8), pp. 30–1 (Randler, C.,), F1007E-HCB-ENG, reprinted by permission of *Harvard Business Review*, Adapted from 'The early bird really does catch the worm' by Randler, C., 88(7/8) 2010 © 2010 by the Harvard Business School Publishing Corporation, all rights reserved; Extract on p. 214 from Leaders must act like they mean it, *The Sunday Times*, 10/10/2010, Appointments Section, p. 4 (Rea, K.), © Rea, News International Trading Ltd, 10 October 2010; Box on p. 292 from We drive hard but we are loyal, *The Times*, 19/07/2011, p. 37 (Lea, R.,), © Lea, News International Trading Ltd, 19 July 2011; Case Study on p. 378 adapted from *Management of Technology. The Technical Change Audit*, Manpower Services Commission, Action for Results: 5: The Process Module (Boddy, D. and Buchanan. D.A.,) Crown copyright, contains public sector information licensed under the Open Government Licence (OGL) v3.0.http://www.nationalarchives.gov.uk/doc/open-government-licence; Exercise on p. 411 adapted from *OB in Action: Cases and Exercises*, 8th edn, South-Western, a part of Cengage Learning (Wolff, S.B., 2007) pp. 218–19, Exercise, 978-0618-61159-1/0618611592; Exercise on p. 411 from *Organizational Behaviour and Management*, 3rd edn, Thomson (Martin, J., 2005) p. 243, ISBN: 1861529481/978-1861529480, Exercise on p. 411 from *Organizational Behaviour and Management*, 3rd edn, Thomson (Martin, J., 2005) p. 243, reproduced by permission of Cengage Learning EMEA Ltd.; Exercise on p. 444 from *Work and Orgaizational Behaviour*, Palgrave Macmillan (Bratton, J., Callinan, M., Forshaw, C. and Sawchuk, P. 2007) p. 317, John Bratton, Peter Sawchuk, Carolyn Forshaw, Militza Callinan and Martin Corbett, *Work and Organizational Behaviour*, published 2007 Palgrave Macmillan reproduced with permission of Palgrave Macmillan; Box on p. 527 adapted from Banking against Doomsday, *The Economist*, 10/03/2012, p. 67, http://www.economist.com/node/21549931, © The Economist Newspaper Limited, London (10/03/2012); Box on p. 528 from http://media.popularmechanics.com/images/1206airbus_diagramTx.jpg; Exercise 16.2 adapted from Simulating organizational design issues, *Journal of Management Education*, 17 (1), 110–13 (J.W. French 1993), Sage Publications, Exercise 16.2 adapted from Simulating organizational design issues, *Journal of Management Education*, 17(1), 110–13 (J.W. French 1993), Elsevier, reprinted by permission of Sage publications, Inc.; Exercise 17.2 adapted from Organization structure and design: The the Club Ed exercise, *Journal of Management Education*, 22(3), 425–428 (Harvey, C. and Morouney, K. 1998), Elsevier; Box on p. 598 from Heywood, S., De Smet, A. and Webb, A. McKinsey, McKinsey Quarterly, September, pp.1–9.; Box on page 615 adapted from 'When bossy is better for rookie managers', 90(5), *Harvard Business Review* (Sauer, S.J., 2012) p. 30, Figure, F1205B-HCB-ENG, Reprinted by permission of *Harvard Business Review*, Adapted from 'When bossy is better for rookie managers' by Sauer, S.J., 90(5) 2012 © 2012 by the Harvard Business School Publishing Corporation; all rights reserved; Box on p. 655 from Sull, D. McKinsey, McKinsey Quarterly, May, pp.1–10, 2015; Exercise on p. 696 from *Experimental Exercises Management Book*, Addision Wesley (Sashkin, M., Morris, W. C., Hellriege, D., 1987) pp. 73–4, 020111545X, Sashkin, Marshall; Morris, William C.; Hellriegel, Donald, *Experimental Exercises Management Book*, 1st edn, © 1987, reprinted and electronically reproduced by permission or Pearson Education, Inc., Upper Saddle River, New Jersey; Exercise 20.2 from Cognitive reflection and decision making, *Journal of Economic Perspectives*, 19(4), p.27 (Frederick, S. 2005), American Economic Association, Exercise 20.2 from Cognitive reflection and decision making, *Journal of Economic Perspectives*, 19 (4), p.27 (Frederick, S. 2005), American Economic Association and Exercise 20.2 from Cognitive reflection and decision making, *Journal of Economic Perspectives*, 19 (4), p.27 (Frederick, S. 2005), American Economic Association; Exhibit on page 762 adapted from You can't be a good girl and get on in this world, *The Sunday Times News* Review section, 27/11/2011, p. 4 (Mills, E.), © Mills, News International Trading Ltd, 27 November 2011; Exercise on p. 764 adapted from Power and the changing environment, *Journal of Management Education*, 24(2), pp. 288–96 (Barbuto, J.E., 2000), Barbuto, J.E., Power and the changing environment, in *Journal of Management Education*, 24(2), pp. 288–96, © 2000, OBTS Teaching Society for Management Educators, reprinted by permission of Sage Publications.

Photographs

The publisher would like to thank the following for their kind permission to reproduce their photographs:

(Key: b – bottom; c – centre; l – left; r – right; t – top)

123RF.com: Adamson 430, Jon Helgason 679, Imagehit Limited 236tl, Georgios Kollidas 636, Tomwang 230, Wavebreak Media Ltd 457; **Alamy Images:** Caroline Woodham 199, Chris Hennessy 112r, Gary Doak 451, Chad Ehlers 89, Everett Collection Historical 153tl, 153bl, Granger, NYC. 156, Interfoto 742, Paul Doyle 726, Peter Jordan 510, Vario Images GmbH & Co K.G. 32; **Barbara Tversky:** photograph copyright Barbara G Tversky 676b; **Reproduced with kind permission of Dr Belbin** 362; **Bentley Historical Library/ University of Michigan:** 367br; **Bridgeman Art Library Ltd:** South Wall of a Mural depicting Detroit Industry, 1932–33 (fresco), Rivera, Diego (1886–1957)/Detroit Institute of Arts, USA/Gift of Edsel B. Ford/© DACS 466; **Camera Press Ltd:** Fabian Bachrach 262; **Courtesy of Alexandra Milgram:** Stanley Milgram papers, 1927–1993 (inclusive). Manuscripts & Archives, Yale University 404bl, From Obedience © 1965 Stanley Milgram/Stanley Milgram papers, 1927–1993 (inclusive). Manuscripts & Archives, Yale University 404br; **Courtesy of AT&T Archives and History Center:** 325b, 326, Wiring and soldering. Hawthorne plant, circa 1941 327; **Courtesy of Rethink Robotics, Inc.:** 85; **Fotolia.com:** Jesussanz 335tr, 335bl, Robert Kneschke 336, Melpomene 279, Catalin Pop 250, John Takai 182; **Georgetown University:** Stephen Voss 233; **Gerald Ferris:** Florida State University 752; **Getty Images:** AFP/Christof Stache 56, AFP/Franck Fife 324t, Ulrich Baumgarten 143, Bettmann 256, 465b, 744, Bloomberg/Fabrice Dimier 324b, BraunS 367t, Gareth Brown 54, Choja 353, Gary Gershoff/WireImage 508, Martyn Hayhow/AFP 578, Tobias Heyer/Bongarts 426, Hulton Archive 150, 463, Ilbusca 390, Hiroyuki Ito 433, Jon Brenneis/Life Magazine/ The LIFE Images Collection 160, Justin Sullivan 329, Koichi Kamoshida 580, Bryn Lennon 440, Rob Lewine 236tr, Library of Congress 232r, Mansell/The LIFE Picture Collection 747, Robin Marchant 505, Mandel Ngan-Pool 229r, Pixdeluxe 360, Popperfoto 181b, Portugal 2004 96, Mike Powell 727, George Rinhart/Corbis 460, Nicolas Torres/LatinContent 419, Todor Tsvetkov 358, VI-Images 421; **Harvard Business School Archives:** 325t; **Linn Products Limited:** 79; **Mary Evans Picture Library:** 181t, 754; **MIT Sloan School of Management :** 102r, Evgenia Eliseeva 102l; **Motorola:** 112l; **News UK Syndication:** James Glossop xxvii, The Sunday Times Magazine/Andrew Testa 313; **Press Association Images:** Adam Oxford/Demotix/Demotix 406, AP Photo/Michael Sohn 229l, Fort Worth Star-Telegram/ ABACA 3, Gregorio Borgia 179, Hanusa/AP 564, Larry MacDougal 465t, PA Archive 438, The State/ABACA 570, Yuin Schiling 277; **Reprinted with kind permission of Princeton University:** 676t; **Reuters:** 11, Chip East 49, Brendan McDermid 595, Sean Adair 738, Str Old 232l; **Rex Shutterstock:** Geoff Moore 654, Jonathan Player 455t, Mari Tefre/Global Crop Diversity Trust 528, Nick Rogers/Associated Newspapers 184; **Science Photo Library Ltd:** European Space Agency 317, Humanities and Social Sciences Library/New York Public Library 261; **Shutterstock.com:** Alexander Chalkin 292, IQconcept 639, LDprod 193, Pling 77, Pressmaster 365, Wavebreakmedia 427; **Smithsonian Institute:** National Museum of American History 461; **Stanford Graduate School of Business:** Joanne Martin|Fred H. Merrill Professor of Organizational Behaviour, Emerita 119; **SuperStock:** age-fotostock 236bl, Johner 236br; **The Drs. Nicholas and Dorothy Cummings Center for the History of Psychology. The University of Akron:** 181c, 199bl, 289, 367bl, 509tl, 509tr, 509bl, 509br; **The Kobal Collection:** WARNER BROS 84; **2016 Uber Technologies Inc.:** 47; **University of Maryland:** George Ritzer I Distinguished University Professor, University of Maryland 471; **Yale Pictorial Records & Collections:** 540.

All other images © Pearson Education

Student briefing

What are the aims of this text?

Introduce the subject We aim to bring the study of behaviour in organizations to undergraduate and postgraduate students who have little or no social science background.

Link to practice We aim to show how organizational behaviour concepts, theories and techniques can be applied in work and management settings.

Recognize diversity We aim to raise awareness of the range of social and cultural factors that affect behaviour in organizations.

Stimulate debate We aim to promote a challenging, critical perspective, observing that the 'correct' answers to organizational questions, and solutions to problems, rely on values, judgements and ideology, as well as on evidence.

Who are our readers?

Our target readers are students who are new to the social sciences, and to the study of organizational behaviour. This is a core subject on most business and management degree, diploma and masters programmes. Accountants, architects, bankers, computer scientists, doctors, engineers, hoteliers, nurses, surveyors, teachers and other specialists, who have no background in social science, may find themselves studying organizational behaviour as part of their professional examination schemes.

What approach do we adopt?

Social science perspective Our understanding of organizations derives from a range of social science disciplines. Other texts adopt a managerial, psychological or sociological perspective. However, many occupations benefit from an understanding of organizational behaviour. Not all students are going to be managers, psychologists or sociologists.

Self-contained chapters The understanding of one chapter does not rely on others. The material does not have to be read in the sequence in which it is presented. Ideas and theories are developed from the organizational context, to individual psychology, through social psychology, to organizational sociology, politics and management topics. Chapters cover both theory and practice, classic and contemporary.

Challenging ideas Many of the issues covered in this text are controversial, and competing views are explained. The aim is not to identify 'correct answers' or 'best practices', which are often simplistic and misleading. The aim is to raise further questions, to trigger discussion and debate, and to stimulate critical thinking.

Flexible design This book works with many semester-based introductory-level programmes. Our *Springboard* feature suggests sources for more advanced assignment work. Organizational behaviour overlaps with other subjects such as human resource management, and this book is useful for those modules, too.

Comparative analysis   One way to highlight how we behave in organizations is to compare our experience with that of others. As a student, you engage routinely in comparative analysis, on railways and aircraft, in buses, hotels, restaurants and hospitals. Is that management behaviour appropriate? Is that employee response effective? Does our theory help us to understand those behaviours, or not?

Too many theories?

Students who are new to organizational behaviour often complain about the number of different theories. You will see this, for example, in our discussion of motivation, culture, leadership and power. Does this mean that the field is immature? How can all of these theories be 'right'? It does not help that many organizational behaviour theories were first developed decades in the past.

Marc Anderson (2007) argues that different theories are valuable because they help us to fill our 'conceptual toolbox'. We live in a complex world, and we need a variety of tools and perspectives to deal with the many, and changing, issues and problems that we face. This means that one theory could be helpful in one context, but a different perspective could be useful in another setting. An idea that appears to be of limited value today may help us to deal with tomorrow's challenges.

There are no 'right or wrong' theories, or 'one best way'. There are only theories that are more or less useful in helping us to deal with different issues in different settings at different times. We benefit from having 'too many theories'. This is not a problem.

What aids to learning are included?

Learning outcomes   Chapters open with clear learning outcomes.

Key terms   Chapters open with a list of the key terms that are then explained, and these are combined in the Glossary.

Exercises   Each chapter has two learning exercises for tutorial or seminar use, and these can be used in a flexible way.

What would you do?   A problem or incident opens each part of the text, and you are asked to make, and to justify, your decision.

Learning resources   The companion website for this text contains an additional set of resources related to each chapter.

Home viewing   Each chapter identifies a movie which illustrates the topic in a graphic, entertaining and memorable way, for home viewing.

OB cinema   In each chapter movie clips are identified for classroom use, illustrating specific issues, concepts or arguments for analysis.

OB on the web   One or two websites or short videos have been selected for the way in which they illustrate the chapter material.

Stop and think   You are regularly invited to stop, to think through controversial and contradictory issues, to apply ideas and arguments to your own experience, to question your assumptions.

Revision   Each chapter closes with sample examination questions, which can be used for personal study or as tutorial exercises.

Cartoons   In order to make the subject interesting and memorable, we include novel, varied and unusual material such as cartoons, illustrations and research boxes, to change the pace, rhythm and appearance of the text.

"It sort of makes you stop and think, doesn't it."

Source: © Sam Gross/The New Yorker Collection/www.cartoonbank.com

Recap	Each chapter closes with a section summarizing the chapter content with respect to the learning outcomes.
Research assignment	A focused information-gathering project involving either a website search, library exercise, or interviewing, or a combination of methods is included in each chapter.
Invitation to see	The opening of each Part of the text is prefaced with a photograph showing how work and organizations are portrayed; visual images are rarely neutral, and you are invited to 'decode' these pictures, identifying the obvious and more subtle meanings that they promote.
Employability	Employability has been defined as 'a set of achievements, skills, understandings and personal attributes, that make graduates more likely to gain employment and be successful in their chosen occupations, which benefits themselves, the workforce, the community and the economy' (Yorke, 2006, p.8).

Employability and OB

Knowledge of this subject can improve your employability and career prospects. What are employers looking for? A qualification alone may not be enough. Most organizations are also looking for other 'competencies' – behaviours, skills, attributes and experiences that they expect you to have, or to develop, in order to perform effectively at work (Egan, 2011). Research by the Chartered Institute of Personnel and Development (2010) found that employers are looking for evidence of:

- leadership
- people management
- business skills/commercial acumen
- work ethic and results orientation
- customer service skills

- communication – oral and written
- interpersonal skills
- project and programme management
- leading and managing change
- general management skills
- creativity and innovation
- teamworking skills
- problem-solving skills
- self-management
- political and cultural awareness.

Components of critical thinking

Alan Thomas (2003) argues that critical thinking is one aspect of effective management, and identifies four components of the critical thinking process:

1. *Identifying and challenging assumptions about*

   - the nature of management, its tasks, skills and purposes
   - the nature of people and why they behave as they do
   - the nature of organizations
   - learning, knowing and acting
   - values, goals and ends.

2. *Creating contextual awareness by understanding*

   - how management has developed historically
   - how management is conceived of in other societies
   - the implications of different industrial, organizational, economic, political and cultural contexts for management
   - the interrelation between organizations and society.

3. *Identifying alternatives by*

   - becoming aware of the variety of ways in which managing and organizing can be undertaken

   - inventing and imagining new ways of managing and organizing
   - specifying new goals and priorities.

4. *Developing reflective scepticism by*

   - adopting a questioning, quizzical attitude
   - recognizing the limitations of much that passes for knowledge
   - knowing how to evaluate knowledge claims
   - developing a resistance to dogma and propaganda
   - being able to distinguish systematic argument and reasoned judgement from sloppy thinking, simplistic formulae and sophistry.

What is the difference between critical and uncritical thinking? When we are thinking uncritically, we accept common-sense assumptions at face value without checking their validity; we deny or ignore the influence of context on beliefs and practices; we do not look for and evaluate alternatives; and we cling rigidly and unquestioningly to dogmas and authoritative pronouncements.

Critical thinking is an attitude of mind which emphasizes the constant need to ask 'why?'.

From an organizational behaviour perspective, we can add the following:

- knowledge of how organizations are managed
- critical thinking; research, analysis and synthesis
- prioritizing and decision making
- appetite for learning; learning to learn
- understand cross-cultural issues and differences.

A CIPD (2013, p.26) survey of 460 UK employers also found that they were also looking for well-developed 'workplace and basic life skills'. These skills include office etiquette, time-keeping, reliability, self-organization, understanding dress codes and work ethic, along with office skills such as telephone techniques, customer service, interpersonal skills, teamworking and showing respect for colleagues. These responses reflect a traditional concern that higher education focuses more on theory and academic excellence than on practical skills, and knowledge of how business works. One response to this survey said:

> The working hard ethic, respect, timekeeping, acceptable work behaviour, problem-solving, proactivity, ability to organize themselves, desire for work – these are key work skills that university courses seem to forget – they concentrate too much on theoretical knowledge and don't prepare youngsters for the workplace, so it is a shock for some. (CIPD, 2013, p.27)

What are your strengths and limitations as far as potential employers are concerned? To help you to think about how to increase your value to employers, we have developed the *employability assessment* matrix. Each chapter asks you for an action plan to develop your profile in relation to the ideas, concepts, frameworks, behaviours, methods and other issues that you have covered while studying that topic. This includes this text and wider reading, tutorial discussion, class presentations, assignment work and critical viewing (visual literacy). We hope that you will find this useful in developing your knowledge, skills and behaviour repertoire. You can do this working alone, or in association with your instructor, helping you to develop your employability.

These competencies overlap with each other; this is not a rigid framework. Different commentators interpret these competencies in different ways, and different employers attach varying degrees of importance to them (Rothwell and Arnold, 2007). What matters, however, is the importance that *you* attach to these competencies with respect to the development of *your* career. The table on the next page shows how our chapters broadly map onto the 20 competencies, grouped for convenience under four main headings – personal qualities, leadership qualities, practical skills and other attributes.

Internships: all work and no pay

One way to improve your employability is to accept an internship – temporary work experience, lasting a few weeks or months, often unpaid. Some internships involve routine manual work, but many organizations provide valuable development opportunities. Google recruits 3,000 interns every year. The European Commission in Brussels and Luxembourg recruits 1,400 *stagiaires* for five months of work with them. The large professional services consultancies – Deloitte, EY, KPMG and PricewaterhouseCoopers – together employ over 30,000 interns a year. The Indian technology company Infosys invites 150 interns to Bangalore each year.

Benefits to employers include free labour, the reputational advantages that come from making a contribution to society and the local community, and the opportunity to assess candidates for permanent positions. Benefits to interns include the chance to acquire new knowledge and skills, to experience work in a particular organization and sector, to extend personal networks and to assess potential employers. Over a third of graduate vacancies in Britain are now filled from organizations' own internship programmes, according to one market research company. From an analysis of the CVs of its members, the online social networking service LinkedIn found that a quarter of interns took full time jobs in the organizations where they did their placements. More than half of the investment banking recruits at Goldman Sachs and Morgan Stanley are recruited from those organizations' own intern programmes (*The Economist*, 2014).

If you plan to follow this route, choose your internship with care. To make the most of the experience, identify how you can use the internship to develop your personal and leadership qualities, practical skills and other attributes. This will be an even more powerful development opportunity if you use the *employability assessment* matrix to identify the specific competencies that you can enhance in relation to the topics covered in this text.

Competencies and chapters

Competencies that will improve your employability

Personal qualities:

self-management	6 Personality
work ethic/results orientation	2 Environment: Gen Y, Gen C
appetite for learning	5 Learning
interpersonal skills	7 Communication; 8 Perception
creativity and innovation	19 Change

Leadership qualities:

leadership	18 Leadership
people management	9 Motivation; 14 Work design
leading and managing change	3 Technology; 19 Change
project management	17 Organizational architecture: 19 Change
general management skills	all chapters relate to this

Practical skills:

commercial/business acumen	2 Environment: corporate responsibility
customer service skills	1 Explaining organizational behaviour
communication skills	7 Communication
problem solving skills	What would you do? feature
teamworking skills	11 Group structure; 12 Individuals in groups; 13 Teamworking

Other attributes:

political awareness	21 Conflict; 22 Power and politics
understand cross-cultural issues	4 Culture
how organizations work	all chapters relate to this
critical thinking	Student briefing; 1 Explaining organizational behaviour
prioritizing, decision making	20 Decision making

Why should we pay attention to these transient images? We see them once and rarely feel the need to refer back to them. Street advertisements and internet banners are displayed for brief periods before being updated. The photographs in magazines and newspapers are just illustrations, contextualized with a brief caption, and it is the accompanying text that matters. The images in television and street advertising are clearly contrived to attract our attention, and they cannot mislead us in that respect.

Visual images are rarely, if ever, neutral. They are not 'just' illustrations. They usually tell a story, present a point of view, support an argument, perpetuate a myth, or maybe create, reinforce or challenge a stereotype. Images carry messages, sometimes obvious, sometimes subtle, sometimes clear, sometimes confusing. Visual imagery is thus a valuable source of information which we often overlook. Visual research methods have been widely used in sociology and anthropology for many years (Bateson and Mead, 1942; Collier and Collier, 1986), but organizational researchers have been slow to exploit the possibilities (Warren, 2009). There has, however, been a recent growth of interest in the potential of visual methods in social science more generally, and in organizational behaviour (Prosser, 1998; Emmison and Smith, 2000; Buchanan, 2001; Mitchell, 2009). The edited collection by Emma Bell et al. (2014) indicates just how mature this field has become, and illustrates the significant and innovative contributions that visual methods can make.

We would therefore like to encourage students to adopt a more critical perspective on visual images of organizational behaviour. You will find at the beginning of each Part of the book a short section titled *Invitation to see*, displaying photographs showing aspects of work and organizations. Visual information constitutes data, in the same way that interviews and survey questionnaires provide data, and which also therefore requires interpretation.

The aims of *Invitation to see* are to:

1. encourage students to look at the organizational world, and the actors who populate it, in an entirely different way;

2. demonstrate the value of visual data in offering insights into human and organizational behaviour;

3. introduce and develop the concept of interpreting or 'decoding' visual images.

Photographs can be seen, read, interpreted or decoded in three main ways.

Reality captured	Images can be seen as captured fragments of reality, frozen in time, indisputably accurate renditions of scenes and actors. This is how photography was regarded when it was invented, and many commentators concluded that 'art is dead'. An artist could never hope to capture reality as accurately as a photograph, so why bother? This perspective is reflected in the saying 'the camera doesn't lie'.
Reality fabricated	Photographs can instead be regarded as social and technological constructs, which reveal as much about the photographer as they do about the image. The photographer selects the scene, a camera, a lens, which in combination determine properties of the image, such as sharpness, contrast, lighting, grain and depth of field. More critically, the photographer selects the angle and framing of a shot, determining what is included, and also selects the moment to open the shutter and capture the image. Viewers see only what the photographer wants them to see. What is outside the frame, and the sequence of events before and after the shutter was fired, remain unseen. Digital photography allows many further possibilities to manipulate images after they have been captured. This perspective implies that 'the camera and the computer lie for the photographer'.

Multiple realities   How an image is interpreted by viewers, independent of the photographer's intent, is also significant. For the cover of this book, we wanted an image that had no direct association with organizations, factories, office buildings, managers, collaborative teams, aggressive animals, or any other typical organizational metaphor. There is a key question concerning whose interpretation of an image is correct – that of the photographer, or that of the viewer? Both points of view are valid, and are of equal interest. As discussed in Chapter 2, the idea that texts can have many interpretations also applies to visual images. The viewer does not have to know the photographer's intent, which may be inferred from the image and its caption. Photographers cannot predict the interpretations which viewers will place on their work, but it is those interpretations that condition the viewer's response. This perspective implies that 'what the camera produces is for us to determine'.

With *invitation to see*, three questions are significant:

1. What are you being invited to see here? What did the *photographer* intend this image to convey? Does it tell a story, present a point of view, support an argument, perpetuate a myth, reinforce a stereotype, challenge a stereotype?

2. What does this image convey to *you*, personally? How do you interpret this? What do you think this means? Do you agree with what is being said here? Is the message inaccurate or misleading, perhaps insulting? Does this image carry meanings which the photographer may not have intended?

3. How do *others* interpret this image? Do they decode it in different ways? How can differences of interpretation of the same image be explained?

This photograph appeared in *The Times* (22 January 2015), illustrating an article about Vicki Tough and her career in industrial abseiling, described in the article header as 'an unconventional route to breaking through the glass ceiling'. We are told that one of Vicki's first assignments involved being lowered through a porthole in an oil tanker in a Newcastle shipyard. The article describes this kind of work as very dirty and extremely dangerous.

Vicki Tough by James Glossop/The Times, 22 January 2015

'You're hanging around all day, but I don't find work is boring'

Here is one decoding of this image:

> Here is a young woman with a happy smile, looking confidently and directly at the camera. She is clearly enjoying her work, despite the fact that this appears to be physically demanding and dangerous, dangling in an abseil harness high above the ground. We cannot see where her feet are placed, but this looks as though she is 'free abseiling' (which can be even more demanding), rather than 'walking' down a wall which provides support and stability. The image caption tells us that this is her full-time job, her chosen career. But we think of this as 'men's work', and the yellow 'high visibility' helmet, and black/grey overalls with reinforcements at the knees and elbows reinforce that view; these are 'men's clothes'. This image, therefore, shatters the stereotype that women cannot do work like this.

What else does this image suggest?

> The woman has clearly posed for this photograph, which appears to be a 'publicity stunt'. The scene has been carefully set up in a clean, safe building (a training facility perhaps?). She is not inside the dirty, smelly hold of an oil tanker. In her dark overalls and yellow helmet, she has been posed against some bright red scaffolding to bring contrasting colours to the photograph. To support the idea that this is a 'setup', her hands, face and overalls are clean. Dangerous work? She is firmly tethered with strong ropes, and appears to be relaxed as well as smiling. This is not a dangerous situation at all (although this is scary if one has not tried abseiling before). Photographed alone, she seems to be a 'maverick', in a role where it is unusual to find a woman – and this is a rare and unusual way in which to 'break through the glass ceiling'. The image can thus be interpreted as reinforcing conventional stereotypes of 'men's work' and 'women's work'.

It is possible to reach different interpretations of this image. The message lies, in part, in the photograph, but also depends on the perceptions of the viewers. This image can be 'decoded' as both contradicting and reinforcing stereotypes related to men's work and women's work. It is of course also possible to read too much into such an image. The key questions are, how do *you* read this image, what story does it tell *you*, what are *you* being invited to see here?

References

Ackroyd, S. and Thompson, P. (1999) *Organizational Misbehaviour*. London: Sage Publications.

Alvesson, M. and Ashcraft, K.L. (2009) 'Critical methodology in management and management and organization research', in David A. Buchanan and Alan Bryman (eds), *The Sage Handbook of Organizational Research Methods*. London: Sage Publications.

Anderson, M.H. (2007) 'Why are there so many theories?', *Journal of Management Education*, 31 (6): 757–76.

Bateson, G. and Mead, M. (1942) *Balinese Character: A Photographic Analysis*. New York: New York Academy of Sciences, Special Publications 2.

Bell, E. and Davison, J. (2013) 'Visual management studies: empirical and theoretical approaches', *International Journal of Management Reviews*, 15 (2): 167–84.

Bell, E., Warren, S. and Schroeder, J. (eds) (2014) *The Routledge Companion to Visual Organization*, Abingdon, Oxon and New York: Routledge.

Billsberry, J., Charlesworth, J. and Leonard, P. (eds) (2012) *Moving Images: Effective Teaching with Film and Television in Management*. Charlotte, NC: Information Age Publishing.

Boozer, J. (2002) *Career Movies: American Business and the Success Mystique*. Austin, TX: University of Texas Press.

Buchanan, D.A. (2001) 'The role of photography in organizational research: a re-engineering case illustration', *Journal of Management Inquiry*, 10 (2): 151–64.

Champoux, J.E. (2005) *Our Feature Presentation: Organizational Behaviour*. Mason, OH: Thomson South-Western.

Champoux, J.E. (2006) 'At the cinema: aspiring to a higher ethical standard', *Academy of management Learning and Education*, 5 (3): 386–90.

Champoux, J.E. (2007) *Our Feature Presentation: Human Resource Management*. Mason, OH: Thomson South-Western.

Chartered Institute for Personnel and Development (CIPD) (2010) *Learning and Talent Development: Annual Survey Report 2010*. London: Chartered Institute for Personnel and Development.

Chartered Institute of Personnel and Development (CIPD) (2013) *Resourcing and Talent Planning: Annual Survey Report*. London: Chartered Institute of Personnel and Development.

Collier, J. and Collier, M. (1986) *Visual Anthropology: Photography as a Research Method*. Albuquerque: University of New Mexico Press.

Davis, G. (2015) 'Addressing unconscious bias', *McKinsey Quarterly*, February: 1–4.

Doherty, E.M. (2011) 'Joking aside, insights to employee dignity in "Dilbert" cartoons: the value of comic art in understanding the employer–employee relationship', *Journal of Management Inquiry*, 208 (3): 286–301.

Egan, J. (2011) *Competence and Competency Frameworks Factsheet*. London: Chartered Institute for Personnel and Development.

Ezzedeen, S.R. (2013) 'The portrayal of professional and managerial women in North American films: good news or bad news for your executive pipeline?', *Organizational Dynamics*, 42 (4): 248–56.

Emmison, M. and Smith, P. (2000) *Researching the Visual: Images, Objects, Contexts and Interactions in Social and Cultural Inquiry*. London: Sage Publications.

Hassard, J.S. and Buchanan, D.A. (2009) 'From *Modern Times* to *Syriana*: feature films as research data', in D.A. Buchanan and A. Bryman (eds), *The Sage Handbook of Organizational Research Methods*. London: Sage Publications.

Hassard, J. and Holliday, R. (eds) (1998) *Organization-Representation: Work and Organizations in Popular Culture*. London: Sage Publications.

Holt, R. and Zundel, M. (2014) 'Understanding management, trade, and society through fiction: lessons from *The Wire*', *Academy of Management Review*, 39 (4): 576–85.

Huczynski, A. and Buchanan, D. (2004) 'Theory from fiction: a narrative process perspective on the pedagogical use of feature film', *Journal of Management Education*, 28(6): 707–26.

Huczynski, A. and Buchanan, D. (2005) 'Feature films in management education: beyond illustration and entertainment', *Journal of Organizational Behaviour Education*, 1 (1): 73–94.

Hunt, C.S. (2001) 'Must see TV: the timelessness of television as a teaching tool', *Journal of Management Education*, 25 (6): 631–47.

Mitchell, C. (2009) *Doing Visual Research*. London: Sage Publications.

Muir, K. (2014) 'This big bad wolf has me howling', *The Times*, 17 January, p.7.

Phillips, N. (1995) 'Telling organizational tales: on the role of narrative fiction in the study of organization', *Organization Studies*, 16 (4): 625–49.

Prosser, J. (ed.) (1998) *Image-Based Research: A Sourcebook for Qualitative Researchers*. London: Falmer Press, Taylor & Francis.

Rothwell, A. and Arnold, J. (2007) 'Self-perceived employability: development and validation of a scale', *Personnel Review*, 36 (1): 23–41.

Smith, G.W. (2009) 'Using feature films as the primary instructional medium to teach organizational behavior', *Journal of Management Education*, 33 (4): 462–89.

Soetaert, R. and Rutten, K. (2014) 'Rhetoric and narratives as equipment for living: spinning in Borgen', *Journal of Organizational Change Management*, 27 (5): 710–21.

The Economist (2014) 'The internship: Generation i', 6 September, pp.59–61.

Thomas, A.B. (2003) *Controversies in Management* (2nd edn). London: Routledge.

Thompson, P. and McHugh, D. (2009) *Work Organization: A Critical Approach* (4th edn). Basingstoke: Palgrave.

Tyler, C.L., Anderson, M.H. and Tyler, J.M. (2009) 'Giving students new eyes: the benefits of having students find media clips to illustrate management concepts', *Journal of Management Education*, 33 (4): 444–61.

Warren, S. (2009) 'Visual methods in organizational research', in D.A. Buchanan and A. Bryman (eds), *The Sage Handbook of Organizational Research Methods*. London: Sage Publications, pp.566–82.

Wilson, F. (2013) *Organizational Behaviour and Work: A Critical Introduction* (4th edn). Oxford: Oxford University Press.

Yorke, M. (2006) *Employability in Higher Education: What It Is – What It Is Not*. Heslington, York: The Higher Education Academy.

Zaniello, T. (2003) *Working Stiffs, Union Maids, Reds, and Riffraff: An Expanded Guide to Films About Labor*. Ithaca, NY and London: ILR Press/Cornell University Press.

Zaniello, T. (2007) *The Cinema of Globalization: A Guide to Films About The New Economic Order*. Ithaca, NY and London: ILR Press/Cornell University Press.

Part 1 **The organizational context**

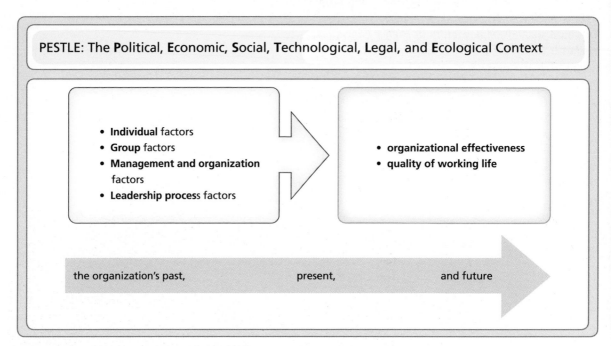

PESTLE: The **P**olitical, **E**conomic, **S**ocial, **T**echnological, **L**egal, and **E**cological Context

- **Individual** factors
- **Group** factors
- **Management and organization** factors
- **Leadership process** factors

→

- **organizational effectiveness**
- **quality of working life**

the organization's past,   present,   and future

A field map of the organizational behaviour terrain

Introduction

Part 1, The organizational context, explores four topics:

1. Different ways to explain organizational behaviour, contrasting traditional variance explanations with contemporary process explanations.

2. How the wider environment of the organization affects internal structures and working practices, including demographic trends, ethical behaviour, and corporate social responsibility.

3. How new technologies, and 'the second machine age' (robotics, machine intelligence), are changing the nature of jobs and organizations, including the automation of knowledge work.

4. Aspects of organizational culture, and different ways to understand this concept, and the links from culture to organizational change and performance.

The second decade of the twenty-first century is a time of severe economic and geopolitical turbulence and uncertainty, accompanied by rapid developments in new technologies. The ability of organizations to anticipate shocks, trends, and opportunities, and to respond rapidly in appropriate ways, are clearly vital to performance and survival. Organizations must be designed and managed – 'built to change' – in order for these degrees of responsiveness and adaptability to happen effectively.

The subject matter of organizational behaviour spans a number of levels of analysis – individual, group, organization, and the wider environment, or context. Part 1 explores key aspects of the organizational context. These include the nature and pace of social and technological change, and the pressures on management to be seen to be acting ethically and exercising corporate social responsibility. Organizations develop their own distinctive cultures, which are different from, while clearly linked to, the wider national cultures in which they operate.

A recurring theme in this text concerns the design of jobs, and the organization and experience of work. The organization of work reflects a number of influences, at different levels of analysis. We explain how the experience and organization of work is influenced by:

- *contextual* factors, in Chapter 2
- *technological* factors, in Chapter 3
- *psychological* factors, in Chapter 9
- *social psychological* factors, in Chapter 13
- *historical* factors, in Chapter 15
- *power and political* factors, in Chapter 22.

Invitation to see

Press Association Images/Fort Worth Star-Telegram/ABACA

Workers assemble Motorola Moto X smartphones at a factory in Texas, for sale in Europe. A photo similar to this appeared in the *Financial Times*, 15 January 2014, p.16, at the head of an article titled 'Google to roll out Moto X in Europe'

1. **Decoding**: Look at this image closely. Note in as much detail as possible what messages you feel that it is trying to convey. Does it tell a story, present a point of view, support an argument, perpetuate a myth, reinforce a stereotype, challenge a stereotype?

2. **Challenging**: To what extent do you agree with the messages, stories, points of view, arguments, myths, or stereotypes in this image? Is this image open to challenge, to criticism, or to interpretation and decoding in other ways, revealing other messages?

3. **Sharing**: Compare with colleagues your interpretation of this image. Explore explanations for differences in your respective decodings.

You're the employee: what would you do?

I am the managing director of a small firm that trades in a high-pressure, fast-moving market. We take pride in our leading edge management practices, and in getting results. Our new 'Generation C' recruits – who I'm told are always 'connected, communicating, clicking' – have an average age of around 20. I am now 45; a lot has changed since I was young, and attitudes to work in particular. We are finding it more difficult to attract new staff, and they seem to need a lot of counselling in the first few months to help them to see beyond the job to the future of the company in this challenging environment. Our motivation strategy involves basic salary with performance-related bonuses. Most of our new staff are quite happy with their basic earnings.

This new Generation C seems to have higher expectations, wanting more challenging work, and greater responsibility, which is admirable. But they seem to expect too much too soon, without putting in the effort. I find this strange, because I worked my way to the top through hard graft. How can I motivate our new staff? You work alongside them, and you are not so much older than they are. What would you do?

Chapter 1 Explaining organizational behaviour

Key terms

organizational behaviour

organization

controlled performance

organizational dilemma

fundamental attribution error

organizational effectiveness

balanced scorecard

quality of working life

positivism

operational definition

variance theory

constructivism

process theory

evidence-based management

human resource management

employment cycle

discretionary behaviour

big data

data analytics

Learning outcomes

When you have read this chapter, you should be able to define those key terms in your own words, and you should also be able to:

1. Explain the importance of understanding organizational behaviour.

2. Explain and illustrate the central dilemma of organizational design.

3. Understand the need for explanations of behaviour in organizations that take account of relationships between factors at different levels of analysis.

4. Understand the difference between positivist and constructivist perspectives, and their implications for the study of organizational behaviour.

5. Understand the difference between variance and process theories and their uses in understanding organizational behaviour.

6. Explain the development and limitations of evidence-based management.

7. Recognize the range of applications of organizational behaviour theory, and contributions to human resource management policy and practice.

What is organizational behaviour?

Why did that happen?

It was a bad experience. You ordered a soft drink and a sandwich. The person who served you was abrupt and unpleasant, did not smile, ignored you, did not make eye contact, and continued their conversation with a colleague instead of asking if you wanted anything else. They slapped your change on the counter rather than put it in your hand, then turned away. You have used this café before, but you have never been treated so rudely. You leave feeling angry, deciding never to return.

How can you explain the unusual behaviour of the person who served you?

Organizational behaviour the study of the structure and management of organizations, their environments, and the actions and interactions of their individual members and groups.

Let's put it this way: if you have a limited understanding of organizational behaviour, then you have a limited understanding of one of the main sets of forces that affect you personally, that influence the society and culture in which you live, and which shape the world around you. Organizations affect everything that you do – sleeping, waking, dressing, eating, travelling, working, relaxing, studying – everything. This chapter explores how we can explain the behaviour of people in organizations. First, let's define what organizational behaviour means.

The definition of a field of study defines the issues, questions and problems that it explores. Organizational behaviour covers environmental (macro) issues and group and individual (micro) factors (Heath and Sitkin, 2001). We live in an organized world. Look at your clothes, phone, food, residence, iPad – we are affected in many ways by organizations of different kinds.

Table 1.1: The top six in 2015

Organization (country)	Number of employees (million)
Walmart (US)	2.10
McDonald's	1.90
Sinopec (China)	1.02
Hon Hai Precision Industry (Taiwan)	1.20
G4S (UK)	0.62
United States Postal Service (US)	0.60

Some organizations are large and powerful. Table 1.1 lists the six largest private sector organizations in the world in 2015, in terms of number of employees (www.Wikipedia.org). Some public sector organizations are also big employers. For example, in 2015 the US Department of Defense had 3.2 million employees; the Chinese People's Liberation Army 2.3 million; the UK National Health Service 1.7 million; the Indian Railways had 1.4 million. The study of organizational behaviour thus has direct practical implications for those who work in, manage, seek to subvert, or interact in other ways with organizations, whether they are small and local, or large and international.

The term organizational behaviour was first used by Fritz Roethlisberger in the late 1950s, because it suggested a wider scope than human relations (Wood, 1995). The term behavioural sciences was first used to describe a Ford Foundation research programme at Harvard in 1950, and in 1957 the Human Relations Group at Harvard (previously the

leak (or 'kick') were missed. Kicks must be detected and controlled in order to prevent blowouts. By the time the *Deepwater Horizon* crew realized that they were dealing with a kick, it was too late for the blowout preventer to stop an explosion. Oil was already in the riser pipe, and heading for the surface.

To create this disaster, eight factors had combined, all involving aspects of management.

1. Leadership

There was conflict between managers and confusion about responsibilities. After a BP reorganization in April 2010, engineering and operations had separate reporting structures. This replaced a project-based approach in which all well staff reported to the same manager.

2. Communication

Those making decisions about one aspect of the well did not always communicate critical information to others making related decisions. The different companies on the rig did not share information with each other. The BP engineering team was aware of the technical risks, but did not communicate these fully to their own employees or to contractor personnel.

3. Procedures

BP did not have clear procedures for handling the problems that arose. The last-minute redesign of procedures in response to events caused confusion on the rig. It would have been more appropriate to stop operations temporarily to catch up.

4. Training and supervision

BP and Transocean had inadequate personnel training, supervision and support. Some staff were posted to the rig without prior assessment of their capabilities. Individuals made critical decisions without supervisory checks. BP did not train staff to conduct and interpret pressure test results. Transocean did not train staff in kick monitoring and emergency response.

5. Contractor management

Subcontracting was common industry practice, but with the potential for miscommunication and misunderstanding. In this case, information about test results and technical analyses did not always find its way to the right person. BP's supervision of contractors was weak, and contractors did not feel able to challenge BP staff decisions, deferring to their expertise.

6. Use of technology

The blowout preventer may have failed, in part, due to poor maintenance. Drilling techniques were much more sophisticated than the technology required to guard against blowouts. Well-monitoring data displays relied on the right person looking at the right data at the right time.

7. Risk management

BP and Transocean did not have adequate risk assessment and management procedures. Decisions were biased towards saving costs and time. The Macondo well risk register focused on the impact of risks on time and cost, and did not consider safety.

8. Regulation

The Minerals Management Service was responsible for safety and environmental protection, and for maximizing revenues from leases and royalties – competing goals. MMS revenues for 2008 were $23 billion. Regulation had not kept pace with offshore drilling technology development. MMS lacked the power to counter resistance to regulatory oversight, and staff lacked the training and experience to evaluate the risks of a project like *Deepwater Horizon*.

Organizational and management failures caused this disaster. This pattern can be seen in other serious events, accidents and catastrophes in different sectors.

Organizations can mean different things to those who use them and who work in them, because they are significant personal and social sources of:

- money, physical resources, other rewards;
- meaning, relevance, purpose, identity;
- order and stability;
- security, support and protection;
- status, prestige, self-esteem, self-confidence;
- power, authority, control.

Organizational dilemma how to reconcile inconsistency between individual needs and aspirations, and the collective purpose of the organization.

The goals pursued by individual members of an organization can be different from the purpose of their collective activity. This creates an **organizational dilemma** – how to design organizations that will achieve overall objectives, while also meeting the needs of those who work for them. One study asked manufacturing workers whether or not they agreed that managers and employees shared the same interests in their businesses (Noon and Blyton, 2007). The proportion of workers who agreed were 24 per cent in The Netherlands, 36 per cent in Britain and 42 per cent in Norway.

Organizations are social arrangements in which people control resources to produce goods and services efficiently. However, organizations are also political systems in which some individuals exert control over others. Power to define the collective purposes of organizations is not evenly distributed. One of the main mechanisms of organizational control is the hierarchy of authority. It is widely accepted (often with reluctance) that managers have the right to make the decisions while lower-level employees are obliged to comply, or leave.

Health service management dilemmas

The UK National Health Service (NHS) held a boat race against a Japanese crew. After Japan won by a mile, a working party found the winners had eight people rowing and one steering, while the NHS had eight steering and one rowing. So the NHS spent £5 million on consultants, forming a restructured crew of four assistant steering managers, three deputy managers and a director of steering services. The rower was then given an incentive to row harder. They held another race and lost by two miles, so the NHS fired the rower for poor performance, sold the boat and used the proceeds to pay a bonus to the director of steering services.

From Patrick Kidd (2014, p.13)
© The Times, 30 December 2014, reproduced with permission.

A concern with performance leads to rules and procedures, and to jobs that are simple and repetitive. This makes it easier to plan, organize and coordinate the efforts of large numbers of people. This efficiency drive, however, conflicts with the desire for freedom of expression, autonomy, creativity and self-development. It is difficult to design organizations that use resources efficiently, and are also effective in developing human potential. Many of the 'human' problems of organizations arise from conflicts between individual needs, and the constraints imposed in the interests of collective purpose. Attempts to control and coordinate human behaviour are thus often self-defeating.

That is a pessimistic view. Organizations are social arrangements, designed by people who can also change them. Organizations can be repressive and stifling, but with thoughtful design, they can also provide opportunities for self-fulfilment and expression.

How eighteenth century pirates solved the organizational dilemma

Martin Parker (2012) notes that life on navy and merchant ships in the early eighteenth century was vicious and unsanitary. Sailors had poor food, their pay was low, and they enjoyed highly unequal shares of the treasure. Discipline was cruel, violent, and often sadistic. A voyage could be regarded as successful if half the crew survived.

Source: www.CartoonStock.com

Pirates, on the other hand, developed a radical alternative approach to work organization based on more democratic and egalitarian principles.

On pirate ships, written 'articles' gave each man a vote, and most had an equal share of the stores and the plunder, apart from senior officers. Crew members could earn extra rewards for joining boarding parties, and pirate vessels operated injury compensation schemes. There were clear rules, with graded punishments for theft, desertion and fighting on board: 'being set ashore somewhere where hardships would ensue, slitting the nose and ears, a slow death by marooning on an island or a quick death on board' (p.42). Weapons were to be kept clean, and no boys or women were allowed on board. In addition, authority depended on consent. Pirate captains had to win a vote by their crew for their position, and only had absolute authority during a conflict. Contrary to the popular image, pirate ships often cooperated with each other in pursuit of a prize. For seafarers, therefore, piracy could be a more attractive alternative than the legitimate alternatives. While naval and merchant ships often had to 'press' their crew members into service by force, many pirates were ex-merchant seamen.

Parker thus argues that the boundaries between legitimate and illegal organizations and activities (including outlaws and the mafia) are not always as clear as they appear to be. Eighteenth century pirates solved the organizational dilemma, and could meet both individual and organizational needs more effectively than the 'legal' competition.

A field map of the organizational behaviour terrain

How can behaviour in organizations be explained? To answer this question systematically, we will first develop a 'field map' of the terrain (see Figure 1.1). Organizations do not operate in a vacuum, but are influenced by their wider context, represented by the outer box on the field map. One approach to understanding context is 'PESTLE analysis', which explores the **P**olitical, **E**conomic, **S**ocial, **T**echnological, **L**egal and **E**cological issues affecting the organization and its members.

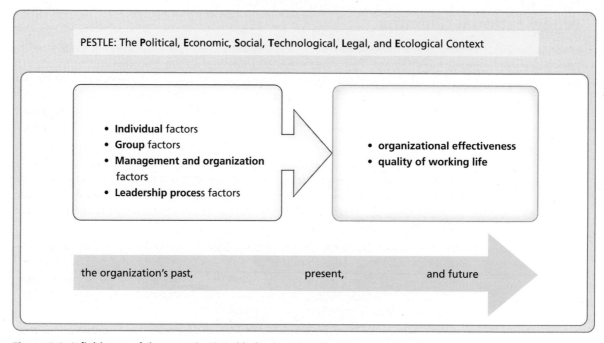

PESTLE: The **P**olitical, **E**conomic, **S**ocial, **T**echnological, **L**egal, and **E**cological Context

- **Individual** factors
- **Group** factors
- **Management and organization** factors
- **Leadership process** factors

- **organizational effectiveness**
- **quality of working life**

the organization's past,   present,   and future

Figure 1.1: A field map of the organizational behaviour terrain

The map explains two sets of outcomes: organizational effectiveness, and quality of working life. There are four sets of factors which can explain those outcomes. These concern individual, group, structural and management process factors. Finally, organizations are not static. Organizations and their members have plans for the future which influence actions today. Past events also shape current perceptions and actions. We need to explain behaviours with reference to their location in time.

As well as helping to explain organizational behaviour, this model is an overview and a guide to the content of this book. You will find this model again at the beginning of each Part of the book, to help you to locate each topic in the context of the subject as a whole.

STOP AND THINK   The atmosphere just isn't the same any more, and the place is losing customers. Staff in the restaurant or bar that you use are less helpful and friendly than they once were. The quality of service that you receive has fallen sharply. Why?

Use the field map in Figure 1.1 to find possible explanations for this poor performance. Can you blame the context, technology, individuals, teamworking, organizational structure, changes to the culture, management style? Maybe the cause lies with a combination of these factors?

Remember the unhelpful person in your café? In situations like these, we often assume that the person is to blame, and we overlook the context in which they work. This tendency to blame the individual is known as the fundamental attribution error, a term first discussed by Lee Ross (1977).

Fundamental attribution error
the tendency to emphasize explanations of the behaviour of others based on their personality or disposition, and to overlook the influence of wider contextual influences.

In some circumstances, the individual may be to blame, but not always. If we are not careful, the fundamental attribution error leads to false explanations for the behaviour of others. We must also be aware of how the social and organizational context can affect behaviour, and the influence of unseen and less obvious factors. To help overcome this attribution bias, Figure 1.1 includes individual factors, and suggests other possible explanations for the behaviour of our shop assistant.

- *Context factors (PESTLE)*: Maybe the store is facing competition, sales have collapsed, the store is closing next month, and the loyal shop assistant is bitter about being made redundant (economic factors). Perhaps closure is threatened because the local population is falling, and reducing sales (social issues).

- *Individual factors*: Maybe the shop assistant is not coping with the demands of the job because training has not been provided (learning deficit). Maybe this assistant is not suited to work that involves interaction with a demanding public (personality traits). Or perhaps the shop assistant finds the job boring and lacks challenge (motivation problem).

- *Group factors*: Maybe the employees in this unit have not formed a cohesive team (group formation issues). Maybe this shop assistant is excluded from the group (a newcomer, perhaps) and is unhappy (group structure problems). The informal norm for dealing with awkward customers like you is to be awkward in return, and this assistant is just 'playing by the rules' (group norms).

- *Structural factors*: Perhaps the organization is bureaucratic and slow, and our assistant is anxiously waiting for a long-standing issue to be resolved (hierarchy problems). Maybe there is concern about the way in which work is allocated (work design problems). Perhaps the unit manager has to refer problems to a regional boss (decision-making issues), who doesn't understand local issues.

- *Management process factors*: Maybe the autocratic unit manager has annoyed our shop assistant (inappropriate leadership style), or the assistant is suffering 'initiative fatigue' following organizational changes (change problems). Perhaps the assistant feels that management has made decisions without consulting employees who have useful information and ideas (management decision-making problems).

These are just some examples; maybe you can think of other contextual, individual, group, structural and management process factors. This list of possible causes for your bad experience illustrates a number of features of explanations of organizational behaviour.

First, we almost always need to look beyond the person, and consider factors at different levels of analysis: individual, group, organization, management, the wider context.

Second, it is tempting to look for the single main cause of behaviour. However, behaviour can be influenced by many factors which in combination, and over time, contribute to organizational effectiveness and the experience of work.

Third, while it is easy to address these factors separately, in practice they are often linked. Our employee's damaging behaviour could be the result of falling sales which jeopardize job security (context), and encourage an autocratic supervisory style (management), leading to changes in working practices (process), which affect existing jobs and lines of reporting (structure) and team memberships (group), resulting in increased anxiety and reduced job satisfaction (individual). These links are not shown in Figure 1.1 because they can become complex (and would make the diagram untidy).

Organizational effectiveness
a multi-dimensional concept defined differently by different stakeholders, including a range of quantitative and qualitative measures.

Fourth, we need to consider the factors that we want to explain. The term organizational effectiveness is controversial, because different stakeholders have different ideas about what counts as 'effective'. A stakeholder is anyone with an interest, or stake, in the organization.

STOP AND THINK Consider the institution in which you are currently studying. List the internal and external stakeholders. Identify how you think each stakeholder would define organizational effectiveness for this institution. Why the differences?

Balanced scorecard an approach to defining organizational effectiveness using a combination of quantitative and qualitative measures to assess performance.

Quality of working life an individual's overall assessment of satisfaction with their job, working conditions, pay, colleagues, management style, organizational culture, work–life balance, and training, development and career opportunities.

Organizational effectiveness can be defined in different ways. For commercial companies, effectiveness often means 'profit', but this raises other issues. First, timescale is important, as improving short-term profits can damage future performance. Second, some organizations forgo profit in order to increase market share, or to secure survival and growth. Shareholders want a return on investment, customers want quality products or services at reasonable prices, managers want high-flying careers, employees want decent pay, good working conditions, job security, and development and promotion opportunities. Environmental groups want to protect wildlife, reduce carbon dioxide emissions and other pollution, reduce traffic and noise levels, and so on.

One approach to establishing organizational effectiveness is the balanced scorecard. This involves determining a range of quantitative and qualitative performance measures, such as shareholder value, internal efficiencies, employee development, and environmental concerns.

The phrase quality of working life has similar problems, as we each have different needs and expectations. Quality of working life is linked to organizational effectiveness, and also to most of the other factors on the left-hand side of our map. It is difficult to talk about quality of working life without considering motivation, teamwork, organizational design, development and change, human resource policies and practices, and management style.

What kind of model is this? The 'outputs' overlap with the 'inputs', and the causal arrow runs in both directions. High motivation and group cohesiveness lead to organizational effectiveness, but high performance can increase motivation and teamwork. The 'outputs' can influence the 'inputs'. Can an 'effect' influence a 'cause'? Logically, this is the wrong way around.

Home viewing

Management at the Belgian manufacturing company Solwal need to cut costs due to competition from Asia. This is the background to the movie *Two Days, One Night* (2014, directors Jean-Pierre and Luc Dardenne) which reveals some of the consequences of the global financial crisis. Sandra Bya (played by Marion Cottilard) has been off work, suffering from depression. During her absence, Mr Dumont, the senior manager, decides that in Sandra's section they need only 16 workers and not 17. He calculates that the company can either pay the €1,000 annual bonuses for 16 employees, or cancel the bonuses and Sandra (the 17th employee) stays. The staff vote 13 to 3 in favour of their bonuses. Sandra learns about this on the Friday before returning to work. However, one of Sandra's colleagues persuades Dumont to hold another ballot on Monday morning. Sandra is married with two children, and badly needs her job. Her husband persuades her to speak to the 13 colleagues who voted for the bonuses, to ask them to change their minds. She has only two days in which to do this. Sandra soon discovers that her colleagues have financial problems of their own.

How do you feel about Dumont's decision to let his employees decide whether to keep their bonuses, or to keep Sandra? At the end of the movie, how do you feel about Dumont's proposal for giving Sandra her job back? Is it inevitable that, in a financial crisis, organizational and individual needs cannot both be satisfied? What other steps could management have taken in these circumstances?

The problem with social science

What can social science offer to organizational behaviour? The contribution of social science to the sum of human knowledge in general is often regarded with scepticism. The natural sciences do not have this problem. What is the problem with social science?

We can put people on the moon, deliver movies to your computer, send pictures to mobile phones on which you can watch television, genetically engineer disease-resistant crops, perform 'keyhole' surgery, and so on. Natural science has also given us technologies with which we can do enormous damage. Textbooks in electrical engineering, naval architecture, quantum mechanics and cardio-vascular surgery tell the reader how things work, how they go wrong and how to fix them. Students from these disciplines often find psychology, sociology and organizational behaviour disappointing because these subjects do not always offer clear practical guidance. Social science often raises more questions than it answers, and draws attention to debates, conflicts, ambiguities and paradoxes, which are left unresolved. Natural science gives us material technology. Social science has not given us a convincing social engineering, of the kind which, say, would reduce car theft, or eliminate terrorism. Nevertheless, managers expect organizational research to resolve organizational problems.

The goals of science include description, explanation, prediction and control of events. These four goals represent increasing levels of sophistication. Social science, however, seems to struggle in all of these areas. Table 1.2 summarizes the problems.

STOP AND THINK   You discover that one of your instructors has a new way to improve student performance. She gives students poor grades for their first assignment, regardless of how good it is. This, she argues, stimulates higher levels of student performance in subsequent assignments.

This is an example of 'social engineering'. To what extent is this ethical?

Table 1.2: Goals of science and social science struggles

Goals of science	Practical implications	Social science struggles
Description	Measurement	Invisible and ambiguous variables People change over time
Explanation	Identify the time order of events Establish causal links between variables	Timing of events not always clear Cannot always see interactions
Prediction	Generalizing from one setting to another	Uniqueness, complexity and lack of comparability between settings
Control	Manipulation	Ethical and legal constraints

These 'struggles' only arise if we expect social science to copy natural science practices. If the study of people and organizations is a different kind of enterprise, then we need different procedures. Social science is just a different kind of science.

Description

Natural and social science differ in what they are attempting to describe. Natural science describes an objective reality. Social science describes (or documents) how people understand and interpret their circumstances. Objective reality is stable. People's perceptions change.

The first goal of science, however, is description, and to achieve this, social science has only three methods: observation, asking questions and studying documents. Documents can include blogs, emails and texts, websites, diaries, letters, company reports, committee minutes, or publications. Physicists and chemists, for example, use only one of these methods – observation. Metals, chemicals and interstellar objects do not respond well to interrogation, or send text messages, and do not publish autobiographies in the style that has become popular, for example, with corporate chief executives.

There are different modes of observation. The researcher can observe informal discussion in a cafeteria, join a selection interview panel, follow candidates through a training programme, or take a job with an organization in order to experience what it is like to work there. Our understanding of the management role, for example, is based largely on observation, but this has limitations. What can we say about someone's perceptions and motives just by observing them? We could shadow somebody for a day or two, and make guesses. Eventually we will need to ask them some questions.

How do we study phenomena that cannot be observed directly, such as learning (Chapter 5)? We do this through inference. As you read this text, we would like to think that you are learning about organizational behaviour. However, if we could open your head as you read, we would struggle to find 'the learning process' (neurophysiology has begun to understand memory processes). The term 'learning' is a label for an invisible (to a social scientist) activity whose existence we can assume.

Some changes must take place inside your head if learning is to occur. Neurophysiology can help to track down the processes involved, but it is not clear how an improved understanding of the neurology and biochemistry of learning would help us to design better job training programmes. The procedures for studying learning by inference are straightforward. We can examine your knowledge of this subject before you read this text, and repeat the test afterwards. If the second set of results is better than the first, then we can infer that learning has taken place. Your ability to perform a particular task has changed, and we can use that change to help us identify the conditions that caused it. In this way, we can study the effects of different inputs to the learning process – characteristics of the teachers, learners, physical facilities, and the time and other resources devoted to the process. We can study variations in methods, materials and timing. Our understanding of the learning process can thus develop systematically. From this knowledge, we can begin to suggest improvements.

STOP AND THINK The manager of a major high street retail store in your area has asked you, a researcher, to assess the level of job satisfaction among sales staff. You cannot speak to staff, because that would affect sales. Can you do this assessment by observation? What will you look for?

Questions can be asked in person in an interview, or through self-report questionnaires. The validity of responses, as a reflection of the 'truth', is questionable for at least three reasons:

First, our subjects may lie. People planning a robbery, or who resent the intrusion of a researcher, may give misleading replies. There are ways in which we can check the accuracy of what people tell us, but this is not always possible or convenient.

Second, our subjects may not know. The mental processes related to our motives typically operate without conscious effort. Most of us struggle through life without constantly asking 'why am I here?', and 'what am I doing?' The researcher gets the answers of which the person is aware, or which seem to be appropriate in the circumstances.

Third, our subjects may tell us what they think we want to hear. People rarely lie to researchers. They create problems by being helpful. Easier to give a simple answer than a complex history of intrigue and heartbreak. The socially acceptable answer is better than no answer at all. Researchers must be aware of the social context in which information is collected.

Explanation

A second goal of science is explanation. We can often infer that one event has caused another even when the variables are not observable. If your test score is higher after reading this text than before, and if you have not been studying other materials, then we can infer that this text has caused your score to improve. The sequence of events is not easily established. We might assume, for instance, that satisfaction leads to higher job performance. However, we also know that good performance makes people more satisfied. Which comes first? Which way does the causal arrow point?

The laws that govern human behaviour seem to be different from those that govern the behaviour of natural phenomena. Consider, for instance, the meteorological law, 'clouds mean rain'. This law holds good right around the planet. The cloud does not have to be told, either as a youngster or when it approaches hills, about the business of raining. Compare this situation with the social law, 'red means stop'. A society can choose to change this law, to 'blue means stop', because some people are red–green colour blind (and thus cause hideous accidents). The human driver can deliberately jump the red light, or have a lapse of concentration and pass the red light accidentally. Clouds cannot vote to change the laws that affect them, nor can they break these laws, or get them wrong by accident.

We are not born with pre-programmed behavioural guides, although it appears that we are equipped from birth to learn certain behaviours, such as language (Pinker, 2002). We have to learn the rules of our particular society at a given time. Different cultures have different rules about relatively trivial matters, such as how close people should stand to each other. We also have rules about how and when to shake hands and for how long the shake should last, about the styles of dress and address appropriate to different occasions, about relationships between superior and subordinate, between men and women, between elderly and young. Even across the cultures of Europe, and of the Pacific Rim, there are major differences in social rules, both between and within countries.

We cannot expect to discover laws governing human behaviour consistently across time and place. Social and cultural norms vary from country to country, and vary across subcultures in the same country. Our individual norms, attitudes and values also vary over time and with experience, and we are likely to answer a researcher's questions differently if approached a second time.

Prediction

A third goal of science is prediction. Social science can often explain events without being able to make precise predictions (Table 1.3). We may be able to predict the rate of suicide in a given society, or the incidence of stress-related disorders in an occupational group. However, we can rarely predict whether specific individuals will try to kill themselves, or suffer sleep and eating disorders. This problem is not critical. We are often more interested in the behaviour of groups than individuals, and more interested in tendencies and probabilities than in individual predictions and certainties.

There is a more fundamental problem. Researchers often communicate their findings to those who have been studied. Suppose you have never given much thought to the ultimate reality of human existence. One day, you read about an American psychologist, Abraham Maslow, who claims that we have a basic need for 'self-actualization', to develop our capabilities to their full potential. If this sounds like a good idea, and you act accordingly, then what he has said has become true, in your case. His claim has become true. This may be because he has given you a fresh view of human experience, or because he has given you a label to explain an aspect of your intellectual makeup.

Table 1.3: **We can explain – but we cannot confidently predict**

We can explain staff turnover in a supermarket in terms of the repetitive and boring nature of work	but we cannot predict which individual staff members will leave, or when they will choose to do so	**Individual** factors
We can explain the factors that contribute to group cohesiveness in an organization	but we cannot predict the level of cohesion and performance of particular groups	**Group** factors
We can explain why some types of organizational structure are more adaptable in the face of external change than others	but we cannot predict the performance improvements that will follow an organizational structure change	**Structure** factors
We can explain how different management styles encourage greater or lower levels of employee commitment and performance	but we cannot predict which managers will achieve the highest levels of commitment and performance in a given setting	**Management** factors

Some predictions are thus self-fulfilling. Simply saying that something will happen can either make it happen, or increase the likelihood of it happening. The statement from a government spokesperson that 'there is no need for motorists to start panic-buying petrol' will always trigger panic-buying by motorists, thus creating the fuel shortages that the statement was designed to avoid. Equally, some predictions are intentionally self-defeating. Many of the disastrous predictions of economists, about budget deficits and interest rate movements, for example, are designed to trigger action to prevent those prophecies from coming true. In an organization, one could predict that valuable employees will leave if a given management style continues, in the hope that this will lead to a change in style.

Control

A fourth goal of science is control, or the ability to change things. Social science and organizational research findings are often designed to encourage change. The natural scientist does not study the order of things in order to be critical, or to encourage that order to improve itself. It is hardly appropriate to evaluate, as good or bad, that gas expands when heated, or the number of components in a strand of DNA. Social scientists, on the other hand, are often motivated by a desire to change aspects of society and organizations. For that purpose, we need to understand how things currently work, and the strengths and weaknesses of those arrangements. Such understanding, therefore, is not necessarily a useful end in itself. Social science can be critical of the social and organizational order that it uncovers, because that order is only one of many that we are able to create.

As we said earlier, we do not have a social technology that enables us to manipulate other people. Perhaps we should be grateful for this. However, Table 1.4 identifies organizational interventions that are designed to control aspects of employee behaviour.

It is important to recognize that our judgements and our recommendations are based not only on evidence, but also on values. Social science has been criticized as 'ideology in disguise'. However, if one studies organizations in order to change and improve them, then we cannot escape that criticism. Our improvement is not necessarily your improvement.

Table 1.4: Interventions to control organizational behaviour

Organizational intervention	Attempts to control
Staff training and development programmes (Chapter 5, Learning)	Employee knowledge and skills
Psychometric assessments (Chapter 6, Personality)	The types of people employed
Employee communications (Chapter 7, Communication)	Employee understanding of and compliance with management-inspired goals
Job redesign (Chapter 9, Motivation)	employee motivation, commitment and performance
Teambuilding (Part 3)	Levels of team cohesion and performance
Reorganization – structure change (Part 4)	Ability of the organizational to respond to external turbulence
Organizational change (Chapter 19, Change)	Speed of change and reduction of conflict and resistance
Organizational culture change (Chapter 4, Culture)	Values, attitudes, beliefs and goals shared by management and employees
Human resource management (Chapter 1, Explaining OB)	high employee performance
Leadership style (Chapter 18, Leadership)	Commitment to an overarching vision

STOP AND THINK

You are a management consultant studying repetitive clerical work in an insurance company. The staff are bored, unhappy and demotivated. Your study shows how work redesign can improve things by giving them variety and autonomy in their jobs. However, managers claim that their work system is cost-effective, and produces the service which customers want, while allowing them to keep their staff under control.

As the management consultant with the evidence, how would you resolve this disagreement, and persuade management to implement your recommendations? What do you think are your chances of being successful?

Explaining organizational behaviour

Positivism a perspective which assumes that the world can be understood in terms of causal relationships between observable and measurable variables, and that these relationships can be studied objectively using controlled experiments.

We need to look again at how social science tries to explain things. The natural sciences are based on an approach known as **positivism**. The term 'scientific' is often used to mean a positivist approach that is objective and rigorous, using observations and experiments to find universal relationships.

Heat a bar of metal, and it expands. Eat more salt, and your blood pressure rises. The factor that causes a change is the *independent* variable. The effect to which it leads is the *dependent* variable. These are also known as the *causal* and *outcome* variables. Salt is the independent (causal) variable; blood pressure is the dependent (outcome) variable. Those variables can be measured, and those causal relationships are universal and unchanging. To measure something, you need an **operational definition** – a method for quantifying the variable.

The operationalization of temperature and blood pressure involves thermometers and monitors. Questionnaires are often used as operational definitions of job satisfaction and

Operational definition the method used to measure the incidence of a variable in practice.

Variance theory an approach to explaining organizational behaviour based on universal relationships between independent and dependent variables which can be defined and measured precisely.

Constructivism a perspective which argues that our social and organizational worlds have no ultimate objective truth or reality, but are instead determined by our shared experiences, meanings, and interpretations.

management style. With those measures, we can answer questions about the effects of different management styles on employee satisfaction, and job performance. That assumes that human behaviour can be explained with the methods used to study natural phenomena.

Our field map of the organizational behaviour terrain (Figure 1.1) can thus be read as a 'cause and effect' explanation. Manipulate the independent variables on the left, and you alter the values of the dependent variables – organizational effectiveness and quality of working life – on the right. This kind of explanation is known as a **variance theory**: do variations in management style cause varying levels of job satisfaction; do varying personality traits cause variations in levels of job performance?

Although positivism and variance theory have been successful in the natural sciences, many social scientists argue that this approach does not work in the social and organizational world. Positivism assumes that there is an objective world 'out there' which can be observed, defined and measured. In contrast, **constructivism** argues that many aspects of that so-called objective reality are defined by us. 'Reality' depends on how we see it, on how we *socially construct* it (Berger and Luckmann, 1966).

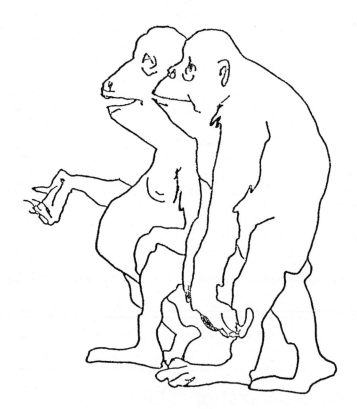

. . . and then he raises the issue of, 'how many angels can dance on the head of a pin?', and I say, you haven't operationalized the question sufficiently – are you talking about classical ballet, jazz, the two-step, country swing . . .

What does it mean to say that 'reality is *socially constructed*'? Suppose you want to measure aggression at student functions. As a positivist, you first have to decide what counts as 'aggression'. Your *operational definition* could be an 'aggressiveness index' which you use to count observable behaviours such as raised and angry voices, physical contact, pain and injury, and damage to property. You might find, for example, that some functions are more aggressive than others, that aggressiveness is higher later in the evening, that female students are just as aggressive as male students, and so on.

Now, suppose you observe one male student shout at and punch another on the arm. The second student responds angrily and pushes the first student away. A table is shaken, drinks are spilled, glasses are broken. Your 'aggressiveness index' just increased by five or six points. In talking to the students, however, they describe their actions as friendly, fun, playful; a typical Friday night. The other members of their group agree. This *socially constructed* version of events, for actors and observers, actually involves friendship. Your operational definition is misleading. What matters is how those involved interpret their own actions. Of course, in a different social or organizational setting, raised voices, physical violence and damaged property will be understood as aggression. The interpretation of those behaviours is not consistent from one context to another. Temperatures of 45 degrees Celsius, or blood pressure readings of 180 over 90, will always be 'high', wherever you are.

Constructivism argues that we are *self-interpreting* beings. We attach meaning and purpose to what we do. Chemical substances and metal bars do not attach meaning to their behaviour, nor do they give interviews or fill out questionnaires. So, human behaviour cannot be studied using methods that apply to natural objects and events. As a constructivist, our starting point must lie with how others understand, interpret and define their own actions, and not with definitions that we create for them. The organizational behaviour variables in which we are interested are going to mean different things, to different people, at different times, and in different places.

Variance theory, therefore, is not going to get us very far. To understand organizational issues, we have to use process theory (Mohr, 1982; Langley et al., 2013).

Process theory shows how a sequence of events, in a given context, lead to the outcomes in which we are interested. Those outcomes could concern individual satisfaction, the effectiveness of change, organizational performance, the resolution of conflict. Outcomes are often generated by *combinations* of factors *interacting* with each other. If salt raises your blood pressure, half that salt will reduce the pressure by a measurable amount. If leadership is necessary for the success of organizational change, it does not make sense to consider the implications of half that leadership.

The Macondo Well blowout described earlier is a good example of a process explanation. This disaster was caused by a combination of factors over time: confused leadership structures, poor communication, lack of procedures, mismanagement of contractors, poor maintenance and use of technology, inadequate risk management, an ineffective regulatory system. No single factor was to blame as they all contributed to the sequence of disastrous events and to the tragic outcomes.

Process theory is helpful when we want to understand:

- complex and messy social and organizational problems;
- situations that are affected by a large number of different factors which are difficult to define and measure, and which change with time and context;
- factors which do not have independent effects, but combine and interact with each other;
- sequences of events where the start and end points are not well defined;
- interesting outcomes which are themselves difficult to define and measure.

Variance theory offers *definitive* explanations where the links between causes and outcomes do not change. The values of the causal variables always predict the values of the outcome variables (this temperature, that volume). Process theories offer *probabilistic* explanations. We can say that combinations of factors are more or less likely to generate the outcomes of interest, but not always.

Process theory
an approach to explaining organizational behaviour based on narratives which show how several factors, combining and interacting over time in a particular context, are likely to produce the outcomes of interest.

STOP AND THINK

Hospital managers are concerned that patients with serious conditions wait too long in the emergency department before they are diagnosed and treated.

How would a positivist approach this problem?

How would a constructivist approach this problem?

The positivist wants to observe and record patient numbers, waiting and treatment times, staffing levels, bed numbers, the availability of resources. The constructivist wants to talk to doctors, nurses and ambulance crews, to find out how they feel about working here and what they think the problems are. Which approach is more likely to resolve the waiting times problem, and why?

Table 1.5 summarizes the contrasting perspectives on which explanations for organizational behaviour can be based. What are the implications for our field map of organizational behaviour? Seen from a *positivist* perspective, that model encourages the search for consistent causal links: this organizational structure will improve effectiveness and adaptability, that approach to job design will enhance performance and quality of working life. The positivist is looking for method, for technique, for universal solutions to organizational problems.

Table 1.5: Positivism versus constructivism

	Perspective	
	Positivism	**Constructivism**
Description	Accepts information that can be observed and quantified consistently	Accepts qualitative information, and relies on inference; studies local meanings and interpretations
Explanation	Uses variance theories. Relies mainly on observable quantitative data and measurements. Seeks universal laws based on links between independent and dependent variables	Uses process theories. Relies mainly on qualitative data and self-interpretations. Develops explanatory narratives based on factors combining and interacting over time and in context
Prediction	Based on knowledge of stable and consistent relationships between variables. Predictions are deterministic	Based on shared understanding and awareness of multiple social and organizational realities. Predictions are probabilistic
Control	Aims to shape behaviour and achieve desired outcomes by manipulating explanatory variables	Aims at social and organizational change through stimulating critical self-awareness

Seen from a *constructivist* perspective, our field map suggests other questions: how do we define and understand the term 'organization', and what does 'effectiveness' mean to different stakeholders? What kind of work experiences are different individuals looking for, and how do they respond to their experience, and why? The constructivist argues that explanations may apply only to a small part of the social and organizational world, and that explanations may have to change as the context changes, with time. Constructivists seek to trigger new ideas and change by stimulating self-critical awareness.

This field map, therefore, does not set out causal links across the organizational behaviour terrain. This is just one way to picture a complex subject quickly and simply. We hope that it also gives you a useful overview, and helps you to organize the material in this text. It also serves as a reminder to consider the range of interacting factors that may explain what we observe, and that it is often helpful to look beyond what may appear to be the main and obvious explanations.

Research and practice: evidence-based management

Do managers use organizational research evidence to inform their plans and decision making? Given the problems facing social science in the areas of prediction and control, do the kinds of evidence and explanation that social science produces help managers in their task? Is research useful when applied to real world organizations and problems?

When the late Peter Drucker was asked why managers fall for bad advice and fail to use sound evidence, he didn't mince words. 'Thinking is very hard work. And management fashions are a wonderful substitute for thinking' (Pfeffer and Sutton, 2006, p.219).

Sara Rynes et al. (2014, p.317) admit that 'when students or practitioners look to the research base to answer practical questions, they often find that much of our research evidence isn't all that impressive'. There is a well-known gap between academic research and organizational practice, and it is not difficult to explain why. Researchers publish their work in academic journals. Most managers do not read much, and few read academic publications. Many researchers follow lines of enquiry that do not focus on the problems that organizations and their managers are facing. Research and practice also work on different timescales. A manager with a problem wants to solve it today; a researcher with a project could take two to three years to come up with some answers.

What does evidence-based management look like?

'Here is what evidence-based management looks like. Let's call this example, a true story, "Making Feedback People-Friendly". The executive director of a health care system with 20 rural clinics notes that their performance differs tremendously across the array of metrics used. This variability has nothing to do with patient mix or employee characteristics. After interviewing clinic members who complain about the sheer number of metrics for which they are accountable (200+ indicators sent monthly, comparing each clinic to the 19 others), the director recalls a principle from a long-ago course in psychology: human decision makers can only process a limited amount of information at any one time. With input from clinic staff,

a redesigned feedback system takes shape. The new system uses three performance categories – care quality, cost, and employee satisfaction – and provides a summary measure for each of the three. Over the next year, through provision of feedback in a more interpretable form, the health system's performance improves across the board, with low-performing units showing the greatest improvement' (from Rousseau, 2006, p.256).

In this example a *principle* (we can process only a limited amount of information) is translated into *practice* (give feedback on a small set of critical performance metrics using terms people understand).

Basing decisions on evidence should be better than relying on habit, bias and false assumptions. Jeffrey Pfeffer and Robert Sutton (2006) are particularly critical of 'pay for performance' schemes used to motivate people to higher levels of achievement. For example, the UK government has considered paying hospital surgeons according to their success in their operating theatres. Schemes like this assume that (a) job performance depends on motivation, (b) staff are motivated by money, (c) performance can be measured in a consistent and reliable way, and (d) employees work alone, and are not dependent on the contributions of others. These assumptions are all false. You may hate your job, but work harder in order to get a good reference when you leave. 'Performance' can have several aspects, some of which are subjective ('quality of care'). The emphasis on financial benefits overlooks the importance that most of us attach to intrinsic rewards and doing a good job. The surgeon in an operating theatre is heavily dependent on cooperation from many colleagues, all of whose efforts affect the patient's well-being. Paying some members of staff more than others is divisive if the scheme is seen as unfair, and that will lower everyone's performance.

Pfeffer and Sutton (2006) argue that, while pay for performance schemes are popular, there is no evidence that they work – except where our four assumptions are correct. There is evidence that these schemes actually lower performance. Managers aware of this evidence would avoid the costs of pay for performance schemes, and find better ways to motivate staff (see Chapter 9).

This argument, inspired by evidence-based medicine, has led to an **evidence-based management** movement. There is an Evidence-Based Management Collaborative, based at Carnegie Mellon University in America. EBMgt has a Wikipedia entry; check it out. EBMgt is a seductive idea. It uses the language of 'scientific evidence' and 'causally interpretable data'. It is attractive to researchers who want to influence practice, and is attractive to

Evidence-based management systematically using the best available research evidence to inform decisions about how to manage people and organizations.

managers looking for independent legitimation for their decisions and actions. (Evidence-based decision making is explored in more depth in Chapter 20.) But does it work as intended?

The similarities between medicine and management have been exaggerated. Medicine may advise with confidence to 'take pill, cure headache', but there are few such general solutions to organizational problems. There is no such thing as 'best practice' because this depends on local circumstances. Management interventions vary according to the context. Usually, a number of initiatives or solutions are implemented at the same time. It is rare to see one solution aimed at a single problem. Medical and managerial decisions differ in other significant respects, too; doctors treating headaches do not have to consider the impact of their decisions on organizational politics.

Best practice or next practice?

Susan Mohrman and Edward Lawler (2012, p.42) argue that:

> The major challenge for organizations today is navigating high levels of turbulence. They operate in dynamic environments, in societies where the aspirations and purposes of various stakeholders change over time. They have access to ever-increasing technological capabilities and information. A key organizational capability is the ability to adapt as context, opportunities, and challenges change.
>
> Evidence-based best practice means doing what worked in the past. To respond effectively to new challenges, we need to focus also on 'next practice'.

Christine Trank (2014) identifies two other problems with EBMgt. First, academic articles are designed to persuade. They are open to interpretation and are not simply neutral ways of sharing information. Different readers can come to different conclusions from the same evidence. Second, she criticizes the prescriptive 'what works' approach of EBMgt because 'It points towards a more technocratic than professional practice: one in which scientific research is translated to narrow action rules that are applied as routines, rather than one in which considerable autonomy is granted to knowledgeable practitioners using judgement and values to decide on action' (Trank, 2014, p.384). Those involved in professional work, she argues, must be able to use their judgement and to ignore 'action rules' based on what worked in the past, elsewhere, but which may not work here and now.

David Denyer and David Tranfield (2009, p.687) prefer the terms 'evidence-informed' and 'evidence-aware'. Rob Briner et al. (2009) note that research evidence is only one factor in most professional decisions, and may not be the most important – stakeholder preferences, context and judgement are also involved. If the term is used rigidly, however, EBMgt may *underestimate* the contributions of research to practice. For Alan Bryman and David Buchanan (2009, p.711) contributions include:

- developing new perspectives, concepts and ideas;
- suggesting how current arrangements could be redesigned;
- confronting social and organizational injustices;
- highlighting significant issues, events and processes;
- surfacing issues that might remain hidden;
- broadcasting voices that might remain silent;
- demonstrating the potential consequences of different actions.

Organizational research can therefore shape practice by suggesting, in creative and positive ways, how problems are understood in the first place, and how they are approached. While we can rarely say, 'here is the solution to your problem', we can often say, 'here is a way to understand your problem, and to develop solutions that will work in this context'.

Source: Cartoon Bank

*"I think you should be more
explicit here in step two."*

Human resource management: OB in action

**Human resource
management** the
function responsible for
establishing integrated
personnel policies to
support organizational
strategy.

One area where organizational behaviour (OB) contributes to evidence-based practice is **human resource management** (HRM – or personnel management). These subjects are often taught separately, with distinct topics and methods, but there is overlap. OB is concerned with micro- and macro-organizational issues, at individual, group, corporate and contextual levels of analysis. HRM develops and implements policies which enhance quality of working life, and encourage commitment, engagement, flexibility and high performance from employees in the context of corporate strategy.

Employment cycle
the sequence of stages
through which all
employees pass in each
working position they
hold, from recruitment
and selection, to
termination.

In designing those policies, HRM (or simply HR) can be seen as 'organizational behaviour in practice'. This applies to all stages of the **employment cycle** (Figure 1.2) – stages that you will encounter at various points in your career. At the end of this cycle, 'termination' can mean that the employee has resigned, retired, been made redundant, or been fired.

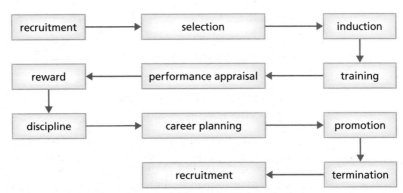

Figure 1.2: The employment cycle

To show the links between OB and HRM, Table 1.6 maps the OB topics covered in this text against areas of HRM practice. The basic model of HRM (Figure 1.3) says that, *if you* design your people policies in a particular way, *then* performance will improve. In terms of the concepts we introduced earlier, HRM policies are *independent variables*, and the quality of working life and organizational effectiveness are *dependent variables*. However, as we will see, a process perspective is more appropriate for explaining relationships between HR policies and organizational outcomes.

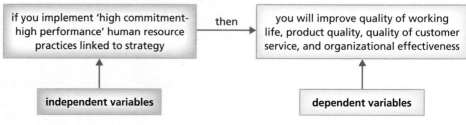

Figure 1.3: The basic model of HRM

Table 1.6: Human resource management and organizational behaviour

HRM functions	issues and activities	OB topics
Recruitment, selection, induction	Getting the right employees into the right jobs; recruiting from an increasingly diverse population; sensitivity to employment of women, ethnic minorities, the disabled, the elderly	Environmental turbulence; PESTLE analysis; personality assessment; communication; person perception; learning; new organizational forms
Training and development	Tension between individual and organizational responsibility; development as a recruitment and retention tool; coping with new technologies	Technology and job design; new organizational forms; learning; the learning organization; motivation; organizational change
Performance appraisal and reward	Annual appraisal; pay policy; fringe benefits; need to attract and retain staff; impact of teamwork on individual pay	Motivation; expectancy theory; equity theory; group influence on individual behaviour; teamworking
Managing conduct and discipline	Sexual harassment, racial abuse, drug abuse, alcohol abuse, health and safety; monitoring misconduct; using surveillance; formulation and communication of policies	Surveillance technology; learning; socialization; behaviour modification; organizational culture; managing conflict; management style
Participation and commitment	Involvement in decisions increases commitment; design of communications and participation mechanisms; managing organizational culture; tap ideas, release talent, encourage loyalty	Communication; motivation; Organizational structure; organizational culture; new forms of flexible organization; organizational change; leadership style
Organizational development and change	The personnel/human resource management role in facilitating development and change; flexible working practices	Organizational development and change; motivation and job design; organizational culture and structure; leadership

The Bath model of HRM

The Bath People and Performance Model (Purcell et al., 2003) is shown in Figure 1.4. This more detailed model focuses on the *processes* through which HR policies influence employee behaviour and performance. For people to perform beyond the minimum requirements of a job, three factors, Ability, Motivation and Opportunity (AMO), are necessary:

Factor	Employees must
Ability	have job skills and knowledge, including how to work well with others
Motivation	feel motivated to do the work, and to do it well
Opportunity	be able to use their skills, and contribute to team and organizational success

If one of these factors is weak or missing, then an individual's performance is likely to be poor. You may have the ability and the motivation, but if your supervisor prevents you from sharing ideas with colleagues and insists on 'standard procedure', then you will probably not 'go the extra mile'.

Discretionary behaviour freedom to decide how work is going to be performed; discretionary behaviour can be positive, such as putting in extra time and effort, or it can be negative, such as withholding information and cooperation.

Most employees have some choice over how, and how well, they perform their jobs. This is known as **discretionary behaviour**.

Sales assistants, for example, can decide to adopt a casual and unsympathetic tone, or they can make customers feel that their concerns have been handled in a competent and friendly way. Negative, uncaring behaviours are often a response to an employee's perception that the organization no longer cares about them. When one member of staff annoys a customer, and management finds out, then that employee has a problem. However, if staff collectively withdraw their positive discretionary behaviours, this affects the performance of the whole organization, and management have a problem.

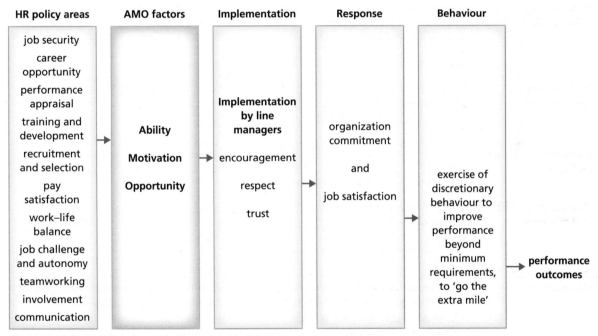

Figure 1.4: The Bath People and Performance Model

Source: adapted from Purcell et al. (2003, p.7). Reprinted by permission of the Chartered Institute of Personnel and Development.

What encourages employees to 'go the extra mile'? The answer lies in the model's *process theory*, which explains performance outcomes in terms of a combination of factors:

1. Basic HR policies are required to produce the Ability, Motivation and Opportunity that are key to any level of performance.

2. The line managers who 'bring these policies to life', have to communicate trust, respect and encouragement, in the way that they give directions, and respond to suggestions.

3. The combination of HR policies with line management behaviours must lead to feelings of job satisfaction and commitment, or the policies themselves will have little impact on behaviour and performance.

4. People tend to use positive discretionary behaviours when they experience pride in their organization, and want to stay there. Commitment and job satisfaction thus encourage employees to use discretionary behaviour to perform better.

How can HR help an organization to make money?

Ed Catmull was the co-founder of Pixar, the animation studio that made the *Toy Story* films. When Pixar began making *Toy Story 2*, Catmull was stunned to discover that his production staff refused to work on the sequel because the creatives had left them feeling 'disrespected and marginalized – like second-class citizens' on the first film. On the first film, everything – budgets, schedules and even ideas – had to be communicated through the appropriate line manager. 'If an animator wanted to talk to a modeller, he had to go through the proper channels', Catmull said. By abolishing that rule – and encouraging a free flow of information – Pixar improved morale. A simple HR fix facilitated the making of two more *Toy Story* films that between them generated well over £1 billion in box office revenues (from Mendoza, 2015, p.31).

While those policies must be in place, it is the *process* of implementing them that matters. The same policies, with inconsistent or half-hearted management, can lower commitment and satisfaction, and positive discretionary behaviours will be withdrawn. The policies central to this model are:

1. *Recruitment and selection* that is careful and sophisticated.
2. *Training and development* that equips employees for their job roles.
3. *Career opportunities.*
4. *Communication* that involves two-way information sharing.
5. *Involvement* of employees in management decision making.
6. *Teamworking.*
7. *Performance appraisal* and development.
8. *Pay* that is equitable and motivating.
9. *Job security.*
10. *Challenge and autonomy.*
11. *Work–life balance.*

This suggests that a *positive bundle* of policies which reinforce each other will have more impact than the sum of individual policies. On the other hand, a *deadly combination* of other policies can compete with and weaken each other: for example, financial rewards based on individual contributions, with appraisal and promotion systems which encourage teamworking.

Big data and the HR contribution

There is compelling evidence for the link between 'high performance' human resource management and organizational performance. On commercial grounds alone, surely this evidence has made an impact on practice? Stephen Wood et al. (2013) report the findings from a survey of 87,000 UK businesses. They found that adoption of high performance practices varied from sector to sector, and between larger and smaller employers. Innovative organizations, and those in competitive markets for premium quality goods and services were more likely to be adopters than those producing basic goods. In the UK, the use of all high performance practices declined between 2007 and 2011. These 'best practices' are not as common in practice as they are in textbooks.

That low impact of HR policies may now change, due to the contributions of 'big data' and 'data analytics'. The increasing 'digitization' of services and processes allows organizations to capture large amounts of information concerning those who use them. Every time you use a search engine, visit a website, make an online purchase, receive or make a call or send a text on your mobile phone, make a payment using your smartphone, transfer funds online, or drive a motor car equipped with a GPS system, the companies which provide these products and services collect information about you, your location, your movements, and your habits and preferences.

For example, Gerry George et al. (2014, p.321) note that 'a participant in a Formula 1 car race generates 20 gigabytes of data from the 150 sensors on the car that can help analyse the technical performance of its components, but also the driver reactions, pitstop delays, and communication between crew and driver that contribute to overall performance'. Before the computers and the internet were available, information of this kind was difficult, if not impossible, to capture, store, or analyse. It is also possible to analyse social behaviour patterns and networks, by mapping patterns of movements in the workplace, using sensors or badges, and the frequency of meeting room usage using remote sensors to record entry and exit patterns. Are the 'right' people communicating and coordinating their activities with each other? How is this reflected in performance? The information required to answer such questions, across a whole organization, is now available in near real time.

Big data information collected, often in real time, from sources such as internet clicks, mobile transactions, user-generated content, social media, sensor networks, sales queries, purchases.

The volume of information now available to commercial businesses and to government agencies is so vast that it is known as big data.

These large amounts of detailed information allow organizations to explore and to predict patterns and trends in individual and group behaviours, such as consumer choices, traffic patterns, or the outbreak and spread of diseases. To reveal those patterns and trends, statistically and visually, more powerful computational tools have been developed, known as data analytics.

Data analytics the use of powerful computational methods to reveal and to visualize patterns and trends in very large sets of data.

Data analytics are contributing to human resource management policies by providing objective information on which to base decisions and to solve HR-related problems. 'Human capital analytics' can provide insights into an organization's workforce, the HR policies and practices that support them, and workforce characteristics such as knowledge, skills and experience (Chartered Institute for Personnel and Development, 2015). Bruce Fecheyr-Lippens et al. (2015) describe how a leading healthcare organization used these methods to improve employee engagement, saving more than US$100 million. Analysis showed that pay discrepancies had caused job dissatisfaction which led to high staff turnover. Using predictive analytics, another company saved $20 million on bonuses while cutting staff turnover by half. Analysis showed that the main reasons why staff left concerned lack of investment in training and inadequate recognition. The expensive retention bonuses were having no impact. The consulting company McKinsey believed that staff defections were due to performance ratings or compensation. Analytics showed, however, that the key factors were a lack of mentoring and coaching. The 'flight risk' across the company fell by up to 40 per cent once coaching and mentoring were improved (Fecheyr-Lippens et al., 2015, p.2).

STOP AND THINK   There is compelling evidence to show that 'high performance' HR practices do work, and can improve financial returns. They have been widely publicized in management journals. So why do you think these management practices are not more widely used?

HR – business partners and working the pumps

The human resource function is traditionally the 'employees' champion', but it is also responsible for ensuring that employment practices fit the company's commercial strategy. These roles involve the use of 'hard' and 'soft' HR practices. Hard HR aims to control costs. Soft HR aims to maintain motivation and commitment. In a recession, the need to control costs can conflict with the staff desire for job security. How does HR work in this situation? Research from Ireland suggests some answers.

Hard HR	Soft HR
Cut pay and bonuses	Improve communications
Reduce headcount	Engage and involve staff
Cut working time	Training, talent management, Redeployment
Control recruitment and promotion	Larger pay cuts for higher paid staff
Measure productivity	In-sourcing
Reduce costs	Build motivation and commitment

Ireland has suffered the most serious economic crisis in its history, with a shrinking economy, rising unemployment, a high rate of company insolvencies, a fall in earnings in both private and public sectors, and the need for an internationally financed rescue package. The traditionally good partnership relations between Ireland's employers, trade unions and government collapsed in 2009 when they failed to agree on pay and economic priorities. How does the HR function operate in this situation?

A team from University College Dublin and Queen's University Belfast surveyed 450 managers and ran focus groups with a further 30 (Roche, 2011). They found that the influence of HR had grown, as companies relied more on the function's expertise. HR had developed a dual role, as 'business partners', helping senior managers with strategy, and 'working the pumps', helping line managers to implement changes.

Do hard times mean hard responses? Some companies, such as Dublin Airport Authority, introduced 'tiered' pay cuts that were deeper for staff on higher salaries, and seen to be fair. Most companies froze recruitment, wages and salaries. But the recession also put a priority on communications, to make sure that everyone understood the commercial situation. Employee engagement was also important as a source of ideas for responding to the crisis.

In other words, the HR response to recession involved *bundles* of hard and soft practices. The hard part of the bundle dealt with the short-term business agenda. But companies were also aware of the need to maintain employee motivation and commitment beyond the recession.

Vario Images GmbH & Co K.G./Alamy

RECAP

1. **Explain the importance of an understanding of organizational behaviour.**

   - Organizations influence almost every aspect of our daily lives in a multitude of ways.

   - If we eventually destroy this planet, the cause will not lie with technology or weaponry, but with ineffective organizations and management practices.

2. **Explain and illustrate the central dilemma of organizational design.**

   - The organizational dilemma concerns how to reconcile the inconsistency between individual needs and aspirations, and the collective purpose of the organization.

3. **Understand the need for explanations of behaviour in organizations that take account of combinations of, and relationships between factors at different levels of analysis.**

   - The study of organizational behaviour is multi-disciplinary, drawing in particular from psychology, social psychology, sociology, economics and political science.

   - Organizational behaviour involves a multi-level study of the external environment, and internal structure, functioning and performance of organizations, and the behaviour of groups and individuals.

   - Organizational effectiveness and quality of working life are explained by a combination of contextual, individual, group, structural, process and managerial factors.

   - In considering explanations of organizational behaviour, systemic thinking is required, avoiding explanations based on single causes, and considering a range of interrelated factors at different levels of analysis.

4. **Understand the difference between positivist and constructivist perspectives, and their respective implications for the study of organizational behaviour.**

   - A positivist perspective uses the same research methods and modes of explanation found in the natural sciences to study and understand organizational behaviour.

   - It is difficult to apply conventional scientific research methods to people, because of the 'reactive effects' which come into play when people know they are being studied.

   - A constructivist perspective assumes that, as we are self-defining creatures who attach meanings to our behaviour, social science is different from natural science.

   - A constructivist perspective believes that reality is not objective and 'out there', but is socially constructed.

   - A constructivist approach abandons scientific neutrality and seeks to stimulate social and organizational change by providing critical feedback and encouraging self-awareness.

5. **Understand the distinction between variance and process explanations of organizational behaviour.**

   - Variance theory explains organizational behaviour by identifying relationships between independent and dependent variables which can be defined and measured. Variance theories are often quantitative, and are based on a positivist perspective.

   - Process theory explains organizational behaviour using narratives which show how many factors produce outcomes by combining and interacting over time in a given context. Process theories can combine quantitative and qualitative dimensions, and can draw from positivist and constructivist traditions.

6. **Explain the development and limitations of evidence-based management.**

   - The concept of evidence-based management is popular, but the links between evidence and practice are complex; evidence can shape the ways in which problems are understood and approached, rather than offering specific solutions.

7. **Recognize the breadth of applications of organizational behaviour theory, and contributions to human resource management practice.**

   - The Bath model of human resource management argues that discretionary behaviour going beyond minimum requirements relies on having a combination of HR policies.

   - High performance work practices increase organizational profitability by decreasing employee turnover and improving productivity, but they are not widely adopted.

Revision

1. How is organizational behaviour defined? What topics does this subject cover? What is the practical relevance of organizational behaviour?

2. Describe an example of organizational *mis*behaviour, where you as a customer were treated badly. Suggest possible explanations for your treatment.

3. Hospital managers are concerned that patients with medical emergencies wait too long in the casualty department before they are diagnosed and treated. Which approach, positivist or constructivist, is more likely to resolve this problem, and why?

4. How can evidence, concepts, theories and models from organizational behaviour contribute effectively to organizational practice? Give examples.

Research assignment

Organizations affect all aspects of our lives. Buy a small notebook. Starting on Friday morning when you wake up, and ending on Sunday night when you go to bed, keep a list of all the organizations with which you have had contact over this period.

'Contact' includes, for example, a radio programme that you listen to at breakfast, a television station that you watch, the shops that you visit, the bank with whose card you make payments, the companies who run the buses, trains and taxis that you use. Which companies make the food and drinks that you consume? Also, which cinemas, bars, nightclubs, sports and social clubs did you visit? Religious and educational establishments? Medical facilities or emergency services that you have used (you never know)? Check your mail: which organizations have written to you? Do you have any utility or council tax bills to pay, and from which organizations do you get these services? Have you dealt with any charity requests? Have you checked your internet service provider and social networking organizations? What companies made your computer and mobile phone? Which companies designed the browser and other software that you are using? Whose advertisements have you watched?

Every time you do anything or go anywhere over these three days, stop and ask: which organizations am I interacting with in some way? – and record the names in your notebook. Then on Sunday night, or first thing Monday morning:

1. Total the number of organizations with which you have had contact on each of the three days – Friday, Saturday and Sunday.

2. Remove any duplicates and assign a number to each organization on your remaining list.

3. Devise a categorization scheme for your numbered organizations, including as many of them as possible; private/public, profit/charitable; goods/services. Use as many categories as you need. Some organizations may not 'fit' your scheme, but this is not a problem. How many organizations were in each category?

4. Consider what this list of organizations reveals about you and your lifestyle. Be prepared to share your conclusions with colleagues.

Springboard

Alan Bryman and Emma Bell (2015) *Business Research Methods* (4th edn). Oxford: Oxford University Press. Authoritative account of methods in management and organizational research.

Stella Cottrell (2011) *Critical Thinking Skills: Developing Effective Analysis and Argument* (2nd edn). Basingstoke: Palgrave Macmillan. Explores the nature and application of critical thinking.

Lyman W. Porter and Benjamin Schneider (2014) 'What was, what is, and what may be in OP/OB', *Annual Review of Organizational Psychology and Organizational Behavior*, 1: 1–21. Fascinating account of the history of organizational behaviour from the mid-twentieth century; reviews current status, with recommendations for the future. Available at www.annualreviews.org/journal/orgpsych

Shaun Tyson (2014) *Essentials of Human Resource Management* (6th edn). London: Routledge. Introductory text exploring how HR has developed new approaches in response to global recession, increasing competition, and the need for corporate agility.

 ## OB cinema

Antz (1998, directors Eric Darnell and Tim Johnson). This clip (7 minutes) begins immediately after the opening credits with Z (played by Woody Allen) saying 'All my life I've lived and worked in the big city' and ends with General Mandible (Gene Hackman) saying, 'Our very next stop Cutter'. This is the story of a neurotic worker ant, Z 4195, who wants to escape from his insignificant job in an authoritarian organization – the ant colony.

1. Using the field map of the organizational behaviour terrain as a guide, identify as many examples as you can of how individual, group, structural and managerial process factors influence organizational effectiveness and quality of working life in an ant colony.

2. What similar examples of factors affecting organizational effectiveness and quality of working life can you identify from organizations with which you are familiar?

 ## OB on the web

Search YouTube for 'The Corporation (6/23): The Pathology of Commerce'. This short clip (47 seconds) from the movie *The Corporation* is presented by Dr Robert Hare who is a consultant to the FBI on psychopaths. He argues that corporations have all the characteristics of psychopaths. Do you find his argument convincing? What are the implications of this viewpoint?

CHAPTER EXERCISES

1. Best job – worst job

Objectives
1. To help you to get to know each other.
2. To introduce you to the main sections of this organizational behaviour course.

Briefing
1. Pair up with another student. Interview each other to find out names, where you both come from, and what other courses you are currently taking.

2. In turn, introduce your partner to the other members of the class.

3. Two pairs now join up, and the group of four discuss:

What was the worst job that you had? What made it so bad?
What was the best job that you ever had? What made it so good?

4. Appoint a scribe, to record the recurring themes revealed in group members' stories about their best and worst jobs. Appoint also a group spokesperson.

5. The spokespersons then give presentations to the whole class, summarizing the recurring features of what made a job good or bad. As you listen, use this score sheet to record the frequency of occurrence of the various factors.

Factors affecting job experience		
Factors	**Examples**	**(✓) if mentioned**
Individual factors	Pay: reasonable or poor Job training: comprehensive or none Personality: clashes with other people Communication: frequent or little	
Group factors	Co-workers: helping or not contributing Conflict with co-workers Pressure to conform to group norms Staff not welded into a team	
Structural factors	Job tasks: boring or interesting Job responsibilities: clear or unclear Supervision: too close or little Rules: too many or insufficient guidance	
Management factors	Boss: considerate or autocratic Decisions: imposed or asked for opinions Disagreements with managers: often or few Changes: well or poorly implemented	

2. Management versus workers

Rate each of the following issues on this five-point scale, in terms of whether you think managers and workers have shared, partially shared, or separate interests (from Noon and Blyton, 2007, p.305):

share identical interests   1   2   3   4   5   have completely separate interests

- health and safety standards
- basic pay
- introducing new technology
- levels of overtime working
- designing interesting jobs
- bonus payments
- flexible working hours
- equal opportunities
- company share price
- developing new products and/or services
- redundancy

Explain why you rated each of these issues in the way that you did.

Employability assessment

With regard to your future employment prospects:

1. Identify up to three issues from this chapter that you found significant.
2. Relate these to the competencies in the employability matrix.
3. Decide what actions you need to take to maintain and/or develop those competencies under each of the four headings of the employability matrix.

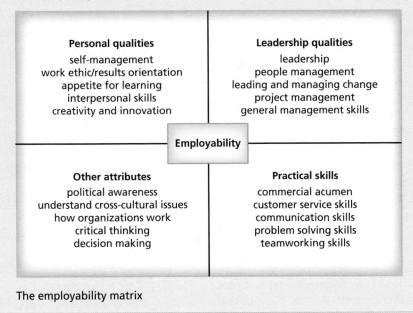

Personal qualities
self-management
work ethic/results orientation
appetite for learning
interpersonal skills
creativity and innovation

Leadership qualities
leadership
people management
leading and managing change
project management
general management skills

Employability

Other attributes
political awareness
understand cross-cultural issues
how organizations work
critical thinking
decision making

Practical skills
commercial acumen
customer service skills
communication skills
problem solving skills
teamworking skills

The employability matrix

References

Berger, P. and Luckmann, T. (1966) *The Social Construction of Reality*. Harmondsworth: Penguin Books.

Briner, R.B., Denyer, D. and Rousseau, D.M. (2009) 'Evidence-based management: concept cleanup time?', *Academy of Management Perspectives*, 23 (4): 19–32.

Bryman, A. and Buchanan, D.A. (2009) 'The present and futures of organizational research', in David A. Buchanan and Alan Bryman (eds), *The Sage Handbook of Organizational Research Methods*. London: Sage Publications, pp.705–18.

Chartered Institute for Personnel and Development (2015) *HR Analytics Factsheet*. London: Chartered Institute for Personnel and Development.

Clegg, S.R., Hardy, C., Lawrence, T. and Nord, W.R. (eds) (2006) *The Sage Handbook of Organization Studies* (2nd edn). London: Sage Publications.

Denyer, D. and Tranfield, D. (2009) 'Producing a systematic review', in David A. Buchanan and Alan Bryman (eds), *The Sage Handbook of Organizational Research Methods*. London: Sage Publications, pp.671–89.

Fecheyr-Lippens, B., Schaninger, B. and Tanner, K. (2015) 'Power to the new people analytics', *McKinsey Quarterly*, 1 (March): 61–63.

George, G., Haas, M. and Pentland, A.S. (2014) 'Big data and management', *Academy of Management Journal*, 57 (2): 321–26.

Heath, C. and Sitkin, S.B. (2001) 'Big-B versus Big-O: what is *organizational* about organizational behavior?', *Journal of Organizational Behavior*, 22 (1): 43–58.

Kidd, P. (2014) 'Ben's bum steer', *The Times*, 30 December, p.13

Langley, A., Smallman, C., Tsoukas, H. and Van de Ven, A.H. (2013) 'Process studies of change in organization and management: unveiling temporality, activity, and flow', *Academy of Management Journal*, 56 (1): 1–13.

Mendoza, M. (2015) 'What we're aiming to do is develop the iPod of moisturizers', *Work*, 4 (Spring): 26–31.

Mohr, L.B. (1982) *Explaining Organizational Behaviour: The Limits and Possibilities of Theory and Research.* San Francisco, CA: Jossey Bass.

Mohrman, S.A. and Lawler, E.E. (2012) 'Generating knowledge that drives change', *Academy of Management Perspectives*, 26 (1): 41–51.

Morgan, G. (2006) *Images of Organization* (3rd edn). London: Sage Publications.

National Commission on the BP Deepwater Horizon Oil Spill and Offshore Drilling (2011) *Deep Water: The Gulf Oil Disaster and the Future of Offshore Drilling.* Washington, DC: National Commission.

National Commission on the BP Deepwater Horizon Oil Spill and Offshore Drilling (2011) *Macondo: The Gulf Oil Disaster: Chief Counsel's Report.* Washington, DC: National Commission.

Noon, M. and Blyton, P. (2007) *The Realities of Work* (3rd edn). Basingstoke: Palgrave.

Oakley, D. (2015) 'Top executives' wage gap stretches to 150 times that of the average worker', *Financial Times*, 13/14 June, p.19.

Parker, M. (2012) *Alternative Business: Outlaws, Crime and Culture.* London and New York: Routledge.

Pfeffer, J. and Sutton, R.I. (2006) *Hard Facts, Dangerous Half-Truths, and Total Nonsense: Profiting from Evidence-Based Management.* Boston, MA: Harvard Business School Press.

Pinker, S. (2002) *The Blank Slate: The Modern Denial of Human Nature.* London: Allen Lane The Penguin Press.

Purcell, J., Kinnie, N., Hutchinson, S., Rayton, B. and Stuart, J. (2003) *Understanding the People and Performance Link: Unlocking the Black Box.* London: Chartered Institute of Personnel and Development.

Roche, B. (2011) 'HR's recession', *People Management*, July, pp.32–35.

Roethlisberger, F.J. (1977) *The Elusive Phenomenon: An Autobiographical Account of My Work in the Field of Organizational Behaviour at the Harvard Business School.* Boston, MA: Harvard University Press.

Ross, L. (1977) 'The intuitive psychologist and his shortcomings: distortions in the attribution process', in L. Berkowitz (ed.), *Advances in Experimental Social Psychology.* New York: Academic Press, pp.173–220.

Rousseau, D.M. (2006) 'Is there such a thing as "evidence-based management"?', *Academy of Management Review*, 31 (2): 256–69.

Rynes, S.L., Rousseau, D.M. and Barends, E. (2014) 'Change the world: teach evidence-based practice', *Academy of Management Learning and Education*, 13 (3): 305–21.

The Economist (2015) 'Lexington: capitalism in America', 27 June, p.44.

Trank, C.Q. (2014) 'Reading evidence-based management: the possibilities of interpretation', *Academy of Management Learning and Education*, 13 (3): 381–95.

Wood, J. (1995) 'Mastering management: organizational behaviour', *Financial Times Mastering Management Supplement (part 2 of 20)*.

Wood, S., Burridge, M., Green, W., Nolte, S., Rudloff, D. and Ni Luanaigh, A. (2013) *High Performance Working in the Employer Skills Surveys.* London: UK Commission for Employment and Skills.

Chapter 2 **Environment**

Key terms

environment

stakeholders

environmental uncertainty

environmental complexity

environmental dynamism

post-modern organization

environmental determinism

strategic choice

environmental scanning

globalization

PESTLE analysis

scenario planning

ethics

ethical stance

corporate social responsibility

Learning outcomes

When you have read this chapter, you should be able to define those key terms in your own words, and you should also be able to:

1. Understand the mutual interdependence between the organization and its environment.

2. Appreciate the strengths and limitations of PESTLE analysis of organizational environments.

3. Explain contemporary organizational responses to environmental turbulence.

4. Apply utilitarianism, theory of rights and theory of justice to assess whether or not management actions are ethical, and recognize the limitations of those criteria.

5. Understand the concept of corporate social responsibility, and the practical and ethical implications of this concept for organizational behaviour.

Why study an organization's environment?

The competitive environment today

Mark Frissora, chief executive of the car rental company Hertz, explains the impact of technology:

> I've never seen a more volatile business environment than the one we are operating in today. Technology and social media have completely changed the concept of competitive advantage. For a long time, companies could test and experiment; they could pilot a new concept or product, but they could keep it confidential. Now, whatever you do and say is almost instantly transferable to your competitors. Pricing strategies, marketing strategies, anything you pilot, even in a small market, immediately gets into your competitors' hands on a global basis. Unless you can patent something, the first-mover advantage, at least the way we learned about it in business school, lasts a very short period of time. What used to be a two-year competitive advantage is two minutes today. This is all due to the increased use of the Internet, social media, and other technology-based advances.

From Kirkland (2013, p.2)

Environment issues, trends and events outside the boundaries of the organization, which influence internal decisions and behaviours.

An organization must interact with the outside world, with its **environment**. That environment has become more volatile, uncertain, complex and ambiguous ('VUCA'). Organizational effectiveness and survival thus depend on monitoring and understanding these trends and developments, and on responding appropriately. The study of the organizational environment is critical.

The work of any organization – local café, city hospital, multinational motor car company – can be described in terms of 'import–transformation–export' processes. The car plant imports staff, materials, equipment and energy, which it transforms into vehicles, which are exported to customers through direct sales or a dealer network. Organizations are constantly involved in exchanges with their suppliers, customers, regulatory agencies and

Stakeholders anyone who is concerned with how an organization operates, and who will be affected by its decisions and actions.

other **stakeholders**, including their employees.

The environment for a motor car plant in the twenty-first century is complex. Energy costs are difficult to predict, and are sensitive to geopolitical events. Hybrid, electric and semi-autonomous vehicles are weakening demand for traditional cars. The engineering skills of car manufacturers have become less significant than electronic expertise, as engine management, safety, entertainment, communications, navigation and other driver-assist systems are computerized. Where in the world should motor car manufacturing plants be located? In 2015, the Japanese carmaker Toyota planned to build new plants in Mexico and China, having built one in Thailand in 2013 (Inagaki, 2015).

Cost competition has encouraged the use of 'lean manufacturing' methods, which affect work organization and quality of working life. The concern with pollution caused by internal combustion engines which burn petrol and diesel oil has encouraged the development of cleaner engines and electrically powered cars to reduce carbon emissions. The volume of traffic in many cities has driven local governments to consider road pricing, congestion charges and taxes to encourage the use of public transport. These are just some of the factors in the environment of a car plant, forcing constant adjustments to ways of thinking about the business. This means constantly reviewing strategy, organization structure, use of resources, management decisions, job design and working practices.

STOP AND THINK   What factors, trends or developments in the external environment of retail food stores – Sainsbury's, Tesco, Waitrose, Walmart – are affecting their behaviour and working practices?

What are the main factors in the environment of your college or university? How are those factors influencing management actions – and how are these affecting you?

The working world in 2020

What will work and management and organizations be like in 2020? A report from the Chartered Management Institute (2014, p.24) outlines the trends that are probably going to shape the future:

- Technology is transforming the ways in which organizations function. By 2020, everybody will have six different devices that will be connected to the internet, in addition to smart buildings and cars. There will be more connected devices on the planet than people.

- People skills will become even more important to managers who will lead teams whose members work flexibly, in a range of locations, connecting with each other online in flat and less hierarchical organization structures.

- With access to big data and data analytics (see Chapter 1), managers will have tools for analysing staff emails and social media profiles, allowing them to assess the intelligence and emotional stability of potential recruits, the engagement of existing staff, and to manage performance and retention more effectively.

- Diversity will become an even more important business imperative. Nearly 1 billion women are likely to join the global workforce over the next decade. By 2020, women are expected to take up 56 per cent of the net increase in jobs in the UK.

- The proportion of black, Asian and other ethnic minorities in the UK population will rise to 20 per cent by 2051.

- Many of the young people joining companies today will live to 100 years old and will be working until they are about 85.

What are the implications of these trends and developments? Managers need to develop a culture that prioritizes ethics, social responsibility, sustainability and flexibility.

Figure 2.1 outlines the argument of this chapter: 'the world out there' influences 'the world in here'.

Figure 2.1: External environment–organization links

Social science texts annoy readers from other disciplines by first presenting a model, and then showing that it is wrong, which we will do here. There are three reasons for using this approach:

1. It is helpful to begin simple and work up to complex.

2. If we construct an argument using basic assumptions, then introduce more complex and realistic assumptions, the thinking behind the model is exposed more clearly.

3. Models like Figure 2.1 are just 'one point of view', and are open to challenge.

Fast and furious: forces affecting the auto industry

In their interview with Bill Ford, the great-grandson of Henry Ford and the executive chairman of Ford Motor Company, Hans-Werner Kass and Thomas Fleming (2015, pp.65–6) asked him about the forces that were influencing the pace of change in the auto industry:

The pace of change is accelerating and I love it. I think it's the most interesting time in my 35 years at Ford. It used to be that the auto industry, and the car itself, were part of a self-contained ecosystem. If there were breakthroughs, they were developed within the industry. It was a much more controlled environment and not nearly as dynamic as today's. In fact, I think we ended up being rather insular as an industry, and on balance it was not a good thing. That's all been turned on its head; we now have disruption coming from every angle, from the potential ways we fuel our vehicles to the ownership model. We have a whole generation that just wants access to vehicles as opposed to ownership – for example, through services such as Uber, Zipcar, and RelayRides.

Even the dealership model is changing, with Tesla selling directly to consumers. In terms of connectivity, so much of the technology is being developed outside the auto industry. Whether it's vehicle-to-vehicle and vehicle-to-infrastructure communication, semiautonomous and fully autonomous driving, or connecting to the cloud – these are all major trends coming at us fast and furiously.

Understanding the dynamics of the environment is central to organizational survival. Organizations which are 'out of fit' have to change, or go out of business: still making CDs now that subscription-based music streaming services such as Spotify, Beats and Tidal are available; still printing books now that tablets and e-book readers are commonplace; still machining components now that we have 3D printing technology. As the complexity and pace of environmental change seem to have increased, organizations that are able to adapt quickly to new pressures and opportunities are likely to be more successful than those which are slow to respond. However, the organization that jumps in the wrong direction – improving existing products and services, for example – may be in trouble; but it is interesting to note that vinyl records ('LPs'), once regarded as obsolete, have become popular again. One concern for organizational behaviour, therefore, has been the search for 'fit' between the internal properties of the organization, and features of the external environment.

The search for 'fit'

Environmental uncertainty the degree of unpredictable turbulence and change in the political, economic, social, technological, legal and ecological context in which an organization operates.

Many commentators argue that the internal structures and processes of an organization should reflect, or 'fit' the external environment. What does this mean? One factor that affects most organizations is environmental uncertainty.

Most managers feel that the pace of events is increasing, and that they lack a clear view of the way ahead, the nature of the terrain, obstacles, or the final destination. How can organizations be adaptable enough to cope with continuous and unpredictable change? Robert Duncan defined uncertainty as the lack of adequate information to reach an unambiguous decision, and argued that environmental uncertainty has two dimensions (Duncan 1972, 1973, 1974, 1979). One dimension concerns the degree of *simplicity* or complexity. The other is the degree of *stability* or dynamism:

Environmental complexity the range of external factors relevant to the activities of the organization; the more factors, the higher the complexity.

Simple–complex	The number of different issues faced, the number of different factors to consider, the number of things to worry about
Stable–dynamic	The extent to which those issues are changing or stable, and whether they are subject to slow movement or to abrupt shifts

Environmental dynamism the pace of change in relevant factors external to the organization; the greater the pace of change, the more dynamic the environment.

External factors can include customers, suppliers, regulatory bodies, competitors and partners in joint ventures. Duncan argued that the 'stable–dynamic' dimension is more important in determining environmental uncertainty. Complexity means that you have many issues to consider. Dynamism, on the other hand, is more difficult to manage because you don't know what is going to happen next. Plotting these two dimensions against each other gives us the typology in Figure 2.2. This typology can be applied to the organization as a whole, or to particular business units and departments.

STOP AND THINK Which type of environment would you prefer to work in; stable/simple or dynamic/complex, and why? Share your choice with a colleague. You will have to consider this question every time you apply for a job.

degree of complexity

	low – simple	high – complex
low – stable	small number of similar external factors changing slowly: beer distributor florist	large number of different external factors changing slowly: insurance company university
high – dynamic	small number of similar external factors changing frequently: fashion designer book publisher	large number of dissimilar external factors changing frequently: airline bank

degree of dynamism

Figure 2.2: Duncan's typology of organizational environments

External environments do not *determine* internal structures and processes. Our *perception* is selective, paying attention to some factors and filtering out others. The same environment may be perceived differently by different managers, even in the same sector. It is management perceptions which affect decisions about organization strategy, structures and processes. Igor Ansoff (1997) has developed this argument, summarized in Table 2.1.

Table 2.1: Ansoff's typology of environments

Level	Environmental change	Organization strategy	Management attitude
1	**Repetitive** Little or no change	**Stable** Based on precedent	**Stability seeking** Rejects change
2	**Expanding** Slow incremental change	**Reactive** Incremental change based on experience	**Efficiency driven** Adapts to change
3	**Changing** Fast incremental change	**Anticipatory** Incremental change based on extrapolation	**Market driven** Seeks familiar change
4	**Discontinuous** Discontinuous but predictable change	**Entrepreneurial** Discontinuous new strategies based on observed opportunities	**Environment driven** Seeks new but related change
5	**Surprising** Discontinuous and unpredictable change	**Creative** Discontinuous new and creative strategies	**Environment creating** Seeks novel change

He identifies five types of environment based on the turbulence being experienced, from 'repetitive' at one extreme, to 'surprising' at the other. Read the first two columns of his table *vertically*, working up and down the scale from 'repetitive' at one extreme to 'surprising' at the other. Go to level 1, the repetitive environment, and read the table *horizontally*. Ansoff argues that we can identify the most appropriate strategy and management attitude for that environment. In a stable environment, strategy should be based on precedent. What worked in the past will work in future. In a repetitive environment, the management attitude concerns stability. Change could ruin the business:

environment is repetitive, with no change $\longrightarrow$ strategy should be stable and based on precedent $\longrightarrow$ management should seek stability, reject change

Now go to level 5, to the surprising, discontinuous and unpredictable environment, and again read across the row. As you might expect, the recommended strategy is creative, based on new approaches, and not on what the organization has done in the past. The management attitude has to be novelty-seeking, seeking to influence the environment in creative ways. Holding on to past precedents in this context will ruin the business:

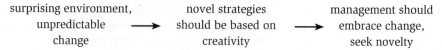

surprising environment, unpredictable change → novel strategies should be based on creativity → management should embrace change, seek novelty

Now read the other three middle rows, again working *across* the table, noting the strategy and management implications for each of the other levels of change. Once that argument and the practical implications are clear, try reading the organization strategy column *vertically*. This can be read as a strategy scale, from stability (precedent driven) at one extreme to creativity (novelty driven) at the other. The final column works in the same way, with a management attitude scale, from stability (rejecting change) to creativity (embracing novelty).

Ansoff (1997) distinguishes between *extrapolative* and *discontinuous* change, shown by the separation in Table 2.1 between levels 3 and 4. Where change is extrapolative, the future can be predicted, more or less, following (extrapolating from) current trends. When change is discontinuous, our ability to predict is limited. Most managers today would probably claim that their organizations operate in discontinuous and/or surprising environments.

Ansoff makes unkind comments about managers who have been successful in organizations with extrapolative environments. He claims that they may lack the skills, knowledge, experience and attitudes to deal with discontinuous change. Success in a discontinuous environment requires entrepreneurial vision and creativity, anticipating change. He suggests that 'Managers incapable of developing an entrepreneurial mindset must be replaced' (Ansoff, 1997, p.76).

STOP AND THINK Does your educational institution face extrapolative or discontinuous change? To what extent is the institution's strategy and management attitude appropriate to that level of change?

Apply this analysis to yourself. What level of environmental change are you subject to, and how does this affect your behaviour?

Our updated model is in Figure 2.3. The stimulus of external change prompts organizational responses. The scale, dynamism and complexity of environmental stimuli encourage an adaptive, environmentally responsive organizational 'paradigm', described as the post-modern organization.

Post-modern organization
A networked, information-rich, delayered, downsized, boundary-less, high-commitment organization employing highly skilled, well-paid autonomous knowledge workers.

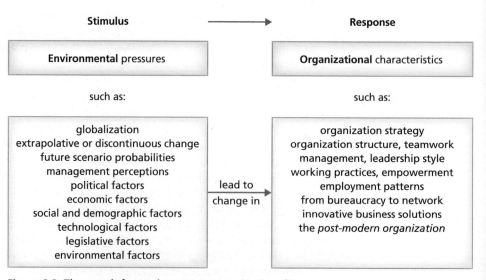

Stimulus	→	Response
Environmental pressures		**Organizational** characteristics
such as:		such as:
globalization extrapolative or discontinuous change future scenario probabilities management perceptions political factors economic factors social and demographic factors technological factors legislative factors environmental factors	lead to change in	organization strategy organization structure, teamwork management, leadership style working practices, empowerment employment patterns from bureaucracy to network innovative business solutions the *post-modern organization*

Figure 2.3: The search for environment–organization 'fit'

Stewart Clegg (1990, p.181) describes the post-modern organization:

Where the modernist organization was rigid, post-modern organization is flexible. Where modernist consumption was premised on mass forms, post-modernist consumption is premised on niches. Where modernist organization and jobs were highly differentiated, demarcated and de-skilled, post-modernist organization and jobs are highly de-differentiated, de-demarcated and multiskilled.

The claim is that bureaucracy, macho managers and boring jobs are being replaced by flexible organizations with participative, supportive managers and interesting, multi-skilled, jobs.

STOP AND THINK

Have you experienced, or observed, a flexible, boundary-less, post-modern organization with skilled and autonomous employees?

Have you experienced, or observed, the opposite – a bureaucratic organization with poorly paid, boring and unskilled jobs that are controlled by autocratic managers?

Environmental determinism
the argument that internal organizational responses are primarily determined by external environmental factors.

We promised that, having built a model, we would knock it down. There are four flaws in the reasoning in Figure 2.3. The first problem concerns environmental determinism.

We know that internal organizational arrangements are affected by many factors: the dynamics of the senior management team, their approach to decision making, employee suggestions, past experience. We also know that, whatever the reality 'out there', what really matters is how the environment is understood and interpreted 'in here'. This means that an environmental 'stimulus' is just one stimulus among many, and that this is not guaranteed either a response, or the expected response.

The second problem concerns assumptions about organizational boundaries. Can we say clearly what is 'out there' and what is 'in here'? Organizations are involved in a constant process of exchange with the environment, importing staff and resources, exporting goods and services. Employees are members of the wider society, whose values and preferences are thus 'inside' the organization. Many organizations operate in collaboration with suppliers and competitors, to share the costs, for example, of developing new materials, processes and products. Some organizations – gymnasiums, motoring assistance – treat customers as 'members'. The boundaries between organizations and their environments are often blurred.

Strategic choice
the ability of an organization to decide on the environment, or environments – that is, sectors, and parts of the world – in which it will operate.

The third problem is one of interpretation. We are considering 'environment' and 'organization' as separate domains. However, an organization chooses and influences its environment; this is a matter of strategic choice (Child, 1997). European motor car companies can choose whether or not to manufacture and sell their cars in China. A restaurant changes its environment (customers, suppliers, competitors) when the owners choose to stop selling fast food and move into gourmet dining. In other words, the external environment is *enacted*: the organization creates and to some extent even becomes its own environment, rather than being 'given' or 'presented with' that environment.

The final problem concerns continuity. The model suggests a picture of rapid and radical change. However, we know that is not the case. We can identify many continuities, environmental and organizational. The German Weihenstephan Brewery was founded in 1040, the Swedish company Stora in 1288, Oxford University Press in 1478, Beretta in 1530, Sumitomo in 1590, Lloyd's in 1688, Sotheby's in 1744, Guinness in 1759, Royal Dutch Shell in 1833, Nokia in 1865. We are familiar with the arguments for constant change. However, organizations that live long and prosper are also valuable: they establish community links, provide continuity of employment across generations, and also offer a sense of social cohesion and communal solidarity (de Geuss, 1999). One set of responses to environmental pressures thus involves organizational adaptation, or reinvention, in order to survive; the telecommunications company Nokia began by making paper, and has since been involved in making rubber boots, raincoats, cables, television sets and studded bicycle tyres (Skapinker, 2015).

Analysing the organization's environment

Environmental scanning techniques for identifying and predicting the impact of external trends and developments on the internal functioning of an organization.

Identifying current and future factors 'out there' which could affect an organization often produces a long list. The first problem, therefore, is to identify all of those factors. The next challenge is to predict their impact. The methods used to analyse the environment are known as environmental scanning techniques.

Environmental scanning involves collecting information from different sources: government statistics, websites, newspapers and magazines, specialist research and consulting agencies, demographic analysis, market research, focus groups. There are three major trends affecting most organizations; technology, globalization and demographics.

Technology

Technology is probably the most tangible and visible aspect of environmental change. The pace of development appears to be unchecked. Three years ago, the previous edition of this text described social networking and cloud computing as 'new'; these are now established and 'old'. Successful new business models based on smartphone 'apps' may be relatively new as this text is being developed, but will be old when you read this. Most of us use our own devices and online services for personal and social, as well as for work purposes; we are no longer dependent on our employing organization's technology (which can often be more cumbersome and slow).

Applications of computing affect almost all aspects of our lives: how we entertain ourselves, how we buy goods and services, how we communicate. These developments have increased the number of 'knowledge workers' whose value depends more on what they know than on what they can do. Software design, creative problem solving and 'back office' support do not depend on location, and these kinds of knowledge work can be outsourced to countries where rates of pay are lower. A focus on computing, however, overlooks developments in other fields, such as new materials, and in healthcare where the pace of development of new drugs, treatment regimes and medical equipment seems to be as rapid as in computing, but attracts less attention.

STOP AND THINK

What new technologies, materials, medical treatments, services, processes, and so on, have affected your life and work recently?

In what ways? For better, or for worse?

Technology affects organizational behaviour in many ways, and on many levels: the design and delivery of products and services, corporate strategies, modes of communications and information exchange, the day-to-day work of individuals. These implications are explored in depth in Chapter 3.

Globalization

In the twenty-first century, developed Western economies see both threats and opportunities in the economic growth of countries such as Brazil, Russia, India and China – the so-called BRIC economies. Those economies have lower labour costs, and some are attractive locations for manufacturing operations and customer service call centres. There is a

Smartphones and the on-demand economy

© 2016 Uber Technologies, Inc.

The smartphone is creating new businesses and business models, which are changing the organization of work and careers by using 'apps' to link service providers rapidly with potential customers. One well-known example is *Uber*, a taxi service founded in San Francisco in 2009 and now operating in over 50 countries. With the *Uber* app on your phone, you can find a taxi or a 'rideshare'

within minutes. *Handy* and *Homejoy* provide customers with self-employed home helps. *Instacart* purchases and delivers groceries. *Washio* offers a laundry service. *BloomThat* delivers flowers. *TaskRabbit* will find a last-minute gift. *SpoonRocket* delivers restaurant-quality meals. *Medicast* and *Axiom* will send you a doctor or a lawyer, respectively. These new app-based business models do not need offices or costly computers, there are no full-time employees, and transaction costs are low. Algorithms link those with needs to those who have the capacity to meet them. Location is not necessarily important, say for organizations that need a specialist to do some computer programming, or to develop a legal brief. This way of working will not suit all potential providers, especially those who prefer stability and predictability in their employment. However, this approach is attractive to those who want to use their spare time to generate income from freelancing, and who are happy working for Me plc (based on *The Economist*, 2015).

Globalization the intensification of worldwide social and business relationships which link localities in such a way that local conditions are shaped by distant events.

widespread perception that 'outsourcing' manufacturing and service operations in this way is happening at the expense of jobs in Europe and North America. The term given to these trends and developments is **globalization** (Giddens, 1990).

Richard Dobbs et al. (2014) explore the implications of the three forces identified in this section: globalization, technology and connectivity, and ageing populations. Each of these forces alone is driving major changes, but in combination, the consequences will be radical. The consulting company McKinsey estimates that half of world economic growth between 2010 and 2025 will come from organizations based in over 400 cities in emerging markets – cities that few people in the West have heard of: Tianjin (China), Porto Alegre (Brazil), Kumasi (Ghana).

Video case: globalization to localization?

This four-minute *Financial Times* video analyses changes in the nature of trade, globalization, and 'hyperglobalization'. Shawn Donnan (world trade editor, *Financial Times*) explains how 'the digital era' is influencing trading patterns, encouraging the local provision of goods and services. What are the disadvantages and benefits of these trends, for individuals, organizations, and national economies?

Home viewing

Syriana (2006, director Stephen Gaghan) comes with the slogan 'everything is connected', and offers insights into globalization. The film is set in the fictional Gulf state of Syriana, and is based on relations between the global oil industry and national politics, illustrating the links between

power and wealth, between political, organizational and personal actions, between the decisions of corporate executives and the fate of workers. The action shifts between America, the Middle East and Europe. Friends are enemies; colleagues are crooks. One character observes, 'Corruption ain't nothing more than government intrusion into market efficiencies in the form of regulation. We have laws against it *precisely* so we can get away with it. Corruption is our protection. Corruption is what keeps us safe and warm. Corruption is how we win'. George Clooney plays Bob Barnes, a CIA agent hunting Middle Eastern terrorists. His role is to prevent the ageing Emir and his idealistic son from finalizing a deal with China, and not America ('I want you to take him from his hotel, drug him, put him in the front of a car, and run a truck into it at 50 miles an hour'). *Syriana* attributes the radicalization of young immigrant Muslims from Pakistan, and their suicide terrorist attack on an oil tanker, to the casual way in which a global oil company treats its employees. George Clooney won an Oscar for his part in this movie. Identify positive and negative examples of globalization in action, and assess whether the advantages outweigh the disadvantages, from the viewpoint of this film.

Source: www.cartoonstock.com

STOP AND THINK

How does globalization affect you personally?

In what ways could globalization influence your working life and your career?

What are the personal benefits and disadvantages?

Globalization is an uneven process. Many people around the world do not have access to the goods and technologies that contribute to the experience of globalization for affluent members of developed economies. Many societies and groups reject the dislocation that globalization can bring, and object to the spread of Western culture, signified most clearly by brand labels. Western organizations (from fast food outlets to national embassies) have become terrorist targets, as well as focal points for the demonstration of anger over perceived attempts to impose Western values on other cultures.

Barbie is a globalization icon

Chip East/Reuters

Barbie is one of the most profitable toys in history, selling at a rate of two per second, and generating over US$1 billion in annual revenues for the Mattell Corporation based in Los Angeles (Giddens and Sutton, 2009, p.135). Sold in 140 countries, she is a global citizen, but she is global in another sense, too. Although she was designed in America, she has never been made there, and was first manufactured in Japan in 1959 (where wages were low at the time), and has since been made in other low-wage countries in Asia. The only components of Barbie which come from America are the cardboard packaging, and some paints. Her body and wardrobe come from elsewhere across the planet:

Component/ manufacturing stage	Source
Designs, pigments, oils, moulds	United States
Cardboard packaging	Made in United States with pulp from Indonesia
Oil for her plastic parts	Saudi Arabia
Refined oil and PVC plastic pellets	Taiwan
Injection moulding	China, Indonesia, Malaysia
Nylon hair	Japan
Cotton dresses	China
Distribution	Hong Kong

The sign on the box may say 'made in China', or Indonesia, or Malaysia. But Barbie crosses many geographical boundaries on her journey from the designer's sketchpad to the customer. Look at the products that you own and use. Where do they come from? Choose one of your favourite items and see if you can identify where in the world its components were made.

The cross-border spider's web of global production and supply

'Victor and William Fung, owners of Li and Fung, a Hong Kong-based company that helps orchestrate these supply chains, have said that this network has "ripped the roof off the factory". Suppliers can now be anywhere. They use the example of a pair of shorts they made for an American retailer. The buttons came from China, the zips from Japan, the yarn was spun in Bangladesh and woven into fabric and dyed in China, and the garment was stitched together in Pakistan. Yet every pair of shorts has to look as if it were made in one factory'.

Demographics

Demographic changes pose some of the most difficult challenges for management in the twenty-first century. The workforce in industrialized economies is ageing. The proportion of the population who have retired from employment is growing relative to the proportion of the population still in work. An ageing population is one consequence of people living longer and having fewer children. This is an accelerating

Generations

Veterans, born 1925 to 1942; also known as the silent generation, matures, traditionalists

Baby Boomers, born 1946 to 1964; also just called Boomers

Generation X, born 1965 to 1979, also known as baby busters, the thirteenth, lost generation

Generation Y, born 1980 to 1994; also known as millennials, nexters, echo boomers

Generation C, born since 1995; Connected, Communicating, always Clicking

These dates are approximate – different commentators disagree (Parry and Urwin, 2011).

global phenomenon. One measure is the percentage of the population aged 65 or over: in the past, that was around 3 to 4 per cent. However, in developed economies today, those over 65 comprise around 15 per cent of the population, and this could reach 25 per cent on average by 2050 (Chand and Tung, 2014). According to one estimate, around half of all the humans who have ever been over 65 are alive today, and that by 2035, over 1.1 billion people – 13 per cent of the world's population – will be above 65 (*The Economist*, 2014a). In the UK, these percentages are:

Year	% of population age 65 or over
1985	15
2010	17
2035*	23

*UK Office of National Statistics estimate: www.statistics.gov.uk

In 2010, there were 10 million people aged 65 or over in the UK. Over 30 per cent of the workforce was over 50 in 2015 (CIPD, 2015). The average age of the UK population is also increasing:

Year	Average age
1985	35
2010	40
2035*	42

*UK Office of National Statistics estimate: www.statistics.gov.uk

An ageing population has social consequences. The Boomers who were born after the Second World War (which ended in 1945), were celebrating their 60th birthdays (and thinking about retirement) from around 2006. Boomers have been called a 'silver tsunami' sweeping across affected countries (*The Economist*, 2010). The novel *Boomsday*, by Christopher Buckley (2007), tells of the anger of younger generations whose taxes pay for the pensions, health and welfare of elderly Boomers.

The silver tsunami has other consequences. How will organizations fill the gaps as Boomers retire, taking their knowledge and experience with them, while the numbers of skilled youngsters are shrinking. Some older workers – 'nevertirees' – have decided to carry on working, and organizations will also have to learn how to manage them. Will older workers adapt to new technologies and working practices, and be willing to be managed

How to handle 'grumpy Boomers'

We tend to think of each generation, such as 'Baby Boomers', or 'Gen Y', as having a distinct set of attitudes and values. A study of Canadian knowledge workers, by Linda Duxbury and Michael Halinski (2014), suggests that this picture is too simple: there can be as much diversity within a generational group as between generations. Boomers, born between 1946 and 1964, will retire between 2010 and 2030. The problem is that, with an ageing population, Boomers will leave the workforce just as the numbers of employees to replace them is falling. Using a survey that measured commitment, and intention to quit work, the research identified four categories of older workers:

disengaged-exiters	organizations will benefit if they quit
engaged-high-performers	organizations want to retain their services
retired-on-the-job	organizations could benefit if they were 're-engaged'
exiting-performers	organizations want to retain their skills and experience

For the organization, disengaged-exiters and engaged-high-performers are not problems. The former will not be a loss if they leave, and the latter will continue to be committed and perform well. The other two groups are more difficult; those who are retired-on-the-job are not contributing as much as they could, and it is costly to replace the exiting-performers.

The main difference between exiting-performers and engaged-high-performers was workload. Those who were planning to exit worked longer hours, and worked more often at home, reporting higher levels of overload than any other group. Those who were retired-on-the-job had moderate levels of job satisfaction, and had mixed views of management and organizational culture.

What are the practical implications? Organizations that want to discourage committed but grumpy Boomers from leaving need to address workload issues; reduce hours and overtime, and introduce flexible working. On the other hand, a focus on skills development, supportive management and organizational culture is necessary to renew the commitment of those who have retired-on-the-job.

by youngsters? These are new problems, with little research or experience on which to draw. Approaches to managing older workers include:

- exit interviews to capture their wisdom
- mentoring systems in which Boomers coach their replacements
- phased retirement rather than a sudden stop
- shorter working weeks with flexible hours
- calling on pools of retired staff for special projects
- working during busy periods, punctuated by 'Benidorm leave'.

A recent survey of over 1,000 managers found that most organizations had not yet developed their age management policies (Pickard, 2010). Younger managers find it difficult to manage older workers, who have different drives, and need flexibility (to care for elderly parents and grandchildren, for example). Management styles have to be consultative, drawing on the experience of older workers for whom money is probably not the main or only motivator. Another useful practice is intergenerational mentoring; Boomers welcome the chance to mentor and support Gen Ys, who can share their potentially better understanding of social networking technologies.

There is a common perception that older workers are less motivated, do not perform well, are more costly and have a reduced ability to learn. Research has shown all of those perceptions to be false. Part of this negative stereotype also says that older workers are more resistant to change – a view that contributes to age discrimination. However, a study of 3,000 German workers in 93 companies by Florian Kunze et al. (2013) found that older employees were *less* resistant to change than younger colleagues. One explanation is that older workers may have better strategies for coping with and adapting to changing organizational environments.

Nevertirement and nevertirees

Barclays Wealth is a bank for 'high net worth' people (www.barclayswealth.com). To find out more about their customers' future plans, they surveyed 2,000 wealthy individuals, who had at least £1 million of assets to invest. They found that, rather than planning a conventional retirement, many planned to go on working (Leppard and Chittenden, 2010):

In Britain, 70 per cent of those under 45 said that they will always want to be involved in some form of commercial or professional work. In other words, 'nevertirement' could become more popular, and this may not apply just to the wealthy. Organizations will need to develop human resource policies and working practices to deal effectively with this trend. The number of people in Britain working beyond retirement age rose to over 800,000 in 2010. In that year, there were around 724,000 people aged 18 to 24 out of work. If the elderly don't retire, but carry on working, will this contribute to youth unemployment?

Country	% planning to work beyond retirement age
Saudi Arabia	92
United Arab Emirates	91
Qatar	91
South Africa	88
Latin America	78
UK	60
Ireland	59
USA	54
Japan	46
Spain	44
Switzerland	34

Generation Y are the children of the Boomers. Most of the student readers of this text will be Gen Ys. Do Boomers and Gen Ys want different things from work? Sylvia Ann Hewlett and colleagues suggest that these groups actually share a number of attitudes, behaviours and preferences (Hewlett et al., 2009). Their findings are based on surveys of around 4,000 college graduates, followed by focus groups and interviews. They found that Boomers and Gen Ys both want flexible work arrangements and opportunities to give something back to society. Both of those factors were more important than pay. The motives of Boomers are summarized in Table 2.2.

Table 2.2: Portrait of Baby Boomers: what makes them 'tick'?

Staying in harness	42% predict they will continue working after age 65 – and 14% say they will never retire because they enjoy their work which is related to their identities
Long runways	47% see themselves as being in the middle of their careers – global recession is also encouraging them to delay retirement
From 'me' to 'we'	55% are members of external volunteer networks – the idealism of the 1960s lives on, and they volunteer time to environmental, cultural, educational and other causes
Familial obligations	71% say they care for the elderly – in addition to looking after elderly parents, they contribute financial support to their own children
Yearning for flexibility	87% say that flexible working is important – they want to pursue other interests as well as work, and look for autonomy and flexibility in their jobs

Source: based on Hewlett et al. (2009).

The rewards from work that Boomers regard as important are:

1. high-quality colleagues;
2. an intellectually stimulating workplace;
3. autonomy regarding work tasks;
4. flexible work arrangements;
5. access to new experiences and challenges;

Source: http://seldomlogical.com

6. giving back to the world through work;

7. recognition from the company or the boss.

Dan Matthews (2015) argues that because Gen Y live in an interactive and collaborative world where feedback is instant and open, they expect to find those features at work. They want to be involved, will share their views whether invited to or not, and are happy working with many communication channels. However, they can be more difficult to manage than other groups, because they are more interested in personal development than in the organization. Change is not threatening, but an opportunity to gain intrinsic (personal) and extrinsic (material) rewards. Managers thus have to spend time communicating with Gen Y on their own terms. Matthews argues, however, that this investment produces returns, by developing Gen Y views on smarter ways of doing things, flexible working, and the devices and services that they prefer to use. Treated with respect, Gen Y can contribute positively to organizational transformation; ignored, they can create problems.

The world of Generation Y

Generation Y, or 'millennials', were born in the 1980s and 1990s. By 2025, it is estimated that they will comprise 75 per cent of the global workforce. From a management perspective, therefore, it is important to understand their values and expectations:

- Generation Y looks for ethical employers, opportunities for progression, a good work–life balance and interesting work; almost half (45 per cent) choose workplace flexibility over pay.

- More than half (57 per cent) of Generation Y in the UK intend to leave their jobs within one or two years of joining.

- They tend to be independent and resist micromanagement, but they want feedback and coaching.

- They are comfortable with technology and social networks, creative and open-minded, multiculturally aware, confident, able to collaborate and ethical.

- More than three-quarters (77 per cent) of Generation Y view formal management qualifications to be the most effective method of learning and development.

- Many want to be entrepreneurs; more than a quarter (27 per cent) of 16- to 30-year-olds in the UK claimed in a study in 2012 that they were considering setting up a business.

- However, they can also display a strong sense of entitlement, an inability to communicate face-to-face, a lack of decision-making skills, a poor sense of awareness, a low work ethic, and can appear overconfident.

- Generation Y lacks a global mindset: just one UK student studies abroad for every 15 international students in the UK (from CMI, 2014, p.20).

Boomers and Gen Y want to serve a wider purpose, want opportunities to explore their interests and passions, and say that flexible working and work–life balance are important to them. They also share a sense of obligation to the wider society and the environment. (Gen Xs are far less likely to find those obligations important.) It is also significant that both groups say that financial gain is not their main reason for choosing an employer. They are interested in other forms of reward: teamwork, challenge, new experiences, recognition. Human resource practices need to emphasize teamwork and collaboration, flexible working, phased retirement, project work, short-term assignments, opportunities to support external causes and eco-friendly work environments.

On the grid 24/7: here comes Generation C

Gareth Brown/Getty Images

make up over 40 per cent of the population in America, Europe and the BRIC countries (Friedrich et al., 2011). Gen C will be:

On the grid 24/7: Connected around the clock is normal. Global mobile phone and internet use are predicted to increase as follows:

	2012	2020
Mobile phone users	4.6 billion	6 billion
Internet users	1.7 billion	4.7 billion

Social animal 2.0: With a range of personal relationships driven by social networks, voice channels, online groups, blogs, electronic messaging. This will create fast-moving business and political pressures as information and ideas spread more widely, more quickly.

Generation C is the label being given to those born after 1990. The 'C' stands for connected, communicating, content-centric, computerized, community oriented and always clicking. This is the first generation to have grown up with the internet, social media and mobile handheld computing, for whom 24/7 mobile and internet connectivity are taken for granted, and freedom of expression is the norm. These technologies encourage more flexible forms of working, and less hierarchical organizations, and they are blurring the boundaries between work and personal life. By 2020, Gen C will

There are organizational consequences. Most Gen C employees will bring their own computers to work rather than use corporate resources. There will probably be more work done by virtual project groups, with fewer face-to-face meetings, and less frequent travel.

Other demographic trends that will affect many organizations include global migration, triggered in part by wars, improved communications and transport, and in Europe by new rules concerning harmonization and labour mobility. This contributes to a richer ethnic, cultural and religious mix in a given workforce, and puts a premium on the ability to manage this diversity of values, needs and preferences. An ageing population is also contributing to widespread labour and skill shortages.

Further trends include 'the hourglass economy', divided between educated and skilled knowledge workers, who are in demand, and poorly educated, untrained and poorly paid manual and clerical workers, for whom there are fewer job opportunities. Lifestyles and values are changing, affecting the formation and composition of households, patterns of living and consumption, trends in leisure and education, and preferences in working patterns. Social values also change. Environmental concern, expressed in punitive fines for organizations which create toxic waste, and in public protests, over new roads and airports, for example, were uncommon before the 1980s, but are now routine. These concerns contribute to the corporate social responsibility movement, explored later in this chapter.

Where is everyone?

Labour and skill shortages are a global problem. The magazine *Work* (2014, published by the Chartered Institute for Personnel and Development) used several public information sources to produce the following picture:

Canada	estimated that 25 per cent of Canadian miners will be eligible for retirement in 2023
United States of America	report in 2014 attributed an annual loss of $1.4bn in farm income to labour shortages
United Kingdom	cybersecurity skills gap could take 20 years to address
Germany	predicted shortage of 500,000 nurses by 2030 being met by recruitment from China
Chile	retailers cannot recruit staff who can earn higher wages in mining
South Africa	workforce management company Adcorp reported in 2014 that 470,000 vacancies were unfilled because applicants lacked the right skills
Russia	future growth harmed and wages increased by inflexible education system
Africa	in 2013 there were more Ethiopian doctors in Chicago than in Ethiopia
Japan	April 2014, labour shortages caused 123 branches of the restaurant chain Sukiya to close on a single day
Australia	one in three butchers reported no suitable applicants for vacancies advertised in 2013

STOP AND THINK

In what ways do your values differ from the values of your parents?

In what ways will your lifestyle differ from that of your parents?

In what ways will your experience of work differ from that of your parents?

How will your values and expectations as an employee make life easier or more difficult for the organizations that are likely to employ you?

PESTLE and scenario planning

PESTLE analysis
an environmental scanning tool identifying Political, Economic, Social, Technological, Legal and Ecological factors that affect an organization.

One approach to environmental scanning is **PESTLE analysis**. This is a simple, structured tool which helps to organize the complexity of trends in technology, globalization, demographics and other factors. Pestle analysis provides an audit of an organization's environment and is used to guide strategic decision making and plan for possible future contingencies (Morrison and Daniels, 2010).

Figure 2.4 illustrates a typical range of PESTLE trends and pressures. The details under each heading are for illustration, and they are not comprehensive. The best way to approach environmental scanning is to do an analysis yourself. This will almost certainly reveal that the neat categories in the model overlap in a rather untidy way in practice. Many legislative changes are politically motivated. Ecological concerns reflect changing social values and preferences. Some technology developments (electric cars) are encouraged by economic and ecological issues (the cost of oil and CO_2 emissions). However, the aim of the analysis is to identify external environmental factors, their interrelationships, and their impact. It is less important to get them into the 'correct' boxes.

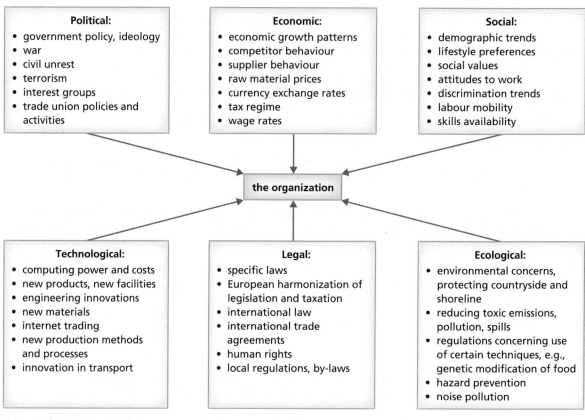

Political:
- government policy, ideology
- war
- civil unrest
- terrorism
- interest groups
- trade union policies and activities

Economic:
- economic growth patterns
- competitor behaviour
- supplier behaviour
- raw material prices
- currency exchange rates
- tax regime
- wage rates

Social:
- demographic trends
- lifestyle preferences
- social values
- attitudes to work
- discrimination trends
- labour mobility
- skills availability

the organization

Technological:
- computing power and costs
- new products, new facilities
- engineering innovations
- new materials
- internet trading
- new production methods and processes
- innovation in transport

Legal:
- specific laws
- European harmonization of legislation and taxation
- international law
- international trade agreements
- human rights
- local regulations, by-laws

Ecological:
- environmental concerns, protecting countryside and shoreline
- reducing toxic emissions, pollution, spills
- regulations concerning use of certain techniques, e.g., genetic modification of food
- hazard prevention
- noise pollution

Figure 2.4: PESTLE analysis

BMW's 2017 production line project

AFP/Getty Images

The BMW 7-series motor car is made at Dingolfing, in Lower Bavaria. Production managers were concerned about how to maintain the plant's productivity with an ageing workforce. Older workers tend to have longer sickness absences, and have to work harder to keep up their output. The average age of the plant's workers was expected to rise from 39 to 47 by 2017. So, management set up a pilot project, staffing one of the lines (making rear axle gearboxes) with a 'year-2017 mix' of 42 workers with an average age of 47. Could this '2017' group achieve the same productivity as lines with younger employees? (Loch et al., 2010).

The '2017 line' workers identified 70 changes. These were complemented by job rotation, to balance the workload on individuals, and strength and stretching exercises which were developed by a physiotherapist, but a volunteer from the group then took over. Most changes concerned ways to reduce wear and tear on the workers, which also reduced sickness absence.

Examples of changes	Cost	Benefits
Wooden flooring	€5,000	Reduce knee strain and static electric shocks
Orthopaedic footwear	€2,000	Reduce strain on feet
Magnifying lenses	€1,000	Reduce eyestrain, minimize errors
Barbershop chairs	€1,000	Enable short breaks; work while seated
Manual hoisting cranes	€1,000	Reduce back strain
Angled monitors	No cost	Reduce eyestrain
Adjustable work tables	No cost	Less physical effort; quick to adjust
Large-handled tools	No cost	Reduce strain on arms
Stackable containers	No cost	Less physical effort
Larger typeface on screens	No cost	Reduce eyestrain, minimize errors

Senior managers identified the problem; production managers set up the experiment; production line workers created the solution. This pilot was initially dismissed as 'the pensioners' line'. However, for a capital investment of €20,000, productivity rose 7 per cent in one year, to the same level as lines staffed by younger workers.

The original line target was 440 gearboxes a shift. This was increased to 500 in 2008, then to 530 in 2009. With zero defects, and absenteeism below the plant average, the company now cites the line as a model of productivity, with similar projects in plants in Liepzig (Germany) and Steyr (Austria).

STOP AND THINK

Choose an organization with which you are familiar: hospital, supermarket, university or college, the place you worked last summer.

Make a list of the political, economic, social, technological, legislative and ecological factors that affect that organization.

What practical advice would you give to the management of this organization?

How would you assess the practical value of this exercise to the organization?

PESTLE analysis raises a number of issues.

First, it is difficult to escape from the argument that the organization must pay attention to PESTLE trends and developments. The organization which fails to respond to those external factors will quickly run into difficulties.

Second, the long list of external factors, even under these neat headings, can be intimidating. Identifying which are most significant, and then predicting their impact, can be difficult.

Third, a full understanding of external factors can involve the analysis of a substantial amount of different kinds of data, and this takes time. How about analysing demographic trends in south-central Scotland, for example, or pan-European regulations affecting the food and drink industry, or forthcoming information technology software innovations, or collating the results of surveys concerning lifestyle changes and consumption patterns across South East Asia. The time spent on these analyses has to be balanced against the need for a rapid response.

Environmental complexity makes prediction hazardous. We can predict demographic trends with some accuracy, with respect to mortality, and gender and age profiles. We can normally predict economic trends with some confidence in the short to medium term, two to three years. Trends in social values and lifestyles, politics, technological innovation, or the impact of new technology, cannot be predicted with much confidence – although that does not stop journalists and others from making the attempt. Environmental scanning can mean a lot of informed guesswork and judgement.

PESTLE analysis has two strengths, and four weaknesses:

Strengths

1. The analysis encourages consideration of the range of external factors affecting internal organizational arrangements and business planning.

2. The analysis is a convenient framework for ordering a complex and bewildering set of factors, helping an organization plan for future opportunities and threats.

Weaknesses

1. This analysis can identify many factors which may not be significant. It is difficult to strike a balance between identifying all factors, and those which are important.

2. It is difficult to anticipate 'defining events', such as wars, terrorist attacks, new discoveries, economic collapse, and major political or financial crises which shift country boundaries or radically change government policies.

3. This analysis can involve the time-consuming and expensive collection of data, some of which may be available, and some of which may have to be researched.

4. The time spent in information gathering and analysis may inhibit a rapid and effective response to the very trends being analysed.

Scenario planning in a high-risk world

Terrorism is not the only unexpected risk that might ruin a business. Outbreaks of infectious diseases such as SARS and MERS can be equally damaging. In the past, says Bain's (a management consultancy firm) Mr Rigby, managers were reluctant to draw up plans in case they frightened employees and customers. Now, he says, 'it's a necessity'. The new concern with geopolitical risks has led to a revival of scenario planning. Pioneered in the 1970s by Pierre Wack at Royal Dutch/Shell (which includes three different forecasts of the global economy in its strategic planning), scenario planning became unfashionable because the geopolitical climate appeared to be benign. Now, however, it has become popular as a way to help managers to think about and plan for future uncertainties (Cave, 2008; The Economist, 2004). An international survey of over 2,000 executives found that the main perceived threats to economic growth are geopolitical instability and political leadership transitions (McKinsey, 2015).

Another study, produced for the annual World Economic Forum (Marsh, 2015) identified the ten global risks of highest concern to executives over the next ten years:

interstate conflicts	terrorist attacks
extreme weather events	natural catastrophes
water crises	spread of infectious diseases
unemployment or underemployment	energy price shock
data fraud or theft	misuse of technologies

The top three risks in terms of *likelihood* were interstate conflict, extreme weather events, and failure of national governance. The top three in terms of *impact* were water crises, spread of infectious diseases and weapons of mass destruction. Alec Marsh (2015, p.8) advises, 'Take these and build plausible scenarios assuming that one of them happens. Next, ask what would happen if a second event occurred at the same time'. Scenario planning can help to assess the risk landscape, and can also help organizations to prepare for what could happen.

Scenario planning
the imaginative
development of one
or more likely pictures
of the dimensions
and characteristics
of the future for an
organization.

Environmental analysis with PESTLE is used for **scenario planning**, a technique developed by the oil company Royal Dutch/Shell in the 1970s (Wilkinson and Kupers, 2013) and also known as the 'Shell method'. Scenarios are not predictions, but 'plausible stories' about the future, and are designed to break the habit of assuming that the future will look much like the present, and to encourage creative discussion of issues and developments that might otherwise be overlooked.

Scenario planning combines environmental scanning with creative thinking, to identify the most probable future scenario as a basis for planning and action. In the field of corporate strategy, scenario planning is used to explore 'best case, worst case' possibilities, and to encourage 'out-of-the-box' and creative 'blue skies' thinking. Environmental scanning is a useful predictive tool, particularly when allied with scenario planning, and as a guide to creative decision making. This is also a useful framework which exposes the range of external environmental influences on internal organizational behaviour, and highlights the relationships between those external factors.

Work in 2020: colourful scenarios

The consultancy company PricewaterhouseCoopers used scenario planning to explore the future of work (Arkin, 2007). They developed three possible scenarios for 2020:

Orange world   Big companies have been replaced by networks of small specialized enterprises. People work on short-term contracts exploring job opportunities online through portals developed by craft guilds.

Green world   Demographic change, climate and sustainability are key business drivers. Employment law, employee relations and corporate responsibility are vital in this heavily regulated environment.

Blue world   Huge corporations are like mini-states providing staff with housing, health, education and other welfare benefits. Human capital metrics are sophisticated, and people management is as powerful as finance.

What if none of these models turns out to be correct? Is this a waste of time? Sandy Pepper, the project leader, argues that: 'You can respond more quickly to what does happen if you have trained yourself to think in a more innovative, lateral way about the future'.

We can now update our model. Figure 2.5 shows the links between external environmental pressures and internal organizational responses in more detail.

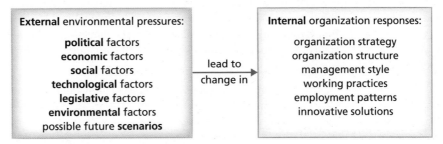

Figure 2.5: External environment–organization link detailed

This model relies on a number of basic assumptions:

- That all the relevant data can be identified, collected and analysed.
- That the analysis will lead to accurate forecasts, and to realistic future scenarios.
- That the analysis will be consistent, and not pull the organization in different directions.
- That the kinds of internal organizational responses indicated by the analysis can be implemented at an appropriate pace.

Ethical behaviour

Organizations and managers are expected to behave ethically. The emphasis on this aspect of organizational behaviour has increased in the twenty-first century, for two reasons. The first concerns a number of high-profile corporate scandals (Enron, Worldcom). The second concerns increasing media scrutiny of organization and management practices, focusing on environmental issues, use of low-cost labour and other potentially unethical behaviours (such as bribery). These concerns are not new, but they are seen as more important and attract more attention than they have done in the past.

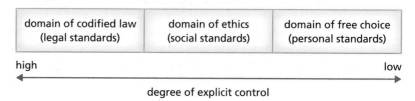

<table>
<tr><td>domain of codified law
(legal standards)</td><td>domain of ethics
(social standards)</td><td>domain of free choice
(personal standards)</td></tr>
</table>

high   low

⟵————————————————————————————————⟶

degree of explicit control

Figure 2.6: Three domains of action

Richard Daft (2008) distinguishes between the 'domain of codified law', and the 'domain of free choice'. In the domain of law, our behaviour is decided by legislation. Individuals are not allowed to murder or to steal, and organizations must conform with accounting, tax, health and safety, and employment legislation. If we do the wrong thing, we end up in court, or in jail; organizations can be fined, and in some cases senior managers can be imprisoned. In the domain of choice, we can do what we like: smoke cigarettes, eat unhealthy food, take as little exercise as we choose. Organizations can decide which businesses to be in, where to locate their headquarters, which markets to expand.

Are we ever really 'free to choose' our behaviour? Daft (2008, p.139) points out that, even where there are no laws to guide our behaviour, there are 'standards of conduct, based on shared principles and values about moral conduct that guide an individual or company'. We have to decide whether or not to comply with those norms. The domain of ethics thus sits between the domain of law and the domain of choice (Figure 2.6). We may have to take responsibility for our actions in a courtroom (domain of codified law), in the court of our own conscience (domain of free choice), or in the court of social judgement (domain of ethics).

We need to distinguish between *individual* ethics and *business* ethics. The behavioural choices facing individuals and organizations are different, and the criteria against which we judge those actions may also be different. Gerry Johnson, Kevan Scholes and Richard Whittington (2008) explore questions of individual and business ethics using a three-level framework which includes the ethics of the individual manager, the organization's ethical stance, and the organization's approach to corporate social responsibility:

Level 1: individual ethics
This concerns the decisions and actions of individual managers, and the ethical principles behind their behaviour.

Level 2: the organization's ethical stance
This concerns the extent to which the organization's minimum obligations to stakeholders and to society at large will be exceeded.

Level 3: corporate social responsibility
This focuses on how the organization puts its ethical stance into practice, by addressing different stakeholder interests.

Individual ethics

Managers should surely act ethically. However, there is no consensus on what constitutes 'ethical' behaviour. Different commentators use different criteria with regard to decisions

Ethics the moral principles, values and rules that govern our decisions and actions with respect to what is right and wrong, good and bad.

over what is right, and what is wrong. Those differences lead to conflicting judgements about the same behaviour. As a result, **ethics** is a controversial subject.

Gerald Cavanagh, Dennis Moberg and Manuel Velasquez developed a template to distinguish ethical from unethical management actions (Cavanagh et al., 1981; Velasquez et al., 1983). Their perspective is based on three ethical frameworks: utilitarianism, individual rights, and natural justice (Table 2.3). They suggest that these criteria should be combined to reach ethical judgements.

Utilitarianism

A utilitarian perspective judges behaviour in terms of outcomes; this is the classic 'ends justifies means' argument. This approach considers the 'balance sheet' of benefits and costs to those involved. Behaviour is ethical if it achieves 'the greatest good of the greatest number'. However, in even modestly complex settings, with several stakeholders, and actions with a range of consequences, calculating the costs and benefits can be challenging.

Rights

This perspective judges behaviour on the extent to which fundamental individual rights are respected. This includes the right of free consent, the right to privacy, the right to freedom of conscience, the right of free speech, the right to due process in the form of an impartial hearing. The ethical decision depends on whether or not individual rights have been violated.

Table 2.3: Ethical frameworks

	Strengths	**Weaknesses**
Utilitarianism	Encourages efficiency Parallels profit maximization Looks beyond the individual	Impossible to quantify variables Can lead to unjust resource allocation Individual rights may be violated
Rights	Protects the individual Establishes standards of behaviour independent of outcomes	May encourage selfish behaviour Individual rights may become obstacles to productivity and efficiency
Justice	Ensures fair allocation of resources Ensures democratic operation, independent of status or class Protects the interests of the under-represented in the organization	Can encourage a sense of entitlement that discourages risk and innovation Some individual rights may be violated to accommodate justice for majority

Source: adapted from *Organizational Dynamics*, Vol. 12, No 2, Velasquez, M., Moberg, D.J. and Cavanagh, G.F., Organizational statesmanship and dirty politics: ethical guidelines for the organizational politician, p.72, © 1983, with permission from Elsevier.

Justice

This perspective judges behaviour on whether or not the benefits and costs flowing from an action are fairly, equitably and impartially distributed. Distributive justice states that rules should be applied consistently, those in similar circumstances should be treated equally, and individuals should not be held responsible for matters beyond their control. As with the utilitarian view, these issues are awkward to resolve in practice, as judgements of consistency, similarity and responsibility are subjective and vary from one setting to another.

These three perspectives produce a 'decision tree' for deciding whether an action is ethical or not (Figure 2.7). First, 'gather the facts', then ask about benefits, rights and justice. The framework also introduces circumstances which could justify unethical behaviour in some settings. 'Overwhelming factors' are issues that justify setting aside ethical criteria. Some actions may have 'dual effects', with positive and negative outcomes, and the negatives may be acceptable if they are outweighed by the positives. 'Incapacitating factors' may prevent the decision maker from applying ethical criteria. For example, managers can be constrained by the views and actions of colleagues, and may be pressured into behaviour that they would not choose themselves. Individual managers may not have enough information on which to reach a judgement. Finally, the individual may doubt the relevance of one or more ethical criteria to a given setting. The right to free speech, for example, may not apply if this involved releasing information that would be damaging to others.

As a result, we have several escape routes which allow actions that would be prohibited by the three criteria. The urgency of the case, time pressures, resource constraints, penalties for inaction, and so on, can all be called upon as overwhelming, dual, or incapacitating factors.

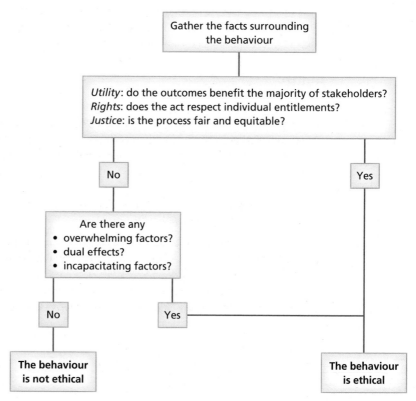

Figure 2.7: The ethical decision tree

STOP AND THINK

Sam and Bob: Sam and Bob are research scientists in the General Rubber product development laboratory. Sam, who is introvert, quiet and serious, is more technically proficient; his patents have earned the company around $6 million over the past ten years. Bob does not have the same expertise, his output is 'solid though unimaginative', and he is extrovert and demonstrative. The rumour is that Bob will be moved into an administrative role. The lab offers a $300,000 fund each year for the best new product idea. Sam and Bob both submit proposals, which are assessed as having equal merit. Sam takes no further action, but Bob conducts a publicity campaign, about which he tells Sam in advance, promoting the advantages of his proposal to those who might influence the final decision. Informal pressure builds to decide in Bob's favour (Cavanagh et al., 1981).

Is Bob's behaviour ethical? Does the ethical decision tree help you to reach a decision?

Manyika et al. (2013) also argue that the nature of work will change, with millions requiring new skills. Some jobs will be automated (service work, for example), and computing power will complement other human skills such as creativity and decision making. Advanced and developing economies will be affected in different ways; energy storage will make electric vehicles more competitive in the former, and will provide developing countries with access to electricity and the internet. The benefits from these technologies will thus not be evenly distributed.

Martin Hirt and Paul Willmott (2014, p.1) note that that computerization is 'profoundly changing the strategic context: altering the structure of competition, the conduct of business, and, ultimately, performance across industries'. They identify three opportunities for organizations:

- *enhancing interaction*, between customers, suppliers, employees and other stakeholders, as consumers come to prefer tailored, mixed-media, digital online communication channels;
- *improving management decisions*, by processing 'big data' and information from 'the internet of things', and thus being able to personalize marketing allocations, and reduce operational risks by sensing equipment breakdowns;
- *creating new business models*, such as crowdsourcing product development, and peer-to-peer customer service.

One of the 12 technologies identified by Manyika et al (2013) is robotics. Robots left movie screens and the pages of science fiction long ago, and they are developing rapidly in the twenty-first century. One driving force, sponsored by the US Pentagon, has been the Defence Advanced Research Projects Agency (DARPA) which organized the Darpa Robotic Challenge (DRC), first held in 2013. Teams were each given $1 million with which to improve their robots and compete again the following year. The estimated cost of the DRC is $80 million, and is based on the belief that robots have many further military, commercial and household benefits. A review of the robotic technology available in 2014 demonstrated the wide range of applications – laboratory assistance, hospital trolley pusher, care for the elderly, carpet cleaning, aerial photography and remote controlled weaponry (Morton, 2014).

Will robots humans at an accelerating pace? Discussion of this issue at the World Economic Forum in Davos in January 2015 estimated that 45 per cent of jobs in the United States would be replaced by robots and other forms of automation over the next 20 years, with the middle tier of jobs disappearing (Tett, 2015). The Forum also concluded that income inequality would get worse.

Robots have traditionally been seen as automating manual work, replacing human effort. Although that trend will continue, robots are now being designed to work alongside humans, in ways that can complement each other's abilities. For example, meet Sawyer (picture opposite). This is a 'cobot', one of a new generation of collaborative robots that are designed to work safely alongside employees. Made by an American company, Rethink

Video case: automation, jobs and history

This six-minute *Financial Times* video is presented by Cardiff Garcia, US editor of FT Alphaville. Garcia considers the future of the labour market as robots threaten to take over more jobs. New technologies are fundamentally different from 'old' technology, and the pattern of replacement and compensation mechanisms that has avoided unemployment in the past may no longer work. Are we creating a divided society? On the one hand, a skilled, employed, affluent elite. On the other, those who are either unemployed or in poorly paid menial jobs.

Computerizing Lego

Lego, the highly profitable (and privately owned) Danish toy manufacturer, famous for its coloured bricks, is not immune from computerization. The company's traditional business model is simple, transforming plastic that costs $1 a kilo into Lego box sets which sell for $75 a kilo. However, children increasingly play games on iPads and smartphones, and Lego's sales growth slowed after 2010. How can Lego compete in the evolving digital world?

Lego's first experiment with the online game *Lego Universe* was not successful. They then developed a partnership with a Swedish company Mojang, which designed *Minecraft*, a popular computer game based on virtual landscapes resembling Lego building blocks. Lego now sells sets based on the game. Another partnership involved TT Games, to develop video games based on Lego ranges such as *Star Wars* and *Legends of Chima*. *The Lego Movie*, made in collaboration with Warner Bros in 2014, generated $500 million when it was released. In partnership with Google, *The Lego Movie* was accompanied by a video game, new construction sets (the giant Sea Cow pirate ship and the hero Emmet Brickowski), and a website (www.buildwithchrome.com). The sequel is scheduled for 2017. Another innovation was *Lego Fusion*. Items built with Lego bricks are captured using a smartphone or tablet which imports them into a 3D digital online world where users can play using their own designs. Lego was one of the most-watched brands on YouTube. Emphasizing the continuing importance of the physical brick, and physical play, Lego's chief executive, Jørgen Vig Knudstorp, explained, 'I see digital as an extra experience layer' (Milne, 2014). With record sales and earnings, Lego became the world's most popular and most profitable toymaker in 2015; the company estimates that, on average, every person on earth owns 102 Lego bricks (Milne, 2015).

The Kobal Collection/Warner Bros

Robotics, Sawyer has a single arm, and can perform a range of tasks in electronics manufacturing such as machine tending and circuit board testing. Another cobot, from Universal Robots, a Danish company, is called UR3, and is a small table-top device that can assemble, polish, glue and screw components, and pack eggs.

In other words, our understanding of what constitutes a robot is changing, to include a much wider range of clever machines that can perform many more functions. Organizations are using cobots to handle jobs that used to need human dexterity and eyesight, and also to deal with problems caused by labour shortages and rising wages. Cobots can also do things that humans find physically difficult or unpleasant. These new cobots are light and easy to move between tasks, and do not require specialist programming skills to operate. This means that they can be used by smaller organizations, which could not afford larger and more expensive traditional robots (Powley, 2015). Rather than be seen as a threat to job security, cobots can work with and help employees in various ways. Faced with an ageing workforce, cobots could enable companies to retain the services of older workers.

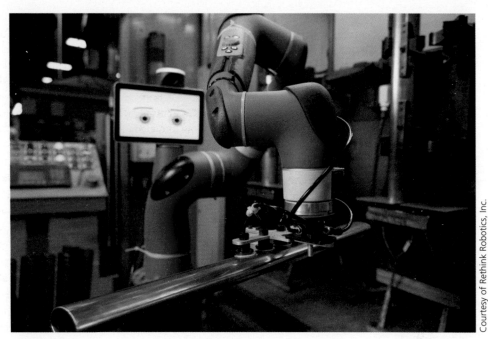

Courtesy of Rethink Robotics, Inc.

Sawyer the cobot

Automating knowledge work

John Markoff (2015) argues that there is a choice between using artificial intelligence (AI) to automate jobs and replace people, and developing 'intelligence augmentation' (IA) systems that make people more effective. As computerization develops, therefore, will knowledge workers be free to deal with more complex and demanding tasks, making them more productive and valuable? Or, like manual workers, will knowledge workers also be replaced by machines?

Automation began with simple routine tasks, in manufacturing and office administration. It is more difficult to automate tasks where adaptability, flexibility, judgement and sophisticated cognitive skills are required, such legal writing, driving a car and managing people. In many professions, computer systems have been used as tools which complement rather than replace human skills and knowledge. However, computerization costs are falling, and computing capabilities are growing: artificial intelligence, speech recognition, pattern matching, machine learning, machine vision, data mining, data analytics, text mining, image processing, problem-solving skills, mobile robotics, drones and wearable technology. More tasks can now be performed efficiently and economically by machine. The traditional advantages of skilled labour are being diluted, through the combination of computing power, clever software and access to very large amounts of information.

Artificial intelligence and big data allow more knowledge work to be automated, such as:

- automating routine communication tasks such as answering customer calls;
- extending the capabilities of professionals, such as doctors and lawyers, with machine learning systems that can identify connections that humans could miss;
- providing automatic content creation and synthesis;
- increasing the consistency of tasks such as searching and analysing information (Chui et al., 2013, p.19).

Carl Frey and Michael Osborne (2013) also note that work can be classified as routine (repetitive) or non-routine (varied, requiring flexibility). The former follows explicit rules or procedures, and the latter is more difficult to codify because of the many exceptions. Work can also be classified in terms of whether manual (physical) or cognitive (intellectual) capabilities are more important. In the past, work that was more easily codified was more readily automated. Now, computerization can handle non-routine work as well. Table 3.2 identifies some of the non-routine manual and cognitive tasks that can now be computerized, thus putting the jobs of some knowledge workers at risk.

Table 3.2: How computerization will affect non-routine tasks

Non-routine work that can now be computerized	
Manual tasks	**Cognitive tasks**
Elderly care	Driving a car in city traffic
Equipment maintenance	Deciphering poor handwriting
Maintaining wind turbines	Financial trading
Quality screening vegetables	Fraud detection
Hospital surgery	Medical diagnostics

Frey and Osborne (2013, p.23) identify three 'bottlenecks' that are preventing or delaying further computerization. These concern the problems that computers still have with tasks that involve perception and manipulation, creative intelligence and social intelligence:

- *Complex perceptual and manipulation tasks*: identifying objects and their properties in a cluttered environment.
- *Creative intelligence tasks*: music, sculpture, jokes, recipes, creative writing.
- *Social intelligence tasks*: negotiating, persuading, caring, counselling, therapy.

These bottlenecks suggest that many non-routine professional tasks cannot be automated. That is not necessarily the case, as Frey and Osborne (2013, p.23) observe:

> Beyond these bottlenecks, however, we argue that it is largely already technologically possible to automate almost any task, provided that sufficient amounts of data are gathered for pattern recognition. Our model thus predicts that the pace at which these bottlenecks can be overcome will determine the extent of computerization in the twenty-first century.

As decisions come to rely more on 'big data', when will 'thinking machines' with artificial intelligence be able to take over top management jobs? Rik Kirkland (2014) argues that data analytics software with pattern-matching capabilities may be able to solve some problems better than senior managers who rely instead on personal experience and intuition. However, he concludes that, because computers are not good at innovating, top executives will still be required for their creative abilities, leadership skills and strategic thinking. Andrew McAfee commented:

> I've still never seen a piece of technology that could negotiate effectively. Or motivate and lead a team. Or figure out what's going on in a rich social situation or what motivates people and how you get them to move in the direction you want. These are human abilities. They're going to stick around. (Kirkland, 2014, p.72)

The work of chief executives and other senior managers requires a high degree of social intelligence, dealing with senior colleagues and other officials to discuss future plans and strategies, coordinate activities, resolve problems, and to negotiate and approve contracts and agreements. Consequently, most management, business and finance occupations where social intelligence is necessary face a low risk of being affected by computerization, as with many jobs in education, healthcare, the arts and media. Engineering and science occupations where high degrees of creative intelligence are required are also 'low risk'. Lawyers are 'low risk', but paralegals and legal assistants are 'high risk'. In general, high skill–high wage occupations are least susceptible to computerization (Keen, 2015).

What can domain newbies do?

'In 2012, a team of four expert pathologists looked through thousands of breast-cancer screening images, and identified the areas of what's called mitosis, the areas which were the most active parts of a tumour. It takes four pathologists to do that because any two only agree with each other 50 percent of the time. It's that hard to look at these images; there's so much complexity. So they then took this kind of consensus of experts and fed those breast-cancer images with those tags to a machine-learning algorithm. The algorithm came back with something that agreed with the pathologists 60 percent of the time, so it is more accurate at identifying the very thing that these pathologists were trained for years to do. And this machine-learning algorithm was built by people with no background in life sciences at all. These are total domain newbies' (Kirkland, 2014, p.69).

Martin Dewhurst and Paul Willmott (2014) also ask whether algorithms could take over from the board of directors. They conclude that, although 'brilliant machines' working with 'big data' will become decision-making aids, 'senior executives will be able to make the biggest difference through the human touch. By this we mean the questions they frame, their vigour in attacking exceptional circumstances highlighted by increasingly intelligent algorithms, and their ability to do things machines can't. That includes tolerating ambiguity and focusing on the "soft" side of management' (Dewhurst and Willmott, 2014, p.77). They also argue that rich information and more powerful analysis tools will empower lower-level managers who will have more decision-making autonomy. This means that senior executives can spend less time on day-to-day management, and focus on longer-term strategic issues, and on solving major problems when the need arises.

Use your soft skills

'Humans have and will continue to have a strong comparative advantage when it comes to inspiring the troops, empathizing with customers, developing talent, and the like. Sometimes, machines will provide invaluable input, as Laszlo Bock at Google has famously shown in a wide range of human-resource data-analytics efforts. But translating this insight into messages that resonate with organizations will require a human touch. No computer will ever manage by walking around. And no effective executive will try to galvanize action by saying, "we're doing this because an algorithm told us to"' (Dewhurst and Willmott, 2014, p.82).

New ways of working

Nonstandard work employment that does not involve a fixed working schedule at the same physical location for an extended time.

Computerization, and in particular the mobile internet and cloud technology, has encouraged the development of various forms of **nonstandard work**. These are jobs which do not involve turning up at the same place and time every day to work under supervision with the mutual expectation that this arrangement will be permanent. Various labels are used for nonstandard work: alternative, contingent, contract, disposable, e-lance, freelance, telecommuting, workshifting. In a nonstandard job, your place of work is just as likely to be in your home, or a coffee shop. For some, the world has become a virtual office. Census data suggest that, in America, 10 per cent of the working population have nonstandard jobs, and that these are more common for high skill–high pay knowledge workers such as independent contractors, researchers and consultants, managers and other professionals. The same trend applies in Britain, Australia, Canada, Europe, Japan and parts of Asia (Ashford et al., 2007). The exercise of knowledge, creativity and problem-solving skills requires more freedom and flexibility than traditional bureaucracy allows, and computerization has made this possible.

Many of us prefer nonstandard work because it is flexible and varied, free from direct management supervision and organization politics, is often better paid, and gives us

STOP AND THINK What for you are the benefits and disadvantages of nonstandard work? If you know someone who has a nonstandard job, ask them how they feel about it. Would their experience encourage you to find nonstandard work?

a lifestyle in which we can more easily combine work with personal and family interests. These preferences have been linked to the expectations of Generation Y – the Netgeneration – born since 1980 and who have grown up with today's technology. Gen Y does not have a monopoly on these preferences and lifestyles, which are also characteristic of many Gen Xers and Baby Boomers (see Chapter 2). One of the challenges created by these trends concerns managing a *blended workforce*, in which standard and nonstandard employees work in collaboration, but with different working conditions and lifestyles.

Home viewing

In the movie *Ex Machina* (2015, director Alex Garland), Caleb (played by Dohmnall Gleeson) wins a company competition; the prize is to spend a week in the house of the chief executive Nathan (Oscar Isaac). Nathan wants Caleb to test his creation, Ava (Alicia Vikander), an artificially intelligent humanoid robot. Is she really intelligent? Does she have consciousness? Will there come a time when we will not be able to distinguish between human and robot? What does this movie suggest may be the benefits and dangers of artificial intelligence?

What motivates those who design and manufacture these machines? The theme of *Ex Machina* is similar to that of *I Robot* (2004, director Alex Proyas) in which Chicago cop Del Spooner (Will Smith) investigates the possibility that a robot has overridden its programming and committed murder. In 2015, the famous physicist Stephen Hawking predicted that artificially intelligent machines will eventually take over from their inferior human creators. In your assessment, is that a possibility, or is that claim exaggerated?

There are many personal and organizational advantages. Working from home does not need expensive office space. There is no distracting office 'chit chat'. The time, costs and frustrations of travel to work are cut. Many organizations report increased efficiency, productivity, work turnaround, accuracy, speed of response and morale. Where location is not important, an organization can use people whom they might not otherwise employ. For the employee, there is freedom to arrange the working day without supervision, and you become your own boss.

Workshifters

Workshifter: someone who works from coffee shops, hotels, airports, home, anywhere.

Workspace, not workplace: that's the new mantra of forward-thinking companies where business leaders know that it's not where their employees work, but how they work that makes the difference. Whether they are in an airport departure lounge, a conference centre, a client's offices, or simply in the study or spare bedroom of their own home, a new breed of employee – a group sometimes referred to as 'workshifters' – is increasingly demanding access to corporate information from a huge variety of physical locations.

In fact, say workshifters, flexibility is key to their job satisfaction. In a recent survey of 3,100 mobile workers at over 1,100 enterprises worldwide, almost

Chad Ehlers/Alamy

two-thirds (64 per cent) reported improved work/life balance and more than half (51 per cent) say that they feel more relaxed because of more flexible working arrangements.

At BT, for example, flexible workers are judged to be 20 per cent more productive than their office-based colleagues. At American Express, teleworkers handle 26 per cent more calls and produce 43 per cent more business. Bosses at Dow Chemicals, meanwhile, have calculated that average productivity has increased by around 38 per cent since the introduction of its flexible work programme. In all these cases, contributing factors seem to be fewer interruptions and more effective time management, because better connectivity means less time is wasted while sitting on a train, for example, or in the odd free hour between conference sessions. (© Twentyman, News International Trading Ltd, 6 October 2011)

From Twentyman (2011)

Could the office become a 'dead concept' in the second machine age? Are organizations 'ditching the desk'? A survey by a meetings room booking agency found that (Bounds, 2015):

- three-fifths of workers say that they do not need to be in an office to be productive;
- 60 per cent of professionals work outside the office;
- on average office desks are unoccupied for over 60 per cent of the time.

Tablets, phablets, iPads, smartphones, Wi-Fi, broadband, mobile internet and cloud storage have reduced the need for daily travel to a specific place of work. In 1998, there were 2.9 million 'homeworkers' in the UK (working at home, or using home as a base). By 2014, that had risen to 4.2 million – about 14 per cent of the working population (Office of National Statistics: www.ons.gov.uk). In 2015 the public relations agency M&C Saatchi removed most of the desks and desktop computers in its London offices, to encourage staff to work 'free range' anywhere (Spanier, 2015, p.11). The flexibility of working from home can lead to higher job satisfaction and better work–life balance.

However, not being seen in the office can create problems. Kimberly Elsbach et al. (2010) interviewed 39 managers in offices in California, to explore their observations and assessments of their staff. They found that homeworkers who were high performers were nevertheless promoted less often than their colleagues who turned up for work. The researchers' explanation for this concerns 'passive face time' – the amount of time that you are seen at work, without talking to anyone. This means being observed sitting at a desk, working in a public area, or attending meetings. Face time can be *expected* (normal working hours), or *extracurricular* (arriving early, leaving late). If you have lots of expected face time, you are likely to be seen as more responsible, dependable, reliable, trustworthy and conscientious. Put in some extracurricular face time, and you may also be seen as more committed, dedicated, devoted and caring. For example, managers in interviews said:

'So this one guy, he's in the room at every meeting. Lots of times he doesn't say anything, but he's there on time and people notice that. He definitely is seen as a hardworking and dependable guy.'

'Working on the weekends makes a very good impression. It sends a signal that you're contributing to your team and that you're putting in that extra commitment to get the work done.' (Elsbach et al., 2010, p.745)

Observers use passive face time at work to assess employees' characteristics, and in particular how responsible and committed they are. As a manager, you need to be aware of this when evaluating performance, and give more weight to employee output and other contributions. As an employee, you need to be aware that working at home can improve your work–life balance, but can also damage your career, by affecting your status, performance evaluations, salary increases and chances of promotion.

Along with the flexibility, freedom and work–life balance, nonstandard work has disadvantages:

- high set-up costs (but hardware and software costs are falling);
- employees are not able to share equipment and other office facilities;
- lack of face-to-face social interaction, sharing of ideas, team spirit;
- employees lose touch with organizational culture and goals;
- management cannot easily monitor and control activity;
- some customers, partners and suppliers are reassured by a 'conventional' office.

Despite the working style choices which increasing computerization has created, does that daily commute to work now sound more worthwhile?

The social matrix

Social technology is a massive technological and social phenomenon – but its power as a business tool is still being discovered. Never before has a communications medium been adopted as quickly or as widely as social media. It took commercial television 13 years to reach 50 million households, and Internet service providers took three years to sign their 50 millionth subscriber. But it took Facebook just a year and Twitter even less time to reach the same milestone.

Socially enabled applications will become ubiquitous, allowing liking, commenting, and information sharing across a large array of activities. We will live and conduct business in a social matrix, where virtually all resources can be found – collaborators, talent, customers, funders. The social matrix will enable new forms of organization that are only just becoming apparent. (Chui et al., 2013, p.3)

The Internet at first offered 'flat' applications, with which users could not interact; communications were one-way only. The social networking service Facebook was launched in 2004, and we now have many internet-mediated tools that allow two-way, real-time communication, collaboration and co-creation. In 2015, Facebook claimed over 1 billion users; LinkedIn had 300 million; over 250 million people used Twitter; Pinterest had over 70 million users. WeChat, the Chinese mobile text and messaging service had around 440 million active users, which is more than the population of the United States. These tools allow us to create and share information, ideas, pictures, music and videos. The mobile internet and cloud storage mean that we can do this where and when we want, without having to rely on traditional corporate computing. Social media and mobile technologies are 'low friction' tools: they are everywhere, easy to use, and flexible. Another feature is their rapid development; much of this chapter will be out of date before this text is published.

Social matrix an environment in which any online activity can be social, influencing actions, solving problems, innovating and creating new types of organizations that are not constrained by traditional boundaries.

Social media are radically changing the ways in which we interact with each other, develop our relationships, share experiences and form opinions. These networking tools have also changed the ways in which organizations interact with and gather information about their customers. We now live and work in a social matrix in which any interaction or activity can become social (Chui et al., 2013, p.3). Crowdsourcing can help to solve problems. Crowdfunding can support new business ideas. Collaboration and knowledge sharing can be encouraged through social networks. Customers can be attracted by the 'social' features of new products and services, which they can help to improve. Facebook 'likes' can be used to identify what products people are buying and to improve retail merchandising and marketing, for example.

A study by McKinsey Global Institute concluded that social media could increase the productivity of knowledge workers by 20 to 25 per cent, as people would spend much less time looking for information (Chui et al., 2013). In January 2015 Facebook launched a corporate version of its social networking platform, called Facebook at Work. A number of corporate 'partners' were asked to experiment with its possibilities, to discover if this could increase employee productivity by sharing ideas through posts, groups and messages. This development was triggered by the observation that Facebook's own staff were using the network instead of email for internal communication. This new platform sought to address organizational concerns over data security, intellectual property and privacy. Unlike 'personal' Facebook, information shared on Facebook at Work belongs to the employer, and employees who leave will not have access to their corporate account (Kuchler, 2015).

Collaborative potential

'Kraft Foods, which had launched an internal social network in 2011, saw the potential to raise the level of collaboration and knowledge sharing across the corporation by investing in a more powerful social networking platform. The new system supports microblogging, automatic content tagging, and easy creation and maintenance of subgroups for communities of practice (e.g., pricing experts). This has accelerated knowledge sharing, leading to shorter development cycles, as well as quicker responses to actions of competitors.

'Firms are exploring using social media tools to reduce email, which is responsible for more than a quarter of the typical office worker's time. French IT services provider Atos SE pledged in 2011 to become a "zero email" company by 2014 and aims to boost employee productivity by replacing email with a collaborative social networking platform' (from Chui, 2013, p.5).

Social media are in widespread use, especially by younger employees. These technologies could thus make significant contributions to organizational effectiveness. Jonny Gifford (2013) argues that the main ones are:

Efficient communication: increase efficiency of communication and knowledge transfer, getting the right information to the right people.

Employee voice: seeking employee views, giving employees a platform.

Networking and collaboration: creating meaningful connections with people we would otherwise not know, and facilitating collaboration.

Learning and development: the use of social media to support e-learning and development and to encourage self-directed learning.

Recruitment and job hunting: social networking sites are now widely used for recruitment; employers and job-seekers use social media to check each other to inform their choices.

These applications promise to transform internal communications and staff engagement, recruitment and learning. Social media could be central in encouraging more open, communicative, egalitarian, collaborative and responsive organizational cultures. However, ease of communications can also generate information overload. How are organizations actually using social media? Marketing and customer services have already been affected. Social media allow consumers to share opinions of brands to a wider audience than word-of-mouth can reach. Consumers are therefore 'hyper-informed' when making purchasing decisions. Customer service is also being transformed, with half of US customers using social media to raise complaints or ask questions; a third of social media users say that they prefer this channel to the phone when dealing with customer service issues (Bannon, 2012). Organizations must be sensitive to these trends, and respond accordingly.

The use of social media in relation to employee engagement, productivity, innovation and communication, however, are more diffuse. The applications listed above allow organizations to tailor information to individuals and groups. The organization can communicate with large numbers of people at the same time, regardless of location, thus creating dialogue concerning particular topics and problems, and encouraging networks and collaboration. Social networking sites can also reveal (to potential employers) information about candidates' abilities and characteristics, and also display (to potential employees) an organization's culture, goals and priorities, such as attitude to corporate social responsibility, for example.

Social media drivers

A survey of executives found that the main drivers of social media adoption were (Matthews, 2015):

1. responding faster to changing needs
2. optimizing business processes
3. increasing revenue and profits
4. attracting the best talent in a competitive market
5. better-engaged employees.

Signs of the social networking times.

In 2011, the consulting company McKinsey held a contest to find companies using social media in innovative ways, to improve management methods and engage frontline employees (McKinsey & Company, 2011). Demonstrating the uses and benefits of these tools, here are some of the winners:

The Dutch Civil Service. Dutch government employees faced bureaucratic hurdles, such as having to book meeting rooms in their own buildings through an external agency, which took time and generated costs. Following a frustrated tweet from one member of staff, a group formed, and used open-source software to develop their own reservation system. This now covers over 50 offices and over 550 workplaces in government buildings across the country.

Essilor International. Essilor is a global manufacturer of ophthalmic lenses, and has a training programme with personal and Web 2.0 approaches to share best practices across 102 sites in 40 countries. It now takes one year to reach the level of skill that once took three years, and social networking allows coaching across different locations. A lens-processing centre in Thailand developed a game to teach new employees how to understand the shape of a particular type of lens, and this game is now also used in Brazil.

Best Buy. Best Buy is a consumer electronics retailer with 1,500 locations and 100,000 employees. To ensure that top management understood what frontline staff learned from customers, the company created an online feedback system which allowed everyone to see the customer information gathered in all the stores. This influenced a range of practices, from improving shop signs, to complex decisions about implementing a national promotion. This was a fast, flexible and inexpensive way of responding to 'the voice of the customer'.

Cemex. Cemex is a large Mexico-based cement company, which developed an approach to employee collaboration called Shift. This helped to reduce the time taken to introduce new products and process improvements. Shift uses wikis, blogs, discussion boards and web-conferencing to help employees around the world collaborate with each other. For example, 400 employees working on ready-mix products helped to identify which worked well, and which were obsolete, slimming the product line and updating the global catalogue. Now, with over 500 active communities, Shift is used to solve local problems, using global resources, as well as storing and sharing the knowledge that is generated.

Those organizations may be rare examples. A survey of 2,100 UK employees and 590 human resource managers suggests that the development of novel uses of social media has been slow and that few employees used these tools for work (Gifford, 2013). Only one-quarter of the organizations surveyed allowed staff to connect personal smartphones and tablets to the organization's IT network. Employees are probably more sophisticated in the use of social media tools in their private lives than are employers with regard to organizational applications. Where organizations were using these technologies, they were more likely to be targeting external (customers, other stakeholders) rather than internal audiences. Applications of 'employee voice' were superficial, with management seeking employee views, but not necessarily being more responsive or open to influence as a result. There was limited corporate support for BYOD (bring your own device) practices.

A study in 2013 examined how chief executives in American organizations used four social networks: Twitter, LinkedIn, Facebook and Google Plus. Around 30 per cent were LinkedIn members, but participation in other networks was 'dismal'. Linda Pophal (2014, p.23) concludes, 'It appears that few CEOs and other senior executives are familiar with, or convinced of, the benefits of communicating via social media'. Access to social networking and mobile technology is not a barrier; a perceived lack of organizational relevance is.

Antisocial media

One large UK bank had a company intranet, which gave staff the opportunity to give feedback to senior management. During a major reorganization, which involved cutting costs, and the closure of many branches with job losses, the bank's human resources director decided to assess staff morale. He posted an intranet article which praised employees' commitment and flexibility. Staff were asked to leave comments, and hundreds responded. Most of the feedback was negative:

'If you want promotion do every extracurricular task that you can. Don't worry about the quality of the work as it is irrelevant.'

'Either execs are lying, or somewhere down the line people are misrepresenting what is being communicated from above.'

'Why should we trust you after what you did on pensions?'

Most complaints concerned the decision to close the generous final salary pension scheme. This happened at the same time as the chief executive was awarded a large pension contribution as part of his multi-million-pound annual package, and was seen as showing double standards. Staff also criticized the excessive bureaucracy and lack of top management support. The corporate intranet makes it easy for management to capture staff feedback. That feedback, however, may be unfavourable, particularly when management actions are seen as inconsistent, or unfair.

There are three challenges to the further development of these technologies:

1. Finding ways to exploit social media effectively, to achieve organizational goals. Those goals may include external relationships and reputation, and internal culture change to improve engagement, information sharing, collaboration and the organization's ability to respond rapidly to trends and new ideas.

2. Finding the best 'fit' between new online tools and the social system of the organization, including the needs, interests and preferences of employees. Socio-technical system design has become more important in this context, given the pace of technology development.

3. Designing and redesigning effective socio-technical systems when, as noted earlier, the technologies involved are moving targets. The number and nature of digital tools and social networking sites are constantly evolving. Individuals and organizations are still developing an understanding of how they can be used effectively, for personal and corporate benefit.

The development of *enterprise-specific* social networks may help to realize the potential of these technologies. Employees can be involved in two-way discussions using a secure 'gated' corporate networking platform, for incubating ideas and feeding these to senior management. This can also be used to facilitate ad hoc communication and collaboration. Social networking can be a more engaging medium than traditional communication tools, to send corporate messages, quickly capture employee reactions, to check that messages have been understood, and for information-sharing in general. A corporate social network could strengthen the sense of shared purpose, by celebrating achievements, reinforcing mission and values, and strengthening identification with the organization. From a study of seven organizations with internal networks, Gifford (2014) offers this advice:

• Enterprise networks need a clear rationale or purpose if they are to be used and become embedded. They need to support day-to-day activities.

• The process of identifying uses is better developed bottom-up, coming from staff. But effective uses need to be identified and replicated if they are to spread and be sustained.

• It helps if there is a key individual, or a team of 'community champions' guiding and encouraging the use of social media until this reaches critical mass.

• Enterprise social networks are time-efficient ways for senior managers to engage with large numbers of staff and to increase their visibility. However, the effects will be negative if senior management challenge or criticize comments with which they disagree.

• Social networks should be self-managed and not censored; policies should be 'light touch' (with an expectation that posts will be 'respectful'); negative comments should be dealt with frankly and openly; employees should be informed if comments have caused offence.

Social media offer a range of powerful, flexible, 'information-rich' communication channels, which appear to have valuable uses. Organizations that have experimented with these technologies have achieved significant benefits. Most of the tools are public, and require little skill to use. In order to develop beneficial applications, it also seems that innovation and experimentation will be necessary in order to tailor these new methods to local conditions and organizational goals.

Four challenges

The second machine age will transform many sectors and jobs, public and private sector, and will generate social and economic benefits. New disruptive technologies will improve quality of working life, health and healthcare, and the environment. However, there seem to be at least four challenges that governments and organizations will need to address: the problems of growing inequality and skill shortages, and the increasing risks of cybercrime and technological unemployment.

Inequality

As more routine manual tasks are automated, in manufacturing, services and office work, demand for unskilled employees will fall. This could create a 'two-tier society' with growing inequality. There will be a well-paid elite, of owners, 'supermanagers' and professionals who have valuable skills and knowledge, and whose capabilities are complemented by technology. The rest will be unemployed, or will have poorly paid, routine tasks that machines are still unable to do (dog walking, cleaning). Those in the middle will be squeezed out. Inequality can be socially and politically dangerous, especially if it is visible and extreme, and those who do not belong to the elite believe that they have been treated unfairly. Extreme pay inequality generates grievances and protests.

CHAPTER EXERCISES

1. Into the matrix

Objectives

1. To encourage breadth of thinking about a topic, in this case the social matrix.
2. To develop skills in producing a wide-ranging and balanced assessment.
3. To consider the extent to which technology determines or facilitates the outcomes or impacts that it produces.

Briefing

The issue for debate is: What are the individual, organizational, and social benefits and dangers of living and working in a social matrix?

Divide into groups of three. Your group's task is to think of as many relevant points as you can concerning the issue for debate. List these points on a flipchart for presentation. Time allowed: 10 to 15 minutes.

Present your points in plenary. Your points will be awarded 'quality marks' for relevance, importance, plausibility, and creativity. If your argument for a point is particularly impressive or original, you can win more quality marks. The group with the highest quality marks will be declared the winner. Time allowed depends on number of groups: up to 45 minutes.

Consider two of the main benefits and two of the main dangers that you have identified. To what extent are these inevitable consequences of the social matrix? To what extent do these consequences depend on how individuals and organizations decide to use the technologies that are involved?

2. Old McDonald's Farm

Objective

To explore the integration of social and technical aspects of an organization (Marcic, 1995).

Briefing

Organizations are socio-technical systems. This means that technology – equipment, machines, processes, materials, layout – has to work alongside people – structures, roles, role relationships, job design. You can't design an organization to suit the technology while ignoring the people, because that would be ineffective. Similarly, designing an organization just to suit the people, while ignoring the requirements of the technology, would be equally disastrous. The concept of socio-technical system design means that the social system and the technical system have to be designed so that they can work with each other.

Old McDonald's farm

Let's consider Old McDonald's farm. On this farm, he had no pigs, cows, or chickens. He had only corn, planted in long rows that grew all year round. McDonald had a perfect environment for growing corn. The soil was rich, and the climate was perfect, 12 months every year.

McDonald's rows were so long that at one end of the row, the soil was being prepared for planting, while the next section on that row was being planted, the next section was growing, and the next was being harvested. McDonald had four of these long rows.

McDonald is a progressive and scientific farmer. He is concerned about both productivity and quality. He had an industrial engineer study the amount of effort required to complete the work in each function on each row. He found that two employees were required per section, on each row, fully employed in that function all year round. Therefore, he employed eight workers on each row.

Initially, Mr McDonald had only four rows, A, B, C and D, and a total of 32 people. But he decided to expand, adding two more rows. This added 16 more workers. Now he had 48 employees. Until this time, he had only one supervisor responsible for directing the work of all 32 employees on the initial four rows. Now he decided that there was too much work for one supervisor. He added another.

Mr McDonald now had to decide whether to reorganize the work of his managers and employees. He decided to talk to his two supervisors, Mr Jones and Mr Smith, who had very different ideas.

Mr Jones insisted that the only intelligent way to organize was around the technical knowledge, the functional expertise. He argued that he should take responsibility for all employees working on the first two sections, soil preparation and planting, on all rows. Mr Smith, he acknowledged, had greater expertise in growing and harvesting, so he would take responsibility for all employees in the last two sections. They would each have an equal number of employees to supervise.

Mr Smith had a different idea. He argued that, while some specialized knowledge was needed, it was more important for the employees to take responsibility for the entire growing cycle. This way, they could move down the row, seeing the progress of the corn. He argued for organizing the employees into teams by row.

	Soil prep	Planting	Growing	Harvesting
Row A				
Row B				
Row C				
Row D				
Row E				
Row F				

Mr McDonald has hired you as a consultant to help him with his organizational design. The questions that he wants you to answer are:

1. How will you organize employees on the farm, and how will you assign responsibility to Smith and Jones? You can recommend any assignment that you like, but the numbers of employees that are required will stay the same.

2. What socio-technical principles support your recommendations? Why is your approach better than the alternatives?

If you were one of Mr McDonald's employees, which approach to organizational design would you prefer, and why?

Employability assessment

With regard to your future employment prospects:

1. Identify up to three issues from this chapter that you found significant.
2. Relate these to the competencies in the employability matrix.
3. Decide what actions you need to take to maintain and/or develop those competencies under each of the four headings of the employability matrix.

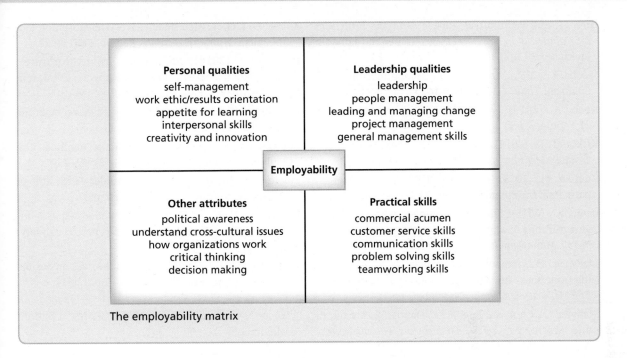

The employability matrix

References

Andrew, P., Ip, J., Worthington, J. and Brooke, C. (2014) *Fast Forward 2030: The Future of Work and the Workplace*. Los Angeles: CBRE/Genesis.

Ashford, S.J., George, E. and Blatt, R. (2007) 'Old assumptions, new work: the opportunities and challenges of research on nonstandard employment', *The Academy of Management Annals*, 1 (1): 65–117.

Avent, R. (2014) 'The third great wave', *The Economist Special Report: The World Economy*, 4 October, pp.1–18.

Bannon, D. (2012) *The Social Media Report*. New York: Neilsen Holdings.

Bounds, A. (2015) 'Desk-bound offices a "dead concept"', *Financial Times*, 21 April, p.4.

Brynjolfsson, E. and McAfee, A. (2014) *The Second Machine Age: Work, Progress, and Prosperity in a Time of Brilliant Technologies*. New York and London: W.W. Norton & Company.

Chui, M., Manyika, J., Bughin, J., Brown, B., Roberts, R., Danielson, J. and Gupta, S. (2013) *Ten IT-Enabled Business Trends for the Decade Ahead*. New York: McKinsey & Company/McKinsey Global Institute.

Dewhurst, M. and Willmott, P. (2014) 'Manager and machine: the new leadership equation', *McKinsey Quarterly*, September, pp.76–83.

Elsbach, K.D., Cable, D.M. and Sherman, J.W. (2010) 'How passive 'face time' affects perceptions of employees: evidence of spontaneous trait inference', *Human Relations*, 63 (6): 735–60.

Emery, R.E. and Trist, E.L. (1960) 'Socio-technical systems', in C.W. Churchman and M. Verhulst (eds), *Management Science, Models and Techniques, Volume 2*. London: Pergamon Press, pp.83–97.

Frean, A. (2011) 'Financial terrorists pose grave risk to US', *The Times*, 2 February, p.9.

Frey, C.B. and Osborne, M.A. (2013) 'The future of employment: how susceptible are jobs to computerization?', Oxford: University of Oxford Department of Engineering Science.

Gifford, J. (2013) *Social Technology, Social Business?* London: Chartered Institute for Personnel and Development.

Gifford, J. (2014) *Putting Social Media to Work: Lessons from Employers*. London: Chartered Institute for Personnel and Development.

Gottlieb, J. and Willmott, P. (2014) *McKinsey Global Survey Results: The Digital Tipping Point*. New Jersey and London: McKinsey & Company.

Gratton, L. (2011) *The Shift: The Future of Work is Already Here*. London: Collins.

Hirt, M. and Willmott, P. (2014) *Strategic Principles for Competing in the Digital Age*. Taipei and London: McKinsey & Company.

Jacobs, E. (2015) 'Advice for the second machine age', *Financial Times*, 31 March, p.14.

Keen, A. (2015) *The Sunday Times News Review*, 22 February, p.2.

Kirkland, R. (2014) 'Artificial intelligence meets the C-suite', *McKinsey Quarterly*, September, pp.66–75.

Kuchler, H. (2015) 'Facebook at Work opens to trial partners', *The Financial Times*, 14 January, p.8.

Lewis, G. (2015) 'She's the employee who could cost you millions... and she's not even a real person', *People Management*, January, pp.8–10.

McKinsey & Company (2011) 'Social technologies on the front line: The Management 2.0 M-Prize winners', *The McKinsey Quarterly*, September, pp.1–4.

Manyika, J., Chui, M., Bughin, J., Dobbs, R., Bisson, P. and Marrs, A. (2013) *Disruptive Technologies: Advances That Will Transform Life, Business and the Global Economy*. New York: McKinsey & Company/ McKinsey Global Institute

Marcic, D. (1995) *Organizational Behavior: Experience and Cases* (4th edn). St Paul, MN: West Publishing.

Markillie, P. (2012) 'Manufacturing and innovation: special report', *The Economist* (supplement), 21 April.

Markoff, J. (2015) *Machines of Loving Grace: The Quest for Common Ground between Humans and Robots*. New York: Ecco Press.

Matthews, D. (2015) 'Digital transformation in the workplace', *The Times Raconteur Supplement*, 9 April, pp.4–6.

Milne, R. (2014) 'Lego: King of the castle', *Financial Times*, 10 July, p.13.

Milne, R. (2015) 'Lego shores up title of most profitable toymaker', *Financial Times*, 26 February, p.18.

Morey, T., Forbath, T. and Schoop, A. (2015) 'Customer data: designing for transparency and trust', *Harvard Business Review*, 93 (5): 96–107.

Morse, G. (2006) 'High fidelity: Ivor Tiefenbrun on tapping talent', *Harvard Business Review*, 84 (11): 28.

Morton, O. (2014) 'Immigrants from the future', *The Economist Special Report on Robots*, 29 March, pp.1–16.

Pennington, C. (2015) 'App can help you sweet-talk the boss', *The Sunday Times*, 3 May, p.8.

Pophal, L. (2014) 'How to sell social media to the C-suite', *Communication World*, 31 (2): 22–25.

Powley, T. (2015) 'Robots rub shoulders with human buddies', *Financial Times*, 19 March, p.27.

Robertson, D. (2011) 'Cyber bandits under suspicion for wiping billions off companies', *The Times*, 31 January, pp.12–13.

Spanier, G. (2015) 'Companies ditch the desk as flexible workers stretch out', *The Times*, 22 April, p.11.

Stewart, I., De, D. and Cole, A. (2014) *Technology and People: The Great Job-Creating Machine*. London: Deloitte LLP.

Tett. G. (2015) 'The changing face of employment', *Financial Times*, 30 January, p.23.

The Economist (2011) 'The war on terabytes', 31 December, pp.49–50.

Townsend, K. (2011) 'The evolving threat landscape', *The Times, Raconteur on IT Supplement*, 6 October, pp.4–5.

Trist, E.L. and Bamforth, K.W. (1951) 'Some social and psychological consequences of the longwall method of coal-getting', *Human Relations*, 4 (1): 3–38.

Twentyman, J. (2011) 'Workspaces: the new word for workplace', *The Times, Raconteur on IT Supplement*, 6 October, p.17.

Upton, D.M. and Creese, S. (2014) 'The danger from within', *Harvard Business Review*, 92 (9): 94–101.

Walton, R.E. and Susman, G.I. (1987) 'People policies for the new machines', *Harvard Business Review*, 65 (2): 98–106.

Chapter 4 **Culture**

Key terms

organizational culture

surface manifestations of organizational culture

organizational values

basic assumptions

organizational socialization

pre-arrival stage of socialization

encounter stage of socialization

role modelling

metamorphosis stage of socialization

integration (or unitary) perspective on culture

differentiation perspective on culture

fragmentation (or conflict) perspective on culture

strong culture

weak culture

internal integration

external adaptation

social orientation

power orientation

uncertainty orientation

goal orientation

time orientation

Learning outcomes

When you have read this chapter, you should be able to define those key terms in your own words, and you should also be able to:

1. Account for the popularity of the concept of organizational culture among managers and researchers.

2. List, describe, and give examples of Schein's three levels of organizational culture.

3. Distinguish the stages of organizational socialization.

4. Contrast managerial and social science perspectives on organizational culture.

5. Assess the link between organizational culture and organizational performance.

6. Distinguish between different types of organizational culture.

7. Distinguish different dimensions of national culture.

Why study organizational culture?

Organizational culture can be thought of as the personality of an organization. It is also often referred to as corporate culture. It deals with how things are done in a company on a daily basis. It affects how employees perform their work; how they relate to each other, to customers, and to their managers. Organizational culture affects not only task issues – how well or badly an organization performs, but also emotional issues – how workers feel about their work and their companies.

Banking cultures of concern

Can you name a bank that has been reported as being involved in some financial irregularity in recent years? Perhaps it is easier to name one that has not. Banks have been accused of rash lending, tax evasion, financial mis-selling, attempts to manipulate the London Inter-bank Offer Rate (Libor) and the foreign exchange (forex) markets, and even of money laundering. CCP Research Foundation estimated that since 2010, the world's largest banks have spent over $300 billion on litigation (Shotter, 2015). Some have admitted their misdemeanours and been fined, sued, forced to make reparations, or all three. When challenged by the media or an investigating parliamentary committee, their senior managers claim that the problem was caused by a small group of staff or an isolated individual employee ('a bad apple') who has now resigned, been dismissed, or else is being retrained.

However, the prevalence of such misconduct within the banking industry around the world suggests that this form of organizational behaviour cannot be explained solely in terms of individual factors. Instead, it is necessary to ask questions about the ethics of the banking industry in general, and about the cultures of the individual banks in particular. Peter Day (2012) argued that the banking industry's culture had changed from doing 'what is right' to doing what is OK by the lawyers and compliance officers or, as he puts it, 'doing what you can get away with'. If banking culture is the problem, then changing it has to be the solution. Two main changes have been proposed:

More women. The UK Parliamentary Committee on Banking Standards reported that 'The culture on the trading floor is overwhelmingly male' and called for a better gender balance in investment banks (Thompson and Jain, 2013). The argument is that research shows that high levels of male testosterone fuel a greater willingness to take risks, so you can reduce both by increasing the number of women on the trading floor. Others argue that physiological diversity is more important, so you need older males as well as women.

More training. Over a quarter of a million employees of some of the major international banks have been undergoing training to reinforce work codes, company values, desired employee behaviour, and positive corporate culture. However, there is scepticism that managers can successfully monitor, measure, and maintain adherence to corporate values, especially when competitive pressures mount (Hill, 2013).

A study by André Spicer and colleagues (2014) concluded that the 'toxic' and 'aggressive' culture inside British banks which led to the aforementioned scandals would take a generation to change. Poor standards have so far cost the UK banking industry £38.5 billion in fines and customer compensation. The messages from top banking executives about culture change are still not reaching frontline staff. 'Culture change initiatives particularly in the large institutions, remain relatively fragile', concludes the report.

If there are so many 'bad apples' then just culture training them may not be enough or even appropriate. Banks need to change their 'barrels' by modifying their organization structures, and changing their processes of staff recruitment, promotion, day-to-day decision making, and particularly staff remuneration. The chief executive of one bank reported that it had completely overhauled the way that its employees' performance was measured and how they were being incentivized (Arnold, 2014). Rather than blaming 'bad apples', it may be more appropriate to ask what the senior 'barrel-makers' are doing (Zimbardo, 2007).

Organizational culture has been a popular topic since the early 1980s. First adopted by senior executives and management consultants as a quick-fix solution to virtually every organizational problem, it was later adopted by researchers as an explanatory framework with which to understand behaviour in organizations (Alvesson, 2001). Ann Cunliffe (2008) states that organizational culture is important because it:

- shapes the image that the public has of an organization;
- influences organizational effectiveness;
- provides direction for the company;
- helps to attract, retain and motivate staff.

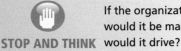

STOP AND THINK   If the organization that you are currently studying at or working in were a person, would it be male or female? How old would it be? Where would it live? What car would it drive?

Rise of organizational culture

Organizational culture the shared values, beliefs and norms which influence the way employees think, feel and act towards others inside and outside the organization.

Organizational culture remains a controversial concept. Some writers argue that just as one can talk about French culture, Arab culture, or Asian culture, so too it is possible to discuss the organizational culture of the British Civil Service, McDonald's, Microsoft, or of Disney. It is generally recognized that organizations have 'something' (a personality, philosophy, ideology, or climate) which goes beyond economic rationality, and which gives each of them their own unique identity. Organizational culture has been variously described as 'the way we do things around here' (Deal and Kennedy, 1982), 'how people behave when no one is watching', and 'the collective programming of the mind' (Hofstede, 1980, 2001).

The current debates about culture are traceable to the early 1980s when two books catapulted the concept to the forefront of management attention, *In Search of Excellence*, written by Tom Peters and Robert Waterman (1982); and Terrence Deal and Allan Kennedy's (1982) *Corporate Cultures*. These publications suggested that a strong organizational culture was a powerful lever for guiding workforce behaviour. Other factors also stimulated an interest in culture:

- Japan's industrial success during the 1970s and 1980s.
- Increasing globalization placed organizational culture into sharp focus alongside national culture.
- The assumption that organizational performance depended on employee values being aligned with company strategy.
- The contentious view that management could manipulate culture to achieve organizational (change) objectives.
- The belief that intangible (soft) factors such as values and beliefs impacted on financial (hard) ones such as profits.

Originally introduced to managers by consultants, it was not long before academics started to take an interest in organizational culture as well. Edgar Schein (2004), a business school professor, was among the first to refine the concept, seeking to measure it for research purposes. Research attention turned to the meanings and beliefs that employees assigned to organizational behaviour, and how these influenced the ways in which they themselves behaved in companies (Schultz, 1995).

Culture: surface manifestations, values and basic assumptions

Surface manifestation of organizational culture culture's most accessible forms which are visible and audible behaviour patterns and objects.

Edgar Schein's (2004) model is widely accepted and considers organizational culture in terms of three levels, each distinguished by its visibility to, and accessibility by individuals (Figure 4.1). Schein's first level is the surface manifestation of organizational culture, also called 'observable culture'. It refers to the visible things that a culture produces. It includes both physical objects and also behaviour patterns that can be seen, heard or felt. These all 'send a message' to an organization's employees, suppliers, and customers.

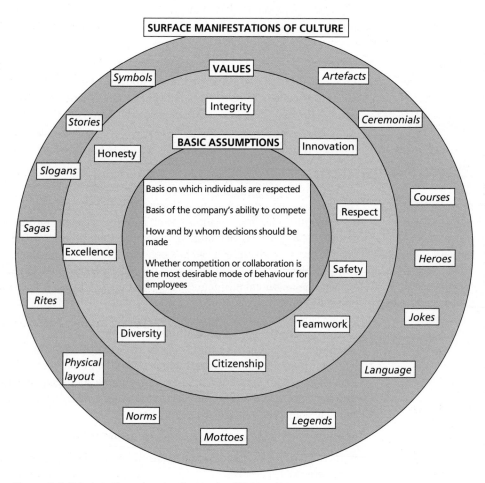

Figure 4.1: Schein's three levels of organizational culture

Source: adapted from *Organizational Behaviour and Analysis: An Integrated Approach*, Rollinson, D., Pearson Education Limited, © Pearson Education Limited 2008.

The surface level of culture is the most visible. Anyone coming into contact with it can observe it. Its constituent elements are defined below and illustrated in Table 4.1:

1. *Artefacts* are material objects created by human hands to facilitate culturally expressive activities. They include tools, furniture, appliances and clothing.

2. *Ceremonials* are formally planned, elaborate, dramatic sets of activities of cultural expression, e.g. opening events, prize-givings, graduations, religious services.

3. *Courses* and workshops are used to instruct, induct, orient and train new members in company practices.

4. *Heroes* are characters, living or dead, who personify the values and beliefs; who are referred to in company stories, legends, sagas, myths and jokes; and who represent role models that current employees should emulate.

5. *Jokes* are humorous stories intended to cause amusement, but their underlying themes carry a message for the behaviour or values expected of organizational members.

6. *Language* is the particular form or manner in which members use vocal sounds and written signs to convey meaning to each other. It includes both specialist technical vocabulary related to the business (jargon), as well as general naming choices.

7. *Legends* are handed-down narratives about wonderful events based on company history, but embellished with fictional details. These fascinate employees and invite them to admire or deplore certain activities.

8. *Mottoes* are maxims adopted as rules of conduct. Unlike slogans, mottoes are rarely, if ever, changed.

9. *Norms* are expected modes of behaviour that are accepted as the company's way of doing things, thereby providing guidance for employee behaviour.

10. *Physical layout* concerns things that surround people, providing them with immediate sensory stimuli, as they carry out culturally expressive activities.

11. *Rites* are elaborate, dramatic sets of activities that consolidate various forms of cultural expression into one event. They are formally planned events such as annual staff performance reviews.

12. *Sagas* are historical narratives describing the unique accomplishments of groups and their leaders. They usually describe a series of events that are said to have unfolded over time and which constitute an important part of an organization's history.

13. *Slogans* are short, catchy phrases that are regularly changed. They are used for both customer advertising and also to motivate employees.

14. *Stories* are narratives describing how individuals acted and the decisions they made that affected the company's future. Stories can include a mixture of both truth and fiction.

15. *Symbols* refer to any act, event, object, quality or relationship that serves as a vehicle for conveying meaning.

Table 4.1: Examples of surface manifestations of organizational culture at Motorola and Rolls Royce

Manifestation	Examples	
	Motorola	**Rolls Royce**
1. Artefacts	Name badges, stationery, T-shirts, promotional items, celebratory publications	Name badges. Standard work wear, issued to all staff levels in the organization. Each polo shirt is customized with the wearer's name
2. Ceremonials	Annual service dances, annual total customer satisfaction competition	Fun days, sporting events, commemorative shows
3. Courses	Basic health and safety course	Induction courses to orient new starts to RR principles
4. Heroes	Paul Galvin, Joseph Galvin – founders	Henry Rolls, Charles Royce – founders
5. Jokes		'The Right Way, The Wrong Way and the Rolls-Royce Way' – humorous, self-deprecating comments about the evolution of certain ways of going about things, but also a reminder of the importance of individuality and identity

(Continued)

Table 4.1: *Continued*

Manifestation	Examples	
	Motorola	**Rolls Royce**
6. Language	Employees known as 'Motorolans'. Role-naming conventions and communications remind everyone of their responsibilities as Motorolans	Divisional/departmental naming – job roles defined within particular naming structures
7. Legends	The first walkie-talkies. First words communicated from the moon via Motorola technology	Commemorative window in tribute to the Rolls-Royce Spitfire's contribution to World War II
8. Mottoes	Total Customer Satisfaction, Six Sigma Quality, Intelligence Everywhere, Engineering Intelligence with Style	Centre of Excellence Trusted to Deliver Excellence
9. Norms	Ethics, Respect, Innovation	Code of Business Conduct – Quality, Excellence, Ethics, Respect
10. Physical layout	Semi-open plan – cubed group set up – Junior managers have separate offices beside staff; senior managers have corporate offices distanced from most employees	Open plan layouts – applies to both offices and work cells where possible
11. Rites	Badges – initially the identity badge, but then the service badge, given at five-year intervals, has a great deal of kudos	Length of Service Acknowledgement – rite of passage
12. Sagas	Motorola's time-lined history used repeatedly to demonstrate its influence on the world.	The 1970s bankruptcy saga
13. Slogans	*Hello Moto* – Modern reinvention of how the Motorola name came into being – a fusion of 'Motor' (representing a car) plus 'Hola' representing Hello in Spanish, to emphasize communications on the move	
14. Stories	About a particular vice-president who fell asleep at a very important customer meeting. A cautionary tale about what not to do!	Impact of a particular shop floor visit and how the feedback to quality managers changed thinking and processes. The tale is cautionary about how misunderstandings can generate unnecessary panics
15. Symbols	Motorola 'M' brand – known as the *emsignia*  	The Rolls-Royce brand – RR

Source: personal communications. Rolls-Royce logo © Chris Hennessey/Alamy.

STOP AND THINK Think about an organization of which you have personal experience. Provide examples of as many of the 15 surface manifestations of organizational culture as you can.

Organizational values the accumulated beliefs held about how work should be done and situations dealt with, that guide employee behaviour.

Schein's second level of culture concerns **organizational values**. These:

- represent something that is explicitly or implicitly desirable to an individual or group;
- influence employees' choices from available means and ends of action;
- reflect their beliefs as to what is right and wrong, or specify their general preferences.

Organizational values are the accumulated beliefs held about how work should be done and situations dealt with (Adler and Gundersen, 2008). They can be consciously or unconsciously held; they are often unspoken, but guide employees' behaviours. They can be encapsulated either in phrases or in single words such as:

Citizenship	Diversity	Excellence
Honesty	Integrity	Innovation
Respect	Safety	Teamwork

Values are said to provide a common direction for all employees, and to guide their behaviour. 'People way down the line know what they are supposed to do in most situations because the handful of guiding values is crystal clear' (Peters and Waterman, 1982, p.76). Motorola has two key values – 'uncompromising integrity' and 'constant respect for people'. The Central Intelligence Agency's (CIA) core values, shown on its website, state that 'quiet patriotism is our hallmark'; 'we pride ourselves on our extraordinary responsiveness to the needs of our customers'; staff 'embrace personal accountability'; put 'country first and agency before self', and they learn from their mistakes because they 'reflect on their performance'. Additionally, CIA employees 'seek and speak the truth', but they add, only 'to our colleagues and our customers'. You can go to the website of any large, private, public or voluntary organization – Microsoft, the British National Health Service or Amnesty International – and locate their values in their vision or mission statement. Two well-known companies' values, Google's and IKEA's, are listed in Table 4.2.

Table 4.2: Corporate values

Google's 10 things we know to be true	IKEA's nine fundamental doctrines
1. Focus on the user and all else will follow	1. The product range is our identity
2. It's best to do one thing, really, really well	2. The IKEA spirit – a strong and lively reality
3. Fast is better than slow	3. Profit gives us resources
4. Democracy on the web works	4. To reach good results with small means
5. You don't need to be at your desk to need an answer	5. Concentration of energy is important for our success
6. You can make money without doing evil	6. Simplicity is a virtue
7. There's always more information out there	7. The different way
8. The need for information crosses all borders	8. To behave responsibly is a privilege
9. You don't need a suit to be serious	9. Most things still remain to be done – a glorious future
10. Great just isn't good enough	

Source: based on Bock (2015, p.31) and Stenebo (2010, p.135).

Sources of values

Values distinguish one organization from another, but where do they come from? One source of values is the views of the original founder, as modified by the company's current senior management (Schein, 1983). Originally, a single person or group of people, has an idea for a new business, and brings in other key people to create a core group who share a common vision. This group then creates an organization, recruits others, and begins to build a common history. Stephen Robbins and Timothy Judge (2013) suggest that a company's current top management acts as its 'culture carriers'. Thus 'organizational' values are really always the values of the current company elite (senior managers). This is similar to the way that 'organizational goals' actually represent the preferred aims of chief executives and their management teams (see Figure 4.2).

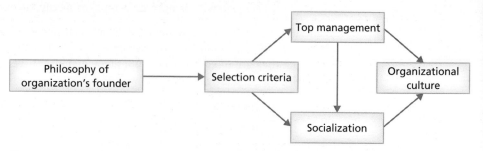

Figure 4.2: Where does organizational culture come from?

Source: Robbins, Stephen P., Judge, Timothy A., *Organizational Behavior*, 15th, © 2013. Printed and electronically reproduced by permission of Pearson Education, Inc., Upper Saddle River, New Jersey.

Home viewing

The film *Steve Jobs* (2015, director Danny Boyle) is a biographical drama based on the life of the co-founder of Apple Inc. It depicts the launches of three iconic company products – Macintosh (1984), Next (1998) and the iMac (1998). As you watch the film, look out for examples of Jobs' values and beliefs. How might these have influenced the development of Apple's organizational culture?

In a sense, therefore, organizational values are always backward looking, despite being developed to contribute to the future development of the company. For an organizational culture to form, a fairly stable collection of people need to have shared a significant history, involving problems, which allows a social learning process to take place. Organizations that have such histories possess cultures that permeate most of their functions (Schein, 2004). Company values come in lists. They are to be found printed in company reports, framed on company walls, and published on organizational websites.

Football culture

Emmanuel Ogbonna and Lloyd Harris (2014) studied an English Premier League football club's attempt to modernize its culture. They identified five factors that perpetuated the existing cultural norms, values and beliefs that impeded club executives' attempts to change it. These were:

Historical legacy. The club's rich history and past success guided daily activities and, it was believed, would bring future success. The philosophy of life and football of a past manager credited with reviving club fortunes came to be adopted by the club. The new value of 'professional commercialism' was questioned, and putting profits ahead of winning trophies was seen as a betrayal of this manager. Despite a lack of success, this historical legacy hampered current executives' attempts to change core values, introduce individual performance management matrices, and to radically restructure pay and working conditions.

Symbolic expressions. The club museum exhibits were full of symbolic imagery and meanings. Cups, trophies and player strips all stressed team spirit, tradition, fan loyalty, togetherness and passion. Ex-players were disproportionately represented in the museum exhibits, and others acted as guides, sharing their stories of the past. All these symbolic expressions created a bridge between the present and the past. The museum reinforced the existing culture, preventing executives implementing their desired changes.

Subculture dynamics. Several different sub-cultures were brushing up against each other within the organization. The team, and all those associated with it, were revered and respected, and their sub-culture dominated the club. The team manager's preferences concerning new stadium location and the purchase of a player prevailed over those of the executives. The team sub-culture did not accept the executives' redefinition of success, and it embodied the belief that success would return by continuing with past values and recipes.

Employment practices. Traditionally, the club's new managers had been internal appointments. Despite attempts to introduce new, more systematic recruitment practices, informal approaches were continued. The choice of an external manager was opposed by the team sub-culture, but was accepted when an ex-player who was unlikely to work with executives to undertake radical transformation was appointed

as assistant manager. These human resource practices impeded executives' culture change efforts.

Key stakeholders. Three classes of supporters existed. While the 'casual' and 'club-connected' ones engaged with the club, it was the die-hard fans that had the greatest influence. They possessed an encyclopaedic knowledge of club history, had a variety of match rituals, and were the opinion leaders with whom the club wanted to have good relations. They associated with the team rather than the club's management; saw their role as continuing the club's traditions, and therefore resisted the proposed changes by means of protest marches and radio phone-ins which embarrassed the club's executives.

Discussing the relationship between junior-level employees and corporate values, Chris Grey recounted the experience of one of his MBA students, a senior manager in a supermarket chain, a company known to be an exemplar of successful culture management. The staff had been subject to a multimillion-pound culture training initiative, and he wanted to discover the extent of their 'buy-in' to the company's culture values. To what extent did frontline staff subscribe to these corporate values? He found that not only did staff did not believe in these values, but three-quarters of them claimed never to have even *heard* of these values! (Grey, 2009, p.74).

STOP AND THINK

Can you list any of the values of the organization that you work for currently or have done so in the past? Would knowing their values change your way of working?

Basic assumptions
invisible, preconscious, unspoken, 'taken-for-granted' understandings held by individuals within an organization concerning human behaviour, the nature of reality and the organization's relationship to its environment.

Finally, basic assumptions are the deepest level of culture, and are the most difficult to comprehend. They are the set of shared but unspoken suppositions about the best way to do things within a company. They relate to the nature of reality and the organization's relationship with its environment. Towards the start of the animated film *Chicken Run* (2000), Mrs Tweddie the farmer responds to her husband's suspicion that the chickens are planning to escape by saying 'They're chicken's you dolt! Apart from you, they're the most stupid creatures on this planet. They don't plot, they don't scheme, and they are not organized!' Here, Mrs Tweddie's 'basic assumptions' are blinding her to reality and preventing her from taking appropriate action (Ambrosini et al., 2012).

Over time, a company's values, beliefs and attitudes become so ingrained and well-established that they cease to be articulated or debated by employees. Instead of being discussed, they become 'baked' into the fabric of an organization's culture. These basic assumptions begin with the founder's thinking, and then develop through a shared learning process. A company's basic assumptions often relate relate to:

Quality	Economy	Predictability
Stability	Excellence	Responsibility
Morality	Profitability	Innovativeness

As employees act in accordance with company values, beliefs and attitudes, these become embedded as basic assumptions. Because they are invisible, they are difficult to pin down (Notter and Grant, 2011). Staff who are judged not to share these basic assumptions may be regarded as outsiders, become ostracized, and perhaps even be 'performance managed' out of the company.

Organizational socialization

Organizational socialization the process through which an employee's pattern of behaviour, values, attitudes and motives is influenced to conform to those of the organization.

The ultimate strength of a company's culture depends on the employees' shared agreement on their company's core values and their emotional attachment to them (Gordon and DiTomaso, 1992). One learns about these through **organizational socialization**. This is the process through which an employee's pattern of behaviour, values, attitudes and motives are influenced to conform to those of the organization's (see Figure 4.3). It includes the careful selection of new company members, their instruction in appropriate ways of thinking and behaving; and the reinforcement of desired behaviours by senior managers.

Figure 4.3: Dimensions addressed in most socialization efforts

Source: Colquitt et al. (2009, p. 558) from Chao, G.T., O'Leary-Kelly, A.M., Wolf, S., Klein, H.J. and Gardner, P.D., Organizational socialization: its content and consequences, *Journal of Applied Psychology*, Vol. 79, No 5, pp. 730–43, American Psychological Association, (APA), reprinted with permission.

Socialization is important because, as John van Maanen and Edgar Schein (1979) argue, if the culture of the organization is to endure, new recruits have to be taught to see the organizational world as their more experienced colleagues do. Socialization involves newcomers absorbing the values and behaviours required to survive and prosper in an organization. It reduces the variability of behaviour by instilling employees with an understanding of what is expected of them, and how they should do things. By providing both internal guidance and a shared frame of reference, socialization standardizes employee behaviour, making it predictable for the benefit of senior management. Richard Pascale (1985) distinguished seven key steps in the process of organizational socialization. These are shown in Figure 4.4.

Selection: Trained recruiters carefully select entry-level candidates. They determine their traits using psychometric selection methods. The entrants are not 'oversold' on a particular position, because the companies rely on applicants 'deselecting' themselves, that is, withdrawing from the application process, if they find that the organization's values do not fit in with their own. This is also referred to as the **pre-arrival stage of socialization**.

Pre-arrival stage of socialization the period of learning in the process that occurs before an applicant joins an organization.

Induction experiences: Once working, the organization encourages new entrants to adopt the company's beliefs and values. It can do this by having them attend induction courses, assigning them to an existing employee who 'shows them the ropes' (buddy system), or

perhaps anticipates environmental changes. In contrast, if a company has a predictable and relatively static environment, it will need a strong but less adaptable culture. A study by Jose Garmendia (2004) into companies in the health insurance industry confirmed that a strong culture had a positive impact on organizational performance (results), but only if that culture was adapted to the firm's environment and interacted proactively with it.

STOP AND THINK   Organizational culture influences how employees dress for work. Think about what clothes your bosses and co-workers wear at your current or recent workplace. How do your university lecturers dress? What do their dress choices tell you about the culture of these organizations?

Types of organizational culture

Various writers have produced different culture typologies, all of which assume that, rather like different personality type classifications (e.g. introvert, extrovert), an entire organization (like an individual) can be assigned to a single culture type category on the basis of its possession of certain unique cultural traits. Perhaps the most popular organizational culture typology is Charles Handy's (1993). His classification is based on the degree of centralization and formalization, and is shown in Figure 4.6. Centralization refers to how much power and authority is concentrated at the top of the organization; and formalization concerns the extent to which rules, procedures and policies govern organizational activities.

- *Power* cultures have a single, dominant individual who exerts their will; controlling by recruiting those of a similar viewpoint; and operating with the minimum of rules. It is represented symbolically by a web. It works on precedent, anticipating desires of those at the centre. Decisions are based on a balance of power rather than logic, and there is little emphasis on discussion to reach consensus. For example, small companies run by their founder-owners.

- *Role* culture organizations emphasize the importance of rules, procedures, role expectations and job descriptions. It is represented symbolically by a Greek temple. Managers within them operate 'by the book', on the basis of their position in the hierarchy and their role, and in a depersonalized way. It is based on its functional departments and specialties, and its operations are driven by logic and rationality. This culture is characteristic of bureaucracies.

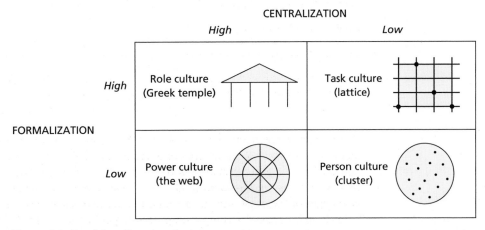

Figure 4.6: Handy's culture typology
Source: based on Handy (1993).

- *Person* culture organizations are focused on individuals. It is represented symbolically by a cluster. They exist for the benefit of their members, and may include a 'star performer'. Control is exercised only by mutual consent, and the organization is seen as being subordinate to individuals. This type of culture is typical of originations such as rock bands and classical music quintets, as well as small, start-up IT firms, architects' partnerships and barristers' chambers.

- *Task* cultures are job or project oriented. It is represented symbolically by a lattice. The task is specified at the top, but then the emphasis shifts to finding the resources and getting the job done through using individuals' enthusiasm and commitment, working as a team. Influence within this culture is based on expertise, rather than position or personal power. Such cultures are found in client-focused agencies such as advertising companies and management consultancies.

National cultures

The culture of a nation is affected by many variables. Laurent (1989) argues that national culture is more powerful and stable than organizational culture. Brooks (2003) saw organizational culture being partly the outcome of societal factors, some of which are identified in Figure 4.7. National cultural stereotypes are well established: Scots are mean; Americans are brash; Germans are humourless; French are romantic; and Japanese are inscrutable. Researchers have studied how national cultures might affect organizational cultures in specific country settings. For example, there is much known about the processes and outcomes of multicultural teams (Stahl et al., 2010). Attempts to establish a common organizational culture in a multinational firm can be undermined by the strength of a national culture. An organization's culture, while having unique properties, is necessarily embedded within the wider norms and values of the country in which its office and facilities are located, and is affected by the personal values that employees bring with them to work.

Figure 4.7: Factors affecting national culture

Source: from *Organizational Behaviour: Individuals, Groups and Organization*, Brooks, I., Pearson Education Limited © Pearson Education Limited 2003.

Vanhoegaerden (1999) felt that an awareness and understanding of national cultural differences was crucial for everybody in the organization. He suggested two reasons as to why these have been neglected. First, many people believed that, underneath, everybody was fundamentally the same. This belief is reinforced by the impression that national cultures are merging. The success of global companies such as Disney and Coca-Cola, among others, can wrongly convince us that the countries in the world are becoming more alike. However, the political upheavals, economic crises, military conflicts and human suffering reported on TV screens every evening challenges this view and shows that cultures remain very different.

Second, the convergence that appears to exist does so at only a superficial level, and many deep cultural differences remain. Blaise Pascal (1623–1662), the French mathematician and

CERN: organizational culture and national cultures

The European Organization for Nuclear Research is better known by its original, French acronym CERN, which stands for the *Conseil Européen pour la Recherche Nucléaire*. The organization is the world's largest particle physics research centre and home to the Large Hadron Collider (LHC) housed in a 27 km tunnel that straddles the Franco-Swiss border near Geneva. It is the place where, in 1989, the World Wide Web was invented by Sir Tim Berners-Lee, a British scientist, and where in 2012, the Higgs boson (the 'God particle') was discovered, which explains how the universe began.

CERN receives £700 million a year of funding from 21 member states including Israel. It has over 2,500 permanent employees, but visiting scientists from 113 countries increase numbers to 14,000 people. In its staff canteen Nobel Prize winners with their plastic trays sit alongside students. Anna Cook, its head of recruitment, says that within CERN, collaboration between different cultures is paramount. 'We've got Indians working alongside Pakistanis, Israelis working beside Palestinians. I think the mission – "science for peace and looking for the answers to fundamental questions of the universe" – unites people.' In her view, other organizations can achieve a similar culture but they need to embrace diversity by having a management board comprising people from different cultures, nationalities and backgrounds' (*Financial Times*, 2015).

philosopher noted that 'There are truths on this side of the Pyrenees, which are falsehoods on the other'. Even an archetypal global brand like McDonald's encounters cultural obstacles as it covers the world. When it opened in Japan, it found that Ronald McDonald's clown-like white face did not go down well. In Japan, white is associated with death and was unlikely to persuade people to eat Big Macs. The company also found that Japanese people had difficulty in pronouncing the 'R' in Ronald, so the character had to be renamed *Donald* McDonald.

Home viewing

Outsourced (2007, director John Jeffcoat) tells the story of Todd Anderson (played by Josh Hamilton), a 32-year-old manager of a Seattle customer call centre whose entire order fulfilment department is outsourced to India. Despite facing unemployment, he accepts a temporary job to go there to train his replacements. What does he learn about Indian culture? As you watch, each time you notice a culturally specific practice, tradition, taboo, behaviour, attitude, assumption or approach, pause the film and make a note of it. How many items do you end up with on your list? What issues does the film raise about the effect of cultural difference at work; the relationships between employees from different backgrounds; and the global economy's impact on national and personal identity?

Penalty shootouts, national culture and high status

The English national football team's history of bungled penalties has become a national disgrace. Penalty shootouts were first used as a tie-breaker in European Championships in 1976 and in the World Cup in 1982. England is at the bottom of the international league with only a 66 per cent success rate, just below that of The Netherlands (67 per cent). It has been eliminated from five international tournaments since 1990. In contrast, Germany, four-time winners of the World Cup, has won all its shootouts in that competition, and has a success rate of 93 per cent over the two competitions. However, it is the Czechs who are the masters of the penalty shootout with an overall 100 per cent success rate. Penalty-taking makes particular demands of footballers. Although the match itself is a team game, the penalty kick is an individual endeavour. It looks simple, but the stakes are incredibly high. It is more a test of nerve than athleticism. What can explain the national teams' varying success rates?

Superficially, one might speculate that it has something to do with national cultures. Maybe countries with collectivist national cultures perform better than those with individualistic ones. Geir Jordet (2009) investigated whether national differences in variables associated with *pressure* on players could explain national differences in penalty shot performance by players from teams of approximately the same standard. He identified countries whose national teams had the highest status by having previously won the World Cup or the European Championship, and whose team included players from UEFA European domestic league winners/Champions league (CL).

England has a high status national team. It is a country that had the highest average CL wins at the time of the shootout; and had the most internationally merited players in the shootout; but has the longest time without winning a title. This suggests that expectations on the England players are high and they experience extraordinary pressure. Jordet's research indicates that if you are an England player and have a highly favourable view of yourself; if your fans have high expectations of you; if you are in a high-pressure situation (a penalty miss means your team's instant defeat); and you fear recriminations from an unforgiving media if you fail, then a common response to such an ego-threat is to engage in escapist strategies. These include rushing to take the penalty as quickly as possible (quick response time) and avoiding looking at the goalkeeper (avoidance behaviour). Both have been associated with poor shootout performance. When the pressure builds, the lessons appear to be: emphasize the positive incentives rather than the costs of failure and, if possible, avoid the Germans and the Czechs (*The Economist*, 2014b; Jordet, 2009).

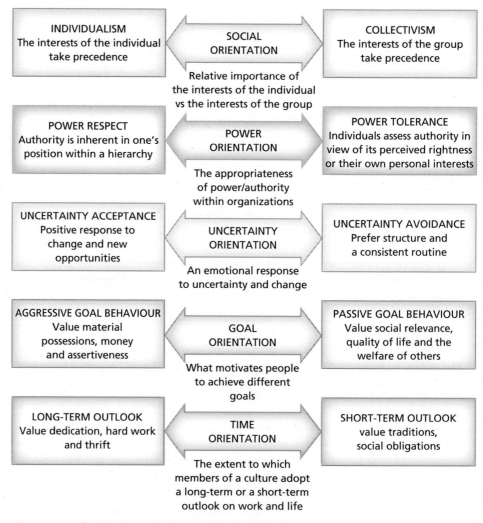

Figure 4.8: Hofstede's five dimensions of national culture

Source: from Griffin, Ricky W., Pustay, Michael W., *International Business*, 5th edition, © 2007, p.102. Reprinted and electronically produced by permission of Pearson Education, Inc., Upper Saddle River, New Jersey.

5. **Assess the link between organizational culture and organizational performance.**

   - Few research studies have been conducted which explicitly test a causal link between an organization's culture and its economic performance.

   - Those that have been conducted do not illustrate any direct causal relationship between a 'strong' culture and high economic performance suggesting, at a minimum, that other, mediating variables may be more significant.

   - There is anecdotal data as well as a logical argument, to suggest that organizations possessing a strong culture at a time of required change, may be less flexible, less able to change, and hence less likely to perform well economically.

6. **Distinguish between different types of organizational culture.**

   - Handy categorized the cultures of organization using a four-type framework: role, power, task and person

7. **Distinguish different dimensions of national culture.**

   - Hofstede suggested that national culture could be differentiated along five dimensions: power distance; uncertainty avoidance; individualism–collectivism; and masculinity–femininity and short term–long term perspectives.

   - The GLOBE framework for assessing national culture incorporates and extends Hofstede's dimensions and includes: assertiveness; future orientation; gender differentiation; uncertainty avoidance; power distance; individualism/collectivism; in-group collectivism; performance orientation; humane orientation.

Revision

1. Is organizational culture capable of being managed or do chief executives have to tolerate the culture that they inherit?

2. How can culture help or hinder an organization's effectiveness?

3. What guidance does the research into national culture offer managers working around the world for global corporations?

4. To what extent, and in what ways, might a national culture affect an organization's own culture?

Research assignment

First, familiarize yourself with the list of Schein's 15 surface manifestations of culture as shown on pages 110–11. Use this list to (a) interview a manager and obtain examples of as many of the surface manifestations of culture as they are able to provide you with. (b) For each manifestation, ask your manager what purpose it serves within their organization. (c) Ask them what external and internal factors have moulded the organization's culture into what it is today. (d) Fit your organization into Handy's organizational culture typology justifying your choice with examples from the company concerned.

Springboard

Lazlo Bock (2015) *Work Rules*. London: John Murray. The author describes Google's culture and how its human resource managements practices have contributed to it.

Vas Taras, Piers Steel and Bradley Kirkman (2011) 'Three decades of research on national culture in the workplace: do the differences still make a difference?', *Organizational Dynamics*, 40 (3): 89–198. This article discusses the effect of national culture on employee attitudes and behaviour.

Hugh Willmott (1993) 'Strength is ignorance, slavery is freedom: managing culture in modern organizations', *Journal of Management Studies*, 30 (5): 515–52. A classic article in which the author proposes that culture is a particular form of control which operates, not by external regulation, but by shaping the identity (internal world) of an organization's employees.

Fleming, P. (2013) 'Down with Big Brother: the end of corporate culturalism?', *Journal of Management Studies*, 50 (3): 515–52. Twenty years on, the author reflects on Willmott's classic article; and considers the role of resistance. He argues that companies use 'biopower' and not just cultural control, which encourages other types of dissent.

 ## OB cinema

Dead Poets Society (1989, director Peter Weir): DVD track 1, 0:00:53–0:04:44 (4 minutes)

To establish context, many films begin with shots of an organization to communicate its culture. The clip begins with the opening credits of the film, and ends after Mr Keating has been introduced, sits down and there is a shot of an outside scene.

1. Which surface manifestations of Welton Academy's culture are being communicated here?

2. What values can you infer about Welton Academy's organizational culture from viewing this clip?

	Example from Welton Academy culture
1. *Artefacts* are material objects created to facilitate culturally expressive activities. They include tools, furniture, appliances and clothing.	
2. *Ceremonials* are formally planned, elaborate, dramatic sets of activities of cultural expression.	
3. *Courses* and workshops are used to instruct, induct, orient and train new members, and to recognize the contributions of existing ones.	
4. *Heroes* are characters, living or dead, who personify the values and beliefs; who are referred to in company stories.	
5. *Jokes* are humorous stories intended to cause amusement but whose underlying themes may carry a message about behaviour or values.	
6. *Language* is the particular form or manner in which members use vocal sounds and written signs to convey meaning to each other.	
7. *Legends* are handed-down narratives about wonderful events based on history, but embellished with fictional details.	
8. *Mottoes* are maxims adopted as rules of conduct which are rarely, if ever, changed.	
9. *Norms* are expected modes of behaviour that are accepted as the company's way of doing things.	
10. *Physical layout* concerns things that surround people, providing them with sensory stimuli.	
11. *Rites* are elaborate, dramatic sets of activities that consolidate various forms of cultural expression into one event.	
12. *Sagas* are historical narratives describing the unique accomplishments of a group and its leaders.	
13. *Slogans* are short, catchy phrases that are regularly changed.	
14. *Stories* are narratives describing how individuals acted and the decisions they made that affected the company's future.	
15. *Symbols* refer to any act, event, object, quality or relation that serves as a vehicle for conveying meaning.	

OB on the web

Can you deduce an organization's culture from its videos? Insert 'Google culture' into YouTube and view some of the videos displayed. Using just these video clips, describe what you think are the main features of the company's culture.

How do national cultural differences get in the way of communication? Insert 'Cultural differences' into YouTube, and view a selection of these video clips. Identify which verbal and non-verbal behaviours differ most between cultures (e.g. dress, etiquette) and which might cause offence if they are inappropriate.

CHAPTER EXERCISES

1. Surface manifestations

Objectives
1. Understand how organizational structure and processes affect organizational culture.
2. Speculate how the organizational culture might affect your views and behaviours as an employee.

Briefing
Examine the three clusters of descriptions as directed by your instructor. For each one:
1. Decide what 'message' each one sends to employees about the organization's culture.
2. Speculate on the reactions and behaviours it might encourage or discourage among employees.

Descriptions
1. Companies want their employees to have creative ideas.
   (a) Company A hires only the smartest people and then immediately after appointment sends them on creativity workshops.
   (b) Company B has a rigorous selection procedure. Its expensive and elaborate three-day assessment centre selection approach focuses on determining each applicant's level of creativity.
   (c) Company C has a staff restaurant with only six-seater tables to allow different staff to meet; its rest areas have whiteboards on the walls; and there are suggestion boxes in every main corridor

2. Companies have different approaches to employees' work spaces.
   (a) Company A encourages staff to personalize their workspaces by decorating them with photos, toys and other items brought from home. Staff are free to come to work dressed as they like.
   (b) Company B has open space work areas for all staff. They wear business dress and address each other by their first names. Managers do not have their own offices or secretaries. The conference suite is used for staff meetings to which secretarial and support staff are invited. Recycling boxes are located throughout the building.
   (c) Company C believes messy desks demonstrates a lack of personal organization; it operates a paperless office system and requires managers to enforce a 'clear surface' policy. Non-business-related items in workspaces are considered unprofessional and are banned. 'Dress-down Fridays' were introduced by senior management after much discussion, some time ago.

3. Companies have different approaches to employees' errors.

    (a) In company A, an employee's mistake is discussed at a team meeting, recorded on the employee's file, and senior management is informed for possible disciplinary action.

    (b) In Company B, the manager identifies errors made by subordinates, talks to the individuals, shows them where they went wrong, and what he should do in the future.

    (c) In Company C, employees discuss their mistakes with their managers. The manager assists the subordinate to analyse their error, helps them learn from it, and agrees an action plan for future improvements.

2. National culture etiquette

Objectives
1. To recognize the similar ways in which national cultural values are shared.
2. To understand differences between national cultures

Briefing
1. Students form into small groups based on their country of origin (e.g. China, USA, Japan) or region (e.g. Scandinavia, Eastern Europe, South America, Middle East).

2. Individually, identify an experience that you had after coming to this country that you found surprising, unusual, upsetting, puzzling, irritating, pleasing or significant in some way.

3. Each group then prepares:

    (a) A list of 'student experiences' about this country.

    (b) Do's and Don'ts guide for a person visiting their country or region for the first time, so as to avoid embarrassment or causing offence when interacting with its nationals.

Your guide should cover:

- business situations (e.g. visiting company offices, attending business meetings) and social situations (e.g. being invited to the person's home and meeting their family)

- verbal behaviour (e.g. choice of words, mode of speech, conversation topics) and non-verbal behaviour (e.g. dress, greetings, gifts).

Nominate a speaker and present your group members' experiences and their guide to the other class members.

Employability assessment

With regard to your future employment prospects:

1. Identify up to three issues from this chapter that you found significant.

2. Relate these to the competencies in the employability matrix.

3. Decide what actions you need to take to maintain and/or develop those competencies under each of the four headings of the employability matrix.

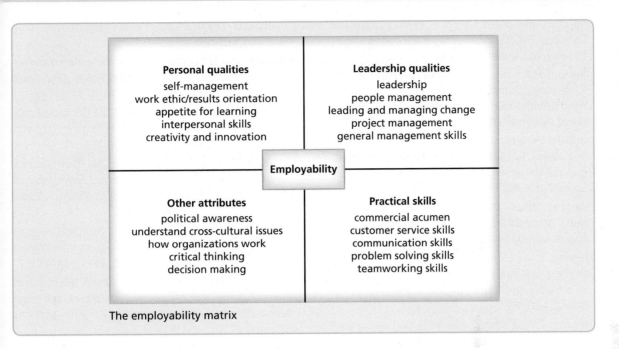

Personal qualities
self-management
work ethic/results orientation
appetite for learning
interpersonal skills
creativity and innovation

Leadership qualities
leadership
people management
leading and managing change
project management
general management skills

Employability

Other attributes
political awareness
understand cross-cultural issues
how organizations work
critical thinking
decision making

Practical skills
commercial acumen
customer service skills
communication skills
problem solving skills
teamworking skills

The employability matrix

References

Adler, N.J. and Gundersen, A. (2008) *International Dimensions of Organizational Behaviour* (5th edn). London: International Thomson.

Alvesson, M. (2001) *Understanding Organizational Culture*. London: Sage Publications.

Ambrosini, V., Billsberry, J. and Collier, N. (2012) 'To boldly go where few have gone before', in J. Billsberry, J. Charlesworth and P. Leonard (eds.), *Moving Images: Effective Teaching with Film and Television in Management*. Charlotte, NC: Information Age Publishing, pp.171–91.

Arnold, M. (2014) 'Banks failing to shed aggressive sales culture report warns', *Financial Times*, 26 November, p.2.

Bains, G. (2015) 'Leadership across cultures', *Harvard Business Review*, 93 (5): 30–31.

Barney, J.B. (1986) 'Organizational culture: can it be a source of sustained corporate advantage?', *Academy of Management Review*, 11 (3): 656–65.

Barney, J.B. (1991) 'Firm resources and sustained competitive advantage', *Journal of Management*, 17 (1): 99–120.

Becker, H. (1982) 'Culture: a sociological view', *Yale Review*, 71: 513–27.

Bock, L. (2015), *Work Rules*. London: John Murray.

Boyce, A.S., Nieminen, L.R.G., Gillespie, M.A., Ryan, A.M. and Denison, D.R. (2015) 'Which comes first, organizational culture or performance? A longitudinal study of causal priority with automobile dealerships', *Journal of Organizational Behaviour*, 36 (3): 339–59.

Brooks, I. (2003) *Organizational Behaviour: Individuals, Groups and Organization* (2nd edn). Harlow, Essex: Financial Times Prentice Hall.

Burman, R. and Evans, A. (2008) 'Target zero: a culture of safety', in R. Oddy (ed.), *Defence Aviation Safety Centre Journal*. RAF Bentley Priory, Stanmore: MoD Aviation Regulatory and Safety Group, pp.22–27.

Chatman, J.A., Caldwell, D.F., O'Reilly, C.A. and Doerr, B. (2014) 'Parsing organization culture: how the norm for adaptability influences the relationship between culture consensus and financial performance in high technology firms', *Journal of Organizational Behaviour*, 35 (6): 785–808.

CIPD (2013) *Employee Outlook:Focus on Rebuilding Trust in the City*. London: Chartered Institute of Personnel and Development.

Colquitt, J.A., LePine, J.A. and Wesson, M.J. (2009) *Organizational Behaviour: Improving Performance and Commitment in the Workplace*. London: McGraw Hill.

Congdon, C. and Gail, C. (2013) 'How culture shapes the office', *Harvard Business Review*, 91 (5): 34–35.

Costas, J. (2012) 'We are all friends here: reinforcing paradoxes of normative control in a culture of friendship', *Journal of Management Inquiry*, 21 (4): 377–395.

Cunliffe, A.L. (2008) *Organization Theory*. London: Sage Publications.

Day, P. (2012) 'What's gone wrong with the bank?', *BBC News Online*, 24 July, www.bbc.co.uk/news/business-18915060

Deal, T.E. and Kennedy, A.A. (1982) *Organization Cultures: The Rites and Rituals of Organization Life.* Reading, MA: Addison Wesley.

Denison, D.R., Haaland, S. and Goelzner, P. (2004) 'Corporate culture and organizational effectiveness: is Asia different from the rest of the world?' *Organizational Dynamics*, 33 (1): 98–109.

Dorfman, P., Javidan, M., Hanges, P., Dastmalchian, A. and House, R. (2012) 'GLOBE: a twenty year journey into the intriguing world of culture and leadership', *Journal of World Business*, 47 (4): 504–18.

Financial Times (2015) 'Collaboration is winning formula in world of competitive science', Executive Appointments, 28 May, p.3.

Fleming, P. and Spicer, A. (2004) 'You can checkout anytime, but you can never leave: spatial boundaries in a high commitment organization', *Human Relations*, 57 (1): 75–94.

Fleming, P. and Spicer, A. (2007) *Contesting the Corporation: Struggle, Power and Resistance in Organizations.* Cambridge: Cambridge University Press.

Fleming, P. and Sturdy, A. (2011) 'Being yourself in the electronic sweatshop: new form of normative control', *Human Relations*, 64 (2): 177–200.

Furnham, A. and Gunter, B. (1993) 'Corporate culture: definition, diagnosis and change', in C.L. Cooper and I.T. Robertson (eds.), *International Review of Industrial and Organizational Psychology*, vol. 8. Chichester: John Wiley, pp.233–61.

Gagliardi, P. (1986) 'The creation and change of organizational cultures: a conceptual framework', *Organization Studies*, 7 (2): 117–34.

Garmendia, J.A. (2004) 'The impact of company culture on company performance', *Current Sociology*, 52 (6): 1021–38.

Goffee, R. and Jones, G. (2003) *The Character of a Corporation: How Your Company's Culture Can Make or Break Your Business.* London: Profile Business.

Gordon, G.G. and DiTomaso, N. (1992) 'Predicting corporate performance from organizational culture', *Journal of Management Studies*, 29 (6): 783–98.

Grey, C. (2009) *A Very Short, Fairly Interesting and Reasonably Cheap Book About Studying Organizations.* London: Sage.

Handy, C. (1993) *Understanding Organization* (4th edn). Harmondsworth, Middlesex: Penguin Books.

Hill, A. (2013) 'Bankers back in the classroom', *Financial Times*, 17 October, p.16.

Hofstede, G. (1980) *Culture's Consequences: International differences in Work-related Values.* Beverley Hills, CA: Sage Publications.

Hofstede, G. (1986) 'Editorial: the usefulness of the concept of organization culture', *Journal of Management Studies*, 23 (3): 253–57.

Hofstede, G. (1991) *Cultures and Organizations.* London: McGraw-Hill.

Hofstede, G. (2001) *Culture's Consequences: International Differences in Work-related Values* (2nd edn). London: Sage Publications.

Hofstede, G. and Bond, M. (1988) 'The Confucian connection: from cultural roots to economic growth', *Organizational Dynamics*, 16 (4): 4–21.

House, R.J., Hanges, P.J., Javidan, M., Dorfman, M. and Gupta, V. (eds) (2004) *Culture, Leadership and Organizations: The GLOBE Study of 62 Societies.* Thousand Oaks, CA: Sage Publications.

Javidan, M. and House, R.J. (2001) 'Cultural acumen for the global manager: lessons from the Project GLOBE', *Organizational Dynamics*, 29 (4): 289–305.

Jordet, G. (2009) 'Why do English players fail in soccer penalty shootouts? A study of team status, self-regulation and choking under pressure', *Journal of Sports Sciences*, 27 (2): 97–106.

Kellaway, L. (2013) 'Kellaway's history of the office: why did offices become like home?', BBC Radio 4, 2 August.

Knights, D. and Willmott, H. (1987) 'Organizational culture as management strategy: a critique and illustration from the financial services industry', *International Studies of Management and Organization*, 17 (3): 40–63.

Kotter, J.P. and Heskett, J.L. (1992) *Corporate Culture and Performance.* New York: Free Press.

Kunda, G. (1992) *Engineering Culture: Control and Commitment in a High Tech Corporation.* Philadelphia, PA: Temple University Press.

Laurent, A. (1989) 'A cultural view of organizational change', in P. Evans, Y. Doz and A. Laurent (eds), *Human Resource Management in International Firms.* London: Macmillan, pp.83–94.

Lawson, E. and Price, C. (2003) 'The psychology of change management', *The McKinsey Quarterly*, (2), pp.31–41.

Luthans, F. (1995) *Organizational Behaviour* (7th edn). New York: McGraw Hill.

Martin, J. (1992) *Cultures in Organizations: Three Perspectives.* Oxford: Oxford University Press.

Mayo, E. (1933) *The Human Problems of an Industrial Civilization.* New York: Macmillan.

Mayo, E. (1945) *The Social Problems of an Industrial Civilization.* Cambridge, MA: Harvard University Press.

Mesmer-Magnus, J., Glew, D.J. and Viswesvaran, C. (2012) 'A meta-analysis of positive humour in the workplace', *Journal of Managerial Psychology*, 27 (2): 155–90.

Miller, D. (1994) 'What happens after success: the perils of excellence', *Journal of Management Studies*, 31 (3): 325–58.

Meyer, E. (2014) 'Navigating the cultural minefield', *Harvard Business Review*, 92 (5): 119–23.

Chapter 5 **Learning**

Key terms

learning

behaviourist psychology

cognitive psychology

feedback (learning)

positive reinforcement

negative reinforcement

punishment

extinction

Pavlovian conditioning

Skinnerian conditioning

shaping

intermittent reinforcement

schedule of reinforcement

cybernetic analogy

feedforward interview

intrinsic feedback

extrinsic feedback

concurrent feedback

delayed feedback

behaviour modification

socialization

behavioural modelling

provisional selves

behavioural self-management

learning organization

single-loop learning

double-loop learning

tacit knowledge

explicit knowledge

knowledge management

Learning outcomes

When you have read this chapter, you should be able to define those
key terms in your own words, and you should also be able to:

1. Explain the characteristics of the behaviourist and cognitive
   approaches to learning.

2. Explain and evaluate the technique of behaviour modification.

3. Explain the socialization process, and assess the practical relevance
   of this concept.

4. Explain and evaluate the technique of behavioural self-
   management.

5. Describe features of knowledge management and the learning
   organization.

Why study learning?

In an economy dominated by knowledge work and rapid, unpredictable change, the ability to learn, and to continue learning, for individuals and organizations, is crucial. Technologies are developing at such a pace in the 'second machine age' that skills and knowledge which are required today may have little value tomorrow (as we explored in Chapter 3). Individual learning ability is therefore important in terms of employment, performance, job security and career. Organizations also need to recruit staff who have appropriate skills and knowledge, and then to ensure that those capabilities are kept up to date. Learning theory thus affects many areas of management practice:

- the induction of new recruits;
- the design and delivery of job training and development;
- the design of payment systems;
- how supervisors evaluate employee performance and provide feedback;
- methods for modifying employee behaviour;
- creating a learning organization;
- the design and operation of knowledge management systems.

Learning is a fundamental topic in psychology but, as we will see, is divided between behaviourist and cognitive theories. The learning organization, an idea which has become popular, combines structures and policies to encourage learning, with individual and corporate benefits. Some larger companies regard learning as so important that they have established their own corporate universities.

What will you need to learn?

In 2014, research involving 200 business leaders and young people from Asia, Europe and America by the consulting company CBRE found that:

Young workers are breaking the unwritten rules of hierarchy and of who talks to whom. They are losing verbal skills but have the ability to maintain large networks, absorb more information and filter out non-essential material to avoid overload. They draw from rich and varied sources and forms of media to tell compelling stories in unique ways. However, there are concerns that young workers are not developing valuable interpersonal skills. Said one participant: We need to tease this generation out of the isolation of their devices to collaborate. There will be a competitive advantage to organizations that nurture the discipline of knowing when to switch devices off and talk face to face. (Andrew et al., 2014, p.3)

How does this finding apply to you – and to your future employability and career?

Knowledge can be an asset more important than equipment and materials, where understanding of processes – the 'how to' of making products and providing services – is critical. Competitive advantage means knowing *how to* make products, *how to* innovate rapidly, *how to* bring new products and services quickly to the marketplace, knowing *how to* meet changing customer needs. The capacity to learn and to develop new knowledge affects an organization's ability to grow and survive, as technologies, customer requirements, government policies and economic conditions change.

Delivering profit

Norbert Dentressangle was a French transport company, with 12,800 employees in its logistics division in the UK. Their lorries were a common sight on Europe's roads. This was not a 'hi-tec' organization: most employees were packing operatives and drivers, who delivered goods to stores such as M&S and Tesco. Why should an organization like this invest in learning and development (L&D), especially in a difficult and competitive market with a need to cut costs? From 2012, however, the company actually increased its L&D investment. Chris Dolby, L&D manager for the logistics division explained:

> Our competitors use the same sorts of warehouses and similar methods so ultimately the difference between us and them is our people. We have to be more effective, more reliable and closer to our customers. We don't have huge layers of management. We empower people to manage their team and make decisions as if it was their own mini business. For them

to be able to do that we have to train and develop them. (Chynoweth, 2013, p.19)

The company's training programmes were attended by 7,200 staff in 2012. Driver training programmes led to a 30 percent reduction in road accidents. Frontline staff with management potential could apply to join the company's 'fast track' graduate training scheme. During that scheme, one employee, initially hired to stack shelves and pick stock, generated £120,000 of savings by making the customer returns process more efficient. The company's annual management development programme cost £78,000 for 30 participants, who each had to implement a cost savings project. Projects in 2012 saved £1.1 million, through consolidating routes and changing the ways in which empty trailers were managed. Asked about the value of L&D, Dolby said:

> It's all about delivering performance that improves the bottom line. It's not pink and fluffy. It's about hard-nosed strategy that delivers profit. (Chynoweth, 2013, p.19)

The learning process

How do we learn? How do we come to know what we know, and to do what we are able to do? These questions lie at the heart of psychology, and it is not surprising that we are faced with different approaches to these questions. This variety maintains controversy, excitement and interest in the subject, and also helps to generate new thinking. The ability to learn is not unique to human beings. Animals also learn, as dog owners and circus fans can confirm. One feature that seems to distinguish us from animals is our ability to learn about, adapt to, survive in and manipulate our environment for purposes that we ourselves define. Animals can adapt to changes in their circumstances, but their ability to manipulate their environment is limited, and they appear to have little choice over their goals. In addition, animals have developed no science, technology or engineering – or social science.

We hope that when you have finished reading this text you will be able to say that you have learned something. The test is whether or not you will be able to do things that you could not do before. You should know what the study of organizational behaviour involves, and you should be able to tell others what you know and think about it. You should be able to complete assignments and answer questions that you could not tackle before. We can describe this process as learning.

Learning the process of acquiring knowledge through experience which leads to a lasting change in behaviour.

This definition of learning emphasizes durability and experience. Behaviour can be changed temporarily by many factors, in ways that do not involve learning. Other factors which change our behaviour are maturation (in children), ageing (in adults), drugs and fatigue. Our interest is with lasting behaviour change. This can involve procedural learning, or 'knowing how', concerning your ability to carry out skilled actions, such as horse riding or painting a picture. Or this can involve declarative learning, or 'knowing that', such as the history of our use of the horse, or the contribution of the European Futurist movement in the early twentieth century to contemporary art.

From neurological research, we know which areas of the brain are involved in learning and memory processes, although our understanding of these processes is incomplete. The study of learning, however, is not confined to brain surgery. We can *infer* that learning has taken place by examining changes in your behaviour. If we assume that behaviour does not alter spontaneously, for no reason, then we can look for experiences that could cause behaviour change. These experiences may be internal, or they may be sensory, from the environment. The task of inferring whether or not learning has taken place may be an obvious one, but observable behaviour may not always reveal learning.

Changes in behaviour can be measured using a 'learning curve', one example of which is shown in Figure 5.1, concerning the development of manual skills.

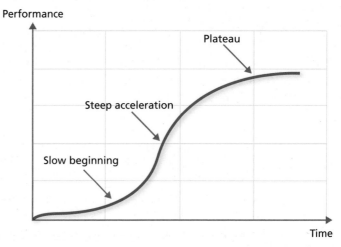

Figure 5.1: The typical manual skills learning curve

Neuroscience says: less coffee, no late-night computer games, more exercise

Neuroscience is the study of brain activity, using tools such as magnetic resonance imaging to explore how mental processes relate to emotions and behaviours. One area where neuroscience has started to develop fresh insights concerns the study of learning. These findings have implications for organizational practice. Paul Howard-Jones (2014) argues that neuroscience will help us to:

• understand how the brain is capable of learning continuously, at all ages;

• be aware of the flexibility, or 'neuroplasticity' of the brain and how it can reorganize and develop with experience;

• learn skills that support the development of further learning;

• improve learning through exercise and other physical activity.

Research has shown how the development of basic literacy and 'number sense' at school builds a platform for learning work-related skills. The skill and knowledge requirements for many jobs are increasing, and individuals and organizations will need to keep up with the pace of environmental and technological change. However, computer-based 'brain training' can improve our ability to retain information, which is in turn a predictor of academic and professional achievement, and helps us to solve problems more effectively.

Neuroscience studies have shown links between exercise, cognitive function and learning. The ability to learn and speed of recall, for example, are higher in teenagers and adults who are physically fit. Studies have also shown how financial rewards for completing a learning task *reduce* motivation by removing the fun and intrinsic value of the task. Contrary to popular belief, caffeine may keep you awake, but it suppresses cognitive function, and interferes with learning. Caffeine can also cause sleep disruption, and reduce the efficiency of our learning further.

One piece of bad news is that playing computer games late at night can also lead to sleep disorders and interfere with learning. However, research shows that video games can help to improve our ability to switch our visual attention, ignore irrelevant visual cues, and to infer the probable outcomes of different actions. These learning effects may be due to the way in which games stimulate the brain's reward and pleasure centres.

One study found that a specially designed video game improved the performance of air force cadet pilots, and another study showed that surgeons who played video games made over 30 per cent fewer errors in a test of their surgical skills (skill using Nintendo Wii may be linked to ability to perform laparoscopic or 'keyhole' surgery). The 'gamification' of learning is not currently well understood, however, and may apply to some skills but not to others.

Insights from neuroscience research are likely to have a growing impact on organizational learning. However, we should be cautious. This report concludes, 'We should see neuroscience as a new area of insights to be carefully combined with those from other perspectives, rather than a silver bullet solution' (Howard-Jones, 2014, p.14).

The learning can be plotted for one person, for a group of trainees, or even for a whole organization. The curve in Figure 5.1 suggests that:

1. Learning is not a smooth process, but changes in pace over time, until a stable peak performance is eventually reached.

2. The learner's ability develops slowly at first, then accelerates and develops more quickly, before finally reaching a plateau.

Learning curves for manual skills often follow this profile, but cognitive skills can develop in the same way. The shape of a learning curve depends on the characteristics of the task and of the learner. It is often possible to measure learning in this way, to compare individuals with each other, and to establish what constitutes good performance. If we understand the factors influencing the shape of the curve, we can develop ways to make learning more effective.

STOP AND THINK

Draw your own learning curve for this organizational behaviour course.

Why is it that shape? What would be your ideal learning curve look like?

How could you change the shape of your learning curve?

The experiences that lead to changes in behaviour have a number of important features.

First, the mind is not a passive recorder of information picked up through the senses. We can often recall the plot of a novel, for example, but remember very few of the author's words. This suggests that we do not record experiences in a straightforward way.

Second, we are usually able to recall events in which we have participated as if we were another actor in the drama. We are able to reflect, to see ourselves 'from outside', as objects in our own experience. At the time when we experienced the events, those cannot have been the sense impressions that we picked up. Reflection is a valuable capability.

Behaviourist psychology a perspective which argues that what we learn are chains of muscle movements; mental processes are not observable, and are not valid issues for study.

Cognitive psychology a perspective which argues that what we learn are mental structures; mental processes can be studied by inference, although they cannot be observed directly.

Third, new experiences do not always lead to behaviour change. Declarative learning, for example, may not be evident until we are asked the right questions. Our experiences must be processed in some way if they are to influence our behaviour in future.

Fourth, the way in which we express our drives depends on a mix of genetics and experience. We have innate drives, which are seen in behaviour in different ways, depending on a combination of factors. Our innate makeup biases our behaviour in certain directions, but these predispositions can be modified by experience.

This chapter examines two approaches to learning, based on behaviourist ('stimulus-response') psychology and cognitive ('information processing') psychology. These perspectives are in many respects contradictory, but they can also be seen as complementary. Summarized in Table 5.1, these perspectives have different implications for organization and management practice.

Table 5.1: Behaviourist and cognitive perspectives

Behaviourist, stimulus-response	Cognitive, information processing
Studies observable behaviour	Studies mental processes
Behaviour is determined by learned sequences of muscle movements	Behaviour is determined by memory, mental processes and expectations
We learn habits	We learn cognitive structures
We solve problems by trial and error	We solve problems with insight and understanding
Routine, mechanistic, open to direct research	Rich, complex, studied using indirect methods

---

Video case: rise of neuroscience in executive education

This five-minute *Financial Times* video explains why neuroscience has become a popular aspect of management education. Tara Sward from the MIT Sloan School of Management describes how sleep, nutrition and physical wellbeing can measurably affect our thinking ability (IQ) and productivity.

The behaviourist approach to learning

John Broadus Watson (1878–1958)

The American psychologist John B. Watson (1878–1958) introduced the term *behaviourism* in 1913. He was critical of introspection, a popular technique at that time, in which subjects were asked to talk about their experiences and thought processes, to explore their minds, and to describe what they found there. Instead, Watson wanted objective, 'scientific' handles on human behaviour, its causes and its consequences. This took him, and many other psychologists, away from the intangible contents of the mind to study relationships between visible stimuli and visible responses. That is why behaviourist psychology is also known as 'stimulus-response psychology'.

Behaviourism assumes that what lies between the stimulus and the response is a mechanism that will be revealed as our knowledge of the biochemistry and neurophysiology of the brain develops. This mechanism relates stimuli to responses in a way that governs behaviour. We can thus study how stimuli and responses are related without understanding the nature of that mechanism. Behaviourism argues that nothing of *psychological* importance happens between stimulus and response. Cognitive psychology argues that something of considerable psychological importance happens here.

The oldest theory of learning states that actions that are experienced together tend to be associated with each other (touching a flame, pain). We use knowledge of the outcomes of past behaviour to do better in future (don't touch flames). You learn to get higher assignment grades by finding out how well you did last time and why. We cannot learn without feedback. Behaviourists and cognitive psychologists agree that experience affects behaviour, but disagree over how this happens.

Feedback (learning) information about the outcomes of our behaviour.

Feedback can be rewarding or punishing. If a particular behaviour is rewarded, then it is more likely to be repeated. If it is punished or ignored, it is likely to be avoided in future. This is known as the 'law of effect', which states that we learn to repeat behaviours that have favourable consequences, and avoid those that have neutral or undesirable outcomes. Using this knowledge, rats can be trained to run through mazes with a combination of food pellets and electric shocks.

Positive reinforcement the attempt to encourage desirable behaviours by introducing positive consequences when the desired behaviour occurs.

Behaviourism makes subtle distinctions relating to reward and punishment, illustrated in Table 5.2. With **positive reinforcement**, desired behaviours lead to positive consequences. With **negative reinforcement**, the undesirable outcomes continue until the desired behaviour occurs. As one-off **punishment** follows undesirable behaviour, this is different from negative reinforcement. Where behaviour has no positive or negative outcomes, this can lead to the **extinction** of that behaviour, as it comes to be seen as unimportant.

Table 5.2: Reinforcement regimes

	Behaviour	Reinforcement	Result	Illustration
Positive reinforcement	Desired behaviour occurs	Positive consequences are introduced	Desired behaviour is repeated	Confess, and stick to your story, and you will get a shorter prison sentence
Negative reinforcement	Desired behaviour occurs	Negative consequences are withdrawn	Desired behaviour is repeated	The torture will continue until you confess
Punishment	Undesired behaviour occurs	A single act of punishment is introduced	Undesired behaviour is not repeated	Fail to meet your scoring target and we kick you off the team
Extinction	Undesired behaviour occurs	Day's work not counted towards bonus	Undesired behaviour is not repeated	Ignore an individual's practical jokes used to gain attention

STOP AND THINK   Some airlines, concerned about the cost of fuel, want to encourage passengers to carry less luggage (a lighter plane uses less fuel). One approach is to allow passengers with hand luggage only to skip the check-in queues. Another is to charge passengers extra for each item of luggage that they check in.

Which reinforcement regimes are being used to teach passengers to travel light?

Behaviour modification in practice

David Boddy (2013, p.458) reports the following communication from a call centre manager:

> In our call centre, staff are rewarded when behaviour delivers results in line with business requirements. Each month, staff performance is reviewed against a number of objectives, such as average call length, sales of each product, and attention to detail. This is known as Effective Level Review and agents can move through levels of effectiveness ranging from 1 to 4, and gain an increase in salary after six months of successful reviews. Moving through effective levels means that they have performed well and can mean being given other tasks instead of answering the phone. The role can become mundane and repetitive so the opportunity to do other tasks is seen as a reward for good performance. Thus it reinforces acceptable behaviour.
>
> Conversely, staff who display behaviour that is not desirable cannot move through these levels, and repeated failure to do so can lead to disciplinary action. This can be seen as punishment rather than behaviour modification. People can become resentful at having their performance graded every month, particularly in those areas where it is their line manager's perception of whether or not they have achieved the desired results.

Which reinforcement regimes does this call centre manager describe?

Negative reinforcement the attempt to encourage desirable behaviours by withdrawing negative consequences when the desired behaviour occurs.

Punishment the attempt to discourage undesirable behaviours through the application of negative consequences, or by withholding a positive consequence, following the undesirable behaviour.

Extinction the attempt to eliminate undesirable behaviours by attaching no consequences, positive or negative, such as indifference and silence.

Pavlovian conditioning a technique for associating an established response or behaviour with a new stimulus.

The development of associations between stimuli and responses occurs in two different ways, known as **Pavlovian conditioning** and **Skinnerian conditioning**. Pavlovian conditioning, also known as classical and as respondent conditioning, was developed by the Russian physiologist Ivan Petrovich Pavlov (1849–1936).

The best-known response which Pavlov studied concerned a dog salivating at the sight of food. Pavlov demonstrated how this could be associated with a completely different stimulus, such as the sound of a bell. Dog owners are trained today in classical conditioning methods. If you show meat to a dog, it will produce saliva. The meat is the stimulus, the saliva is the response. The meat is an *unconditioned* stimulus; the dog salivates naturally, and the saliva is an *unconditioned* response. Unconditioned responses are also called reflexes. Your lower leg jerks when you are struck just below the kneecap; your pupils contract when light is shone into your eyes. These are typical human reflexes. Humans also salivate, another unconditioned response, at the sight and smell of food.

Source: PEANUTS © 1989 Peanuts Worldwide LLC. Dist by Universal Uclick. Reprinted with permission. All rights reserved.

Suppose we ring a bell before we show the meat to the dog. Do this often enough, and the dog will associate the bell with the meat. Soon, it will salivate at the sound of the bell, without food being present. The bell has become a *conditioned* stimulus, and the saliva is now a conditioned response. The dog has learned from experience to salivate at the sound of a bell as well as at the sight of food. It does not have to be a bell. All manner of stimuli can be conditioned in this way. Pavlov discovered this form of conditioning by accident. His research was initially concerned with salivation, but he observed that his dogs salivated at the sight and sound of his laboratory assistants, before they were given their meat. He found this more interesting, and changed the focus of his research.

Home viewing

Pavlov has influenced Hollywood. In *The Truman Show* (1998, director Peter Weir), Truman Burbank (played by Jim Carrey) is adopted as a child by a television network. He believes that he is living a normal life, but he is actually a prisoner in an immense domed city-sized soundstage, simulating the town of Seahaven, where he is surrounded by actors who play members of his family, teachers and employers. As in the *Big Brother* television series, his every action is broadcast to viewers around the world, 24 hours a day, and has created a multimillion-dollar franchise for the network. If Truman were to quit, network profits would collapse. To stop him from leaving, the production team devise a plan based on Pavlovian conditioning. As you watch this movie, note how Truman's original conditioning is achieved. How does this conditioning affect Truman's daily life? How does he overcome his conditioning in his attempt to escape from Seahaven?

Suppose we now stop giving the meat to the dog after the bell. The dog will continue to salivate at the sound of the bell alone, expecting the bell to signal the arrival of food. If we continue to do this, however, the volume of saliva produced falls, and the association between the conditioned stimulus and conditioned response eventually suffers *extinction*.

Can you recognize conditioned responses in your own behaviour?

Is there a particular song, or a smell (perfume or aftershave, or food cooking), that makes you think of another person, another place, another time, another experience?

Ivan Petrovich
Pavlov (1849–1936)

Burrhus Frederic
Skinner (1904–1990)

Skinnerian conditioning is also known as instrumental and as operant conditioning, discovered by the American psychologist Burrhus Frederic Skinner (1904–1990). With instrumental conditioning, new behaviours or responses become established through association with particular stimuli.

Where the consequence of a behaviour is desirable to the individual, then the frequency of that behaviour is likely to increase. Given a particular context, any behaviour that is rewarded or reinforced will tend to be repeated in that context. Skinner put a rat into a box (known as a 'Skinner box') with a lever which, when pressed, gave the animal food. The rat is not taught to press the lever in the box. However, wandering around the box, the rat eventually moves the lever. It may sit on it, knock it with its head, or push it with a paw. That random behaviour is reinforced with food, and so it is likely to happen again.

Skinnerian conditioning is also called instrumental conditioning because it concerns behaviours that are a means to getting some material reward. Skinner's rat has to be under the influence of some drive before it can be conditioned in this way. His rats were hungry when they went into his box, and their behaviour thus led to a desired reward.

CRAIG SWANSON © WWW.PERSPICUITY.COM

Skinnerian conditioning
a technique for associating a response or a behaviour with its consequence.

Where do the terms respondent and operant conditioning come from? Respondent conditioning comes from Watson's stimulus-response psychology which stated that there was no behaviour, or no response, without a stimulus to set it in motion. One could thus condition a known response to a given stimulus. Such responses are called respondents. Knee jerks, pupil contractions and salivation are well known and clearly identified responses that are amenable to conditioning.

Skinner, on the other hand, observed that animals and humans do behave in the absence of specific stimuli, such as a rat wandering around in his Skinner box. He argued that most human behaviour is of this kind. Behaviours that do not have identifiable stimuli are called operants. Operant conditioning thus explains how new behaviours are established,

Shaping the selective reinforcement of chosen behaviours in a manner that progressively establishes a desired behaviour pattern.

Intermittent reinforcement a procedure in which a reward is provided only occasionally following correct responses, and not for every correct response.

such as pressing that lever to get food. Respondent conditioning does not alter the animal's behaviour (the dog always did salivate when it thought that food was coming), only the behaviour's timing. Skinner also developed the technique of shaping, or the selective reinforcement of desired behaviours. He was able to get pigeons to play ping-pong and to walk in figures of eight – demonstrating how spontaneous behaviours can be shaped by operant conditioning. You can see a demonstration on YouTube by searching for 'BF Skinner Foundation – Pigeon Ping Pong Clip'.

Skinner studied numerous variations on the operant conditioning theme. One concerned the occasional reward of desired behaviour rather than delivering rewards in a continuous and regular way. This is closer to real life than a laboratory experiment. Why, for example, do gamblers keep playing when they lose most of the time? Why do anglers continue to fish when they are catching nothing? There are many such examples of the power of intermittent reinforcement. Behaviour can be maintained without regular and consistent reinforcement every time that it occurs.

Automating behaviour modification

B.J. Fogg (2009) argues that technology can be used to modify people's behaviour, by 'automating persuasion'. One persuasive technology is the fuel gauge in a Toyota Prius. This measures engine efficiency, and encourages owners to change their driving behaviour to get more miles per gallon. The games that come with the Nintendo Wii tell families to 'get off the couch and start moving'. Fogg's five rules for designing automated persuasion are:

1. *Target a simple behaviour*. 'Reduce stress levels' is a complex and ambitious goal; persuading people to stop and stretch for 20 seconds when prompted is more realistic, anyone can do it, and the success rate is measurable.

2. *Understand what is preventing the target behaviour*. The reason always concerns lack of motivation, lack of ability or lack of a trigger to perform the behaviour. In other words, **B**ehaviour change depends on **M**otivation, **A**bility, and a **T**rigger:

3. *Choose the right technology channel*. Email, online video, e-commerce websites, social networks, text messages – these are simple and direct. Installed software and specialist devices can make target behaviours simpler and increase ability.

4. *Start small and fast*. Sophisticated ideas take time to design, and users may reject the complexity. Creating a simple, focused persuasive experience with a clear goal is inexpensive, can be implemented quickly, and is easy to change if it doesn't work.

5. *Build on small successes*: Getting people to stretch for 20 seconds is not a sexy project. However, Fogg's trial had a 70 per cent compliance rate, and the prompt was expanded to include relaxation techniques – again with high compliance.

The trigger, therefore, lies in the technology. Once a simple approach is working, it can be expanded. Get people to repeat the behaviour routinely, on a fixed schedule. Increase the difficulty of the behaviour. Reach more people. Target other simple behaviours. Target less persuadable groups. Automating behaviour modification is inexpensive, and it works.

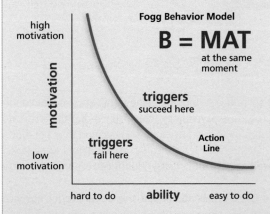

Source: © 2007 BJ Fogg; www.behaviormodel.org.
For permissions contact BJ Fogg.

Schedule of reinforcement the pattern and frequency of rewards contingent on the display of desirable behaviour.

The pattern and timing of rewards for desired behaviour is known as the **schedule of reinforcement**. The possible variation in schedules of reinforcement is limitless, and Skinner investigated the effects of a number of these (Ferster and Skinner, 1957). However, there are two main classes of intermittent reinforcement, concerning interval schedules and ratio schedules, which are described in Table 5.3 (based on Luthans and Kreitner, 1985), contrasted with continuous reinforcement.

Skinner claimed that one could explain the development of complex patterns of behaviour with the theory of operant conditioning. This shows how behaviour is shaped by our environment, by our experiences, and by the selective rewards and punishments that we receive. Thinking, problem solving and the acquisition of language, he argued, are dependent on these simple conditioning processes. Skinner rejected the use of 'mentalistic' concepts and 'inner psychic forces' in explanations of human behaviour because these were not observable, were not researchable, and were therefore not necessary to the science of human psychology. Why use complicated and unobservable concepts when simple and observable phenomena provide adequate explanations?

Skinner's influential work led to the development of programmed learning, a technique of instruction designed to reinforce correct responses in the learner and to let people learn at their own pace. The *behaviour modification* techniques described later are also based on his ideas. As the behaviour of a conditioned animal is consistent and predictable, this can also be used to test the effects of drugs.

Table 5.3: Schedules of reinforcement

Schedule	Description	Effects on responses	Example
Continuous	Reinforcement after *every correct response*	Establishes high performance, but can lead to satiation; rapid extinction when reinforcement is withheld	Praise
Fixed ratio	Reinforcement after a *predetermined number* of correct responses	Tends to generate high rates of desired responses	Incentive payments
Variable ratio	Reinforcement after a *random number* of correct responses	Can produce a high response rate that is resistant to extinction	Commission on sales
Fixed interval	Reinforcement of a correct response after a *predetermined period*	Can produce uneven response patterns, slow following reinforcement, vigorous immediately preceding reinforcement	Weekly payments
Variable interval	Reinforcement of a correct response after *random periods*	Can produce a high response rate that is resistant to extinction	Prizes

Reinforcing desired behaviour is generally more effective than punishing undesirable behaviour. However, C.C. Walters and J.E. Grusek (1977), from a review of research, suggested that punishment can be effective if it meets the following conditions:

- the punishment should be quick and short;
- it should be administered immediately after the undesirable behaviour;
- it should be limited in its intensity;
- it should be specifically related to behaviour, and not to character traits;
- it should be restricted to the context in which the undesirable behaviour occurs;
- it should not send 'mixed messages' about what is acceptable behaviour;
- penalties should take the form of withdrawal of rewards, not physical pain.

STOP AND THINK

To what extent should the criteria for effective punishment be used by managers when disciplining employees in an organizational context?

The cognitive approach to learning

**Norbert Wiener
(1894–1964)**

Cybernetic analogy
an explanation of the
learning process based
on the components and
operation of a feedback
control system.

**Feedforward
interview** a method
for improving employee
performance by focusing
on recent success and
attempting to create the
same conditions
in the future.

Why should we look only at observable stimuli and responses in the study of psychology? Is it not possible to study the internal workings of the mind in indirect ways, by inference? Behaviourism seems to be unnecessarily restrictive, excluding those characteristics that make us interesting, different and, above all, human.

How do we select from all the stimuli that bombard our senses those to which we are going to respond? Why are some outcomes seen as rewarding and others as punishments? This may appear obvious where the reward is survival or food and the punishment is pain or death. However, with intrinsic or symbolic rewards this is not always clear. To answer these questions, we have to consider states of mind concerning perception and motivation.

The rewards and punishments that behaviourists call reinforcement work in more complex ways than conditioning theories suggest. Reinforcement is always knowledge, or *feedback* (defined earlier), about the success of past behaviours. Feedback is information that can be used to modify or maintain previous behaviours. This information has to be perceived, interpreted, given meaning and used in decisions about future behaviours. The feedback has to be processed. This is why cognitive learning theories are called information processing theories.

This approach draws concepts from the field of cybernetics which was established by the American mathematician Norbert Wiener (1954). He defined cybernetics as 'the science of communication in the animal and in the machine'. One central idea of cybernetics is the notion of the control of system performance through feedback. Information processing theories of learning are based on what is called the **cybernetic analogy**.

The elements of a cybernetic feedback control system are outlined in Figure 5.2.

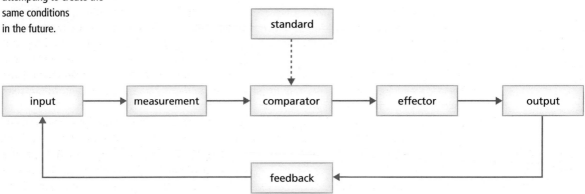

Figure 5.2: Elements of cybernetic feedback control

Feedback – or feedforward

The aims of appraisal interviews are to give employees feedback on past performance, and provide guidance to help them to improve in future. However, there are problems with this approach. It is often seen as an annual ritual in which the main purpose is to complete the paperwork as quickly as possible. If the feedback is negative, focusing on mistakes, shortfalls and weaknesses, this can trigger a defensive response, and reduce the motivation to change behaviour. Job satisfaction and organizational commitment are also damaged where employees feel that the feedback is biased, unfair, inaccurate or politically motivated.

Marie-Hélène Budworth et al. (2015) suggest an alternative: the **feedforward interview**. A traditional appraisal focuses on what went wrong and what the employee has to do in order to improve. A feedforward interview explores what has been positive in the employee's experience, focusing on strengths and successes. The appraiser does not have to act as judge or critic, and provides no negative feedback in this process

A feedforward interview begins by asking the employee to describe occasions when their performance was successful. The interviewer then explores situations where the individual and the organization both benefit. The employee is then asked to identify the difference between their goals and the current state. This leads finally to the employee setting goals to reduce this discrepancy. As employees identify their own performance goals, and what they have to do to achieve them, the motivation to change is higher that it would be if those goals and behaviour changes were imposed.

Budworth et al. (2015) describe how the sales and customer service unit in a business equipment organization compared the effects of traditional appraisals with feedforward interviews. All 25 managers were randomly assigned to a traditional or a feedforward approach. Those who were to use feedforward were trained in the method, but employees were not aware of this. About half of the employees (70) were given a feedforward interview, and the other 75 had a traditional appraisal. After the appraisals, employee performance was assessed using a behavioural observation scale, with items such as 'this individual completes projects before deadlines' and 'this person actively finds ways to improve this business'. The feedforward interview not only improved performance more than traditional appraisals, but that improvement was lasting. Citing a survey of 5,000 employees which found that less than one-third felt that a traditional appraisal helped them to improve performance, Budworth et al. (2015) conclude that feedforward could be more effective than feedback.

Consider a domestic heating control system. The temperature standard is set on a thermostat, and a heater (effector) starts to warm up the room. The output of the system is heated air. Changes in temperature are measured by a thermometer. The temperature of the room is continually compared with the standard. When the room reaches the required temperature the effector is switched off, and when the room cools it is switched on again.

The cybernetic analogy says that this control loop is a model of what goes on in the mind. For standard, read motive, purpose, intent or goals. The output is behaviour. Our senses are measuring devices. Our perception is the comparator which organizes and imposes meaning on the sensory data which control behaviour in pursuit of our goals. We each have an internal representation or 'schema' of ourselves and our environment. This internal representation is used in a purposive way to determine our behaviour, and is also known as the individual's *perceptual world* (see Chapter 8).

We make plans to achieve our goals. These plans are sets of mental instructions for guiding the required behaviour. Within the master plan (get an educational qualification) there are likely to be a number of sub-plans (submit essays on time; pass examinations; make new friends). The organization of our behaviour is hierarchical – a concept which is also seen in computer programs where routines and subroutines are 'nested' within each other.

We can also use information on how we are doing – feedback – to update our internal representation and to refine and adapt our plans. Feedback can either be self-generated or come from an external source: it can be either **intrinsic** or **extrinsic**.

Independent of the source and nature of the feedback, timing is also important. Feedback can arrive during or after the behaviour that we are learning: it can be either **concurrent** or **delayed**.

Intrinsic feedback is invariably concurrent. When you throw rings over pegs at the fair to win a soft toy, the intrinsic concurrent visual feedback means that you know immediately how well (or how badly) you are performing. Some extrinsic feedback is also concurrent – from a driving instructor, for example. However, for your next course assignment, feedback from your lecturer is going to be delayed. Instructors cannot provide concurrent feedback on your essay or project, but the longer the delay, the less effective the feedback is likely to be.

Feedback, rewards and punishments, and knowledge of results, have a *motivating* effect on behaviour, as well as a reinforcing effect. Opportunities to learn new skills and knowledge, to understand more, and to develop more effective ways of coping with our environment can be intrinsically motivating. The American psychologist Robert W. White (1959) suggests that we have a motive to develop 'competence', which gives us satisfaction. As our discussion of the *learning organization* shows, the 'urge towards discovery' and the

Intrinsic feedback information which comes from within, from the muscles, joints, skin and other mechanisms such as that which controls balance.

Extrinsic feedback information which comes from our environment, such as the visual and aural information needed to drive a car.

Concurrent feedback information which arrives during our behaviour and which can be used to control behaviour as it unfolds.

Delayed feedback information which is received after a task is completed, and which can be used to influence future performance.

'will to understand' have triggered a search for novel organizational forms in which individual and organizational learning are encouraged.

STOP AND THINK From your own experience, identify an example of each of the four varieties of feedback. What changes in that feedback would be required for you to be able to improve your performance (on this course, at sport, whatever)?

Behaviourism in practice

Behaviour modification
a technique for encouraging desired behaviours and discouraging unwanted behaviours using operant conditioning.

Behaviourism led to the development of **behaviour modification** techniques, first used to treat mental and learning disorders and phobias, and for psychiatric rehabilitation and accident and trauma recovery. These methods are now used in many organizational settings.

As developed by Fred Luthans (Luthans and Kreitner, 1985; Luthans et al., 1998), organizational behaviour modification, or OBMod, has five steps:

1. *Identify* the critical, observable and measurable behaviours to be encouraged.
2. *Measure* the current frequency of those behaviours, to provide a baseline against which to measure improvement.
3. *Establish* the triggers or antecedents for those behaviours, and also establish the consequences – positive, neutral and negative – that follow from those behaviours.
4. *Develop* a strategy to strengthen desired behaviours and weaken dysfunctional behaviours through positive reinforcement (money, recognition) and feedback; punishment may be necessary in some cases, for example to inhibit unsafe behaviour.
5. *Evaluate* systematically the effectiveness of the approach in changing behaviour and improving performance compared with the original baseline measurement.

Behaviour modification is attractive to managers who can manipulate the reinforcement of employee behaviours. The method focuses on behaviour rather than on internal mental states and processes. Desirable behaviours include speaking politely to customers, attending training, helping colleagues, or, in a hospital, washing hands to reduce infections. Undesirable behaviours include lateness, making poor quality items and being rude to customers. OBMod uses reinforcement to eliminate undesired behaviour and encourage desired behaviour. Suppose a manager wants work assignments completed on time, with few submitted beyond the deadline. The OBMod options are summarized in Table 5.4.

Table 5.4: Behaviour modification options

Procedure	Operationalization	Behavioural effect
Positive reinforcement	Manager praises employee each time work is completed on schedule	Increases desired work behaviour
Negative reinforcement	Unpaid overtime continues to be mandatory until work is completed on schedule, then overtime is rewarded	Increases desired work behaviour
Punishment	Manager asks employee to stay late when work is not handed in on time	Eliminates or decreases undesired behaviour
Extinction	Manager ignores the employee when work is handed in late	Eliminates or decreases undesired behaviour

Fred Luthans and colleagues (1998) describe how OBMod improved productivity in a Russian textile mill. For performance improvements, workers were given extrinsic rewards including American products such as adults' and children's clothing, and food that was difficult to get in Russia. They were also given 'social rewards' (attention, recognition, feedback) for specific actions such as checking looms, undertaking repairs, monitoring fabric quality and helping others. This approach was welcome, and led to significant increases in performance (Luthans et al., 1998, p.471). Asking the workers for ideas on how improve performance got no response; the culture and political climate prevented them from making suggestions which would criticize methods and colleagues. Luthans concludes that OBMod 'fits' Eastern European organizational cultures where it has wide applicability.

OBMod, MRSA and ICUs

Adverse events cost the UK health service £2 billion a year, and hospital-acquired infections cost a further £1 billion. Human error seems to be the main cause, but research shows that organizational culture and management systems can encourage undesirable behaviour. Could behaviour modification techniques be used to improve patient safety?

Dominic Cooper et al. (2005) describe a hospital OBMod programme designed to reduce infections, such as MRSA (methicillin-resistant *staphylococcus aureus*). The usual methods include screening, isolation, cleaning, monitoring, training, awareness-raising and improved policies and protocols, but that wasn't enough to solve the problem. Two intensive care units (ICUs) were involved, employing 140 doctors, nurses, healthcare assistants and administrative staff. The units had many visitors, including physicians, other hospital staff, family members and friends. The programme focused on two behaviours. The first was hand-washing, to reduce the spread of infection; research shows that doctors wash their hands on less than 10 per cent of appropriate occasions. The second concerned the accuracy and completeness of nursing documents which record patients' conditions.

Staff were briefed on the aims and conduct of the programme, to engage them in problem solving and in generating ideas (such as installing a sink at the entrance where visitors could wash). Staff were asked to identify their main concerns, and what they saw as the most common undesired behaviours. A project coordinator and eight observers were trained in behaviour modification methods; how to observe, how to give feedback, how to set improvement goals. A checklist of 36 desired behaviours was developed, so that observers could record compliance, which they did by standing at the central nursing station for 20 minutes at a randomly chosen time each day. Observation data were analysed weekly, posted on a feedback chart, and discussed in group feedback meetings.

The results showed significant changes in behaviour which along with other methods reduced MRSA infections by 70 per cent. With fewer MRSA patients, there was extra ICU capacity, reduced laboratory costs, less overtime and temporary staff costs, and reduced costs of complaints. These outcomes were attributed to motivation to provide quality care (goals), and to the weekly performance data (feedback) which let staff know that they were doing a good job. Apart from the time that staff spent training, observing and in meetings, the programme costs came to only a few hundred pounds for clerical materials and cleaning items.

OBMod has the following characteristics:

- It applies to clearly identifiable and observable behaviours, such as timekeeping, absenteeism, carrying out checks and repairs, and the use of particular work methods.
- Rewards are contingent on the performance of the desirable behaviours.
- Positive reinforcement can take a number of forms, from the praise of a superior to cash prizes, to food, to clothing.
- Behaviour change and performance improvements can be dramatic.
- The desired modification in behaviour may only be sustained if positive reinforcement is continued (although this may be intermittent).

STOP AND THINK

How do you feel about being given food, t-shirts and praise for working harder?

Do you regard this approach as practical, or as demeaning – and why?

Cognitive perspectives in practice

Socialization the process through which individual behaviours, values, attitudes and motives are influenced to conform with those seen as desirable in a given social or organizational setting.

Albert Bandura
(b.1925)

Behavioural modelling learning how to act by observing and copying the behaviour of others.

When people join an organization, they give up some personal freedom. That is part of the price of membership. Employees thus accept that an organization can make demands on their time and effort, as long as these demands are seen to be legitimate. Other members of the organization have to teach new recruits what is expected of them. The process through which recruits are 'shown the ropes' is called socialization. Cognitive psychologists regard behaviour modification as simplistic, and turn to more complex social explanations and methods for organizational behaviour change.

This perspective draws on social learning theory which is based on assumptions about human psychology different from those behind OBMod techniques. One of the most influential advocates of social learning theory has been Albert Bandura (1977, 1986), who showed that we learn new behaviours by observing and copying others, through behavioural modelling. We copy the behaviour of others, and we do not need rewards or punishments to encourage us to do this. However, if the behaviours that we copy are successful (rewarded or reinforced by positive results), then we are more likely to continue to act in that way. Our capabilities for reflection and self-determination are central in this perspective. We construct, through observation and experience, internal models of our environment, and plan courses of action accordingly. The ways in which we model ourselves on others is particularly apparent in children, and we continue to copy or imitate others as adults.

Bandura's argument that we learn through social experience, through observation and modelling, does not deny the importance of reinforcement. Behavioural modelling involves the four processes of attention, retention, production and reinforcement outlined in Figure 5.3. Suppose we choose to base some of our behaviours (how to handle a job interview, how to make new friends) by modelling ourselves on someone who is successful in those areas. Suppose that our new approach does not lead to the desired results: we don't get the job, we fail to establish relationships. Without reinforcement, we abandon those new behaviours and look for other models. If our new methods are successful, however, we will use them again.

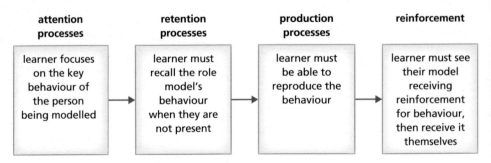

Figure 5.3: The behavioural modelling process
Source: based on Weiss (1990).

When we get a new job, we have to learn how to 'fit in', and this means following the norms and rules that are considered to be appropriate in the organization and work group. From her study of financial analysts and consultants, Herminia Ibarra (1999; Ibarra and Barbulescu, 2010) shows how we adapt to new roles by experimenting with

Provisional selves
from observing others, the experiments that we make with the ways in which we act and interact in new organizational roles.

provisional selves, which are based on the role models that we see around us. This process, she found, has three stages:

Observing: we watch other people to see how they behave and respond.

Experimenting: we try out some of those behaviours to see how they work for us.

Evaluating: we use our own assessment and feedback from others to decide which behaviours to keep, and which to discard.

Our observations of role models in a new setting can cover a range of issues: physical appearance, personal style, ways of interacting, displays of skill. This does not mean that we just copy others. We choose the behaviours that we feel are credible, and that are consistent with how we see ourselves, and also consistent with how we want others to see us – as competent, creative, enthusiastic, trustworthy. We do this by experimenting, keeping those actions that we like, and discarding those that do not work, or which are inconsistent with our self-image. Comments from Ibarra's (1999) interviewees illustrate this:

> There are a good half dozen to a dozen senior people I'd view as mentors. I think up until director, you're building your skills, you're trying on different styles, like different clothes, almost. You try and figure out what styles fit your personality and fit what you're good at. And then that's how you should try to go after business. (p.777)

> I've been out with X and watched him in action. He's very aggressive in new business – one of the best in the firm. He has a very charismatic personality, which is something you can't teach. I don't think I could really replicate his style. I'm not as outgoing, but I think the attitude and persistence are things that I have. (p.775)

> I don't have an aggressive personality. I have been told I need to improve. I have adjusted to it by becoming more assertive over time. Just watching P was good. She is very vocal, asks lots of questions, always makes sure she has a point to make, is very assertive. Now I do like she does. (p.780)

STOP AND THINK   Think of two people who you have observed recently – one a real person, the other a character in a film or a television programme. How have they influenced you? Which of their behaviours have you adopted? How did that work out?

The dark side of socialization

New recruits have to learn the behaviours and attitudes that will help them to 'fit in', and to perform their jobs well. Many organizations have formal induction programmes. Informal socialization – observing, and getting information and feedback from co-workers – is also important. However, as well as introducing newcomers to desired organizational norms, informal processes can encourage unsafe and risky behaviours, such as drinking alcohol at work.

Songqi Liu and colleagues (2015) studied 57 supervisors and 147 recently appointed members of sales and client service staff in two manufacturing companies in China. The roles of the service staff included contacting and visiting new and existing customers, to discuss their needs for products and services, to negotiate sales and to resolve complaints. The researchers used interviews and questionnaires to find out about staff drinking habits in relation to clients.

The new client service staff quickly learned that 'drinking alcohol is an effective and legitimate means to improve job performance' (p.334). Why? Alcohol creates a more relaxed and friendly atmosphere, lowers inhibitions and encourages the free and open exchange of information. Some cultures have a tradition of closing a deal with a drink. After observing existing employees and external clients, new recruits began 'performance drinking'. The consumption of alcohol in work meetings was acceptable, because it improved business relationships, increased sales and helped individual careers. The long-term damage to health was less important than the need to conform with the job expectations.

How does social learning theory apply to organizational settings? Organizations encourage different standards concerning:

- what counts as good work performance;
- familiarity in social interactions at work;
- the amount of deference to show to superiors;
- dress and appearance;
- social activities after work;
- attitudes to work, colleagues, managers, unions, customers.

You have to learn these standards, and the related attitudes and behaviours, to become an accepted member of the organization. You do not have to believe that the organization's standards are appropriate. In order to 'fit in', what matters is that you behave *as if* you believe in those norms. Socialization methods often involve formal induction programmes combined with mentoring and buddy systems, corporate videos and podcasts, 'face-to-face' challenge meetings with senior executives, and 'master classes' run by top performers. Socialization can also be informal, achieved without planned intervention, by giving rewards such as praise, encouragement and promotion for 'correct' behaviour. Newcomers also 'learn the ropes' just by watching colleagues. This may be supported by negative reinforcements and punishments, like being ignored, ridiculed or fined for behaviour that is 'out of line'. We quickly learn what attitudes to take, what style of language to use, what 'dress code' to obey, where to take lunch and with whom, and so on.

STOP AND THINK   Remember when you first joined this college or university; how did you feel about the formal socialization or induction process? To what informal socialization were you exposed? Which had the greater impact on your behaviour, the formal or the informal processes?

Managed socialization in action

Social learning theory argues that we learn correct behaviours through experience and through the examples or *role models* that other people provide. While this can happen naturally, some companies prefer not to leave it to chance, and to manage the process instead. For example, some companies use a 'buddy system', pairing new recruits with established employees. However, if you get a job with the American computer software company Trilogy, based in Austin, Texas, you will be sent to Trilogy University (TU) for three months, to join an orientation programme modelled on Marine Corps basic training (Tichy, 2001). This is an intense and intimidating 'boot camp', designed to challenge recruits, most of whom are university graduates with an average age of 22. Trilogy wants to familiarize them with appropriate knowledge and skills, and also with the company's 'vision and values'. Run over three months, for up to 200 recruits at a time, the boot camp has three stages.

Month one

New recruits are assigned to a section, of about 20 people, and to an instruction track. The section leader is an experienced Trilogy employee, and the tracks resemble work in the company. Along with functional training, the recruits are assessed on a series of increasingly challenging assignments, which mirror real customer problems, but with reduced timescales. Students are stretched beyond the point of failure in order to introduce company values including humility, creativity, innovation, teamwork, customer problem solving and risk taking. Another goal is to develop lasting, trusting relationships with colleagues.

Month two

Recruits are asked to develop 'a frame-breaking great new business idea'. Teams of three to five have to generate an idea, create a business model, build the product, design a marketing plan and present the results to the Chief Executive. These projects are real, and many are funded. Recruits are expected to learn about the need to set priorities, assess probabilities and measure results. Failure to generate a successful idea is not punished.

Month three

Most recruits move on to business-related 'graduation projects', and leave TU as they find sponsors willing to take them on. Graduation involves a meeting with the recruit, the new manager and the section leader, at which the recruit's abilities are reviewed, their career objectives are examined and the manager's three- to five-year goals for the recruit (including further skill development) are agreed. Most graduates find a home in the company, but those few who cannot find a sponsor have to leave.

Since 1995, when TU was founded, recruits' projects have generated revenues of $25 million, and formed the basis for $100 million in new business for the company. Innovative ideas include internet-based motor car retailing, and a website which allows shoppers to put products from several different internet retailers into a single purchase. In addition, the section leaders assigned for three months to inspire, mentor and develop the new recruits improve their own leadership and change agency skills.

Of course, organizations do not rely on socialization alone in order to equip employees with appropriate knowledge and skills. Most use a combination of other formal and informal learning and development methods. A survey of 550 human resource professionals in the UK in 2015 found that the five most common learning and development methods in use were (CIPD, 2015a):

- on-the-job training;
- in-house development and internal peer-to-peer knowledge-sharing programmes;
- coaching by line managers or colleagues;
- online e-learning courses;
- external conferences, workshops and events.

These methods were expected to grow in popularity, except external conferences. On the other hand, formal education, off-site instructor-led training, external conferences and the use of MOOCs (Multiple Online Open Learning Courses) were expected to decline. The survey also revealed that on-the-job training was thought to be the most effective learning practice. Online and mobile learning, off-site instructor-led training and external events were considered to be the least effective (CIPD, 2015b, p.11). Given the difficult domestic and global economic conditions at the time of this survey, organizations felt it appropriate to use internal resources to support learning and development instead of more expensive external providers. It is also interesting that technology-based methods were thought to be among the less effective learning and development methods. However, the developments in learning technology which respondents said would have the most impact over the next five years included mobile learning, virtual classrooms, social media and webinars.

Behaviour modification versus socialization

Is behaviour modification a useful approach to learning at work and the development of appropriate behaviours? The evidence suggests a qualified 'yes'; there are two qualifications.

First, behaviour modification needs careful planning to identify specific behavioural goals, and procedures for reinforcing the behaviours that will achieve those goals. The method can be effective when behaviour and reinforcement are clearly identified and linked: wear your seat belt and we'll give you cash. The method is less effective when this relationship is vague: demonstrate your commitment and we will consider you for promotion.

Second, the 'rewards for good behaviour' method appears broadly consistent with American (and perhaps Eastern European) cultural values and aspirations. The transfer of this approach to other cultures could be a problem. The most often cited practical examples are American.

You are responsible for training the new shelf-stacker in your local supermarket. What combination of behaviour modification and socialization techniques will you use, and how will you apply these?

Behaviour modification is manipulative, often ignores internal needs and intrinsic rewards, and can be a threat to individual dignity and autonomy. It can be seen as a simplistic and transparent attempt to manipulate others, prompting cynicism rather than behaviour change. The technique thus has limitations. However, OBMod requires the communication of goals and expectations in unambiguous terms. Many would argue that such clarity is desirable. Fred Luthans and Robert Kreitner (1985) summarize the problems with behaviour modification:

1. Appropriate reinforcers may not always be available, in routine work settings, for example.

2. We do not all respond in the same way to the same reinforcers; what one person finds rewarding may be of little consequence to someone else.

3. Once started, a behaviour modification programme has to be sustained.

4. There may not be enough extrinsic motivators (health care benefits, bonuses) available.

They also argue, however, that the technique has made significant contributions:

1. Behaviour modification techniques put the focus on observable employee behaviour and not on hypothetical internal states.

2. The method shows how performance is influenced by outcomes that depend in turn on the individual's behaviour.

3. It supports the view that positive reinforcement is more effective in changing employee behaviour than punishment.

4. It is possible to show a clear causal link to performance, which is often hard to establish with other behaviour change methods, such as job enrichment.

Social learning is dependent on the cultural context, and is a process rather than a specific technique. Socialization, in contrast, is more flexible. American socialization techniques, for example, may be quite different from Swedish, Belgian, Nigerian, Malaysian or Spanish ones. Socialization is a process that takes place anyway, planned or not. The issue concerns appropriate socialization, with respect to organizational culture and behavioural preferences. Because it is a 'natural' process, with no clear financial or other benefit from investing in its operation, it may be difficult to persuade management to give socialization the attention and resources that this requires. Table 5.5 summarizes the contrasts between behaviour modification and socialization.

Table 5.5: Behaviour modification versus socialization

Behaviour modification	Socialization
Feedback needed in both approaches for behaviour to change	
Planned procedure	Naturally occurring, even if also planned
Stimulus determines responses	Individual needs determine responses
Externally generated reinforcements	Internally generated reinforcements
Focuses on observable behaviour	Focuses on unobservable internal states
Focus on tangible rewards and punishments (money, other material rewards)	Focus on intangible rewards and punishments (social inclusion, self-esteem)
Clear links between desired behaviour and consequences	Intangible links between desired behaviour and consequences
Compliance required by external agent	Conformity encouraged by social grouping

However, as the following section shows, some organizations have introduced the methods of the learning organization. This is an attempt to socialize an organization's members with respect to attitudes and behaviours related to the acquisition and development of new knowledge, creativity, innovation, flexibility and readiness for change.

Behavioural self-management (BSM)

Management attempts to modify the behaviour of others raises ethical questions. Self-improvement, however, is acceptable and fashionable. Fred Luthans and Tim Davis (1979) developed the technique of **behavioural self-management** for individual use.

BSM combines the behavioural focus of OBMod with the cognitive processes central to social learning theory. It is not merely a form of self-imposed behaviour modification. Social learning theory argues that we actively process stimuli and consequences, in a self-monitoring fashion, whereas behaviourism sees our behaviour shaped by rewards and punishments.

BSM involves the following steps (Kreitner et al., 1999):

1. *Identify the undesirable behaviour* that you want to change, develop or improve.

2. *Manage the situational cues* which trigger desired behaviour. Avoid situations which trigger the target behaviour; seek situations which encourage desired behaviour instead. Use 'reminders and attention focusers' such as notes stuck in prominent places, and 'self-observation data' recording success and lapses. Set personal contracts, establish behavioural goals; post records of these in prominent places.

3. *Provide cognitive support* for the new behaviour. There are three ways to do this. First, through *symbolic coding*, using visual images and acronyms to support the desired behaviour (KISS – Keep It Simple Stupid, and MBWA – Management By Walking Around).

Second, through *mental rehearsal* of the desired behaviour (a technique used by many successful sports people). Third, through *self-talk*, which is positive and supportive of the desired behaviour change.

4. *Develop self-reinforcement*, which is within your control, and which is delivered only on condition that the desired behaviour change is achieved. This can be strengthened by arranging also for positive reinforcement from supportive friends and colleagues.

This web of situational cues, cognitive support and self-reinforcement can be a powerful combination in helping to eliminate target behaviours and establish desired behaviours in their place. Using this technique, Rakos and Grodek (1984) report how American college students successfully modified behaviour problems concerning smoking, lack of assertiveness, poor study habits, overeating, sloppy housekeeping, lack of exercise and moodiness. Luthans and Davis (1979) describe how the technique was used to deal with management behaviour problems such as overdependence on the boss, ignoring paperwork, leaving the office without notifying anybody, and failing to fill out expense reports.

Apply behavioural self-management to yourself. Target a behaviour of current personal significance; drinking, smoking, overeating, excessive clubbing, inappropriate study habits. Establish a pattern of situational cues, cognitive support and self-reinforcement. Set a timescale, and use your experience to assess the power and relevance of this technique.

The learning organization

Behavioural self-management a technique for changing one's own behaviour by systematically manipulating cues, cognitive processes and contingent consequences.

The concept of the **learning organization** is based on the work of Chris Argyris and Donald Schön (Argyris and Schön, 1974, 1978; Argyris, 1982). This is an organization that helps individuals to learn and to perform more effectively.

The learning organization concept has become significant for several reasons:

- the production of goods and services increasingly involves sophisticated knowledge;
- knowledge is, therefore, as valuable a resource as raw materials;
- many organizations have lost knowledgeable staff through retirements and delayering;
- 'second machine age' technologies are knowledge intensive;
- some knowledge can have a short life span, made obsolete by innovation;
- flexibility, creativity and responsiveness are now prized capabilities;
- knowledge can thus be a source of competitive advantage for an organization.

Ikujiro Nonaka and Hirotaka Takeuchi (1995) argue that the ability to create knowledge and solve problems is a 'core competence' for most organizations. For them, everyone is a knowledge worker. Anyone dealing with customers is a source of intelligence on customer perceptions of products, services and pricing. These 'boundary workers' are often poorly paid (receptionists, porters, sales staff), and their customer intelligence is overlooked as their positions are distant, in terms of physical location and organization structure, from management.

Why should organizations invest in learning and development?

Employee learning and development is often treated as a corporate luxury, and can be one of the first budget items to be cut in a recession. To control costs, some organizations focus their investment on 'high potential' and 'high performing' individuals. Others, however, take a more inclusive 'whole workforce' approach. Investment in learning and development can produce a number of returns:

- commercial benefit by improving individual and group performance;
- enhance employee engagement and develop human capital;
- support the management of change, organizational adaptability and agility;
- support the organization's corporate social responsibility goals;
- improve retention and motivation by offering personal career development;
- develop skills that will be needed in future.

Most organizations face major environmental, cultural and technological changes (Chapters 2 and 3). Generation Y, or 'millennials', born between the early 1980s and the early 2000s, have high expectations of personal development through work, and are more likely to see themselves belonging to a professional skills network, than to one employer. Keeping staff skills and knowledge up to date in this uncertain, complex and volatile context has thus become more important. Given these trends, which learning strategy is more appropriate: a 'high performers' focus or a 'whole workforce' approach, and why? (based on CIPD, 2015a).

A survey of employers in 2015 found that 54 percent adopted a 'whole workforce' approach to talent management, and 35 per cent focused instead on high potential staff (CIPD, 2015b, p.20).

Learning organization
an organizational form that enables individual learning to create valued organizational outcomes, such as innovation, efficiency, environmental alignment and competitive advantage.

Karl Weick and Frances Westley (1996, p.440) argue that the concepts of 'organization' and 'learning' are contradictory. Organization implies structure, order, stability. Learning implies change, variety, disorganization. Can these concepts be combined successfully?

STOP AND THINK

An organization doesn't exist without its members. How can an organization 'learn'?

The idea of the learning organization was popularized by Peter Senge whose book *The Fifth Discipline* (1990) was an international best-seller. Senge argues (1990, p.4) that work at all levels must become more 'learningful', by applying the five 'learning disciplines' in Table 5.6.

Table 5.6: Five learning disciplines

Learning discipline	Explanation
1. Personal mastery	*Aspiration*, concerning what you as an individual want to achieve
2. Mental models	*Reflection and inquiry*, concerning the constant refinement of thinking and development of awareness
3. Shared vision	*Collective commitment* to a common sense of purpose and actions to achieve that purpose
4. Team learning	*Group interaction*, concerning collective thinking and action to achieve common goals
5. Systems thinking	*Understanding interdependency and complexity* and the role of feedback in system development

Senge's argument is – have realistic goals, challenge your assumptions, commit to a shared vision, teamworking is good. The application of these 'disciplines', however, is problematic, and is linked to our discussion of socialization, to encouraging the 'correct' attitudes, values and beliefs among employees at all levels. The most important learning discipline is 'the fifth discipline', systems thinking, which means understanding how complex organizations function, and how they can be changed to work more effectively. The theory is:

> [T]he practice of organizational learning involves developing tangible activities: new governing ideas, innovations in infrastructure, and new management methods and tools for changing the way people conduct their work. Given the opportunity to take part in these new activities, people will develop an enduring capability for change. The process will pay back the organization with far greater levels of diversity, commitment, innovation and talent. (Senge et al., 1999, p.33)

In other words, the manager who wants commitment, flexibility and creativity from employees must provide them with lots of learning opportunities.

Some commentators argue that a learning organization helps its members to learn. Others claim that the organization itself learns. How can this be? Silvia Gherardi (1997, p.542) treats the term learning organization as a metaphor which regards an organization as a biological entity, as 'a subject which learns, which processes information, which reflects on experiences, which is endowed with a stock of knowledge, skills and expertise'. Gherardi supports the view that organizations learn with experience, the proof lying with visible changes in an organization's behaviour. For example, in the development of manufacturing processes, the staff hours required to produce a unit of output decrease with accumulated experience, even though the staff change. Another example concerns the ways in which organizations evolve and adapt to 'fit' their environment, introducing internal structural changes in response to environmental opportunities and pressures.

Is yours a learning organization?

A survey tool for deciding if you have a learning organization has been developed by David Garvin et al. (2008). They felt that while others had provided a compelling vision of the learning organization, they had not developed a practical approach to implementing the idea. The effective learning organization, they argue, has three building blocks. Here are the three blocks and their components, with a sample of the survey questions which employees are asked to rate in order to measure how well the learning organization functions:

Block 1: Supportive learning environment

Psychological safety	'In this unit, it is easy to speak up about what is on your mind'
Appreciation of differences	'Differences in opinion are welcome in this unit'
Openness to new ideas	'In this unit, people are interested in better ways of doing things'
Time for reflection	'Despite the workload, people in this unit find time to review how the work is going'

Block 2: Concrete learning processes and practices

Experimentation:	'This unit experiments frequently with new ways of working'
Information collection	'This unit frequently compares its performance with that of competitors and best-in-class organizations'
Analysis	'This unit engages in productive conflict and debate during discussions'
Education and training	'In this unit, time is made available for education and training activities'
Information transfer	'This unit regularly shares information with networks of experts within and outside the organization'

Block 3: Leadership that reinforces learning

'My managers invite input from others in discussion'

'Managers acknowledge their limitations with respect to knowledge, information, or expertise'

'My managers listen attentively'

These three blocks overlap with and reinforce each other, but measuring an organization's performance in each area identifies areas of excellence and opportunities for improvement.

Organizations also have available to them several different types of knowledge, not all of which are dependent on individual expertise (Gherardi, 1997, p.547). This includes learning from past experience through assessment and evaluation, and learning from the experience of other organizations. There is also knowledge 'built in' to equipment and raw materials, with formulae, ingredients, recipes, known properties and so on. Standard operating procedures can usually be found in instruction manuals, forms and job descriptions – all ways of codifying knowledge. Many organizations also possess patents and property rights.

Carlsberg puts learning on tap

Carlsberg shut its entire Leeds brewery for one day for staff to be given additional training. The move was designed to give health and safety advice to 170 staff at the Danish lager firm, update them on new technology and hold wellness and personal development sessions. Such a large-scale initiative marks a change of thinking for Carlsberg.

Natalie Steed, change manager, HR, told *People Management* (30 October 2008, p.8) that 'Stopping production for training is rare in manufacturing, if not unprecedented. But feedback from staff told us it was what they wanted, and having all the trainers on site on a single day meant we could spend our training budget in the most effective way.'

Usually, training at the company is conducted in groups of eight people, which is as many as can be spared at any one time. Shutting the plant gave them time to go beyond the bare essentials, explained Steed. 'It's given us the time to carry out things we've always wanted to do – particularly around health and well-being – rather than just doing what we have to do', she said.

The day was a boost for learning at all levels. Engineers, who typically have high-level degrees, were given the chance to carry out a 'skills gap analysis' to identify areas to improve. It was also an opportunity to promote Carlsberg's new learning centre, where staff can pursue courses in numeracy, literacy and basic IT skills. The learning day idea is now set to be repeated in Carlsberg's other UK brewery, in Northampton.

Single-loop learning the ability to use feedback to make continuous adjustments and adaptations, to maintain performance at a predetermined standard.

Double-loop learning the ability to challenge and to redefine the assumptions underlying performance standards and to improve performance.

Karl Weick and Frances Westley (1996) argue that organizational learning is best understood in terms of *organizational culture*. Culture includes values, beliefs, feelings, artefacts, myths, symbols, metaphors and rituals, which taken together distinguish one organization or group from others. Organizations are thus 'repositories of knowledge' independent of their members (Schön, 1983, p.242). Organizations which accumulate stocks of codified, documented knowledge, independent of their members, can thus be said to learn.

Weick and Westley (1996) note how different organizational forms are better equipped for learning. The post-modern organization (Chapter 2) adapts to environmental change in an innovative and responsive way. This is an organizational form associated with creative thinking and rapid learning, and has also been described as 'adhocracy'. Bureaucracy, on the other hand, is concerned with efficiency, division of labour, rigid chain of command, and with clear distinctions and rationality.

How can 'organizational learning' be understood? Argyris and Schön (1974) developed the distinction between **single-loop learning** and **double-loop learning** (see Figure 5.4).

The concept of single-loop learning comes from cybernetics, where control systems are designed around norms, standards, procedures, routines and feedback. As previously discussed, the classic example of cybernetic control is the thermostat which, by detecting temperature variations, takes action to correct deviations from a set norm.

In single-loop learning, the system maintains performance at that norm, and is unable to 'learn' that the norm is too high or too low. It cannot 'learn how to learn', to challenge and rethink its assumptions and values. Limited to making small-scale changes, single-loop learning is not really learning at all.

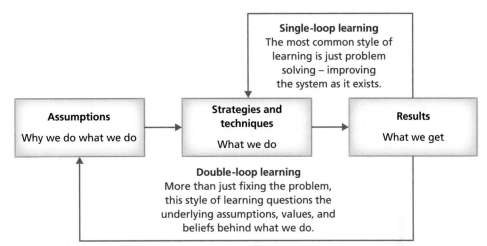

Tacit knowledge
knowledge and understanding specific to the individual, derived from experience, and difficult to codify and to communicate to others.

Figure 5.4: Single- and double-loop learning
Source: http://selfleadership.com/blog/topic/leadership/relfecting-and-learning-2009-to-2010/

STOP AND THINK Let us assume that you are learning during your organizational behaviour course. Is this single-loop learning, or double-loop learning? Which of these two types of learning should you be engaged in?

Learning how to learn involves double-loop learning. This means challenging assumptions, beliefs, norms, routines and decisions, rather than accepting them and working within those limitations. In single-loop learning, the question is, how can we better achieve that standard of performance? With double-loop learning, in contrast, the question becomes, is that an appropriate target in the first place?

Explicit knowledge
knowledge and understanding which is codified, clearly articulated and available to anyone.

When we learn, we acquire knowledge – of organizational behaviour, gardening, guitar playing, accountancy, electrical engineering, and so on. Knowledge, however, is a difficult term to define clearly. For Nonaka and Takeuchi (1995), there are two types of knowledge, tacit knowledge and explicit knowledge.

Mobile learning at BP

The energy company BP found that many staff did not understand how the different parts of the company's business – refining, drilling, logistics – fitted together. Instead of running tutor-led courses, Claire Churchard (2015) describes how BP developed innovative mobile methods instead.

First, BP developed a *3D aerial schematic*, giving staff an interactive birds' eye view of the links between the upstream and downstream parts of the business. Viewers clicked on the different areas to discover more, through factsheets with infographics, and five-minute video animations. All this could be accessed on iPads, anywhere, and at any time.

Second, the *Build your own oil company* game allowed players (learners) to navigate around a 3D world and to discover energy reserves over four continents. One of the consultants working with the BP learning team said, 'People come to this game out of choice rather than have it pushed onto them. And we've found that people want to play this'.

Third, BP also produced *videos* which staff could watch on their smartphones. To share experience and support those moving into new roles, for example, one video series featured leaders discussing the advice that they would have given to themselves at different points in their careers.

Fourth, *text and video-animated checklists* proved to be popular mobile learning tools, including 'top eight leadership mistakes' and 'six things that affect decision making'.

Other organizations planning this approach should listen to what the company itself learned. Nick Shackleton-Jones, BP's director for online and informal learning, said: 'People like learning online but they won't use anything that is not easy to find or beautifully designed and useful. And if it meets all of these criteria people will tell their colleagues about it and share it on social media'.

Tacit knowledge includes insights, intuition, hunches and judgements, and concerns the individual's unarticulated mental models and skills. Tacit knowledge tends to be personal, specific to particular contexts, and difficult to communicate. For example, if you are able to drive a motor car with a manual gear shift, then you will know where to position your foot to 'slip the clutch' and prevent the car from rolling on a slope. You will be able to move your foot to that position, accurately and consistently, without much conscious thought. However, expect to run into difficulties when you try to explain this tacit skill to a learner driver.

Explicit knowledge on the other hand is articulated, codified, expressed, available to anyone. Nonaka and Takeuchi argue that the Japanese emphasize tacit knowledge, while Westerners emphasize explicit, formal, codified knowledge. In Western cultures, tacit knowledge is undervalued because it is intangible and difficult to measure. However, tacit and explicit knowledge are complementary. Nonaka and Takeuchi are thus concerned with 'knowledge conversion' in which tacit knowledge is made available to the organization, on the one hand, and organizational knowledge becomes the individual's tacit knowledge, on the other (Nonaka et al., 1999).

Knowledge management the conversion of individual tacit knowledge into explicit knowledge so that it can be shared with others in the organization.

Organizational learning is related to, but is different from **knowledge management**.

Table 5.7 summarizes the main positive and negative aspects of the learning organization, and its related concepts of intellectual capital and knowledge management.

Table 5.7: Learning organization positives and negatives

Learning organization positives	Learning organization negatives
A rich, multi-dimensional concept affecting many aspects of organizational behaviour	A complex and diffuse set of practices, difficult to implement systematically
An innovative approach to learning, to knowledge management, and to investing in intellectual capital	An attempt to use dated concepts from change management and learning theory, repackaged as a management consulting project
A new set of challenging concepts focusing attention on the acquisition and development of individual and corporate knowledge	A new approach for encouraging employee compliance with management directives in the guise of 'self-development'
An innovative approach to organization, management and employee development	An innovative approach to strengthening management control over employee behaviour
Innovative use of technology to manage organizational knowledge through databases and the internet or intranets	A technology-dependent approach which ignores how people actually develop and use knowledge in organizations
Exponential growth in computing power and the ability to analyse very large sets of data	Growing concerns about breaches of privacy and increased surveillance of employees

Knowledge management and the learning organization are fashionable ideas. Their popularity has been strengthened by trends discussed in Chapter 3: developments in computing power, 'big data', machine intelligence, and 'deep learning'. Other supportive trends include the growth of knowledge work, and the realization that ideas generate competitive advantage. Given the negatives summarized in Table 5.7, it will be interesting to see how these approaches develop through the twenty-first century.

 RECAP

1. **Explain the characteristics of the behaviourist and cognitive approaches to learning.**

   - Behaviourism argues that we learn chains of muscle movements. As mental processes are not observable, they are not considered valid issues for study.

   - Cognitive psychology argues that we learn mental structures. Mental processes are important, and they are amenable to study although they cannot be observed.

   - In behaviourist theory, feedback contributes to learning by providing reinforcement; in cognitive theory, feedback provides information and is motivational.

2. **Explain and evaluate the technique of behaviour modification.**

   - Respondent (or Pavlovian, classical) conditioning is a method by which an established response (good work performance) is associated with a new stimulus (supervisory encouragement).

   - Operant (or Skinnerian, instrumental) conditioning is a method by which a behaviour (good work performance) is associated with a new consequence (bonus payment).

   - Positive reinforcement, negative reinforcement, punishment and extinction condition the target by manipulating the consequences of desirable and undesirable behaviours.

   - Behaviour modification works well when rewards are linked clearly to specific behaviours, but does not work well when these links are ambiguous and vague; this manipulative approach may not be acceptable in some cultures.

3. **Explain the socialization process, and assess the practical relevance of this concept.**

   - Social learning theory argues that we learn values, beliefs and behaviour patterns through experience, through observation and modelling.

   - Socialization can be informal – this happens anyway – or it can be formally organized through induction and training programmes.

4. **Explain and evaluate the technique of behavioural self-management.**

   - Behavioural self-management involves identifying the behaviour you want to change, altering the situational cues which trigger that behaviour, and establishing support and reinforcement for your new behaviour.

5. **Describe the characteristics of the learning organization.**

   - A learning organization is characterized by its approach to strategy, to environmental scanning, to the use of information, to the creation of learning opportunities, and to the creation of structures that are flexible and enable employee learning, in contrast to rigid bureaucratic organizations in which learning is the employee's responsibility.

   - The learning organization concept became popular as managers recognized the strategic need for more highly skilled and trained, flexible and creative workforces.

   - Knowledge management is a technology-based approach to making tacit knowledge available more widely, through individual and corporate databases, building on developments in computing power and 'big data' analysis techniques.

Revision

1. What part do feedback and reinforcement play in the cognitive and behaviourist approaches to learning?

2. Describe and illustrate the technique of organizational behaviour modification, and identify the advantages and disadvantages of this technique.

3. What is the difference between feedback and feedforward? With regard to performance appraisal, what are the advantages and disadvantages of these approaches?

4. What are the advantages and disadvantages of the learning organization in practice, first from a management perspective, and then from an employee perspective? Why should there be any contradiction between these viewpoints?

Research assignment

Review your understanding of social learning theory, behaviour modelling, and the concept of provisional selves. How do these approaches explain the ways in which new employees learn about the organization and their job? Interview a manager, a supervisor or team leader, and a frontline employee in an organization of your choice. Find out how each of those three individuals learned about the organization and their work when they first joined (and/or when they moved to a new job in another part of the organization). Collect examples of behaviour modelling, and of their experiments with provisional selves. How effective were those methods in helping the new employee to 'fit in'? What other methods and sources of information did those individuals use in order to help them to 'fit in'? From this evidence, what are the strengths and limitations of behaviour modelling and provisional selves as an explanation of how new employees are socialized by organizations?

Springboard

Chris Argyris (1982) *Reasoning, Learning, and Action*. San Francisco: Jossey Bass. Classic text on the nature of individual and organizational learning.

Amy C. Edmondson (2010) *Teaming: How Organizations Learn, Innovate, and Compete in the Knowledge Economy*. San Francisco: Jossey Bass. Argues that teams are key. Factors preventing team learning include fear of failure, groupthink, power structures and information hoarding. Leaders can help by encouraging reflection, psychological safety and the sharing of ideas. Examples drawn from Bank of America, Children's Hospital and Verizon.

Raymond A. Noe, Alena D.M. Clarke and Howard J. Klein (2014) 'Learning in the twenty-first century workplace', *Annual Review of Organizational Psychology and Organizational Behavior*, 1: 245–75. Review of current trends in developing 'human capital resources' to gain competitive advantage, including learning based on social media.

OB cinema

A Clockwork Orange (1971 and 2000, director Stanley Kubrick) DVD track (scene) 19,1:06:57 to 1:11.40 (6 minutes). Clip begins with doctor introducing herself: 'Good morning. My name is Dr Branom'. Clip ends with Dr Branom (played by Madge Ryan) saying, 'Dr Brodski is pleased with you. You've made a very positive response'.

This movie is based in a future totalitarian state in which the Droog (thug) Alex (played by Malcolm McDowell) is subjected to aversion therapy to cure him of his addiction to violence, rape, drugs and classical music. Fiction? Aversion therapy was used to 'treat' homosexuals in the 1960s. An extremely violent film for its time, Kubrick removed it from circulation in 1974 when it was accused of triggering copycat crimes. The film was released on the anniversary of Kubrick's death, in 2000. In this clip (which contains violence and nudity):

1. To what conditioning and reinforcement regime is Alex subjected?

2. How effective is this in changing his behaviour?

3. Does society have a moral right to interfere with individual behaviour in this way?

 OB on the web

Search YouTube for 'Big Bang Theory – operant conditioning'. In this five-minute clip from the comedy series, Sheldon uses operant conditioning methods to change the behaviour of Leonard's girlfriend, Penny. Leonard complains about this, but Sheldon's tactics are working. Are you aware of having your own behaviour conditioned in this way? Can you use this method on your friends? What ethical issues are raised by such attempts to manipulate the behaviour of others?

CHAPTER EXERCISES

1. Reinforcement and behaviour

Objective   To examine the effects of positive and negative reinforcement on behaviour change.

This exercise takes about half an hour, and although it can be used with any size of group, it works particularly well with large classes (Marcic, 1995, pp.61–63 and 122–23).

Exercise overview   Two or three volunteers will receive reinforcement from the rest of the class while performing a simple task. The volunteers leave the room while the class is being briefed. The instructor identifies an object which the student volunteers must find when they return to the room. This object should be unobtrusive, but it should be clearly visible to the class: a piece of paper stuck to the wall, a briefcase or bag in the corner, a mark on the wall. The instructor specifies the reinforcement regime that will apply when each of the volunteers comes back into the room.

Negative reinforcement regime: the class will hiss, boo, make sarcastic comments, and throw harmless items at the first volunteer when they are moving away from the chosen object, and sit silently when they are moving towards it.

Positive reinforcement regime: the class will smile, cheer, applaud and make encouraging comments with compliments when the second volunteer is moving towards the chosen object, and sit silently when they move away.

Combined reinforcement regime: the class will cheer when the third volunteer approaches the object and boo when they move away from it.

Nominate one student to record the time that it takes each of the volunteers to find the object.

Exercise sequence   1. The first volunteer is brought back into the room, and instructed: Your task is to find and touch a particular object in the room. The class will help you, but you cannot ask questions, and they cannot speak to you. The first volunteer continues to look for the object until it is found, with the class giving negative reinforcement.

2. The second volunteer is brought back into the room, and is given the same instruction, to look for the object, with the class giving positive reinforcement.

3. The third volunteer is brought back into the room, and is instructed to find the object with the class giving a combination of negative and positive reinforcement.

Class discussion

• Ask the volunteers how they each felt during this exercise. What were their emotional responses to the different kinds of reinforcement they received?

• What effects did the different reinforcement regimes have on the behaviour of the volunteers?

• Which reinforcement regime do you think is most common in today's organizations? What are the likely effects on motivation and productivity?

2. Branto bakery

Branto Bakery is a large company producing a range of bakery products for major supermarkets. Analysis by the human resource management department shows that the sales and administration departments have the highest rates of absenteeism and poor timekeeping. Interestingly, each of these departments also has individuals with the best absence and punctuality records. The managing director has asked the two department heads to address these absence and timekeeping problems. Alan Anderson, head of sales, has decided to adopt a behaviour modification approach. Barbara Brown, head of administration, has chosen to develop a socialization approach with current and new staff. As an external management consultant, you have been hired to give advice.

1. Design either a behaviour modification programme for Anderson, or a socialization plan for Brown, that will reduce absenteeism and improve timekeeping in their departments.

2. Explain the elements of your plan, how it will address their problems, and how it will be implemented.

3. Assess the strengths and weaknesses of your plan in the short term, and in the long term.

Employability assessment

With regard to your future employment prospects:

1. Identify up to three issues from this chapter that you found significant.

2. Relate these to the competencies in the employability matrix.

3. Decide what actions you need to take to maintain and/or develop those competencies under each of the four headings of the employability matrix.

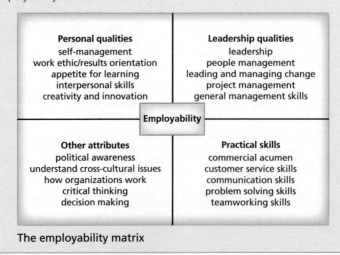

The employability matrix

References

Andrew, P., Ip, J., Worthington, J. and Brooke, C. (2014) *Fast Forward 2030: The Future of Work and the Workplace*. Los Angeles: CBRE/Genesis.

Argyris, C. (1982) *Reasoning, Learning, and Action*. San Francisco: Jossey Bass.

Argyris, C. and Schön, D. (1974) *Theory in Practice*. San Francisco: Jossey Bass.

Argyris, C. and Schön, D. (eds) (1978) *Organizational Learning: A Theory of Action Perspective*. Cambridge, MA: Addison-Wesley.

Bandura, A. (1977) *Social Learning Theory*. Englewood Cliffs, NJ: Prentice-Hall.

Bandura, A. (1986) *Social Foundations of Thought and Action: A Social Cognitive Theory*. Englewood Cliffs, NJ: Prentice-Hall.

Boddy, D. (2013) *Management: An Introduction* (6th edn). Harlow, Essex: Financial Times Prentice Hall.

Budworth, M.-H., Latham, G.P. and Manroop, L. (2015) 'Looking forward to performance improvement: a field test of the feedforward interview for performance management', *Human Resource Management*, 54 (1): 45–54.

Churchard, C. (2015) 'BP reveals unconventional approach to mobile learning', *People Management*, 15 May, www.cipd.co.uk/pm/peoplemanagement/b/weblog/archive/2015/05/15/cipd-l-amp-d-show-2015-bp-reveals-unconventional-approach-to-mobile-learning.aspx

Chynoweth, C. (2013) 'Our L&D strategy isn't pink and fluffy – it's about saving millions of pounds', *People Management*, December, pp.18–19.

CIPD (2015a) *Learning and Development Strategy Factsheet*. London: Chartered Institute for Personnel and Development.

CIPD (2015b) *Learning and Development Annual Survey Report 2015*. London: Chartered Institute for Personnel and Development.

Cooper, D., Farmery, K., Johnson, M., Harper, C., Clarke, F.L., Holton, P., Wilson, S., Rayson, P. and Bence, H. (2005) 'Changing personnel behavior to promote quality care practices in an intensive care unit', *Therapeutics and Clinical Risk Management*, 1 (4): 321–32.

Ferster, C.S. and Skinner, B.F. (1957) *Schedules of Reinforcement*. New York: Appleton-Century-Crofts.

Fogg, B.J. (2009) 'The new rules of persuasion', *RSA Journal*, Spring, pp.24–28.

Garvin, D.A., Edmondson, A. and Gino, F. (2008) 'Is yours a learning organization?', *Harvard Business Review*, 86 (3): 109–16.

Gherardi, S. (1997) 'Organizational learning', in Arndt Sorge and Malcolm Warner (eds), *The Handbook of Organizational Behaviour*. London: International Thomson Business Press, pp.542–41.

Howard-Jones, P. (2014) *Fresh Thinking in Learning and Development: Neuroscience and Learning*. London: Chartered Institute for Personnel and Development.

Ibarra, H. (1999) 'Provisional selves: experimenting with image and identity in professional adaptation', *Administrative Science Quarterly*, 44 (4): 764–91.

Ibarra, H. and Barbulescu, R. (2010) 'Identity as narrative: prevalence, effectiveness, and consequences of narrative identity work in macro work role transitions', *Academy of Management Review*, 35 (1): 135–54.

Kreitner, R., Kinicki, A. and Buelens, M. (1999) *Organizational Behaviour*. London: McGraw-Hill.

Liu, S., Wang, M., Bamberger, P., Shi, J. and Bacharach, S.B. (2015) 'The dark side of socialization: a longitudinal investigation of newcomer alcohol use', *Academy of Management Journal*, 58 (2): 334–55.

Luthans, F. and Davis, T.R.V. (1979) 'Behavioural self-management: the missing link in managerial effectiveness', *Organizational Dynamics*, 8 (1): 42–60.

Luthans, F. and Kreitner, R. (1985) *Organizational Behaviour Modification and Beyond* (2nd edn). Glenview, IL: Scott, Foresman.

Luthans, F., Stajkovic, A., Luthans, B.C. and Luthans, K.W. (1998) 'Applying behavioural management in Eastern Europe', *European Management Journal*, 16 (4): 466–74.

Marcic, D. (1995) *Organizational Behavior: Experiences and Cases* (4th edn). St Paul, MN: West Publishing.

Nonaka, I. and Takeuchi, H. (1995) *The Knowledge Creating Company*. New York: Oxford University Press.

Nonaka, I., Umemoto, K. and Sasaki, K. (1999) 'Three tales of knowledge-creating companies', in Georg von Krogh, Johan Roos and Dirk Kleine (eds), *Knowing in Firms: Understanding, Managing and Measuring Knowledge*. London: Sage Publications, pp.146–72.

Rakos, R.F. and Grodek, M.V. (1984) 'An empirical evaluation of a behavioural self-management course in a college setting', *Teaching of Psychology*, October, pp.157–62.

Schön, D.A. (1983) *The Reflective Practitioner*. New York: Basic Books.

Senge, P. (1990) *The Fifth Discipline: The Art and Practice of the Learning Organization*. New York: Doubleday Currency.

Senge, P., Kleiner, A., Roberts, C., Ross, R., Roth, G. and Smith, B. (1999) *The Dance of Change: The Challenges of Sustaining Momentum in Learning Organizations*. London: Nicholas Brealey.

Tichy, N.M. (2001) 'No ordinary boot camp', *Harvard Business Review*, 79 (1): 63–70.

Walters, C.C. and Grusek, J.E. (1977) *Punishment*. San Francisco, CA: Freeman.

Weick, K.E. and Westley, F. (1996) 'Organizational learning: affirming an oxymoron', in S.R. Clegg, C. Hardy and W.R. Nord (eds), *Handbook of Organization Studies*. London: Sage Publications, pp.440–58.

White, R.W. (1959) 'Motivation reconsidered: the concept of competence', *Psychological Review*, 66 (5): 297–333.

Wiener, N. (1954) *The Human Use of Human Beings: Cybernetics and Society*. New York: Avon Books.

Chapter 6 Personality

Key terms

personality	idiographic
psychometrics	self-concept
chronotype	generalized other
type	unconditional positive regard
trait	thematic apperception test
nomothetic	need for achievement
type A personality	projective test
type B personality	reliability
Big Five	predictive validity

Learning outcomes

When you have read this chapter, you should be able to define those key terms in your own words, and you should also be able to:

1. Distinguish between type, trait and self-theories of personality.

2. Identify the strengths and limitations of formal approaches to personality assessment.

3. Explain the relationship between personality and stress, and identify individual and organizational stress management strategies.

4. Compare the advantages and disadvantages of questionnaires and projective tests as measures of personality.

5. Evaluate the benefits and problems of psychometric assessment as a management decision-making tool, particularly in selection.

6. Assess your own personality.

Why study personality?

Personality the psychological qualities that influence an individual's characteristic behaviour patterns, in a stable and distinctive manner.

We want to know what kind of person we are, to understand our strengths and weaknesses. Work seems to have become more pressured and intense, and personality affects how we deal with stress. Employers want to know whether you can do the job, work in a team, 'fit' with the organization culture, and be open to training. Methods for assessing **personality** are used as part of the selection process by 40 per cent of UK organizations (CIPD, 2013). **Psychometrics** – the measurement of personality and other individual capabilities – is now a multimillion pound industry.

Latin roots

per sonare	to speak through	*persona grata*	an acceptable person
persona	an actor's mask; a character in a play	*persona non grata*	an unacceptable person

---

Psychometrics the systematic testing, measurement and assessment of intelligence, aptitudes and personality.

It is widely believed that that personality is related to job performance and career success. Most of us believe that we are 'good judges of character'. In a selection interview, this often means that you are not going to get the job unless 'your face fits', even if you have the capabilities. Psychometrics offer to support selection decisions with objective data.

An internet search for 'psychometrics' produces many hits. Here, we explain two approaches to personality assessment; *nomothetic* and *idiographic*. Nomothetic methods form the basis for most psychometrics, using 'tick box' questionnaires which are easy to administer and to score. Idiographic methods use open-ended approaches to capture an individual's unique characteristics; these take more time, and are more difficult to score and to interpret. Quantitative, nomothetic methods appear to be more objective. However, these approaches rely on different assumptions. Our assessment should rely on the validity of these assumptions, and not on how easy the methods are to use.

The term *psychometrics* covers a range of assessments of aptitude, intelligence, integrity and personality. When measuring aptitude or intelligence, we can use the term 'test', because for those characteristics, a high score is usually better than a low score. When measuring personality, however, the term 'assessment' is more appropriate. There are no 'correct' answers in a personality assessment, and a high score cannot be said to be better or worse than a low score.

Oops! Is there an 'accident prone' personality?

The luxury cruise liner *Costa Concordia* ran aground off the Tuscany coast in January 2012. Discussing incidents like this, Adrian Furnham (2012) identifies six personality factors that can make some people (such as a ship's captain) more prone to accidents than others:

defiant–compliant	defiant individuals have problems with authority, they don't like being told what to do, which makes them accident prone
panicky–strong	in a crisis, the person who is cool and confident can prevent others from panicking and making mistakes
irritable–cheerful	people who are easily upset, get depressed and lose their tempers can annoy those around them and become indecisive

distractible–vigilant	people who get bored quickly are inattentive, and more likely to make mistakes; vigilance is needed to avoid accidents
reckless–cautious	some people just don't listen to warnings
arrogance–self-confidence	arrogant individuals are less willing to learn and more likely to make bad decisions – but overconfident people don't listen to others either

Costa Concordia cruise liner aground off the Tuscany coast, January 2012

You may want to avoid working (and sailing) with people who are defiant, panicky, irritable, easily distracted, reckless and arrogant. Watch the news for stories about people involved in 'high-profile' accidents. The press often describe their characters; do they fit this profile?

In addition to selecting job applicants, psychometric assessment has several other useful applications:

- assessment of suitability for promotion;
- assessment for redeployment purposes;
- evaluation of training potential;
- team and leadership development;
- vocational guidance, career counselling;
- recruiting graduates with limited work experience;
- redundancy counselling.

Psychometrics often complement informal and subjective methods, and can help managers to make better-informed judgements about people. However, psychometrics have been criticized for being unfair and misleading, in gender and cultural terms, as well as being poor predictors of job performance. If you want to improve your scores, or to cheat on an assessment, you will find many 'how to' websites and popular psychology books to help you do just that.

Defining personality

The concept of personality helps to identify our unique characters and to measure and understand differences between individuals. Personality describes behaviours which are stable and enduring, and which distinguish one individual from others.

Stability

Personality theory deals with behaviour patterns that are consistent in different contexts, and over time. We are less interested in behaviours that occur briefly and on rare occasions. Mood swings, and behaviours caused by illness, or drugs, are not stable and are not personality characteristics, unless they become permanent. However, there is a problem. Personality seems to be flexible. The manager who is loud and autocratic in the office can be caring and supportive at home. The 'stable' behaviours which we exhibit depend, in part, on social context. Some personality features (as with allergies) may only appear in particular social and physical settings.

Distinctiveness

Personality theory is concerned with the pattern of dispositions and behaviours unique to the individual, and is less concerned with properties that all or most other people share. You may be aggressive towards waiters, friendly with librarians, deferential to professors, and terrified of mice. You may share many of these dispositions with a friend whose hobby is breeding mice.

Some psychologists argue than personality is inherited, determined by genetics and the biochemistry and physiology of the brain. Evidence suggests, for example, that because measures of job satisfaction are fairly stable over time and across jobs, a predisposition to be content with or to be frustrated at work may have a genetic component. In this view, your personality is fixed at birth, if not before, and life's experiences do little to alter it.

Others argue that our characters are shaped by environment, culture and social factors, and that our feelings and behaviour patterns are learned. Social learning theory argues that we acquire new behaviours by observing and imitating others. Motivation theory shows how job satisfaction can be influenced by changes in supervisory style and the design of jobs. Every society has distinctive ways of doing things. We cannot possibly be born with this local knowledge. In this view, your personality is flexible, and changes with experience. Psychological well-being may depend on such adaptability.

Chronotype a cluster of personality traits that can affect whether someone is more active and performs better in the morning or in the evening.

The controversy over the effects of heredity and environment on personality is known as the 'nature–nurture' debate. Few psychologists hold the extreme views set out here. Both genetic *and* situational factors influence behaviour. The argument concerns the emphases to be given to these factors, how to measure them, and how they interact. In the twentieth century, 'nurture' was the more fashionable view. In the twenty-first century, evidence from biology, genetics and neurophysiology has shifted attention towards 'nature'. These theoretical debates affect management practice. Can personality assessment help us to make better predictions about an individual's future job performance?

Are you a morning person or a night owl – and does it matter?

Christoph Randler (2010) argues that those who are most energetic and proactive in the morning (they get up early), are more likely to have successful careers than those who are at their best in the evening. You can adjust your **chronotype** with training, but Randler argues that it is difficult to make major changes. His research on university students showed that morning people, on average:

- get better grades in school and go to better colleges
- have better job opportunities

- anticipate and try to minimize problems
- perform better at work, are paid better, and have greater career success.

The personality traits associated with these chrono-types are:

Morning people	Evening people
Agreeable	Creative
Optimistic	Intelligent
Stable	Humorous
Proactive	Extraverted
Conscientious	Pessimistic
Satisfied with life	Neurotic and depressed

Evening people can be smart, creative, funny and out-going, but Randler notes that 'they're out of sync with the typical corporate schedule'. Most organizational timetables are tailored to morning people. The evidence suggests that the population is evenly split between morning and evening types, but that after age 50, most of us become morning types.

Is your chronotype geared for career success? If not, what can you do about that?

Types and traits

Type a descriptive label for a distinct pattern of personality characteristics, such as introvert, extravert, neurotic.

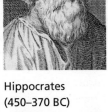

Hippocrates (450–370 BC)

Descriptions of the structure of personality have focused on the concepts of *type* and *trait*. One of the most straightforward ways of analysing personality is to classify people in terms of personality **types**.

One of the first personality theorists was Hippocrates ('The father of medicine'), who lived in Greece around 400 BC. He claimed that personality type or 'temperament' was determined by bodily 'humours', which generated the behaviour patterns shown in Table 6.1.

Table 6.1: Hippocrates' type theory of personality

Body humour	Temperament or type	Behaviours
Blood	Sanguine	Confident, cheerful, optimistic, active
Phlegm	Phlegmatic	Sluggish, apathetic
Black bile	Melancholic	Depressed, sad, prone to ill-founded fears
Yellow bile	Choleric	Aggressive, excitable, irritable

William H. Sheldon (1898–1970)

Although his terms are still in use today, there are problems with Hippocrates' theory. First, there is no evidence to confirm these relationships between body chemistry and behaviour. Second, personal experience suggests that there are more than four types of people in the world.

William Sheldon (1942) argued that temperament was related to physique, or 'somato-type' (see Figure 6.1). Your personality type thus depends on your 'biological individuality', your body size and shape (and on how many hamburgers you eat).

Once again, this appealing typology it is not a good predictor of behaviour. Can you think of an endomorph who is introverted and intellectual? Are you friendly with a mesomorph who is a relaxed gourmet – or an ectomorph who is sociable and assertive?

Carl Gustav Jung (1875–1961)

Type theory was further developed by the Swiss psychologist, Carl Gustav Jung (1875–1961), who explored psychological preferences for extraversion or introversion, for sensation or intuition, for thinking or feeling, and for judging or perceiving (Jung, 1953, 1971). At the heart of this theory lie four personality types, plotted across the sensation–intuition and thinking–feeling dimensions, shown in Figure 6.2. The mother and daughter team of Katherine Briggs and Isabel Myers (Myers, 1962, 1976; Myers and McCaulley, 1985) used Jung's theory to develop the Myers–Briggs Type Indicator (MBTI), the world's most popular

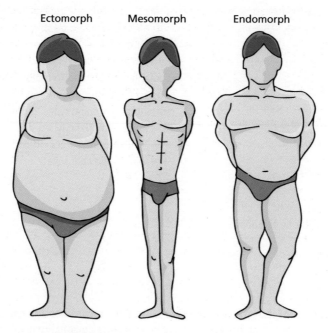

Figure 6.1: Somatotypes

Source: John Takai/fotolia.com

personality assessment. The MBTI makes Jung's theory easier to understand, and to use, by rating personal preferences on four scales:

Introvert	←——————→	Extravert
Sensing	←——————→	**iNtuiting**
Thinking	←——————→	**Feeling**
Judging	←——————→	**Perceiving**

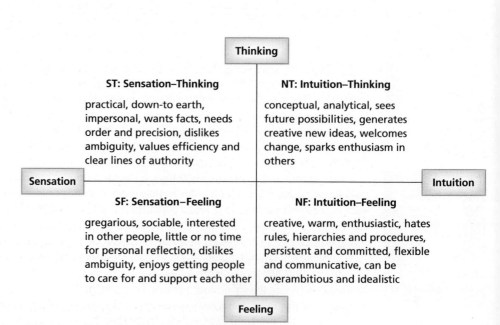

Thinking

ST: Sensation–Thinking

practical, down-to earth, impersonal, wants facts, needs order and precision, dislikes ambiguity, values efficiency and clear lines of authority

NT: Intuition–Thinking

conceptual, analytical, sees future possibilities, generates creative new ideas, welcomes change, sparks enthusiasm in others

Sensation | **Intuition**

SF: Sensation–Feeling

gregarious, sociable, interested in other people, little or no time for personal reflection, dislikes ambiguity, enjoys getting people to care for and support each other

NF: Intuition–Feeling

creative, warm, enthusiastic, hates rules, hierarchies and procedures, persistent and committed, flexible and communicative, can be overambitious and idealistic

Feeling

Figure 6.2: Jung's personality type matrix

This approach assigns each individual to one side or other of each dimension, establishing 16 personality types, each known by its letter code; iNtuiting is known by the letter N to avoid confusion with introversion. If you are ENFP, you have been typed as Extravert, Intuitive, Feeling and Perceiving. It is useful to remember, however, that these are preferences and tendencies; you are not trapped in those categories. Although we may prefer impersonal analysis (T), we can when appropriate use emotional judgements (F); we may prefer to focus on the immediate and concrete (S), but also be able when appropriate to consider imaginative opportunities (N).

The MBTI is used in many organizational contexts, including management development programmes exploring self-awareness and personal development. It is also used with problem-solving and decision-making groups which need a complementary personality mix; intuitive types need sensing types, feeling types need thinking types. See Belbin's (1993) theory of group composition (Chapter 11).

A personality type (e.g. extravert) is a category whose members are expected to have the same pattern of behaviours (i.e. active, impulsive, risk taking, sociable). A personality trait, on the other hand, is a predisposition to behave in a particular way. The trait approach, however, does not expect someone who is active and impulsive necessarily to be risk-taking and sociable – but they could be. In contrast with types, traits allow us to explore the complexity and variation in personality. Individuals belong to types, traits belong to individuals. You fit a type, you have a trait – and the traits that you have may or may not allow us to categorize you as belonging clearly to one personality type or another.

Other examples of traits include shyness, excitability, reliability, moodiness, punctuality. The study of traits in personality assessment, and of how traits cluster to form 'super traits', is associated with the nomothetic approach in psychology.

Trait a relatively stable quality or attribute of an individual's personality, influencing behaviour in a particular direction.

Nomothetic an approach to the study of personality emphasizing the identification of traits, and the systematic relationships between different aspects of personality.

A genetic test for 'personality'

By Leslie Hook

What can you learn from your DNA, and how much do you really want to know? Companies exist that are prepared to tell you about your potential medical conditions or your ancestry based on a cheek swab. Now Karmagenes, a start-up based in Geneva in Switzerland, proposes to go further and tell you about your personality.

Co-founder Kyriakos Kokkoris, who holds a PhD in microbiology, argues: "You can cheat a theoretical personality test by how you answer the questions, but you can't cheat your DNA." It is an appealing proposition in an age where every other self-help book promises to tell you more about who you really are.

He and his co-founders developed an algorithm that matches specific genetic regions to personality traits, drawing on published research. Their test scores 14 characteristics they have defined such as spontaneity, risk-taking, confidence and self-awareness. The company slogan is "meet yourself". Mr Kokkoris and his wife have taken the test, and he even tested his son at three months old.

Karmagenes' success will hinge on consumers' acceptance of the idea that personality is determined by genetics, which is controversial. Personalities are a mix of nurture and nature: but Mr Kokkoris says that by knowing their predisposition users of the Karmagenes kit can remedy "weaknesses" or focus on strengths. "My DNA says I am 'low social', but after 11 years abroad, I can talk to anyone," says Mr Kokkoris.

In the US, companies offering DNA tests to assess health risks have been censured by regulatory authorities. That has not stopped Karmagenes dreaming big: Mr Kokkoris talks about financial advice, professional guidance, even matchmaking, eventually being based on DNA data.

Source: Hook, L. (2015) A genetic test for 'personality', *Financial Times*, 1 July, p.16.

Nomothetic means 'law setting or law giving'. This approach assumes that personality is inherited and that environmental factors have little effect. This sits on the nature side of the nature–nurture debate, and uses the following procedures. First, the main dimensions on which personality can vary are identified. Trait approaches assume that there is a common set of dimensions – temperament, character, predispositions – on which we can all be assessed, and also assumes that your personality can be measured and compared with others on the same dimensions.

Source: Drew Fairweather

Second, the personalities of groups of people are assessed, using self-report questionnaires based on 'forced choice' questions: 'true' or 'false', 'yes' or 'no', or 'strongly agree' to 'strongly disagree'.

Third, your personality profile is constructed across the traits measured. Your score on each dimension is compared with the average and the distribution of scores for the whole group. This allows the assessor to identify individuals around the norm, and those with characteristics that deviate from the norm. Your personal score has little meaning beyond the scores of the population with which you are being compared. You cannot have 'high' or 'low' scores; you can only have scores that are high or low when compared with others.

Fourth, the group may be split into subgroups, say by age, sex or occupation. This produces other reference points, or norms, against which individual scores can be compared. One may find, for example, that successful Scottish male managers tend to be introverted, or that women under the age of 30 who work in purchasing roles have low scores on shyness. This approach is impersonal. It is difficult to use the results to predict the behaviour of individuals, even those with 'extreme' scores, because they are only extreme in comparison with others. It may be possible, however, to judge the behavioural tendencies and preferences of groups.

It may seem odd that one approach to individual personality assessment relies on studies of large groups. However, through this method, it is possible to find out what is normal or average – in the statistical sense – and then to compare individuals with that. Individuals who 'deviate from the norm' are not social outcasts. However, assessments based on this method are often used as a guide to the personality profiles of individuals, especially in employment selection.

One of the most influential trait theories was developed by Hans Jurgen Eysenck (1970, 1990). His research explored how personality varies on two key dimensions – the extraversion–introversion or 'E' dimension, and the neuroticism–stability or 'N' dimension. However, unlike Jung, Eysenck sought to identify trait clusters. Eysenck's model offers a way of linking types, traits and behaviour, arguing that personality structure is hierarchical. Each individual possesses more or less of a number of traits – trait 1, trait 2, trait 3, and so on. Research shows how individuals who have a particular trait,

Hans Jürgen
Eysenck
(1916–1997)

say trait 1, are more likely to have another, say trait 3, than people who do not have trait 1. In other words, traits tend to 'cluster' in patterns. These clusters identify a 'higher order' of personality description, which Eysenck refers to as personality types, or 'super traits', as Figure 6.3 illustrates.

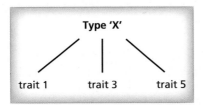
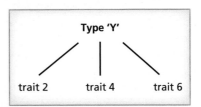

Figure 6.3: A hierarchical model of personality types and traits

This does not mean that everyone with trait 1 has a Type 'X' personality. It means that questionnaire analysis has shown that those who score highly on trait 1 are also more likely to have high scores on traits 3 and 5, putting them into the Type 'X' category. The result of an individual assessment using this approach is a personality profile across several traits, not necessarily labelling them as any one personality type. Eysenck's approach identifies two main sets of types of trait clusters. The E dimension runs from extravert to introvert. The N dimension runs from neuroticism to stability.

Extraverts are tough-minded individuals who need stimulation. They are sociable, like parties, are good at telling stories, enjoy practical jokes, have many friends, but do not enjoy studying on their own. **Introverts** are tender-minded, have strong emotions, and do not need intense stimuli. They are quiet, prefer books to people, are reserved, plan ahead, distrust impulse, appreciate order, lead careful sober lives, suppress emotions, are pessimistic, worry about moral standards, and are reliable.

Neurotics are emotional, unstable and anxious, have low opinions of themselves, feel that they are unattractive failures, tend to be disappointed with life, and are pessimistic and depressed. They feel controlled by events, by others and by fate. **Stable** people are 'adjusted', self-confident, optimistic, realistic, solve their own problems, have few health worries, and have few regrets about their past.

Home viewing

Glengarry Glen Ross (1992, director James Foley) is based in a Chicago real-estate office. To boost flagging sales, the 'downtown' manager Blake (played by Alec Baldwin) introduces a sales contest. First prize is a Cadillac Eldorado, second prize is a set of steak knives, third prize is dismissal. The sales staff include Ricky Roma (Al Pacino), Shelley Levene (Jack Lemmon), George Aaronow (Alan Arkin) and Dave Moss (Ed Harris). In the first ten minutes of the film, note how Blake in his 'motivational talk' fits the stereotype of the extravert, competitive 'macho' salesman (warning: bad language). How does his 'pep talk' affect the sales team? Should salespeople copy Blake's stereotype? What is Blake's view of human nature? This part of the movie shows how identity is constructed through a 'performance'. This contrasts with a view of identity as genetically determined.

Most of us have a trait profile between these two sets of extremes. Is one personality more desirable than another? Extraverts may be sociable and friendly, but they can also be unreliable. Introverts, on the other hand, are reliable, but they would rather read a book than talk to you. Those with extreme scores have what Eysenck calls an 'ambiguous gift'. It is important to be aware of your personality, and to appreciate what others could see as strengths and weaknesses.

Would you pass an integrity test?

Employers want staff who are conscientious, dependable and honest. Many companies use integrity tests to identify those who could pose risks, such as dishonesty, cheating, lying, stealing, drug abuse, racism, sexism, and violent and criminal behaviour. After using integrity testing in 600 of its 1,900 stores, one American retailer reported a 35 per cent drop in the loss (or theft) of stock in its stores, while losses rose by over 10 per cent in stores that did not use integrity testing (Arnold and Jones, 2006). Paul Whitely (2012) at the University of Essex Centre for the Study of Integrity has developed a test that asks you to rate the following ten items using these scores and ratings:

1. never justified   2. rarely justified
3. sometimes justified   4. always justified

a. avoiding paying the fare on public transport

b. cheating on taxes if you have a chance

c. driving faster than the speed limit

d. keeping money you found in the street

e. lying in your own interests

f. not reporting accidental damage you've done to a parked car

g. throwing away litter in a public place

h. driving under the influence of alcohol

i. making up things on a job application

j. buying something you know is stolen

If your score is	this means
up to 15	you are very honest and really want to do the right thing
15 up to 19	your integrity is above average but you don't mind bending the rules
20 up to 24	you are relaxed about breaking the rules when it suits you
25 and above	you don't believe in rules and it's easy to break them when it suits you

A survey in 2011 found that just under 50 per cent of UK respondents scored up to 15, and only 5 per cent scored over 25. The average was 16. There was high tolerance for keeping money found in the street, exceeding the speed limit and lying in one's own interests. Faking job applications, dropping litter, buying stolen goods and drunk driving were condemned. There were no differences depending on affluence, education or occupational status. Women had slightly higher scores than men.

Younger people were more relaxed about 'low level' dishonesty. For example, while 75 per cent of those over 65 regarded making false statements on a job application as never justified, only 33 per cent of those under 25 took that view, with similar views about telling lies. Comparison with a survey from 2000 showed that the percentage of respondents saying that a behaviour is never justified had fallen for eight out of the ten indicators. Attitudes to dropping litter have not changed much, but on the whole we appear to be more tolerant now of low level dishonesty than we were ten years ago.

Declining integrity is a problem. Societies in which trust and integrity are strong have better economic performance. This effect may apply to organizations in a world increasingly sensitive to corporate social responsibility. Remember – it is easy to cheat on these tests, and to give yourself a higher integrity score, especially if you are low in integrity.

Personality Types A and B

Type A personality
a combination of emotions and behaviours characterized by ambition, hostility, impatience and a sense of constant time pressure.

Another influential type theory links personality to stress. Meyer Friedman and Ray Rosenman (1974) identified two 'behaviour syndromes' called **Type A** and **Type B personality** (see Table 6.2).

Friedman and Rosenman found that Type A personalities were three times more likely to suffer heart disease than Type Bs. The typical Type A thrives on long hours, high workload and tight deadlines. These are socially and organizationally desirable characteristics, as are competitiveness and a high need for achievement. However, the extreme Type A may not be able to

Table 6.2: Type A and Type B personality characteristics

Type A personality characteristics	Type B personality characteristics
Competitive	Able to take time out to enjoy leisure
High need for achievement	Not preoccupied with achievement
Aggressive	Easygoing
Works fast	Works at a steady pace
Impatient	Seldom impatient
Restless	Not easily frustrated
Extremely alert	Relaxed
Tense facial muscles	Moves and speaks slowly
Constant feeling of time pressure	Seldom lacks enough time
More likely to suffer stress-related illness	**Less likely to suffer stress-related illness**

Type B personality
a combination
of emotions
and behaviours
characterized by
relaxation, low focus on
achievement and ability
to take time to enjoy
leisure.

relax long enough to stand back from a complex problem to make an effective and comprehensive analysis, and may lack the patience and relaxed style required in some management roles. Another problem is that impatience and hostility can increase the stress levels in those who have to work with them. Like the extravert, a Type A personality can appear to have many desirable aspects, but this behaviour syndrome can be dysfunctional for the individual, and for others.

Friedman and Rosenman argue that a Type A can change into a Type B, with awareness and training, and they suggest a number of personal 're-engineering strategies':

- keep reminding yourself that life is always full of unfinished business;
- you only 'finish' when you die;
- learn how to delegate responsibility to others;
- limit your weekly working hours;
- schedule time for leisure and exercise;
- take a course in time management skills.

The problem, of course, is that the extreme Type A personality – the person most at risk – can never find time to implement these strategies.

STOP AND THINK

Are you a Type A or a Type B? Do you suffer from: alcohol abuse, excessive smoking, dizziness, upset stomach, headaches, fatigue, sweating, bad breath? If 'yes', these could be stress responses to your Type A behaviour. Expect your first heart attack before you are 45.

If you don't suffer stress-related symptoms, perhaps you are a Type B. Do you think that your relaxed, casual behaviour will damage your career prospects?

Whichever your response, what are you going to do about it?

Stress management: individual and organizational

The work of Friedman and Rosenman shows a relationship between personality and health. Negative emotional states such as depression, hostility and anxiety are linked to heart disease, respiratory disorders such as asthma, headaches and ulcers. People in highly stressful jobs, in which they have little or no autonomy, have a 23 per cent higher risk of a heart attack (Boseley, 2012). Stress is also caused by individual factors; difficulty in coping with change, lack of confidence, poor time management, poor stress management skills. In a UK survey in 2014, 56 per cent of employees said that their work was 'very or fairly stressful'; in 2013–2014, 11.3 million working days were lost due to stress, depression or anxiety, costing employers an estimated £26 billion a year (Martindale, 2015).

Stress has many causes other than personality. Any condition that requires an adaptive response is known as a stressor. The pace of life and constant change generate stress by increasing the range and intensity of the demands on our time. Typical stressors that arise in organizations are:

- *inadequate physical working environment*: noise, bad lighting, poor ventilation, lack of privacy, extremes of heat and cold, old and unreliable equipment;

- *inappropriate job design*: poor co-ordination, poor training, lack of information, rigid procedures, inadequate staffing, high workloads, no challenge, little use of skills, no responsibility or participation in decision making, role ambiguity;

- *poor management style*: inconsistent, competitive, crisis management, autocratic management, excessive time pressures placed on employees;

- *poor relationships*: with superiors, with colleagues, with particular individuals, lack of feedback, little social contact, racial and sexual harassment;

- *uncertain future*: job insecurity, fear of unemployment or redeployment, few promotion opportunities, low-status job;

- *divided loyalties*: conflicts between personal aspirations and organizational requirements, conflict between job and family and social responsibilities.

Stress – or pressure – can also be arousing and exciting, and can enhance our sense of satisfaction and accomplishment, and improve our performance. The term *eustress* describes this positive aspect of stress. The prefix 'eu' is Greek for 'good'. This contrasts with *distress*, which means the unpleasant, debilitating and unhealthy side of stress.

Stress can be episodic. When dealing with life's problems, we get anxious, cope with the problem, and then relax again. Some events can be extremely stressful, such as the death of a relative, or a prison sentence. Other stressful experiences include getting a poor exam grade, being fined for speeding, or arguing with a friend, but these trigger less extreme responses. Each of these episodes on its own is unlikely to cause lasting damage. However, when several of these episodes occur around the same time, the health risk is increased.

Stress can be chronic. This happens when we face constant stress, with no escape, and this can lead to exhaustion and 'burnout'. This may be due to the unfortunate coincidence of several unrelated episodes. However, chronic stress also arises from the enduring features of our personal, social and organizational circumstances. If we are always under pressure, always facing multiple unrealistic demands, always having difficulties with our work, our colleagues, and our relationships, then the health risk from stress is likely to increase.

There are three other factors moderating the impact of stressors:

Condition: You are better able to cope with stress if you are in good health.

Cognitive appraisal: If you believe that you are not going to cope with a particular event, this belief can become a 'self-fulfilling prophecy'.

Hardiness: Hardiness is an outlook on life characterized by a welcoming approach to change, commitment to purposeful activity, and a sense of being in control. This combination increases ability to deal with to stress.

Stress has many symptoms which, taken on their own, do not appear significant and are not threatening if they are temporary. Occasional headaches are not cause for concern. Many of the symptoms of stress also have other causes, so they can be overlooked, and stress is not recognized, and is not treated. Table 6.3 identifies typical signs of stress (from Ayling, 2015).

Source: Jantoo

Stress can have emotional consequences: anxiety, fatigue, depression, frustration, nervousness, low self-esteem. Extreme stress can lead to mental breakdown and suicide. Stress also affects behaviour in other ways, from 'comfort tricks' involving alcohol and other drugs and excess eating, to accident-proneness and emotional outbursts. Stress affects our ability to think, and interferes with learning, concentration, decision making, attention span and reaction to criticism. Physiological responses to stress include increased heart rate and blood pressure, sweating and 'hot and cold flushes'.

The consequences of stress can be costly. The performance of stressed employees can be poor, and stress causes absenteeism, staff turnover, accidents and sabotage. Stress damages relationships (poor relationships can cause stress in the first place), and commitment to work and the organization falls.

Table 6.3: The signs of excessive pressure and stress

Work performance	Regression
Declining, inconsistent Performance	Crying
Uncharacteristic errors	Arguments
Loss of control over work	Undue sensitivity
Loss of motivation, commitment	Irritability, moodiness
Indecision	Over-reaction to problems
Lapses in memory	Personality clashes
Increased time at work	Sulking
Lack of holiday planning, usage	Immature behaviour

Withdrawal	Aggressive behaviour
Arriving late to work	Malicious gossip
Leaving early	Criticism of others
Extended lunches	Vandalism
Absenteeism	Shouting
Resigned attitude	Bullying or harassment
Reduced social contact	Poor employee relations
Elusiveness, evasiveness	Temper outbursts

Other behaviours	Physical signs
Out-of-character behaviour	Nervous stumbling speech
Difficulty relaxing	Sweating
Increased alcohol consumption	Tiredness, lethargy
Increased smoking	Upset stomach, flatulence
Lack of interest in appearance, Hygiene	Tension headaches
Accidents at home or work	Hand tremor
Reckless driving	Rapid weight gain or loss
Unnecessary risk-taking	Constantly feeling cold

There are two broad strategies for reducing stress; *individual emotion-focused* strategies, and *organizational problem-focused* strategies.

Individual emotion-focused strategies improve resilience and coping skills and include:

- consciousness-raising to improve self-awareness;
- exercise and fitness programmes;
- self-help training, in biofeedback, meditation, relaxation, coping strategies;
- time management training;
- development of other social and job interests.

Organizational problem-focused strategies deal directly with the stressors and include:

- improved selection and training;
- staff counselling;
- improved organizational communications;
- job redesign and enrichment strategies;
- development of teamworking.

It is not always helpful to 'blame' the individual for their experience of and response to stress, despite the known link to personality. Stress is also caused by organizational factors. While individual resilience can be improved, the need for problem-focused organizational solutions is inescapable. Figure 6.4 summarizes the argument of this section, in terms of the causes of stress, factors that moderate the experience of stress, stress symptoms and coping strategies.

Built to rush: pressure and stress are good for you

In his book *Rush: Why You Need and Love the Rat Race*, Todd Buchholz (2011a) argues that speed, stress and competition at work add to our health and happiness. Taking it easy makes us unhealthy, depressed and miserable. Buchholz is a Harvard economics professor and a former White House economic adviser. He has no time for 'work–life balance', lazy vacations or yoga retreats. Instead, he emphasizes the benefits of activity. As we are 'built to rush', pressure and stress drive us to perform better, and competition encourages creativity and innovation.

Friedman and Rosenman (1974) argued that people with Type A personalities have problems with their health and with making good decisions. In contrast, Buchholz cites an Australian study, involving 9,000 people, which found that those with a passive lifestyle, who spent four or more hours a day 'de-stressing' in front of the television, had an 80 per cent higher chance of developing heart disease than those who spent less than two hours a day channel hopping:

> In your bloodstream is an enzyme called lipoprotein lipase. It's a friendly enzyme because it draws fat to your muscles, where it can be burned as fuel. But sitting on your bum leaves fat in your bloodstream, where it might as well clog into formations that spell out 999.

> We want to feel that rush of dopamine when we face a new challenge at work. We need that push of forward momentum in order to be creative. And we need it much more than we need mantras, deep breathing or the murmur that comes when we try to snooze through life. (Buchholz, 2011b, p.21)

Research has also shown that cognitive abilities – speed and clarity of thought – decay in people after they retire from work.

Competition is beneficial. At Apple, teams of designers and engineers were encouraged to compete with each other to persuade Steve Jobs which features to include in new iPhones and iPads. Buchholz is critical of the 'Edenists' who argue for a simpler, happier lifestyle. What would you rather do when you have finished reading this chapter: go relax, or rush on to the next task?

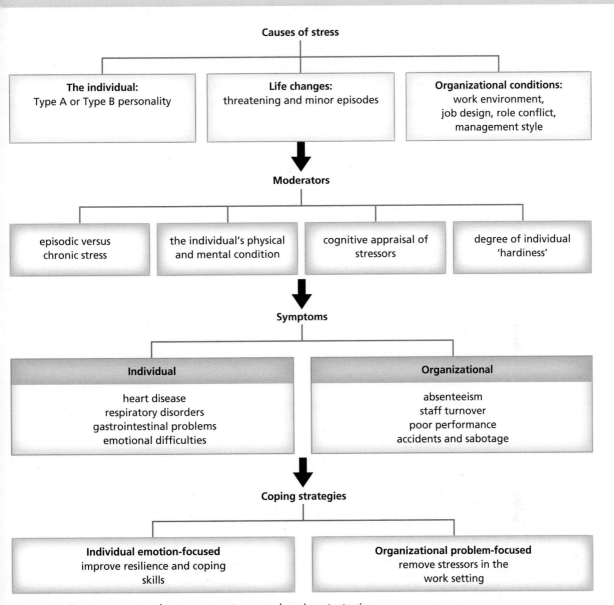

Figure 6.4: Stress causes, moderators, symptoms, and coping strategies

Video case: hurry sickness – an epidemic affecting executives

This six-minute *Financial Times* video contradicts the argument of Todd Buchholz (2011) that we are 'built to rush'. Richard Jolly from London Business School claims that we are suffering from an epidemic of 'rushing around doing things', which stops us from reflecting and focusing on priorities. Managers need new competencies, shifting the focus from human capital (personal knowledge and skill) to social capital – being able to get things done through other people.

The Big Five

Big Five consistent trait clusters that capture the main dimensions of personality; Openness, Conscientiousness, Extraversion, Agreeableness and Neuroticism.

Building on Eysenck's work, work on trait clusters has focused on the Big Five (Costa and McCrae, 1992). This is now broadly accepted as a common descriptive system. Research has consistently reproduced these dimensions in different social settings and cultures, with different populations, with different forms of data collection, and in different languages.

Table 6.4: The Big Five personality trait clusters

High ⟵————————————————————⟶ **Low**

explorer (O+) creative, curious, open-minded, intellectual	**Openness** rigidity of beliefs and range of interests	*preserver* (O–) conventional, unimaginative, narrow-minded
focused (C+) organized, self-disciplined, achievement-oriented	**Conscientiousness** desire to impose order and precision	*flexible* (C–) disorganized, careless, frivolous, irresponsible
extravert (E+) outgoing, sociable, talkative, assertive	**Extraversion** level of comfort with relationships	*introvert* (E–) reserved, quiet, introverted
adapter (A+) good-natured, trusting, compliant, soft-hearted	**Agreeableness** the ability to get along with others	*challenger* (A–) rude, quarrelsome, uncaring, irritable, uncooperative
reactive (N+) anxious, depressed, self-conscious	**Neuroticism** tendency to maintain a balanced emotional state	*resilient* (N–) calm, contented, self-assured

High ⟵————————————————————⟶ **Low**

The Big Five (which spell OCEAN) are not personality types. These are sets of factors, 'super traits', which describe common elements among the sub-factors or traits which cluster together. Costa and McCrae identify six traits under each of the five headings, giving 30 traits in total. You can find a summary of The Big Five trait clusters in Table 6.4. You can profile your own personality using the assessment exercise at the end of this chapter.

Openness is based on six traits: fantasy, aesthetics, feelings, actions, ideas, values. These run on a continuum from 'explorer', at one extreme, to 'preserver' at the other:

Explorer (O +) traits are useful for entrepreneurs, architects, change agents, artists and theoretical scientists. *Preserver* (O–) traits are useful for finance managers, stage performers, project managers and applied scientists. Those in the middle (O) are labelled 'moderates' who are interested in novelty when necessity commands, but not for too long.

Conscientiousness: competence, order, dutifulness, achievement striving, self-discipline, deliberation. This continuum runs from 'focused' to 'flexible':

Focused (C +) traits are useful for leaders, senior executives and other high achievers. *Flexible* (C–) traits are useful for researchers, detectives and management consultants. Those in the middle (C) are 'balanced', and find it easy to move from focus to being flexible, from production to research.

Extraversion: warmth, gregariousness, assertiveness, activity, excitement-seeking, positive emotions. This continuum runs from 'extravert' to 'introvert':

Extravert (E +) traits are useful in sales, politics, and the arts. *Introvert* (E–) traits are useful for production management, and in the physical and natural sciences. Those in the middle (E) are 'ambiverts' who move easily from isolation to social settings.

Agreeableness: trust, straightforwardness, altruism, compliance, modesty, tender-mindedness. This continuum runs from 'adapter' to 'challenger':

Adapter (A+) traits are useful in teaching, social work and psychology. *Challenger* (A−) traits are useful in advertising, management and military leadership. Those in the middle (A) are 'negotiators' who move from leadership to followership as the situation demands.

Neuroticism, or 'negative emotionality': worry, anger, discouragement, self-consciousness, impulsiveness, vulnerability. This continuum runs from 'reactive' to 'resilient':

Reactive (emotional) or 'N+' traits are useful for social scientists, academics, and customer service professionals, but extreme reactivity interferes with intellectual performance. *Resilient* (unflappable) or 'N−' traits are useful for air traffic controllers, airline pilots, military snipers, finance managers and engineers. Those in the middle (N) are 'responsives', able to use levels of emotionality appropriate to the circumstances.

Those trait clusters may be appropriate to particular occupations. Does success in your chosen career, however, depend on your personality? Research suggests the following relationships:

Conscientiousness	is positively related to salary, promotions and job status in most occupations
Neuroticism	is negatively related to performance, salary and status
Extraversion	findings are inconsistent, linked to performance, salary and job level in some studies, but not in others; may depend on type of work
Openness and agreeableness	do not correlate consistently with job performance; these attributes could contribute to lower performance in some jobs
Openness	shown to reduce the performance of rugby referees
Agreeableness	seems to interfere with management potential

Research has also shown that purchasing habits are related to The Big Five personality traits (*The Economist*, 2013, p.86). For example, extraverts are more likely to respond to a mobile phone advert that promises excitement, than to one that emphasizes convenience or security. Extraverts tend to prefer Coca-Cola, and agreeable people tend to prefer Pepsi. Organizations could thus develop more effective marketing strategies if they understood their customers' personalities, but customers are likely to ignore corporate requests to submit to personality assessments. Some researchers, however, believe that your personality profile can be assessed in other ways.

LDprod/Shutterstock.com

A group at IBM's research centre in California has developed software that analyses streams of 'tweets', looking for words that indicate the tweeter's personality, values and needs. Extraverts use words like 'bar', 'restaurant' and 'crowd' more frequently. Neuroticism is associated with terms such as 'awful', 'lazy' and 'depressing'. Agreeableness is associated with 'summer' and 'unusual'. Word use can also be linked to values (what you think is important – loyalty, accuracy, self-development) and needs (what you feel you cannot live without – excitement, control, acceptance). Armed with this information, companies can design their advertising specifically for you. The researchers analysed the tweets of 90 million users over three months. They claim to be able to produce a fairly accurate individual personality profile from 50 tweets, and a comprehensive profile from 200 tweets. When you next tweet somebody may be following your every word, but not in the way that you intended.

Is personality linked to success in management? Using The Big Five personality assessment, Joanna Moutafi et al. (2007) studied 900 British managers, from ten organizations, in retailing, telecoms, manufacturing, consultancy, accounting and legal services. They reached three conclusions:

Conscientiousness was positively related to management level. This suggests that you are more likely to be promoted if you are capable, sensitive, effective, well-organized, thorough, dependable, reliable, ambitious and hard-working. However, it may also be the case that high-level jobs encourage the development of those characteristics.

Neuroticism was negatively related to management level. This means that you are less likely to be promoted if you appear nervous, tense, anxious, stress-prone, unhappy, depressed, shy and unable to cope. People with those characteristics may avoid jobs with high levels of responsibility, but the stress in those management roles may increase neuroticism.

Extraversion was positively related to management level. This implies that you are more likely to be promoted if you are dominant, confident, assertive, energetic, determined, outgoing and sociable. The researchers note that 'Management is an extraverted activity. Managers attend meetings, give talks and socially interact all day long, which are activities more easily handled by extraverts than introverts' (Moutafi et al., 2007, p.277).

Psychometric tests of cognitive abilities tend to be good predictors of job performance, while measures of personality traits are poorer predictors. This particular study suggests, however, that personality assessment could be useful in selecting people for management roles.

Automating personality assessment

Most of us believe that we are good judges of the personalities of others. However, this could be another human cognitive skill that computers perform better. Wu Youyou et al. (2015) compared human and computer-based judgements of the personalities of 86,200 participants, who first completed a Big Five personality assessment: openness, conscientiousness, extraversion, agreeableness, neuroticism. The researchers also designed a computer model using Facebook Likes, which indicate 'positive associations' with a range of issues: products, brands, websites, sports, music, books, restaurants. The participants' personalities were then rated on The Big Five by Facebook friends.

The computer model was a more accurate judge, needing only 100 Likes in order to perform better than a human judge (300 Likes if the human assessor was a spouse). On average, Facebook users each have 227 Likes. Computers may be better judges because they can store and analyse volumes of information which are difficult for humans to retain, and their assessments are not biased by emotions and motives. Why should Facebook Likes be linked to personality? The researchers explain: 'Exploring the Likes most predictive of a given trait shows that they represent activities, attitudes, and preferences highly aligned with The Big Five theory. For example, participants with high openness to experience tend to like Salvador Dali, meditation, or TED talks; participants with high extraversion tend to like partying, Snookie (reality show star), or dancing' (Wu Youyou et al., 2015, p.1037).

Automated, accurate, inexpensive personality assessment could have several uses: tailoring marketing messages, matching candidates to jobs, adjusting services to customers. However, the personal information that can be collected from your 'digital footprint' can also be used to influence and manipulate, raising questions of privacy.

In the movie *Her* (2013, director Spike Jonze), the writer Theodore Twombly (played by Joaquin Phoenix) falls in love with Samantha (Scarlet Johansson), who is his computer's artificially intelligent operating system. Samantha understands and responds to Theodore in a more helpful and effective way than his friends. The researchers conclude that their findings could turn this fiction into reality.

The development of the self

Idiographic an approach to the study of personality emphasizing the uniqueness of the individual, rejecting the assumption that we can all be measured on the same dimensions.

The nomothetic approach to the study of personality has been criticized by those who advocate an **idiographic** approach, which contrasts sharply in perspective and implications.

Idiographic means 'writing about individuals'. Psychologists using this perspective begin with a detailed picture of one person, aiming to capture their unique richness and complexity. This is a valuable way of deepening our understanding, but does not produce universal laws of behaviour.

The idiographic approach makes the following assumptions:

- First, each individual has unique traits that cannot be compared with the traits of others. Your sensitivity and aggression are not necessarily the same as my sensitivity and aggression. Idiographic research produces in-depth studies of normal and abnormal individuals, with information from interviews, letters, diaries and biographies, including what people say and write about themselves.

- Second, we are not just biological machines powered by heredity. We are socially self-conscious. Our behaviour patterns are affected by our experience, and by reflection and reasoning, not just by instinct and habit.

Self-concept the set of perceptions that we have about ourselves.

- Third, we behave in accordance with the image that we have of ourselves – our **self-concept**. We learn about ourselves through our interactions with others. We take the attitudes and behaviours of others and use those to adjust our self-concept and our behaviour.

- Fourth, as the development of the self-concept is a social process, this means that personality can change with social experiences. The development of personality is not the inevitable result of genetic inheritance. It is through interaction with others that we learn to understand ourselves as individuals. We cannot develop self-understanding without the (tacit) help of others. In this view, 'human nature' is a fluid concept. This contrasts with the argument that human nature is largely influenced by biology and genetics. This perspective, therefore, is on the nurture side of the nature–nurture debate.

The mind's ability to reflect on its own functions is an important capability. We experience a world 'out there' and we can experience ourselves in that world, as objects that live and behave in it. We can observe, evaluate and criticize ourselves in the same conscious, impersonal way that we observe, evaluate and criticize others, and we can experience shame, anxiety or pride in our own behaviour. Our capacity for reflection allows us to evaluate past and future actions and their consequences.

The American psychologist Charles Horton Cooley introduced the concept of the 'looking glass self'. Our mirror is the other people with whom we interact. If others respond warmly and favourably towards us, we develop a 'positive' self-concept. If others respond with criticism, ridicule and aggression, we develop a 'negative' self-image. The personality of the individual is thus the result of a process in which the individual learns to be the person they are. Most of us learn, accept and use most of the attitudes, values, beliefs and expectations of the society in which we are brought up.

In other words, we learn the stock of knowledge peculiar to our society. Red means stop. Cars drive on the left-hand side of the road (in Australia and Britain). An extended hand is a symbol of respect and friendship, not of hostility or aggression. These examples, on their own, are trivial. Taken together, these make up our 'recipe knowledge' of how society works. The taken-for-granted 'rules' that govern our behaviour are created, recreated and reinforced through our ongoing interactions with others based on shared definitions of our reality. We interact with each other successfully because we share this understanding. What we inherit from our parents cannot possibly tell us how to behave in a specific culture. We have to learn how to become *persona grata* through social interaction.

If we all share the same ideas and behaviours, we have a recipe for a society of conformists. This is not consistent with the evidence, and the theory does not imply this. George Herbert Mead (1934) argued that the self has two components:

I   the unique, individual, conscious and impulsive aspects of the individual

Me   the norms and values of society that the individual learns and accepts, or 'internalizes'

Generalized other
what we think other people expect of us, in terms of our attitudes, values, beliefs and behaviour.

Mead used the term **generalized other** to refer to the set of expectations that we believe others have of us. 'Me' is the part of self where these generalized attitudes are organized. 'Me' refers to the mental process that enables us to reflect on our own conduct. 'Me' is the self as an object to itself.

The 'I' is the active, impulsive component of the self. Other people encourage us to conform to current values and beliefs. Reflective individuals adjust their part in the social process. We can initiate change by introducing new social values. Patterns of socially acceptable conduct are specified in broad and general ways. There is plenty of scope for flexibility, modification, originality, creativity, individuality, variety and change.

STOP AND THINK

List the ten words or phrases that best describe the most important features of your identity.

These features could concern your social roles, physical characteristics, intellectual qualities, social style, beliefs and particular skills.

Then make a second list, putting what you regard as the most important feature at the top, and ranking all ten items with the least important at the bottom.

Starting at the bottom of your list, imagine that these items are removed from your personality one by one. Visualize how you would be different without each personality feature. What difference does its absence make to you?

This is the start of the process of establishing your *self-concept*. How much more or less valid is this approach than one based on forced choice questionnaires – and why?

Figure 6.5 illustrates what Carl Rogers (1947) called the 'two-sided self'.

Our self-concept gives us a sense of meaning and consistency. But as our perceptions and motives change with new experiences and learning, our self-concept and our behaviour also change. Personality in this perspective, therefore, is not stable; the self-concept can be reorganized. We have perceptions of our qualities, abilities, attitudes, impulses and so on. If these perceptions are accurate, conscious, organized and accepted, then we can regard our self-concept as successful because it will lead to feelings of comfort, freedom from tension and psychological adjustment. Well-adjusted individuals thus have flexible images of themselves, and are open to change through new experiences.

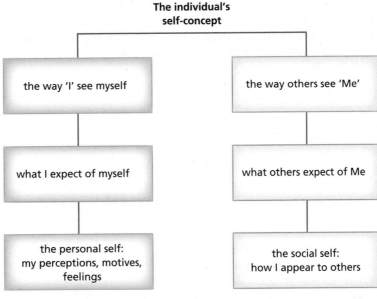

Figure 6.5: The two-sided self

Personality disorders can be caused by a failure to bring together experiences, motives and feelings into a consistent self-concept. We usually behave in ways consistent with our self-images, but when we have new experiences or feelings that are inconsistent we either:

- recognize the inconsistency and try to integrate the two sets of understanding – the healthy response; or
- deny or distort one of the experiences, perhaps by putting the blame onto someone or something else – an unhealthy defence mechanism.

Unconditional positive regard unqualified, non-judgemental approval and respect for the traits and behaviours of the other person (a term used in counselling).

Rogers argued that at the core of human personality is the desire to realize fully one's potential. To achieve this, the right social environment is required, one in which we are treated with **unconditional positive regard**. This means that one is accepted for whatever one is; one is valued, trusted and respected, even in the face of characteristics which others dislike. In this environment, the individual is likely to become trusting, spontaneous and flexible, with a rich and meaningful life and a harmonious self-concept. However, this is very different from the type of social environment in many contemporary organizations. Most of us face highly conditional regard, in which a narrow range of thoughts and behaviours is accepted.

Should you be true to yourself?

Leaders and managers are advised to be 'authentic' if they are to be effective. What does that mean in practice? 'Authenticity' means genuine, original, not a copy. For the individual, this means behaving in ways that are consistent with one's 'true self'. Herminia Ibarra (2015) argues, however, that a rigid self-concept is a problem when we are constantly faced with radical work and organizational changes, and where we want to change our behaviour to improve our performance. With an increasingly diverse workforce, many of us have colleagues whose norms and expectations are different from our own. It can be difficult to choose between what is expected of us, and what feels authentic.

Ibarra (2015) describes how two contrasting psychological profiles lead to different ways of managing our self-concept:

→

- *Chameleons* are able and willing to adapt to the demands of different situations without feeling that they are faking. They 'try on' different styles to find a fit with the context.

- *True-to-selfers* say what they really think and feel, even if that is not consistent with the expectations and demands of the situation.

There are problems with both of these profiles. Adaptable chameleons may have fast-track careers, but they can be seen as insincere and immoral. True-to-selfers may stay in their comfort zones and not change their behaviour to meet new demands. Ibarra cites the example of a manager who took on a more responsible position. She believed in transparent, collaborative leadership, and openly shared her anxieties about her role with her new staff. However, those employees were looking for a confident leader to take charge. Instead of building trust, her 'authenticity' damaged her credibility.

Instead, Ibarra (2015, p.58) advises managers and leaders to develop an *adaptively authentic* profile. This involves 'playing' with different approaches:

> When we adopt a playful attitude, we're more open to possibilities. It's OK to be inconsistent from one day to the next. That's not being a fake; it's how we experiment to find out what's right for the new challenges and circumstances we face.

There are three ways to develop an adaptively authentic profile. First, adapt the styles and behaviours of others, by borrowing selectively from a large number of varied role models. Second, set learning goals, stop protecting our 'comfortable old selves', and do not expect to get everything right first time. Third, keep under review the personal narratives – the stories and images that we have of ourselves – and edit or drop these when we find ourselves in new situations. For example, the 'friendly team player and peacekeeper' image may not be helpful in a demanding new leadership assignment, and a bolder, more adventurous narrative may be appropriate. Ibarra (2015, p.59) concludes:

> The only way we grow as leaders is by stretching the limits of who we are – doing new things that make us uncomfortable but that teach us through direct experience who we want to become. Such growth doesn't require a radical personality makeover. Small changes – in the way we carry ourselves, the way we communicate, the way we interact – often make a world of difference in how effectively we lead.

Thematic apperception test an assessment in which the individual is shown ambiguous pictures and is asked to create stories of what may be happening in them.

Need for achievement a concern with meeting standards of excellence, the desire to be successful in competition, the motivation to excel.

Compared with nomothetic methods, an idiographic approach appears to be a complex, untidy view of personality and its development. It has influenced research, but has had little impact on contemporary psychometrics. Any approach to studying your self-understanding with questions worded by someone else is not going to work. You may reject that wording as not relevant to *your* self-concept.

We need another route into the mind. Well, we can ask people to write and to talk about themselves. Such methods are in common use, including free association, interpretation of dreams, and the analysis of fantasies. Here the individual has freedom of expression and responses are not tied to given categories. The researcher's job is to identify themes that reveal an individual's preoccupations, interests and personality. One technique is the thematic apperception test, or TAT.

This label breaks our rule about not describing personality assessments as 'tests'. However, we have to be consistent with the literature. This is how the TAT works. First, you are told that you are about to take a test of your creative writing skills. Then you are shown photographs or drawings, typically including people, and asked to write an imaginative story suggested by what you see. The images do not imply any particular story. The contents of your imaginative accounts are then assessed in various ways. One of these concerns your need for achievement. This is not a test of your imaginative writing at all.

STOP AND THINK

Write an imaginative story (100 words) about what is happening in this picture:

Caroline Woodham/Alamy

Henry Alexander Murray (1893–1988)

Projective test
an assessment based on abstract or ambiguous images, which the subject is asked to interpret by projecting their feelings, preoccupations and motives into their responses.

The assessment procedure first involves deciding whether any of the characters in your story have an achievement goal. In other words, does somebody in your story want to perform better? This could involve doing something better than someone else, meeting or exceeding a self-imposed standard of excellence, doing something unique, or being involved in doing something well. Points are scored for the presence of these features in your story. The more achievement imagery, the higher your score.

The TAT is widely used in psychological research, occupational choice, psychiatric evaluation and screening candidates for high-stress jobs. The test was invented by Henry Murray and Christiana Morgan in the 1930s, and was later developed by David McClelland (1961; McClelland et al., 1976) as a means of measuring the strength of need for achievement. The TAT is also used to measure the needs for power and affiliation, using similar scoring procedures, but looking for different imagery. In the original full test, you are asked to write stories about 31 pictures.

What can short, creative stories about ambiguous pictures tell us about your distinctive and stable personality characteristics? The thematic apperception test is a projective test.

The label 'projective' is used because subjects project their personalities into the stories they write. The Rorschach test is a form of projective assessment which uses random ink-blots instead of pictures or photographs. McClelland argues that it is reasonable to assume that the person with a strong concern with achievement is likely to write stories with lots of achievement imagery and themes. The evidence seems to support this view.

Need for achievement is important in an organizational context. People with low need for achievement are concerned more with security and status than with personal fulfilment, are preoccupied with their own ideas and feelings, worry more about self-presentation than their performance, and prefer bright Scottish tartans. People with high need for achievement tend to have the following characteristics:

- They prefer tasks in which they have to achieve a standard of excellence rather than simply carrying out routine activities.
- They prefer jobs in which they get frequent and clear feedback on how well they are doing, to help them perform better.
- They prefer activities that involve moderate risks of failure; high-risk activities lead to failure, low-risk activities do not provide opportunities to demonstrate ability.
- They have a good memory for unfinished tasks and do not like to leave things incomplete.
- They can be unfriendly and unsociable when they do not want others to get in the way of their performance.
- They have a sense of urgency, appear to be in a hurry, to be working against time and have an inability to relax.

- They prefer sombre Scottish tartans with lots of blues and greens (Buchanan tartan has lots of red and yellow); unobtrusive backgrounds allow them to stand out better.

Organizations want employees with drive, ambition and self-motivation. Can the TAT be used to identify them? Unfortunately, it is not a good assessment for this purpose. Although the detailed scoring is not obvious to the untrained, the definition of achievement imagery is close to popular understanding. So, when you know what the 'test' is all about, it is easy to fake your score – the same problem that we have with objective questionnaires.

The TAT faces other problems as an organizational selection tool. The output of the assessment is hard for the untrained eye to regard as 'objective data'. The scoring procedure involves subjective interpretation. Expensive training is required in the full technical procedure to produce judges who can reach reliable assessments. With an objective questionnaire, anyone with the scoring key can calculate the results quickly and accurately.

McClelland argues that need for achievement can be increased by teaching you the scoring system, thus helping you to write high scoring stories, and by encouraging you to see life more clearly in achievement terms. McClelland and colleagues have used this approach with senior managers, entrepreneurs, police officers and social workers, and the first application outside America was with Indian businessmen in 1963. The TAT can thus be used to assess, and also to change personality.

Nomothetic versus idiographic

These contrasting perspectives on personality are summarized in Table 6.5.

Table 6.5: Nomothetic versus idiographic

The nomothetic approach	The idiographic approach
Positivist bias	Constructivist bias
Generalizing; emphasizes the discovery of laws of human behaviour	Individualizing; emphasizes the richness and complexity of the unique individual
Based on statistical study of large groups	Based on intensive study of individuals
Uses objective questionnaires	Uses projective assessments (tests) and other written and spoken materials
Describes personality in terms of the individual's possession of traits, and trait clusters or personality types	Describes personality in terms of the individual's own understanding and interpretation of their identity
Personality is composed of discrete and identifiable elements	Personality has to be understood as an indivisible, intelligible whole
Personality is primarily determined by heredity, biology, genetics	Personality is primarily determined by social and cultural processes
Personality is given and cannot be altered	Personality is adaptable, open to change through experience

How can we choose between these perspectives? We can look at the logic of the arguments, and consider the evidence. We can resort to practical uses and assess how these methods can treat personality disorders, or analyse and predict behaviour. These forms of judgement miss the point that these approaches are based on very different views of human nature. The evidence is such as to leave us debating for a considerable time without resolution. We need to use criteria such as:

- Which theory is more aesthetically pleasing?
- Which approach 'feels' right?
- How does each approach fit with my world view?

Another approach is to see these perspectives as complementary. They offer two broad research strategies, each of which is capable of telling us about different aspects of human psychology. What each alone reveals is interesting, but partial. Perhaps we should use both approaches and not concentrate on one alone. However, contemporary employee assessment and selection methods ignore this advice, using mostly nomothetic methods.

Selection methods

Personality assessment almost always contributes to employee selection. This may be an informal, personal judgement ('does their face fit?'), but, as mentioned earlier, organizations have increasingly turned to formal psychometric methods. Choosing the right candidate for a job, or for promotion, is a critical decision. Incorrect decisions lead to frustrated employees and poor performance. Selection procedures are costly and time-consuming, and it is expensive to repeat them to recover from errors.

A selection (or a promotion) decision is a prediction about the candidate's future performance. Predictions are based on an understanding of the demands of the job, and on information about the candidates. Traditionally, candidate information has come from application forms, references and interviews. The application form provides background, but is impersonal. Referees notoriously reveal only good things about candidates. Research suggests that interviews can also be unreliable, and are not suitable for all occupations: what would you think of the football team captain who selected players on the basis of how well they performed in an interview?

Psychometrics

Psychometrics, the systematic testing, measurement and assessment of intelligence, aptitudes and personality, promise to improve the objectivity of selection and promotion decisions by collecting information that has predictive power. Psychometric applications developed rapidly during the late twentieth century, and there are now thousands of tests and assessments in use.

When choosing a psychometric assessment, for any purpose, two criteria are particularly important: reliability and predictive validity.

Reliability the degree to which an assessment delivers consistent results when repeated.

If the same group of people is given the same assessment on two or more occasions, and the results are the same or similar, then the assessment can be described as reliable. This is known as 'test–retest reliability'. The validity of an assessment concerns the extent to which it actually measures what it sets out to measure. There are different types of validity:

Predictive validity the extent to which assessment scores accurately predict behaviours such as job performance.

- *Face validity*: does it look right?
- *Construct validity*: does it relate to other similar measures?
- *Predictive validity*: will it tell us how well someone will perform on the job?

In employee selection, predictive validity is particularly important. So, can we predict job performance from personality assessments? No single method can accurately predict how well an individual will perform in a specific role. Most employers use several methods for gathering information about candidates. A survey of 460 public and private sector organizations in the UK by the Chartered Institute for Personnel and Development (2013, p.19) found that interviews were still a common selection method, and that competency-based interviews were the most popular across all sectors. Although face-to-face interviews were preferred, 56 per cent of employers were using telephone interviews, and nearly one-third also used video or Skype interviews. The survey findings are summarized in Table 6.6.

Table 6.6: The popularity of different selection methods

Selection method	% of organizations using
Competency-based interview	82
Interview based on application form and CV	71
Tests for specific skills	55
Literacy and/or numeracy tests	45
General ability tests	45
Assessment centres	43
Personality and aptitude questionnaires	42
Group exercises, such as role-playing	28
Pre-interview references	22
Online tests	22

More than half of the organizations surveyed used social media in their recruitment process, but less than a fifth had a social media strategy. Social media were used mainly to attract candidates (86 per cent), but only 6 per cent used social media to screen candidates' online profiles. Three-fifths of those organizations which did not use social media in this context felt that it would benefit them to do so. Over 80 per cent said that social media use had strengthened their employer brand and increased the number of applicants from which they could select. And 75 per cent said that social media had reduced their recruitment costs (Chartered Institute for Personnel and Development, 2013, p.5).

Approaches to selection vary from country to country. Employers in Britain and America rely on interviews, but graphology (handwriting analysis) is more widely used in France. Assessment centres are popular in Britain, Germany and The Netherlands. Blood group is a selection criterion in Japan.

Selection methods differ in their validity, or ability to predict job performance. The 'perfect' method would be right every time, and would have a validity coefficient of '1'. Random selection with a pin would score '0'. Studies show that structured interviews score 0.6, assessment centres 0.4, personality assessments 0.4 and unstructured interviews 0.3. Graphology (handwriting assessment) and astrology both score 0 (Rees and French, 2010, p.178). Any method with a validity coefficient of less than 0.5 is going to be wrong more often than it is right. Second, personality assessments have relatively low predictive validity. The average cost of filling a vacancy is around £5,000 for senior managers and directors, and £2,000 for other employees, so selection errors can be expensive, and these figures do not consider costly errors that the wrong person could make (Chartered Institute of Personnel and Development, 2013, p.4).

STOP AND THINK At your next job interview, you are asked, 'Why should we employ you?' The first part of your answer concerns your knowledge and skills. The second part of your answer concerns your personality. What are you going to say? Will this help you to get the job?

Does size matter?

Nick Seybert (2013) claims that companies whose chief executives have large signatures perform worse than those led by CEOs with small signatures. How can that be? This conclusion is based on an analysis of ten years of annual reports of 400 large American companies.

A large signature is an indicator of narcissistic personality traits such as dominance and high self-esteem (i.e. outsized ego), and those were associated with overspending, lower return on assets and (paradoxically) higher CEO pay relative to that of industry peers. Narcissistic individuals tend to dominate discussions, ignore criticism and belittle employees. Don't we want leaders to be hard-charging, dominant and confident? Yes, and some are successful (Steve Jobs is an example – but he was also a genius and a visionary). Seybert (2013, p.33) notes that 'Most people who have grandiose ideas about their own abilities and refuse input from others make worse decisions', and he concludes (p.32):

[W]hen an annual report has a big CEO signature on it – as measured by the area of a box drawn around the signature's end points, and controlling for name length – a firm will, on average, spend more on capital goods, R&D, and acquisitions than its industry peers, yet show worse sales growth over the next three to six years.

The results of personality assessments are rarely used as the sole basis of a selection decision. While these may give further useful information, along with other selection methods, personality assessments are not always good predictors of performance because:

- people are flexible and multifaceted, and can develop new skills and behaviours and adapt to new circumstances; personality assessment captures a part of the whole at one point in time;
- most jobs are multifaceted in their demands on skill and knowledge, and traits which enhance competence in one task may not improve overall job performance;
- job performance usually depends on many factors that are not related to personality such as luck, training, payment systems, physical facilities, supervisory style, organization structure, company policies and procedures, and organization culture and norms;
- most jobs change over time, so predictions based on current measures are unreliable;
- nomothetic methods work with large samples, against which individual profiles can be compared; these methods are not designed to make predictions about individuals, although that is how they are often used;
- in clinical and research settings, most people give honest answers about personality, but these assessments are easy to falsify when a job or promotion is at stake.

New, improved interview techniques

It can be difficult to predict the future job performance of candidates using traditional unstructured interviews. Interviewees prepare, and good social skills can influence interviewers who do not have time to gather more information. Interviews can be improved by training interviewers in questioning techniques, effective probing of responses, taking notes (many interviewers do not do this), using structured rating scales, and not making any decisions until after the interviews are over. However, there are four other types of interview technique which can improve the process (Brittain, 2012):

Interview technique	Features (and drawback)
Structured competency interview	Interview questions focus on key competencies and behaviours, answers are matched with desired criteria, questions tailored to individual candidates (may be seen as unfair)
Career history interview	Interviewer guides candidate through key events in their career, what they achieved and how, what failures they have experienced and what they learned, reveals behaviour patterns leading to success (takes time)
Pseudo-clinical psychology interview	Interviewer asks candidate to describe childhood memories and experiences, as these affect work behaviour in adult life (may be seen as not relevant)
Conversational interview	Similar to structured competency approach, interviewer adopts the style of a peer who is taking an interest in the candidate's role and aspirations, and allows conversation to flow naturally (needs a highly trained interviewer)

Interviews provide valuable, but partial information about candidates. It is helpful to draw on information from other sources as well, such as aptitude tests and business simulation methods. Structured, competency-based or situational interviewing has relatively high predictive validity (CIPD, 2013) Candidates may also be presented with work-based problems, and asked how they would respond. Imagine that you have applied for a job as an emergency telephone operator. Your interviewer asks you this question:

A friend calls you. She is upset. Her child has been injured. She begins to tell you, in a hysterical manner, about how difficult it is to get baby-sitters, what the child is wearing, what words the child can speak, and so on. What would you do?

Your answer is rated for communication skills, emotional control and judgement, and is compared with the actual behaviour of high-level performers in this occupation. It is difficult for you to cheat or to practise responses to a structured competency interview, because you do not know what behaviours are being sought by assessors. Companies using these methods report a high success rate.

Assessment centres

Assessment centres were developed during the Second World War by British War Office Selection Boards. Groups of around six to ten candidates are brought together for one to three days. They are presented, individually and as a group, with a variety of exercises, tests of ability, personality assessments, interviews, work samples, team problem solving and written tasks. Their activities are observed and scored. This is useful for selection and promotion, staff development, talent spotting, and for career guidance. The evidence suggests that this combination of techniques improves the probability of selecting and promoting appropriate candidates.

Assessment centres are expensive to design and run. Qualified assessors are necessary, and a lack of top management commitment to the process can give assessors and candidates inappropriate signals. Methods must be tailored to each organization's needs. The focus on observable and measurable aspects of behaviour overlooks less easily assessed skills. Advocates argue that the information collected is comprehensive and comparable, and candidates have opportunities to demonstrate capabilities unlikely to appear in interviews. The self-knowledge gained can also be valuable to candidates. It has been claimed that a well-designed assessment centre using a variety of methods can achieve a predictive validity of 0.8 with respect to job performance (CIPD, 2013).

Selection at Google

Every year, between 1 and 3 *million* people apply to work for Google, which hires several thousand of them, making it more selective than Harvard, Yale or Princeton universities. Because only 10 per cent of applicants will become top performers, Google has to separate the exceptional from the rest. Alan Eustace, Senior Vice President for Knowledge, says: 'A top notch engineer is worth three hundred times or more than an average engineer' (Bock, 2015, p.62). Selection is so important to Google that, in the beginning, it took over six months to appoint anyone; each applicant had 15 to 25 interviews. Each new recruit consumed 250 hours of employee time.

Selection aims to predict how well candidates will perform when they join a team. Google looks for five attributes: engineering ability, general cognitive ability, leadership, role-related knowledge and 'Googleyness'. These attributes are assessed using structured interviews, and assessments of cognitive ability, conscientiousness and leadership. Each job has attributes to test for, and interview questions are designed to predict performance. Google also uses work sample tests to identify problem-solving ability: 'Write an algorithm to do this'. By 2013, despite recruiting even more staff, the amount of time spent on each hire was reduced by 75 per cent. But there is one final reviewer of every job applicant – Larry Page, the co-founder and current Chief Executive of Google.

RECAP

1. **Distinguish between type, trait and self theories of personality.**

   - Type theories (Hippocrates, Sheldon, Jung) *classify* individuals using a limited number of personality categories.

   - Trait theories, based on a nomothetic perspective (Eysenck, Costa and McCrae), *profile* the individual's personality across a number of different facets.

   - Self-theories, based on an idiographic perspective (Cooley, Mead), *describe* unique individual personalities.

2. **Identify the strengths and limitations of formal methods of personality assessment.**

   - Formal methods offer objective and comprehensive assessments of personality. But they are impersonal, based on group norms, and don't capture individual uniqueness.

   - Formal methods provide objective information about job candidates, but the links between personality assessment scores and job performance are often weak.

3. **Compare the advantages and disadvantages of questionnaires and projective tests as measures of personality.**

   - Objective questionnaires are easy to score and offer quantitative rigour. But they can only be interpreted using group norms; individual scores are meaningless.

   - Projective tests capture the richness and uniqueness of the individual. But they have complex scoring, are subjective, and individual results cannot easily be compared.

4. **Explain the relationship between personality and stress, and identify appropriate individual and organizational stress management strategies.**

   - Type A personalities (competitive, impatient) are more stress prone than Type B personalities (easy-going, relaxed).

   - Individuals can develop physical and psychological resilience and coping skills.

   - Management has to reduce or remove work-related stressors (job design, management style, adverse working conditions, excessive workload).

5. **Evaluate the benefits and problems of psychometric assessment as a tool to assist management decision making, particularly in selection.**

   - Psychometrics offer objective, systematic, comprehensive and quantitative information. They are also useful in career guidance, counselling and development.

   - Individual scores are meaningless outside the context of group norms.

   - It is difficult to predict job performance from a personality profile.

   - Personality assessment can identify strengths in specific areas of competence.

6. **Assess realistically the main characteristics of your own personality.**

   - Current thinking profiles personality on 'the Big Five' trait clusters of Openness, Conscientiousness, Extraversion, Agreeableness and Neuroticism (OCEAN). Self-theories argue that the self-concept is what is important, not your test scores.

Revision

1. What is psychometrics, and what are the main applications? What are the benefits and drawbacks of psychometric assessment in organizational contexts?

2. What is 'personality' and why is this term difficult to define clearly?

3. What is the difference between 'type' and 'trait' theories of personality? Using at least one example of a trait theory, explain the benefits and problems associated with this approach to personality assessment.

4. Explain the distinction between nomothetic and idiographic views of personality. What are the advantages and drawbacks of these methods?

Research assignment

Interview two managers who are involved in selecting candidates for jobs in their organizations. Choose two different types of organization; large and small, or public and private sector, or manufacturing and retailing. First ask them (a) what selection methods do they use, (b) why they use those methods, and (c) what in their experience are the strengths and weaknesses of these methods. Then ask them for their judgement concerning the relative importance of personality as a predictor of a candidate's job performance. If they use psychometrics, find out the extent to which the scores influence selection decisions. Your report will cover the following issues:

1. Describe the range of selection methods used by these organizations.

2. If the two managers reported using different methods, how can this be explained? Was this due to personal preferences, to the nature of the work for which candidates were being chosen, or to the differing nature of the organizations?

3. Summarize the strengths and weaknesses of their methods. Is their experience-based assessment consistent with the evidence presented in this chapter? Based on the evidence concerning selection methods, what advice would you give to these managers?

4. Prepare a brief assessment of the importance placed on personality by those managers in their selection processes, compared with the evidence concerning our ability to predict job performance using personality assessment scores.

Springboard

Tomas Chamorro-Premuzic and Adrian Furnham (2010) *The Psychology of Personnel Selection*. Cambridge: Cambridge University Press. Comprehensive exploration of theories, techniques and controversies, and guidelines for choosing assessments and how they can predict job performance.

Kathy Daniels and Lisa Ayling (2011) *Stress and Mental Health at Work*. London: Chartered Institute of Personnel and Development. Explains the nature and significance of stress, identifies the symptoms, and outlines strategies for managing stress along with legal issues.

Kevin Dutton and Andy McNab (2014) *The Good Psychopath's Guide to Success*. London: Bantam Press. Argues that there are good and bad psychopaths; the former display or conceal ruthlessness, fearlessness, conscience and empathy depending on the situation. Psychopathy is one of the 'Dark Triad' of personality characteristics which includes narcissism and Machiavellianism.

Neal Schmitt (2014) 'Personality and cognitive ability as predictors of effective performance at work', *Annual Review of Organizational Psychology and Organizational Behavior*, 1: 45–65. Assesses the advantages and limitations of cognitive testing and personality assessment in employee selection, based on recent research.

 OB cinema

The Imitation Game (2014, director Morten Tyldum) is based on the true story of Alan Turing (played by Benedict Cumberbatch), one of the founders of computing science and artificial intelligence. During the Second World War, Turing worked as a cryptanalyst for the UK Government Code and Cypher School at Bletchley Park. The movie shows how Turing and his team broke the German communications code, Enigma. Turing was arrogant, antisocial, solitary, literal-minded and showed little

References

Arnold, D.W. and Jones, J.W. (2006) 'Who the devil's applying now?', www.crimcheck.com/employment_testing.htm (no longer available).

Ayling, L. (2015) *Stress in the Workplace Factsheet*. London: Chartered Institute for Personnel and Development.

Belbin, R.M. (1993) *Team Roles at Work*. Oxford: Butterworth Heinemann.

Bock, L. (2015) *Work Rules: Insights from Inside Google That Will Transform How You Live and Lead*. London: John Murray.

Boseley, S. (2012) 'Work stress can raise risk of heart attack by 23%, study finds', *The Guardian*, 14 September, p.5.

Brittain, S. (2012) 'Interviewing skills: building a solid structure', *People Management*, April, pp.30–33.

Buchholz, T.G. (2011a) *Rush: Why You Need and Love the Rat Race*. New York: Hudson Street Press.

Buchholz, T.G. (2011b) 'Stressing the benefits', *RSA Journal*, Autumn, pp.20–21.

Chartered Institute of Personnel and Development (2013) *Resourcing and Talent Planning: Annual Survey Report*. London: Chartered Institute of Personnel and Development.

Costa, P. and McCrae, R.R. (1992) *NEO PI-R: Professional Manual*. Odessa, FL: Psychological Assessment Resources.

Eysenck, H.J. (1970) *The Structure of Human Personality* (3rd edn). London: Methuen.

Eysenck, H.J. (1990) 'Biological dimensions of personality', in L.A. Pervin (ed.), *Handbook of Personality, Theory and Research*. New York: Guilford Press, pp.244–76.

Friedman, M. and Rosenman, R.F. (1974) *Type A Behaviour and your Heart*. New York: Knopf.

Furnham, A. (2012) 'Signs that you are sailing with Captain Catastrophe', *The Sunday Times*, Appointments section, 29 January, p.3.

Ibarra, H. (2015) 'The authenticity paradox: why feeling like a fake can be a sign of growth', *Harvard Business Review*, 93 (1/2): 52–59.

Jung, C.G. (1953) *Collected Works*. New York: Bollingen Series/Pantheon.

Jung, C.G. (1971) *Psychological Types (The Collected Works of C.G. Jung, Volume 6)*. Princeton, NJ: Princeton University Press (first published 1923).

Kerbaj, Richard (2014) 'Dyslexic spies sharpen GCHQ's senses', *The Sunday Times*, 21 September, p.4.

Lewis, G. (2014) 'Business is still scared of autism', *People Management*, December, pp.32–3.

McClelland, D.C. (1961) *The Achieving Society*. Princeton, NJ: Van Nostrand Reinhold.

McClelland, D.C., Atkinson, J.W., Clark, R.A. and Lowell, E.L. (1976) *The Achievement Motive* (2nd edn). New York: Irvington.

Martin, A., Woods, M. and Dawkins, S. (2015) 'Managing employees with mental health issues: identification of conceptual and procedural knowledge for development within management education curricula', *Academy of Management Learning and Education*, 14 (1): 50–68.

Martindale, N. (2015) 'How to avoid workplace stress to stay focused', *The Times Raconteur Supplement*, 24 March, pp.8–9.

Mead, G.H. (1934) *Mind, Self and Society*. Chicago, IL: University of Chicago Press.

Moutafi, J., Furnham, A. and Crump, J. (2007) 'Is managerial level related to personality?', *British Journal of Management*, 18 (3): 272–80.

Myers, I.B. (1962) *The Myers–Briggs Type Indicator Manual*. Princeton, NJ: Educational Testing Service.

Myers, I.B. (1976) *Introduction to Type* (2nd edn). Gainesville, FL: Centre for Applications of Psychological Type.

Myers, I.B. and McCaulley, M.H. (1985) *Manual: A Guide to the Development and Use of the Myers-Briggs Type Indicator*. Palo Alto, CA: Consulting Psychologists Press.

Randler, C. (2010) 'The early bird really does get the worm', *Harvard Business Review*, 88 (7/8), pp.30–31.

Rees, G. and French, R. (2010) *Leading, Managing and Developing People* (3rd edn). London: Chartered Institute of Personnel and Development.

Rogers, C.R. (1947) 'Some observations on the organization of personality', *American Psychologist*, 2 (9): 358–68.

Seybert, N. (2013) 'Size does matter (in signatures)', *Harvard Business Review*, 91 (5), 32–3.

Sheldon, W. (1942) *The Varieties of Temperament: A Psychology of Constitutional Differences*. New York: Harper & Row.

The Economist (2013) 'No hiding place', 25 May, p.86.

Whitely, P. (2012) 'Are Britons getting more dishonest', *University of Essex Centre for the Study of Integrity Working Paper*, Essex, January.

Youyou, W., Kosinski, M. and Stillwell, D. (2015) 'Computer-based personality judgements are more accurate than those made by humans', *Proceedings of the National Academy of Sciences*, 112 (4): 1036–40.

Chapter 7 **Communication**

Key terms

social intelligence

communication process

coding

decoding

perceptual filters

noise

feedback (communication)

non-verbal communication

power tells

high context culture

low context culture

impression management

emotional intelligence

communication climate

Learning outcomes

When you have read this chapter, you should be able to define those key terms in your own words, and you should also be able to:

1. Describe the dimensions of social intelligence, and explain the importance of this capability.

2. Understand the components of the interpersonal communication process.

3. Identify the main barriers to effective interpersonal communication.

4. Understand different questioning techniques, conversation controls and listening skills.

5. Explain the nature and significance of non-verbal communication cues and clusters.

6. Understand the nature and mechanisms of impression management skills and techniques.

7. Assess the concept of emotional intelligence and its practical significance.

8. Explain how corporate communication can influence understanding and encourage compliance with management directions.

Why study communication?

People management skills

To understand the attributes that employers look for in graduates, the Chartered Management Institute ran a series of workshops and a national survey. The employers said:

- Graduates need to know how to have a difficult conversation about performance. They must also be able to manage a project, work in a team, and communicate and persuade – both orally and in writing.

- Nearly two-thirds (65 per cent) of employers agree that graduates lack the interpersonal skills necessary to manage people.

- The ability to communicate is the most important skill that a graduate can possess, according to employers. This is followed by problem-solving, team-building and motivational skills.

(Chartered Management Institute, 2014, p.8)

Communication is central to understanding organizational behaviour for several reasons:

- the effectiveness of communication affects individual careers and organizational performance;
- very few people work alone, and the job of most managers involves interacting with other people, often for more than 90 per cent of their time;
- communication is seen as a problem in many organizations;
- in an increasingly diverse society, sensitivity to the norms and expectations of others is vital to effective cross-cultural communication;
- new technology is radically changing how, what and when we communicate.

Everything significant that happens in an organization involves communication; hiring and training staff, giving feedback, purchasing supplies, solving problems, dealing with customers, deciding strategy. However, many factors can interfere with communication: hierarchy, power and status differences, job design, the nature of (part-time, temporary) employment, physical layouts and rules.

Communications are improved if you are able to 'feel' what others are feeling. Can you 'read' what's happening in complex social settings? Do you use that understanding to manage your relationships? If so, then you have social intelligence. Despite modern communications technology, personal interactions, one-to-one, face-to-face (F2F), or 'face time' are still important, perhaps even more so. Our ability to interact effectively with others was first described as social intelligence in 1920 by Edward Thorndike, but the idea was seen then as just another aspect of general intelligence.

For Daniel Goleman (2007), social intelligence is a special set of capabilities, including social awareness (what we sense about others) and social facility (how we act on that awareness). Each of these dimensions has four components (Table 7.1).

Social intelligence
the ability to understand the thoughts and feelings of others and to manage our relationships accordingly.

Table 7.1: Social intelligence

Social awareness	Primal empathy	'Reading' others' emotions intuitively from small clues (such as a brief facial expression)
	Attunement	Understanding the other person through complete and sustained attention and careful listening
	Empathic accuracy	Explicit understanding, through observation and inference, of what someone feels and thinks
	Social cognition	Knowing how the social world works, what is expected, reading the social signals
Social facility	Synchrony	Smoothly orchestrating our interactions with the right gestures (smiles, nods, posture, timing)
	Self-preservation	Ability in interactions to trigger desired emotional responses in others, charisma
	Influence	Shaping the outcomes of interactions with tact and control, tuning actions to fit the circumstances
	Concern	Capacity for compassion, sharing others' emotions, elation or distress

Globalization means that we often find ourselves working with people from other countries and cultures. Cultures have different norms concerning how conversations are handled, appropriate greetings, degree of formality, the use of eye contact, suitable topics for discussion, physical distance between speakers, and the interpretation of gestures.

Social intelligence is crucial in a culturally diverse world. Goldman Sachs, a US bank, trains its Japanese staff to communicate more effectively with colleagues from other countries. Social norms in Japan encourage holding back in meetings, acting with modesty, and avoiding 'behind the scenes' lobbying – the opposite of expectations in Western organizations (Nakamoto, 2012).

Can social intelligence be improved with training? Ken Rea (2010), who teaches acting at the Guildhall School of Music and Drama in London, tells this story:

> Recently, when I was coaching a senior manager of a multinational, he confided, 'When I speak in a meeting people cut me off. They don't seem to listen to my ideas. Then another person in the meeting will have the same idea and they will all listen to her. If I could fix that, I'd be happy'. We did a role play where he had to ask his chief executive for more resources. I sat in as the chief executive. He sat hunched.
>
> Now, when you sit like that, you are not going to be breathing properly and it will affect your voice, which will sound monotonous. It will also affect how you feel. He soon had a scowl on his face. I asked him to sit up, then to send out a more friendly energy. When we looked at the video recording afterwards, he was amazed. He never realised what negative signals he had been sending out. Suddenly he could see why people were cutting him off: there was absolutely no commitment to his message. He could see it in his body and hear it in his voice. But by sitting up straight and projecting a friendly energy, suddenly the voice brightened and became more powerful. The eyes came alive, and there on the screen was the commitment to what he was saying. Nobody would cut off this person. He walked out of the room a different man.
>
> © Rea, News International Trading Ltd, 10 October 2010

Social media and other digital tools appear to have made communication simpler. However, Karin Moser (2013) argues that difficulties arise if we do not consider the differences between virtual and F2F settings. Virtual communications offer fewer social and non-verbal cues, and provide limited information about the context in which others are working. The anonymity of virtual media reduces our awareness of the effect of our behaviour on others. People may be unhappy to collaborate with people in locations where the norms, rules and subcultures are different.

Communication is not a 'soft' function

The American consulting company Towers Watson (2013) argues that communication is key to organizational performance. Three factors now put a premium on 'communication effectiveness':

- **Workforce**: increasingly diverse workforce, with rising expectations of the employment deal.

- **The stakes**: the competitive advantage to be gained from 'discretionary effort' – the willingness of employees to 'go the extra mile' to improve company performance.

- **Shorter timelines**: the need to communicate rapidly, driven by developments in technology and globalization, tighter resources and increased concerns for security.

From a global survey of 650 organizations, they found that those with effective communication practices were three times more likely to show superior financial performance, compared with those which did not use those practices. The best practices were:

1. helping employees to understand the business;
2. educating employees about organization culture and values;
3. providing information on financial objectives and organizational performance;
4. integrating new employees;
5. communicating how employee actions affect customers;

6. providing information about the value of individuals' total compensation package;

7. asking for rapid feedback from employees about their opinions of the company.

Towers Watson also argues that effective organizations categorize employees into groups based on the value of their skills and on personal characteristics. This employee 'segmentation' means that communication strategy can be tailored to focus on behaviours that are critical to performance. The most effective companies pay close attention to employees when they are planning change, evaluating culture, and assessing readiness and the impact of change. Middle and frontline managers need to be good at: articulating what employees need to do differently to be successful, communicating what change means to individual employees, and creating a sense of ownership about change initiatives.

Thomas J. Allen demonstrated in the 1970s that the frequency with which we communicate depends on distance (see Allen and Henn, 2006). At that time, we were four times more likely to communicate regularly with someone who was two metres away from us than with someone who was 20 metres away, and we rarely communicated with colleagues on separate floors or in other buildings. He expressed this finding in 'the Allen curve' (Figure 7.1).

Does distance matter in today's digitally connected world? Yes it does. Research by Ben Waber et al. (2014) shows that the Allen curve is still valid, and that proximity seems to have become more important as the technology has developed. In one of their studies, engineers sharing an office were 20 per cent more likely to communicate digitally than those who worked at other locations. When close collaboration was necessary, colleagues in the same location sent four times the volume of emails compared with those in other locations, leading to faster project completion times. Waber et al. (2014, p.73) conclude, 'out of sight, out of sync'.

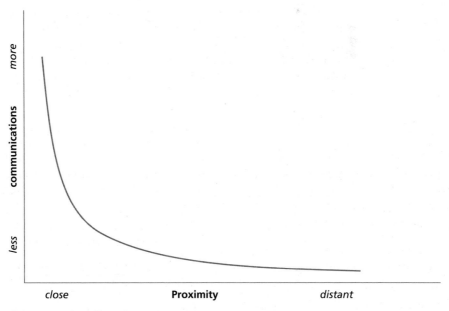

Figure 7.1: The Allen curve

Moser (2013, p.29) offers advice on how to manage virtual collaboration effectively:

1. Set rules for communication etiquette; always confirm receipt of message, use proper address and greeting in every message; find acceptable compromises in multicultural contexts.

2. If in doubt, communicate – as you would if the person were sitting next to you.

3. Increase transparency (about goals, tasks, rules) – because this helps to build trust.

4. Train staff in the differences between F2F and virtual communications.

5. Assess staff language skills, as virtual media are more heavily based on written communication, and those who are not good writers may be disadvantaged.

Instead of making our communication easier, Moser (2013, p.29) argues that,

> Virtual work requires much more frequent and elaborate communication and thus much more effort compared to traditional work settings. Things that literally work 'without saying' in a face-to-face context need to be made explicit, discussed and agreed on in a virtual work context. This is only possible if there is an awareness of the central differences in working face-to-face versus virtually, and if the employees have both the motivation and the ability to engage in that extra effort.

Interpersonal communication

Conversation: a competitive sport in which the first person to draw breath is declared the listener.

Communication process the transmission of information, and the exchange of meaning, between at least two people.

In most cultures, conversation is a social imperative in which silences are discouraged (Finland is different). Normally, as soon as one person stops talking, another takes their turn. The currency of conversation is information. We ask you the time. You tell us the time. Information has been transmitted. Interpersonal communication has been achieved. However, the **communication process** is often more subtle and interesting.

We will first focus on interpersonal communication. A more detailed study would recognize the importance of other aspects of communication, including the use of different media, networks and inter-organizational communication. The principles that we will explore, however, have wide application. For the moment, let us focus on 'one-on-one' or 'F2F' communication.

STOP AND THINK

We all have experience of ineffective communication. Either the other person misunderstood what you had to say, or you misunderstood them. Remember the last time this happened: what went wrong? What caused that communication to fail? Share your analysis with colleagues to see whether there are common causes.

We do not receive communication passively. We have to interpret or decode the message. To the extent that we interpret communication from others in the manner they intended, and they in turn interpret our messages correctly, then communication is effective. However, communication is an error-prone process.

Interpersonal communication involves much more than the transfer of information. Pay attention to the next person who asks you what time it is. You will often be able to tell how they are feeling, and about why they need to know, if they are in a hurry, perhaps, or if they are anxious or nervous, or bored with waiting. In other words, their question has a purpose or a meaning. Although it is not always stated directly, we can often infer that meaning from the context and from their behaviour.

The same considerations apply to your response. Your reply suggests, at least, a willingness to be helpful, may imply friendship, and may also indicate that you share the same concern as the person asking the question (we are going to be late; when will this film start?). However, your reply can also indicate frustration and annoyance: 'five minutes later than the last time you asked me!' Communication thus involves the transmission of both information and meaning.

Coding the stage in the interpersonal communication process in which the transmitter chooses how to express a message for transmission to someone else.

Decoding the stage in the interpersonal communication process in which the recipient interprets a message transmitted to them by someone else.

Perceptual filters individual characteristics, predispositions and preoccupations that interfere with the effective transmission and receipt of messages.

This process of exchange is illustrated in Figure 7.2, which shows the main elements of interpersonal communication. This model is based on the work of Claude Shannon and Warren Weaver (1949), who were concerned with signal processing in electronic systems, rather than with organizational communication. At the heart of this model, we have a transmitter sending a message to a receiver. We will assume that the channel is face-to-face, rather than text, telephone or email. It is useful to think of the way in which the transmitter phrases and expresses the message as a *coding* process; the transmitter chooses words, and also how the message will be expressed (loud and with exasperation, quiet and in a friendly manner, for example). The success of our communication depends on the accuracy of the receiver's *decoding*; did they understand the language used, and appreciate the exasperation or friendship? We each have our own *perceptual filters* which can interfere with accurate decoding, such as predispositions to hear, or not to hear, particular types of information, and preoccupations which divert our attention elsewhere.

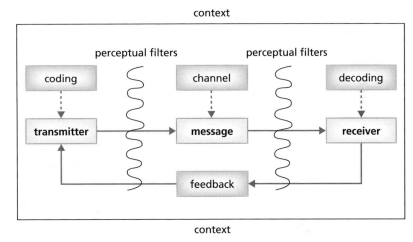

Figure 7.2: Exchanging meaning: a model of the communication process

There are many ways in which coding and decoding can go wrong. For example, without a shared 'codebook', some common words can lead to misunderstandings:

Term	Popular use	Dictionary definition
decimate	devastate	cut by 10 per cent
exotic	colourful, glamorous	from another country
aggravate	to annoy, to irritate	to make worse
clinical	cold, impersonal	caring, at the bedside of the sick
avid	enthusiastic	greedy

STOP AND THINK

Which communication skills do employers value most? Which communications skills are taught most often on business school programmes?

Studies have found that listening is the workplace communication skill most valued by employers, followed by conversing (interviewing, for example), and then presenting. However, a study of business schools found that they had their priorities the other way round, concentrating on students' presentation skills, followed by conversing, and paying little attention to listening skills (Brink and Costigan, 2015).

How does your programme prioritize these skills? Do you need to speak to your instructors about this? How can you fill gaps in your skills development for yourself?

Decoding UK civil service jargon

As a British tourist visiting another country, what help will you get from the UK Foreign Office when something goes wrong? Here is a guide to what you can expect (Burgess, 2015):

What they say	What they mean
'offered consular assistance'	'we've told them our phone number'
'receiving consular assistance'	'they've spoken to us and been told that it's nothing to do with us, especially at weekends'

The Home Office also has its own code to indicate when something is going to happen (Kidd, 2015):

What they say	What they mean
'quickly'	two weeks
'almost there'	four weeks
'as fast as humanly possible'	nine weeks
'by the summer'	before the end of November
'it will take a while'	never

Language is also used to 'soften' or to disguise unpleasant events. Employees being made redundant, for example, may be 'given the pink slip', 'downsized', 'demised', 'right-sized', 'delayered', invited to 'take gardening leave', to 'spend more time with the family', or to 'put their careers on hold'. They may also be 'transitioned out of the company', 'repositioned', invited to 'develop their careers elsewhere', but are rarely 'fired'. In some organizations, there are no 'problems and difficulties', only 'challenges and opportunities'. Do students 'fail' exams, or do they experience 'deferred success'.

The communication process is made more complex by the perceptual filters which affect what we say, and which in turn affect what we hear and how we hear it. When you asked what time it was, did you 'hear' the frustration or friendship in the response? Or did you simply focus on the information, because that was more important to you? The transmitter of a message has motives, objectives, personality traits, values, biases and prejudices, which colour the content and expression of communication. We decide the information we wish to reveal, and which to withhold from others, but our filtering is not always conscious. Similarly, at the receiving end, filtering can affect what is heard, what is decoded, what is not decoded, and the way in which the message is understood.

The physical, social and cultural context also affect the communication process. The casual remark by a colleague across a café table ('we could all be redundant by Christmas') may be dismissed. The same casual remark by a colleague across an office desk could cause alarm. An innocent gesture in one culture causes offence in another. The style and content of our conversation often depends on our relationships with others. Status differences colour our communication. We do not reveal to the boss what we discuss with colleagues. The style and content of communication can change in a striking manner when normal organizational relationships are 'suspended', such as during an office party.

Noise factors outside the communication process which interfere with or distract attention from the transmission and reception of the intended meaning.

Anything that interferes with a communication signal is called **noise** by electronics experts.

Communication suffers from noise, a term which covers more than just the sound of machinery and other people talking. Noise includes coding and decoding problems and errors, perceptual filters, and any other factors that damage the integrity of our chosen channel, including issues arising from our relationships with others. Our motives, emotions and health can constitute noise; coding and decoding are affected by anxiety, pressure, stress, and by enthusiasm and excitement.

Our past experiences also affect the way in which we see things today, and lead us to filter what we transmit and what we receive. Communication stumbles when transmitter and receiver have different frames of reference, and do not share experience and understanding, even where they share a common language. We make judgements about the honesty, integrity, trustworthiness and credibility of others, and decode their messages and act on them (or not) accordingly. People in an organizational setting may have time to reflect, or they may be under time pressure, or 'communication overload'.

There is a final aspect of our communication model which we have to consider: feedback.

Feedback (communication) processes through which the transmitter of a message detects whether and how that message has been received and decoded.

When we communicate face to face, we can usually tell if the other person likes us, if they agree with us, and if they are interested in what we have to say – or not. How do we know this? Well, they may say, 'that's interesting', or 'I disagree', or 'I have to catch my flight'. We can also tell from cues such as the tone of their replies, their facial expression, body posture and limb gestures. We will explore the coding and decoding of *non-verbal communication* (body language) later in the chapter.

When we communicate face to face, we get instant feedback, from what others say, and how they say it. This helps us to exchange information more effectively. Communication can be awkward where feedback is delayed, or absent. We ask a question, see the other person look annoyed or puzzled, see that we have not worded our question correctly, and 'recode' the message. Face to face, if we pay attention, this works well. With more formal and distant forms of communication, feedback can be partial, delayed or non-existent, and we need to be more careful about our coding.

STOP AND THINK

With whom do you communicate often? What prevents effective communication in your experience? How can you improve the effectiveness of your communication?

The communication process is prone to errors arising on both sides of the exchange. We cannot confidently assume that receivers will always decode our messages in a way that gives them the meaning that we wanted to send. Communication is also central to organizational effectiveness, and this has practical implications. We assume that organizations function better where:

- communications are open;
- relationships are based on mutual understanding and trust;
- interactions are based on cooperation rather than competition;
- people work together in teams; and
- decisions are reached in a participative way.

These features, however, are not universal, and do not feature in all countries or cultures. The main barriers to effective organizational communication are:

Power differences	Research consistently shows that employees distort upward communication, and that superiors often have a limited understanding of subordinates' roles, experiences and problems.
Gender differences	Men and women use different conversational styles which can lead to misunderstanding; men tend to talk more and give information while women tend to listen and reflect more.
Physical surroundings	Room size and layout influence our ability to see others and our readiness to participate in conversations and discussions.
Language	Even within one country, variations in accent and dialect can make communication difficult.
Cultural diversity	Different cultures have different norms and expectations concerning formal and informal conversations; lack of awareness of those norms creates misunderstanding.

Maureen Guirdham (2002) offers this advice for improving communications:

Face to face	When we are able to speak to someone directly, we can use the feedback to check the coding and decoding, and to correct mistakes and misunderstanding.
Reality checks	We should not assume that others will decode our messages in the way we intended, and we should check how our messages have been interpreted.
Place and time	The right message delivered in the wrong place or at the wrong time is more likely to be decoded incorrectly, or ignored; choose the time and place with care.
Empathetic listening	See things from the other person's point of view, consider the thinking that may have led to their behaviour, decode the message the way they might decode it, listen attentively to feedback.

Verbal communication

The word 'verbal' also causes decoding problems. Verbal means 'in words', which can be either spoken or written. 'Verbal agreement' and 'verbal warning' can thus refer either to oral or to written communication, and both are contrasted with non-verbal communication.

Questioning techniques

How do we get the information we want from a conversation? We do this by using different questioning techniques. The main types of question are shown in Table 7.2. The first basic distinction in questioning strategy is between closed and open questions. Closed questions invite a factual statement in reply, or a simple yes or no response. Open questions invite the person responding to give us more information. Predict the different response to these two questions:

Will you have dinner with me this evening?

What are you doing this evening?

Table 7.2: Questioning techniques

Question types	Illustration	Uses
Closed	Did you enjoy the movie?	To get a 'yes' or 'no' answer; to obtain factual information; to establish conversation control
Open	What did you think of that movie?	To introduce a subject; to encourage further discussion; to keep the other person talking
Probe	Can you tell me more about that?	To follow up an open question; to get more information; to demonstrate interest
Reflective	You thought the acting was poor?	To show interest and concern; to encourage further disclosure of feelings
Multiple	What did you think of the movie, and wasn't the star excellent in that role, and didn't you think that the ending was predictable?	Confuses the listener; gives them a choice of question to which to respond
Leading	You didn't see anyone leaving the house?	To get the answer that you expect to hear (so, why ask?)
Hypothetical	What would happen if . . .?	To encourage creative thinking

When we are lying, we may unconsciously send non-verbal 'deceit cues', which include rapid shifts in gaze, fidgeting in our seats, long pauses and frequent speech corrections. When lying, it is important to control these cues, ensuring that verbal and non-verbal messages are consistent. Similarly, when we want to emphasize the sincerity or strength of our feelings, it is important that the non-verbal signals we send are consistent with the verbal message.

Lie detectors

Adrian Furnham (2005) identifies several (UK) verbal and non-verbal 'lie detectors'. However, in other cultures, these cues may constitute normal interpersonal behaviour and may *not* signal deceit.

Verbal cues

Response latency	The time between the end of a question and the start of a reply. Liars take longer, hesitate more.
Linguistic distance	Not saying, 'I', but talking in the abstract: for example, 'one might believe that . . .'
Slow, uneven speech	As an individual tries to think through their lies. They might also suddenly talk quickly, attempting to make a sensitive subject appear less significant.
Too eager to fill gaps in conversation	Liars keep talking when it is unnecessary, as if a silence signifies that the other person does not believe them.
Too many pitch raises	Instead of the pitch dropping at the end of a reply, it is lifted in the same way as asking a question.

Non-verbal cues

Too much squirming	Someone shifting around in their seat is signalling their desire not to be there.
Too much eye contact, rather than too little	Liars tend to overcompensate. They need to look at you to monitor how successful they are being.
Micro-expressions	Flickers of surprise, hurt or anger that are difficult to detect. Sudden facial expressions of pain are often giveaways.
An increase in comfort gestures	These often take the form of self-touching, particularly around the nose and mouth.
More stuttering and slurring	Including what are known as 'Freudian slips'.
A loss of resonance in the voice	It tends to become flatter and more monotonous.

STOP AND THINK

Say out loud exactly the same sentence, 'This is a really interesting textbook', in two different ways, with opposite meanings.

Non-verbal communication is a 'relationship language' (Guirdham, 2002, p.184). This is how we communicate trust, boredom, submission, dislike and friendship without revealing our feelings directly. For example, when someone wants to signal liking or friendship, they will turn their body towards you, look you straight in the face, establish eye contact, look away infrequently, and nod and smile a lot, keeping their hands and arms by their sides or in front of them. This pattern or combination of behaviours is called an *open or positive* non-verbal cluster. When decoding non-verbal communication, it is important to note the pattern of behaviours.

**Luckily for Karen, her management training had included
a session on detecting negative body language.**

Source: Mike Seddon

The typical *closed or negative* non-verbal behaviour cluster, indicating disagreement or dislike, involves turning your body away, folding your arms tightly, crossing your legs so that they point away from the other person, loss of eye contact, wandering gaze, looking at someone else or at the door (suggesting a desire to leave), and a lack of nods and smiles. If you are observant, you can often tell that someone does not like what you are saying before they talk to you about it. The context is also important. We adopt closed postures when we are unwell, anxious or cold.

Interpreting gesture clusters

Cluster signals	Indicating
Flexible open posture, open hands, display of palms and wrists, removing jacket, moving closer to other person, leaning forward in chair, uncrossed arms and legs, smiling, nodding, eye contact	Openness
Rigid, closed posture, arms and legs tightly crossed, eyes glancing sideways, minimal eye contact, frowning, no smiling, pursed lips, clenched fists, head down, flat tone of voice	Defensiveness
Drumming fingers, head cupped in palm of hand, foot swinging, brushing or picking lint from clothing, body pointing towards exit, repeatedly looking at watch, the exit, a book	Boredom, impatience
Small inward smile, erect body posture, hands open and arms extended outwards, eyes wide and alert, lively walk, expressive and well-modulated voice	Enthusiasm
Knitted forehead, deadpan expression, tentative nodding or smiling, one slightly raised eyebrow, strained voice, saying 'I understand' while looking away	Lack of understanding
Blank expression, phoney smile, tight posture, arms stiff at side, sudden eye shifts, nervous tapping, sudden mood shifts, speech toneless and soft or too loud and animated	Stress

The dilation and contraction of our pupils is beyond our direct control, unlike our hand movements; but our eyes also send non-verbal information. Our pupils dilate in low light, and when we see something or someone interesting. Dilation conveys honesty, openness and sexual attraction. Our pupils also dilate when we are relaxed, and when consuming alcohol and other drugs. Context is again critical to accurate decoding. Contracted pupils can signify low lighting conditions, or lack of interest, distrust, hostility, stress, sorrow, or a hangover. It is only possible to decode pupil dilation or contraction with reference to other non-verbal clues, and to the context.

Someone who is anxious usually displays 'self-manipulation': stroking lips or an ear lobe, playing with hair. Anxiety can also be signalled by shifting direction of gaze. Some friendship signals can be amusing to observe. When we meet someone to whom we are attracted, we often use 'preening gestures': smoothing our clothes, stroking our hair, straightening our posture. Watch a group of friends and you will often see them standing, sitting, and even holding cups or glasses in an almost identical manner. This is known as 'posture mirroring'. You can often spot the 'outsider' as the one not using the posture. Friendship groups copy each other's gestures, known as 'gesture mirroring'.

Power tells non-verbal signals that indicate to others how important and dominant someone is, or how powerful they would like us to *think* they are.

We also use non-verbal communication to show how important we are with **power tells** (Chapter 22).

The power tells that dominant people display include using open postures and invasive hand gestures, smiling less, looking away while speaking, speaking first and dominating the conversation, and interrupting others. Signals which suggest a submissive attitude include modifying your speech to sound like the other person, hesitations (lots of 'ums' and 'ers'), close postures and self-comfort gestures such as clasping your hands, and touching your face and hair (Collett, 2004).

Leading politicians also use non-verbal gestures to signal their dominance (Kirton, 2014). As a 'positive power gesture', Angela Merkel (Germany) grips and then pats the shoulder of political colleagues. To signal that he is confidently in control, Barack Obama (USA) holds his hands in front of him, palms facing inwards, as if holding an invisible brick. Political leaders also tend to speak with a deeper voice (Margaret Thatcher, UK), walk with a sense of purpose to appear young and energetic (Ronald Reagan, USA), and make eye contact while shaking hands (Bill Clinton, USA).

AP Photo/Michael Sohn

Mandel Ngan-Pool/Getty Images

Saying 'sorry' without saying anything

In Japan, the way in which bosses bow indicate how sorry the company is for mistakes, such as Toyota's recall of 8 million cars in 2010 due to faulty accelerator pedals.

A slight bow from the waist, not held for very long, indicates a mild apology.

A deeper bow, at an angle of about 45 degrees, and lasting for about one and a half seconds, suggests contrition, without accepting personal responsibility.

A full 90-degree bow, held for up to seven seconds, indicates personal and/or official responsibility for an incident that has caused significant damage, and for which the person is asking forgiveness.

The most extreme form of bow involves kneeling with one's head on the floor for perhaps 30 seconds. This indicates that 'The law may punish me, but that does not cover how sorry I am'.

When Toyota recalled its cars, the company president Akio Toyoda performed a 25-degree bow, suggesting that he was 'quite sorry': 'In bowing terms, it holds the same apology value as you might get from a waiter who had forgotten your order' (Lewis and Lea, 2010).

Cultural differences in communication style

The use and interpretation of non-verbal communication differ from culture to culture. In Japan, smiling and nodding implies understanding, but not necessarily agreement. In Australia, raising the pitch of your voice at the end of a sentence signifies openness to challenge or question, not a lie. In some Asian cultures, it is impolite to give superiors direct and prolonged eye contact; a bowed head signals deference and not lack of self-confidence or defensiveness. People from northern European cultures prefer a lot of personal space and rarely touch each other. French, Italians and Latin Americans stand closer together and touch more often to indicate agreement and friendship.

Simple gestures must also be used with care. Make a circle with your thumb and forefinger, extending the other three fingers. How will this be interpreted? In America, and to scuba divers, it means 'OK'. In Japan, it means money. In France, it means zero or nothing. In some Arab countries, it signifies a curse. In Germany and Brazil, it is obscene.

High context culture a culture whose members rely heavily on a range of social and non-verbal clues when communicating with others and interpreting their messages.

Low context culture a culture whose members focus on the written and spoken word when communicating with others and interpreting their messages.

Edward Hall (1976, 1989) distinguished between high context culture and low context culture.

High context culture	Low context culture
Establish relationship first	Get down to business first
Value personal relations and goodwill	Value expertise and performance
Agreement based on trust	Agreement based on legal contract
Slow and ritualistic negotiations	Fast and efficient negotiations

China, Korea, Japan and Vietnam are high context cultures, where people tend to take a greater interest in your position, your business card, your dress, material possessions and other signs of status. Written and spoken communications are not ignored, but they are secondary. Agreements can be made on a handshake, on someone's word.

North America, Scandinavia, Switzerland and Germany are low context cultures, where people pay secondary attention to non-verbal messages. People in German organizations tend to be preoccupied with detailed written rules, and Americans like to have precise legal documents. Agreements are not made until the contract is in writing, and it is signed.

These categorizations reflect tendencies and are not absolute. Most countries have subcultures with very different norms. In addition, men tend to be more high context than women, but this observation does not apply to all men or to all women. Nevertheless, it is easy to see how misunderstanding can arise when high and low context cultures meet, unless those communicating are sensitive to their respective differences. You can reduce these misunderstandings with the following four rules (Robbins et al., 2010, p.307):

1. *assume that others are different*, unless you can establish otherwise; we tend to assume that others are more like us than they often are, so you are less likely to make a mistake if you assume difference until you can prove similarity

2. *use description and avoid evaluation*, until you have had time to observe and understand the perspectives of the other culture, or cultures, as interpretations and evaluations are based on cultural background rather than on what you observe

3. *practice empathy*, putting yourself in the other person's position, understanding their values, background and experience, and frames of reference

4. *treat interpretations as working hypotheses*, and keep testing and questioning your conclusions and explanations, using feedback and checking with colleagues.

Aboriginal culture and communication

Australian Aboriginal culture uses verbal and non-verbal communication in ways that are different from European and North American communication styles (Nelson-Jones, 2000):

- Aborigines value brevity in verbal communication rather than detailed elaboration, and simple 'yes' and 'no' replies are common.

- There is no word for 'thank you' in Aboriginal languages. People do things for you as an obligation.

- In some Aboriginal tribes, it is unlawful to use the name of a dead person.

- The terms 'full-blood', 'half-caste', 'quarter-caste', 'native' and 'part-Aborigine' are regarded as offensive by Aborigines.

- Long silences in Aboriginal conversation are common and are not regarded as awkward.

- To some Aboriginal people, it is not acceptable to look another straight in the eye.

- Some Aboriginal groups do not allow men and women to mix freely.

- Aborigines feel that it is not necessary to look at the person who is speaking to them.

- Aborigines do not feel that it is necessary to attend meetings (an interview, for example) at specific times.

How do these norms and preferences compare with the communication style of your culture?

Impression management

Impression management the processes through which we control the image or impression that others have of us.

We usually send and receive non-verbal messages unconsciously. However, it is possible to control the non-verbal signals that we send, and to be aware of and to read the cues that others are giving to us. This level of attention and control can be difficult to sustain, but it can be important in organizational settings, especially where we want to control the image or impression that others have of us. We can do this through impression management techniques, based originally on the work of Erving Goffman (1959).

Paul Rosenfeld and colleagues (2001) note that our impression management methods are rich and varied, including:

- what we do and how we do it;
- what we say and how we say it;
- the furnishings and arrangement of our offices;
- our physical appearance including clothes and makeup;
- non-verbal communication such as facial expressions or postures.

Effective impression management means being consciously aware and in control of the cues that we send to others through verbal and non-verbal channels. This suggests that we consciously seek to manipulate the impression or perceptions that others have of us.

STOP AND THINK

Is impression management simply a form of deceit? What in your view are the ethical problems raised by the advice that we should consciously manipulate the impression that others have of us through verbal and non-verbal communication?

Do you use, or do you avoid, impression management methods when you are deciding what to wear to go to parties, clubs, job interviews, lectures?

As with conversation controls, we can use impression management to manipulate the behaviour of others. We do this, for example, by 'giving off' the impression that we are friendly, submissive, apologetic, angry, defensive, confident, intimidating, and so on. The more effectively we manage our impression, the greater the control we can achieve in social interaction, and the greater our power to pursue our preferred outcomes over others.

Some people regard impression management as acting. However, we manage our impression all the time. It is hardly possible to avoid sending signals through, for example, our dress, posture, facial expressions, gestures, tone and pitch of voice, and even location in a room. We can distinguish between conscious (by implication more effective) and unconscious (by implication less effective, or misleading) impression management. Conscious impression management has many advantages. Interactions run more smoothly when we give the correct signals to others who in turn accurately decode these signals of our attitudes and intents. Impression management is a critical skill in many organizational contexts, such as counselling, and in selection, appraisal and disciplinary interviews.

The ethics of impression management

At first, Richard Nixon vowed he would not debate John Kennedy. He had little to gain from such an encounter, and much to lose. As vice-president, he was better known than the young senator and universally considered a heavyweight. But in the end his fear of appearing fearful overcame his caution. It was a mistake. The camera is unkind to men who look shifty.

At the first debate in 1960, Nixon was not feeling well. After hearing Kennedy turn down the offer of makeup, he turned it down too, although it might have covered his five o'clock shadow. Kennedy got his aides to apply makeup when Nixon wasn't looking, and presented a tanned and handsome face to the nation. Nixon looked like a sweaty corpse. Radio listeners thought he did well. But on television, Kennedy won by a mile (*The Economist*, 2008).

In your judgement, was John F. Kennedy's behaviour ethical at that debate in 1960?

Reuters/Str Old

Library of Congress/Getty Images

Home viewing

Catch Me If You Can (2003, directed by Steven Speilberg) is a comedy drama based on the true story of the forger and confidence trickster Frank Abagnale Jr (played by Leonardo Di Caprio) and the FBI agent Carl Hanratty (Tom Hanks) who finally apprehends him, but not before Frank has committed millions of dollars-worth of fraud. Frank is a master of the art of impression management, effortlessly convincing others that he is, at various stages in his 'career' a newspaper journalist, high school teacher, airline pilot, doctor and lawyer. He is so convincing that, when he does at one point decide to reveal the truth, his fiancé's father (Martin Sheen) does not believe him. Note examples of how Frank combines non-verbal communication, courtship techniques, avoidance of lie detection cues, paralanguage and gesture clusters to manage the impression that he wants to convey.

Most practical advice concerns how to make a good impression, for example in a job interview. Andrew DuBrin (2011, pp.76–7) identifies tactics for creating a *negative* impression of yourself. Here are the tactics that you should avoid:

- mumbling, putting your hand over your mouth, not using facts to persuade someone;
- writing business email messages in the style that teenagers use when texting and tweeting;
- appearing immature, unprofessional and uninterested;
- ignoring colleagues while they are talking, by looking at your watch, taking a mobile phone call, checking text messages;
- making immature excuses for being late – 'my alarm clock broke', 'the traffic was bad';
- denying rather than apologizing for your own mistakes;
- appearing unenthusiastic and bored when others talk about their problems;
- when asked a job-related question, you reply, 'I don't know, I haven't googled it yet'.

Deborah Tannen
(b.1945)

Do men and women use impression management tactics in different ways? Deborah Tannen (1990, 1995) argued that girls and boys learn different linguistic styles – characteristic speaking patterns – which create communication barriers, and affect career prospects. Her research found that, while girls learn to develop rapport, boys learn that status is more important. Girls focus on a small group of friends, emphasizing similarities, and playing down ways in which someone could be better than others. Girls tend to be modest, less self-assured and ostracize those who claim superiority. Boys play in large groups, emphasize status and leadership, display their knowledge and abilities, challenge others, take 'centre stage' by telling jokes and stories, and try to acquire status in their group by giving orders. This childhood learning follows girls and boys into adult life.

Tannen's arguments are still valid. Kathryn Heath et al. (2014) studied successful and ambitious women who said that they were not being taken seriously in critical high-level meetings. They were ignored, and found it hard to break into the conversation, so their ideas were overlooked. Men are aware of this problem. After a meeting, one male manager said to a female colleague, 'Stop acting like a facilitator. Start saying what you stand for'. The researchers analysed feedback that had been collected on 1,100 female executives, surveyed 250 female managers in Fortune 500 organizations, and interviewed 65 top male and female executives from large multinational companies.

The research found that, although men and women agreed on the problems, they disagreed on the causes. For example, men said that they were concerned that women would respond negatively to criticism. Women, on the other hand, complained that they did not get feedback, even when they asked for it. Men said that women should be more concise when making a point. Women said that they did not want to repackage old ideas or to state the obvious. Men observed that women were more emotional than men, but women said that 'it's not emotion – it's passion'. Heath et al. (2014, pp.120–1) suggest three steps to help women become more comfortable and effective in what are still male-dominated settings:

- *Groundwork*: Ideas are tested, and decisions are taken in informal meetings that happen before the main meeting. That is why men often arrive for meetings early and leave late, to sound people out, and build alliances. Women need to do this, too, to 'master the pre-meeting'.

- *Preparation*: Women prefer formal presentations, which men avoid. However, key points, relevant comments and interesting questions can be written down in advance, and 'off-the-cuff' remarks can be rehearsed. Women should '*prepare* to speak spontaneously'.

- *Emotion control*: Although passion can be persuasive, when women felt passionate about an idea, men saw 'too much emotion'. Women must appear to be in command, speak with an even tone, accept that confrontation is not personal, and avoid signalling frustration.

The differences between women and men are not always as clear as this brief discussion suggests. Research findings are often expressed in terms of averages, tendencies and predispositions. Many women do not fit the Tannen profile. Heath et al. (2014, p.119) suggest that 'men with more reserved personalities' will find their advice useful, along with members of racial and ethnic minorities.

Emotional intelligence

Emotional intelligence the ability to identify, integrate, understand and reflectively manage one's own and other people's feelings.

Non-verbal communication is one way in which we display emotion. While often embarrassing, an open show of emotion can sometimes be desirable. Emotions are a key source of motivation. Inability to display and share feelings can be a handicap. Sharing feelings of frustration and anger can be as important in an organizational setting as showing positive feelings of, for example, praise, satisfaction and friendship. The ability to handle emotions can be regarded as a skill, which can be developed with training, but some regard this skill as a personality dimension (see Chapter 6).

The concept of emotional intelligence (EQ) was first developed by Peter Salovey and John D. Mayer (1990) who argued that the concept of 'rational' intelligence ignores emotional competencies.

The concept was popularized by Daniel Goleman (2005; Goleman et al., 2013), who argues that EQ is more important to career success than technical skills or rational intelligence. Goleman's dimensions of EQ are summarized in Table 7.5.

Table 7.5: The five dimensions of emotional intelligence

Dimension	Definition	Hallmarks
1. **Self-awareness**	The ability to recognize and understand your moods, emotions and drives, and the effect you have on others	Self-confidence, realistic self-assessment, self-deprecating sense of humour
2. **Regulating feelings**	The ability to control your disruptive moods and impulses; the propensity to suspend judgement, to think before acting	Trustworthiness and integrity, comfortable with ambiguity, openness to change
3. **Motivation**	A passion to work for reasons beyond status and money; a propensity to pursue goals with energy and persistence	High achievement need, optimism even in the face of failure, organizational commitment
4. **Empathy**	The ability to recognize and understand the emotional makeup of others; skill in dealing with the emotional responses of others	Expertise in building and retaining talent; cross-cultural sensitivity; service to clients and customers
5. **Social skills**	Effectiveness in managing relationships and building networks; ability to find common ground, to build rapport	Effectiveness in leading change; persuasiveness; expertise in building and leading teams

Goleman claims that EQ gives us an advantage, at work and in social relationships, but that it is particularly important for top management, where conventional notions of intelligence are taken for granted. At senior levels, high EQ is a mark of the 'star performer'. There are several EQ assessments, and some commentators argue that EQ can be developed with experience and training.

"I keep a cold pack in my desk drawer to help me cool my emotions before I approach an argumentative student."

Source: Jantoo

However, EQ is a controversial concept. Different commentators use different definitions, and there is no agreed measure, although there are lots of questionnaires which say that they do this. From their review of the research, Frank Walter et al. (2011) conclude that EQ can help to explain behaviour, but that this is only one factor that affects an individual's job performance, and that we should treat exaggerated claims for the power of EQ with caution. Along with personality and functional skills, cognitive ability – traditional intelligence – is also important, even in jobs that are emotionally demanding (Smedley, 2014). Take the short emotional intelligence test below.

Who is about to explode?

Test your emotional intelligence. Look carefully at the microexpressions in each of these four portraits. Can you tell which one is about to 'blow'?

What clues did you use to reach that judgement?

(From *People Management*, December 2014)

Imagehit Limited/123RF.com

Rob Lewine/Getty Images

age-fotostock/SuperStock

Johner/SuperStock

Organizational communication

Many managers regard communication as a problem, and many employees feel that they are not fully informed about management plans. Employee communication has become more important, partly due to the volume of other information available through the internet, and because expectations, to be kept informed and to contribute ideas have increased.

A survey of 100 UK organizations in 2010 found that only 40 per cent had formal communication strategies. Companies with formal strategies were four times more likely to agree that this contributed to their success. The main goals of internal communication were keeping staff informed of changes and strategies, staff engagement, and providing updates on policies and procedures. Only one organization used communications to encourage new ideas and innovation. The most popular communication methods were department meetings, one-on-one meetings with line managers, team meetings, letters and memos, and email. Social media were unpopular: online video, instant messaging, internal blogging, wikis, Skype and podcasts were used by very few organizations, probably because these are seen as personal communication methods (Wolff, 2010).

There was no one best method. Face-to-face was seen as more successful than print or computer-based methods. Intranet sites were useful for providing information on policies, procedures and legal requirements. Top management briefings were considered best in terms of employee engagement, opinion surveys the best way to encourage feedback, and meetings with line managers the best way to improve individual performance.

One key management problem is to persuade employees to work in the interests of the organization as a whole. However, the interests of individuals and organizations do not always coincide. How can employee behaviour be channelled in the desired directions? In their seminal contribution to organizational behaviour, James March and Herbert Simon (1958) argued that management cannot change behaviour directly, or alter people's personalities. It is more effective and practical, they argue, to influence the premises on which people make their own decisions about how to behave.

Thirteen points for an effective communication strategy

1. Convince top management that communication is important.

2. Build alliances across the organization to support initiatives.

3. Recognize that no one method will be effective.

4. Use a mix of approaches and use all available channels where relevant.

5. Target communication to the audience; different methods for shop floor and managers.

6. Respect cultural diversity and vary approaches accordingly.

7. Make sure that messages are consistent, over time and between audiences.

8. Ensure clarity of message and keep things simple.

9. Train managers in communication skills.

10. Develop and sustain two-way communication, dialogue and feedback.

11. Ensure that employees feel that they can say what they think without discomfort.

12. Ensure that communication is built into the planning stages of all activities.

13. Review initiatives to check what has worked, what hasn't, and why.

(Cannell, 2010)

"Let's work on your communication style."

Source: 123RF

How can management influence the premises – the underlying assumptions – which affect the decisions of employees? For example, pay can be based on attendance, time-keeping and work rate (through piece rates and bonuses). Company rules, how these are enforced, and the terms in which they are expressed are also ways of 'signalling' or 'coding' desirable and undesirable behaviours. Desirable behaviours can be reinforced through the appraisal system which, in a retail store for example, can evaluate employee behaviours such as 'expresses ideas clearly, keeps others informed, shares knowledge, provides timely communication, listens and responds to customers'.

STOP AND THINK

How does your educational institution use rewards and sanctions to influence the decisions that you make about the nature and direction of your studies? What 'signals' do teaching staff send in order to communicate how they expect you to behave?

These 'signalling systems' are saying 'behave this way and you will be rewarded and/or promoted, but behave that way and you will be overlooked for promotion – or fired'. These systems are often complemented by the organization's vision and mission statements, and by statements of corporate values.

Better communication is often advocated by management consultants as a cure for many organizational problems such as low morale, high absenteeism and turnover, labour unrest and conflict, low productivity and resistance to change. This advice is based on the theory that, if people understand what is going on, then they will be more likely to follow management directions. A well-presented argument supported with compelling evidence should result in consensus and compliance. Is that always the case?

Organizations use a range of mechanisms for communicating with employees, such as:

- the management chain of command;
- regular meetings with senior and/or middle managers;
- in-house newspapers and magazines;
- company intranet;
- noticeboards;
- videos and in-house television;
- conferences and seminars;
- employee reports;
- team briefings;
- email, texts, blogs, podcasts.

Those are traditionally one-way, top-down modes of communication. Two-way exchanges are more effectively achieved through methods such as:

- social media (see Chapter 3);
- 'speak out' programmes in which problems are taken to counsellors;
- suggestion or 'bright ideas' schemes;
- open door policies;
- the appraisal system;
- quality circles;
- attitude surveys;
- interactive email (where managers guarantee to reply).

OB on the web

Search YouTube for video clips concerning 'body language' and 'impression management'. There are many to choose from. One of the best (which explores both of these topics) is 'Body language – indicators of interest' (15 minutes). These clips mostly offer tips and techniques, and 'do's and don'ts' for leaders and job interviewees in particular. Select two videos on each topic, based on how interesting and relevant they appear to you. As you watch, make notes on how you can improve your impression management and body language, particularly with regard to improving your employability. Note the behaviours that you could use, but also what to avoid.

CHAPTER EXERCISES

1. Impression management checklist

Objective   1. To assess aspects of the way in which you deal with other people.

Briefing   As you read each of the following 18 statements, ask yourself whether or not it applies to you, and answer (tick) 'yes' or 'no' accordingly. You will of course occasionally feel that you want to answer 'sometimes'. But try in each case to decide where your personal preferences, strengths and priorities really lie. You don't always get to sit on the fence. This is not a test with right or wrong answers. It is designed for personal reflection and group discussion (based on Snyder, 1987, p.179).

		Yes	No
1.	I find it hard to imitate the behaviour of other people.		
2.	At parties and gatherings, I do not attempt to do or say things that others will like.		
3.	I can only argue for ideas which I already believe.		
4.	I can make impromptu speeches even on topics about which I have almost no information.		
5.	I guess I put on a show to impress or entertain others.		
6.	I would probably make a good actor.		
7.	In a group of people, I am rarely the centre of attention.		
8.	In different situations and with different people, I often act like very different persons.		
9.	I am not particularly good at making other people like me.		
10.	I'm not always the person I appear to be.		
11.	I would not change my opinions or the way I do things in order to please someone or win their favour.		
12.	I have considered being an entertainer.		
13.	I have never been good at games like charades, or acting.		
14.	I have trouble changing my behaviour to suit different people and different situations.		
15.	At a party I let others keep the jokes and stories going.		
16.	I feel a bit awkward in company and do not show up quite as well as I should.		
17.	I can look anyone in the eye and tell a lie with a straight face, if for an appropriate reason.		
18.	I may deceive people by being friendly when I really dislike them.		

Scoring   You get either one point or zero, depending on how you responded to each statement. Simply add up the number of points you got.

Statement	Score		Your score
	Yes	No	
1	0	1	
2	0	1	
3	0	1	
4	1	0	
5	1	0	
6	1	0	
7	0	1	
8	1	0	
9	0	1	
10	1	0	
11	0	1	
12	1	0	
13	0	1	
14	0	1	
15	0	1	
16	0	1	
17	1	0	
18	1	0	
	Total:		

Interpretation

A score of 13 or more implies strong impression management skills:

Awareness: you are consciously aware of your own and other people's feelings and behaviour, and of how you affect others.

Flexibility: you are able to adjust what you say and do to match other people's expectations, and to achieve your goals.

Control: you are able consciously to control your behaviour, and thus to control other people; you probably enjoy this.

A score of 7 or less implies weak impression management skills:

Awareness: you are not always aware of your own or other people's feelings and behaviour, or of how you affect others.

Flexibility: you are unable to adjust what you say and do to match other people's expectations, and to achieve your goals.

Control: you are unable consciously to control your behaviour, and may feel uncomfortably manipulated at times.

A score between 8 and 12 implies moderate impression management skills. Read over the interpretations, and judge your strengths for yourself. Which way would you like to go – up or down?

Analysis   Whatever your own score, consider the following key issues:
1. To what extent are impression management skills learnable and to what extent are we born with them?
2. Is it unethical to adjust your behaviour in order to modify the feelings and behaviours of others?
3. Regardless of your own impression management score, in what ways would it benefit you to be more aware of how other people use these skills? Give specific examples.

2. How would you respond?

Objectives   1. To analyse the practical uses of questioning techniques and conversation controls.
2. To explore appropriate management options in dealing with employee grievances.

Briefing   Individually, read each of the three cases and choose your preferred responses.
For groups of three or four. As a group:

1. Decide the objective of the interaction with this person; what do you, as this person's supervisor, want to achieve by the end of the conversation?
2. What are the key issues relevant to the individual, team and organization in this situation?
3. Which is the best response of the four offered, and why?
4. Develop a fifth response, if you think that is desirable, and explain its strengths.
5. Plenary: Each group presents and explains its conclusions to the group as a whole.
6. Debriefing: Your instructor will lead a discussion of the implications of the different responses in each case, and of the key learning points from this exercise.

Here are statements from employees, directed at you, their immediate supervisor.

Situation A: Assistant Supervisor, age 30, computer manufacturing plant

'Yes, I do have a problem. I'd like to know more about what happened with the promotions last month. Charlie got the supervisor's job in motherboard assembly and I didn't even know he was interested. Why did you give the job to him? I would like to know more about what you think of my promotion prospects here. I've been doing this job for about three years now, and I've been with the company for almost five years. I haven't had any complaints about my work. Seems to me I've been doing a pretty good job, but I don't see any recognition for that. What do I have to do to get promoted round here?'

1. You'll make a great supervisor, Bill, but give it time. I'll do what I can to make your case. Don't be discouraged, OK? I'm sure you'll get there soon, you'll see.

2. So, you're not sure about how the company regards your work here?

3. I understand how you feel, but I have to admit it took me five years to make supervisor myself. And I guess I must have felt much the same way you do today. But we just have to be patient. Things don't always happen when we'd like them to, do they?

4. Come on, you've been here long enough to know the answer to that one. Nobody got promoted just by waiting for it to happen. Get with it, you've got to put yourself forward, make people stand up and take notice of your capabilities.

Situation B: Secretary, age 45, insurance company headquarters

'Can I ask you to do something about the calendars that Mr Johnson and Mr Hargreaves insist on displaying in their offices? They are degrading to women and I find them offensive. I know that some of the other secretaries who work on their floor feel exactly the same way as I do. I have to work with these men and I can't stay out of their offices. Don't we have a company policy or something? I'm surprised you've allowed it to go on this long as it is.'

1. You and some of the other secretaries find these calendars insulting?

2. Look, you're taking this all too seriously. Boys' toys, that's all it is, executive perks. Doesn't mean anything, and there's nothing personal behind it at all. You've no cause for concern.

3. You're right, I don't like that either, but we're talking about their own offices here, and I think that they have the right, within reason, to make their own decisions about what pictures to put on the walls, same as you and I do.

4. I'll see if I can't get a chance to have a quiet word with them sometime next week, maybe try to persuade them to move their calendars out of sight, OK? I'm sure they don't mean anything by it.

Situation C: Personnel Officer, age 26, local authority

'I've just about had it. I can't put up with this kind of pressure for much longer. We just don't have the staff to service the level of requests that we're getting and still do a good job. And some of the people we have to deal with! If that old witch in administration calls me one more time about those files that went missing last week, she's going to get a real mouthful in return. How come you let your department get pushed around like this?'

1. You're not alone. Pressure is something that we've all had to endure at some time. I understand that, it comes with the territory. I think it's about developing the right skills and attitudes to cope.

2. You're right, this is a difficult patch, but I'm sure that it will pass. This can't go on for much longer, and I expect you'll see things start to come right at the end of the month.

3. Well, if you can't stand the heat, I suppose you just have to get out of the kitchen. And please don't refer to people who are senior to you in this organization in that manner ever again.

4. Let me check – this is not about Mrs Smith in admin is it? You're saying the strain is such that you're thinking of leaving us?

Employability assessment

With regard to your future employment prospects:

1. Identify up to three issues from this chapter that you found significant.

2. Relate these to the competencies in the employability matrix.

3. Decide what actions you need to take to maintain and/or develop those competencies under each of the four headings of the employability matrix.

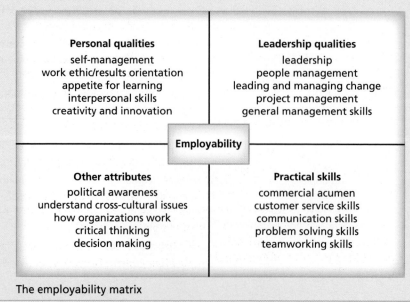

The employability matrix

References

Allen, T.J. and Henn, G. (2006) *The Organization and Architecture of Innovation: Managing the Flow of Technology*. London: Routledge.

Brink, K.E. and Costigan, R.D. (2015) 'Oral communication skills: are the priorities of the workplace and AACSB-accredited business programs aligned?', *Academy of Management Education & Learning*, 14 (2): 205–21.

Burgess, K. (2015) 'TMS diary', *The Times*, 4 March, p.11.

Burne, J. and Aldridge, S. (1996) 'Who do you think you are?', *Focus Extra*: 1–8.

Cannell, M. (2010) *Employee Communication Factsheet*. London: Chartered Institute for Personnel and Development.

Collett, P. (2004) 'Show and tell', *People Management*, 10(8): 34–35.

Chartered Management Institute (2014) *21st Century Leaders: Building Practice Into the Curriculum to Boost Employability*. London: Chartered Management Institute.

De Jorio, A. (2001) *Gesture in Naples and Gesture in Classical Antiquity* (Adam Kenton, Trans.). Bloomington, IN: Indiana University Press.

DeSteno, D. (2014) 'Who can you trust?', *Harvard Business Review*, 92 (3): 112–15.

DuBrin, A.J. (2011) *Impression Management in the Workplace: Research, Theory, and Practice*. New York and London: Routledge.

Evans, M. (2008) 'Charming the locals: a soldier's guide', *The Times*, 11 February, p.14.

Feldman, D.C. and Klich, N.R. (1991) 'Impression management and career strategies', in K. Giacalone and P. Rosenfeld (eds), *Applied Impression Management: How Image Making Affects Managerial Decisions*. London: Sage Publications, pp.67–80.

Furnham, A. (2005) *The Psychology of Behaviour at Work* (2nd edn). Hove, Sussex: Psychology Press/Taylor & Francis.

Gibb, J.R. (1961) 'Defensive communication', *Journal of Communication*, 11 (3): 141–48.

Goffman, E. (1959) *The Presentation of Self in Everyday Life*. New York: Doubleday Anchor.

Goleman, D. (2005) *Emotional Intelligence: Why It Can Matter More Than IQ*. London: Bloomsbury Publishing (first published 1995).

Goleman, D. (2007) *Social Intelligence: The New Science of Human Relationships*. London: Hutchinson.

Goleman, D., Boyatzis, R.E. and McKee, A. (2013) *Primal Leadership: Unleashing the Power of Emotional Intelligence*. Cambridge, MA: Harvard Business Press.

Guirdham, M. (2002) *Interactive Behaviour at Work* (3rd edn). Harlow, Essex: Financial Times Prentice Hall.

Hall, E.T. (1976) *Beyond Culture*. New York: Doubleday/Currency.

Hall, E.T. (1989) *Understanding Cultural Differences*. Yarmouth, ME: Intercultural Press.

Heath, K., Flynn, J. and Holt, M.D. (2014) 'Women, find your voice', *Harvard Business Review*, 92 (6): 118–21.

Kidd, P. (2015) 'TMS diary', *The Times*, 3 March, p.11.

Kirton, H. (2014) 'Reach for the brick', *People Management*, October, p.31.

Larker, D.F. and Zakolyukina, A.A. (2012) 'Detecting deceptive discussions in conference calls', *Rock Center for Corporate Governance, Working Paper Series No.83*. Stanford, CA: Stanford University.

Lewis, L. and Lea, R. (2010) 'Toyota chief bows to pressure over pedal defect', *The Times*, 6 February, p.13.

March, J. and Simon, H.A. (1958) *Organizations*. New York: Wiley.

Moser, K. (2013) 'Only a click away? – What makes virtual meetings, emails and outsourcing successful', in *CMI Management Articles of the Year 2013*. London: Chartered Management Institute, pp.25–30.

Nakamoto, M. (2012) 'Cross-cultural conversations', *Financial Times*, 12 January, p.16.

Nelson-Jones, R. (2000) *Introduction to Counselling Skills: Text and Activities*. London: Sage Publications.

Pease, A. (2014) *Body Language: How to Read Others' Thoughts by Their Gestures*. London: Manjul Publishing.

Quirke, B. (2008) *Making the Connections: Using Internal Communication to Turn Strategy into Action*. Aldershot: Gower Publishing.

Rea, K. (2010) 'Leaders must act like they mean it', *The Sunday Times, Appointments Section*, 10 October, p.4.

Robbins, S.P., Judge, T.A. and Campbell, T.T. (2010) *Organizational Behaviour*. Harlow, Essex: Financial Times Prentice Hall.

Rosenfeld, P., Giacalone, R.A. and Riordan, C.A. (2001) *Impression Management: Building and Enhancing Reputations at Work*. London: Thomson Learning.

Salovey, P. and Mayer, J.D. (1990) 'Emotional intelligence', *Imagination, Cognition and Personality*, 9: 185–211.

Shannon, C.E. and Weaver, W. (1949) *The Mathematical Theory of Communication*. Urbana, IL: University of Illinois Press.

Smedley, T. (2014) 'Who's the most "intelligent"?', *People Management*, December, pp.24–30.

Snyder, M. (1987) *Public Appearance and Private Realities: The Psychology of Self-Monitoring*. New York: W.H. Freeman.

Tannen, D. (1990) *You Just Don't Understand: Women and Men in Conversation*. New York: William Morrow.

Tannen, D. (1995) 'The power of talk: who gets heard and why', *Harvard Business Review*, 73 (5): 138–48.

The Economist (2008) 'Debating the debates', Lexington, 11 October, p.62.

The Economist (2015) 'James Bond's body language', 24 January, p.40.

Towers Watson (2013) *How the Fundamentals Have Evolved and the Best Adapt: Change and Communication Report 2013–2014*. New York: Towers Watson.

Waber, B., Magnolfi, J. and Lindsay, G. (2014) 'Workspaces that move people', *Harvard Business Review*, 92 (10): 69–77.

Walter, F., Cole, M.S. and Humphrey, R.H. (2011) 'Emotional intelligence: sine qua non of leadership or folderol?', *Academy of Management Perspectives*, 25 (1): 45–59.

Wolff, C. (2010) 'IRS internal communications survey 2012: employer practice', *IRS Employment Review*, June.

Home viewing

In the movie, *The Matrix* (1999, directors Andy and Lana Wachowski) Morpheus (played by Laurence Fishburne) explains the arbitrary nature of reality to Neo (Keanu Reeves). As Morpheus reveals the nature of the Matrix, Neo exclaims, 'This isn't real'. Morpheus replies, 'What is reality?' This occurs around 35 minutes into the film. You may be able to find this 3-minute scene on YouTube by searching for 'The Matrix (1999) Construct scenes'.

control is not always necessary. We can, however, control some aspects of the process simply by being consciously aware of what is happening. There are many settings where such control is desirable and can help us to avoid dangerous and expensive errors. Understanding the characteristics of perception can be useful in many organizational settings – with the design of aircraft instruments and displays for pilots, in the conduct of selection interviews, and in handling disputes and employee grievances.

Perception is a dynamic process because it involves ordering and attaching meaning to raw sensory data. Our sensory apparatus is bombarded with vast amounts of information. Some of this information is internal: feelings of hunger, lust, pain, fatigue. Some of this information comes from people, objects and events in the world around us. We do not passively record these sensory data. We are constantly sifting and ordering this stream of information, making sense of and interpreting it.

Selective attention
the ability, often exercised unconsciously, to choose from the stream of sensory data, to concentrate on particular elements, and to ignore others.

Perception is an information processing activity which involves selective attention.

Our senses – sight, hearing, touch, taste, smell and internal bodily signals or 'kinaesthesia' – each consists of specialist nerves that respond to specific forms of energy, such as light, sound, pressure and temperature changes. There are some forms of energy that our senses cannot detect unaided, such as radio waves, sounds at very low and very high pitch, and infrared radiation. Our sensory apparatus has limitations that we cannot overcome without the aid of special equipment. We are unable to hear sound frequencies above 10,000 hertz, but many animals, including dogs and dolphins, can. We are unable to hear sounds below 30 hertz, but whales can. Owls have much better eyesight than we do.

Home viewing

The Sixth Sense (1999, director M. Night Shyamalan) concerns the attempts by a child psychologist, Malcolm Crowe (played by Bruce Willis), to cure a young boy, Cole (Haley Joel Osment), who is tormented because he sees dead people. Crowe spends so much time with Cole that he ignores his wife Anna (Olivia Williams). However, this film manipulates the perceptions and assumptions of the audience. Once you have watched the film, either reflect on the action, or watch it again. Notice which clues you 'saw', but either ignored or misinterpreted the first time around. Notice how your interpretation of events relied on the assumptions that you made – or the assumptions that you were *expected* to make. Only when you know the full plot of the film can you make 'correct' assumptions and interpretations, based on the same evidence you were given the first time around. What does this movie say about the ease with which your perceptions can be manipulated?

Perceptual threshold
a boundary point, either side of which our senses respectively will or will not be able to detect stimuli, such as sound, light or touch.

The constraints imposed by our sensory apparatus can be modified in certain ways by experience. The boundary, or perceptual threshold, between what we can and cannot detect can be established by experiment. We can explore individual differences in thresholds across the senses, and these thresholds can sometimes be altered by training and experience.

If there is a clock ticking in the room where you study, you will almost certainly not be aware of the sound, until somebody mentions it, or the clock stops. Next time you visit a library, close your eyes for few seconds and pay attention to the background noise that you do not usually hear. But surely you must have heard it, as you must have heard the clock ticking, if your ears were working properly? Our sensory apparatus responds not simply to energy, but to changes in energy levels. Having detected a stimulus, such as a clock or the hum of air conditioning, the nerves concerned become tired of transmitting the same information indefinitely and give up, until the stimulus changes. This explains our surprise at the sudden silence which follows when machinery stops.

Once stimuli become familiar, they stop being sensed. This phenomenon, in which the perceptual threshold is raised, is known as **habituation**.

Habituation the decrease in our perceptual response to stimuli once they have become familiar.

Our sensory apparatus has design limitations which filter out some information, such as x-rays and dog whistles. Perception involves other filtering processes, as the phenomenon of habituation suggests. In particular, information that is familiar, non-threatening and unnecessary to the task in hand is screened out of our conscious awareness.

Stand on the pavement of a busy street and pay attention to as much of the available information as you can: the noise of the traffic, the make, colour and condition of passing vehicles, the smell of rubber tyres and exhaust fumes, the pressure of the pavement on the soles of your feet, the breeze across your face, the aftershave of a passing man, that woman's perfume, the clothes of the man across the street and the type of dog he is walking, an overheard mobile phone conversation. When you think you are taking it all in, start to cross the road. If you get across safely, you will find that your heightened awareness has lapsed, dramatically. You would be mown down fairly quickly if this were not the case. Selective attention allows us to concentrate on the important and significant, and to ignore the insignificant and trivial.

Nancy Adler (2002) offers an excellent example of habituation in our use of language. Read the following sentence, and then quickly count the number of Fs:

> FINISHED FILES ARE THE RESULT OF YEARS OF SCIENTIFIC STUDY
> COMBINED WITH THE EXPERIENCE OF YEARS

Most people who speak English as a second language see all six Fs. Native English speakers usually pick up only three or four, because they tend to miss out the Fs in 'of'. Native speakers have been habituated to skip the 'of' because it does not contribute to the meaning of the sentence.

Perceptual filters individual characteristics, predispositions and preoccupations that interfere with the effective transmission and receipt of messages.

Adler's explanation is that, once we stop seeing the 'ofs', we do not see them again, even when we are looking for them. There is too much information available at any one time for us to pay attention to all of it, so we screen out that which is apparently of little value. The image of the world that we carry around inside our heads can only ever be a partial representation of what is 'really out there'. This leads to the conclusion that our behavioural choices are determined not by reality, but by what we perceive that reality to be. Our perception is influenced by what are called **perceptual filters**.

The internal and external factors which affect selective attention are illustrated in Figure 8.2.

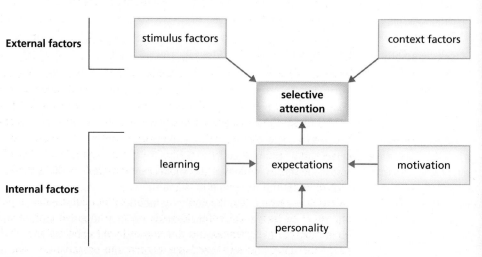

Figure 8.2: The external and internal factors influencing selective attention

The external factors affecting selective attention include stimulus factors and context factors. With respect to the stimulus factors, our attention is drawn more readily to stimuli that are:

large		small
bright		dull
loud		quiet
strong	rather than	weak
unfamiliar		familiar
stand out from surroundings		blend with surroundings
moving		stationary
repeated (but not repetitive)		one-off

Note, however, that we do not merely respond to single features, as this list might imply; we respond to the pattern of stimuli available to us.

STOP AND THINK Identify examples of the ways in which advertisements creatively use stimulus factors to attract our attention, in newspapers, magazines, and on billboards and television.

Our attention is also influenced by context factors. The naval commander on the ship's bridge and the cook in the kitchen may both have occasion to shout 'fire', but these identical statements mean quite different things to those within earshot, and will lead to radically different forms of behaviour (the taking and saving of lives, respectively). We do not need any help to make this crucial distinction, beyond our knowledge of the context.

The internal factors affecting perception include:

- *Learning*. You've heard those instructions before (the pre-flight safety briefing), so are you going to listen to it again? Our past experience leads to the development of expectations or *perceptual sets*, which predispose us to pay attention to some stimuli, and to ignore others.

- *Personality*. How come you (gregarious, sociable) saw the advertisement for the party, but your friend (reserved, shy) did not? Our personality traits predispose us to pay attention to some issues and events and human characteristics and not others.

- *Motivation*. Do you get out of the shower to take a phone call, perhaps expecting a party invitation or a job offer? We are more likely to respond to stimuli that we perceive as important and motivating.

Much of perception can be described as classification or categorization. We categorize people as male or female, lazy or energetic, extrovert or shy. In fact our classification schemes are usually more sophisticated than that. We classify objects as cars, buildings, furniture, crockery, and so on, and we refine our classification schemes further under these headings. However, we are not born with a neat classification scheme 'wired in' with the brain. These categories are learned. They are social constructs. What we learn is often culture bound, or culture specific. The British revulsion at the thought of eating dog (classified as pet), the Hindu revulsion at the thought of eating beef (classified as sacred), and the Islamic aversion to alcohol (classified as proscribed by the Koran), are all culturally transmitted emotions based on learned values.

Problems arise when we and others act as if our culture had a monopoly on 'right thinking' on such issues. Different does not mean wrong. Different people in the same culture have different experiences and develop different expectations. The internal factors – our past experience and what we have learned, our personalities, our motivations – all shape our expectations of the world around us, what we want from it, what will happen in it, and what should happen. We tend to select information that fits our expectations, and pay less attention to information that does not.

Our categorization processes, and the search for meaning and pattern, are key characteristics of perception. This perceptual work is captured by the concept of **perceptual organization**.

Perceptual organization the process through which incoming stimuli are organized or patterned in systematic and meaningful ways.

The principles by which the process of perceptual organization operates were first identified by Max Wertheimer (1880–1943) in 1923. The 'proximity principle' notes that we tend to group together or to classify stimuli that are physically close to each other and which thus appear to 'belong' together. Note how you 'see' three sets of pairs rather than six blobs here:

The 'similarity principle' notes that we classify or group together stimuli that resemble each other in appearance in some respect. Note how you 'see' four pairs here, not eight objects:

Max Wertheimer
(1880–1943)

The fact that we are able to make use of incomplete and ambiguous information, by 'filling in the gaps' from our own knowledge and past experience, is known as the 'principle of closure'. These principles of perceptual organization apply to simple visual stimuli. Of more interest here, however, is the way in which these principles apply to person perception. How often do we assume that people are similar just because they live in the same neighbourhood, or work in the same section of the factory or office building (proximity principle), or just because they wear the same clothes or have similar ethnic origins (similarity principle)? How often do we take incomplete information about someone (he's Scottish) and draw inferences from this (closure principle)? This can cause the spread of false rumours in organizations through what is called 'the grapevine'.

Change blindness: just how selective can we get?

Picture the following, and prepare to be amazed by this famous experiment. You're walking across a college campus when a stranger asks you for directions. While you're talking to him, two men pass between you carrying a wooden door. You feel a moment's irritation, but they move on and you carry on describing the route. When you're finished, the stranger informs you that you've just taken part in a psychology experiment. 'Did you notice anything change after the two men passed with the door?' he asks. 'No', you reply uneasily. He then explains that the man who initially approached you walked off behind the door, leaving him in his place. The first man now comes up to join you. Looking at them standing side by side, you notice that the two are of different height

and build, are dressed differently, have different haircuts, and have different voices.

It sounds impossible, but when Daniel Simons, a psychologist at Harvard University, and his colleague Daniel Levin of Kent State University in Ohio did this experiment, they found that half of those who took part failed to notice the substitution. The subjects had succumbed to what is called 'change blindness'. Rather than logging every detail of the visual scene, says Simons, we are highly selective about what we take in. Our impression of seeing everything is just that – an impression. We extract a few details and rely on memory, or perhaps even our imagination, for the rest (Spinney, 2000).

Video case: what makes a great boss?

This five-minute *Financial Times* video argues that great bosses have a high degree of self-awareness, and awareness of others. Valérie Gauthier from HEC Paris argues that good leaders make full use of all their five senses, of which listening is only one. Sensation and perception are key to anticipation, which is another key leadership skill. How would you benefit from developing your perception in the ways that Valérie Gauthier describes?

Perceptual sets and perceptual worlds

We have shown how the perceptual process selects incoming stimuli and organizes them into meaningful patterns. We have also argued that this processing is influenced by learning, motivation and personality – factors which give rise to expectations, which in turn make us more ready to respond to certain stimuli in certain ways and less ready to respond to others. This readiness to respond is called the individual's **perceptual set**.

Perceptual set
an individual's predisposition to respond to people and events in a particular manner.

Look at this drawing, made in 1915 by the cartoonist W.H. Hill. What do you see? Is she an old woman, or a young woman? Your answer may be influenced by what you are predisposed to see. The reactions of different individuals may not be the same, and it does not make sense to argue over whose perception is correct. Two people can see the same thing, but perceive it in different ways.

Artwork supplied by *The Broadbent Partnership*, London. Reproduced with permission

Old woman or young woman?

Is it ethical?

Sally Power and Lorman Lundsten (2005) studied employee perceptions of ethical behaviour in the workplace. They asked 280 white collar and managerial staff to identify three ethical challenges they experienced at work. 'Ethical' was not defined, as the researchers wanted to find out how employees interpreted the term. The 764 ethical challenges that were reported fell into six categories:

Category	Examples
Honesty	Misreporting financial figures; over-billing; hiding information; not telling the whole truth; stealing through expense reports
Personal issues	Stealing time from employer; lack of integrity; self-interest; acting contrary to company policy

Category	Examples
Complex business issues	Concern about excess corporate profit; environmental issues; competitive practices; sexual harassment; insider trading
Relationships	Taking credit for others' work; favouritism; stealing ideas; inappropriate relationships; backstabbing; threat of job loss
Fairness	Discrimination; taking advantage of customers
Other	Disloyalty; bribes or rebates

These respondents had no difficulties in identifying situations in which ethical or moral principles had been violated. Much of the academic commentary on this issue, however, is less confident about categorizing these behaviours. For example, it is often necessary to balance competing interests, and behaviour perceived as unethical in one context could be appropriate in another setting. The two settings most often described as ethical challenges by respondents in this study involved the treatment of employees by employers, and the treatment of customers by the company and its employees.

Failure to understand the importance of differences in perception creates many difficulties. Employees may perceive that they face chronic problems, while management see these complaints as trivial and temporary. The starting point for resolving such issues must lie with the recognition that different people hold different, but equally legitimate, views of the same set of circumstances. Chapter 1 identified two views of human behaviour. The *positivist* perspective sets out to discover an objective world out there, as it really is. The *constructivist* perspective explores how our world is socially constructed, and how we experience and interpret that world. The argument in this chapter suggests that 'the world out there' is not a good starting point for developing an understanding of human behaviour. We each have a unique version of what is out there and of our own place in it. We each live in our own **perceptual world**.

Perceptual world
the individual's personal internal image, map or picture of their social, physical and organizational environment.

We each have a perceptual world that is selective and partial, and which concentrates on features of particular interest and importance to us. Through the processes of learning, motivation and personality development, we each have different expectations and different degrees of readiness to respond to objects, people and events in different ways. We impose meaning on received patterns of information; the meanings that we attach to objects, people and events are not intrinsic to these things, but are learned through social experience and are coloured by our current needs and objectives.

Our perceptions — that is, the meanings that we attach to the information available to us – shape our actions. Behaviour in an organization context can usually be understood once we understand the way in which the individual perceives that context. Figure 8.3 illustrates the links between available information based on observation and experience, the perception based on that information, and outcomes in terms of decisions with respect to actions. This example explains why employees would ignore apparently reasonable management requests to become 'team players'.

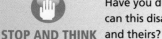

STOP AND THINK   Have you disagreed with someone recently? What did you disagree about? How can this disagreement be explained by differences between your perceptual world and theirs?

To understand an individual's behaviour, therefore, we need to know something of the elements in their perceptual world, and the pattern of information and other cultural

aftershave – because these also contribute to how you are perceived by interviewers. Third, smile, to improve your own self-confidence, and to establish rapport with your interviewer. Finally, with regard to dress, Stevens suggests:

For women	For men
Empire line or shirt dress with cardigan and patent platform court shoes	Single breasted dark suit
	Avoid turn-ups on trousers
Black, boot-leg trousers with shirt and jacket	Conservative tie with colour that blends in rather than stands out
A-line skirt with smart top and peep-toe shoes	
Tailored blazer, to create a streamlined, classic, more formal look	Well-fitting trousers with shirt and blazer when a suit is not necessary

STOP AND THINK

You are a student. What is the popular stereotype of a student? What characteristics are you supposed to have? What behaviours are expected of you? Is this a positive, favourable stereotype, a negative, critical one, or is it balanced? Is this stereotype broadly accurate, as far as you are concerned, or is it biased and false? How do you feel about being stereotyped?

What stereotypes do you have of other groups, occupations and people? Are those positive or negative? To what extent are they based on experience and evidence? How would you expect those others to respond if you revealed your stereotype to them?

Sex, appearance, attractiveness and discrimination

Height of success

Taller women earn more money than their shorter female colleagues because they are perceived as more authoritative, a survey has found. Those standing taller than 5ft 8in are twice as likely to earn more than £30,000 a year, and make an average of £5,000 more annually, according to a poll of over 1,400 women carried out by Opinion Matters and commissioned by retailer Long Tall Sally.

'Research shows that tall people are consistently more successful in the workplace – not only do they earn more but they're also more likely to be in leadership positions', said Arianne Cohen, author of *The Tall Book*. 'As taller people look down when speaking to shorter colleagues, they are instinctively perceived to have confidence – which means they are respected by their colleagues and bosses' (*People Management*, 22 April 2010, p.15).

We said earlier that the perceptual process is concerned with making sense of and explaining the world around us, and the people and events in it. Our need for explanation and understanding is reflected in the way in which we search for the causes of people's actions. Our perceptions of causality are known as **attributions**.

Attribution the process by which we make sense of our environment through our perceptions of causality.

An attribution is a belief about the cause or causes of an event or an action. Attribution theory was developed in the 1950s and 1960s by Fritz Heider (1958) and Harold Kelley (1971). They argue that our understanding of our social world is founded on our continual attempts at causal analysis based on how we interpret experience.

Why is that person successful? Why did that project fail? If we understand the causes of success and failure, we may be able to adjust our behaviour accordingly. Attribution is simply the process of attaching causes or reasons to the actions and events we see. We tend to look for causes either in people's abilities and personalities, or in aspects of the circumstances in which they find themselves. This distinction can be described in terms of internal causality and external causality. We may explain an individual's success, or promotion, with reference to their superior skills and knowledge (internal causality), or with reference to luck, powerful friends and coincidence (external causality).

Research has revealed patterns in our attributions. When we explain our achievements (exam success), we point to our personal capabilities, but when we are explaining our lack of success, we blame our circumstances (poor teaching). This is known as *projection*. We project blame onto external causes that are beyond our control. However, we tend to attribute the behaviour of others to their disposition, that is, to aspects of their personality. We met *the fundamental attribution error* in Chapter 1. This refers to the tendency to exaggerate the disposition and personality of the individual rather than the context in which they find themselves – explaining company success in terms of the chief executive's leadership, rather than the buoyant economy.

Attribution theory can explain aspects of discrimination in organizational settings. For example, sex and appearance affect how we are paid and promoted. In Britain, Barry Harper (2000) studied over 11,000 people (belonging to the long-term National Child Development Study) aged 33 to determine the effects of looks, height and obesity on pay. This study confirmed that attractive people, men and women, earn more, and that tall men earn substantially more. Height is slightly less important for women. Tall men earn 10 per cent more than men of average height, but tall women earn only 5 per cent more. Employers in China prefer taller employees, who are often paid more for the same job than shorter colleagues. Tall Chinese security guards, for example, are more highly paid because they make people feel safer than do short guards (*The Economist*, 2015).

Unattractive men earn 15 per cent less than colleagues with average looks, while unattractive women earn 11 per cent less. Obese women earn 5 per cent less than those of average weight, but obese men are not affected. While widespread, the benefits of height and the costs of being unattractive were more common in 'white collar' occupations. For women, a 15 per cent penalty for being unattractive was most common in secretarial and clerical jobs. Attractive men in customer-facing sales roles earned 13 per cent more, while tall men in 'high touch' positions earned 25 per cent more. Some commentators are critical of 'beauty bias' – putting appearance before capability – and see this as another form of unfair discrimination at work.

Why should appearance affect career progression? Our attributions are related to our stereotypes. We seem to attribute explanations of people's behaviour to aspects of their appearance. Discrimination against particular groups and individuals, on the basis of sex, sexual orientation, age or ethnic background, is now widely recognized. Legislation seeks to address sexual and racial discrimination. Social attitudes towards homosexuals and the elderly in organizational settings do appear, slowly, to be changing. However, attribution research suggests that discrimination, based on our perceptions of causal links between sex, appearance and job performance, are more subtle, and less public.

Hot dogs, old dogs, new tricks

Fast food outlets traditionally employ younger and less experienced staff and managers. With an ageing workforce, the supply of young employees is declining. In America, less than 8 per cent of employees and managers working in food service are over 55, and the main age group for employees is 18–24. As the sector expands, however, and proportion of the workforce in the 55 to 64 range grows, the industry will have to recruit increasing numbers of older staff. But there is a problem. While younger workers are often regarded as less reliable and more accident prone than their older colleagues, research shows that stereotyped perceptions of older workers are more often negative: difficult to train, lacking in creativity, too cautious, resistant to new technology, inflexible. In the hospitality industry, some managers keep older workers out of frontline positions in service areas, believing that they have a negative impact on customer perceptions of the business. Hiring more elderly staff could of course help to overcome that negative stereotype.

"I was hoping by this age to have outlived my usefulness."

Source: © Barbara Smaller/The New Yorker Collection/ www.cartoonbank.com

Robin Depietro and Merwyn Strate (2007) studied the perceptions that American managers in this sector had of older workers. They also asked these managers about the numbers of older workers they expected to employ in future. The 20 managers in this study perceived older workers to be self-motivated, disciplined, loyal and dependable, with good communication skills, lower levels of absenteeism, respect for authority and credibility with customers.

Despite these positive perceptions, only 25 per cent of the managers said that they would prefer to have older workers in their restaurants. Only 10 per cent said that they expected to employ more older workers in future, and 15 per cent said that they expected to employ fewer. Management perceptions, it seems, are not consistent with management actions. Dipietro and Strate (2006, p.183) argue that fast food organizations need to rethink their human resource and organization development policies, to match management perceptions with recruitment practices. There are sound business reasons for this:

There needs to be some thought and planning for how older workers can add some dependability and maturity into restaurants, and can possibly change part of the image of quick service restaurants. Working to actively recruit and hire older employees could add a new dimension and some new markets for quick service restaurants.

With respect to attractiveness, sex, height and weight, we are dealing with factors which cannot have any meaningful impact on performance for most jobs or occupations. The tall, attractive female computer programmer of average weight may be more effective in her job than the short, overweight male programmer with the unremarkable features. A moment's thought, however, would probably lead us to reject height, weight and attractiveness as causal factors here, and lead us to look for differences in education, experience and ability instead. The problem is that we make attribution errors by jumping quickly and unconsciously to judgements of this kind, particularly when we have little information about the other person on which to base a more careful assessment.

Tattoo or not tattoo

Around 20 per cent of people in Britain have a tattoo (including, at the time of writing, the Prime Minister's wife). Some employers, however, have a 'no visible tattoos' policy. There is no law banning discrimination against people with tattoos. Organizations can make up their own rules. There seems to be a conflict, therefore, between individual and organizational rights, between personal freedom and corporate image, and opinions are deeply divided (*People Management*, 2014b). The same concerns apply to facial piercing.

Will facial piercing and visible tattoos affect your job and career prospects? The answer is, yes, probably. Two studies by James McElroy et al. (2014) concluded that job applicants (male and female) with facial piercings were perceived by interviewers as less suitable. The first study involved 200 undergraduate students, who (the researchers thought) were more likely to tolerate piercings than adults. The students were asked to rate candidates for jobs on the basis of their application and a portrait photograph. Some candidates had facial piercings, and

→

some did not. The second study used the same approach with 100 working adults, with similar results, although the students' ratings were more negative than those of the adults. The applicants with facial piercings were perceived as:

- more extraverted;
- less agreeable;
- less conscientious;
- less attractive;
- of more questionable character;
- less competent;
- less sociable;
- not as trustworthy.

Andrew Timming (2015) interviewed 15 service sector managers, and 10 adults with visible tattoos. Half of the tattooed adults were unemployed, including an ex-member of a neo-Nazi skinhead gang with a spider web tattoo on his face and neck. All of the management recruiters expressed 'derision and distaste' for visible tattoos. One described them as a sign of 'questionable behaviour', indicating that people with these characteristics were 'discredited', 'flawed' or 'deficient'. One overriding consideration, however, related to the perception of customers, and tattoos were thus likely to be seen as more acceptable in 'back stage' rather than customer-facing jobs. There are settings, however, where employers want staff with tattoos, to help establish relationships, in social work, the prison service, and in 'trendy' clothing and sportswear stores, for example.

Body modifications are becoming more popular, and many managers have tattoos or piercings themselves, other than in their ears. Many students believe that piercings and tattoos will not affect their job prospects. However, other studies have found that 80 per cent of managers and recruitment interviewers say that they would not hire anyone with piercings or tattoos (McElroy et al., 2014, p.26). Perceptions may be changing, but the negative stigma and prejudice persists. For now, at least, candidates with piercings and tattoos are likely to have more difficulty in getting jobs.

Any aspect of our appearance is a form of *non-verbal communication* (see Chapter 7). We cannot control our age, or height, but these factors, combined with behaviour that is under our control, send signals that others decode in the light of their experiences (age is related to reliability), expectations (tall and handsome means self-confident and knowledgeable) and prejudices (short and overweight women deter customers). This also applies to choice of clothing, which is under our control. Dress can indicate organizational culture, and can contribute significantly to the individual's *impression management*. The way in which we dress can tell others how we want to be seen (as formal, relaxed, creative, businesslike) rather than what we are really like. However, we may not always be aware how others perceive our attempts to manage our impression through our appearance.

Perceptual errors and how to avoid them

As we said at the beginning of the chapter, it is our *perceptions* of circumstances, events and other people which influence our judgements, decisions and actions. However, we have seen how our perceptions can often lead to inaccurate judgements and inappropriate decisions and actions. In order to avoid perceptual errors, we need to be aware of how these can arise, and how we can be misled.

Will you pass the 'posh test'?

You may not get that job even if you have the capabilities. A lot depends on how you are perceived by the person who interviews you. A study by the UK Social Mobility and Child Poverty Commission found that elite law, accountancy and financial services organizations discriminate against working class applicants (Ashley et al., 2015). Although a degree from an elite university was taken as a 'signal for quality', recruiters looked for a number of other characteristics including 'personal style, accent and mannerisms, adaptability, team working and other soft skills' (p.25). These criteria give applicants from middle and upper class backgrounds an advantage. The press accused these companies of using a 'posh test' to choose candidates (Churchard, 2015).

Asked about interviewing applicants with working class backgrounds, one employer said, 'Is there a diamond in the rough out there? It's highly probable, but how much mud do I have to sift through in that population to find that diamond?' (p.45). Speaking of a recent recruit, another employer said,

> She's short of polish. We need to talk about the way that she articulates, the way that she chooses words and the way she pronounces them. It will need some polish because whilst I may look at the substance, you know, I've got a lot of clients and a lot of colleagues who are very focused on the personal presentation and appearance side of it. (p.46)

It is perhaps not surprising that a successful working class candidate admitted to covering up his background, and to adjusting his accent, saying that 'It's about having the skill to adapt to your environment. When I went home, I went back to my old slight twang. When I'm in this environment, I pretend I'm posher than I am' (p.71).

A study by Lauren Rivera (2015) uncovered the same perceptual biases in American banking, law and consulting companies, where graduates from affluent backgrounds get the best jobs. Rivera suggests how less privileged candidates can create the perception that they do fit in, by studying the organization to which they have applied, exploiting connections with 'insiders', not appearing eccentric, preferring team sports (a sign of a 'rounded character'), telling stories about how they 'triumphed against the odds', and showing self-confidence. Style is just as important as substance.

Adrian Furnham (2005) argues that the process of appraising the performance of employees is subject to a number of perception errors. Here are his 'unlucky 13':

1. *Central tendency*: Appraising everyone at the middle of the rating scale.

2. *Contrast error*: Basing an appraisal on comparison with other employees (who may have received undeserved high or low ratings) rather than on established performance criteria.

3. *Different from me*: Giving a poor appraisal because the person has qualities or characteristics not possessed by the appraiser. (People like others who are similar to themselves.)

4. *Halo effect*: Appraising an employee undeservedly well on one quality (performance, for example) because they are perceived highly by the appraiser on another quality (attractiveness, perhaps).

5. *Horn effect*: The opposite of the halo effect. Giving someone a poor appraisal on one quality (attractiveness) influences poor rating on other qualities (performance).

6. *Initial impression*: Basing an appraisal on first impressions rather than on how the person has behaved throughout the period to which the appraisal relates.

7. *Latest behaviour*: Basing an appraisal on the person's recent behaviour, rather than on how they have behaved throughout the appraisal period.

8. *Lenient or generous rating*: Perhaps the most common error, being consistently generous in appraisal, mostly to avoid conflict.

9. *Performance dimension error*: Giving someone a similar appraisal on two distinct but similar qualities, because they happen to follow each other on the appraisal form.

10. *Same as me*: Giving a good appraisal because the person has qualities or characteristics possessed by the appraiser.

11. *Spillover effect*: Basing this appraisal, good or bad, on the results of the previous appraisal, rather than on how the person has behaved during the appraisal period.

12. *Status effect*: Giving those in higher level positions consistently better appraisals than those in lower level jobs.

13. *Strict rating*: Being consistently harsh in appraising performance.

The main sources of errors in person perception thus include:

1. Not collecting enough information.
2. Basing our judgements on information that is irrelevant or insignificant.
3. Seeing what we expect to see and what we want to see, and not investigating further.
4. Allowing early information to colour our judgement, despite later contradictory information.
5. Allowing our own characteristics to influence our judgements of others.
6. Accepting stereotypes without criticism.
7. Attempting to decode non-verbal behaviour outside the context in which it appears.
8. Basing attributions on flimsy and potentially irrelevant evidence.

The steps we need to take to avoid making perceptual errors include:

1. Take more time and avoid instant or 'snap' judgements.
2. Collect and consciously use more information about other people.
3. Develop self-awareness, and an understanding of how our personal biases and preferences affect our perceptions and judgements of others.
4. Check our attributions – the assumptions we make about the causes of behaviour, particularly the links we make between aspects of personality and appearance on the one hand and behaviour on the other.

It's not what you hear, it's the way that you see it

Our perceptions (of someone's intelligence and trustworthiness, for example) can be influenced by factors that have little or no relevance (height and attractiveness). But when we are asked to judge the quality of music, surely nothing else matters apart from the sound – the *auditory* cues. That may not be the case. Experiments conducted by Chia-Jung Tsay (2014) suggest that such judgements depend more heavily on what we see – on *visual* cues.

One experiment involved 118 'novice' participants who had no training in classical music. They were exposed to six-second excerpts from live recordings of international chamber ensemble competitions, and asked to choose which they thought was the winning ensemble in each case. Participants were divided into three groups, with one group watching the video-only version, one hearing the sound-only recording, and the third seeing video-and-sound. Questioned afterwards, over 80 per cent of participants said that, in judging these performances, the sound was critical. However, participants who only saw the recordings quickly identified the winning ensembles. Participants who were given the sound-only, or video-and-sound recordings, were less able to identify which ensembles had won. Participants who watched the full video-and-sound recordings were no better than chance at picking the competition winners.

With video, one can see the passion, the gestures and the group interactions that produce a winning performance. Were the original competition judges influenced as much by what they saw as what they heard? Or perhaps the musical novices in this experiment relied more heavily on those visual cues. Tsay repeated the experiment, this time using 193 experienced professional musicians. Once again, over 80 per cent said that the music was the critical factor. However, as with the novices, the professionals who were shown the video-only recordings were able to identify the winning ensembles; the choices of those who were exposed to sound-only or video-and-sound were no better than chance.

These experiments demonstrate the powerful effect of visual cues on our perceptions and judgements, even in situations where we would expect auditory cues to be more important. Other research has shown that our impressions of the personalities and capabilities of others are influenced by aspects of their appearance. It is therefore important to recognize the visual bias in our perceptions, and to take this into account, particularly when making selection and promotion decisions. Tsay (2014, p.30) concludes: 'This research suggests that the ultimate music ensemble astounds not its listeners, but its viewers.' Does this also apply to 'the ultimate chief executive'?

To improve our understanding of others, we must first have a well-developed knowledge of ourselves – our strengths, preferences, flaws and biases. The development of self-knowledge can be an uncomfortable process. In organizational settings, we are often less able to express our feelings (positive and negative) about other people, due to social or cultural norms, and to the communication barriers erected by status and power differentials. This may in part explain the appeal of training courses in social and interpersonal skills, self-awareness and personal growth designed to help us overcome these problems, to 'get in touch' with others, and to 'get in touch with ourselves'. Training in interpersonal skills often emphasizes openness and honesty, active listening, sensitivity to non-verbal behaviour, and how to give and receive critical and non-evaluative feedback.

 RECAP

1. **Identify the main features of the process of perception.**

   - People behave according to how they perceive the world, not in response to 'reality'.

   - The perceptual process involves the interpretation of sensory input in the light of past experience, and our store of knowledge, beliefs, expectations and motives.

2. **Distinguish between the bottom-up processing of sensory information and the top-down interpretation of that information.**

   - Sensation, or bottom-up processing, determines the data to which we pay attention.

   - Perception, or top-down processing, determines the way in which we organize and interpret perceived information in order to make behavioural choices.

3. **Understand the nature and implications of selective attention and perceptual organization.**

   - Selective attention is influenced by external factors relating to the stimulus and the context, and by internal factors such as learning, personality and motivation.

   - The way in which we organize and interpret sensory data in meaningful ways, even when it is incomplete or ambiguous, is known as perceptual organization.

4. **Give examples of how behaviour is influenced by our perceptions.**

   - We each have our own perceptual world, an internal mental image of our environment.

   - Different cultures lead to differences in perception and consequently in behaviour.

5. **Explain and illustrate the main processes and problems in perception, including false attributions, halo effects and stereotyping.**

   - An attribution is a belief about cause and effect. When speaking about ourselves, we tend to attribute success to personal factors and failure to external factors. When speaking about others, we tend to attribute success and failure to personality features.

   - Making a favourable judgement of someone on the basis of a single positive characteristic is known as the halo effect, and is called the horn effect if the judgement is negative.

   - Assuming that someone possesses a set of personality traits because they belong to a particular social group is known as stereotyping.

6. **Explain some less widely appreciated sources of discrimination at work arising from characteristics of the person perception and attribution processes.**

   - Aspects of behaviour are attributed to appearance, leading to discrimination. You are likely to be paid less at work if you are an overweight or underweight female, a short man, a husband with an overweight wife, and are perceived to be unattractive.

   - The fundamental attribution error leads us to emphasize individual personality and ignore social and organizational context when explaining behaviour.

7. **Suggest techniques for improving perceptual accuracy and avoiding errors.**

   - To avoid mistakes, avoid rapid judgements, take more time, collect more information, be aware of your own prejudices and biases, and develop increased self-awareness.

   - To improve accuracy, expect errors to occur, use as much feedback as you can get, and take small steps rather than radical ones to reduce risks.

Revision

1. Explain the distinction between sensation and perception. What is the significance of this distinction?

2. What is the individual's perceptual world? What factors influence this construct, and how does an understanding of someone's perceptual world help us to understand their behaviour?

3. What is the difference between selective attention and perceptual organization? What factors influence the latter process?

4. How can an organization's selection, appraisal and promotion processes be affected by errors and biases in perception? How can these errors and biases be overcome?

Research assignment

Look carefully at the style of dress and appearance of the instructors in your educational institution, across all the subjects that you are studying. How does their appearance affect your perceptions of their:

- approachability
- subject knowledge
- professionalism
- understanding of the world beyond the academic 'ivory tower'?

Write a report that first identifies specific aspects of your instructors' dress and appearance that lead you to make judgements on those criteria. Conclude your report with advice to instructors on how they could change their dress and appearance to improve the ways in which they are perceived by students on those criteria – to make them appear more approachable, more professional, and so on.

Springboard

E. Bruce Goldstein (2009) *Sensation and Perception* (8th edn). Belmont, CA: Wadsworth Publishing. Introduction to the psychology and physiology of sensation and perception. Illustrates how the senses function, exposing the complexity of perceptual processes.

Daniel S. Hamermesh (2011) *Beauty Pays: Why Attractive People are More Successful.* Princeton, NJ: Princeton University Press. Handsome men earn 4 per cent more than average-looking men, and unattractive men earn up to 13 per cent less. The laws of 'pulchronomics' also apply to women. Attractive workers may attract more customers, so perhaps they should be paid more. Hamermesh argues that those who are unattractive should have legal protection.

Heidi Grant Halvorson (2015) 'Managing yourself: a second chance to make a first impression', *Harvard Business Review*, 93 (1/2): 108–11. Useful advice on what to do if you made a *bad* first impression. Provide positive information. Compliment the person on their fairness and open-mindedness. Make yourself indispensable. Choose the right moments, offering to help when they are under pressure.

 OB cinema

Legally Blonde (2001, director Robert Luketic), DVD track (scene) 8, 0:21:17 to 0:22:46 (3 minutes). Clip begins with the tutor saying, 'OK, welcome to law school'; clip ends with Elle saying, 'Whoever said that orange was the new pink was seriously disturbed'.

This movie tells the story of a blonde sorority queen, Elle Woods (played by Reece Witherspoon), whose boyfriend leaves her to go to Harvard Law School. To get him back, she goes to Harvard, too. Every character in this movie plays a stereotyped role. In this clip, on the law school lawn, Elle and three of her classmates are asked by a tutor to introduce themselves. As you watch the clip, observe the five characters carefully and:

1. Decide on an appropriate stereotype label (e.g. 'absent-minded professor') for each character.

2. Explain why you have chosen that label, based on the evidence that each character provides (what they say, how they say it, appearance, non-verbal behaviour).

3. For each character, identify two adjectives that you think would describe how they would be likely to interact socially with others.

4. Think about each of those characters in an organizational context, assess what you feel would be their strengths and their weaknesses.

 ## OB on the web

Search YouTube for 'The Corporation perception management'. This clip is part of the documentary, *The Corporation* (2006, directors Jennifer Abbott and Mark Achbar).

Watch the first two minutes and ten seconds. The commentators argue that large corporations are not just selling products and services. They are also advertising a way of life, a way of thinking. They are 'manufacturing consent' for their actions and for business norms and values. Is this a form of propaganda? One of the interviewees, the chief executive of a public relations company, explains his profession in terms of 'perception management', arguing that this is a valuable contribution to business and to society.

After you have watched this, identify the ways in which your own perceptions are managed in this way by large organizations. What is your conclusion: is corporate perception management necessary and valuable, or an unacceptable form of manipulation?

CHAPTER EXERCISES

1. Person perception

Objective   To explore factors influencing our perception of other people. Research has shown, for example, that we assess others' characters from their faces. These assessments include how friendly, aggressive, trustworthy and creditworthy another person is. The judgements that we reach based on such apparently limited information often turn out to be correct.

Briefing   1. Break into groups of three.

2. Your instructor will give you five or six photographs of people, taken from recent newspapers and magazines. You have five minutes to work out as much as you can about each of these people, using only what you can see in the picture. Consider characteristics such as their:

- conscientiousness
- sense of humour, fun
- intelligence
- aggressiveness

→

- approachability
- reliability
- other characteristics suggested by the photographs.

3. Prepare a presentation based on your photographs and your assumptions. Explain clearly which items of evidence from the photographs led you to make those assessments.

2. You're the interviewee: what would you do?

You are about to go for a job interview, but first you will be kept waiting in the interviewer's office. During that time, you can observe clues about your interviewer and perhaps about the organization. What clues do you think are significant and revealing? What personal experiences in your own past affect how you observe and make judgements in this setting?

This exercise can be completed in class time, but is more effective if steps 1 to 3 are completed in advance. For a one hour tutorial, time will be tight without preparation.

Step 1   Read *The manager's room description* which follows, to get a feel for the setting in which you find yourself.

Step 2   Complete the analysis sheet.

- In the *data* column, record those observations that you find significant and revealing about the kind of person who occupies this room.
- In the *inferences* column, note the perceptions or conclusions that you reach from your data.
- In the *experiences* column, record past incidents or events, recent or distant, that you think influence your inferences.

Data I observe in the room	The inferences that I make	Based on past experience

Step 3   Using that analysis, construct a profile of your interviewer.

Step 4   Finally, record your answers to the following questions:

1. What is the sex, marital status and ethnic background of the managing director? Identify the data in the room that lead you to your inferences.

2. How would you describe the managing director's character? What are this person's interests? What would you expect this person's management style to be like? Once again, identify the data on which you base these judgements.

3. Given your own personality, do you think that you would be happy working for this person?

4. Explain how your analysis illustrates the concepts of selective attention, perceptual organization, perceptual world, halo effect and stereotyping.

Step 5   Present your findings, according to your instructor's directions.

The manager's room description   You are now in the company offices, top floor, for your job interview. It sounds like your ideal position. As personal assistant, you will be working for the managing director who has asked to interview you. You have arrived on time, but the managing director's secretary apologizes and tells you there will be a delay. The managing director has been called to an important meeting which will take up to 15 minutes. The secretary tells you that you are welcome to wait in the managing director's private office, and shows you in.

You know that you will be alone here for 15 minutes. You look around the room, curious about the person with whom you may be working. The shallow pile carpet is a warm pink, with no pattern. You choose one of six high-backed chairs, upholstered in a darker fabric that matches well with the carpet and curtains, and with polished wooden arms. In the centre of the ring of chairs is a low glass-topped coffee table. On the wall behind you is a large photograph of a vintage motor car, accompanied by its driver in leather helmet, goggles, scarf and long leather coat; you can't make out the driver's face. The window ledge holds four plants arranged equal distances apart; two look like small exotic ferns and the others are a begonia and a geranium in flower.

On the other side of the room sits a large wooden executive desk, with a black leather chair. There are some papers on the desk immediately in front of the chair. A framed copy of the company's mission statement hangs on the wall behind the desk, and below that sits a black leather briefcase with combination locks. The plain grey waste basket by the wall beside the desk is full of discarded paper. There is a thick pile of what looks like committee minutes at the front of the desk, with a pad of yellow 'post-it' notes on the top, and a Mont Blanc pen with the Acme company logo on the barrel. To the side is a laptop computer and a desk lamp. In front of the lamp sits a metal photograph frame holding two pictures. One is of an attractive woman in her thirties with a young boy around eight years old. The other photograph is of a retriever dog in a field to the side of some farm buildings.

On the other side of the desk is a delicate china mug. In front of it lies what looks like a leather-covered notebook or perhaps a diary, and a passport. A copy of the *Financial Times* newspaper sits beside the notebook. You see that there is no telephone on the desk. Behind the desk is a small glass-fronted display case. There are some books lined up on top of the case: *Plugged In: The Generation Y Guide to Thriving at Work*, *The Oxford Concise Dictionary of Quotations*, *Managing Difficult Interactions* and *Leaning In: Women, Work, and the Will to Lead.* Also on top of the case sits a small bronze statue, of a man sitting with his legs crossed in a Yoga position. Inside the case, there are computing systems manuals and books and pamphlets on employment law, many of which deal with race and sex discrimination issues.

You decide to get up and look out the window. There is a three-seater settee under the window, covered in the same fabric as the armchairs with matching scatter cushions in the corners. From the window you can easily see people shopping and children playing in the nearby park. You turn to another table beside the settee. Some magazines sit in front of a burgundy ceramic lamp with a beige shade. There are two recent copies of *The Economist*, and a copy each of *Asia Today*, *Classic CD* and *Fortune*. As you head back to your chair, you notice that the papers on the desk in front of the chair are your job application and curriculum vitae. Your first name, obviously indicating your sex, has been boldly circled. As the Managing Director may return at any moment, you go back and sit in your chair to wait.

Employability assessment

With regard to your future employment prospects:

1. Identify up to three issues from this chapter that you found significant.
2. Relate these to the competencies in the employability matrix.
3. Decide what actions you need to take to maintain and/or develop those competencies under each of the four headings of the employability matrix.

→

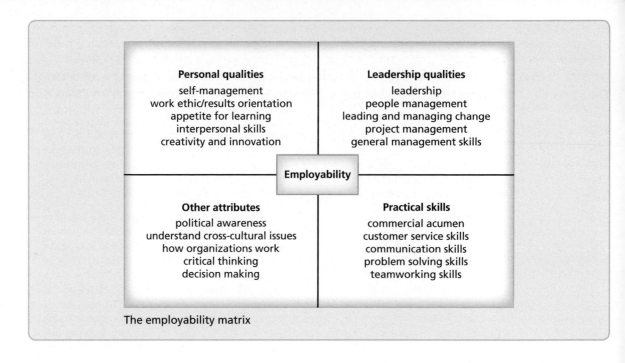

The employability matrix

References

Adler, N.J. (2002) *International Dimensions of Organizational Behaviour* (4th edn). London: International Thomson.

Ashley, L., Duberley, J., Sommerlad, H. and Scholarios, D. (2015) *A Qualitative Evaluation of Non-Educational Barriers to the Elite Professions*. London: Social Mobility and Child Poverty Commission.

Churchard, C. (2015) 'Posh test bars working-class talent from top jobs, finds study', *People Management*, 15 June, www.cipd.co.uk/pm/peoplemanagement/b/weblog/archive/2015/06/15/posh-test-bars-working-class-talent-from-top-jobs-finds-study.aspx

Dipietro, R.B. and Strate, M.L. (2006) 'Management perceptions of older employees in the US quick service restaurant industry', *Journal of Foodservice Business Research*, 9 (2/3): 169–85.

DuBrin, A.J. (2011) *Impression Management in the Workplace: Research, Theory, and Practice*. New York and Abingdon, Oxon: Routledge.

Furnham, A. (2005) *The Psychology of Behaviour at Work*. Hove, Sussex: Psychology Press.

Harper, B. (2000) 'Beauty, stature and the labour market: a British cohort study', *Oxford Bulletin of Economics and Statistics*, 62 (S1): 771–800.

Heider, F. (1958) *The Psychology of Interpersonal Relationships*. New York: John Wiley.

Hong, H. and Liskovich, I. (2015) 'Crime, punishment and the halo effect of corporate social responsibility', Princeton University, Department of Economics.

Kelley, H.H. (1971) *Attribution: Perceiving the Causes of Behaviour*. New York: General Learning Press.

Little, L.M., Major, V.S., Hinojosa, A.S. and Nelson, D.L. (2015) 'Professional image maintenance: how women navigate pregnancy in the workplace', *Academy of Management Journal*, 58 (1): 8–37.

McElroy, J.C., Summers, J.K. and Moore, K. (2014) 'The effect of facial piercing on perceptions of job applicants', *Organizational Behavior and Human Decision Processes*, 125 (1): 26–38.

Nisbett, R.E. and Wilson, T.D. (1977) 'Telling more than we can know: verbal reports on mental processes', *Psychological Review*, 84 (3): 231–59.

People Management (2014a) 'Are these stereotypes true?', July, p.24.

People Management (2014b) 'Is it fair to ban tattoos at work?', October, pp.16–7.

Power, S.J. and Lundsten, L.L. (2005) 'Managerial and other white-collar employees' perceptions of ethical issues in their workplace', *Journal of Business Ethics*, 60 (2): 185–93.

Rivera, L.A. (2015) *Pedigree: How Elite Students get Elite Jobs*. Princeton, NJ: Princeton University Press.

Stevens, M. (2013) 'Dress to impress in seven seconds', *People Management*, 2 April, www.cipd.co.uk/pm/peoplemanagement/b/weblog/archive/2013/04/02/dress-to-impress-in-seven-seconds.aspx

The Economist (2015) 'The rise of China', 25 October, p.64.

Spinney, L. (2000) 'Blind to change', *New Scientist*, 18 November, pp.27–32.

Timming, A.R. (2015) 'Visible tattoos in the service sector: a new challenge to recruitment and selection', *Work, Employment and Society*, 29 (1): 60–78.

Tsay, C.-J. (2014) 'The vision heuristic: judging music ensembles by sight alone', *Organizational Behavior and Human Decision Processes*, 124 (1): 24–33.

Vernon, R.J.W., Sutherland, C.A.M., Young, A.W. and Hartley, T. (2014) 'Modeling first impressions from highly variable facial images', *Proceedings of the National Academy of Sciences*, 111 (32): 3353–61.

Chapter 9 Motivation

Key terms

extreme job	goal-setting theory
boreout	inner work life theory
gig economy	job enrichment
drive	motivator factors
motive	hygiene factors
motivation	vertical loading factors
self-actualization	intrinsic rewards
equity theory	extrinsic rewards
expectancy theory	growth need strength
valence	job diagnostic survey
instrumentality	motivating potential score
expectancy	employee engagement
total rewards	high performance work system

Learning outcomes

When you have read this chapter, you should be able to define those key terms in your own words, and you should also be able to:

1. Understand different ways in which the term motivation is used.

2. Understand how motives and motivation processes influence behaviour.

3. Apply expectancy theory and job enrichment techniques to diagnose organizational problems and to recommend practical solutions.

4. Explain contemporary interest in this field, with respect to extreme jobs, boreout, the gig economy, employee engagement and high performance work systems.

Why study motivation?

A motivated workforce can be a sign of a successful organization. However, we each have a different reason for getting out of bed in the morning. Your motives – from the Latin *movere*, to move – are key determinants of your behaviour. If we understand your motives (desire for more leisure), we can influence your behaviour (take a day off if you finish that assignment). A survey of 50,000 business students in 15 countries (*Financial Times*, 2015) found that their top career goals were to:

1. have work–life balance;
2. be secure or stable in their job;
3. have an international career;
4. be a leader or manager of people;
5. be competitively or intellectually challenged;
6. be entrepreneurial or creative and innovative;
7. be dedicated to a cause or serve a greater purpose;
8. be autonomous or independent;
9. be a technical of functional expert.

Employers concerned with attracting, motivating and retaining college and university graduates should therefore try to provide jobs that lead to these kinds of work and career experiences and opportunities. This pattern is apparently seen in many other countries, too. In other words, look for the job advertisements which suggest that 'we don't pay much, but it's fun'.

A demotivated workforce can be disastrous. When Apple released the iPad in May 2010, pictures of iPhones were burned in Hong Kong and protesters called for a global boycott of Apple products. This followed a series of employee suicides at Foxconn, a contract manufacturer which makes products for Apple and other companies at Foxconn City, an industrial park in Shenzen. Foxconn City has 15 multi-storey manufacturing buildings where there were 12 suicides in one year. These deaths raised questions about 'sweatshop' working conditions.

Inside Foxconn city

Although Foxconn paid the Shenzen minimum wage, employees compared the company facilities to a prison, said that they were forced to work illegal overtime and night shifts, were exposed to hazardous materials, and had their privacy invaded by management. In response to the suicides, the company put nets around its buildings, hired counsellors, and brought in Buddhist monks to pray. The chief executive denied that he was running a 'sweatshop', but Apple, Foxconn and other companies had already suffered 'bad press' (*The Economist*, 2010).

The question of work motivation is particularly significant during a recession, when most organizations want to cut costs. Can employees be motivated without offering more money? Douglas McGregor (1960) set out two sets of motivational propositions, which he called 'Theory X' and 'Theory Y'. To find out which propositions apply to you, complete this questionnaire. Read each pair of statements, and circle the number that reflects your view:

The average person inherently dislikes work	1	2	3	4	5	Work is as natural as rest to people
People must be directed to work	1	2	3	4	5	People will exercise self-discretion and self-control
People wish to avoid responsibility	1	2	3	4	5	People enjoy real responsibility
People feel that achievement at work is irrelevant	1	2	3	4	5	Achievement is highly valued by people
Most people are dull and uncreative	1	2	3	4	5	Most people have imagination and creativity
Money is the only real reason for working	1	2	3	4	5	Money is only one benefit from work
People lack the desire to improve their quality of life	1	2	3	4	5	People have needs to improve their quality of life
Having an objective is a form of imprisonment	1	2	3	4	5	Objectives are welcomed as an aid to effectiveness

Add up the numbers that you circled to give you a score between 8 and 40. If you scored 16 or less, then you subscribe to Theory X. If you scored 32 or more, then you subscribe to Theory Y. Theory X managers believe in giving orders, direct supervision, and in the motivating power of money. Theory Y managers believe in giving autonomy and responsibility, and in the motivating power of interesting jobs. As an employee, which theory would you like to have applied to you at work?

McGregor argued that Theory Y was a more accurate description of most people's attitudes to work, and that the application of Theory X demotivated people. In other words, non-financial rewards can be as powerful, if not more powerful motivators than money, as we also value recognition, jobs with a worthwhile purpose, flexible working and personal development. McGregor died in 1964, but his terminology has entered the language, and his ideas remain influential (Heil et al., 2000).

Video case: catering to the millennials

This four-minute *Financial Times* video argues that millennials – those who became adults around the turn of the twenty-first century – have a distinct motivational profile. Alison Davis-Blake, of the Ross School of Business at the University of Michigan, says that millennials prefer learning by doing, and working in groups. Also, they have shorter attention spans, and a stronger social conscience than other generations. Are you a millennial? Do you fit this profile? Will this influence your career choice?

Show me the money

Hicks Waldron, when he was chief executive of Avon, once said, 'It took me a long while to learn that people do what you pay them to do, not what you ask them to do' (Aguinis et al., 2013, p.242).

Is money a motivator? Surveys often find that money is not a major factor, but pay does affect whether or not somebody will accept a job offer from one organization, and not a competitor. Reviewing the research evidence, Herman Aguinis et al. (2013) thus argue that financial rewards can improve motivation and performance in some ways, but not in others.

Can do: The money helps to attract and retain top performers. Financial rewards also meet basic and higher level needs, from food, shelter and leisure, to group membership, personal development and status (including the purchase of status symbols). Level of pay itself is often seen as an indicator of social status and achievement.

Can't do: The money cannot improve job-related knowledge, skill and abilities, unless it is invested in training and development. Paying someone more highly does not mean that they will become smarter and increase their productivity. Higher pay does not make the work itself more meaningful and interesting – which are known motivating factors. Nor does money affect other powerful motivators such as level of autonomy and degree of participation in decision making.

Finally, generous payments do not always lead to good performance. Those on high salaries may misrepresent results in order to protect their earnings. Employees can reduce their performance ('choke') due to fear of failure when they are offered large sums of money. Well-paid staff can develop a sense of entitlement and react negatively when rewards do not meet their expectations. Money can thus motivate undesirable behaviours. Aguinis et al. (2013, p.243) give this example:

> Green Giant, a producer of frozen and canned vegetables, once rewarded its employees for removing insects from vegetables. It was later found that employees began to bring insects from their homes, placed them in the vegetables, and subsequently removed them to receive the monetary rewards.

Jason Shaw and Nina Gupta (2015) describe how the Pacific Gas and Electric Company gave bonuses to supervisors of crews which kept their repair costs low. This encouraged crews to overlook safety threats, and resulted in an explosion in 2010 which killed eight people and destroyed 38 homes.

In making decisions about financial rewards, therefore, it is important to know when and why money will be effective in improving motivation and performance.

Melpomene/fotolia.com

Extreme jobs, boreout and the gig economy

Extreme job a job
that involves a working
week of 60 hours
or more, with high
earnings, combined with
additional performance
pressures.

Research into work motivation declined in the 1990s. The ideas developed in the mid-to-late twentieth century, however, are still 'current'. Managers still use the terms and tools from earlier research. Three other trends suggest that motivation is still a core issue. One concerns extreme jobs, a second concerns *boreout*, and the third relates to the development of *the gig economy*.

Extreme jobs

Some of us are motivated by the extreme job which involves long hours, frequent travel across different time zones, and multiple other pressures.

The characteristics of extreme jobs include:

- physical presence in the office of at least ten hours a day;
- tight deadlines and fast working pace;
- unpredictable workflow;
- inordinate scope of responsibility;
- frequent travel;
- after-hours work events;
- availability to clients 24/7;
- responsibility for profit and loss;
- responsibility for mentoring and recruiting.

Sylvia Ann Hewlett and Carolyn Buck Luce (2006) found that people in extreme jobs enjoy their work and are fulfilled by it. Answers to the question 'why do you do it?' included adrenaline rush, great colleagues, high pay, recognition, status and power. They cite this example:

> A financial analyst we'll call Sudhir emigrated five years ago from Mumbai, India. He works at a major commercial bank in New York. Summertime, when he puts in 90 hours a week, is his 'light' season. The rest of the year, he works upwards of 120 hours a week – leaving only 48 hours for sleeping, eating, entertaining, and (he smiles) bathing. Sudhir stays late in the office even when he has nothing particularly pressing to do. His get-a-life existence is a hazard of the profession – but worth it: As a 23-year-old with a first job, he is in the top 6 per cent of earners in America. (Hewlett and Luce, 2006, p.49)

There are more men than women in extreme jobs; only 20 per cent of 'extreme job-bers' are female. Long hours and intense pressure are exhausting, and have implications for family life. Women in extreme jobs are concerned that their children are less disciplined, eat more junk food, and watch too much television as a result of their frequent absence. Research has shown that extreme jobs with long hours are associated with higher satisfaction, better career prospects and higher salary, but with also with higher levels of stress, more psychosomatic symptoms, lower family satisfaction and poorer emotional health (Burke and Fiksenbaum, 2009a, 2009b). The motivational impact of extreme jobs needs to be balanced with ways to reduce the long-term personal and domestic costs.

Boreout boredom,
demotivation and
lack of energy and
enthusiasm caused
by uninteresting,
unchallenging and
monotonous work.

Boreout

According to Philippe Rothlin and Peter Werder (2008), demotivation is common, especially among office workers, and is caused by repetitive, uninteresting, unchallenging work, leading to boreout.

They estimate that 15 per cent of office workers are affected; boreout leads to high levels of sick leave and reduces company loyalty. If you suffer boreout, you turn up for work without enthusiasm or energy, and spend your time surfing the internet, chatting to colleagues, and trying to look busy. The journalist Roger Boyes (2007) describes one of his tactics:

> I remember while working for the *Financial Times* in the 1970s that colleagues developed an 'Italian Jacket' system. A spare jacket, kept in the office, would be spread over the back of your chair, a half-drunk cup of coffee would be placed next to the phone – and you could disappear for a couple of hours. The editor would assume that you were briefly somewhere else in the building.

Other tactics include the fake stomach upset which creates time to read magazines in the toilet, and 'fake smokers' who use their 'addiction' as an excuse to escape from their desk. The employee who answers 'yes' to four or more of these questions may be suffering boreout:

1. Do you complete private tasks at work?
2. Do you feel under-challenged or bored?
3. Do you sometimes pretend to be busy?
4. Are you tired and apathetic after work even if you experienced no stress in the office?
5. Are you unhappy with your work?
6. Do you find your work meaningless?
7. Could you complete your work quicker than you are doing?
8. Are you afraid of changing your job because you might take a salary cut?
9. Do you send private emails to colleagues during working hours?
10. Do you have little or no interest in your work?

The gig economy

The nature of work itself is changing, with implications for work motivation. Arun Sundarajan (2015) explains the development of a new mode of working and employment in the gig economy:

Gig economy a system of employment in which freelance workers sell their skills and services, through online marketplaces, to employers on a project or task basis.

> Not so long ago, the only people who looked for 'gigs' were musicians. For the rest of us, once we outgrew our school dreams of rock stardom, we found 'real' jobs that paid us a fixed salary every month, allowed us to take paid holidays and formed the basis for planning a stable future. Today, more and more of us choose, instead, to make our living working gigs rather than full time. To the optimists, it promises a future of empowered entrepreneurs and boundless innovation. To the naysayers, it portends a dystopian future of disenfranchised workers hunting for their next wedge of piecework.

The growth of the gig economy is driven by the development of online platforms such as Airbnb, Fivver, Freelancer, LinkedIn, Monster, Thumbtack, Uber and Upwork. These platforms allow employers who need particular skills and experience to connect with casual workers who can provide those capabilities (Jacobs, 2015). In the gig economy, you can buy a taxi ride, accommodation, software expertise, and shopping and delivery services, for example. If the work that needs to be done is a clearly defined project or task, the organization can hire just the right skills for the right amount of time. This cuts the cost and the delay in hiring permanent staff members.

What would motivate you to work independently? You will be free to innovate and be entrepreneurial, without having to navigate the organizational bureaucracy or deal with the office politics. You will be independent, self-reliant and have access to a wider variety of clients and tasks than you would in a single organization.

There are many jobs where your location is not important: web development, translation services, graphic design, providing legal advice. National borders are not a barrier to employment, with 'e-lancers' in one country selling their services to organizations in another. Andrew Byrne and Richard Walters (2015) note that,

Ukraine's army of freelancers, the fourth-largest in Upwork's global network, earned $61m in 2014. For the mainly western companies that dole out jobs on the website, Ukrainian web and mobile developers are cheap, responsive and easily assessed based on verified reviews by previous clients.

On the other hand, looking for gigs can be lonely, financially insecure, and lead to a blurring of work and home lives – all of which can trigger anxiety. Freelance workers do not have the same workplace benefits as permanent employees, or the organization's protection should things go wrong. Working gigs, there is little or no prospect of a progressive career (Gapper, 2015).

Which do you prefer? The freedom and flexibility of working gigs, or the security and social contact in a conventional organization? Today's theories of work motivation, and the techniques that influence management practice, were developed some time ago. As we will see, however, those 'old' theories can help to explain employee responses to new trends and developments.

Drives, motives and motivation

Motivation can be explored from three distinct but related perspectives:

1. **Goals**. What are the main motives for our behaviour? Wealth, status and power trigger behaviours directed towards their achievement. This perspective views motivation in terms of our desired outcomes or goals. This question is addressed by *content* theories of motivation.

2. **Decisions**. Why do we choose to pursue certain goals? Why do you study hard to earn distinctions while a friend has a full social life and is happy with pass grades? This perspective views motivation in terms of the cognitive decision-making processes influencing an individual's choice of goals. This question is addressed by *process* theories of motivation.

3. **Influence**. How can we get you to work harder? Managers want to motivate employees to turn up on time and be helpful to customers. This perspective views motivation as a social influence process and is addressed by *job enrichment* theories.

Drive an innate, biological determinant of behaviour, activated by deprivation.

Do we inherit our goals, or are they acquired through experience? If our motives are innate, then it would be pointless to attempt to change them. If they are acquired, then they can be altered. Our behaviour is influenced by our biological equipment. We appear to have an innate need for survival. Our needs for oxygen, water, food, shelter, warmth and sex can be overpowering. These needs are triggered by deprivation and are known as **drives**.

Home viewing

Search YouTube for 'Whiplash "good job" motivational scene'; the clip lasts for 3 minutes.

The focal character in *Whiplash* (2014, director Damien Chazelle) is a young drummer, Andrew Neiman (played by Miles Teller) who enrols at the prestigious Shaffer Conservatory of Music. Andrew's goal is to become 'one of the jazz greats', like Buddy Rich. His bandleader and instructor, Terence Fletcher (J.K. Simmons) has high expectations of his students. To push Andrew and others to reach their potential, he uses fear and intimidation, abuse, insults, public humiliation and physical violence. When a student commits suicide as a result of this pressure, Fletcher is fired by the school. However, he defends his methods: 'Truth is, I don't think people understood what I was doing at Shaffer. I wasn't there to conduct. I was there to push people beyond what's expected of them. I believe that is an absolute necessity. Otherwise we're depriving the world of the next Louis Armstrong. The next Charlie Parker. There are no two words in the English language more harmful than "good job"'. At the end of the movie, Andrew plays an outstanding drum solo; to what extent was Fletcher responsible for that performance? What are the advantages and disadvantages of Fletcher's motivational methods? How widely applicable is this approach?

Our drives may not be restricted to basic biological needs. Some psychologists claim that we are active sensation-seekers who have the innate cognitive drives listed in Table 9.1.

Table 9.1: Innate cognitive drives

Curiosity	The need to explore, to play, to learn more
Sense-making	The need to understand the nature of the world around us
Order and meaning	The need for order, certainty, equity, consistency, predictability
Effectance or competency	The need to exert mastery and control over the world around us
Self-understanding	The need to know who and what we are

The drives come with the body. We do not have to learn to be cold, thirsty or hungry. However, we can *override* these drives. Some religious orders inflict celibacy on willing members. Altruism can overcome personal safety needs in extraordinary circumstances. The idea that our behaviour is pre-programmed is too simple. Animal behaviour, in contrast, is triggered largely by instincts. Birds and squirrels cannot override their programming, and remain locked into their niches in nature. The ways in which we, on the other hand, seek to satisfy our drives are innumerable, and vary between individuals and across cultures. David Zweig (2014) describes those who are not interested in public recognition as 'invisibles'. These individuals are motivated instead by the anonymous reward from pride in the vital work that they do, such as designing airport signs, making celebrity brand perfumes, or servicing the band's gear so that concerts run smoothly.

Motive a socially acquired need activated by a desire for fulfilment.

Motives, in contrast, appear to be acquired through experience.

Polygamy is a crime in most Western cultures, but a sign of male achievement, wealth and status in parts of the Arab world. In some Muslim societies, the consumption of alcohol is punished, but gifts of alcohol are the norm in many Western cultures. Our choice of goals and behaviours is influenced by the norms of our society. Those who choose not to conform are often shunned, ridiculed, and sometimes imprisoned. Table 9.2 outlines the distinction between drives and motives.

Table 9.2: Drives versus motives

Drives	Motives
are innate	are learned
have a physiological basis	have a social basis
are activated by deprivation	are activated by environment
are aimed at satiation	are aimed at stimulation

This distinction between innate drives and acquired motives is not clear. The terms 'needs' and 'goals' are also used to refer to both drives and motives. We try to satisfy our biological drives in ways acceptable to our society. The innate drives for competency, sense-making and curiosity are socially prized in most cultures. The constructivist perspective (Chapter 1) argues that human behaviour is purposive; we attach reasons to our goals and behaviours. To understand your motives, and to influence your behaviour, we need to understand why you choose particular outcomes and how you decide to pursue them.

Motivation the cognitive decision-making process through which goal-directed behaviour is initiated, energized, directed and maintained.

Motivation is a broad concept which includes preferences for particular outcomes, strength of effort (half-hearted or enthusiastic) and persistence (in the face of problems and barriers). These are the factors that we have to understand in order to explain your motivation and behaviour. These are the factors which a manager has to appreciate in order to motivate employees to behave in desirable ways.

Content theories

Theories of motivation based on drives and needs are known as content theories, because drives and needs are seen as part of our common 'mental luggage'. The most recent content theory of work motivation was developed by Nitin Nohria, Boris Groysberg and Linda-Eling Lee (2008). Their 'emotional needs' theory claims that we are driven by four basic and innate ('hardwired') drives:

The drive to *acquire*	Obtain scarce goods, develop social status
The drive to *bond*	Form connections with other individuals and groups
The drive to *comprehend*	Satisfy our curiosity, master our environment
The drive to *defend*	Protect against threats, promote justice

From a survey of 700 employees of large companies, they found that an organization's ability to meet the four drives contributes to employee motivation by influencing feelings of involvement, energy and initiative, satisfaction, commitment, and intention to quit (or stay). Fulfilling employees' drive to bond has the greatest impact on commitment, while meeting the drive to comprehend is closely linked to involvement, energy and initiative. However, the best way to improve motivation is to meet all four drives: 'a poor showing on one drive substantially diminishes the impact of high scores on the other three'. How can this framework be used in practice? There is a 'primary lever' linked to each of the drives. These are the organization's reward system, its culture, the way that jobs are designed, and performance management and resource allocation processes. Organizational policies and practices in each of those areas can enhance motivation, as shown in Table 9.3.

Table 9.3: Emotional needs theory and implications for practice

Drive	Primary lever	Management actions
Acquire	Reward system	Differentiate good from average and poor performers Tie rewards clearly to performance Pay as well as your competitors
Bond	Culture	Foster mutual reliance and friendship among co-workers Value collaboration and teamwork Encourage sharing of best practices
Comprehend	Job design	Design jobs that have distinct and important roles in the organization Design jobs that are meaningful and foster a sense of contribution to the organization
Defend	Performance management	Increase the transparency of all processes Emphasize their fairness Build trust by being just and transparent in granting rewards, assignments, and other forms of recognition

This emphasis on organizational factors does not mean that management behaviour is not important. On the contrary, because managers have some control over the way in which company policies are implemented, they can help to meet their employees' drives. For example, a line manager or supervisor can link performance and reward through the use of praise, recognition, favoured assignments, the allocation of bonuses, encouraging teamwork, and making jobs interesting and meaningful. Once again, employees expect their managers to address all four drives, within the constraints of the organization. Managers who fail to fulfil even one drive are rated poorly.

This theory is similar to the framework developed several decades ago by the American psychologist Abraham Maslow (1943, 1954, 1971). Maslow also argued that we have innate needs (including drives and goals), and identified nine of these (Figure 9.1).

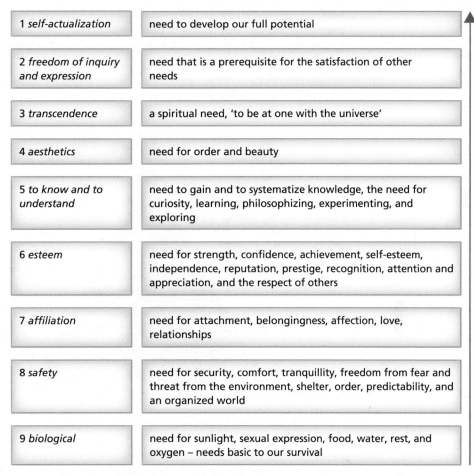

Figure 9.1: Abraham Maslow's needs hierarchy

If our biological and safety needs are not satisfied, we die. If our needs for love and esteem are not satisfied, we can feel inferior and helpless; but if these needs are satisfied, we feel self-confident. **Self-actualization**, Maslow argued, is our ultimate goal, and freedom of inquiry and expression is a prerequisite for this. Aesthetics and the metaphysical concept of transcendence have been largely ignored by management writers and researchers who have focused instead on self-actualization.

Maslow argued that self-actualized people are rare, and that creating the conditions for us to develop our capabilities to this extent was a challenging task. He also argued that these needs are organized in a hierarchy, with lower order biological and safety needs at the bottom, and higher order self-actualization and transcendence needs at the top, as in Figure 9.1.

Self-actualization
the desire for personal fulfilment, to develop one's potential, to become everything that one is capable of becoming.

STOP AND THINK   How could you use Maslow's framework to explain a friend's preference for either the freedom and flexibility of working freelance in the gig economy, or the security and social contact provided by working in a conventional organization?

This hierarchy, Maslow argued, has the following properties:

1. A need is not an effective motivator until those lower in the hierarchy are more or less satisfied. A satisfied need is not a motivator, and we have an innate desire to work our way up the hierarchy.

2. Lack of need satisfaction can affect mental health. Consider the frustration, anxiety and depression that can arise from lack of self-esteem, loss of the respect of others, an inability to sustain relationships, and an inability to develop one's capabilities.

3. The experience of self-actualization stimulates desire for more. Maslow claimed that self-actualizers have 'peak experiences'. When you have had one of these, you want another.

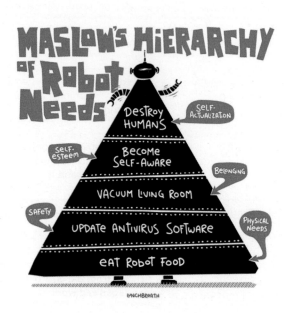

Maslow did not intend this hierarchy to be regarded as rigid, but as a typical picture of how human motivation is likely to develop under ideal conditions.

Maslow's theory has been criticized as reflecting white American middle class values in the mid-twentieth century. However, Louis Tay and Ed Diener (2011) have found that subjective well-being is associated with need fulfilment around the world. They analysed data from the Gallup World Poll which asks about six needs: food and shelter, safety and security, social support, respect and pride, mastery, and self-direction. This poll covers over 60,000 people in 123 countries in eight regions: Africa, East and South Asia, Former Soviet Union, Latin America, Middle East, Northern Europe, South East Asia, and Southern Europe. Need fulfilment was important for well-being in 80 per cent of those surveyed. A survey of 130 bank managers in Bangladesh also found support for Maslow's needs hierarchy (Rahman and Nurullah, 2014). It seems that the needs identified by Maslow may be universal, and independent of culture.

Table 9.4: Nohria and Maslow compared

Nohria's emotional needs	Maslow's hierarchy of needs
Acquire	Biological, esteem
Bond	Affiliation, esteem
Comprehend	Knowing and understanding, Freedom of enquiry
Defend	Safety

Maslow's theory is still valuable, in recognizing that behaviour depends on a range of needs, drives and motives. His ideas still influence management practice concerning rewards, management style and work design. Many techniques such as job enrichment, total quality management, process redesign, self-managing teams, 'new leadership' and engagement have been influenced by his thinking. His framework is also consistent with emotional needs theory (see Table 9.4).

YOUR CALL IS IMPORTANT
to US -- BUT NOT IMPORTANT
ENOUGH FOR US to HIRE
ADDITIONAL STAFF to
tALK to YOU.

RING

SCHWADRON

Source: www.CartoonStock.com

desired. The expectancy and instrumentality (but not valence) of the managers appeared to be mirrored by their CSRs, probably as a result of social learning, as CSRs modelled the attitudes and behaviours of their managers. However, this motivational effect was stronger for charismatic managers, who also affected the valence (desirability of outcomes) of their CSRs. Non-charismatic managers who supported the new technology actually reduced the extent to which their CSRs valued the new tool.

The manager wishing to encourage specific behaviours in subordinates should thus be motivated to engage in those behaviours themselves, and being a charismatic leader also helps.

Goal-setting theory

Goal-setting theory
a process theory of
motivation which argues
that work motivation
is influenced by goal
difficulty, goal specificity
and knowledge of
results.

Goal-setting theory is another process theory of motivation, which attempts to predict and explain work behaviour. However, the main advocate of this approach, Edwin Locke (1968), once argued that 'goal-setting is more appropriately viewed as a motivational technique rather than a formal theory' (Locke, 1975, p.465). Is seems to be both a theory and a technique.

Goal theory has four propositions which are well-supported by research (Locke and Latham, 1990):

1. *Challenging goals* lead to higher levels of performance than simple and unchallenging goals. Difficult goals are also called 'stretch' goals because they encourage us to improve.

2. *Specific goals* lead to higher levels of performance than vague goals such as 'do your best'. It is easier to adjust our behaviour when we know precisely what is required of us. Goals should thus be SMART: specific, measurable, attainable, realistic and time-related.

3. *Participation* in goal setting can improve performance by increasing commitment to those goals, but managerially assigned goals that are adequately explained and justified can also lead to high performance.

4. *Knowledge of results* of past performance is necessary for effective goal achievement. Feedback contains information and is also motivational.

This theory has been tested mainly in situations where short-term targets can be expressed in clear and quantifiable terms. It is unclear if the theory applies to longer-term goals, say over a period of years, as targets are likely to be more qualitative and to change as circumstances alter. It is also uncertain whether this applies where goals are difficult to measure, such as in most types of professional work. Another limitation is the focus on individual goals and performance rather than on teamwork.

Herminia Ibarra (2015) suggests that mobile and wearable devices (smartphones and Fitbits), and other technology tools, are making 'the quantified self' and goal-setting more popular. BetterWorks, in Palo Alto California (www.betterworks.com), designs performance tracking software that allows individuals to set and share goals, log progress on the company dashboard, and get feedback ('cheers' or 'nudges') from colleagues through a smartphone app. This approach is used by Google, Twitter and Intel, and BetterWorks has 50 other customers (*The Economist*, 2015). This does not solve the problem that aspects of work that are difficult to measure ('thinking strategically', for example) may be overlooked by the focus on problems and activities with clear 'OKRs' – objectives and key results. Another problem is that the pursuit of goals interferes with learning; people want to look good by getting results, rather than spending 'downtime' developing new capabilities. Ibarra (2015) explains:

> Imagine this, not too far-fetched situation: a manager sets a goal of 'becoming a better listener'. Aided by polling tools that provide continual, anonymous feedback from his or her direct reports and name badges with sensors that track location, face-to-face interaction, gestures and speech dynamics – technologies that are already available – the manager might realise that listening is easier in the morning, and schedule accordingly. That would be a benefit. But she might also start unconsciously avoiding people with whom listening is harder, in order to keep her numbers up.

Driving people hard

The secret to a happy workforce, says Charles Morgan, the third-generation head of The Morgan Motor Company, is not so much that they work for a family company but that there is a long-term plan and a product of which they can be proud. Morgan, founded in 1910, employs 190 staff in Malvern, Worcestershire, producing 1,000 of its trademark cars a year, which speak of a different age when British automotive design and engineering were at their height.

Alexander Chalkin/Shutterstock

The relaunch (in 2011) of the Morgan three-wheeler, the model that originally made the 101-year-old company's name, should take production up to 1,500 next year. 'We can think in the long term and are very loyal to our staff', Mr Morgan said. 'We drive people hard but this is because we know they enjoy the pressure. We work to task not to the clock but are flexible so people can build up time off. We also have an open-door policy, which means the customer can come and see their car made. That is fairly powerful for staff and increases their satisfaction in a product in which they can be proud. We have made a commitment to launching a new model every year and that brings its own incentives for people, it puts people on their toes and they can see what they are doing next', he said. 'It also helps that when Aston Martin and Bentley were laying off people during the recession, we did not let anyone go. It helps here that people feel they are not working for a company which might make arbitrary decisions based on moves in exchange rates and labour costs', Mr Morgan said (© Lea, News International Trading Ltd, 19 July 2011).

Inner work life theory

Inner work life theory a process theory of motivation which argues that our behaviour and performance at work are influenced by the interplay of our perceptions, emotions, and motives.

Equity, expectancy and goal-setting theories of motivation allow us to make choices, implying a rational, logical, reasoned approach to the decisions that shape our behaviour. They do not allow for the influence of emotions. The **inner work life theory** developed by Teresa Amabile and Steven Kramer (2007) argues that our behaviour and work performance are influenced by the way in which our perceptions, motives and emotions interact with each other, triggered by everyday events.

Our private thoughts and feelings may not be visible to others, but we do not leave them at home when we go to work. To find out how the dynamics of our 'inner work life' can affect performance, Amabile and Kramer asked 238 professionals from 26 project teams to complete a personal diary, in a standard format, every day for the duration of their projects. The researchers sent daily emails to each professional, asking for a description of an event that stood out in their mind that day and how that made them feel (similar to the critical incident method used by Herzberg, described below). This gave the researchers around 12,000 diary entries to analyse, revealing the richness and intensity of people's inner work lives, what they call 'the reality management never sees'.

One of the main implications of this perspective concerns the role of emotions. Neuroscience has shown that cognition (including perception) and emotion are closely linked. Events at work trigger a combination of perceptual, emotional and motivational processes. The way in which these processes interact shapes our behaviour and our performance at work.

The researchers conclude that we perform better when our work experiences include more positive emotions, stronger intrinsic motivation and more favourable perceptions of the work, the team, management and the organization. Positive emotions, perceptions and motivation were also linked to creativity. Productivity, commitment and collegiality also improve when we 'are in a good mood'.

The management implications of this research differ from those of other motivation theories, which emphasize the 'daily pat on the back' and attempts to make work fun. This research suggests instead that the two most important management behaviours involve 'enabling people to move forward in their work' and 'treating them decently as human beings'.

1. Enable progress

The factor that made the difference between 'good days' and 'bad days' for the respondents in this study was a sense of being able to make progress. This could mean achieving a goal, accomplishing a task, solving a problem. The worst days – frustrating, sad, fearful – were characterized by setbacks, and even small delays could have this impact. Managers should:

- provide direct help and do not get in the way;
- make sure that time and other resources are adequate;
- react to successes and failures with a learning orientation;
- set clear and unambiguous goals (as goal theory suggests).

2. Manage with a human touch

Interpersonal relationships are also important, treating people fairly and with respect. These events had almost as much impact as 'enabling progress' on the distinction between good and bad days. Praise in the absence of real progress has little positive impact, and can arouse cynicism. Good progress without recognition leads to anger and sadness.

No play, no stay

If you have fun at work, are you less likely to leave? Michael Tews et al. (2014) studied the relationship between fun and employee turnover in a national restaurant chain in the US. Turnover is a constant problem in this sector, which tends to employ younger workers. The researchers surveyed almost 300 recently employed staff in 20 restaurants. Fun activities included social events, teambuilding tasks, competitions and public celebrations of achievements and milestones. Fun activities on their own, however, had little effect on staff turnover. Staff retention was improved where managers were seen to support the idea of having fun at work, and where the fun involved opportunities to socialize and to develop quality relationships with colleagues. The researchers conclude that 'entry-level employees in the hospitality industry appear to particularly value coworkers who are friendly, outgoing and who socialize with one another, as well as managers who allow and encourage fun on the job' (Tews et al., 2014, p.931). If an organization has problems retaining staff, supporting a workplace environment where staff can have fun together could help to solve the problem.

The social process of motivating others

Motivation can also be seen as a social influence process. The advice in the previous section, about enabling progress and 'managing with a human touch', illustrates this. The general question is, how do we motivate others to do what we want them to do? The question for management is, how do we motivate employees to perform well? Many jobs are still designed using the methods of the American engineer Frederick Winslow Taylor (1911). Taylor's *scientific management* approach to designing jobs (see Chapter 14) is as follows:

1. Decide on the optimum degree of *task fragmentation*, breaking down a complex job into a sequence of simple steps.

2. Decide the *one best way* to perform the work, through studies to discover the most effective method for doing each step, including workplace layout and design of tools.

3. *Train* employees to carry out these simple fragmented tasks in the manner specified.

4. *Reward* employees financially for meeting performance targets.

STOP AND THINK   You are employed on a job in which you repeat the same simple task every 15 seconds, perhaps wiring plugs for lamps, 9.00 am until 5.30 pm, every day (with a lunch break), five days a week. Describe your emotional response to this work.

Is it inevitable that some jobs just have to be like this, given the nature of work and technology, and the need to keep quality high and costs low?

Task fragmentation has advantages:

- employees do not need expensive and time-consuming training;
- repeating one small specialized task makes employees very proficient;
- unskilled work gets lower pay; and
- some of the problems of achieving controlled performance are simplified.

The disadvantages include:

- repetitive work is very boring;
- the individual's contribution to the organization is meaningless and insignificant;
- monotony leads to apathy, dissatisfaction and carelessness; and
- the employee does not develop skills that might lead to promotion.

Job enrichment
a technique for broadening the experience of work to enhance employee need satisfaction and to improve motivation and performance.

Taylor's approach to job design appears logical and efficient, but it creates jobs that do not stimulate motivation or improve performance. Taylor had a simplified view of human motivation, regarding 'lower level' employees as 'coin operated' and arguing that the rewards for working as instructed should be financial. Taylor's methods are more likely to encourage absenteeism and sabotage than commitment and flexibility. Managers are thus interested in theories of motivation as sources of alternative methods for encouraging motivation and high performance. During the 1960s and 1970s, these concerns created the Quality of Working Life (QWL) movement whose language and methods are still influential today. One QWL technique is **job enrichment**.

Motivator factors
aspects of work which lead to high levels of satisfaction, motivation and performance, including achievement, recognition, responsibility, advancement, growth and the work itself.

The concept of job enrichment was first developed by the American psychologist Frederick Herzberg (1966, 1968). However, more recent research suggests that many employees today respond in ways that his theory predicts (Basset-Jones and Lloyd, 2005). To discover what factors affected job satisfaction and dissatisfaction, 203 Pittsburgh engineers and accountants were asked two 'critical incident' questions. They were asked to recall events which had made them feel good about their work, and events which had made them feel bad about it.

Hygiene factors
aspects of work which remove dissatisfaction, but do not contribute to motivation and performance, including pay, company policy, supervision, status, security and physical working conditions.

Analysis of these incident narratives showed that the factors which led to job satisfaction were different from those which led to job dissatisfaction. Herzberg called this a 'two factor theory of motivation', the two sets of factors being **motivator factors** and **hygiene factors**, summarized in Table 9.6. Motivators are also known as (job) content factors, while hygiene factors are known as (organizational) context factors.

Table 9.6: Motivator and hygiene factors

Motivator factors (job content)	Hygiene factors (organizational context)
Achievement	Pay
Advancement	Company policy
Growth	Supervisory style
Recognition	Status
Responsibility	Security
The work itself	Working conditions

Herzberg (1987, p.31) claimed that this pattern of motivation had been identified in Finland, Hungary, Italy, Israel, Japan and Zambia. In South Africa, however, while managers and skilled workers, black and white, produced the expected results, unskilled workers' satisfaction appeared to be dependent on hygiene. Herzberg claimed that 'the impoverished nature of the unskilled workers' jobs has not afforded these workers with motivators – thus the abnormal profile'. He also cites a study of unskilled Indian workers who were 'operating on a dependent hygiene continuum that leads to addiction to hygiene, or strikes and revolution'.

According to this theory, the redesign of jobs to increase motivation and performance should thus focus on motivator or content factors. Improvement in the hygiene or context factors, Herzberg (1968) argued, will remove dissatisfaction, but will not increase motivation and performance. He suggested using **vertical loading factors** to achieve job enrichment.

The way in which a job is designed determines the rewards available, and what the individual has to do to get those rewards. It helps to distinguish **intrinsic rewards** and **extrinsic rewards**.

Intrinsic rewards are valued outcomes within the control of the individual, such as feelings of satisfaction and accomplishment. For some of us, and for some actions, the outcome is its own (intrinsic) reward. Mountaineers, poets, athletes, authors, painters and musicians are usually familiar with the concept of intrinsic reward. Few people ever get paid for climbing hills, and there are few wealthy poets on this planet. *Extrinsic rewards* are valued outcomes that are controlled by others, such as recognition, promotion or pay increases.

The relationships between performance and intrinsic reward are more immediate than those between performance and extrinsic reward. Intrinsic rewards are thus more important influences on our motivation to work. It has long been argued that 'eat what you kill' incentive reward schemes do not work well (Kohn, 1993; Aguinis et al., 2013). Money is not an overriding concern for most people, and 'bribing' people to perform better with cash incentives can be seen as manipulative. Incentive pay schemes also discourage risk taking and creativity, and undermine interest in the job itself. Extrinsic rewards might buy compliance, but they do not encourage commitment.

The Job Characteristics Model (Figure 9.3) describes the job enrichment strategy of Richard Hackman and Greg Oldham (1974; Hackman et al., 1975). This model sets out the links between the features of jobs, the individual's experience, and outcomes such as motivation, satisfaction and performance. The model suggests that jobs can be analysed in terms of five *core dimensions*:

1. *Skill variety*: making use of different skills and abilities.

2. *Task identity*: providing a 'whole' and meaningful piece of work.

3. *Task significance*: how the job affects the work of others.

4. *Autonomy*: the degree of independence and discretion.

5. *Feedback*: providing performance information.

Vertical loading factors methods for enriching work and improving motivation, by removing controls, increasing accountability, and by providing feedback, new tasks, natural work units, special assignments and additional authority.

Intrinsic rewards valued outcomes or benefits which come from the individual, such as *feelings of satisfaction, competence, self-esteem* and *accomplishment*.

Extrinsic rewards valued outcomes or benefits provided by others, such as promotion, pay increases, a bigger office desk, praise and recognition.

Growth need strength a measure of the readiness and capability of an individual to respond positively to job enrichment.

This model also takes into account individual differences in **growth need strength**, which is similar to Maslow's concept of self-actualization.

Growth need strength (GNS) is an indicator of your willingness to welcome personal development through job enrichment. The causal chain, from job redesign through individual experience, to performance outcomes, depends on GNS. With employees whose GNS is low, an enriched job is unlikely to improve their performance.

STOP AND THINK Your instructor offers to enrich your educational experience of studying organizational behaviour, with additional classes and tutorials, further reading, and extra feedback and revision sessions. There is no guarantee, however, that this will increase your course grades. How do you feel about this offer?

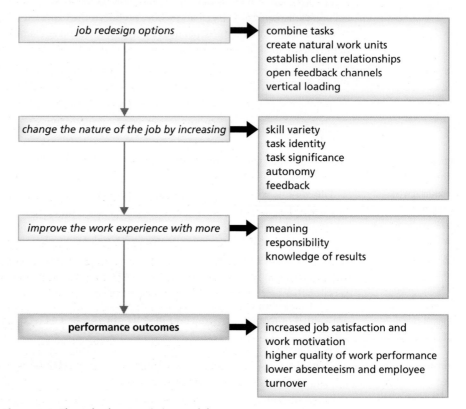

Figure 9.3: The Job Characteristics Model
Source: based on Hackman et al. (1975, p.62).

Job diagnostic survey a questionnaire which assesses the degree of skill variety, task identity, task significance, autonomy and feedback in jobs.

To assess jobs on the core dimensions, Hackman and colleagues developed a questionnaire called the **job diagnostic survey** (JDS).

Skill variety and autonomy are measured in the JDS by questions such as:

How much *variety* is there in your job? That is, to what extent does the job require you to do many different things at work, using a variety of your skills and talents?

How much *autonomy* is there in your job? That is, to what extent does your job permit you to decide *on your own* how to go about doing the work?

Respondents rate their answers to these questions on a seven-point scale. The JDS thus provides *operational definitions* (glossary) of the variables in the model. The core job dimensions are *independent variables*, and critical psychological states and performance outcomes are *dependent variables* (see Chapter 1). Growth need strength is a mediating variable in

Motivating potential score an indicator of how motivating a job is likely to be for an individual, considering skill variety, task identity, task significance, autonomy and feedback.

this causal chain. The JDS can be used to establish how motivating a job is, by calculating the **motivating potential score** (MPS) from answers across groups of employees doing the same job.

The MPS is calculated using the values of the variables measured by the JDS:

$$MPS = \frac{(\text{skill variety} + \text{task identity} + \text{task significance})}{3} \times \text{autonomy} \times \text{feedback}$$

The first part of this equation concerns aspects of the job. The second part concerns how the work is managed. Autonomy and feedback are more important than the other dimensions. The equation reflects this by treating them as two separate components. Only the arithmetic mean of the ratings for skill variety, task identity and task significance is used. If one of the three main components – job aspects, autonomy, feedback – is low, then the MPS will be low. A near-zero rating on either autonomy or feedback, for example, would pull the score down disproportionately (five times zero equals zero). A near-zero rating on task variety, identity or significance would not have much impact on the overall score. The five core dimensions stimulate three psychological states critical to high work motivation, job satisfaction and performance. These critical psychological states are:

1. *Experienced meaningfulness*: the extent to which the individual considers the work to be meaningful, valuable and worthwhile. (Susie Cranston and Scott Keller, 2013, call this the 'meaning quotient', which inspires employees to perform at their peak.)

2. *Experienced responsibility*: the extent to which the individual feels accountable for their work output.

3. *Knowledge of results*: the extent to which the individual knows and understands how well they are performing.

Jobs with high MPS are more likely to lead to the experience of critical psychological states than jobs with low scores. Expectancy theorists argue that all three critical states, and not just one or two, must be present if the personal and work outcomes on the right-hand side of the model are to be achieved. The MPS is only a guide to how motivating a job will be as different employees can have different perceptions of the same job. Those who put a low value on personal growth (revealed by a low GNS score) will not respond as the model suggests. No point, then, in offering them enriched jobs, unless one believes that the experience of personal development can in itself stimulate future growth need.

The model also shows how the motivating potential of jobs can be improved by applying five *implementing concepts*. These (including vertical loading, from Herzberg) are:

1. *Combine tasks.* Give employees more than one part of the work to do, to increase variety and contribution to the product or service.

2. *Form natural work units.* Give employees meaningful patterns of work, to increase individual contribution and task significance.

3. *Establish client relationships.* Give employees responsibility for personal contacts, to increase variety, autonomy, and feedback (see the research box 'Here's looking at you, chef').

Here's looking at you, chef

Scott Berinato (2014) interviewed Ryan Buell, a researcher at Harvard Business School, whose study (with colleagues Tami Kim and Chia-Jung Tsay) found that chefs made better meals when they could see their customers. Using a real cafeteria, and a video-conferencing arrangement, Buell set up four different scenarios. In the first of these, chefs and diners could not see each other. Second, diners could see the chefs. Third, chefs could see the diners. Finally, chefs and diners could see each other. Customers were surveyed about the service and the food. Satisfaction with the food was 10 per cent higher when the chefs could see their customers than when they could

→

not see them. When customers and chefs could all see each other, customer satisfaction was over 17 per cent higher.

Buell argues that seeing the customer makes employees feel more appreciated and satisfied, and more motivated to perform well. The study also showed that it was not just the customers' perception of quality that improved; the food did get better. Buell explained:

> During the experiment we had an observer in the kitchen taking notes and timing service. Normally, chefs would make eggs on the grill in advance, adding them to plates as needed and often overcooking them. When we turned on the screens and the chefs saw the customers, they started making eggs to order more often. … There's something refreshingly human about the idea that just seeing each other can make us more appreciative and lead to objectively better outcomes. (Berinato, 2014, pp.34, 35)

The researchers conclude that 'opening up the work environment' in this way, creating a relationship with the customers, can motivate chefs to higher levels of performance, for little or no cost.

4. *Vertical loading.* Increase autonomy, by giving employees responsibilities normally allocated to supervisors, such as work scheduling, problem solving, training others and recruitment decisions.

5. *Open feedback channels.* Give employees performance summaries and corporate information. Feedback tells people how well they are doing, and provides a basis for improvement.

Job enrichment methods are important in an economic downturn, when costs are cut, jobs are lost and work motivation is imperative. However, is a model from the 1970s relevant today? Maria Karanika-Murray and Georges Michaelides (2015) identify nine workplace characteristics that affect motivation and performance. Three of these support employee *autonomy*: responsibility for decision making, involvement in work planning and role flexibility. Three support *competence*: feedback, appreciation, and supportive management. Three support *relatedness*: social support, trust, and sense of community. These characteristics are similar to the JCM core dimensions of autonomy, variety, feedback, significance and task identity, indicating that the approach is still valid.

Recognizing that individuals have different motivational profiles, attention has also focused on designing and enriching jobs, through three other routes: 'job sculpting', 'job crafting' and 'i-deals'.

Job sculpting first identifies what interests and challenges employees; new technology, developing theories, mentoring others, negotiating and persuading. Jobs, special assignments and career paths can then be 'sculpted' to match those interests, enhance motivation and performance, and discourage people from leaving. Timothy Butler and James Waldroop (1999) describe a bank lending officer, who was good at customer services but was interested in theory and conceptual thinking. He was about to leave the company until it gave him a role in competitive analysis and strategy formulation.

Job crafting involves individuals adapting jobs to fit more closely their skills and interests by making adjustments to activities, time commitment and work intensity, and 'task trading' with colleagues. Amy Wrzesniewski and Jane Dutton (2001) argue that most employees do this naturally. Teams can also craft their work, leading to improved engagement and performance (Tims et al., 2013).

I-deals are personally negotiated – idiosyncratic – work arrangements that differ from those of co-workers, and can include pay and other benefits, work at home arrangements, flexible hours, special projects, and training and development opportunities. Traditionally this approach may have been limited to 'superstars' who had the power to negotiate their own special packages (top musicians and movie stars, for example). Denise Rousseau and colleagues (2006) conclude that these deals are now widespread in many organizations, in response to increasing complexity, and the pace of change.

Invitation to see

News UK Syndication/*The Sunday Times Magazine*/Andrew Testa

No Loafing: Workers at the Greencore factory near Worksop, which produces 3 million sandwiches a week. At some stage, they have probably made your lunch.

The Sunday Times Magazine, March 2015, pp.22–23.

1. **Decoding**. Look at this image closely. Note in as much detail as possible what messages you feel that it is trying to convey. Does it tell a story, present a point of view, support an argument, perpetuate a myth, reinforce a stereotype, challenge a stereotype?

2. **Challenging**. To what extent do you agree with the messages, stories, points of view, arguments, myths, or stereotypes in this image? Is this image open to challenge, to criticism, or to interpretation and decoding in other ways, revealing other messages?

3. **Sharing**. Compare with colleagues your interpretation of this image. Explore explanations for differences in your respective decodings.

You're the manager: what would you advise?

Stan, a member of one of my delivery teams, has recently put on a lot of weight. We are a nationwide furniture producer, and as distribution manager, I have to deal with this issue. Stan's team has complained that he now has problems lifting furniture from the van and carrying it into customers' premises. Normally, Stan is very hard working and willing. However, his level of fitness could increase the risk of injury to his colleagues. For example, another delivery team member recently had to take three weeks off work with a back injury. The team said that this injury happened when he was working with Stan, who was not able to help carry the products. I tried talking to him, but he became angry, and said that this was none of my business, and that his weight wasn't a problem anyway.

I don't think that Stan is capable of doing this job, but there is no other role that I can offer him. The last thing I want to do is to turn this into a formal disciplinary matter, with all the legal implications that would follow. Stan has been a loyal employee, and I want to be fair to him, but without exposing the other delivery team members to health and safety risks? What would you advise?

Chapter 10 **Group formation**

Key terms

group

group dynamics

aggregate

huddle

additive task

conjunctive task

disjunctive task

Hawthorne Effect

Human Relations approach

work passion

formal group

informal group

group self-organization

activities

interactions

sentiments

Learning outcomes

When you have read this chapter, you should be able to define those key terms in your own words, and you should also be able to:

1. List the key characteristics of a group.
2. Distinguish between different types of group tasks.
3. Name the four research phases of the Hawthorne studies.
4. Distinguish between a formal and an informal group.
5. Outline Homans' theory of group formation.
6. Enumerate the five stages of Tuckman and Jensen's model of group development.
7. Summarize Katzenbach and Santamaria's distinction between a team and a single-leader working group.

Why study groups?

Work groups and teams have become a nearly ubiquitous part of contemporary management practice in the majority of organizations in the world. For over two decades, organizations have been restructuring their workforces into groups and teams (Li et al., 2014; Kozlowski and Bell, 2013). Diane Coutu (2009, p.99) observed that:

> a cult has grown up around teams. Even in a society as fiercely independent as America, teams are considered almost sacrosanct. The belief that working in teams makes us more creative and productive is so widespread that when faced with challenging new tasks, leaders quickly assume that teams are the best way to get the job done.

However, Richard Hackman reflecting on his many years of research into groups and teams, concluded:

> I have no question that when you have a team, the possibility exists that it will generate magic, producing something extraordinary, a collective creation of previously unimagined quality or beauty. But don't count on it. Research consistently shows that teams underperform despite the extra resources that they have. That's because problems with co-ordination and motivation typically chip away at the benefits of collaboration. And even when you have a strong and cohesive team, it's often in competition with other teams, and that dynamic can also get in the way of real progress. (in Coutu, 2009, p.100)

While the practical aspects of groups may be significant, as Marion Hampton (1999, p.113) explains, the symbolic ones may be even more important:

> Groups embody many important cultural values of Western society: teamwork, co-operation, a collective that is greater than the sum of its parts, informality, egalitarianism and even the indispensability of the individual member. Groups are seen as having a motivating, inspiring influence on the individual, drawing the best out of him or her, enabling him or her to perform feats that would be beyond him or herself as a detached individual. Groups can have a healing effect on individuals, bolstering their self-esteem and filling their lives with meaning.

According to Vašková, (2007) and the European Foundation (2007):

- 60 per cent of European Union workers perform all or part of their work in teams;
- most teamworking is to be found in the UK and Estonia (81 per cent) and the least in (Lithuania 38 per cent) and Italy (41 per cent);
- most teamwork occurs in industrial rather than service industries;
- teamwork is most often found in larger organizations.

Groups in organizations

Group performance thus affects the success of the organization as a whole. Being able to work productively with others is so important that companies place an emphasis on their recruits being good 'team players'. A recent survey of employers revealed that teamworking was the second most important key skill (60 per cent) that they wanted to develop in their young recruits in their first year on the job (CIPD, 2015). It was slightly behind communication skills (64 per cent).

Researching how graduates could get a job in one of the top management consultancies, investment banks or big law firms, Lauren Rivera (2015) noted that these companies expected their employees to spend extraordinary amounts of time together – learning the ropes in boot camps, working late in the office, having constant work dinners, getting stuck together in airports in godforsaken places. Recruiters told her that they looked for people who could be their friends as well as colleagues, and that selection was like 'picking a team in the playground', so as to create a 'fraternity of smart people' (*The Economist*, 2015).

It has been argued that the modern organization is no longer a collection of individuals, but rather a network of interconnected teams (Kozlowski and Bell, 2013). Group working and teamworking has been an aspect of organizational life for a long time, yet remains controversial. The management literature promotes the benefits of group working, and stresses the commonality of interests between individual workers, organized by management into teams, and the goals of the 'organization as a whole' – that is, those of senior management.

Teams and knowledge production

A study that investigated 19.9 million research papers published over five decades and 2.1 million patents showed that teams increasingly outperform solo authors in the production of knowledge. Research is increasingly done in teams across nearly all fields. Teams typically produce more frequently cited research than individuals do, a trend that that has been increasing over time. Teams now also produce the exceptionally high-impact research, even where that distinction was once the domain of solo authors. These findings apply to sciences and engineering, social sciences, arts and humanities and patents, suggesting that the process of knowledge creation has fundamentally changed (Wuchty et al., 2007).

Critics, in contrast, contend that the extent of employee resistance to management's attempt to establish groups has been underplayed or ignored. Employees also have been less convinced about teamworking. A recent study by Denise Thursfield (2015) of laboratory technicians revealed that when employees enjoy personal responsibility, individual autonomy and accountability in their performance in their work, they dislike and resist management attempts to introduce group working. More generally, David Knights and Darren McCabe (2000) reported that employees in an automobile plant:

- disliked the intrusion that group working had into their personal lives, causing them to distrust management;
- claimed they did not understand the norms of group working and its protocols;
- resented the move away from traditional, individual working.

Loners do the best group work

Susan Cain observed that the modern workplace is all about teams, open plan offices and collective brainstorming. Schools are increasing arranged in teaching 'hubs' rather than individual desks to encourage group learning. However, she suggests that teamwork might actually be stifling the creativity it is intended to encourage. The lone wolf, who likes to sit in an office with the door closed, in order to think, has become an endangered species. Lone geniuses are out, collaboration is in. However research suggests that people are more creative when they have privacy and freedom from interruption. Seventy per cent of American employees inhabit open plan offices. People are in each other's faces all the time, listening to each other's conversations. This constant interaction is exhausting and unproductive according to Cain. Studies show that workers who are constantly interrupted make 50 per cent more mistakes and typically take twice as long to complete tasks. In contrast, some of the most spectacularly creative people in many fields are introverts, who see themselves as individualistic, independent, non-joiners. That puts them out of step with the modern, team-focused workplace. Perhaps it is time to review our approach to people working together in organizations (Cain, 2012; Driscoll, 2012).

Drexler and Forrester (1998) suggest three tests to determine whether a work task should be performed by individuals or by a group:

- *Can be work be done better by more than one person?* This assesses the degree of task complexity and the requirement for diverse skills and perspectives. Rapidly changing conditions can also require numerous people to be involved on a task.

- *Does the work create a common goal for group members?* The group goal must be more than the aggregate of individual goals. While members are responsible for their piece of work, the group is collectively responsible for the whole process, and for collectively producing something that a single member alone cannot. For example, providing a pleasant dining experience in a restaurant.

- *Are the individual members of the group interdependent?* Does the success of the whole depend on the success of each one and vice versa? For example, as in the case a university group student project where all the individual student members receive the same group project grade.

To boldly go … in groups

Perhaps the most fictional aspect of the classic science fiction TV and film series *Star Trek* was how well the crew members got on with each other despite being in such close proximity in the Starship Enterprise for years. Here on Earth, Anatoly Perminov, the head of the Russian space agency, Roskosmos, revealed Russia's intention of building an inhabited space station on the moon by 2032, as a prelude to launching a manned mission to Mars. The estimated duration of a round trip to Mars, including a stay on the surface, is 520 days. This would be as much of a psychological as a technical challenge.

In preparation for this, in June 2010, a Frenchman and a Columbian-Italian, together with three Russians and one Chinese, entered a set of four steel containers which they would occupy together. This was a 17-month simulated mission to Mars designed by Roskosmos and the European Space Agency (ESA) to test the physical and mental requirements of an ultra-long duration spaceflight. The cramped metal construction (see photo), which has no windows, and in which the volunteers lived, was the Mars 500 'spaceship'. It was located in Russia's Institute of Biomedical Problems (IBP). Like the contestants on the TV's show *Big Brother*, the subjects were required to complete tasks, and were monitored to determine the effects of separation and close proximity living. During a similar experiment in IBP's *Mars Flyer* isolation chamber in 1999, two Russian cosmonauts broke into a fist fight, spluttering blood on the module walls. One of them then pressed unwelcome kisses on a Canadian crew member.

Russians psychologists claim that cosmonauts can develop 'space dementia'; become clinically depressed; and suffer from 'asthenization', which causes irritability,

ESA/Science Photo Library

→

low energy and leads crew members to get on badly with each other. Nick Kanas of the University of California investigated interactions between space crew and their mission ground controllers on the ground of *Mir* (the Soviet Union's first space station), *Skylab* (NASA's first station) and the current *International Space Station* (ISS). He found that the way crew coped with stress was to blame the ground staff. They converted tensions on board into feelings that the people on Earth did not care. One Skylab crew became so annoyed with mission control during its 84 days in space that they mutinied, sulked and turned off all communications. Psychologists are unsure whether a Mars mission should be crewed entirely by women (they are less likely to commit suicide or murder each other when irritable); be mixed (the sexes would support each other); or consist of psychologically robust and less libidinous robots. At the start of November 2011, the Mars 500 volunteers emerged after their 17 month, 70 million mile virtual journey complaining of boredom. These studies tell us that group dynamics within a confined space are problematic and need to be better understood (Amos, 2010, 2011; Wood, 2001).

Definitions of groups

Group two or more people, in face-to-face interaction, each aware of their group membership and interdependence, as they strive to achieve their goals.

Interpersonal behaviour builds up into group behaviour that in turn sustains and structures future interpersonal relations. The term **group** is thus reserved for people who consider themselves to be part of an identifiable unit, who relate to each other in a meaningful fashion and who share dispositions through their shared sense of collective identity. Our definition of group emphasizes people seeking to achieve their own goals. Those goals can come in the form of meeting innate needs. Abraham Maslow distinguished a hierarchy of human needs (Chapter 9). Amongst those frequently considered are biological, safety, affiliation, esteem and self-actualization needs. Individuals often join groups to meet their innate needs.

STOP AND THINK

Think of a group that you have joined voluntarily. Which of Maslow's needs are you meeting through your membership of the group?

Group dynamics the forces operating within groups that affect their performance and their members' satisfaction.

Groups affect the behaviour of the individuals who compose them. For this reason, social psychologists study internal **group dynamics**. They ask how members of a group communicate with each other and coordinate their activities; how they influence each other; what roles they play in a group; what kind of relationships they have; which members lead, and which follow; how they balance a focus on their task with social issues; and how they resolve conflicts (see Figure 10.1).

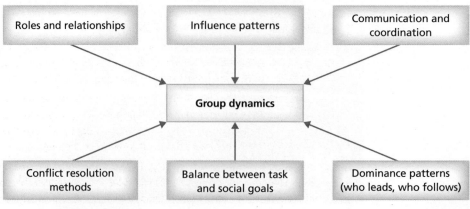

Figure 10.1: Group dynamics

Why would only *one* of the following be considered to be a group? In what circumstances could one of the other aggregates become a group?

a. People riding on a bus

b. Blonde women between 20 and 30 years of age

c. Members of a football team

d. Audience in a theatre

e. People outside an office building smoking

It is important to maintain a distinction between mere aggregates of individuals and what are called groups. The latter are so called because they exist not only through the (often visible) interactions of members, but also in the (not observable) perceptions of their members.

Aggregate a collection of unrelated people who happen to be in close physical proximity for a short period of time.

In the Stop and think example, only the football team would fulfil our criteria for a group, and we can usefully distinguish it from an **aggregate**. Aggregates are individuals who happen to be collected together at any particular time. Like the bus travellers, theatre audience or the smokers, they neither relate to one another in any meaningful fashion, nor consider themselves a part of any identifiable unit, despite their temporary physical proximity. Similarly, our definition excludes classes of people defined by their physical attributes, geographical location, economic status or age, and those who do interact with each other on a regular basis. Thus, a group is unlikely to exceed 12 or so persons. Beyond that number, the opportunity for frequent interaction between members and hence group awareness is considerably reduced.

It is possible for aggregates to be transformed into groups through outside circumstances. At the start of 'disaster movies', strangers fight for their lives on board sinking ships, hijacked aeroplanes and burning skyscrapers. The danger causes them to interact with one another, increasing their awareness of each other, and leads them to see themselves as having common problems. By the end of the film, the survivors demonstrate all the characteristics of the group as defined here. Groups differ in the degree to which they possess the five characteristics discussed below. The more of them that they have, the more a group will be recognized as such, and the more power it will have with which to influence its members.

1. *A minimum membership of two people.* Groups can range from two people to over 30. However, the greater the number of group members, the higher the number of possible relationships between them, the greater the level of communication that is required, and the more complex the structure needed to operate the group successfully.

2. *A communication network.* Each group member must be capable of communicating with every other member. In this communication process, the aims and purposes of the group are exchanged. The mere process of interaction satisfies some of our social needs, and it is used to set and enforce standards of group behaviour.

3. *A shared sense of collective identity.* Each member must identify with the other members of their group, and not see themselves as an individual acting independently. They must all believe themselves to be participants in the group, which itself is distinct from other groups.

4. *Complementary goals.* Members have individual objectives which can only be met through membership of and participation in the group. Their goals may differ but are sufficiently complementary that members feel able to achieve them through participation in the group. They recognize the need to work collectively and not as individuals.

5. *Group structure.* Individuals in the group will have different roles (e.g. ideas person, suggestion provider, compromiser). These roles, which tend to become fixed, indicate what members expect of each other. Norms or rules exist which indicate which behaviours are acceptable in the group and which are not (e.g. smoking, swearing, late coming).

Between a group and an aggregate, there is now a new, third, work arrangement. Management practitioners refer to it as a swarm. Gartner (2010) says that a swarm is characterized by a flurry of collective activity involving anyone who is able to add value to a task. In traditional groups, members know one another and work for the same manager or team leader. In contrast, swarms form quickly, attack a problem or grab an opportunity, and then quickly disperse. They involve members who are not members of the same formal group, and perhaps include those who have never worked together before (CIPD, 2014). However, academic researchers, taking their lead from the famous sociologist Erving Goffman (1963), refer to this work arrangement as a huddle. A **huddle** is defined as an unofficial gathering of two or more individuals convened to discuss work issues. It is impossible to distinguish conceptually between a swarm and a huddle, so the latter term will be employed here. Huddles represent an ad hoc response to action requirements in organizations, and these displace the more structured, bureaucratic group practices.

Huddle a type of short-term, focused social interaction occurring between two or more individuals in an organization which discusses work issues and which enhances learning.

Huddles are low on formality (ignoring rules, behaviour conventions, official roles and authority) and high on task content. They include problem-solving, information-sharing activities and involve collaboration. Quinn and Bunderson (2016) give an example of huddles at the Toyota Motor Company. Huddles (called 'Y-gaya') formed spontaneously to deal with plant problems with speakers' contributions being based on their knowledge rather than on their hierarchical position (MacDuffie, 1997). Huddles can be considered to be ultra-short-term groups. Some huddle memberships begin and end when goals are accomplished in a single interaction. However, task completion may take longer. It is unlikely that those who participate in a huddle would think of themselves as being members of any sort of group or team. Some commentators consider huddles to be more of an 'event' than a type of group.

Size matters

Technological developments have enabled organizations to create ever larger teams to tackle ever larger challenges. The problem is how to motivate and direct their members. With its increased number of employees, Google's co-founder and chief executive, Larry Page, reduced the numbers of products and services being developed. The company now has 30,000 employees, but tasks are still divided up into projects that can be handled by groups of between five and ten people. At Amazon, founder and chief executive Jeff Bezos limits team sizes to those small enough to be fed with two pizzas. Limited numbers improve accountability and goal clarity. In a small group no one can avoid pulling their weight, or claim that they do not know what their goal is. Research by Peter Klimek, a physicist from the Medical University in Vienna, confirmed that the more people there are at a meeting, the harder it is to get consensus. He used a program that simulated decision making by different sized committees. Once they exceed 20 members, it was difficult to reach consensus because too many sub-groups are formed. However, small can also be a problem. A meeting of eight people is the worst total for decision making. It produces neither a consensus nor a majority view, and has the highest probability of becoming deadlocked (Hill, 2012; Taher, 2009).

Once formed, all groups face a number of challenges, irrespective of whether they are government ministers agreeing a policy or university students completing a group project. Ten classic challenges facing groups are listed in Table 10.1, and have a direct effect on the group's success or failure.

STOP AND THINK

What additional challenges do work groups face with the development of social media and other technology-based communication tools?

Table 10.1: Work group challenges

Challenge	Explanation
climate	What atmosphere should pervade a group and how should members relate to one another? e.g. in a university student project group
objective	To what extent do members understand, accept and are committed to the group's objective? e.g. producing a project report that will gain an A-grade
contribution	Are all members expected to be equally involved in the group's activities? Who will contribute what expertise? e.g. is work to be shared equally and completed on time?
task division	How is the group's task to be divided up and shared between its members? e.g. on what basis is work to be divided between members?
information	How is information to be shared between members? What is the best way to inform those who need to know? e.g. regular meetings, emails, social media?
leadership	Should leadership be shared by the group or performed by one person? Should that person be appointed or elected? e.g. should there be a formal leader or should leadership be rotated?
conflict resolution	How should conflict between group members to be managed? Should differences be avoided, accommodated or negotiated? e.g. what happens when members express differences of view?
decision-making	How should the group make decisions? What should happen if there are disagreements? e.g. leader decides or group voting?
member evaluation	How should members' performance be assessed? What happens when individuals fail to meet their obligations? e.g. assessment by the group leader or collectively by peer review?
performance evaluation	How should the performance of group as a whole be assessed and improved? e.g. regular group reviews or member questionnaires?

As the size and complexity of modern organizations has increased, the need to integrate the work of different groups within organizations has also grown. McLaren Racing is well known in Formula 1 competition. The company is divided into four groups – those who conceive the car, those who engineer it, those who manufacture it, and those who race it (Blitz, 2007). There are many benefits of group working:

- They allow organizations to develop and deliver products and services quickly and cost-effectively while maintaining quality.
- They enable organizations to learn and retain that learning, more effectively.
- Cross-functional groups promote improved quality management.
- Cross-functional design groups can undertake effective process reengineering.
- Production time can be reduced if tasks performed concurrently by individuals are performed concurrently by people in groups.
- Group-based organization promotes innovation because of the cross-fertilization of ideas.
- Organizations with flat structures can be monitored, coordinated and directed more effectively, if the functional unit is the group rather than the individual.
- Groups can better handle the rise in organizational information processing requirements caused by increasing complexity than individuals (Mohrman et al., 1995).

Respect and group formation

Naomo Ellemers and her colleagues (2013) argue that the concept of 'perceived respect' involves two elements – a sense of being included in the group (perceived inclusion) and a sense of adding value to the group task (perceived value). They found that:

- Perceived respect was positively related to perceived inclusion and perceived value.

- Perceived inclusion related to positive team identity (morale, ability to perform and persistence).

- Perceived value related to 'willingness to invest in the team' (to give support to, and compensate for colleagues).

- Both positive team identity and willingness to invest were related to group performance (as measured by supervisor ratings).

Because perceived inclusion and perceived value affect group performance in different ways, their importance varies in different situations. In newly formed groups with little identity, it may be most important to foster individuals' sense of inclusion, but when joint effort is required, it is more critical to focus on what they can contribute to the group. This study focused on military teams working on peace-keeping duties in the Balkans but has relevance for employees working closely together, doing highly stressful work with important consequences such as those in the emergency services, crisis management and surgical teams.

Types of group tasks

Borrill and West (2005) reported research that estimated that 88 per cent of the variation in a group's performance could be explained with reference to the task that it was asked to perform. Thus, to fully understand group process or group performance, one has to take account of the task that a group performs. Joseph McGrath's circumplex model shown in Figure 10.2 offers a classification of group tasks. It consists of two axes. The horizontal axis reflects the degree to which a group task entails cognitive (mental) versus behavioural (physical) performance requirements. The vertical axis reflects the degree to which the group task is cooperative or conflicted. The degree of cooperation or conflict in a group is the result of the diversity of perspectives, values or interests of group members that leads to differences in their preferences for alternative outcomes.

McGrath proposes that groups engage in four major processes: 'generate', 'execute', 'negotiate' and 'choose'. Creative tasks such as brainstorming, and planning tasks such as agenda setting, both require idea generation. Execute tasks require physical movement, coordination or dexterity, for example, surgical operations, military missions, athletic contests. Negotiate tasks involve resolving conflicting viewpoints or interests, for example, labour–management industrial disputes. Intellective or problem-solving tasks require choosing correct answers, and decision making or judgement tasks necessitate reaching consensus on a preferred solution. McGrath's model goes on to identify eight different task categories. While some groups only perform one of these eight tasks, others will perform those from several categories (Straus, 1999).

Ivan Steiner (1972) took a different, simpler approach to classifying group tasks, based on the type of interdependence that a group's task created between its members. He distinguished three types of tasks:

Additive task

With this type of task, all group members do basically the same job, and the final group product or outcome (group performance) is the sum of all their individual contributions. The final outcome is roughly proportional to the number of individuals contributing. There is low interdependency between these people. A group working together will normally

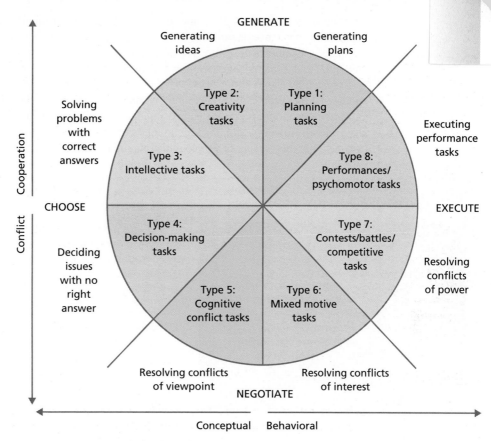

Figure 10.2: McGrath's circumplex model of group tasks

Source: from *Group Dynamics*, Thomson Wadsworth (Forsyth, D.R. 2006) p.14, 0495007293/
978-0495007296 adapted from McGrath, J.E., Groups: Interaction and Performance, 1st ed.,
© 1984, p.61. Reprinted and electronically reproduced by permission of Pearson Education, Inc.,
Upper Saddle River, New Jersey.

perform better than the same number of individuals working alone, provided that all group members make their contribution. Social loafing can, however, reduce performance on an additive task. Examples of additive tasks are tug-of-war contests, crowdsourcing and cricket.

Additive task a task whose accomplishment depends on the sum of all group members' efforts.

Conjunctive task

Conjunctive task a task whose accomplishment depends on the performance of the group's least talented member.

In this task, one member's performance depends on another's. There is high interdependency. Thus, a group's *least* capable member determines performance. A successful group project at university depends on one member finding the information, a second writing it up, and a third presenting it. All three elements are required for success and hence coordination is essential in conjunctive tasks. Groups perform less well on conjunctive tasks than lone individuals. Examples of conjunctive tasks include climbing a mountain, playing chamber music, and running a relay race (Steiner and Rajaratnam, 1961).

Disjunctive tasks

Disjunctive task a task whose accomplishment depends on the performance of the group's most talented member.

In this type of task, once again, one member's performance depends on another's. Again there is high interdependency. However, this time, the group's *most* capable member determines its performance. Groups perform better than their average member on disjunctive tasks, since even the best performer will not know all the answers, and working with others helps to improve overall group performance. Diagnostic and problem-solving activities performed by a group would come into this category. Coordination is important here as well, but in the sense of stopping the others impeding the top performers (Diehl and Stroebe, 1991). Examples of disjunctive task performers are quiz teams (*University Challenge*, pub quiz) and a maintenance team in a nuclear power generating plant.

Research by Glenn Littlepage (1991) on 324 undergraduate students confirmed Steiner's model of group productivity. He found that how productive a workgroup was depended not only on its size, but also on the nature of the task that it was given (additive, conjunctive or disjunctive). However, and in addition, member participation patterns also played a part. It was not only the number of people in a group that mattered, but also what they did.

The handover

AFP/Getty

Yves Morieux of the Boston Consulting Group observed that relay races were often won by teams whose members did not necessarily have the fastest individual times. Members of the medal-winning French women's Olympic relay team explained that, at some point, each had to decide whether to run their guts out, and literally be unable to see straight when they passed the baton, or whether they held something back, to make a better baton change, and thus enable their team mate to run a faster time. The value of this sort of decision making, and each individual's contribution to the team, was beyond measure (Hindle, 2006).

Groups will tend to outperform the same number of individuals working separately when working on disjunctive tasks than on additive or conjunctive tasks. This is provided that the most talented member can convince the others of the correctness of their answer. The attitudes, feelings and conflicts in a group setting might prevent this from happening.

World of Warcraft group dynamics

Bloomberg/Getty

MMORGs (massive multiplayer online role-playing games) such as Activision Blizzard's *World of Warcraft* have become some of the most popular computer games in recent times.

At the start of 2015, the number of its active subscribers passed 10 million. Typically, 40 to 200 players combine into groups (or guilds), getting to know each other and forming their relationships within the game world. Members adopt different roles and responsibilities on behalf of their group, which has to undertake some incredibly difficult tasks. Guild membership often changes as players/ members become fed up with their colleagues, or seek more attractive opportunities elsewhere. The game has become the focus of many scholarly studies which have used qualitative ethnography and quantitative census data analysis. Researchers have examined many aspects of this virtual world including its culture, economic markets and group formation. Irrespective of how strong an individual game character may be, the challenges require that the person works with others, as part of a group, who possess complementary skills, but also weaknesses.

Leading a raiding party of 25 group (guild) members on a six-hour raid on Illidan, the Betrayer's temple fortress, poses many organizational challenges.

These include recruiting, training, assessing, motivating, rewarding and retaining a talented and culturally diverse number of team members and coordinating their efforts. Decision making has to be done quickly but collectively; using limited information; and has long-term implications. The organization must be built and sustained with a volunteer workforce in a digitally mediated environment. That environment features a fluid workforce; self-organized and collaborative work activities; decentralized, non-hierarchical, rotating leadership, which is changed when conditions alter. It is therefore not surprising that companies and management consultants are exploring the potential of online 'group management simulators' to develop managers' group leadership skills (Bainbridge, 2015; Reeves et al., 2008).

The Hawthorne studies

The famous Hawthorne studies consisted of a series of experiments conducted during the 1920s and 1930s. Although they are approaching their centenary anniversary, they are still of interest to us today. This is because they formed the basis of the Human Relations School of Management, which in turn became the basis of organizational behaviour – the subject of this text. The studies revolutionized social science research methods and provided a vocabulary with which to discuss social relations in the workplace which continue to be used to this day.

The studies were conducted at the Hawthorne plant of the Western Electric Company, located in Cicero, Illinois, which manufactured telephones. At that time, factories used natural daylight or candles to illuminate the workspaces of their workers. In an attempt to promote the sales of light bulbs, the company paid for a series of experiments to try to demonstrate a positive correlation between the amount of light and worker productivity. The original experiments therefore examined the effect of physical changes – originally illumination – on worker productivity (Gillespie, 1991).

William J. Dickson (1904–1973)

Later, Professor George Elton Mayo of the Harvard Business School was invited to bring an academic research team into the factory. Team members included Fritz Jules Roethlisberger who later became the first Professor of Organizational Behaviour, holding his post in the Harvard Business School, and William J. Dickson. It was through their book *Management and the Worker* that the results of the Hawthorne studies were communicated to the world (Roethlisberger and Dickson, 1939). The Hawthorne research revolutionized social science thinking.

The illumination experiments (1924–1927)

These explored the relationship between the quality of illumination and efficiency. No correlation was found between production output obtained and the lighting provided. Production even increased when the light intensity was reduced. The conclusion was that lighting was only one of several factors affecting production, and perhaps a minor one. A different study, with fewer workers, was needed to control for the effect of any single variable.

Relay Assembly Test Room experiments (1927–1933)

These experiments focused on the effect of rest pauses and the length of the working day on employees and their attitudes to their work and the company. Six, self-selected female workers, drawn from the regular workforce of the Relay Assembly Department were placed in a separate room for closer observation (Figure 10.3). They had been working a 48-hour week including Saturdays with no tea breaks. A researcher was placed in the room with them and kept a note of what happened (Figure 10.4). He maintained a friendly atmosphere by listening to their complaints, and told them what was going on. A total of 13 time periods were studied during which changes were made to the women's rest pauses, hours of work and refreshment breaks.

Figure 10.3: Relay Assembly Test Room, c. 1929

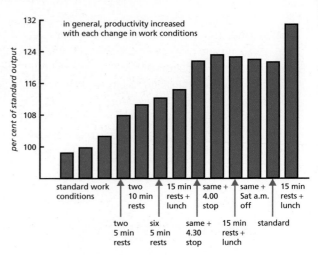

Figure 10.4: Productivity and work conditions

Source: based on data from Roethlisberger and Dickson (1939). From *Behaviour in Organizations*, 6/E by Greenberg/Baron, © 1997. Reprinted by permission of Pearson Education, Inc. Upper Saddle River, NJ.

The results showed a nearly continuous increase in output over those 13 periods. This increase began when employee benefits such as rest periods, served lunches and early finishes were added, but was maintained even when these privileges were withdrawn and the women returned to their normal 48-hour week. The five reasons offered for the increased output were:

1. The motivating effect of acquiring a special status through their selection for and involvement in the experiment.

2. The effect of participation as the women were consulted and informed by the researcher.

3. The effect of observer friendliness which improved their morale.

4. A different and less intensive form of supervision which reduced their stress while increasing their productivity.

5. The self-selected nature of the group creating higher levels of mutual dependence and support appropriate for group working.

Hawthorne Effect
the tendency of people being observed to behave differently than they otherwise would.

The increase in output due to the increased attention paid to employees in this study is now known as the Hawthorne Effect. It is defined as the tendency of people being observed, as part of a research effort, to behave differently than they otherwise would. Mayo and his colleagues became convinced that the women were not solely motivated by money or by improvements in their working conditions. Their attitudes towards and achievement of increased output seemed to be affected by the group to which they belonged. These results led management to study employee attitudes using an interviewing programme.

Interviewing programme (1928–1930)

To find out more about how employees felt about their supervisors and working conditions and how these related to morale, management instituted an interviewing programme involving over 20,000 interviews, which extended to family and social issues. These interviews also revealed the existence of many informal, ganglike groups within the formal working groups. Each had its own leaders and 'sidekicks' who controlled production output. Examining this became the focus of the next experiment.

Bank Wiring Observation Room experiments (1931–1932)

The interviews had revealed that groups exercised a great deal of control over the behaviour of their members. To find out more, a group of men were observed in another part of the company. The Bank Wiring Observation Room consisted of 14 men who were formally organized into three subgroups, each of which contained three wirers and one supervisor. The experiment revealed the existence of two informal groups or 'cliques' within the three formal groups; and that these cliques developed informal rules of behaviour or 'norms', as well as mechanisms to enforce these. This group was operating below its capability and its individual group members were not earning as much as they could. The norms under which the group operated were found to be (Roethlisberger and Dickson, 1939, p.522):

- You should not turn out too much work. If you do, you are a *ratebuster*.
- You should not turn out too little work. If you do, you are a *chisler*.
- You should not tell a supervisor anything that might get a colleague into trouble. If you do, you are a *squealer*.
- You should not attempt to maintain social distance or act officiously. If you are an inspector, you should not act like one.

Figure 10.5: Bank wiring, Hawthorne, 1941

Courtesy of AT&T Archives and History Centre

The researchers discovered that the Bank Wiring Observation Room men were afraid that if they significantly increased their output, the piece rate would be cut and the daily output expected by management would increase. The men could be reprimanded and layoffs might occur. To avoid this, the group members agreed between themselves what was a fair day's output (neither too high nor too low). They enforced this informal output norm through a system of negative sanctions or punishments. These included:

- ridicule as when a group member was referred to as The Slave or Speed King;
- 'binging', which involved striking a norm violator painfully on the upper arm;
- total rejection or exclusion of the individual by the group as a whole.

The social organization of the group controlled the behaviour of its members and protected it from management interference. These results showed that workers were more responsive to the social forces of their peer group than to the controls and incentives of management. Mayo concluded that:

- Work is a group activity and not just an individual activity.
- The social world of the adult is primarily patterned around work activities.

- At work, within their social group, people fulfil their needs for belonging and recognition, which enhances their productivity.

- A worker's complaint is a manifestation of a more basic, often psychological problem.

- Informal groups at work exercise strong social controls over the work habits and attitudes of individual workers.

- Managers need to collaborate with these informal groups to increase cohesion for the company's benefit.

Human Relations approach a school of management thought which emphasizes the importance of social processes at work.

Those conclusions led to the Human Relations approach to management which held that work should be a source of social relationships for individuals, a way of meeting their need for belonging and for group membership, and could even be a focus for their personal identity. As Rose (1988, p.104) noted:

> Within work-based social relationships or groups … behaviour, particularly productivity or cooperativeness with management, was thought to be shaped and constrained by the worker's role and status in a group. Other informal sets of relationships might spring up within the formal organization as a whole, modifying or overriding the official social structure of the factory which was based on purely technical criteria such as division of labour.

STOP AND THINK   Employees in the Bank Wiring Observation Room were subject to group-devised norms which were policed and enforced. Think of a group that you have known, e.g. at school, work, college or socially. What norms did that group have? How did it police and enforce those norms?

Group-oriented view of organizations

In his book *The Social Problems of an Industrial Society*, Elton Mayo proposed a social philosophy which placed groups at the centre of our understanding of human behaviour in organizations (Mayo, 1945). He stressed the importance of informal groups, and encouraged managers to 'grow' them. He discussed *natural groups* of 3–6 workers and *family groups* of between 8 and 30 members. These would develop into one, large, *organized group,* consisting of a plant-wide network of family groups, each with its own natural groups. Mayo's vision was of a community organization in which all or most employees were members of well-knit, natural groups, which were linked together in common purpose. These were not the formal groups discussed earlier. Mayo invited managers to act somewhat like gardeners rather than engineers, and to use their skills, intelligence and experience to deliberately integrate individuals within groups.

Work passion a strong inclination towards a job that they like, and in which they invest their time and energy.

The work-as-community theory reflects the observation that many employees now spend more time at work than previous generations. For many staff, it is the most important thing in their lives. Work passion has been defined as a strong inclination towards a job that they like, and in which they invest their time and energy. Harmonious work passion results from individuals internalizing their favourite work activity into their identity, and voluntarily engaging in it harmoniously, along with other aspects of their lives. In contrast, obsessive work passion, also the result of internalization, is driven by intra- or interpersonal pressures such as a person's need for self-esteem or acceptance, or desire for rewards. Obsessive work passion is in conflict with other life activities and comes at a cost to the individual (Vallerand, 2010; Astakhova and Porter, 2015).

At school, your classes were examples of formal groups. Students were assigned to classes by teachers for specific subjects. Outside classes, at break times, you regularly associated with different students. These were examples of informal groups. In the film *Mean Girls* (2004, director Mark Waters), Cady's map of North Shore High School distinguished 19 different informal groups of students which were reflected in their seating choices in the school cafeteria. These informal groups' names were the Freshmen; Preps; JV jocks; Cool Asians; Varsity jocks; Girls who eat their feelings; Girls who don't eat anything; Desperate wannabees; Burnouts; Sexually active Bandees; and the Plastics (YouTube: *Mean Girls Cafeteria tribes*).

STOP AND THINK

Can you remember the informal student groupings at your school? To which informal group do you belong now at college or university? Search

Researching the social networks of informal groups

Interest in informal employee networks and productivity goes back to the Hawthorne studies. The term *social network* refers to the informal organization developed by the workers themselves, in contrast to the formal organization created by management (see Chapter 12). Using surveys and human observation, Cross and Prusak (2002) studied the social networks that existed within 50 large organizations. Their research revealed a few role-players in the network whose performance was critical to the entire organization. The roles of these individuals included:

- *Central connectors* link most of the people within an informal network to one another. Despite not being formal leaders, they know who possesses the critical information or expertise required to get the work done.

- *Boundary spanners* connect the informal organization with other parts of the company or with similar networks in other organizations. They consult and advise individuals from many different company departments, regardless of their own functional affiliations.

- *Information brokers* keep different subgroups in an informal network together. Failure to communicate across subgroups would lead to their splintering into smaller, less effective segments.

- *Peripheral specialists* are those members within an informal network to whom anyone can turn to for specialized expertise.

More recent work by Maya Orbach and her colleagues (2015) used advances in social sensing technology to collect sensor and digital data to investigate the informal network communication structure within the sales division of a US global manufacturing company. Using sociometric badges to collect data on face-to-face interactions (see Chapter 11, p.361), as well as email and instant messaging logs over a two-month period, the researchers studied individuals' intra-team and inter-team communication with their colleagues to determine the structure of their informal network and its effect on task completion. Their findings showed that the management's expected inter-team workflows did not describe the actual communications that existed between the different teams in the company, suggesting that it did not have a clear idea of how employees accomplished their tasks. Using this new face-to-face sensing technology, the company could change the spatial layout of the workplace and measure the effects of the changes on employee communications.

A formal organization is ostensibly designed on rational principles and is aimed at achieving the collective purpose of the organization. It thus limits employees' behaviour in order to be able to control and predict it. However, the individual brings their hopes, needs, desires and personal goals to their work. While the company may not be interested in these, the employee will nevertheless attempt to achieve their personal ambitions while at work by manipulating the situation to fulfil their unmet needs. Most other staff will generally be seeking to do the same, so it will not be difficult to set up a series of satisfying relationships.

These relationships in turn will lead to the formation of informal groups. Because of our social nature, we have a tendency to form informal groups. The task-oriented, formal groups rarely consider the social needs of their members. Indeed these needs are frequently considered to be dispensable and counterproductive to the achievement of the formal purpose of the organization.

STOP AND THINK Consider how your educational institution contributes to the satisfaction of your social needs while studying through your membership of social groups (class, tutorial groups, self-help and study groups, clubs and societies, sports teams). On the other hand:

- How are other aspects of your institution's structure, rules, procedures and policies blocking your satisfaction?
- How could your institution meet your social needs and those of your fellow students more effectively through different forms of group arrangement – and would these be consistent with good teaching and learning practice?

Group formation

Groups do not suddenly appear out of nowhere. Before being able and willing to contribute as part of a collective, individuals who were previously strangers have to become acquainted with each other in order to establish how best to work together to achieve the common task. George Homans (1951) addressed this question of how groups formed. His three-part model is summarized in Figure 10.7, and we shall examine it in relation to management and workers in organizations.

Environment of group	External system	Internal system	
Physical Technological Social	Required activities Required interactions Required sentiments	Emergent activities Emergent interactions Emergent sentiments	Formation of a group

Figure 10.7: Homans' model of group formation

Group environment

Homans proposed that every group (or *social system* in his model) exists within an environment which affects it physically, technologically and socially. This environment is created by management's decisions in three areas:

- *Physical.* These are the actual surroundings within which a group functions. It includes the spatial arrangement of physical objects and location of human activities, e.g. office architecture and work furniture; placement of workers on an assembly line.
- *Technological.* This includes both material technology (the tools, machinery and equipment that can be seen, touched and heard) that group members use to do their jobs, and the social technology (the methods which order their behaviour and relationships).
- *Social.* This encompasses the norms and values of the group itself, of its managers (e.g. employees as motivated solely by money) and of the organizational culture (stressing mutual support and collaboration or competition, distrust and backstabbing).

Homans argued that a group's environment was created by the organization's management through its design of the physical work place; its purchase of equipment and choices in job design; as well as its choice of strategy, structure and culture.

Homans' group environments

Physically, the context of a group in a call centre differs depending on management's choice of work furniture (see photos below). Each arrangement limits the form and nature of operators' interactions with each other, and requires them to behave in certain ways. Managers can select work furniture to isolate operators, discourage them from interacting with colleagues and thus prevent informal groups from forming. Alison Barnes' study of Australian call centres reported a manager saying 'It's not the sort of place where you can talk to the person beside you or behind you if you're not taking calls … it's not a job where there is a lot of interaction during the day'. Barnes noted that the lack of spaces at work where staff members could meet privately hindered their collective organization. A company policy of 'hot desking' also prevented an operator working with the same group of people.

The technological context of their work requires staff to interact with customers using the telephone

Jesussanz/fotolia.com

Jesussanz/fotolia.com

and computer. In addition, there are the wallboards, with their 6-inch-high LED numbers, which show the number of calls waiting to be answered. These flash faster as the length of the queue increases. Computers monitor how many calls each operator deals with, and how quickly, keeping figures on all staff. The social technology consists of the script and prompt software held in the computer that directs their conversations in certain, required ways. Socially, the norms, values and goals that make up the shared understanding within which the group will function are specific to each group and are influenced by the culture of the call centre organization in which it operates. Barnes (2007, p.253) concluded, 'The design of work in the call centres – the technology such as the automatic call distribution or the focus on statistics – inhibited worker interaction. Designing an office space in order to facilitate employee communication would have been inconsistent with company objectives.'

External system

Homans' external system broadly equates to the concept of the formal organization introduced earlier. Managers have certain requirements or expectations of employees which, from the employees' perspective, are the 'givens' of their jobs. They require individuals to perform certain **activities**; to have certain **interactions** with others; and to have certain **sentiments** or feelings towards their work.

For example, in a supermarket, the physical, technological and social environment is represented by the design and positioning of the checkout stations; the choice of scanning equipment; and the company's 'the customer is always right' policy. The supermarket management wants its checkout operators to scan customers' purchases (activities); greet them, offer to pack their bags, and say goodbye to them (interactions). They are also

Activities in Homans' theory, the physical movements, and verbal and non-verbal behaviours engaged in by group members.

Interactions

in Homans' theory, the two-way communications between group members.

Sentiments

in Homans' theory, the feelings, attitudes and beliefs held by group members towards others.

expected to have positive attitudes and feelings towards their customers and their employer (sentiments). Homans prefaced each of these elements with the term 'required' (*required activities, required interactions* and *required sentiments*) and referred to them collectively as the *external system*.

Each of these three elements reinforces each other. The more activities that employees share, the more frequent will be their interactions, and the stronger will be their shared activities and sentiments (how much the other persons are liked or disliked). The greater the number of interactions between persons, the more will be their shared activities and the stronger their sentiments towards each other. The stronger the sentiments people have for one another, the greater will be the number of their shared activities and interactions. Persons in a group interact with one another, not just because of spatial or geographical proximity (called propinquity), but also to accomplish goals such as cooperation and problem-solving.

Homans' required activities and interactions

Robert Kneschke/fotolia.com

'At most supermarkets, checkout operators are expected to conform to particular patterns of non-verbal behaviour even when not serving. For example, one checkout operator, Denise (name changed) commented in an interview with the authors that, at her store, not only were the checkouts constantly monitored by closed-circuit television but supervisors regularly patrolled behind the checkouts, preventing any of the operators turning around to talk to fellow operators, by whispering the command "FF", which meant "Face the Front". Denise and her colleagues were required not only to "FF", but also to sit straight at all times; they were strictly forbidden, for example, from putting their elbows on the counter in front of them to relax their backs' (Noon and Blyton, 2007, p.189).

Internal system

Homans' internal system broadly equates to the concept of the informal organization introduced earlier. This is another, different set of group members' activities, interactions and sentiments that emerge from the physical – technological – social environment, and as a result of the required activities, required interactions and required sentiments themselves. Homans prefaced each of these elements with the term 'emergent' (*emergent activities, emergent interactions* and *emergent sentiments*) and referred to them collectively as the *internal system*. They represent the creation of informal groups within the organization.

These emergent activities can occur in addition to, or in place of the required activities, and are not required by the organization's management. For example, if the job is repetitive (technological context), operators might see how quickly they can perform it (emergent activity), so as to give their work more challenge. If employees are in close proximity to each other (physical context), they might relieve their boredom by talking to each other (emergent interaction) even though company rules forbid it. Group members may come to view customers as a nuisance and develop anti-customer feelings (emergent sentiments). For Homans, the relationship between the external and internal systems was crucial.

- *The internal and the external systems are interdependent.* A change in one system will produce a change in the other. For example, the replacement of a management-selected team leader (external system) can impact on the activities between the group members (internal system). Similarly, the sentiments of group members (internal system) can affect the way they do their work (external system).

- *The environment and the internal and external systems are interdependent.* Changes in the environment produce changes in the external (formal) and internal (informal) work organization. Individuals and groups will modify what they do and how they do it, to respond to the changes they perceive.

Homans' model of group formation established the basis for our understanding of group behaviour. First, it highlights how the environment within which a group functions (the physical dispersion of staff; the technology that they use; and their social context), helps or hinders the process of group formation. Second, it highlights how this management-created environment imposes the required activities, required interactions and required sentiments on individuals and groups in an organization, and then how these in turn stimulate the emergent activities, emergent interactions and emergent sentiments that are not required by the external system.

Self-forming groups

Ross Smith, director of testing at Lync, a company producing audio-visual conferencing and instant messaging systems, is responsible for a team of 85 software engineers. He was asked to reorganize his existing team so as to allow next-generation product testing to begin. The engineers needed to be smart, but their work, while it was intense, complex and technical, was not intrinsically interesting. Smith had to keep them focused and motivated. He decided to let the team lead the reorganization, a process which became known as 'WeOrg'. Rather than have the four managers who reported directly to him pick their team members, Ross decided that the 85 individual staff, acting as free agents, should choose which of the four teams they wanted to join.

The team leaders were not allowed to offer their members more money, but could give them career development opportunities, new technologies to work on, and new work colleagues to work with. Initially the engineers were sceptical and had to be convinced that the managers were serious in accommodating everyone's choices. WeOrg took longer than anticipated as employees took time to find the 'right team fit', researching the jobs and interviewing prospective bosses. Ultimately staff found themselves in acceptable if not ideal roles, and a subsequent survey revealed that 95 per cent of them 'liked' or 'somewhat liked' the allocation method. In most organizations, senior executives design structures, define roles, and allocate people to them. While being an efficient method, it ignores the fact that individuals have their own skills and motivations, and it can lead to skill-underutilization, staff demotivation and increased labour turnover. The WeOrg approach involves greater staff participation, but is more time-consuming and requires a great degree of manager–employee trust (Birkinshaw, 2013).

Group development

Groups of whatever type do not come into existence fully formed. Bruce Tuckman and Mary Ann Jensen (1977) suggested that groups pass through five clearly defined stages of development which they labelled forming, storming, norming, performing and adjourning (Figure 10.8). Of course not all groups develop through all the stages and some get stuck in the middle and remain inefficient and ineffective. Progress through the stages may be slow, but appears to be necessary and inescapable.

1. Forming

This is the orientation stage, at which the set of individuals has not yet gelled. The individual asks 'How do I fit in?' and the group asks 'Why are we here?' Everyone is busy finding out about each other's attitudes and backgrounds, and establishing ground rules. Members are also keen to fix their personal identities in the group and make a personal impression on the others. In the personal relations area, members are *dependent* on some leader to provide them with structure in the form of ground rules and an agenda for action. Task-wise, they seek *orientation* as to what they are being asked to do, what the issues are, and whether everyone understands the task.

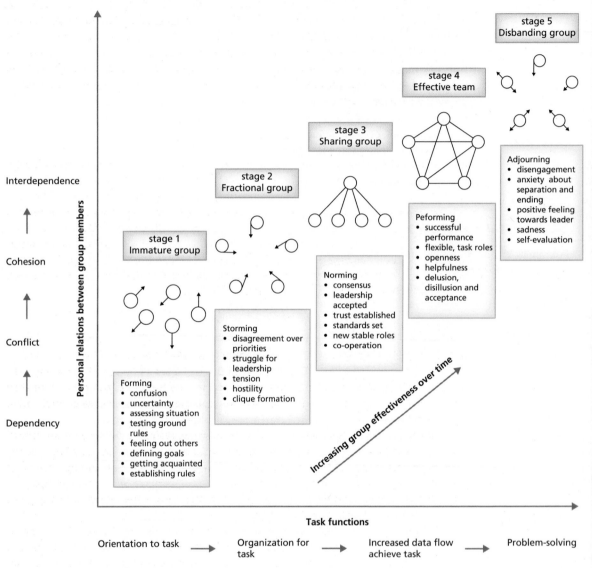

Figure 10.8: Stages of group development

Source: based on Tuckman and Jensen (1977) and Jones (1973).

2. Storming

This is a conflict stage in the group's life and can be an uncomfortable period. The individual asks 'What's my role here?' and the group asks 'Why are we fighting over who's in charge and who does what?' Members bargain with each other as they try to sort out what each of them individually, and as a group, want out of the group process. Individuals reveal their personal goals and it is likely that interpersonal hostility is generated when differences in these goals are revealed. Members may resist the control of other group members and may show hostility. The early relationships established in the forming stage may be disrupted. The key personal relations issue in this stage is the management of *conflict*, while the task function question is *organization* – how best to organize to achieve the group objective.

References

Ackroyd, S. and Thompson, P. (1999) *Organizational Misbehaviour*. London: Sage Publications.

Astakhova, M.N. and Porter, G. (2015) 'Understanding the work passion: the mediating role of organizational identification and moderating role of fit at work', *Human Relations* 68 (8): 1315–1346.

Amos, J. (2010) 'Cosmonauts chosen for Mars test, *BBC News*, 10 May.

Amos, J. (2011) 'Simulated Mars mission "lands" back on Earth', *BBC News*, 4 November.

Bainbridge, W.S. (2015) 'World of Warcraft', in *The International Encyclopedia of Digital Communication and Society*. Chichester: Wiley, pp.1–4.

Barnes, A. (2008) 'The construction of control: the physical environment and the development of resistance and accommodation within call centres', *New Technology, Work and Employment*, 22 (3): 246–59.

Birkinshaw, J. (2013) 'Reorganizing from the bottom up: Microsoft Lync engineers chose teams', *Financial Times*, 24 January, p.12.

Blitz, R. (2007) 'Winning formula', *Financial Times Magazine*, 11 August, pp.22–23.

Bock, L. (2015) *Work Rules*. London: John Murray.

Borrill, C. and West, M. (2005) 'The psychology of effective teamworking', in N. Gold (ed.), *Teamwork*. London: Palgrave Macmillan, pp.136–60.

Cain, S. (2012) *Quiet: The Power of Introverts in a World that Can't Stop Talking*. New York: Crown Publishing.

Catmull, E. (2008) 'How Pixar fosters collective creativity', *Harvard Business Review*, 86 (9): 64–72.

CIPD (2014) *Research Report: L&D: New Challenges, New Approaches*, December. London: Chartered Institute of Personnel and Development.

CIPD (2015) *Research Report: Learning to Work: Survey Report*. London: Chartered Institute of Personnel and Development.

Cohen, A.R., Fink, S.L., Gadon, H. and Willits, R.D. (1995) *Effective Behaviour in Organizations* (6th edn). Homewood, IL: Irwin.

Coutu, D. (2009) 'Why teams don't work', *Harvard Business Review*, 87 (5): 99–105.

Cross, R. and Prusak, L. (2002) 'The people who make organizations go – or stop', *Harvard Business Review*, 80 (6): 104–12.

Diehl, M. and Stroebe, W. (1991) 'Productivity loss in idea generating groups: tracking down the blocking effect', *Journal of Personality and Social Psychology*, 61 (3): 392–403.

Drexler, A.B. and Forrester, R. (1998) 'Teamwork – not necessarily the answer', *HR Magazine*, 43 (1): 55–58.

Driscoll, M. (2012) 'Do not disturb: loners do the best work', *The Sunday Times*, 22 January, p.8.

Ellemers, N., Sleebos, E. and Stam, D. (2013) 'Feeling included and valued: how perceived respect affects positive team identity and willingness to invest in the team', *British Journal of Management*, 24 (1): 21–37.

European Foundation for the Improvement of Living and Working Conditions (2007) *Fourth European Working Conditions Survey*, http://eurofound.europa.eu

Gartner (2010) *Gartner Says the World of Work Will Witness 10 Changes During the Next 10 Years*, www.gartner.com/newsroom/id/1416513

Gersick, C.J. (1988) 'Time and transition in work teams', *Academy of Management Journal*, 31 (1): 9–41.

Gersick, C.J. (1989) 'Marking time: predictable transitions in task group', *Academy of Management Journal*, 32 (2): 274–309.

Gillespie, R. (1991) *Manufacturing Knowledge: A History of the Hawthorne Experiments*. Cambridge: Cambridge University Press.

Goffman. E. (1963) *Behaviour in Public Places; Notes on the Social Organization of Gatherings*. New York: Free Press of Glencoe.

Greenberg, J. and Baron, R.A. (1997) *Behaviour in Organization* (6th edn). Englewood Cliffs, NJ: Pearson/Prentice Hall.

Hampton, M.M. (1999) 'Work groups', in Y. Gabriel (ed.), *Organizations in Depth*. London: Sage Publications, pp.112–38.

Hayes, N. (1997) *Successful Team Management*. London: International Thomson Business Press.

Hill, A. (2012) 'We should stop trying to change the world', *Financial Times*, 27 March, p.14.

Hindle, T. (2006) 'Take a deep breath', *The Economist, The New Organization: A Survey of the Company*, 21 January, pp.5, 6 and 8.

Hochschild, A.R. (1997) *The Time Bind: When Home Becomes Work and Work Becomes Home*. New York: Owl Books.

Homans, G.C. (1951) *The Human Group*. London: Routledge and Kegan Paul.

Jones, J.E. (1973) 'Model of group development', in *The 1973 Annual Handbook for Group Facilitators*. San Francisco, CA: Jossey Bass, pp.127–29.

Katzenbach, J.R. and Santamaria, J.A. (1999) 'Firing up the front line', *Harvard Business Review*, 77 (3): 107–17.

Knights, D. and McCabe, D. (2000) 'Bewitched, bothered and bewildered: the meaning and experience of teamworking for employees in an automobile plant', *Human Relations*, 53 (11): 1481–518.

Kozlowski, S.W.J. and Bell, B.S (2013) 'Work groups and teams in organizations', in I.B. Weiner, N.W. Schmitt and S. Highhouse (eds), *Handbook of Psychology, Volume 12: Industrial and Organizational Psychology* (2nd edn). London: Wiley, pp.412–69.

Leavitt, H.J. (1975) 'Suppose we took groups seriously', in E.L Cass and F.G. Zimmer (eds), *Man and Work in Society*. London: Van Nostrand Reinhold, pp.67–77.

Li, N., Kirkman, B.I. and Porter, C.O.L.H. (2014) 'Toward a model of team altruism', *Academy of Management Review*, 39 (4): 541–65.

Likert, R. (1961) *New Patterns of Management*. New York: McGraw-Hill.

Littlepage, G.E. (1991) 'Effects of group size and task characteristics on group performance: a test of Steiner's model', *Personality and Social Psychology Bulletin*, 17 (4): 449–56.

Mayo, E. (1945) *The Social Problems of an Industrial Civilization*. Cambridge, MA: Harvard University Press.

MacDuffee, J.P. (1997) 'The road to root cause: shop-floor problem-solving at three auto assembly plants', *Management Science*, 43 (4): 479–502.

McGrath, J.E. (1984) *Groups: Interaction and Performance*. Upper Saddle River, NJ: Prentice Hall.

Mintzberg, H. (2009) 'Rebuilding companies as communities', *Harvard Business Review*, 76 (7/8): 140–143.

Mohrman, S.A., Cohen, S.G. and Mohrman, A.M. (1995), *Designing Team-Based Organizations*. San Francisco, CA: Jossey Bass.

Murphy, H. (2015) 'The office as somewhere you enjoy', *Financial Times*, 10 March, p.7.

Noon, M. and Blyton, P. (2007) *The Realities of Work* (3rd edn). Basingstoke: Palgrave.

Orbach, M., Demko, M., Doyle, J., Waber, B.N. and Pentland, A. (2015) 'Sensing informal networks in organizations', *American Behavioural Scientist*, 59 (4): 508–24.

Ouchi, W.G. and Johnson, A.M. (1978) 'Type Z organizations: stability in the midst of mobility', *Academy of Management Review*, 3 (2): 305–14.

Peters, T. (1987) *Thriving on Chaos: Handbook for a Management Revolution*. London: Macmillan.

Quinn, R.W. and Bunderson, J.S. (2016) 'Could we huddle on this project? Participant learning in newsroom conversations', *Journal of Management* 42 (2): 386–418.

Reeves, B., Malone, T.W. and O'Driscoll, T. (2008) 'Leadership online labs', *Harvard Business Review*, 86 (5): 58–66.

Reimers, J.M. and Parsons, G. (2003) 'Case study: *Remember the Titans* (2000) to examine power, servant leadership, transformational leadership, followership and change', *Journal of Behavioural and Applied Management*, 5 (2): 152–165.

Rivera, L.A. (2015) *Pedigree: How Elite Students Get Elite Jobs*. Princeton, NJ: Princeton University Press.

Roethlisberger, F.J. and Dickson, W.J. (1939) *Management and the Worker*. Cambridge, MA: Harvard University Press.

Rose, M. (1988) *Industrial Behaviour and Control*. Harmondsworth, Middlesex: Penguin Books.

Smith, G.W. (2009) 'Using feature films as the primary instructional medium to teach organizational behaviour', *Journal of Management Education*, 33 (4): 462–89.

Steiner, I. (1972) *Group Process and Productivity*. New York: Academic Press.

Steiner, I. and Rajaratnam, N.A. (1961) 'A model for the comparison of individual and group performance scores', *Behavioural Science*, 6 (2): 142–47.

Straus, S.G. (1999) 'Testing a typology: an empirical validation of McGrath's (1984) group task circumplex', *Small Group Research*, 30 (2): 166–87.

Taher, A. (2009) 'Number's up for "unlucky" eight', *The Sunday Times*, 11 January, p.7.

The Economist (2015) 'Schumpeter: how to join the 1 per cent', 16 May, p.73.

Thursfield, D. (2015) 'Resistance to team working in a UK research and development laboratory', *Work, Employment and Society* 29 (6): 989–1006.

Tuckman, B.W. and Jensen, M.A.C. (1977) 'Stages of small group development revisited', *Group and Organizational Studies*, 2 (4): 419–27.

Vallerand, R.J. (2010) 'On passion for life activities; the dualistic model of passion', *Advances in Experimental Social Psychology*, 42: 97–103.

Vašková, R. (2007) *Teamwork and High Performance Team Organization*. European Foundation for the Improvement of Living and Working Conditions, www.eurofound.europa.eu/observatories/eurwork/articles/working-conditions/teamwork-and-high-performance-work-organisation

Wood, W.S. (2001) 'Can we go to Mars without going crazy?' *Discover Magazine*, 5 May, http://discovermagazine.com/2001/may/cover

Wuchty, S., Jones, B.F. and Uzzi, B. (2007) 'The increasing dominance of teams in production of knowledge', *Science*, 316 (5827): 1036–38.

Chapter 11 **Group structure**

Key terms

team player

person–group fit

collective fit

group structure

group process

power

formal status

social status

sociometry

sociogram

communication network analysis

communigram

communication pattern analysis

communication pattern chart

Interaction Process Analysis

task activity

maintenance activity

social role

team role

distributed leadership

virtual team

global virtual team

networked individualism

Learning outcomes

When you have read this chapter, you should be able to define those key terms in your own words, and you should also be able to:

1. List the six dimensions of group structure.

2. Identify the sources of power within a group.

3. Distinguish between two common uses of the concept of status.

4. Understand how emotional relationships within a group can be represented symbolically.

5. Distinguish between communication network analysis, communication pattern analysis and Interaction Process Analysis (IPA).

6. Distinguish between task, relationship and individual roles within a group.

7. Differentiate between Belbin's team roles.

8. Give examples of three leadership styles identified by White and Lippitt.

9. Distinguish between a task and a socio-emotional group leader.

10. List the four key dimensions of a virtual team.

11. Identify the benefits and problems associated with virtual teams.

Why study group structure?

Organizations are keen to employ people who work well together. Nicky Binning, head of experienced hire and global mobility at KPMG, an international advisory firm says that,

> There is now such a pace of change that it almost doesn't matter what you have done in the past … It is the ability to understand what is in front of you, and work collaboratively that counts. You have to work together as a team because it is likely that you are facing something that you have never faced before. (cited by Tieman, 2012, p.1)

An individual from a function like marketing may be delegated to participate in various teams which can be face-to-face, project, huddling, virtual, cross-cultural or a combination of these. Increasingly, members of one firm may be required to create a joint team with those of another company, in order to meet a client's needs. A study of 600 organizations into teamworking around the world by Pam Jones, director of Ashridge Business School's Performance Through People programme found that 75 per cent of the teams were dispersed geographically; 30 per cent were spread across time zones; and half were 'virtual' and rarely met (cited Tieman, 2012, p.1).

David Aguado and his colleagues (2014) observed that successful teamwork required its members to deploy specific competencies to enable them to effectively interact with each other; synchronize their contributions; deal constructively with conflict; and function as a unified whole so as to achieve the group objective. They should become an 'expert team' and not merely a 'group of experts'. Those who possess these competences are called **team players**. This is a person who works willingly in cooperation with others for the benefit of the whole team. A team player is humble; does not pursue personal glory, values the performance of the group over individual recognition; is committed to a common goal, and to achieving it selflessly.

Team player a person who works willingly in cooperation with others for the benefit of the whole team.

Companies invest a great deal of time and effort during the selection process to find applicants who are good 'team players'. Michael Stevens and Michael Campion (1994, 1999) listed the knowledge, skills and attitudes (KSAs) needed by team member for team success. As Table 11.1 shows, these are divided into interpersonal and self-management clusters, each with its own sets of particular KSAs.

STOP AND THINK Companies want to hire applicants who are good team players. At your job interview, you claim to be one. What evidence would you provide to support your claim?

Table 11.1: Knowledge, skills and abilities possessed by team players

Interpersonal KSAs

1. Conflict resolution
   Recognizes the types and sources of conflict; encourages functional and discourages dysfunctional conflict; employs win–win negotiation strategies.

2. Collaborative problem-solving
   Identifies situations in which participative group problem-solving is appropriate; judges the appropriate degree of participation; and overcomes obstacles to ensure it happens.

3. Communication
   Understands and uses decentralized communication networks; achieves consistency in verbal and non-verbal communication; and correctly interprets others' non-verbal communication.

These data were compared with team performance and used to identify which communication patterns contributed to successful teamwork. The same patterns were in found in different teams, irrespective of their type or their goals. Successful call centre teams and successful senior management teams shared certain 'data signatures' allowing the researchers to predict team success without actually having to meet their members. Three aspects of communication were found to affect team performance most. *Energy* was the number and nature of exchanges between team members; and *engagement* was the distribution of energy between team members. If all team members had relatively equal and reasonably high energy with one another, then engagement would be strong. *Exploration* concerned members' communication with those outside their team. Successful, creative teams oscillated between 'exploration for discovery' and 'engagement

for integration' of ideas gathered from outside. The authors concluded that 35 per cent of variation in a team's performance could be accounted for by the number of face-to-face exchanges.

Sociometric Solutions, a commercial firm, has commercialized the use of 'badge technology' to discover social dynamics at work. They monitor how employees move around the workplace. One of its clients, Bank of America, discovered that its most productive workers were those who were allowed to take their coffee breaks together, during which time they 'let off steam' and shared tips about dealing with frustrated customers. It used this finding to introduce collective staff breaks, thereby raising performance by 23 per cent, and reducing the amount of stress in workers' voices by 19 per cent (Kuchler, 2014). Badges have also been used in informal network research as described by Orbach et al. (2015).

Role structure

Social role the set of expectations that others hold of an occupant of a position.

It is a short step from identifying the types of oral contributions that individuals make in their groups to determining their team member roles. The occupants of every position in a group are expected to carry out certain functions when group members interact with one another. The expected behaviours associated with a position within the group constitute the social role of the occupant of that position. **Social role** is the concept that relates the individual to the prescriptive dictates of the group. People's behaviour within an organization is structured and patterned in various ways. An understanding of role helps us to explain how this happens.

Social role refers to the set of expectations that others hold of an occupant of a position in an organizational structure, e.g. shop manager, bishop, head of the production department, etc. These role expectations presume attitudes, relationships and behaviours. A role is similar to a script that actors are given. The same actor changes their roles, and can act out different parts in front of different audiences. Different roles are played out by different members of a group. By totalling the columns in the oral interaction score sheet shown earlier, you can see how group members contributed to the group discussion. Bales found that individuals played different roles within their groups, and that this was a universal feature of face-to-face interaction in groups. As the group deals with its problems, individual members begin to 'specialize' in certain types of behaviours, thereby taking on different 'roles' within the group.

Group member roles

Within a group activity, such as a staff meeting or a tutorial discussion, some individuals will show a consistent preference for certain oral behaviours and not for others, for example, expressing their opinion, asking for information from others. How an individual chooses to expresses him- or herself leads them to be seen to be playing a particular role within their group. Kenneth Benne and Paul Sheats (1948) distinguished three categories of roles played by members of a group and these are shown in Table 11.3.

Table 11.3: Benne and Sheats' roles commonly played by members of a group

Task	Relationships	Individual
Initiator-contributor	Encourager	Aggressor
Information seeker	Harmonizer	Blocker
Opinion seeker	Compromiser	Recognition seeker
Information giver	Gatekeeper and expeditor	Self-confessor
Opinion giver	Standard setter	Dominator
Evaluator-critic	Observer and commentator	Help seeker
Energizer	Follower	Special interest pleader
Procedural technician		Playboy/cougar
Recorder		

Source: based on Benne and Sheats (1948).

The first of these are *task roles*, which are principally directed towards achieving a group's task. The second category, *relationship roles*, are concerned with building and maintaining good relations between group members so as to ensure the group as a whole can work together. Both of these categories of roles help the group to achieve its objective. In contrast, the third category, *individual roles*, impedes the group's efforts to achieve its aims. They have also been called 'self-interested roles' because they advance only the interests of the individual member, rather than those of the group as a whole. Back in 1948, Benne and Sheats labelled the last of these roles 'playboy'. However, both male and female members of a group ('playboys' and 'cougars') are equally capable of enjoying themselves at the cost of impeding the achievement of their group's task.

Team role an individual's tendency to behave in preferred ways which contribute to, and interrelate with, other members within a team.

Belbin's team role theory

A widely used framework for understanding roles within a group or team was developed by Meredith Belbin and was based on research conducted at the Administrative Staff College, Henley (Belbin, 1993, 1996, 2010). He distinguished nine team roles. Each **team role** makes its own, distinctive contribution to the performance of the team. These can be grouped under three headings:

Action roles	Social roles	Thinking roles
• Shaper	Coordinator	Plant
• Implementer	Teamworker	Monitor–Evaluator
• Completer–Finisher	Resource investigator	Specialist

Raymond Meredith Belbin (b.1926)

Belbin (1996) argued that:

1. Within an organization people are generally appointed to a functional role on the basis of their ability or experience, e.g. marketing. They are rarely selected for personal characteristics that would fit them to perform additional tasks within a team. In an ideal world, a person's functional role and their team role would coincide.

2. The personal characteristics of an individual fit them for some roles within a team, while limiting the likelihood that they will be successful in other roles. For Belbin, therefore, team roles are *individual preferences* based on personality, and not the *expectations of others*, as discussed earlier in this chapter with respect to social role.

3. Individuals tend to adopt one or two team roles fairly consistently.

4. The roles that individuals are naturally inclined towards can be predicted through personality assessments and a team role questionnaire.

5. In an ideal ('dream') team, all the necessary roles are represented, and the preferred roles of members complement each other, thereby avoiding 'gaps' – i.e. there is team role balance. This does not mean that every team has to consist of nine people. A single member can 'double up' and play several roles, thereby enabling the overall size of the team to be reduced.

6. The assessment, selection, placement and guidance of individual employees by management is the way to improve team effectiveness. Once management knows employees' team role preferences, it can use them to compose balanced teams in which all the required role preferences are represented.

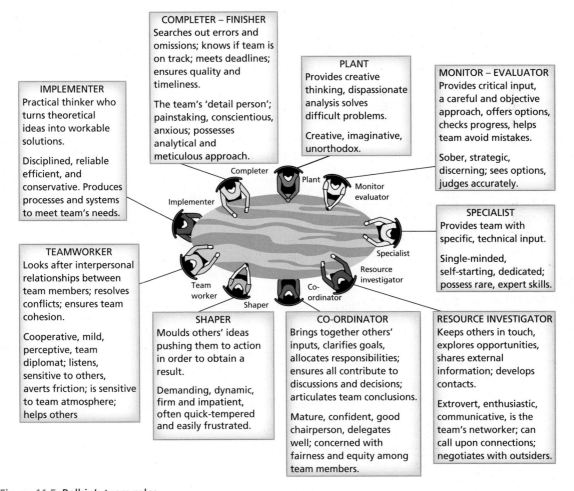

Figure 11.5: Belbin's team roles

Source: adapted from Matthewman et al. (2009); based on Belbin (1981).

STOP AND THINK   Belbin argued that a balanced team was one in which all nine of his roles were represented. What factors, inside or outside the organization, other than team role preferences, are likely to affect the success or failure of a team within an organization?

Critique of team role theory

Belbin's theory has received a great deal of critical assessment, some of which has been summarized by Aitor Aritzeta et al. (2007). Belbin Associates (2009) have themselves offered a response to some of the questions raised about their team roles model. The main criticisms of the theory are:

- It is difficult to devise measures of team success that can be objectively related to team composition. It is difficult to say that a given team succeeded because it possessed all nine roles or failed because it lacked some of them.

- How individuals see their team roles is influenced as much by the roles that they habitually play, and what is expected of them in such roles. Thus the questionnaire scores reflect not only an individual's personality traits, but also their social learning of roles.

- The theory takes an excessively psychological perspective on role, neglecting the sociological dimension of the social position they habitually adopt, and what is expected of them in such positions by others.

- The theory does not sufficiently take into account differences in the type of task that the team is being asked to perform. Additive, conjunctive and disjunctive tasks may require different combinations of team roles to achieve success.

- Team performance is affected by a variety of different factors such as strategy and leadership, structure and management style, interpersonal skills and company resources. Focusing exclusively on team composition leads to ignoring these other critical factors.

- The concepts of team role and personality have become intertwined, being treated as interchangeable, rather than as separate but interrelated.

Because of its widespread popularity, team role theory continues to generate interest and research. According to Belbin, a balanced team, i.e. one in which all nine roles are present, will perform better than an unbalanced one in which roles are duplicated or missing. Simona Lupuleac and her colleagues (2012) studied 32 teams containing 145 members working on development projects. They found a statistical relationship between team role balance and team motivation (preparedness to work hard and make a contribution to their team) and thus confirm the value of the theory for designing teams.

Nicoleta Meslec and Petru Curşeu (2015) investigated the impact of team role balance on group processes (communication, coordination and planning) and group outcomes (group cohesion, perceived performance). They studied 459 students at a Dutch university. They concluded that although balanced teams performed significantly better in the initial phases of group development, the effect disappeared towards the end of the group project and thus did not predict group performance at later points in time. Moreover, it linked negatively with group processes and outcomes. Finally, Nel Mostert (2015) studied 730 employees in the R&D teams of a fast-moving consumer goods company over a seven-year period. He found that:

- most project team leaders were Shapers;
- each team had its own unique team innovation culture;
- all team members benefited from knowing each other's team roles;
- in an R&D environment, Plants, Resource investigators and Specialists produced the most creative team combination.

Home viewing

In the film *The Internship* (2013, director Shawn Levy), Google summer interns form themselves into small teams to compete with one another. One of these teams, 'Team Lyle', consists of six members – Lyle, Neha, Yo-Yo, Stuart, Nick and Billy. Team members have to work effectively together to meet the challenges set for them. Identify which individuals play which of Belbin's team roles, on which occasions, with what result.

Gervase Bushe and Alexandra Chu (2011) noted that unstable team membership greatly impedes team performance. A fluid team is defined as a collection of individuals who are made responsible for an outcome by their organization, but whose membership changes. Fluid teams have been widespread in health care, aviation (flight crews) and are increasingly common in engineering, product development, and sales and customer support. Among the reasons for team membership changes are upsizing and downsizing; different skill requirements at different times; the desire for flexible personnel allocation; and staff career development opportunities. The authors identified four problems and suggested solutions to each of these, as summarized in Figure 11.6.

Unstable membership creates barriers to effective team functioning because of . . .	Solutions	For increased
Loss of individual knowledge	• Create generalized roles and prescribed processes for teams. • Use standardization of skills for coordination. • Create a few stable roles which act as knowledge resources for others.	Efficacy
Lack of shared mental models	• Reduce task interdependence. • Substitute simple structures and knowledge management. • Increase understanding of coordination needs of other roles.	
Low individual commitment to group success	• Design motivating roles. • Design peer transparency into work.	Belonging
Lack of cohesion	• Build identification and cohesion through the pools of expertise that form more stable groups. • Build loyalty to higher level groups and the organization as a whole.	

Figure 11.6: Problems and solutions for fluid teams

Source: reprinted from *Organizational Dynamics*, 40(3), Bushe, G.R. and Chu. A., Fluid teams: solutions to the problems of unstable team membership, pp.181–88 (p.183, Figure 2 Problems and solutions for fluid teams) © 2011, with permission from Elsevier.

What makes a team smarter – more women?

Pressmaster/Shutterstock.com

Anita Woolley and Thomas Malone (2011) gave subjects aged 18 to 60 standard individual intelligence tests and assigned them randomly to teams. Teams were asked to complete brainstorming, decision making, visual puzzle and problem solving tasks, and were then given a collective (team) intelligence score based on their performances. It was found that there was little correlation between a group's collective intelligence and the IQs of its collective members. However, if a group included more women, its collective intelligence rose. This collective group intelligence was not found to correlate with group satisfaction, group cohesion, group motivation or individual intelligence. The teams that had members with higher IQs did not achieve higher team scores, but those which had more women did. So, are brainy people overrated and are women the true key to team success?

The researchers concluded that gender did make a difference. The traditional argument is that diversity is good and that you should have a mixture of men and women on your team. However, this research suggests that the more women the better. Why? The explanation runs as follows. Studies of excellently performing groups report that members listen to each other; share constructive criticism; have open minds; are not autocratic. These are all aspects of what is called *social sensitivity*, and women in general score higher in tests of social sensitivity than do men. So what is important is to have people high in social sensitivity whether they are men or women. If you don't know the sensitivity of an individual, then choose a female, as she is likely to have more of it. This study showed that intelligence tests used to predict individuals' performances on a range of tasks could also predict group performance. A group's collective intelligence can be increased by changing its membership or increasing incentives for collaboration.

Leadership structure

There are many jobs to be done in a group if it is to be both productive and satisfying for its members. The emergence of a leader within any group is a function of its structure. Usually, a group makes a leader of the person who has some special capacity for coping with the group's particular problems. They may possess physical strength, shrewdness, or some other relevant attribute. The leader and the members all play roles in the group. Through them, a group atmosphere is created which enables communication, influence and decision making to occur. In much of the management literature, leadership is considered exclusively as a management prerogative.

The relationship between the group's leader and the followers may be thought of as one of social exchange. The leader provides rewards for the group by helping its members to achieve their own and the group's goals. They in turn reward the leader by giving the individual heightened status and increased influence. However, members can withdraw that influence at any time if they feel that the leader is no longer worthy of their respect. Viewed as a social exchange process, the leader has power in terms of their ability to influence the behaviour of those around them. Nevertheless, it is the group members who give the leader the power to influence them.

Distributed leadership the collective exercise of leadership behaviours, often informal and spontaneous, by staff at all levels of an organization.

It has been found that the type of leadership exercised affects group performance and member satisfaction. Activities are performed and actions are taken by the leader. There has been an increasing interest in **distributed leadership** within a group as opposed to individual leadership (see Chapter 18). One can distinguish between a leader and acts of leadership. If we accept Raymond Cattell's (1951) view that the leader is any group member who is capable of modifying the properties of the group by their presence, then we can acknowledge that any member of the group can perform acts of leadership, and not just a single, designated individual. The group leadership approach considers the characteristics of small groups, seeking to understand the organizational context in which they exist, and the objectives that they seek to achieve. It seems therefore more useful to view leadership as a set of behaviours that change their nature depending on circumstances, and which switch or rotate between group members as circumstances change, rather than a static status associated with a single individual.

Research by Robert Bales and Philip Slater (1956) into newly constituted groups found that two leaders regularly emerged. One was the *task leader* who specialized in making suggestions, giving information, expressing opinions and generally contributing to helping the group achieve its objective. The other was the *socio-emotional leader* who helped maintain relationships between group members, allowing them to express their ideas and positive feelings (see earlier distinction between group activities). This person made jokes, and released tensions in the group, and helped to maintain the group as a functioning entity. Although there was some rivalry, the two group leaders, *task* and *socio-emotional*, typically cooperated and worked together well.

Lynda Gratton and her colleagues (2007) confirmed this distinction 50 years later when investigating teams which demonstrated high levels of collaboration. They found that the

Revision

1. Select any two groups with which you are familiar. Contrast them in terms of any group structure dimensions that are relevant – power, communication, liking, roles and leadership. Suggest possible reasons for the similarities and differences that you have highlighted.

2. Describe situations in which a (i) team role analysis and (ii) a sociogram would be relevant to improve a group's functioning. How would you apply these two techniques? How would you use the results?

3. Critically assess the strengths and weaknesses of Belbin's team role theory as a guide for the manager wishing to construct a team that will be effective.

4. Identify some of the problems of virtual teamworking for (a) the companies which establish them, and (b) the individuals who work in them. How might these problems be overcome?

Research assignment

Studies suggest that employees spend many hours each week in meetings. Get invited to a real meeting that will last at least 30 minutes. Consult the box 'Analysing oral interactions in a group' on page 359, making several copies of the oral interaction score sheet that you will find there. Read and follow the instructions detailed in the box. After 30 minutes of silently observing and scoring, excuse yourself and leave the meeting quietly. After you have added up your scores, write a brief report which comments on (a) the way this group as a whole was working, (b) the roles played by its individual members, and (c) the adequacy of your scoring sheet and its underlying assumptions. Make recommendations as to how your group members' interactions could be improved.

Springboard

Lucy Gilson, Travis Maynard, Nicole Jones Young, Matti Vartiainen and Marko Hakonen (2015) 'Virtual teams research: 10 years, 10 themes and 10 opportunities', *Journal of Management*, 41 (5): 1313–37. The authors review and summarize the last ten years of empirical research on virtual teams. A good starting point for a student project on the topic.

Nir Halvey, Eileen Chou and Adam Galinsky (2011) 'A functional model of hierarchy: why, how and when vertical differentiation enhances group performance', *Organizational Psychology Review*, 1 (1): 32–52. The authors identify five ways in which the rank ordering (hierarchy) of individuals within a group facilitates its success.

Selin Kesebir (2012) 'The superorganism account of human sociality: how and when human groups are like beehives', *Personality and Social Psychology Review*, 16 (3): 233–61. The author contrasts groups with beehives emphasizing the role of individuals within the collectivity.

John Mathieu, Scott Tannenbaum, Michael Kukenberger, Jamie Donsbach and George Alliger (2015) 'Team experience and orientation: a measure of construct validity', *Group & Organizational Management*, 40 (1): 6–34. The authors review nine team role models from 1948 to 2006 before offering their own TREO model.

 ## OB cinema

Network (1976, director Sidney Lumet), DVD track 16, 1:48:00–1:53:00 (5 minutes). This film is set in the US television industry. Because of his falling ratings, the Union Broadcasting System (UBS) fires its leading news anchorman Howard Beale (played by Peter Finch). Beale's on-air behaviour then becomes increasingly bizarre, after he promises to kill himself on television. Initially, his ratings

→

skyrocket as he becomes the 'Mad Prophet of the Airways', but they then decline, affecting UBS's other programmes and its revenue. The clip begins as network executives assemble for a meeting, and ends with Diana saying 'let's kill the son-of-a-bitch'. Hackett (played by Robert Duvall) sits at the desk and begins the meeting by describing the problem.

Listen to the discussion between the six individuals in the room. Each time one of them speaks, decide into which of the six oral categories if fits, and indicate this by putting a dot, under their name. Continue until the clip has finished.

| B
Joe | C
Man in chair | D
Man in armchair | E
Herb (standing) | F
Diana |

A
Hackett

Oral interaction score sheet

Oral category	Meeting participants						
	A Hackett	B Joe	C Main in chair	D Man in armchair	E Herb (standing)	F Diana	TOTAL
Proposing							
Building							
Supporting							
Disagreeing							
Giving • information • opinions • suggestions							
Seeking • information • opinions • suggestions							
TOTAL							

Bergiel, B.J., Bergiel, E.B. and Balsmeier, P.W. (2008) 'Nature of virtual teams: a summary of their advantages and disadvantages', *Management Research News*, 31 (2): 99–110.

Bowditch, J.L. and Buono, A.F. (2001) *A Primer on Organizational Behaviour*. New York: Wiley.

Bushe, G.R. and Chu, A. (2011) 'Fluid teams: solutions to the problems of unstable team membership', *Organizational Dynamics*, 40 (3): 181–88.

Cattell, R. (1951) 'New concepts for measuring leadership in terms of group syntality', *Human Relations*, 4 (2): 161–68.

Courtright, S.H., Stewart, G.L. and Ward, M.M. (2012) 'Applying research to save lives: learning from health care training approaches in aviation and health care', *Organizational Dynamics*, 41 (4): 291–301.

Dahl, R.A. (1957) 'The concept of power', *Behavioural Science*, 2 (3): 201–215.

Dimitrova, D. and Wellman, B. (2015) 'Networked work and network research: new forms of teamwork in the triple revolution', *American Behavioural Scientist*, 59 (4): 443–56.

Dennis, J.D., Meola, D. and Hall, M.J. (2013) 'Effective leadership in a virtual workforce', *T + D*, 67 (2): 46–52.

Ferrazzi, K. (2014) 'Managing yourself getting virtual teams right', *Harvard Business Review*, 92 (12): 120–23.

French, J.R.P. and Raven, B.H. (1958) 'The bases of social power', in D. Cartwright (ed.), *Studies in Social Power*. Ann Arbor, MI: Institute for Social Research, University of Michigan Press, pp.150–67.

Foushee, H.C. (1984) 'Dyads and triads at 35,000 feet: factors affecting group process and air crew performance', *American Psychologist*, 39 (8): 885–93.

Gilson, L.L., Maynard, M.T., Jones Young, N.C., Vartiainen, M. and Hakonen, M. (2015) 'Virtual teams research: 10 years, 10 themes and 10 opportunities', *Journal of Management*, 41 (5): 1313–37.

Gould, R.V. (2002) 'The origin of status hierarchies: a formal theory and empirical test', *American Journal of Sociology*, 107 (5): 1143–78.

Gratton, L., Voight, A. and Erickson, T. (2007) 'Bridging fault lines in diverse teams', *Sloan Management Review*, 48 (4): 22–29.

Greenberg, J. and Baron, R.A. (1997) *Behaviour in Organizations* (6th edn). Englewood Cliffs, NJ: Prentice Hall.

Halgin, D.S., Gopalakrishnan, G.M. and Borgatti, S.P. (2015) 'Structure and agency in networked distributed work: the role of work engagement', *American Behavioural Scientist*, 59 (4): 457–74.

Halvey, N., Chou, E.Y. and Galinsky, A.D. (2011) 'A functional model of hierarchy: why, how and when vertical differentiation enhances group performance', *Organizational Psychology Review*, 1 (1): 32–52.

Hogg, M.A. and Vaughan, G.M. (2008) *Social Psychology* (5th edn). Harlow: Pearson/Prentice Hall.

Huffman, B.J. and Kilian, C.M. (2012) '*The Flight of the Phoenix*: interpersonal aspects of project management', *Journal of Management Education*, 36 (4): 568–600.

Jarvenpaa, S.L. and Leidner, D.E. (1999) 'Communication and trust in global virtual teams', *Organization Science*, 10 (6): 791–815.

Kilduff, M. and Krackhardt, D. (2008) *Interpersonal Networks in Organizations*. Cambridge: Cambridge University Press.

Kristof-Brown, A.L., Seong, J.Y., Degeest, D.S., Par, W.-W. and Hong, D.-S. (2014) 'Collective fit perceptions: a multilevel investigation of person–group fit with individual-level and team-level outcomes', *Journal of Organizational Behaviour*, 35 (7): 969–89.

Kuchler, H. (2014) 'Data pioneers watching us work', *Financial Times*, 18 February, p.12.

Lupuleac, S., Lupulaec, Z.-L. and Rusu, C. (2012) 'Problems of assessing team role balance – team design', *Procedia Economics and Finance*, 3: 935–940.

Malhotra, A., Majchrzak, A. and Rosen, B. (2007) 'Leading virtual teams', *Academy of Management Perspectives*, 21 (1): 60–70.

Meslec, N. and Curşeu, P.L. (2015) 'Are balanced groups better? Belbin roles in collaborative learning groups', *Learning and Individual Differences*, 39: 81–88.

Milanovich, D.M., Driskell, J.E., Stout, R.J. and Salas, E. (1998) 'Status and cockpit dynamics: a review and empirical study', *Group Dynamics*, 2 (3): 155–67.

Moreno, J. L. (1953) *Who Shall Survive?* (2nd edn). New York: Beacon Press.

Mostert, N.M. (2015) 'Belbin – the way forward for innovation teams', *Journal of Creativity and Business Innovation*, 1: 35–48.

Newing, R. (2007) 'The great enabler: trust', Understanding the Culture of Collaboration Supplement, *Financial Times*, 29 June, pp.18–19.

O'Leary, M.B., Mortensen, M. and Woolley, A.W. (2011) 'Multiple team membership: a theoretical model of its effects on productivity and learning for individuals and teams', *Academy of Management Review*, 36 (3): 461–478.

Orbach, M., Demko, M., Doyle, J., Waber, B.N. and Pentland, A. (2015) 'Sensing informal networks in organizations', *American Behavioural Scientist*, 59 (4): 508–24.

Pentland, A. (2012) 'The new science of building teams', *Harvard Business Review*, 90 (4): 60–70.

Piazza, A. and Castellucci, F. (2014) 'Status in organization and management theory', *Journal of Management*, 40 (1): 287–315.

Rainie, L. and Wellman, B. (2012) *Networked: The New Social Operating System*. Cambridge, MA: MIT Press.

Sauder, M., Lynn, F. and Podolny, J.M. (2012) 'Status: insights from organizational psychology', *Annual Review of Sociology*, 38: 267–83.

Shapiro, D.L., Furst, S.A., Speitzer, G.M., and Von Glinow, M.A. (2002) 'Transnational teams in the electronic age: are teams' identity and high performance at risk', *Journal of Organizational Behaviour*, 23 (4): 455–67.

Shaw, M.E. (1978) 'Communication networks fourteen years later', in L. Berkowitz (ed.), *Group Processes*. New York: Academic Press, pp.351–61.

Siakas, K. and Siakas, E. (2015) 'A contemporary team process management model to enhance multicultural virtual team performance', *International Journal of Networking and Virtual Organizations*, 15 (1): 65–79.

Shin, Y. (2005) 'Conflict resolution in virtual teams', *Organizational Dynamics*, 34 (4): 331–45.

Stevens, M.J. and Campion, M.A. (1994) 'The knowledge, skill and ability requirements for teamwork: implications for human research management', *Journal of Management*, 20 (2): 503–30.

Stevens, M.J. and Campion, M.A. (1999) 'Staffing work teams: development of a selection test for teamwork settings', *Journal of Management*, 25 (2): 207–28.

Tarnow, E. (2000) 'Self-destructive obedience in the airplane cockpit and the concept of obedience optimization', in T. Blass (ed.), *Obedience to Authority: Current Perspectives on the Milgram Paradigm*. Mahwah, NJ: Erlbaum, pp.111–124.

Tichy, N. and Fombrun, C. (1979) 'Network analysis on organizational settings', *Human Relations*, 32 (11): 923–65.

Tieman, R. (2012) 'From teamwork to collaboration', *Financial Times*, Executive Appointments, 15 March, p.1.

Weaver, A.C., Callaghan, M., Cooper, A.L., Brandman, J. and O'Leary, K.J. (2015) 'Assessing interprofessional teamwork in inpatient medical oncology units', *Journal of Oncology Practice*, 11 (1): 19–22.

White, R. and Lippitt, R. (1960) *Autocracy and Democracy*. New York: Harper and Row.

Woolley, A. and Malone, T. (2011) 'Defend your research: what makes a team smarter? More women', *Harvard Business Review*, 89 (6): 32–33.

Zander, L., Mockaitis, A.I. and Butler, C.L. (2012) 'Leading global teams', *Journal of World Business*, 47 (2): 592–603.

Zander, L., Zetting, P. and Mäkelä, K. (2013) 'Leading global virtual teams to success', *Organizational Dynamics*, 42 (3): 228–37.

Zigurs, I. (2002) 'Leadership in virtual teams: oxymoron or opportunity?', *Organizational Dynamics*, 31 (4): 339–51.

Chapter 12 **Individuals in groups**

Key terms

social identity	free rider
self-concept	group norms
social categorization	pivotal norms
self-categorization	peripheral norms
self-esteem	group sanction
social representations	ostracism
shared frame of reference	conformity
social influence	obedience
social facilitation	group cohesion
social inhibition	group socialization
synergy	organizational socialization
social compensation	deindividuation
choking	compliance
social loafing	conversion

Learning outcomes

When you have read this chapter, you should be able to define those key terms in your own words, and you should also be able to:

1. Explain the basic principles of social identity theory and social representation theory.
2. Distinguish between social facilitation and social loafing.
3. Understand how groups use norms to regulate the behaviour of their members.
4. Understand the process of group socialization of individuals.
5. Explain why individuals conform to the dictates of their group.
6. Distinguish between conformity and obedience, and between compliance and conversion.

Why study individuals in groups?

The enthusiasm of management for groups and teams in the workplace is tempered by the research of social scientists who see them possessing a darker side, one which becomes evident when manifested in the behaviour of some mobs and crowds on the street. They are seen as taking over the individual's mind, depressing intelligence, eliminating moral responsibility and forcing conformity. A group can cause its members a great deal of suffering and despair and can perpetuate acts of great cruelty.

There is now extensive research evidence which demonstrates the power of groups to affect the behaviour of their members. This was originally conducted by Elton Mayo at the Hawthorne plant in the 1920s. Since that time, managements have harnessed this power by creating groups and teams which police and discipline their own members, keeping their behaviour in line with organizational (management) objectives. While the power of the group to affect the perceptions, performance and behaviour of its individual members is well established, there has also been a growing body of research that shows how a lone individual can influence a majority.

The individual and the group

Henri Tajfel and John Turner (1986) argued that as long as individuals see themselves as more important than their group, then the latter cannot function effectively. Participants have to identify themselves as group members, treating the group's values as their own. Such an attitudinal 'switch' and commitment, facilitates the long-term existence and success of their group. This question of how much an individual should be part of the group (for their own well-being, for that of their group, and for the organization) and how much separate from it (to remain creative, critical and for their own mental health) is a continuing debate in the literature.

Social identity that part of the self-concept which comes from our membership of groups and which contributes to our self-esteem.

Let us first consider some theories which seek to explain the relationship between the individual and their group. Tajfel and Turner developed social identity theory that holds that a person's self-concept is based not only on their individual characteristics or personal identity (*I am reserved, I am interested in music, I have blond hair*), but also on their group membership (*I am French, I work for ABC corporation, I am a member of the accounting profession*). They then compare themselves to other individuals and groups. People have a strong tendency to mentally organize things and people, including themselves, into categories. To the extent that we associate ourselves with groups, that is, categorize ourselves, we have social identities. Social identities, developed through group membership, are an important part of how we define ourselves.

Self-concept the set of perceptions that we have about ourselves.

Group formation can be seen as an adaptive process as one moves from feeling and thinking as an individual (personal identity), to feeling and thinking as a member of a group (social identity). Group identity holds that group membership affects people's sense of who they are. The groups or social categories to which we belong (e.g. student course member, management team member, parent or sports club secretary) are an integral part of our self-concept. Our own self-concept is the way in which we see ourselves, the set of perceptions that we have about ourselves. It affects both how we feel about ourselves and how we act within a group. This is because joining a group lowers our self-awareness and raises our group awareness. The roles that we play within different groups, especially those that are important to us, influence and shape our attitudes and behaviours.

Social identity is therefore that part of an individual's self-concept that comes from their membership of a group and it fulfils two functions. First, it defines and evaluates a person (e.g. 'she's a member of the design team'). Such definition and evaluation is done both by others and by the person themselves. Second, it prescribes appropriate behaviour for them. They think and behave in characteristically 'design team' ways. How this happens is through social comparison.

According to Tajfel, in order to evaluate your own opinions and abilities, you not only compare yourself with other individuals with whom you interact, but you also compare

the same grade as all the others, without having contributed anything whatsoever to the team's final report.

Free riding dooms a team to ineffectiveness and is abhorrent to team members for three reasons. It violates an equity standard – members who have contributed baulk at others who receive the same benefits, despite having contributed nothing. It violates a social responsibility standard – everyone should contribute their fair share. Finally, it violates a reciprocity standard – members should exchange their contributions with each other. The basic strategy for management to counteract free-riding is to broaden the individual's concept of self-interest and arrange matters so that an individual's personal goals are attained by the achievement of the group's collective goal (Albanese and Van Fleet, 1985).

Avoiding free riders

Towards the start of the film *The Internship* (2013) the large aggregate of Google summer interns rapidly form themselves into small groups to compete with one another. The members of the winning group will be offered permanent jobs. If you had to choose fellow students (whom you did not know) to join you for a student group project, all of whose members would be awarded the same project grade, how would you choose whom to include and exclude?

Wayne Neu (2015) studied how business school undergraduates did this. He found that they wanted to find individuals who would be willing to do their share of the group's work (no free riders); who would help the group achieve a high project grade; and who would not cause them anxiety, uncertainty, anger or stress. Essentially, they wanted a person whom they could trust, and that trustworthiness was primarily signalled to them by a person's reliability, communicativeness, cooperativeness and flexibility. Their personality was also held to be important, and four of the 'Big Five' traits – conscientiousness, agreeableness, extroversion and openness (see Chapter 6) – were sought. However, personal attributes such as personality and trustworthiness can only deduced indirectly. So how do you decide whom to invite to join your group? The answer is that in the group member selection process, students use external, directly observable, physical and behavioural cues. In order of importance, these were:

Physical cues

- Clothing attributes – include those wearing business school casual clothing.
- Hair attributes – include those who are well-groomed, clean-cut and clean-shaven men.
- Tool attributes – include those already possess tools and supplies relevant to the team's task (writing instruments, paper, planner, textbook, laptop).
- Body art attributes – avoid students with piercings or tattoos.
- Physique – avoid men who are too physically fit.

Behavioural cues

- Smiling – avoid non-smilers.
- Class behaviours – include those who attend lectures regularly, listen to the lecturer, take notes, use a highlighter pen, write in a planner.
- Socializers – include those who socialize with fellow students before a class.
- Participation – include those who ask or respond to questions and comment thoughtfully.

Making inferences about classmates based on which social category you place them in rather than on individual merit is stereotyping. How many of these physical and behavioural cues would you use to help you decide whom to approach or avoid during student project group formation?

STOP AND THINK Have you had experience of social loafing or free riding in your educational or work context? What advice would you give to your instructor or manager to remove it?

p influences on individuals' behaviour

...rms an expected mode of behaviour or belief that is established either formally or informally by a group.

Pivotal norms socially defined standards relating to behaviour and beliefs that are central to a group's objective and survival.

Elton Mayo originally noted the existence of group norms, and their enforcement through sanctions, during the Bank Wiring Observation Room studies at the Hawthorne works. The men there restricted their output to conform to a group-agreed norm or standard. In another study which has now become a classic in experimental social psychology, Muzafer Sherif (1936) showed how group norms emerged.

Sherif's work showed that in a situation where doubt and uncertainty exist and where first-hand information is lacking, a person's viewpoint will shift to come into line with those of other group members. In essence this situation leads to the creation of a group norm. This occurs quickly among group members who have had little previous experience of the group's work. It also occurs among those who have had experience, although more slowly. Few of the subjects who took part in Sherif's experiments felt conscious that others had influenced their judgements. Sherif's work suggested that in order to organize and manage itself, every group developed a system of norms. Norms are behavioural expectations and they serve to define the nature of the group. They express the values of the members of the group and provide guidelines to help the group achieve its goals. A group may develop their norms both consciously and unconsciously.

Sherif's study of the emergence of group norms

Muzafer Sherif (1936) placed a group of three subjects in a darkened room and presented them with a small spot of light on a wall for them to view. He then asked them to track the apparent movement of the spot, and to say, aloud, each in turn, the direction in which they thought that the light was moving. The apparent movement is

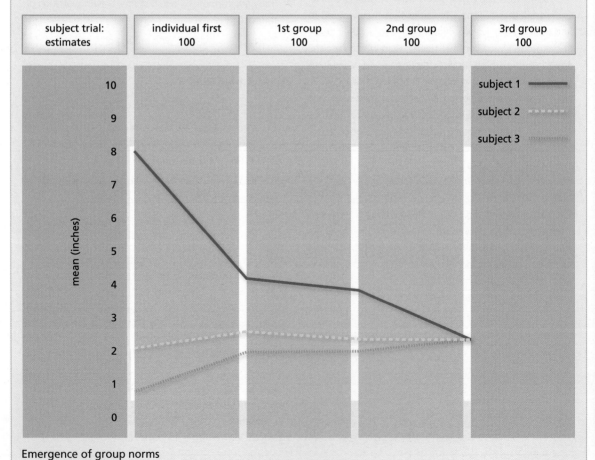

subject trial: estimates	individual first 100	1st group 100	2nd group 100	3rd group 100

Emergence of group norms

ultimately exercised by the group members themselves, it was managers who *initiated* peer control by prescribing the norms of appropriate behaviour for the groups; *authorizing* it by delegating control facilities to groups; and *facilitating* it by structuring group work patterns. The role of group members was to accept, participate in and maintain peer control once it was in place. The authors quote a section from James Barker's research to illustrate this process. This involves a group member, Martha, observing one of her fellow group members, Phil, once again arriving late for work. She gathers two other group members, Diego and Mary, and together they confront Phil. The exchange goes as follows:

[Martha said,] 'Look Phil, we don't like the pattern you're setting here. You've been late and you're going to get yourself into trouble'. Phil starts to say something, but Mary cut him off. 'You're a member of our team. We expect you to support us all... You can't

be hanging back.' Diego followed: 'You've got to support us. We all support each other. When you're late, the rest of us have to work harder'... But Mary held the floor: 'No, you look. This is a bad pattern you have going here... If you're not going to do what we need you to do... we have to do something. Don't make us do that'. Phil looked at them, then looked away. 'OK, OK'. (Barker, 1999, pp.80–1)

In this example, 'employees arriving at work on time' is a management-instituted norm. However, while management authorizes the use of peer pressure by explicitly transferring the responsibility for exercising control over individual tardiness to the group, the decision to exercise that pressure lies with the group. While such pressure can be applied by individual members, as in this example, it is often done in collaboration with fellow group members, acting on behalf of the whole group.

Conformity a change in an individual's belief or behaviour in response to real or imagined group pressure.

Obedience a situation in which an individual changes their behaviour in response to direct command from another.

Conformity with norms tends to increase under certain conditions. An increase in conformity is associated with a decrease in the size of the group; and also with an increase in the group's homogeneity, visibility and a stable experience. Members who perceive themselves to be of low status in the group will tend to conform more, and feel that they have to 'earn' the right to be deviant. High conformers are also those who feel that they are not fully accepted by the others. Diagnosing a team's norms and its members' conformity to them can help to explain group behaviour. Conformity can be contrasted with **obedience**, a situation in which individuals change their behaviour in response to a direction from others.

If you want to deviate from a group norm you have several options. You can attempt to persuade others to your viewpoint, and thus alter the group norm. Of course, the other members may respond by persuading you to conform to the existing norm. The higher your status, the more power you will have in the group and the more you will be able to change the behaviours and beliefs of the other members (and the less likely they will be to change your own). What other options are there? If the group is of little importance to you, and if you are free to leave the group, you will do so. Conversely, if you are of little importance to the group, you may be forced either to conform to its norms or else be rejected by its members. If, however, your presence is important to your group (e.g. because you possess high status, power, popularity or special skills), then the group may tolerate your deviant behaviour and beliefs in order to avoid the threat of losing you as a valued member.

In the film comedy *Galaxy Quest* (1999), five unemployed actors whose sci-fi TV series has been discontinued, earn a living through public appearances at fan conventions, shopping mall dedications and supermarket openings. One member of the group, Jason Nesmith (played by Tim Allen) is regularly late at these events. He was the fictional captain of the Starship Protector in the TV show, and is the character most loved by the fans. Because of his popularity and fan appeal, the other group members are forced to tolerate his continued late arrival. Hence, the power that a group has to influence its members towards conformity to its norms depends on three main factors:

- The positive and negative sanctions (rewards and punishments) that the group has at its disposal.
- The member's desire to avoid negative sanctions such as social and physical punishments or expulsion from the group.
- The degree of attraction that the group has for an individual member and the attraction that group members have for each another.

Group cohesion the number and strength of mutual positive attitudes between individual group members.

The last item on the list concerning mutual attraction is called **group cohesion**. It refers to the number and strength of mutual positive attitudes towards group members. Table 12.3 shows the contributors to and consequences of group cohesion (Pearce et al., 2002). The widely cited research conclusion is that cohesion has a moderating, positive relationship on group performance (Greer, 2012; Gully et al, 1995).

Table 12.3: Group cohesion – contributors and consequences

Contributors to group cohesion	Consequences of group cohesion
Small size	Group success
Past success	Member satisfaction
External threat	Higher group productivity
Common goals	More cooperative behaviour between individuals
Difficulty of entry	Increased interaction between members
Stable membership	Lower group productivity
Opportunity to interact with others	Greater conformity by members
Attractiveness of group to individuals	Members' evaluations become distorted
Fairness of rewards between members	Increased group influence over members
Members' agreement about their statuses	

STOP AND THINK

Consider a group of which you are a member, and its norms and sanctions. Reflect on a situation in which a member (perhaps yourself) broke a norm and received a negative sanction.

Assess the positive and negative outcomes of this occurrence for the individual group member concerned and for the group as a whole.

Having established a set of norms and the sanctions to enforce them, a group has to communicate these to new members. The new group member 'learns the ropes', and is shown how to get things done, how to interact with others, and how to achieve a high social status within the group. An important aspect of achieving such status is to adhere to the group's rules or norms. Initial transgressions will be pointed out to the new member gently. However, the continued violation of norms by a group member puts at risk the cohesion of the group. When there is disagreement on a matter of importance to the group, the preservation of group effectiveness, harmony and cohesion requires a resolution of the conflict. Hence pressure is exerted on the deviating individual through persuasive communication to conform. The name given to this 'educational' process which the new member undergoes is **group socialization** and it occurs within most groups in all types of organizations (Figure 12.8).

Group socialization the process whereby members learn the values, symbols and expected behaviours of the group to which they belong.

If new recruits are thoroughly socialized, they are less likely to transgress group norms and require sanctions to be administered. However, while such pressure to go along with the majority of other members may be beneficial in many respects for the group, it also carries costs. If conformity is allowed to dominate, and individuals are given little opportunity to present different views, there is the danger of the group collectively making errors of judgement, leading them to take unwise decisions. Consider the concept of groupthink, which, through internal conformity and external group pressure, leads individual members collectively to make poor group decisions (this is discussed in Chapter 20).

It is important to remember that while a work group will be attempting to get its new member to adopt its own values, symbols and expected behaviours, the organization which recruited the person will be endeavouring to do the same (see Table 12.4).

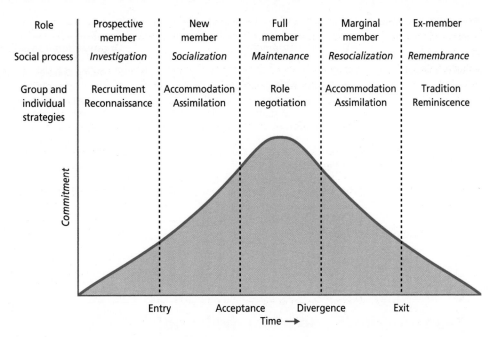

Figure 12.8: A model of the process of group socialization

Source: adapted from *Advances in Experimental and Social Psychology*, Volume 15, L. Berkowicz, (ed.), Socialization in small groups: temporal changes in individual–group relations by Moreland, R.L. and Levine, J.M., pp.137–92. © 1982, Academic Press, with permission from Elsevier. Reproduced with permission from Hogg & Vaughan, *Social Psychology* © 2011 Pearson Australia, p.290.

Home viewing

Ratatouille (2007, director Brad Bird) is an animated film about Remy, a young rat who wants to become a chef. It includes a short sequence which opens with a young man, Alfredo Linguini, cutting vegetables and Colette Tatou, the staff's only female chef, immediately correcting his behaviour. It ends with the characters thanking each other for giving and receiving advice. This short sequence illustrates a range of concepts in the encounter stage of organizational socialization. Can you identify them? (Champoux, 2012).

Table 12.4: Comparison of stages group of development to stages of socialization

	Group development	Organizational socialization
Stage 1: Orientation	1. Forming • Establish interpersonal relationships • Conform to organizational traditions and standards • Boundary testing in relationships and task behaviours	1. Getting in (anticipatory socialization) • Setting of realistic expectations • Determining match with the newcomer
Stage 2: Redefinition	2. Storming • Conflict arising because of interpersonal behaviours • Resistance to group influence and task requirements	2. Breaking in • Initiation to the job • Establishing interpersonal relationships • Congruence between self and organizational performance appraisal

(Continued)

Table 12.4: *Continued*

	Group development	Organizational socialization
Stage 3: Coordination	3. Norming • Single leader emerges • Group cohesion established • New group standards and roles formed for members	3. Settling in (role management) • The degree of fit between one's life interests outside work and the demands of the organization • Resolution of conflicts at the workplace itself
Stage 4: Formalization	4. Performing • Members perform tasks together • Establishing role clarity • Teamwork is the norm	

Source: from Gordon (1993, p.184)

Teamworking? – _do_ make me laugh!

American firms such as Southwest Airlines, Ben & Jerry's, Sun Microsystems, Facebook and eBay invest a lot of time and resources in play, humour and in making their workplaces fun for their employees. Kingston, a technology company, lists among its six values 'Having fun' – working in the company of friends'. Today's young workers (18–25), known as *Generation C* (Connected, Communicating, always Clicking) want to play and have fun at work. Google, Microsoft and other firms have created campus-style work environments which address employee demands for play, fun and a relaxed workplace. In addition, increasing numbers of people, especially in knowledge-intensive industries, are employed in jobs which require successful cooperation, collaboration and creativity. Such groups are a source of value to the company and are hard to duplicate. In order to motivate, resolve conflicts and inspire group members (and stop them from leaving), companies have increasingly used play, fun and humour as management motivational tools.

Some business journals such as *The Economist* (2010, p.84) take a negative view of fun in organizations. It writes that:

> These days many companies are obsessed with fun. They are software firms in Silicon Valley which have installed rock-climbing walls in their reception areas and put inflatable animals in their offices. They fear that the cult of fun has spread like some disgusting haemorrhagic disease. Acclaris, an American IT company has a 'chief fun officer'. TD Bank, the American arm of Canada's Toronto Dominion, has a 'Wow' department that dispatches costume-clad teams to 'surprise and delight' successful workers. Red Bull, a drinks firm, has installed a slide in its London office.

Managers hope that 'fun' will make workers more engaged and creative.

However, researchers disagree with this negative view of play and fun. Sørensen and Spoelstra (2011) contrast 'serious play' as an engine of business with the view that work and play are indistinguishable in post-industrial organizations. They concluded that 'It pays to play'. Studies also show that humour, defined as amusing communications that produce positive emotions and cognitions in the individual, group or organization, does create a positive mental state that acts as a social lubricant. When used in groups, their members experience positive emotions that make interactions between them more effective and efficient, leading the group to bond faster. Humour is thus an important contributor to group effectiveness because it positively affects group cohesiveness, communication and creativity. It reduces stress; and fosters *esprit de corps*.

Humour produces an increase in physical and psychological energy leading workers to expend more effort in challenging tasks, and ensures good communication by inducing positive feelings. It reduces listener resistance, making the listener more receptive to the message that management sends. This more persuasive message also tends to be more interesting to its recipients, requiring less repetition and explanation by management. It also reduces social distance between supervisors and subordinates. From a group's point of view, joking and teasing serve as a foundation of group culture, and are used to communicate group values, beliefs and expectations to its new members. Humour reaffirms the reason for the formation of a group, emphasizes shared values, indicates appropriate behaviour and aids the development of group norms.

Thus, while critics may laugh at what may seem to be a management fad, the research suggests that play, fun and humour appear to be effective in building high morale and cohesion, good communication patterns and strong social bonds, especially among groups of young employees. It may therefore be management which has the last laugh! (*The Economist*, 2010; Romero and Pescosolido, 2008; Sørensen and Spoelstra, 2011; www.kingston.com)

Organizational socialization the process through which an employee's pattern of behaviour, values, attitudes and motives is influenced to conform to that of the organization.

Some companies, such as Disney, are famous for, and invest much time, money and effort into getting their new employees to adopt the 'company way' of doing things. This equivalent process is called organizational socialization (see Chapter 4). If the picture of organizational life that the newcomer is presented with by the organization is congruent with the picture held by the workforce, they will accept it. If not, the newcomer is more likely to adopt the picture held by their own work group, as these are the people with whom they will spend most of their time.

Why do members conform to group pressure? Group norms increase the predictability of the behaviour of others, and reduce the chances of individuals embarrassing each other when interacting – for example, when speaking at social events. Complying with group norms may be of such personal benefit to us that we are willing to abide by them. In so doing, we suppress our own personal desires and reduce our individual freedoms. Moreover, we also punish those who violate the group's norms and reward those who do not. Additionally, individuals have a desire for order and meaning in their lives. They view uncertainty as disturbing and as something that should be reduced to the absolute minimum. Norms, and the adherence to norms, help us 'make sense' of seemingly unconnected facts and events; provide us with explanations of 'what's going on'; and allow us to feel in control of the situations in which we find ourselves. The earliest experimental studies into conformity to group norms were carried out by Solomon Asch (1951, 1952, 1956). He found that those subjects who yielded to group pressure did so for different reasons. He distinguished three types of yielding:

1. *Distortion of perception.* These subjects seem to have convinced themselves that they actually did see the lines the way the other group members stated their judgements. Yielding at the perceptual level was rare, and occurred primarily among those who displayed a lack of trust in themselves. They were unaware that their estimates had been displaced or distorted by the majority.

2. *Distortion of judgement.* These subjects yielded either because they were unsure that they understood the task set for them, or because they did not want to 'spoil the experiment'. They suffered from primary doubt and lack of confidence. The factor of greatest importance was their decision that their perceptions were inaccurate, and that those of the majority were correct. Distortion of judgement occurred frequently.

3. *Distortion of action.* The subjects did not suffer a modification of perception, nor did they conclude that they were wrong. They yielded because they feared being excluded, ostracized or considered eccentric. These subjects suppressed their observations, and voiced the majority position with a full awareness of what they were doing.

Asch's experiment was replicated more than 30 years later, this time with five individuals using PCs who were told that they had been linked together (Doms and van Avermaet, 1981). Whereas Asch had found that the number who refused to conform to the group in any trial was just 25 per cent, in a repeat study 69 per cent of the subjects made no errors. Maybe a computer-mediated communication environment reduces our tendency to conform to a unanimous group position.

STOP AND THINK   Think of an occasion when you have given an opinion or supported a decision contrary to your own feelings and judgement, but consistent with those around you at the time. How can you live with yourself for acting in such a socially compliant and submissive manner? What is your pathetic excuse for having done so?

Asch's study of conformity

In the early 1950s, Solomon E. Asch constructed a laboratory experiment into individual conformity in groups.

The situation

Seven men sat around a table supposedly to participate in a study on visual perception.

The subject

Only number 6 (second from the right) was a real subject. The remainder were Asch's paid accomplices.

The task

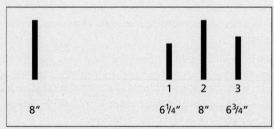

The task was an easy one: to judge which of three lines was equal in length to one they had seen earlier.

The problem

In experimental conditions, the accomplices had been instructed to lie about which line was correct. Under pressure, the subject (no. 6) showed signs of conflict, of whether to conform to the group judgement or give the response he judged to be correct.

The results

Members making at least one error	76%
Times average member conformed	37%
Members who never conformed	24%
Members who conformed over 10 times	11%
Members who made at least one error when tested alone	5%

Based on Asch (1951)

Milgram's 'electric shock' experiments

Stanley Milgram
(1933–1984)

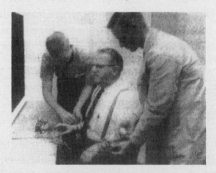

Volunteer subject, accomplice 'learner' and accomplice experimenter

A study by Stanley Milgram showed that a group can pressure an individual to defy authority. Would you torture another person simply because you were told to do so by someone in authority? Of course not, you would probably refuse with little hesitation. In a series of now famous and highly controversial experiments, Stanley Milgram examined people's level of obedience to authority. The research involved ordinary people of different ages, sexes, races and occupations. First, groups of psychiatrists, postgraduate students and social science lecturers were asked by Milgram to predict how many of the research subjects would actually obey the experimenter's order. There was a high agreement that virtually all subjects would refuse to obey. Only one in a hundred would do it, said the psychiatrists, and that person would be a psychopath.

Milgram's experiment involved volunteer subjects participating in a learning experiment. They were to act as teachers of people who were trying to learn a series of simple word pairs. As teachers they were told to punish the student when he failed to learn by giving him an electric shock. At the start the shocks were small in intensity but every time the learner made a mistake, the teacher was told to increase the size of the shock. In carrying out the experiments Milgram found that two out of every three subjects tested administered the electric shocks up to a level which was clearly marked 'fatal' simply because an authority figure told them to do so. In fact, no electric shocks were ever actually given although the volunteer 'teachers' believed that the learners were really receiving the shocks they administered. An earlier experiment by Asch had shown that it only needed one other person to agree with a deviant for the conformity effect to be counteracted. In one variation of his experiment, Milgram placed two of his accomplices alongside the subject, so that the testing of the wired-up learner would be done by a group and not by a single subject. This experimental situation is thus similar to Asch's.

The experiment began with one of the accomplices administering the shocks. The first accomplice then refused to continue, argued with the experimenter, and withdrew sitting in the corner of the room. The second accomplice then took over, continued for a bit, and then refused just as the previous one had done. The real subject now remained to administer the shocks. Milgram repeated this procedure 40 times, each with a different subject. In 30 of these 40 cases, he found that once the subjects had seen their group colleagues defy the experimenter, they also defied him. When group pressure for such defiance was lacking, only 14 subjects defied the authority figure. Milgram concluded that peer rebellion is a very powerful force in undercutting the experimenter's authority. A replication of Milgram's experiment by Jerry Burger revealed that things had not changed greatly in the intervening 45 years. A total of 70 per cent of his participants (compared to Milgram's 82.5 per cent) were prepared to continue delivering shocks after the learner had cried out in pain at 150 volts. Men and women did not differ in their rates of obedience (Milgram, 1973; Burger, 2009; Blass, 2007).

Deindividuation

Deindividuation
an increased state of anonymity that loosens normal constraints on individuals' behaviour, reducing their sense of responsibility, and leading to an increase in impulsive and antisocial acts.

Social facilitation explains how groups can arouse individuals and stimulate their performance, while social loafing shows that groups can diffuse and hence diminish individual responsibility. Together, arousal and diffused responsibility combine to decrease normal social inhibitions and create deindividuation. **Deindividuation** refers to a person's loss of self-awareness and self-monitoring. It involves some loss of personal identity and greater identification with the group.

The writings of Gustave Le Bon led to the theory of deindividuation which was first proposed by Leon Festinger, Albert Pepitone and Theodore Newcombe (1952). However, it is Marion Hampton (1999, p.112) who neatly captures the experience of deindividuation when she writes:

There are moments when we can observe ourselves behaving irrationally as members of crowds or audiences, yet we are swept by the emotion, unable to check it. In smaller groups too, like committees or teams, we may experience powerful feelings of loyalty, anxiety or anger. The moods and emotions of those around us seem to have an exaggerated effect on our own moods and emotions.

Edward Diener (1980) considered self-awareness (i.e. awareness of oneself as an object of attention) to be the crucial element in the deindividuation process. The environmental conditions which reduce self-awareness and thereby trigger deindividuation, as well the consequences of deindividuation, are summarized in Figure 12.9.

The influence of the crowd

Adam Oxford/Demotix/Demotix/Press Association Images

Gustave LeBon stated that the crowd is 'always intellectually inferior to the isolated individual … mob man is fickle, credulous, and intolerant showing the violence and ferocity of primitive beings'. He added, 'by the mere fact that he forms part of an organized crowd, a man descends several rungs in the ladder of civilization. Isolated he may be a cultivated individual, in a crowd he is a barbarian – that is a creature acting by instinct' (LeBon, 1908, p.12). The street rioting that started in the Tottenham neighbourhood of London in 2011 quickly spread across the capital, and then to other English cities – Manchester, Birmingham, Liverpool and Nottingham – on the following four nights. The police were pitted against mocking, mobile and mostly young gangs of violent looters. In his book *The Crowd*, originally published in 1895, LeBon hypothesized that humans had a two-part personality. The upper half was conscious, unique to each individual and contained dignity and virtue. The lower half, in contrast, was unconscious, was shared with everyone else, and contained bad desires and instincts. *The Economist* (2011a, 2011b) newspaper reported that 'As long as looters are part of a street mob they feel strong and invulnerable. Once individuals are arrested in large numbers … powerful peer pressure and the groupthink that goes with them are broken'. LeBon attributed this primitive behaviour to three things:

Anonymity: Individuals cannot be easily identified in a crowd.

Contagion: Ideas and emotions spread rapidly and unpredictably.

Suggestibility: The savagery that is just below the surface is released by suggestion.

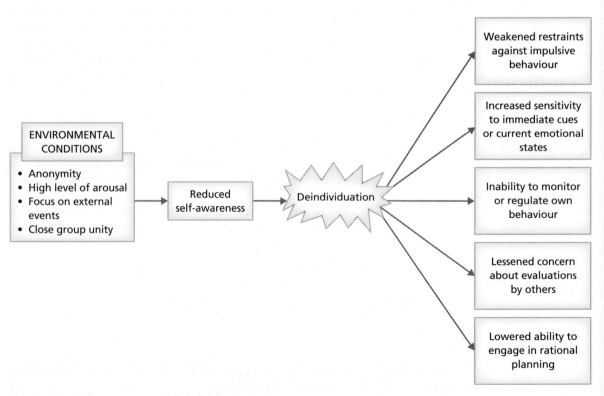

Figure 12.9: Self-awareness and deindividuation

Source: reproduced with permission from Hogg & Vaughan, *Social Psychology* © 2011 Pearson Australia, p.424.

Anonymity within a crowd or large group lessens inhibitions. Warriors in a tribe paint their faces and wear masks. When attention is drawn away from the individual in a crowd or group situation, their anonymity is increased, and they are more likely to abandon their normal restraints and to lose their sense of individual responsibility. This can lead to anti-social behaviour such as attacking a policeman during protest demonstrations. In military organizations, members have always worn uniforms; and companies now provide their staff with corporate clothing. While this may get them to identify more closely with their organizations, it can also increase their anonymity.

STOP AND THINK   Think about a group to which you belong and with which you identify. Write down what this group means to you, and list some of the things that you have said or done that show that you identify strongly with this group.

Now, think about a group to which you belong, but with which you do not identify. Again write down what the group means to you and this time give examples of your lack of identification with that group.

A great number of different factors influence conformity to norms (see Figure 12.10). The personality characteristics of individuals play a part in predisposing them to conform to group norms. The kind of stimuli eliciting conformity behaviour is also important. That people conform to norms when they are uncertain about a situation was demonstrated by the Sherif experiments. He also discovered that a person with a high degree of self-confidence could affect the opinions and estimates of other group members. Asch found that if even just one confederate in his experiment broke the unanimity with his dissenting voice, then the dramatic effects of conformity were erased, and the experimental subject felt free to give the correct answer that seemed obvious all along. Upbringing (including formal education) also plays an important part. Bond and Smith's (1996) analysis showed a steady decline in conformity since the original Asch studies. Collectivist culture countries show higher levels of conformity than individualist culture countries (see Chapter 4).

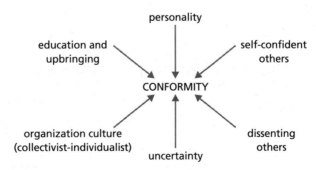

Figure 12.10: Factors influencing conformity to group norms

STOP AND THINK   Is conformity by the individual within organizations a bad thing that should be eliminated or is it a good thing that should be encouraged?

Individual influences on group attitudes and behaviour

So far, the focus has been on the group influencing its members. Does this mean that an individual can never influence their group? Clearly not, since history recounts numerous instances of individuals – revolutionaries, rebels, radical thinkers, religious zealots – who created minority groupings, and as minorities successfully persuaded majorities. Indeed, leadership can be considered an example of minority influence. The underpinning to the process of a minority's influence on a majority is provided by Serge Moscovici's (1980) social influence theory. He used the term **compliance** to describe what happens when a majority influences a minority, through its possession of various kinds of power and its ability to implement positive and negative sanctions. He applied the term **conversion** to describe a minority's persuasion of a majority. The concept of conversion is illustrated every time an employee persuades their company to adopt a new product or create a new division.

Compliance
a majority's influence over a minority.

Conversion
a minority's influence over a majority.

In their review of 143 studies of minority influence, Wood et al. (1994) found that minorities had the ability to change the opinions of those who listened to them, especially if the listeners were not required to publicly acknowledge such a change. Moscovici (1980) stressed the importance of consistency in the conversion process. The individual persuading the group had to stick unswervingly to his or her point of view. Moscovici's research provides us with an understanding of how a minority can influence a majority (Nemeth, 1986). These different writings have been summarized by Huczynski (2004), who listed what the minority influencer of a majority has to do:

Become viable	Take a position that others are aware of; make yourself heard; get yourself noticed; and generally overcome the illusion of unanimity.
Create tension	Motivate those in the majority to try to deal with your ideas.
Be consistent	Stick unswervingly to the same position. Do not take a variety of positions that disagree with the majority.
Be persistent	Restate your consistent position in the face of others' opposition to you.
Be unyielding	Being firm and unyielding involves digging your heels in and not compromising.
Be self-confident	This is conveyed by one's consistency and persistence. It raises self-doubts among the majority leading them to reconsider their position.
Seek defectors	Defections from the majority increase the self-doubt of the remaining majority and free its doubters who may have self-censored themselves to speak out, perhaps encouraging more converts.

In the classic film *Twelve Angry Men* (1957), a jury retires to decide on the guilt or innocence of a youth from a slum background. At the outset, 11 of the 12 jurors are keen to find him guilty without further discussion. Only one member of the jury, played by Henry Fonda, has reservations. He successfully persuades the other 11 jurors to acquit the young defendant. In this example of *conversion*, Fonda uses all the above techniques to achieve his objective.

Teamwork takes longer, and there are many occasions when collaboration is a hindrance rather than a help. Companies therefore need to balance individual autonomy with collective action. We are aware of the downside of individualism in organizations, but teams can be just as destructive, by being strong and controlling, thereby ignoring individuals' voices, learning and contributions. Would the crisis in the financial world have been quite so catastrophic if more people had spoken out in their team meetings about what they knew to be wrongful practices?

well advanced with the project and didn't need his input by this time. Also, we no longer trusted him and did not feel that we could rely on him. I didn't take anything that John said seriously any more, and when he offered to do something, I didn't expect him to do it. He continued to derail our meetings with stories of his weekend parties. He began to complain and make sarcastic comments such as 'Oh, I guess nobody hears me'.

As the project deadline approached, the group agreed to meet at the start and end of the week and then again, over the weekend, for one final time. However, after thinking about the plans just made, John realized that his club's formal dance was scheduled for the same weekend, and he claimed there was no time to work on the project. His statement really annoyed me. Did he expect the rest of us to finish the project for him? Did he really have the nerve to change our plans, just so that he could get drunk all weekend? What were his priorities – university or partying? Suddenly, after this occurred to me, I felt a tremendous pressure. Not only did I and my other team members have to organize everything to finish the project, but we were also the only ones who cared about the quality of the work we produced. We could have talked to John again about his performance, but we never did. We just wanted to get the work done and go home as soon as we could. We decided to speak to the course instructor to see if we could get John removed from our group.

We told John of our intentions and he realized that he would not be able to successfully complete the project on his own, which he would have had to do if he was removed from our group. John agreed to fulfil his duties and, although we had done a large part of the required work that had been assigned to him, he did successfully complete the rest himself.

Adapted from Dr Steven B. Wolff (2009) *OB in Action: Cases and Exercises* (8th edin). Houghton Mifflin, p.318.

Employability assessment

With regard to your future employment prospects:

1. Identify up to three issues from this chapter that you found significant.
2. Relate these to the competencies in the employability matrix.
3. Decide what actions you need to take to maintain and/or develop those competencies under each of the four headings of the employability matrix.

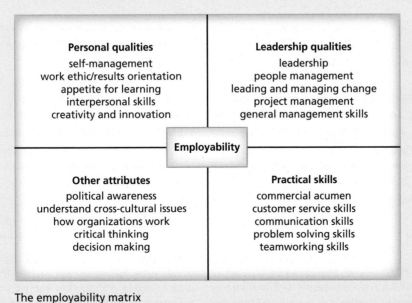

Personal qualities
self-management
work ethic/results orientation
appetite for learning
interpersonal skills
creativity and innovation

Leadership qualities
leadership
people management
leading and managing change
project management
general management skills

Employability

Other attributes
political awareness
understand cross-cultural issues
how organizations work
critical thinking
decision making

Practical skills
commercial acumen
customer service skills
communication skills
problem solving skills
teamworking skills

The employability matrix

References

Albanese, R. and Van Fleet, D.D. (1985) 'Rational behaviour in groups: the free rider tendency', *Academy of Management Review*, 10 (2): 244–55.

Allport, F.H. (1920) 'The influences of the group upon association and thought', *Journal of Experimental Psychology*, 3 (3): 159–82.

Asch, S.E. (1951) 'Effects of group pressure upon the modification and distortion of judgements', in H. Guetzkow (ed.), *Groups, Leadership and Men*. Pittsburgh, PA: Carnegie Press, pp.177–90.

Asch, S.E. (1952) *Social Psychology*. Englewood Cliffs, NJ: Prentice Hall.

Asch, S.E. (1956) Studies of independence and submission to group pressure: a minority of one against a unanimous majority, *Psychological Monograph: General and Applied*, 9 (416): 1–70.

Banyard, P.E., Davies, M.N.O., Norman, C. and Winder, B. (2010) *Essential Psychology: A Concise Instruction*, London: Sage.

Barker, J.R. (1999) *The Discipline of Teamwork: Participation and Concertive Control*. Thousand Oaks, CA: Sage.

Baron, R. and Byrne, D. (2000) *Social Psychology* (9th edn). London: Allyn and Bacon.

Benders, J. (2005) 'Team working: a tale of partial participation', in B. Harley, J. Hyman and P. Thompson (eds), *Participation and Democracy at Work: Essays in Honour of Harvie Ramsey*. London: Palgrave Macmillan, pp.55–74.

Blass, T. (2007) *The Man Who Shocked the World: The Life and Legacy of Stanley Milgram*. New York: Basic Books.

Bond, R. and Smith, P.B. (1996) 'Culture and conformity: a meta-analysis of studies using Asch's (1952b, 1956) line judgment task', *Psychological Bulletin*, 119 (1): 111–37.

Burger, J.M. (2009) 'Replicating Milgram: would people still obey today?', *American Psychologist*, 64 (1): 1–11.

Champoux, J.E. (2012) 'The unique effects of animated film in teaching and learning environments', in J. Billsberry, J. Charlesworth and P. Leonard (eds), *Moving Images: Effective Teaching with Film and Television in Management*. Charlotte, NC: Information Age Publishing, pp.49–62.

Coutu, D. (2009) 'Why teams don't work', *Harvard Business Review*, 87 (5): 99–105.

Di Stefano, G., King, A.A. and Verona, G. (2015) 'Sanctioning in the wild: rational calculus and retributive instincts in gourmet cuisine', *Academy of Management Journal*, 58 (3): 906–31.

De Jong, B.A., Bijlsma, K.M. and Cardinal, L.B. (2014) 'Stronger than the sum of ots parts? The performance implications of peer control combinations in teams', *Organization Science*, 25 (6): 1703–21.

Diener, E. (1980) 'Deindividuation: the absence of self-awareness and self-regulation in group members', in P.B. Paulus (ed.), *Psychology of Group Influence*. Hillsdale, NJ: Erlbaum.

Doms, M. and van Avermaet, E. (1981) 'The conformity effect: a timeless phenomenon?', *Bulletin of the British Psychological Society*, 36 (1): 180–88.

Feldman, D.C. (1984) 'The development and enforcement of group norms', *Academy of Management Review*, 9 (1): 47–53.

Festinger, L., Pepitone, A. and Newcomb, T. (1952) 'Some consequences of deindividuation in a group', *Journal of Abnormal and Social Psychology*, 47 (2 supplement): 382–89.

Frohlich, N. and Oppenheimer, J. (1970) 'I get by with a little help from my friends', *World Politics*, 23 (1): 104–20.

Gaffney, P. (2015) 'The nature and meaning of teamwork', *Journal of the Philosophy of Sport*, 42 (1): 1–22.

George, J.M. (1992) 'Extrinsic and intrinsic origins of perceived social loafing in organizations', *Academy of Management Journal*, 35 (1): 191–202.

Gordon, J. (1993) *A Diagnostic Approach to Organizational Behaviour*. Boston, MA: Allyn & Bacon.

Greenberg, J. (1999) *Managing Behaviour in Organizations* (2nd edn). Upper Saddle River, NJ: Prentice Hall.

Greenberg, J. and Baron, R.A. (1997) *Behaviour in Organizations* (6th edn). Englewood Cliffs, NJ: Prentice Hall.

Greer, L.L. (2012) 'Group cohesion: then and now', *Small Group Research*, 43 (6): 655–61

Guirdham, M. (2002) *Interactive Behaviour at Work*. Harlow, Essex: Financial Times Prentice Hall.

Gully, S.M., Devine, D.J. and Whitney, D.J. (1995) 'A meta-analysis of cohesion and performance: effects of level of analysis and task interdependence', *Small Group Research*, 26: 497–521.

Hampton, M.M. (1999) 'Work groups', in Y. Gabriel (ed.), *Organizations in Depth*. London: Sage Publications, pp.112–38.

Guzzo, R.A. and Dickson, M.W. (1996) 'Teams in organizations: recent research on performance and effectiveness', *Annual Review of Psychology*, 47: 307–38.

Hogg, M.A. and Vaughan, G.M. (2008) *Social Psychology* (5th edn). Harlow: Pearson Education.

Huczynski, A.A. (2004) *Influencing Within Organizations* (2nd edn). London: Routledge.

Ingham, A.G., Levinger, G., Graves, J. and Peckham, V. (1974) 'The Ringelmann effect: studies of group size and group performance', *Journal of Experimental Social Psychology*, 10 (4): 371–84.

Jonsen, K. and Bryant, B. (2008) 'Stretch target', *People Management*, 14 (17): 28–31.

Jordet, G (2009) 'When superstars flop: public status and choking under pressure in international soccer penalty shootouts', *Journal of Applied Sport Psychology*, 21 (2): 125–30.

Jordet, G. and Hartman, E. (2008) 'Avoidance motivation and choking under pressure in soccer penalty shoot-outs', *Journal of Sport and Exercise Psychology*, 30 (4): 450–59.

Karau, S.J. and Williams, K.D. (1993) 'Social loafing: meta-analytic review and theoretical integration', *Journal of Personality and Social Psychology*, 65 (4): 681–706.

Kerr, N.L. (1983) 'Motivation losses in small groups: a social dilemma analysis', *Journal of Personality and Social Psychology*, 45 (4): 819–28.

Kravitz, D.A., and Martin, B. (1986) 'Ringelmann re-discovered: the original article', *Journal of Personality and Social Psychology*, 50 (5): 936–41.

Lam, C. (2015) 'The role of communication and cohesion in reducing social loafing in group projects', *Business and Professional Communication Quarterly*, 78 (4): 454–75.

Latane, B. and Nida, S. (1980) 'Social impact theory and group influence: a social engineering perspective', in P.B. Paulus (ed.), *Psychology of Group Influence*. Hillsdale, NJ: Lawrence Erlbaum Associates, pp.3–34.

Latane, B., Williams, K., and Harkins, S. (1979) 'Many hands make light work: the causes and consequences of social loafing', *Journal of Personality and Social Psychology*, 37 (6): 822–32.

LeBon, G. (1908) *The Crowd: A Study of the Popular Mind*. London: Unwin (first published 1895 by Ernest Benn).

Martin, J. (2005) *Organizational Behaviour and Management* (3rd edn). London: Thomson.

Milgram, S. (1973) *Obedience to Authority*. London: Tavistock Publications.

Moreland, R.L. and Levine, J.M. (1982) 'Socialization in small groups: temporal changes in individual-group relations', in L. Berkowicz (ed.), *Advances in Experimental and Social Psychology, Volume 15*. New York, Academic Press, pp.137–92.

Moscovici, S. (1980) 'Towards a theory of conversion behaviour', in L. Berkowitz (ed.), *Advances in Experimental Social Psychology, Volume.13*. New York: Academic Press, pp.209–39.

Moscovici, S. (1984) 'The phenomenon of social representations', in R.M. Farr and S. Moscovici (eds), *Social Representations*. New York: Academic Press, pp.3–69.

Mumford, S. (2015) 'In praise of teamwork', *Journal of the Philosophy of Sport*, 42 (1): 51–56.

Nemeth, C. (1986) 'Differential contributions of majority and minority influences', *Psychological Review*, 93 (1): 23–32.

Neu, W.A. (2015) 'Social cues of (un)trustworthy team members', *Journal of Marketing Education*, 37 (1): 36–53.

O'Reilly, J., Robinson, S.L., Berdahl, J.L. and Banki, S. (2015) 'Is negative attention better than no attention? The comparative effects of ostracism and harassment at work', *Organization Science*, 26 (3): 774–93.

Pearce, C.L., Gallagher, C.A. and Ensley, M.D. (2002) 'Confidence at the group level of analysis: a longitudinal investigation of the relationship between potency and team effectiveness', *Journal of Occupational and Organizational Psychology*, 75 (1): 115–20.

Robinson, S.L., O'Reilly, J. and Wang, W. (2013) 'Invisible at work: an integrated model of workplace ostracism', *Journal of Management*, 39 (1): 203–31.

Romero, E. and Pescosolido, A. (2008) 'Humour and group effectiveness', *Human Relations*, 61 (3): 395–418.

Schippers, M.C. (2014) 'Social loafing tendencies and team performance: the compensating effects of agreeableness and conscientiousness', *Academy of Management Learning & Education*, 13 (1): 62–81.

Sherif, M. (1936) *The Psychology of Social Norms*. New York: Harper & Row.

Sørensen, B.M. and Spoelstra, S. (2011) 'Play at work: continuation, intervention and usurpation', *Organization*, 19 (1): 81–97.

Steiner, I. (1972) *Group Process and Productivity*. New York: Academic Press.

Tajfel, H. and Turner, J.C. (1986) 'The social identity theory of inter-group behaviour', in S. Worchel and W.G. Austin (eds.), *Psychology of Inter-group Relations* (2nd edn). Chicago, IL: Nelson-Hall, pp.7–24.

The Economist (2010) 'Schumpeter: Down with fun', 18 September, p.84.

The Economist (2011a) 'Under fire', 13 August, p.23.

The Economist (2011b) 'The fire this time', 13 August, pp.21–23.

Triplett, N. (1898) 'The dynamogenic factors in pace-making and competition', *American Journal of Psychology*, 9 (4): 507–33.

Weber, M. (1924) 'Zur Psychophysik der industriellen Arbeit' (first written in 1908/09), in M. Weber (ed.), *Gesammelte Aussatze zur Sociologie und Sozialpolitik von Max Weber.* Tubingen: J.C.B. Mohr, pp.61–255.

Williams, K.D. and Karau, S.J. (1991) 'Social loafing and social compensation: the effect of expectations of co-worker performance', *Journal of Personality and Social Psychology*, 61 (4): 570–81

Wood, W., Lundgren, S., Ouellette, J.A., Busceme, S. and Blackstone, T. (1994) 'Minority influence: a meta-analytical review of social influence processes', *Psychological Bulletin*, 115 (3): 323–45.

Wolff, S.B. (2009) *OB in Action: Cases and Exercises* (8th edn). Boston, MA: Houghton Mifflin.

Zaccaro, S.J. (1984) 'Social loafing: the role of task attractiveness', *Personality and Social Psychology Bulletin*, 10 (1): 99–106.

Chapter 13 Teamworking

Key terms

team	autonomous work team
group	empowerment
team autonomy	Japanese teamworking
advice team	total quality management
quality circles	just-in-time system
action team	external work team differentiation
project team	internal work team differentiation
cross-functional team	external work team integration
production team	team performance
high performance work system	team viability

Learning outcomes

When you have read this chapter, you should be able to define those key terms in your own words, and you should also be able to:

1. Understand why 'team' is a contested concept in the organizational literature.

2. List the nine dimensions of team autonomy.

3. Differentiate between four major types of teams and give an example of each.

4. Discuss the types of obstacles to effectiveness experienced by each type of team.

5. Contrast Western with Japanese concepts of teamworking.

6. List the four main elements in the ecological framework for analysing work team effectiveness.

7. Understand the continuing importance of teamworking.

Why study teamworking?

The modern concept of teamworking goes back to Eric Trist and Kenneth Bamforth (1951) who analysed coal miners' psychological and emotional responses to underground working. Their socio-technical paradigm was developed during the 1960s, but became more widely known through applications in the late 1960s and 1970s. As twenty-first century companies experience increasing challenges and organizations become more diverse, groups of staff are being increasingly formed into teams to achieve organizational goals (Glassop, 2002). Teamworking provides a mechanism to bring together different employees' expertise and skills that are required to complete increasingly complex work tasks in ever shorter time frames. Teams are popular in organizations and are positively perceived by their members, managers and society at large. Companies appear to believe that teams are an effective way of:

- improving performance;
- reducing production costs;
- speeding up innovations;
- improving product quality;
- increasing work flexibility;
- introducing new technologies;
- increasing employee participation;
- achieving better industrial relations;
- meeting the challenge of global competition;
- identifying and solving work-related problems.

Delarue et al. (2008) reviewed the empirical research on the relationship between teamworking and organizational performance and concluded that the evidence suggested that companies which adopted teamworking obtained:

- positive operational outcomes (increased productivity, quality, flexibility); and
- improved worker outcomes in the form of positive worker attitudes (job satisfaction, motivation, commitment) and worker behaviours (lower turnover and absenteeism).

The researchers found that, while in general teams appeared to have had a positive impact on company performance, the link between the two was moderated by organizational factors. For example, company compensation schemes which gave employees a 'team reward' (rather than compensating them individually) were more likely to have an impact on effectiveness by creating interdependencies between team members. A company strategy emphasizing value (rather than cost) which used semi-autonomous teamworking, achieved higher levels of financial performance. Companies which were unionized (rather than non-unionized) were found to benefit more from employees participating in teams, perhaps by providing them with reassurance about continued employment.

Teams at Google

In Douglas Edwards' (2011) account of the early days of Google, he described Urs Hölzle as a key person on the engineering side ('Saint Urs, Keeper of the Blessed Code'):

Urs's most significant accomplishment, however, was building the team that built Google. 'Your greatest impact as an engineer comes through hiring someone who is as good as you or better' he exhorted everybody who would listen, 'because over the next year, they double your productivity. There's nothing else that you can do to double your productivity. Even if you are a genius, that's extremely unlikely to happen'. . . . If you have very good people it gives you a safety net', he believed. 'If there's something wrong, they self-correct. You don't have to tell them. "Hey, pay attention to this." They feel ownership and fix it before you even knew it was broken.' (Edwards, 2011, p.36)

Allen and Hecht (2004) discussed the 'romance of teams', which they defined as a faith in the effectiveness and even superiority of team-based work. The reason that teams are increasingly used, they claim, is because they fulfil not only economic needs but also certain psychological, social and political ones. Teams make people more satisfied and bolster their confidence; they promote the idea that everyone is unique and has something different to contribute to a task, and that individuals should pull together. Teamworking seems to fit in with currently attractive ideas of empowerment, participation and democracy. Thus, despite being inappropriate or ineffective in certain circumstances, teams continue to be used uncritically within organizations (Naquin and Tynan, 2003; Sinclair, 1992). Thus, a reason for studying teamworking is to determine whether or not teams are superior to individuals working alone, and, if so, in which circumstances.

Team working at Copiapó

On 14 October 2010, the last of the 33 Chilean miners who had been trapped for 69 days at the San José gold and copper mine in Copiapó in the Atacama Desert, 2,300 feet below the Earth's surface (two Empire State Buildings deep) was pulled to safety with the help of an unlikely source – the United States' National Aeronautics and Space Administration (NASA). It was a dire situation. While developing their rescue plans, the Chilean government also sought advice and information from other governments and organizations as to how to assist the trapped miners. One of the organizations that responded to the call for assistance was NASA. It quickly formed a team consisting of two medical doctors, a psychologist and an engineer. The team spent three days at the rescue site in Chile assessing the similarities between the miners' plight and life in space.

They gave advice to the rescue team at the mine site. This ranged from warning rescuers not to give the starving men too much food too quickly (which could prove fatal), to suggesting they wear sunglasses when surfacing after two months underground. Most importantly, the NASA team also provided the design for the innovative rescue capsule (nicknamed *Phoenix*) that was used to pull the miners to the surface, and ultimately saved their lives. The four-person NASA team consulted with 20 of their colleagues, and came up with 50 design recommendations. For example, that exterior rollers would cushion the capsule's ride up, reducing both the friction with the tunnel walls, and the possibility of it getting stuck half way. On the day, with remarkable speed – and flawless execution – miner after miner climbed into the capsule, and was hoisted through the rock and saw precious sunlight after the longest underground entrapment in history. Dr Michael Duncan, NASA's deputy chief medical officer stated: 'We were able to bring the knowledge we learned in space to the surface, and under the surface, to help people here on Earth.' The Copiapó incident involved not only very unusual team composition – these occupations, professions and cultures do not normally collaborate in this way; but also as a very unusual team context – rescuing trapped miners – which is not something that is done routinely (National Aeronautics and Space Administration, 2011; Rashid et al., 2013).

Nicolas Torres/LatinContent/Getty Images

The T-word and teamwork design

Team a group whose members share a common goal that they pursue collaboratively and who can only succeed or fail collectively.

The word **team** derives from the old English, Fresian and Norse word for a bridle and thence to a set of draught animals harnessed together and, by analogy, to a number of persons involved in joint action (Annett and Stanton, 2000). It refers to a group whose members share a common goal that they pursue collaboratively; and who can only succeed or fail collectively.

Nicky Hayes saw teams as a sporting metaphor used frequently by managers and consultants. Sainsbury's, a large British supermarket chain, used the employee job title of 'checkout *captain*'. The metaphor stresses both inclusiveness and similarity – members sharing common values and cooperating to achieve common goals; while also emphasizing differences, as various individuals play distinct, albeit equally valuable roles, and have different responsibilities. She wrote:

> The idea of 'team' at work must be one of the most widely used metaphors in organizational life. A group of workers or managers is generally described as a 'team', in much the same way that a company or department is so often described as 'one big family'. But often, the new employee receiving these assertions quickly discovers that what was described as a 'team' is actually anything but. The mental image of cohesion, co-ordination and common goals which was conjured up by the metaphor of the team was entirely different from the everyday reality of working life. (Hayes 1997, p.27)

Jos Benders and Geert Van Hootegem (1999) felt that after decades of experimentation, teams had finally achieved the status of 'good management practice' in Western organizations. The terms 'group' and 'team' are words which are frequently used interchangeably in the management literature. Katzenbach and Smith (1993, p.112) suggest that the key distinction between a work group and a team relates to performance results. They wrote:

> A working group's performance is a function of what its members do as individuals. A team's performance includes both individual results and what we call 'collective work products'. A collective work product is what two or more members work on together . . . [it] reflects the joint, real contribution of team members.

Paul Paulus and Karen van der Zee (2004) explained how, historically, research into groups and that into teams had followed distinct and separate paths, with the literature on groups appearing in psychology textbooks, and that on teams in management textbooks, journals and magazines. They also wrote that 'team is a word for managers' – an appealing word used as a rhetorical strategy through which managers hope to achieve their goals. It conveys the view that we are 'all in it together' and the interests of workers and top management are the same. Other critics have argued that management's promotion of the *team* concept was a union-busting device – a way of threatening the existence of unions as independent institutions promoting workers' interests, and increasing employees' personal insecurity. They imply that, in contrast, **group** is a word used by researchers who study human behaviour in organizations.

Group two or more people, in face-to-face interaction, each aware of their group membership and interdependence, as they strive to achieve common group goals.

Salas et al. (2005) saw teamwork as the set of interrelated thoughts, actions and feelings of each individual team member which combined to facilitate coordinated, adaptive performance that achieved team task objectives, and which allowed members to function as a team and to achieve value-added outcomes. These researchers said that effective teams needed more than just 'task-work' (i.e. individuals interacting with tools, machines and systems). They also needed 'team-work' (i.e. the ability to coordinate and cooperatively interact with each other through a shared understanding of members' knowledge, skills and experiences). Task-work combined with team-work achieved team objectives.

taxi the aircraft, since the nose wheel gear steering is located on that side of the cockpit. The first officer, who starts the engines and who communicates with the control tower, occupies the right-hand seat. The flight engineer sits sideways, facing a panel that allows him to monitor and control the various sub-systems in the aircraft. He is the only one able to reach the auxiliary power unit. In other transportation craft, the relationship of roles to equipment is different. Aeroplane personnel consist of those in the cockpit – flight crew (pilot, co-pilot, flight engineers) – and those outside it – the cabin crew (flight attendants). Between 1959 and 1989, 70 per cent of all severe aircraft accidents were at least partly attributable to flight crew behaviour (Weiner et al., 1993). Thus, it is a more common cause than either pilot error or mechanical failure.

Mending a broken heart

During cardiac surgery, a patient is rendered functionally dead – the heart stops beating, the lungs stop pumping air – while a surgical team repairs or replaces damaged arteries or valves. A week later, the patient walks out of the hospital. The team that performs this task is as important as the technology that allows them to do it. It consists of different specialists – a surgeon, an anaesthetist, a perfusionist (a technician who runs the bypass machine that takes over the functions of the heart and lungs), and a scrub nurse – working closely and cooperatively together. It exemplifies an *action team* where a single error, miscommunication or slow response by any member can result in failure. Individuals are in *reciprocal interdependence* with each other, *mutually adjusting* their actions to match those of fellow members.

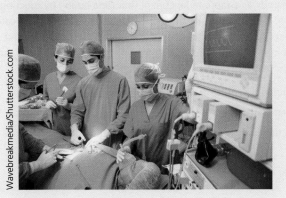

Wavebreakmedia/Shutterstock.com

Amy Edmondson and her colleagues (2001) found that since this type of team performed hundreds of cardiac operations annually, it established a sequence of individual tasks that became very well-defined and routine. Indeed, team members often needed only to look at, rather than speak to, one another, to signal the initiation of the next stage of the procedure. The change from traditional, open-heart surgery procedures to minimally invasive ones involved several changes. The new procedure not only required individual team members to learn new, unfamiliar tasks, but also required a number of familiar tasks to be performed in a different order. Thus, team members had to unlearn old routines before learning new ones. Additionally, the new technology required a greater degree of interdependence and communication between team members. For example, the surgeon had to rely more on team members for essential information (obtained from ultrasound images and digital readouts) than before. This not only disrupted the team's routine but also changed the surgeon's traditional role as order-giver in the operating team's tightly structured hierarchy. Improvements in team performance were found partly to depend on 'the ability of the surgeon to allow himself to become a partner, not a dictator' (Edmondson et al., 2001, p.128). By trying out things that might not work, making mistakes and pointing out problems, learning was accelerated. Such a climate was fostered by the words and actions of surgeons acting as team leaders.

Project teams

Project team a collection of employees from different work areas in an organization brought together to accomplish a specific task within a finite time.

A **project team** consists of individuals who have been brought together for a limited period of time, from different parts of the organization, to contribute towards a management-specified task. The task may be developing a product, refining a service or commissioning a new plant. Once this has been completed, the team is either disbanded, or its members are given new assignments. Project teams are created when:

- creative problem solving is required involving the application of different types of specialized knowledge;

- there is a need to closely coordinate the work on a specific project, such as design and development, or the production and testing of a new product.

Every university has hundreds of project teams that are conducting research. Most of their members are on 2–3 year contracts which span the period of the research project. Team members are recruited on the basis of their specialist knowledge, and their output consists of research reports, books and journal articles.

Cross-functional team employees from different functional departments who meet as a team to complete a particular task.

Within the organizational context, the best known and most common type of project team is the **cross-functional team**. This is a collection of employees who are brought together from different departments (functions) of the company to accomplish a specific task within a finite time. Jack Gordon (1992) reported that in the United States, in organizations with more than 100 employees, 82 per cent had staff working in teams, of which 18 per cent were in cross-functional teams. Another survey, this time by the Hay Group, revealed that approximately 25 per cent of US companies had implemented cross-functional teamworking (Leshner and Brown, 1993). Emmerson, an electronics company based in St. Louis, Missouri, established cross-functional teams in the 1990s to deal with large customers who bought products and services from several of its divisions. Cross-functional teams cut across the company's long-standing boundaries and allowed customers to see Emmerson as a single, integrated supplier rather than a collection of independent divisions (Hindle, 2006; Knight, 2005).

Traditionally, organizations have been divided into functional departments. These have been dubbed 'boxes', 'silos' or 'chimneys' to stress their insularity. By forming teams consisting of people from these different boxes, organizations can break down the boundaries between their functions (e.g. accounting, marketing, research, product design, human resources); improve coordination and integration; release the creative thought of their employees; and increase the speed and flexibility of their responses to customers. Cross-functional teams are established in order to combine a wide range of employee expertise to achieve a more informed and rounded outcome than would otherwise be possible.

Cross-functional teams comprise employees who traditionally work in different departments or work areas. Sometimes, such teams also include customers, suppliers and external consultants. They are supported by their organization's structures, systems and skills which enable the teams to operate successfully as a more independent unit (less bound by functional ties) towards goals which transcend the combined abilities of individual members. Advocates of cross-functional teams claim that they are beneficial to their customers, employees, and to the organization as a whole. Customers obtain more attractive and customized products, and have their needs met more rapidly. Team members benefit through having:

- more challenging and rewarding jobs with broader responsibilities;
- greater opportunities for gaining visibility in front of senior management;
- an increased understanding of the entire processes across the organization;
- a 'fun' working environment;
- closer relationships with colleagues.

The organization gains through:

- increased productivity;
- improved coordination and integration;
- significantly reducing processing times;
- improving market and customer focus;
- reducing the time needed to develop new products;
- improving communications by having boundaries between functions spanned.

Cross-functional teams differ from other types of teams in three important respects:

- They are *representative* in that their individual members usually retain their position back in their 'home' functional department.

- They are *temporary*: they have a finite life, even if their end is years in the future.
- They are *innovative*: they are established to solve non-conventional problems and meet challenging performance standards.

The most common application of cross-functional teams has been in new product development, innovation, and in research and development (R&D). However, they have also been used whenever an organization requires an input of diverse, specialist skills and knowledge. For example, in manufacturing and production; IT development, automation and support; to implement quality, cost, speed improvements and process re-engineering initiatives; to facilitate customer service improvements; and to streamline purchasing and procurement. Recent years have seen the evolution of the global virtual (project) team. These now permeate all levels of most large organizations, often supplementing traditional, face-to-face teams (Cordery et al., 2009; Zander et al., 2012).

Since team members are departmental representatives, they owe their true allegiance to their home, functional department. These members are therefore likely to experience a high degree of pressure and divided loyalties. Their temporary nature also places strains on members who quickly have to develop stable and effective working group processes. Cross-functional teams can therefore have a negative effect on their participants. Organizations and managers need to clearly define cross-functional team assignments in order to maintain order and accountability.

Production teams

Production team
a stable number of individuals who share production goals, and who perform specific roles which are supported by a set of incentives and sanctions.

Typically, a production team consists of individuals who are responsible for performing day-to-day, core operations. These may be product-oriented teams such as those assembling a computer on a factory floor; construction workers placing a bridge in position across a motorway; or teams assembling sound and light systems for a rock concert. The degree of technical specialization required of the team members varies from medium to low, depending on the nature of the duties performed. However, the required degree of coordination, both between the members of each team, and between the team and other work units, is high. It is these other units that are either responsible for providing support activities such as quality control and maintenance, or who provide the inputs to, or receive the outputs of that team.

The focus of 1970s experiments into employee participation and industrial democracy sought to raise productivity by providing employees with more interesting and varied work. In contrast, team-based working innovations of the 1990s represented a greater concern with efficiency and effectiveness. They were stimulated by the need for companies to remain competitive in a fiercely aggressive global environment. The rationale is that in the race to improve service quality or reduce new product cycle times, technology only gives an organization a short-term advantage, and one which can be copied anyway. It is the way that human resources are organized and developed that is more critical.

Team member familiarity

Nearly all commercial airlines now rotate members of their flight crews. Senior pilots on large planes often fly with a different co-pilot on every trip during a month. Airlines do not stick to the same airplane crews because, financially, the airline gets most from its capital equipment and labour by treating each airplane, each pilot and every other crew member as an individual unit, and then uses an algorithm to maximize their utilization.

In consequence, pilots dash through the airports just like passengers, since they have to fly two or three different aircraft, each with a different crew, in a single day.

Team familiarity refers to the amount of previous experience that members have had of working with one another. Robert Huckman and Bradley Staats (2013) studied corporate, healthcare, consulting, military and aviation teams. They found that the degree of familiarity

Adamson/123RF.com

greatly affected team performance, and was a better predictor of team performance than either individual member or project manager experience. They measured how often team members had previously worked together over time. In one study of an Indian software services firm, they found that when team familiarity increased by 50 per cent defects fell by 19 per cent and budget deviations by 30 per cent. How does team familiarity and unfamiliarity affect team performance?

Communication: Differences between members in unfamiliar teams frequently result in poor communication, causing conflict and confusion. Team familiarity obviates the need to learn to communicate with each other, and this speeds up progress towards team goals.

Learning: Unfamiliar teams often fail to tap the knowledge that their members possess since they are unaware of who knows what. Familiarity allows them to become acquainted with what expertise each individual has to help achieve the group task, and encourages them to share it.

Innovation: Since new solutions come from new combinations of existing knowledge, team members must not only share their own knowledge, but also integrate it with that of other members. Team familiarity facilitates this knowledge integration process, increasing the chances of finding innovative solutions.

Change: Teams may be asked to modify goals or change time frames due to outside circumstances which can cause stress and require flexibility. Familiar teams provide a more secure basis from which to meet such challenges.

Organizations develop capabilities that their competitors cannot replicate to gain competitive advantage, and familiar teams are one source of that advantage. Since each team member's performance is dependent on that of the others, competitors cannot replicate an entire team's capabilities by hiring away just one individual member. The US National Transportation Safety Board found that 73 per cent of accidents occurred on crew members' first day of flying together, before individuals had a chance to learn, through experience, how best to operate as a team. A NASA study found that fatigued but familiar crews made about half as many errors as rested but unfamiliar ones. Asked how long it would take for two crew members to work together well on a flight, an airlines operations staff member estimated 5–6 years. Clearly this is not good news from a passenger point of view. Next time you board a plane, ask if the members of this crew have ever flown together before (Coutu, 2009).

Teamwork activities

Whether yours is an advice, action, project or production team, what factors affect its performance? Similar to the 'Big Five' personality traits (see Chapter 6), Eduardo Salas and his colleagues (2005) reviewed past research studies and identified five activities which most affected how well teams performed. These five activities were complemented by three supporting and coordinating mechanisms which allowed team members to engage successfully in Big Five activities.

4. Cohesion

Team cohesion can engender mutual cooperation, generosity and helping behaviour, motivating team members to contribute fully. However, it can also stifle creative thinking as individuals seek to 'fit in' and not to 'rock the boat'. Small group size, similar attitudes and physical proximity of workspaces have all been found to encourage cohesion. Does the level of cohesion aid or impede the team's effectiveness?

Team performance a measure of how well a team achieves its task, and the needs of management, customers or shareholders.

Team viability a measure of how well a team meets the needs and expectations of its members.

Team effectiveness

Team effectiveness is the dependent variable in the Sundstrom et al. framework, and is measured using two criteria – performance and viability. Team performance is externally focused and concerns meeting the needs and expectations of outsiders such as customers, company colleagues or fans. It is assessed using measures such as quantity, quality and time. Meanwhile, team viability is the social dimension, which is internally focused and concerns the enhancement of the team's capability to perform effectively in the future. Team viability indicators include its degree of cohesion, shared purpose, and the level of team member commitment. The two are closely related since there is a possibility that a team may get a job done but self-destructs in the process.

 RECAP

1. **Understand why 'team' is a contested concept in the organizational literature.**
   - Teamworking is being increasingly adopted as a favoured form of work organization in different companies and industries around the world.
   - The different purposes and ways in which managers have introduced this innovation, has meant that the term 'team' is used to describe a wide range of radically different working arrangements.

2. **List the nine dimensions of team autonomy.**
   - Gulowsen's nine dimensions of team autonomy are: selection of the team leader; acceptance of a new member into the team; distribution of work; time flexibility; acceptance of additional work; representation outside the team; production methods (choice of); production goals (output determination); production goals (quality determination).

3. **Differentiate between four major types of teams and give an example of each.**
   - Teams in organizations can be classified as advice (e.g. quality circles); action (e.g. surgery team); project (e.g. cross-functional team); and production (e.g. autonomous work team).

4. **Discuss the types of obstacles to effectiveness experienced by each type of team.**
   - Advice teams frequently lack authority to implement their recommendations. Action teams can fail to integrate their members' contributions sufficiently closely. Project team members can suffer 'divided loyalties' between their team and their home department. Production teams may lack autonomy for job satisfaction.

5. **Contrast Western with Japanese concepts of teamworking.**
   - The Western concept is based upon principles of empowerment and on-line teamworking, while the Japanese concept is based upon management principles of individual working online, and teams advising offline.

6. **List the four main variables in ecological framework for analysing work team effectiveness.**
   - Team development; work team boundaries and organizational context affect team effectiveness.

7. **Understand the continuing importance of teamworking.**
   - Japanese forms of teamworking (Toyotaism) have influenced the production processes used in both manufacturing and service industries all around the world.
   - As a concept, teamworking has an appeal in a management philosophy that stresses egalitarianism, non-hierarchy and inclusiveness within organizations.

Revision

1. Self-managing or autonomous work teams are heavily promoted in the literature. What are the costs and benefits of these to (a) the management that establishes them and (b) the individuals who are members of such teams?

2. What impact can technology have on the behaviour and performance of teams? Discuss positive and negative effects, illustrating your answer with examples.

3. 'Autonomous team is a relative term'. Discuss the concept of team autonomy explaining why similarly labelled teams may, in practice, operate very differently. Consider why management might have difficulty in increasing the autonomy that it gives to a team.

4. Highlight briefly the main differences between West European and Japanese-style teamworking. Then, using references to the literature, consider the positive and negative aspects of both systems for either shop floor workers or management.

Research assignment

Using your library and the internet, locate any relevant research and management literature on effective teamworking and devise a list of best practice 'do's' and 'don'ts', and use it to develop a list of questions. Select an organization; interview a team member, a team leader or a manager responsible for a team. Begin by determining the team's purpose, method of working, performance and the challenges that it faces. Write a brief report assessing the team against your best practice list items from the research literature.

Springboard

Alan Jenkins (1994) 'Teams: from ideology to analysis', *Organization Studies*, 15 (6): 849–60. This is an article defending management's interest in teams.

Journal of Occupational and Organizational Psychology (2004) 77 (4). There continues to be a strong belief in the superiority of teams over individuals among managers, employees and the general public. The first five articles in this issue all discuss the phenomenon of the 'romance of teams'.

Andreas Richter, Jeremy Dawson and Michael West (2011) 'The effectiveness of teams in organizations: a meta-analysis', *The International Journal of Human Resource Management*, 22 (13): 2749–69. Reviews and summarizes past research studies into whether teamworking in organizations is related to organizational effectiveness.

Geert Van Hootegem, Jos Benders, Anne Delarue and Stephen Proctor (2005) 'Teamworking: looking back and looking forward', *International Journal of Human Resource Management*, 16 (2): 167–73. The authors critically assess the popularity of teamworking.

 OB cinema

The Dish (2000, director Rob Sitch): DVD track 8, 0:35:55–0:53:07 (18 minutes sequenced). It is July 1969, and Apollo 11 is heading towards the moon. On earth, the Parkes Radio Telescope in New South Wales, Australia, the largest in the southern hemisphere, has been designated by NASA as the primary receiving station for the moonwalk, which it will broadcast to the world. Then, due to a power cut, it 'loses' Apollo 11! Parkes' director, Cliff Buxton (played by Sam Neill) and his team of scientists – Mitch (Kevin Harrington); Glenn (Tom Long); and Al (Patrick Warburton) – all have to work hard (and quickly) to solve the problem. The clip begins with the lights going out during the dance, and ends with Al saying 'Just enough time to check the generator'.

Identify examples of each of the elements of Sundstrom et al.'s ecological framework for analysing work team effectiveness as the team members deal with the crisis.

Sundstrom framework element	Example
Organizational context	
1. Organizational culture	
2. Task design/technology	
3. Mission clarity	
4. Autonomy	
5. Performance feedback	
6. Rewards and recognition	
7. Physical environment	
8. Training and consultation	
Work team boundaries	
9. External differentiation	
10. External integration	
Team development	
11. Interpersonal processes	
12. Norms	
13. Cohesion	
14. Roles	

 OB on the web

Search YouTube for 'The IT Crowd/Team Players/Channel 4' (1.34 minutes). This short, humorous video clip reminds us of the organizational trend, perhaps even obsession, with teams, teamworking and the necessity to be seen as a team player. Suggest reasons why teams should have become such a popular form of work design. What are the costs to those individuals who prefer to work alone?

CHAPTER EXERCISES

1. Factors affecting team performance

Objectives   1. Identify the various factors that influence a team's success or failure.

2. Practise using Sundstrom et al.'s model as an explanatory framework

Briefing   1. Individually:

(a) Remind yourself of Sundstrom et al.'s ecological framework for analysing team effectiveness (pp.436–41),

(b) Reflect on a situation from your experience where a team of which you were a member (work team, sports team, church team, other) *failed* to achieve its goal and also one where a team of which you were a member *succeeded* in achieving its goal.

   (c) Identify which of Sundstrom's 14 factors (or any others), in your view, contributed to your team's failure or success.

2. Form groups and nominate a spokesperson.

   (a) Go round each member in turn who describes their own experiences of team failure, and identify what they consider might have been the contributing factors.

   (b) After all team members' failures have been shared, the group identifies any recurring factors in the different accounts.

   (c) Groups highlight any 'missing' (non-Sundstrom) factors.

   (d) Each group then discusses what could have been done to avoid the failure in their first examples.

   (e) Go round each member in turn who describes their own experiences of *team success* and identify what they consider to have been the contributing factors.

   (f) After all team members' successes have been shared, the group identifies any recurring factors in the different accounts.

   (g) Groups highlight any 'missing' (non-Sundstrom) factors.

   (h) Each group then discusses how such future success can be ensured in similar teams in the future.

3. The class re-forms. The spokespersons for each group report back:

   (a) identifying the most common factors leading to team failure and suggesting how these could have been avoided;

   (b) identifying the most common factors leading to team success and suggesting how these can be ensured in the future.

2. Land Rock Alliance Insurance

Objectives
1. To evaluate the advantages and disadvantages of teamworking arrangements within an organization.
2. To identify conditions favouring the introduction of different forms of working arrangements.

Briefing
1. Individually, read the case study concerning the two different proposed work arrangements for the processing of the insurance claims at Land Rock Alliance Insurance's offices in Edinburgh.

2. Divide into groups, nominate a spokesperson, and:

   (a) Consider the advantages and disadvantages of Eleanor Brennan's teamworking arrangements for (i) the employees and (ii) the management of the company.

   (b) Consider the advantages and disadvantages of Thomas Campion's proposed work fragmentation arrangements for (i) the employees and (ii) the management of the company.

   (c) Opt for one or other of the two managers' work organization solutions, or suggest a solution of your own.

   (d) More generally, under what conditions in a company is (i) teamworking, and (ii) fragmented task working, likely to be most beneficial?

3. Group spokespersons should be ready to report their group's conclusions to the class.

Background
Since the 1940s, the use of asbestos in building materials and other products has led to many claims for damages as a result of personal injury or wrongful death. The procedure for those making claims is complicated and time-consuming. Insurance companies

Why study work design?

This chapter examines the roots of the design of work (jobs) that we see in today's organizations. Only a handful of management theories can claim to be truly revolutionary, and to have had an enduring and worldwide impact on organizational thought and management practice. Those of Frederick Winslow Taylor and Henry Ford are two of them. Contrary to other texts, which argue that their ideas are no longer relevant to our modern, hi-tech, organizational lives, we contend that both are having a more pervasive impact on society today than they did 100 years ago.

Reports regularly appear in newspapers and magazines whose readers claim that their employers use classic Taylorist techniques to achieve efficiency, and that their performance is constantly being measured (*The Economist*, 2015; Kantor and Streitfeld, 2015). You need only to visit a call centre, a fast food restaurant, attend a university course or think about how the phone in your hand was manufactured to see how the provision of goods and services has been affected by Taylor's and Ford's ideas. Their theories and practices prospered through the twentieth century and are thriving at the start of the twenty-first century. They continue to affect our lives as students, employees, consumers and citizens, even though we may not be aware of it.

HOME VIEWING

Office Space (1998, director Mike Judge) follows the progress of Peter Gibbons (played by Ron Livingston), an employee of the computer company, Initech. His behaviour is driven by the nature of his work and the imminent loss of his job due to downsizing. Peter shows signs of alienation, particularly feelings of powerlessness, meaninglessness and self-estrangement. He tells his hypnotherapist 'Ever since I started working, every single day of my life has been worse than the day before it. So that means that every single day that you see me, that's on the worst day of my life.' What aspects of the design of his job might account for this?

Birth of scientific management

Between 1880 and 1910, the United States underwent major and rapid industrialization, including the creation of its first large corporations like Standard Oil Trust (Esso), United States Steel, General Motors and Ford. These firms used new technologies of production and employed large workforces. The workers in these new factories came from agricultural regions of America or were immigrants from Europe. The fact that they had little knowledge of the English language, possessed few job skills, and had no experience of factory work were major problems for company managers. Scientific management offered a solution, and represented one of the first organizational practices capable of being applied in different companies. It introduced a formal system of industrial discipline.

At the start of the twentieth century, most products were hand-made by skilled operators who used general-purpose machine tools such as lathes. It took these craftsmen years of training to acquire the necessary skills and experience. They could read a blueprint, visualize the final product, and possessed a level of hand-eye coordination and gentleness of touch that allowed them to manufacture the required item (Littler, 1982). However, there were insufficient numbers of them to permit mass production. It was against this background that Frederick Taylor and Henry Ford developed and implemented their ideas. Both shared a belief in **rationalism**, which is the theory that reason is the foundation of certainty in knowledge. They believed that if one understands something, one should be able both to state it explicitly, and to write a law or a rule for it. The purpose of developing and applying rules, laws and procedures is to replace uncertainty with predictability, both in the human and non-human spheres.

Rationalism the theory that reason is the foundation of certainty in knowledge.

Taylorism

Scientific management a form of job design which stresses short, repetitive work cycles; detailed, prescribed task sequences; a separation of task conception from task execution; and motivation based on economic rewards.

Systematic soldiering the conscious and deliberate restriction of output by operators.

Scientific management is also known as *Taylorism* and in this chapter the two terms are used interchangeably. Frederick Winslow Taylor was the world's first efficiency expert. He was born into a wealthy Philadelphia Quaker family in 1856. The city was the industrial heart of 1800s America. It contained many manufacturers who had easy access to the Pennsylvanian coal and iron mines. Taylor became an apprentice machinist in a firm of engineers before joining the Midvale Steel Company in 1878, where he developed his ideas. The company manufactured locomotive wheels and axles, and it was here that he rose to the position of shop superintendent by 1887. In this role, he observed that workers used different and mostly inefficient work methods. He also noticed that few machinists ever worked at the speed of which they were capable. He contrasted natural soldiering (i.e. the inclination to take it easy) with what he labelled systematic soldiering. Taylor attributed systematic soldiering to a number of factors:

- The view among the workers that an increase in output would result in redundancies.
- Poor management controls which enabled them to work slowly, in order to protect their own best interests.
- The choice of methods of work which were left entirely to the discretion of the workers, who wasted a large part of their efforts using inefficient and untested rules-of-thumb.

Soldiering

Robert Kanigel (1997) explained that the word 'soldiering' had nautical roots. It related to soldiers who, when transported by ship, acted as privileged passengers. They were exempt from the work on board that the seamen had to perform. To the sailors, such work avoidance came to be known as 'soldiering'. Frederick Taylor recognized the tendency of workers to take it easy, which he labelled 'natural soldiering'. He considered it unfortunate, but almost excusable. He contrasted this with 'systematic soldiering', which was the organized, collective behaviour of workers in the whole workshop, who restricted their production, prevented their employers knowing how fast they could work, and thus allowed them to pursue their own narrow self-interest. This he considered unacceptable.

Appalled by what he regarded as the inefficiency of industrial practices, Taylor took steps to increase production by reducing the variety of work methods used by the workers. He set out to show how management and workforce could both benefit from adopting his more efficient work arrangements. His objectives were to achieve:

- *efficiency* by increasing the output per worker and reducing deliberate 'underworking' by employees;
- *predictability* of job performance by standardizing tasks and dividing them into small, closely specified subtasks; and
- *control* by establishing discipline through hierarchical authority and introducing a system whereby all management's policy decisions could be implemented.

To achieve these objectives, he implemented his five principles of scientific management:

- A clear division of tasks and responsibilities between management and workers.
- Use of scientific methods to determine the best way of doing a job.
- Scientific selection of the person to do the newly designed job.
- The training of the selected worker to perform the job in the specified way.
- Surveillance of workers through the use of hierarchies of authority and close supervision.

One best way of assembling a *Pret A Manger* sandwich

Jonathan Player/Rex Features

A senior *Pret A Manger* manager explained how to make a sandwich:

It is very important to make sure the same standards are adhered to in every single shop, whether you're in Crown Passage in London, Sauchiehall Street in Glasgow, or in New York. The way we do that is by very, very detailed training. So, for example, how to make an egg mayonnaise sandwich is all written down on a card that has to be followed, and that is absolutely non-negotiable. When somebody joins Pret, they have a 10-day training plan, and on every single day there is a list of things that they have to be shown, from how to spread the filling of a sandwich right to the edges (that is key to us), how to cut a sandwich from corner to corner, how to make sure that the sandwiches look great in the box and on the shelves. So every single detail is covered on a 10-day training plan. At the end of that 10 days the new team member has to pass a quiz, it's called the big scary quiz, it is quite big and it is quite scary, and they have to achieve 90 per cent on that in order to progress. (Boddy, 2014, p.47)

Taylor's approach involved studying each work task. He chose routine, repetitive tasks performed by numerous operatives where study could save time and increase production. Many variables were measured including size of tools, location of tools, height of workers, and type of material worked. His studies tried to answer the question 'How long should it take to do any particular job in the machine shop?' He wanted to replace rules-of-thumb with scientifically designed working methods. Taylor experimented with different combinations of movement and method to discover the 'one best way' of performing any task.

In 1898, Taylor was hired by the Bethlehem Steel Company to improve work methods. For many years, the output of the company's blast furnaces had been moved by 75 pig iron handlers who loaded an average of 12.5 tons per man per day. Taylor estimated that a first-class pig iron handler ought to handle between 47 and 48 long tons per day. Taylor introduced his experimental changes; raised productivity by a factor of four; and increased workers' wages by 60 per cent. The savings achieved with his improved work plan were between $75,000 and $80,000 per annum at 1911 prices. The cost of handling pig iron dropped substantially, and the employed men did the work previously done by many more. Taylor specified what tools workers were to use and how to do their jobs. His 'deal' with his workers was as follows: 'You do it my way, by my standards, at the speed I mandate, and in so doing achieve a level of output I ordain, and I'll pay you handsomely for it, beyond anything you might have imagined'. Taylor said, 'All you do is take orders, give up your way of doing the job for mine' (Kanigel, 1997, p.214). He attempted to align the goals of the workers with those of management.

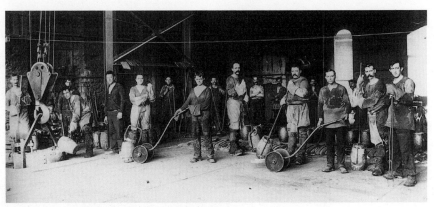

Pig iron handlers at the Bethlehem Steel Works

Initiative and incentive system a form of job design in which management gives workers a task to perform; provides them with the financial incentive to complete it, but then leaves them to use their own initiative as to how they will perform it.

Taylor's scientific management was a powerful and largely successful attempt to take control of the organization of production away from the workers, and to place it in the hands of management. Before Taylor, the use of the initiative and incentive system within the company involved management specifying production requirements, providing workers with incentives in the form of a piece rate bonus, and leaving them to use their own initiative in deciding how best to organize their work. In Taylor's view, not only did this result in wasted effort but also, and more importantly, workers kept their craft secrets to themselves, and worked at a collectively agreed rate that was below their ability. Taylor argued that managers should exercise full responsibility for the planning, coordinating and controlling of work, including selecting the tools to be used (management work), thereby leaving workers free to execute the specified tasks (shop-floor work).

Taylor believed in the application of the principles of science to determine the best way to perform any given task. His 'scientific' approach would end arbitrary management decisions. Management would plan and organize the work, and labour would execute it, all in accordance with the dictates of science. Once his methods had been introduced within a company, trade unions and collective bargaining would, in his view, become redundant. Scientific assessment would eliminate all ambiguity and argument. This and all his other ideas were detailed in his book, *The Principles of Scientific Management* (Taylor, 1911).

Workers were concerned that scientific management just meant 'work speed-up' – that is, more work for less pay. Taylor was adamant that after the implementation of his methods, workers would be rewarded by large pay increases and managers would secure higher productivity and profits. Sometimes workers complained about the inequality of pay increases, such as when a 300 per cent productivity increase resulted in a 30 per cent pay increase. Taylor argued that his approach enabled people to do more work, in less time, using less effort because of the more efficient physical movements. Since they were expending less effort, this had to be taken into account when calculating their wage increases. The efficiency savings also led to the requirement for fewer workers. Would existing workers be redeployed or made redundant? In later years the unions became reconciled with work-study and accepted it, especially if financial benefits followed.

Call centres

Call centres have been extensively studied because they possess many features of Taylorist work design. Researchers have found work in call centres to be pressurized and highly paced, stoked by management's preoccupation with cost minimization and productivity maximization. Most of the jobs were narrowly defined and closely monitored. The time duration of each call taken, the content of the conversation with each customer, and the advice to be given were all closely prescribed.

There was a high level of task fragmentation, scripting and call streaming. Most operators were trained to deal with just one aspect of incoming phone enquiries. Staff were force-fed a diet of standardized calls by automatic systems that matched employees' skill sets.

By packaging knowledge for rapid assimilation during training, call centre firms could train new recruits and plug them into the system in the shortest possible time. Bureaucratic support systems operated to police adherence to the scripts and work targets. Teams within call centres resemble manufacturing industry lean production teams (Taylor et al., 2002; Taylor and Bain, 2007; Ellis and Taylor, 2006).

The quantified workplace

The surveillance of workers, through the use of hierarchies of authority and close supervision, was one of Taylor's five principles. Today, employee behaviour can be tracked at a level of detail that Taylor would not have believed possible. The computers such as those at the Evolv company in San Francisco know, in real time, why employees were hired, how productive they are, and can even follow them to a new job. Evolv analyses more than half a billion 'employee data points' across 13 countries, seeking to identify patterns across companies and industries. These data points range from how often employees interact with their supervisors to how long it takes them to get to the office. This company is a leader in the growing 'quantified workplace' movement. Big data analytics measure how people work, and claim to be able to improve productivity.

Steelcase puts sensors in office furniture and buildings to see how workers interact. Rather than just focusing on junior workers on the call centre floor, this company sees opportunities in creative departments and even in boardrooms where staff time is far more expensive and where efficiency improvements can have a disproportionally large effect on the company. Sensors have become so cheap that they can now be put everywhere. Workplace quantification advocates favour placing them in workspaces where culture clashes occur – for example, in cross-border teams and post-merger groups. Polycom, a video conferencing company, used its monitoring technology to discover that a group in one continent did not understand a team in another.

Fitbits on your wrist, badges embedded with sensor technology, and other wearable devices on your person, together allow your company to track you for 24 hours a day, gathering data on your sleep quality, heart rate, stress, fatigue level, location and web browsing habits. Profusion, a data science consultancy, tracked 171 metrics of 31 staff for ten days. They found they could group employees into clusters ('busy and coping' or 'irritated and unsettled'). Currently devices are being used to make the workforce healthier, safer and more productive. In the future, management may have dashboards showing real-time employee biometrics that are indicators of their performance.

Employees are generally unaware of how much personal information, which they would consider to be private, is already being collected and analysed by their managers, and used to guide staff selection and the management of job performance. For example, their emails and instant messages are routinely monitored, and their work computer and smartphone are accessed by their bosses. No employee has ever won an invasion of privacy case based on an employer monitoring their computer. Whether employee monitoring technology has a positive or negative effect depends on the company culture. A US professor who uses data from Evolv and similar companies to study workplace behaviour believes that constant monitoring signals a 'scary image for the future' and could damage workplace relationships (Kuchler, 2014; Katz, 2015; O'Connor, 2015).

Video case: wearables at work

This eight-minute *Financial Times* video discusses the increases in employee monitoring facilitated by new technology. For the company: What are the problems of obtaining reliable personal data using Fitbit and similar devices? What are the practical, moral and legal problems using this personal employee data? For you: Would you be willing wear a workplace wearable and share your sleep data with your boss? Would you trust your employer not to use the data against you?

Criticisms of Taylorism

Critics of scientific management have argued that:

1. It assumed that the motivation of the employee was to secure the maximum earnings for the effort expended. It neglected the importance of other rewards from work (achievement, job satisfaction, recognition) which later research studies found to be as important.

2. It neglected the subjective side of work – the personal and interactional aspects of performance, the meanings that employees give to work and the significance to them of their social relationships at work.

3. It failed to appreciate the reactions of workers to new procedures and to being timed and closely supervised.

4. It had an inadequate understanding of how individual incentives were affected by an employee's immediate work group. Taylor did attribute 'underworking' to group pressures but misunderstood the way in which these worked. He failed to see that these pressures might just as easily keep production and morale up as down.

5. It ignored the psychological needs and capabilities of workers. The one best way of doing a job was chosen with the mechanistic criteria of speed and output. The imposition of a uniform manner of work can both destroy individuality and cause other psychological problems.

6. It had too simple an approach to the question of productivity and morale. It sought to keep both of these up exclusively by economic rewards and punishments. However, the fatigue studies of Lillian Gilbreth during the 1920s did signal the beginnings of a wider appreciation of the relevant factors that had been ignored by Taylor.

Taylorism in today's HMRC

Bob Carter and his colleagues (2011, 2013) investigated clerical work in the 'back offices' of Her Majesty's Revenue and Customs (HMRC) tax processing centres in the UK. They studied 840 frontline staff who had experienced the application of Taylorism, in the form of lean production (Toyotaism). This impacted on their organization and control of their work; discretion over their task performance; their degree of skill utilization; and the intensity of their work effort. The HMRC had redesigned the work to be completed more efficiently with fewer staff. Time-and-motion techniques were used to appropriate and codify workers' tacit knowledge into written operating procedures and to generate optimum work cycle time targets for individuals and teams.

Originally, staff had operated a system of 'whole-case working' where an administrative officer would deal with all aspects of a tax return – answer phone calls related to it; deal with all its correspondence; ensure compliance with regulations and standards; and complete the job to its conclusion. The targets for work output were the norms of how much work could be completed daily or weekly. Staff enjoyed sufficient autonomy to manage their own workloads within broad parameters. Subsequently, HMRC management introduced a process of work rationalization to increase labour utilization and productivity rates. This involved task fragmentation with core responsibilities being separated out and assigned to specialist offices. Thus some offices become solely responsible for particular parts of the work process, e.g. for corresponding with tax payers or for dealing with phone calls. They dealt with nothing else.

The previously relaxed and relatively high-trust form of work organization was abandoned in the interests of work discipline and flow line efficiency. The lean management concept of 'value-streaming' was implemented in which each worker was assigned responsibility for a single, fragmented task which had been strictly defined by standard operating procedures. The job itself (processing a tax return), was expected to flow efficiently from worker to worker, in an assembly line fashion. These changes to work organization were accompanied by the introduction of set hourly output targets and systematic monitoring of employees' performances. These targets varied from six items an hour for tax letters, to 80 items an hour for opening tax cases. The targets were announced at the start of each shift by line managers, who then patrolled the offices, monitoring individual worker performance, and updated the targets and staff performances on white boards, on an hourly basis. Staff who failed to meet minimum standards were disciplined. Most staff found this new control system degrading and oppressive (Carter et al., 2011, 2013).

STOP AND THINK You have travelled back through time and are able to meet Taylor. What three things would you congratulate him for, and what three things would you criticize him for?

Taylorism in the orchestra

Here is the way in which a Taylorist industrial engineer might report a symphony concert.

For considerable periods the four oboe players had nothing to do. The number should be reduced and the work spread more evenly over the whole concert, thus eliminating peaks and valleys of activity. All the twelve violins were playing identical notes, this seems unnecessary duplication. The staff of this section should be drastically cut. If a larger volume of sound is required, it could be obtained by means of electronic apparatus. Much effort was absorbed in the playing of demisemiquavers; this seems to be an unnecessary refinement. It is recommended that all notes be rounded up to the nearest semiquaver. If this were done, it would be possible to use trainees and lower grade operatives more extensively.

There seems to be too much repetition of some musical passages. Scores should be drastically pruned. No useful purpose is served by repeating on the horns something which has already been handled by the strings. It is estimated that if all redundant passages were eliminated the whole concert time of 2 hours could be reduced to 20 minutes and there would be no need for an intermission. In many cases the operators were using one hand for holding the instrument, whereas the introduction of a fixture would have tendered the idle hand available for other work. Also, it was noted that excessive effort was being used occasionally by the players of wind instruments, whereas one compressor could supply adequate air for all instruments under more accurately controlled conditions. Finally, obsolescence of equipment is another matter into which it is suggested further investigation could be made, as it was reported in the programme that the leading violinist's instrument was already several hundred years old. If normal depreciation schedules had been applied, the value of this instrument would have been reduced to zero and purchase of more modern equipment could then have been considered. (Fulmer and Herbert, 1974, p.27)

Development of Taylorism

Lillian Moller
Gilbreth
(1878–1972)
and Frank
Bunker Gilbreth
(1868–1924)

Contributions of the Gilbreths

Frank Bunker Gilbreth's background resembled Taylor's in that both were practising engineers and managers. Gilbreth's experience was in the construction industry, and his most famous experiments involved bricklayers. He refined the techniques for measuring work, while his wife Lillian, a trained psychologist, focused on the human aspects of work. Together they contributed in three main ways:

- *Motion study*: This refers to the investigation and classification of the basic motions of the body. Taylor had looked mainly at time, and had not focused as closely on motions. Gilbreth rectified this omission and his ideas were published in his book, *Motion Study*, in 1911. To study and improve workers' body movements, Gilbreth attached small electric lamps to workers' hands and left the camera lens left open to track their changing positions, creating *chronocyclegraphic* photographs showing their motion paths. He also used *motion picture cameras* to record workers' motions and times simultaneously.

- *Therbligs*: In his experiments, the elementary body movement was considered to be the building block of every work activity. Gilbreth developed a system for noting such movements, each with its own symbol and colour. These he called 'therbligs' – a variation of his name spelt backwards. Like dance, all the movements of the worker's body performing a particular task were noted down using the therblig notation (see below). Remove an unnecessary therblig or two and efficiency improves and productivity rises. In addition, Gilbreth developed a standard time for each job element, thereby combining time

symbol	name	colour
	search	black
	find	grey
	select	light grey
	group	red
	bold	gold ochre
	transport loaded	green
	position	blue
	assemble	violet
	use	purple
	disassemble	light violet
	inspect	burnt ochre
	preposition	pale blue
	release load	carmine red
	transport empty	olive green
	rest for overcoming fatigue	orange
	unavoidable delay	yellow
	avoidable delay	lemon yellow
	plan	brown

Therblig symbols and colours

Source: Developments in Management Thought, Heinemann (Pollard, H.R. 1974).

Time-and-motion studies measurement and recording techniques used to make work operations more efficient.

study with motion study. Time-and-motion studies are conducted to this day, and are used to improve occupational health, increase productivity and design wage payments systems, whose universal application Gilbreth advocated.

- *Fatigue study*: Lillian Gilbreth's work complemented her husband's. She studied motions to eliminate unnecessary and wasteful actions so as to reduce the fatigue experienced by workers. Since all work produced fatigue, for which the remedy was rest, her aim was to find the best mixture of work and rest to maximize productivity. To do this, she focused on the total working environment, and not just on selecting first-class workers as Taylor had done. She studied jobs to eliminate fatigue-producing elements. Together, the Gilbreths shortened the working day; introduced rest periods and chairs; and instituted holidays with pay (Gilbreth and Gilbreth, 1916).

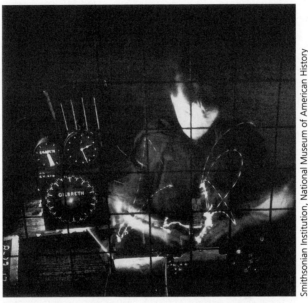

Smithsonian Institution, National Museum of American History

Micromotion studies and chronocyclegraphic models

STOP AND DRINK

Order a glass of coke.

Start position: Sitting at table

Movement 1: Hand to glass (2 seconds)

Movement 2: Grip glass (0.5 seconds)

Movement 3: Lift to horizontal (1 second)

Movement 4: Lift to lips (1 second)

Movement 5: Swallow 0.05 litres of drink (2 seconds)

Movement 6: More arm to horizontal (1 second)

Movement 7: Move glass to table (1 second)

Movement 8: Release grip on glass (0.5 seconds)

Movement 9: Belch (1 second)

End position: Sitting at table

Total time for operation: 10 seconds

Go to your local café with a friend and a stopwatch, and check the above timings.

Adapted from Grey (2009, pp.37–8)

Physiolytics – twenty-first century time-and-motion studies

Physiolytics refers to the practice of linking wearable computing devices with data analysis and quantified feedback to improve performance. James Wilson (2013) argued that the emerging field of physiolytics is creating a twenty-first-century version of Frederick Taylor's time-and-motion studies. Physiolytics grew out of innovations in wearable technologies such as sensors in shoes (e.g. Nike+ used by runners to monitor distance and speed) and smart bracelets (e.g. BodyMedia's FIT). While Taylor examined iron workers individually to obtain generalizable insights, physiolytics goes much further and offers two types of 'scientific management' analyses for company mangers.

Quantifying movements within physical work environments

This analysis is most similar to Taylor's original work in that it focuses on people's movements in various work settings. At a distribution centre in Ireland, Tesco workers move among 87 aisles of three-storey shelves. They wear armbands that track the goods they are gathering. A 2.8-inch display provides analytical feedback, verifying the correct fulfilment of an order or nudging a worker whose order is incomplete. Begun in 2004 by Tesco, its wearables programme operates in its 300 UK locations. Between 2007 and 2012, the number of full-time employees required to run a 40,000-square-foot store fell by 18 per cent. Taylor would have been proud. Managers and shareholders are pleased but workers have complained about the surveillance and the fact that the system only measures speed and not quality of work.

Working with information more efficiently

This analysis makes knowledge work more efficient by analysing the time and motions required to perform a process. Its primary aim is to help employees work smarter, which itself leads to increased efficiency. From the 1990s, Bell Canada equipped its phone technicians with wrist-worn PCs, allowing them to enter data from repair sites without walking back to the computers in their trucks, saving them an hour a day. The US industrial engineering firm Schneider gave its field engineers belt-mounted voice-activated computers, boosting their efficiency by 150 per cent. In 2002, OHS, a British asbestos-remediation firm, equipped its inspectors with belt-mounted computers which contained building blueprints and generated suggestions for navigating rooms efficiently to identify likely trouble spots. This reduced site visit times by 25 per cent, saving each surveyor 480 man-hours a year.

On average, mobile workers check their smart phones more than 150 times daily. Each check takes about 20 seconds and typically requires a sequence of movements (type in password, choose app, enter data). Wearables will replace those steps with *microinteractions* – simple, time-saving gestures. Microsoft is developing armbands that will project keyboards and displays onto wearers' wrists, obviating the need to fumble with a smartphone. In the near future, predictive feedback based on a wearer's movements, through informational and physical contexts, will be an integral part of these tools. By analysing where you are and where you're going, apps will offer contextual data before you ask for it, eliminating search time.

Gantt's contributions

In 1887, Henry Laurence Gantt joined the Midvale Steel Company and became an assistant to the company's chief engineer – F.W. Taylor. Gantt supported Taylor's approach, but humanized scientific management to make it more acceptable (Gant, 1919). He tempered Taylor's work with greater insight into human psychology, and stressed method over measurement. He believed that Taylor's use of incentives was too punitive and lacked sensitivity to the psychological needs of the workers. He believed in consideration for and fair dealings with employees, and felt that scientific management was being used as an oppressive instrument by the unscrupulous. He made three major contributions:

- *Best-known-way-at-present*: Gantt's system was based on detailed instruction cards in the best scientific management tradition. However, he replaced Taylor's 'one-best-way', with his own 'best known way at present'. This involved a much less detailed analysis of jobs than Taylor had suggested.

- *Task-and-bonus payment scheme*: He replaced Taylor's piece-rate wage system with his own task-and-bonus scheme. Each worker was set a task, received a set day rate, and an additional 20–50 per cent bonus.

- *'Gantt Chart'*: He developed a bar chart used for scheduling (i.e. planning) and coordinating the work of different departments or plants. His chart depicted quantities ordered, work progress and quantities issued from store. Although he never patented it, it is still in use today, and bears his name (Figure 14.1).

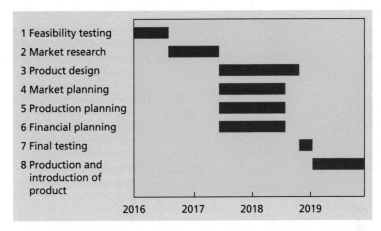

Figure 14.1: Gantt chart for new product development plan beginning 2016

Fordism

Henry Ford
(1863–1947)

Fordism a form of work design that applies scientific management principles to workers' jobs; the installation of single purpose machine tools to manufacture standardized parts; and the introduction of the mechanized assembly line.

By 1920, the name of Henry Ford had become synonymous not only with his Model T motor car, but also with his revolutionary techniques of mass producing it. He moved on from the mechanization and rationalization of work on the individual work piece or object pioneered by Taylor, to mechanizing the flow of objects between workers. The process by which this was done is known as **Fordism**. In this sense, Fordism is distinguishable from Taylorism in that it represents a form of work organization designed for efficient mass production.

Ford established his company in 1903. In the 1890s, it was skilled craftsmen who built motor cars. Ford claimed that there were not enough of them to meet the level of car production that he wanted, and that was why, in his view, the deskilling of work was necessary. Others argue that deskilling made labour easier to control and replace. Ford's goal was 'continuous improvement' rather than the 'one best way'. His objective was to increase his control by reducing or eliminating uncertainty (Ford and Crowther, 1924). Among his major innovations were:

- systematic analysis of all jobs using time-and-motion techniques;
- installation of single-purpose machine tools to manufacture standardized parts;
- introduction of the mechanized assembly line.

Analysing jobs

Ford applied the principles of scientific management to remove waste and inefficiency. He established a Motion Picture Department that filmed work methods in different industries, so as to learn from them. He applied the principles of work rationalization. Employees were allocated simple tasks, all of which had been carefully designed to ensure maximum efficiency. Ford's approach was entirely experimental, very pragmatic, and always open to improvements – try it, modify it, try it again, keep on until it's right. The Ford mechanic, originally a skilled craftsman, became an assembler who tended his machine, only performing low-grade tasks. For example, the wheelwright's job was divided into almost 100 operations, each performed by a different man using specialized equipment.

Installation of single-purpose machine tools to produce standardized parts

Ford used rigid and heavy machine tools, carbon alloy steel tools and universal grinding machines. This ensured that each part was exactly like the next, and hence interchangeable. This facilitated the division of labour and increased certainty. The single-purpose machines that he designed for his factory were called 'farmer machines' because farm boys, coming off the land, could be quickly trained to use them. Their operators did not have to be skilled, just quick. The skill was now incorporated within the machine. This eliminated the need for skilled workers as anybody could now assemble an automobile.

Creation of the mechanized assembly line

Despite the aforementioned innovations, employees could still work at their own speed. In 1913, it still took 90 minutes to assemble a car. To overcome this problem, instead of moving the men past the car, the car was moved past the men. The mechanized assembly line imposed upon employees the working speed that Ford wanted. By 1914, the plant had installed a continuous automatic conveyor that met Ford's technical and philosophical objectives. The engineers arranged work in a logical order. The materials and semi-completed parts passed through the plant to where they were needed. The conveyor belt took radiator parts to assemblers, and then carried their work away to solderers, who finished off the radiators (Gartman, 1979).

After integrating various production processes, Ford's engineers produced a continuously moving line which was fed by overhead conveyors. Each worker was feeding, and being fed by, the assembly line. In 1908, when the Model T was introduced, production ran at 27 cars per day. By 1923, when the River Rouge plant had been completed, daily production had reached 2000 cars. The source of Ford's original idea for the assembly line is disputed. Some stories tell of Henry Ford getting the idea at an abattoir where beef carcasses, suspended from moving hooks, were being disassembled. Other accounts have him visiting a watch plant, and seeing the staged assembly process of timepieces (Collier and Horowitz, 1987).

With a mechanized assembly line, the product went past the worker, instead of the worker having to go around the product. In 1914 Henry Ford estimated that this saved his workers having to walk 50 miles a year. In 2014, at a Little Caesars' restaurant in Salt Lake City, Mark Vadero, an operations specialist, estimated that over a week each worker travelled 26,852 yards making and serving pizzas. He rearranged the store by moving the flour bags and placing the cheese in fridges below the pizza-making stations so that workers did not have to move to grate it. This resulted in a 31 per cent reduction in yards travelled to

Aircraft assembly line

Aircraft manufacturers like Boeing and Airbus have been seeking ways of speeding up production of their planes. In 2014, Boeing and Airbus delivered 723 and 629 aircraft respectively. However, at the end of that year, Boeing had a backlog of orders for 5,789 aircraft (an all-time record), and Airbus had a backlog of 6,386 orders valued at $919.3 billion. At its Renton factory near Seattle, Boeing is using Henry Ford's principles to create a lean manufacturing environment that resembles a Toyota car plant. Aircraft fuselages come in at one end and are hooked onto a moving assembly line. Nose-to-tail, they move along at a rate of two inches a minute through the final assembly process. Out at the other end, roll off complete aircraft with wings, tails, cockpits, toilets, galleys and seats. There are other features of the Toyota system – the visual displays of work in progress, and alarms to stop production if a quality problem emerges. By using two assembly lines, the current version of its 737 is being manufactured at a record rate of 37 a month. Elizabeth Lund, a director of manufacturing, stated: 'A moving line is the most powerful tool available to identify and eliminate waste in a production system … [it] drives efficiency throughout the system because it makes problems visible and creates a sense of urgency to fix the root causes of those problems' (Boeing website, 2006; *The Economist*, 2012; Hollinger, 2015).

Boeing factory

Larry MacDougall /Press Association Images

18,628 – 'if you're walking around, you're not making pizzas' he said, a statement with which Henry Ford would have concurred (Vance, 2014).

Taylor's ambition had always been to remove control of the production process from the workers, and place it into the hands of management. Under Fordism, this was broadly achieved. Ford's objective was to allow unsophisticated workers to make a sophisticated product in volume. He sought to make his workforce as uniform, and interchangeable, as the automobile parts that they handled. He created an authoritarian work regime with closely monitored, machine-paced, short-cycle, unremitting tasks.

First moving assembly line

The photograph below shows men working on the first moving assembly line at Ford's Highland Park factory, 1913.

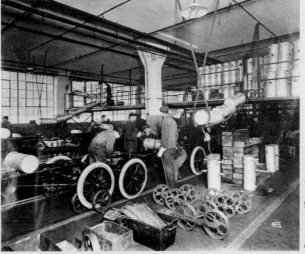

Bettmann/Getty Images

First moving assembly line

Control over the worker was exerted through task specialization and assembly line working. Such control was both invisible and non-confrontational. It was the system not the supervisor that told the employee to work faster. It de-personalized the authority relationship to such a degree that workers were no longer aware that they were being directed. In 1935, Ford's River Rouge plant in Dearborn on the outskirts of Detroit spread over 1,096 acres, had 7.25 million square feet of floor space, possessed 235 acres of glass windows, 90 miles of railway track, employed 100,000 men, and built 2 million cars each year. Little wonder that it was called the *Cathedral of Industry*.

Ford's legacy was twofold. First, he created what came to be defined as the characteristics of **mass production** work:

Mass production a form of work design that includes mechanical pacing of work, no choice of tools or methods, repetitiveness, minute subdivision of product, minimum skill requirements, and surface mental attention.

- mechanical pacing of work;
- no choice of tools or methods;
- repetitiveness;
- minute subdivision of product;
- minimum skill requirements;
- surface mental attention.

Cathedral of Industry

In the 1930s, the Mexican artist Diego Rivera (1886–1957) was commissioned by the Detroit Institute of Art to paint frescos devoted to the city's motor car industry. His panels feature Ford's River Rouge plant. Rivera was an independent artist with a Marxist perspective. He painted the factory workers and the machines that they used, but no completed car. The ethnic mix of the workforce is depicted. The panels show various stages in the production of the automobile. The men in the murals are depicted as sullen and angry, working amid the clamour and din of the machinery around them. The strength shown in their faces was perceived as intimidating by some observers, who accused Rivera of producing left-wing propaganda.

Detroit Industry (South Wall), Diego Rivera, 1932–1933

Rivera, Diego (1886–1957)/Detroit Institute of Arts, USA/Gift of Edsel B. Ford © DACS/ Bridgeman Art Library

Second, he raised people's standard of living. Having shown that something as complicated as a motor car could be built using the techniques of mass production, it was recognized that the manufacture of other, simpler products was also possible – radios, washing machines, refrigerators and vacuum cleaners. Mass production led to mass consumption, giving more people more access to more goods than ever before in human history. In the 50 years to 1970, the standard of living of Americans sky-rocketed. Other countries that adopted Ford's system of manufacturing production also benefited. While Taylorism and Fordism had many similarities, they also had some differences, as Table 14.1 shows.

Table 14.1: Differences between Taylorism and Fordism

	Taylorism	Fordism
Approach to machinery	Organized labour around existing machinery	Eliminated labour with new machinery
Technology and the work design	Took production process as given and sought to reorganize work and labour processes	Used technology to mechanize the work process. Workers fed and tended machines
Pace of work	Set by the workers or the supervisor	Set by machinery – the speed of the assembly line

Critics have argued that Ford destroyed craftsmanship and deskilled jobs. He did indeed change the work process by introducing greater amounts of rigidity and regulation, thereby affecting the skill content of jobs. Others argue that since there were insufficient numbers of skilled workers available to do the original jobs, Ford had to redesign the jobs so that the existing, pre-industrial labour force could cope with them. Was it less a question of forcing a highly-skilled, high-priced employee to accept a cheapened, dead-end job, and more an issue of identifying tasks appropriate for unskilled people to do who would otherwise have performed even less enjoyable, tedious work?

The same critics also assert that short-cycle repetitive jobs have caused worker alienation and stress, and have subjugated human beings to the machine. The assembly line is criticized for exerting an undesirable, invisible control over the workers. Other commentators observe how Fordism has shaped reforms within the British National Health Service. 'Fordism monitors the time doctors and nurses spend with each patient; a medical treatment system based on dealing with auto parts, it tends to treat cancerous livers or broken backs rather than patients in the round' (Sennett, 2008, p.47). The debate over the balance of costs and benefits of Fordism and its precursor, Taylorism, continues to this day.

Toyotaism in hospitals

St. Goran's hospital is not only a jewel in the crown of Sweden's welfare state but also a laboratory for applying business principles in the public sector. It is run by Capio, a private company, and its doctors and nurses are Capio employees who report to the company boss and its board. The hospital uses the Toyota model of lean production, introducing innovations to cut costs. Its contract with the Stockholm County Council to manage the hospital runs to 2021. St. Goran's is organized on Toyotaism's twin principles of 'flow' and 'quality'. Doctors and nurses, previously professionally separated, now sit and work together in teams, and are all responsible for suggesting operational improvements. The emphasis is on collective learning. St Goran's is the medical equivalent of a budget airline. There are six patients to a room, décor is institutional, and the aim is to maximize throughput so as to reduce waiting times and minimize the chances of patients acquiring infections. Private firms in Sweden provide 20 per cent of public hospital care and 30 per cent of public primary care. Both sectors apply lean management to make the best use of resources in a high-cost country (*The Economist*, 2013).

Today, Frederick Taylor's and Henry Ford's legacies are discussed in terms of lean production (or 'lean'), which has become one of the world's most influential management ideas, and is widely promoted for use in manufacturing and service industries, and both the private and public sectors. Lean production is a term used to describe the Toyota Production System (TPS) or *Toyotaism*. TPS's aim is constant improvement, and reduction in costs through the systematic elimination of waste using the assembly line system. For Womack et al. (1990), lean is a scientific discovery that will 'banish waste and create wealth'. Some authors have argued that the adoption of lean manufacturing has allowed employers to remove discretion and silence the voice of workers and unions.

Leo McCann et al. (2015) summarized the numerous criticisms of lean production which can be reduced to the observations that lean is not as radical a break with past practices as its supporters claim. With its heavy standardization, rigid principles, tight statistical control and work intensification, lean creates workplaces which are just as authoritarian and demanding as those in the past. Despite claims that it involves workers in the process of constant improvement thereby increasing their work satisfaction, it actually has no room for any genuine worker involvement. Moreover, much of it involves different forms of employee surveillance and evaluation. Research by Debora Jeske and Alecia Santuzzi (2015) revealed that close, unpredictable or continuous monitoring of individuals via cameras, data entry, chat and phone recording had significant, negative effects on employees' job satisfaction, self-efficacy and commitment to the company. Cavazotte et al. (2014) found that providing legal professionals with smart phones intensified the organization's hold over their employees beyond their regular, 9–5 working hours, reaching out into new settings, time slots and social contexts.

Work design at Foxconn

Jenny Chan (2013) reported on the work design arrangements at Foxconn, a Taiwanese-owned multinational company which employs 1.4 million workers, and is the largest private sector employer in China and one of the largest in the world. It supplies products and components to Apple, HP, Microsoft and other premium brands. Foxconn has adopted a production model based on classical Taylorist and Fordist principles. The production process is so simplified that workers do not require any specialized knowledge or training to do their jobs. Industrial engineers use stop watches and computerized devices to test workers and monitor their smallest movements, in order to make them all rational and planned. If workers are able to meet the quota, then their targets are increased to the maximum possible.

Frontline workers' sitting or standing postures are monitored as much as the work itself. They have to sit in standardized ways, and stools have to be placed in order and cannot be moved beyond a specific point. Each assembly line worker specializes in one specific task and performs repetitive motions at high speed, hourly, daily and for months on end. A worker on the iPhone assembly line described the duration of her work cycle: 'I take a motherboard from the line, scan the logo, put it in an anti-static bag, stick on a label and place it on the line. Each of these tasks takes two seconds. Every ten seconds, I finish five tasks' (p.88). The company's 'advanced' production system removes feelings of accomplishment or initiative towards work. In 2010, 18 employees working for Foxconn attempted suicide. This suicide cluster represents a phenomenon that has no precedent in China's industrial history. Chan wrote that 'Thousands of miles away from the shelves of the Apple store, and ordinarily concealed from consumer concern, lies the reality of alienating toil that, in extreme conditions, contributes to individual tragedies' (p.85).

After Ford: the deskilling debate

The idea of fragmenting work tasks and simplifying jobs was begun by Taylor and developed by Ford. Since that time, has this process of deskilling work continued and been extended to other occupations and types of workers? Or, on the contrary, has work become more complicated, employees been better trained and educated, and jobs made more skilled? Taylor and Ford placed the issue of job skill at the centre of all subsequent discussions about work design. The deskilling debate provides a useful perspective from which to consider the large number of theoretical, empirical and prescriptive writings produced by researchers, managers and consultants.

Two seemingly contradictory trends in work design occurred in the second half of the twentieth century. From the 1950s, both in the United States and Europe, there was a reaction against Taylorism, and an interest in more 'people-oriented' approaches. Labels like human relations, socio-technical systems, quality of working life, organizational development and human-centred manufacturing reflected this inclination. Then, during the 1970s, Japanization, and in particular the success of Japanese 'lean production' manufacturing techniques and Japanese teamworking, became prominent. The contradiction was very apparent. On the one hand, lean production involved many features of Taylorist and Fordist work designs, while on the other, it appeared to incorporate numerous people-oriented features like teamworking. This paradox generated much research and debate.

were being supercharged with digital technology and applied to a wider range of employees. Originally focused on manual workers, Taylorism has now been extended to office, knowledge and service workers, and even to managers themselves. New technology has allowed companies to:

- divide clerical work into routine tasks and outsource them to freelance workers;
- enhance time-and-motion studies through the use of sociometric badges as described earlier;
- introduce peer review software that changes annual performance reviews into continuous employee assessments;
- use drones to measure the progress of building projects;
- strap terminals to warehouse workers' arms to monitor their work efficiency.

A second distinguishing feature of digital Taylorism relates to pay for performance. Frederick Taylor had always been keen that his 'first-class man' who followed his instructions as to how to do the job exactly, and thereby raised his output significantly, should be well rewarded. Wage increases of 30 per cent were not uncommon. Throughout the twentieth century staff appraisals have always distinguished good, average and poor performers. They have rewarded them (or not) with appropriate pay increases. Some get 10 per cent increases, others 5 per cent ones, while others receive written warnings to improve their performance.

For those organizations in the modern era which rely so directly on their workers' brainpower, the employee reward strategies of the past are becoming less relevant. Bill Gates (Microsoft) once said that a great lathe operator commands several times the wage of an average lathe operator, but a great writer of software code is worth 10,000 times the price of an average software writer. This view was echoed by Laszlo Bock, Head of People Operations at Google. In his book chapter entitled 'Pay unfairly', he wrote that 'At Google we have situations where two people doing the same work can have a hundred times difference in their impact and in their rewards' (Bock, 2015, p.241). He went on to cite a situation where one employee received a stock award of $10,000 and another worker in the same area received $1,000,000.

In Taylor's day, workers who did not perform their tasks as instructed or who failed to achieve the required productivity targets were dismissed. This Darwinian 'survival of fittest' approach was popularized by Jack Welch, Chief Executive of General Electric, in the 1980s. His 'vitality curve' used a 20–70–10 performance ranking system that divided the company's 300,000 employees into the top performing 20 per cent, the middle 70 per cent, and the bottom 10 per cent. The last group were fired. The approach has been dubbed 'up or out management' since, as an employee, you either moved up or you moved out! It is also known as 'rank-and-yank' or 'stack ranking', and appears to be back in fashion (*The Economist*, 2015; Hill, 2015).

STOP AND THINK Image that every year, following the publication of the examination results for this course, the worst performing 15 per cent of students are thrown out of the university. Do you think this would improve your motivation to study and your results?

Critics argued that the modern version of scientific management threatens to dehumanize the modern workplace. Specifically:

- Slicing and dicing knowledge jobs limits employees' ability to use their expertise creatively.
- Measuring everything and everyone constantly robs employees of the pleasure from doing their jobs.

- Pushing people to their limits leads to employee burnout and staff turnover – 'burn and churn'.
- Continuous employee peer review and individual rewards work against team work and encourage politically motivated back stabbing.

Digital Taylorism appears set to continue as developments in technology allow firms to measure and monitor their employees in ever more sophisticated ways. The writer concludes that 'The most basic axiom of management is what gets measured gets managed. So the more technology of measurement advances, the more we hand power to Frederick Taylor's successors' (*The Economist*, 2015, p.68).

Employee identification and the pursuit of happiness in a call centre

Most research into call centre working showed that they use Taylorist work designs as described on page 456. However, Sarah Jenkins and Rick Delbridge (2014) studied VoiceTel, a UK multi-client call centre which has won awards for high performance and had a leading market position. The company demonstrated a very different approach which used normative (values-based) controls rather than traditional (Taylorist) bureaucratic or technological controls. Normative control refers to management's attempt to regulate organization members' thoughts, values and emotions, and thus their behaviours.

The owners wanted employees to identify with, and commit to the company. Identification refers to how individuals define themselves through the meanings embedded in the company culture. It focuses on the company practices that shape individuals' constructions of their identity. Identification is important because it is the process through which people come to define themselves, communicate that definition to others, and use it to navigate their lives both inside and outside work. Staff did so, and also expressed great happiness with their employer ('a brilliant place to work') – a most unusual phenomenon for a call centre. Cultural control involves employees internalizing norms and values. At VoiceTel the researchers found this internalization process operated through three employee-identification mechanisms:

Organization value system. Reciprocity, trust and care of employees were the company values espoused and promoted by the firm's owners and were reflected in the way staff were treated. Reciprocal relations were the cornerstone of the people management approach, and the norm of reciprocity formed the basis of the rights and obligations within the company. By caring for employees and valuing their work, it was expected that employees would care for the organization by providing high-quality work.

Social relations. This referred to interactions between employees, employers and clients. The owners achieved employee identity regulation through the company's recruitment ('recruit a friend'); selection of value-sharing job applicants (those who 'go the extra mile'); probation (observation if they 'fitted in'); and the way new recruits were socialized and managed. Regulating identity can be achieved by engendering feelings of belonging and membership and a sense of community, and this shaped and sustained the company's culture.

Nature of work. This related to the content, organization and management within the call centre. The work was characteristic of call centres which use integrated telephone and computer technology. However, there were no scripts or standardized practices governing staff interactions with customers; no electronic monitoring of calls or targets for call-handling times. Workers were organized into fours, each with a supportive team leader who performed a mentoring role. Call workers were given great autonomy in their dealings with clients and had discretion to negotiate service provision. They were expected to act in accordance with company values to achieve company objectives.

 RECAP

1. **Understand how scientific management met the needs of its historical context.**

   - At the start of the twentieth century, European emigration to the United States and internal migration from rural to urban areas produced a large workforce with poor English language skills which lacked work discipline.

- The same period saw the establishment of large corporations, and the development of technology that permitted, for the first time, the mass manufacture of products. These factories required a large workforce.

2. **Describe the main objectives and principles of the scientific management approach.**

   - The objectives are efficiency, by increasing the output per worker and reducing deliberate 'underworking'; predictability of job performance – standardizing tasks by dividing them up into small and closely specified subtasks; and control by establishing discipline through hierarchical authority and introducing a system whereby all management's policy decisions can be implemented.

   - The principles are: a clear division of tasks and responsibilities between management and workers; use of scientific methods to determine the best way of doing a job; scientific selection of employees; the training of the selected worker to perform the job in the way specified; and the surveillance of workers through the use of hierarchies of authority and close supervision.

3. **Enumerate the contributions of the Gilbreths and Gantt to scientific management.**

   - Frank Gilbreth's contributions were micromotion study; the chronocyclegraph; time-and-motion studies; and the 'therbligs' notation system. Lillian Gilbreth contributed fatigue study based on physiological and psychological principles.

- Laurence Gantt supplied the 'best-known-way-at-present' approach to job design; the task-and-bonus payment scheme; and the 'Gantt Chart'.

4. **Understand how Fordism developed out of Taylorism.**

   - Ford developed the analysis of jobs; installed single purpose machine tools to produce standardized parts; and established the mechanically paced assembly line.

5. **Understand the deskilling debate and the contribution of Braverman and Ritzer.**

   - The 'Braverman thesis' holds that there is a long-run tendency for workers and their jobs to become deskilled through fragmentation, rationalization and mechanization.

   - Some argue for the deskilling thesis, while others reject it, claiming that technological developments have upskilled both workers and jobs and created new, high-skill industries.

   - The deskilling debate is often discussed in the context of Ritzer's McDonaldization process, which refers to an approach to work design based on efficiency, calculability, predictability and control.

6. **Provide examples of scientific management in contemporary society.**

   - Apart from fast food restaurants, the process of credit-granting through credit card; semesterization and modularization of university courses; TV programming; food packaging.

Revision

1. Taylorism has been much criticized. What are these criticisms? Which criticisms do you feel are valid and which are not? Give reasons for your assessment.

2. Define five key principles or practices of Taylorism or Fordism. Using examples, explain how these are being used in today's organizations. Discuss how these forms of work organization affect employee behaviour.

3. To what extent are performance-based pay, just-in-time (stock) inventory and business process re-engineering just modern-day applications of Frederick Taylor's scientific management?

4. Identify non-food examples of the McDonaldization process. Analyse them in terms of Ritzer's four key elements.

Research assignment

Visit your local fast food restaurant that uses a Taylorist/Fordist form of work organization. Observe and make notes on the behaviour of its employees, both those at the counter and those in the kitchen. Arrange to talk to one or two crew members – perhaps you already know

→

someone who currently works there, or has done so in the past. Ask them about the best and worst aspects of that job. Relate their answers to the theories and research findings discussed in this chapter. Are the criticisms of fast food restaurants and similar organizations unfair?

Springboard

Christopher Elliott and Gary Long (2016) 'Manufacturing rate busters: computer control and social relations in the labour process', *Work, Employment and Society*, 30 (1): 135–51. The authors provide a detailed case study of the most recent implementation of computer control over manual jobs in a distribution centre and discuss workers' attempts at resistance.

Christina Evans and Leonard Holmes (eds) (2013) *Re-Tayloring Management*. Farnham: Gower. The book contributors consider how Taylor's philosophy is being applied to knowledge workers, the professionalization of management; and the growth of management education. It argues that managers are 'obsessed with control' and challenges the notion that modern management is all about employee engagement or empowerment.

Gerard Hanlon (2016) *The Dark Side of Management: A Secret History of Management Theory*. London: Routledge. Beginning with a consideration of Frederick Taylor, the author offers a critique of management arguing that it ensures that contemporary workers exist in a precarious world without control, democracy or power.

Linzi Kemp (2012) 'Modern to postmodern management: developments in scientific management', *Journal of Management History*, 19 (3): 345–61. The author considers scientific management from the perspective of postmodernism. She looks at examples of scientific management in the measurement of knowledge production, empowerment, total quality management and teamworking.

 ## OB cinema

The Rebel (1961, director Robert Day): DVD track 2, 0:05:00–0:11:30 (7 minutes). In this film, the comedian Tony Hancock plays himself, as a London office worker who finds the routine of his job oppressive. The clip begins with a shot of the office, and ends with the manager saying to Tony, 'Off you go'. As you watch this clip:

1. Identify the design principles underlying the office jobs that Tony and his (all male) colleagues are performing at United International.

2. Complete this matrix, indicating the advantages and disadvantages, to management and to employees, of designing jobs in this way:

	advantages	disadvantages
for management		
for employees		

1. Tony's manager diagnoses his problem and suggests some solutions. How appropriate do you think his suggestions are?

2. Is this movie out of date, because management practice and office technology have changed since the 1960s? Or can you identify jobs that you have personally had, or which you have recently observed, that are designed in the same way? What would be – or what has been – your reaction to work like this?

OB on the web

Search YouTube for 'Time-Motion Study.' It is a 1946, black-and white film demonstrating some of the basic principles of time-and-motion study. Identify any aspect of your work or personal life which would benefit from the application of these principles.

CHAPTER EXERCISES

1. The call centre experience

Objectives
1. To distinguish different forms of control within an organizational context
2. To explain the reasons for the popularity of call centre companies.
3. To identify the problems experienced by call centre employees and how they might be addressed.

Briefing
1. Re-read pages 456–57.
2. Individually consider:
   (a) What is meant by the term, *control* within an organizational context?
   (b) In what different ways does the company that you work for control your behaviour on the job?
3. Form into groups and discuss the following questions:
   (a) What benefits do companies gain from running their call centres?
   (b) What problems does the way that work is organized in a call centre create for its employees?
   (c) How would you improve the quality of working life of call centre employees?

2. Taylor Road order-fillers

Objectives
1. To recognize contemporary examples of Taylorist work design.
2. To explain the reasons for the popularity of these practices.
3. To identify the problems associated with this form of work design.

Taylor Road order-fillers
Taylor Road is a computer-controlled warehouse of a large, multinational company with over 10,000 employees around the world which distributes food products and customer orders. The non-unionized employees receive a wage that is higher than other local manufacturing facilities and twice that of comparable, low-skilled service jobs. With its strict staff selection (95 per cent were males, aged between 20 and 40), and high wages and benefits, the facility enjoys a good reputation in the area. Computer controls direct, monitor and evaluate workers' manual tasks using algorithms.

In a Taylor Road warehouse, a central computer coordinates and individually tailors work for employees. At the start of a shift, each employee receives a wireless mini-computer ('unit'), a headset, and a vehicle for moving goods. They log onto their unit with their personalized settings and passwords. The central computer assigns order-fillers their discrete tasks which come packaged as 'trips'. These are software-generated routes through the warehouse which they have to follow to collect the different parts of customers' orders. Order-fillers are directed to their collection points ('slots') using computer voice-guided instructions. On arrival, the employee confirms the location by speaking a three-digit code printed above the slot. Once the unit 'hears' the code, it

→

responds with the number of cases to be collected from that slot. The order-fillers manually transfer the cases onto their vehicles, and then again speak the correct quantities into their units. If they do not follow this behaviour sequence exactly, the order-fillers are unable to complete a trip.

If they are working at the minimum production rate, each employee would perform this behaviour sequence 1,500 to 2,000 times per shift. On average, each grocery case weighs 18 pounds, so an order-filler would physically lift between 27,000 and 36,000 pounds of goods per shift. The company's industrial engineers have developed a formula which calculates a standard time for each trip. This is based on time study, digitalized maps of the warehouse, size and weight of cases, number of required stops, and fatigue allowances. Thus, every task a worker performs is electronically dispensed and tracked. The collected data is used to maintain the desired level of employee performance. Computer coordination is so good that, in order to function, the warehouse does not require the workers to interact with each other. They might cross paths on two or three occasions during a shift. Thus, the order-filler's task is designed to be repetitive, fatiguing and isolating.

Once he has delivered his load to the dispatch dock, the computer informs the order-filler how quickly he has completed his last trip; updates him on his cumulative shift performance up to that point; lets him know the standard time for his next trip; and tells him the aisle and slot that he has to go to next. To keep their jobs, employees have to maintain a rolling four-week average performance of 95 per cent of standard time, as specified by the formula. Failure to achieve this standard, results in disciplinary warnings, and 3–4 weeks of underperformance leads to dismissal. Employees who survive the first two months of employment generally continue to meet the standard. Each fortnight, workers who have achieved between 105 and 130 per cent performance receive bonuses.

Form into groups and discuss the following questions:

(a) Which examples of Taylorism can you identify here?

(b) How do these practices improve efficiency and productivity?

(c) What problems does the way that work is organized in these warehouses create for its employees?

(d) How might these problems be overcome?

Case based on Elliott and Long (2016)

Employability assessment

With regard to your future employment prospects:

1. Identify up to three issues from this chapter that you found significant.

2. Relate these to the competencies in the employability matrix.

3. Decide what actions you need to take to maintain and/or develop those competencies under each of the four headings of the employability matrix.

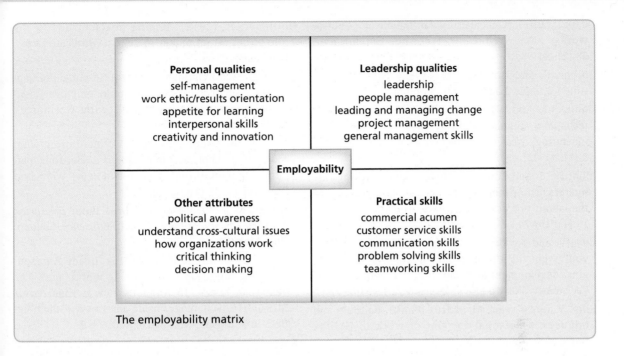

The employability matrix

References

Allan, C., Bamber, G. and Timo, N. (2006) 'Fast-food work: are McJobs satisfying?', *Employee Relations*, 28 (5): 402–20.

Becker, G. (1964) *Human Capital*. New York: National Bureau of Economic Research.

Bock, L. (2015) *Work Rules*. London: John Murray.

Boddy, D. (2014) *Management: An Introduction* (6th edn). Harlow, Essex: Financial Times Prentice Hall.

Boeing website (2006) 'Boeing begins use of moving assembly line for 777 jetliners', News release, 8 November.

Boje, D.M. and Winsor, R.D. (1993) 'The resurrection of Taylorism: total quality management's hidden agenda', *Journal of Organizational Change Management*, 6 (4): 57–70.

Bryman, A. (2011) 'McDonaldization', in M. Tadajewski, P. Maclaran, E. Parsons, and M. Parker (eds), *Key Concepts in Critical Management Studies*. London: Sage, pp.169–73.

Braverman, H. (1974) *Labor and Monopoly Capital: The Degradation of Work in the Twentieth Century*. New York: Monthly Review Press.

Burawoy, M. (1979) *Manufacturing Consent*. Chicago, IL: University of Chicago Press.

Carter, B., Danford, A., Howcroft, D., Richardson, H., Smith, A. and Taylor, P. (2011) '"All they lack is a chain": lean and the new performance management in the British civil service', *New Technology, Work and Employment*, 26 (2): 83–97.

Carter, B., Danford, A., Howcroft, D., Richardson, H., Smith, A. and Taylor, P. (2013) 'Taxing times: lean working and the creation of (in) efficiencies in HM Revenue and Customs', *Public Administration*, 91 (1): 83–97.

Cavazotte, F., Heloisa Lemos, A. and Villadsen, K. (2014) 'Corporate smart phones: professionals' conscious engagement in escalating work connectivity', *New Technology, Work and Employment*, 29 (1): 72–87.

Chan, J. (2013) 'A suicide survivor: the life of a Chinese worker', *New Technology, Work and Employment*, 28 (2): 84–99.

Collier, P. and Horowitz, D. (1987) *The Fords: An American Epic*. London: Futura Collins.

Conti, R.E. and Warner, M. (1993) 'Taylorism, new technology and just-in-time systems in Japanese manufacturing', *New Technology, Work and Employment*, 8 (1): 31–42.

Elliott, C.S. and Long, G. (2016) 'Manufacturing rate busters: computer control and social relations in the labour process', *Work, Employment and Society*, 19 (1): 153:74.

Ellis, V. and Taylor, M. (2006) 'You don't know what you've got till it's gone: recontextualizing the origins, development and impact of call centres', *New Technology, Work and Employment*, 21 (2): 107–22.

Ellis, V. and Taylor, M. (2010) 'Banks, bailouts and bonuses: a personal account of work in Halifax Bank of Scotland during the financial crisis', *Work, Employment and Society*, 24 (4): 803–12.

Etzioni, A. (1986) 'The fast-food factories: McJobs are bad for kids', *The Washington Post*, 24 August.

Felstead, A. (2013) 'Skills at work', *Society Today*, Summer, pp.16–17.

Ford, H. and Crowther, S. (1924) *My Life and Work*. London: William Heinemann.

Fuchs, V. (1968) *The Service Economy*. New York: Basic Books.

Fulmer, R.M. and Herbert, T.T. (1974) *Exploring the New Management*. New York: Macmillan.

Gantt, H. (1919) *Organizing for Work*. New York: Harcourt, Brace and Hove.

Gartman, D. (1979) 'Origins of the assembly line and capitalist control of work at Ford', in A.S. Zimbalist (ed.), *Case Studies on the Labour Process*. London: Monthly Review Press, pp.193–205.

Gilbreth, F.B. (1911) *Motion Study*. New York: Van Nostrand.

Gilbreth, F.B. and Gilbreth, L. (1916) *Fatigue Study*. New York: Sturgis and Walton.

Gould, A.M. (2010) 'Working at McDonald's: some redeeming features of McJobs', *Work, Employment and Society*, 24 (4), pp. 780–802.

Grey, C. (2009) *A Very Short, Fairly Interesting and Reasonably Cheap Book About Studying Organizations* (2nd edn). London: Sage.

Hill, A. (2015) 'Relegation fear works on the pitch but not in the office', *Financial Times*, 5 May, p.12.

Hollinger, P. (2015) 'Boeing beats Airbus to the title of largest jet maker in 2014', *Financial Times*, 13 January.

Jenkins, S. and Delbridge, R. (2014) 'In pursuit of happiness: a sociological examination of employee identification amongst a happy call centre workforce', *Organization*, 21 (6): 867–87.

Jeske, D. and Santuzzi, A. (2015) 'Monitoring what and how: psychological implications of electronic performance monitoring', *New Technology, Work and Employment*, 31 (1): 62–78.

Kanigel, R. (1997) *The One Best Way: Frederick Winslow Taylor and the Enigma of Efficiency*. London: Little Brown.

Kantor, J. and Streitfeld, D. (2015) 'Inside Amazon: wrestling big ideas in a bruising workplace', *The New York Times*, 15 August, www.nytimes.com/2015/08/16/technology/inside-amazon-wrestling-big-ideas-in-a-bruising-workplace.html?_r = 0

Katz, L.M. (2015) 'Big employer is watching', *HR Magazine*, 60 (5): 67–74.

Kuchler, H. (2014) 'Data pioneers watching us work', *Financial Times*, 18 February, p.12.

Littler, C.R. (1982) *The Development of the Labour Process in Capitalist Societies*. London: Heinemann.

Littler, C. and Salaman, G. (1982) 'Bravermania and beyond: recent theories and labour process', *Sociology*, 16 (2): 251–69.

McCann, L., Hassard, J.S., Granter, E. and Hyde, P.J. (2015) 'Casting the lean spell: the promotion, dilution and erosion of lean management in the NHS', *Human Relations*, 68 (10): 1557–77.

Noon, M., Blyton, P. and Morrell, K. (2013) *The Realities of Work* (4th edn). Basingstoke: Palgrave. Macmillan.

O'Connor, S. (2015) 'Wearables at work: the new frontier of staff surveillance', *Financial Times*, 9 June, p.14.

Ritzer, G. (ed.) (2010) *McDonaldization: The Reader* (3rd edn). Thousand Oaks, CA: Pine Forge Press.

Ritzer, G. (2011) *The McDonaldization of Society: An Investigation into the Changing Character of Contemporary Social Life* (6th edn). Thousand Oaks, CA: Pine Forge Press.

SES (2012) *Skills and Employment Survey, 2012*, ESRC Centre for Learning and Life Chances in Knowledge Economies and Societies, www.cardiff.ac.uk/research/projects/view/117804-skills-and-employment-survey- 2012

Sennett, R. (2008) *The Craftsman*. New Haven, CT: Yale University Press.

Suchman, L. (1996) 'Supporting articulation work', in R. Kling (ed.), *Computerization and Controversy* (2nd edn). San Diego, CA: Academic Press, pp.407–23.

Taylor, F.W. (1911) *Principles of Scientific Management*. New York: Harper.

Taylor, P. and Bain, P. (2007) 'Reflections on call centres: a reply to Gluckmann', *Work, Employment and Society*, 21 (2): 349–62.

Taylor, P., Hyman, J., Mulvey, G. and Bain, P. (2002) 'Work organization, control and experience of work in call centres', *Work, Employment and Society*, 16 (1): 133–50.

The Economist (2012) 'Faster, faster, faster', 28 January, p.59.

The Economist (2013) 'Schumpeter: a hospital case', 18 May, p.68.

The Economist (2015) 'Schumpeter: digital Taylorism', 12 September.

Vance, A. (2014) 'The smarter pizza makers', *Bloomberg Businessweek*, 3 October, pp.42–44.

Wilson, H.J. (2013) 'Wearables in the workplace', *Harvard Business Review*, 91 (9): 23–25.

Womack, J.P., Jones, D.T. and Roos, D. (1990) *The Machine that Changed the World: The Triumph of Lean Production*. New York: Macmillan.

Zimbalist, A.S. (1979) *Case Studies on the Labour Process*. London: Monthly Review Press.

Chapter 15 **Elements of structure**

Key terms

organization structure

delegation

work specialization

job definition

job description

organization chart

hierarchy

span of control

line employees

staff employees

authority

responsibility

accountability

line relationship

chain of command

staff relationship

functional relationship

formal organization

informal organization

semi-formal organization

sexuality

sex

gender

role

role conflict

rules

formalization

centralization

decentralization

Learning outcomes

When you have read this chapter, you should be able to define those key terms in your own words, and you should also be able to:

1. Explain how organization structure affects human behaviour in organizations.

2. List the main elements of organization structure.

3. Relate the concept of span of control to that of organizational hierarchy.

4. Identify line, staff and functional relationships on an organization chart.

5. Distinguish between the formal, informal and semi-formal organization of a company.

6. Understand the nature and impact of sexuality on organizational behaviour.

Why study elements of structure?

The structure of an organization is like the skeleton of an animal. The various bones link to each other in specific ways. Different animals have different skeletons. When scientists unearth the remains of an animal and examine its skeleton, they can tell what kind of animal it was. When living, you cannot directly observe an animal's skeleton. It is hidden beneath its skin. However, when a part of the skeleton becomes faulty (e.g. a broken leg), the whole animal cannot perform as normal until the bone heals or has been replaced. What an animal can and cannot do during its life is greatly determined by its skeleton. As Sacha Albers and her colleagues (2016, p.8) explain:

> Formal organizational structures group and connect individuals within an organization. Departments, committees, boards, teams and task forces create temporary or permanent channels for individuals to come together and interact … Role descriptions and task assignments typically specify reporting or supervisory duties and thus create connections among individuals. Essentially then, organization structures establish networks of ties among organizational members.

Employees' attitudes and behaviour can be shaped as much by the structure of the organization within which they work as by the personalities that they possess, and the groups and teams to which they belong. The constraints and demands of the job imposed through the roles that they play can dictate their behaviour, and even change their personalities. For this reason, it is impossible to explain the behaviour of people in organizations solely in terms of individual or group characteristics. Jay Lorsch described organizational structure as management's formal and explicit attempts to indicate to the organization's members what is expected of them. This involves the definition of individual jobs and their expected relationship to each other, as indicated in organizational charts and in job descriptions. In his words, 'this was management's attempt to draw a map of whom they want to do what' (Lorsch, 1977, p.3).

Alan Fox (1966) argued that explanations of human behaviour in organizations must consider structural factors. He was critical of those who insisted on explaining behaviour in organizations exclusively in terms of personalities, personal relationships and leadership. Such explanations are highly appealing to common sense. This is because such variables are directly observable – people say and do things. In contrast, the effects of a company's structure on its employees are generally hidden. The structural approach stands in contrast to the psychologistic approach which holds that it is the individual factors that are the main determinants of human behaviour in organizations.

While corporate strategy specifies the *goals* that a company pursues, organization structure directs the *means* by which these will be achieved. John Child (2015, pp.17–22) noted that an inappropriate structure can obstruct the achievement of organizational goals by causing at least five problems:

1. *Motivation and morale* can fall if inappropriate delegation and spans of control lead to too little or too much responsibility being given to employees. Ill-defined roles and unclear priorities, work schedules and performance standards, all lead to staff not knowing what is expected of them.

2. *Decisions* may be of poor quality and will be made slowly if the company has too many hierarchical levels; if decision makers are separated from each other, and if decision making is over-centralized.

3. *Conflict and lack of coordination*: if the structure does not emphasize a single set of company-wide objectives, departmental priorities may take precedence. Conflict results from a failure to coordinate the activities of individuals, teams and departments, whose work is interdependent.

4. *Changing circumstances* may not be responded to imaginatively if the structure lacks people performing forecasting and planning roles; if it does not give priority to innovation and change; and if there is no top management support or inadequate resources.

5. *Rising costs* may result from many expensive bosses in tall hierarchies with narrow spans of control; and where additional staff are hired to administer excessive rules, procedures, paperwork and targets.

STOP AND THINK   Consider the behaviour of the instructor teaching this course. Identify aspects of their behaviour that you like and do not like. Decide if these positive and negative behaviours are influenced by that person's personality or by the organization structure within which they work?

Organization structuring

Organization structure the formal system of task and reporting relationships that control, coordinate and motivate employees to work together to achieve organizational goals.

At the start of the text, organizations were defined as social arrangements for achieving controlled performance in pursuit of collective goals. One aspect of these 'arrangements' is the creation of a structure. The purpose of organization structure is, first, to divide up organizational activities and allocate them to sub-units; and second, to coordinate and control these activities so that they achieve the aims of the organization.

Because organization structure is an abstract concept, it is useful to begin by listing the seven things that it is concerned with – the elements of structure. These are shown in Table 15.1. Senior management's decisions regarding each element will have a major impact on the employees' work satisfaction and organizational performance, either positively or negatively. A recurring theme running through these decisions is delegation, which refers to managers granting decision-making authority to employees at lower hierarchical levels.

Delegation managers granting decision-making authority to employees at lower hierarchical levels.

Table 15.1: Elements of organization structure

Element	Concerns
Work specialization	Division of work tasks
Hierarchy	Levels of management in the organization
Span of control	Number of workers supervised by a single manager
Chain of command	Reporting relationships
Departmentalization	Grouping of jobs
Formalization	Extent of rules
Centralization	Location of decision making

1. *Work specialization*: To what degree should work tasks in an organization be subdivided into separate jobs? Should there be high specialization, or should workers do several different jobs (low specialization). What are the implications for time, cost of training and employee motivation?

2. *Hierarchy*: Should there be many layers or levels of management (tall hierarchy) or few (flat hierarchy). What are the implications in terms of communication, employee motivation and staff costs?

3. *Span of control*: How many subordinates should a single manager or supervisor be responsible for – many (wide span of control) or few (narrow span of control)?

4. *Chain of command*: To whom should a given individual or group report with respect to their work?

to gravitate towards organizations with tall hierarchies. At one time it was believed that the narrower the span of control was, the greater would be the level of employee productivity. However, research by Theobald and Nicholson-Crotty (2005) suggests that due to negative consequences of a narrow span, it is a moderate span of control that maximizes productivity, as shown in Figure 15.5.

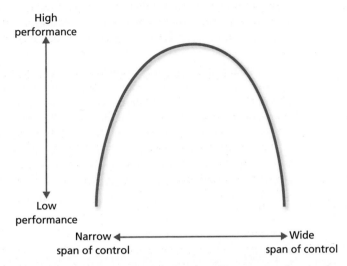

Figure 15.5: Relationship between organizational performance and span of control
Source: based on Theobald and Nicholson-Crotty (2005).

The graph in Figure 15.5 shows that organizational performance and span of control both increase to the point at which the supervisor or manager is no longer able to coordinate or monitor the large number of subordinates they are responsible for. Companies differ, and each seeks to find the span best for it. For example, Wal-Mart sets different spans of control – narrow for store managers so as to ensure standardization, and wide for merchandizing managers at headquarters in order to implement best practices (Simons, 2005). To recap, an organization structure performs three functions. First, it designates the formal reporting relationships, specifying both managers' spans of control and the number of hierarchical levels. Second, it groups together individuals into departments. Finally, it specifies systems within the firm, to ensure that the communication, coordination and integration between different departments is effective.

Line, staff and functional relationships

Line employees
workers who are directly responsible for manufacturing goods or providing a service.

Staff employees
workers who occupy advisory positions and who use their specialized expertise to support the efforts of line employees.

Within an organization, one can distinguish two classes of workers. First, there are the line employees who contribute directly to the provision of goods or services to the customer. In a motor car company this refers those who assembly the car (production) and who sell the car (sales). They are considered to be the primary organizational functions. Line employees are shown on an organization chart which depicts their positions in the organization's structure, and shows the relationships between them. The line structure is the oldest and most basic framework for an organization, and all other forms are modifications of it. It is indispensable if the efforts of employees are to be coordinated. It provides channels for upward and downward communication, and links different parts of the company together with the ultimate source of authority.

The second class of workers are called staff employees. They contribute indirectly to the provision of goods or services to the customer. These individuals occupy advisory positions and use their specialized expertise to support the efforts of line employees. Staff employees work in departments such as purchasing, human resources, information technology and legal. These are considered to be secondary organizational functions. A firm may provide line managers with advice by establishing a separate department headed by staff specialists. This is a modification of the basic line structure, and is referred to as a *line-and-staff structure*. The staff departments and the staff employees within them perform their tasks through the line structure, and not independently of it.

Within any organization structure, individuals occupying different positions will have different relationships with one another. These relationships can be labelled *line*, *staff* and *functional*.

To explain the differences between these types of relationships, it is first necessary to introduce and define the concepts of authority, responsibility and accountability. You cannot be held accountable for an action unless you are first given the authority to do it. In a situation where your manager delegates authority to you, they remain responsible for your actions to senior management. Authority is vested in organizational positions, not in the individuals who occupy them. Military personnel salute the rank, not the person holding it. Authority is accepted by subordinates who comply because they believe the position holder has a legitimate right to exercise the authority. Authority flows down the vertical hierarchy of the organization, along the formal chain of command.

Authority the right to guide or direct the actions of others and extract from them responses that are appropriate to the attainment of an organization's goals.

Responsibility the obligation placed on a person who occupies a certain position in the organization structure to perform a task, function or assignment.

Accountability the obligation of a subordinate to report back on their discharge of the duties for which they are responsible.

Reverse accountability

Traditional accountability refers to the obligation of a subordinate to report back to their boss on their discharge of the duties for which they are responsible. Reverse accountability is the opposite. Gary Hamel (2011) gives the example of an Indian IT services company with thousands of employees that has a management model built on the principle of reverse accountability. Every employee rates their boss and their boss's boss, and their ratings are published online. When reviewing and updating their corporate strategies, the company shares it with its 8,000 employees who become involved, commenting on and helping to build the strategy. It has a complaints system which, if you disagree with your boss's decision or feel that you have been treated unfairly, allows you to complete a complaint form (which is visible throughout the organization) which can only be closed down by you. Your manager then has to address your complaint, either fixing it or explaining the situation. Any complaint that is not resolved within 24 hours is escalated to the next level of management. In this way, bosses report back to their subordinates on the discharge of their duties.

Line relationship one in which a manager has the authority to direct the activities of those in positions below them on the same line.

A line relationship is one in which a manager has the authority to direct the activities of those in positions below them on the same line on an organization chart. Line managers can 'tell' their subordinates on their own line what to do. Such relationships are depicted with vertical lines on the chart, and these connect positions at each hierarchical level with those above and below it. It is this set of manager–subordinate relationships that are collectively referred to as the organization's chain of command. Using the analogy of a river, the line relationships are the designated channels through which authority flows from its source at the top of the organizational pyramid, through the middle management ranks, down via the supervisors, to employees at the desk or on the factory floor. Thus the most junior employee has some linkage to the most senior manager. All non-managerial employees have some authority within their jobs, which may be based on custom and practice or formally defined in their job descriptions.

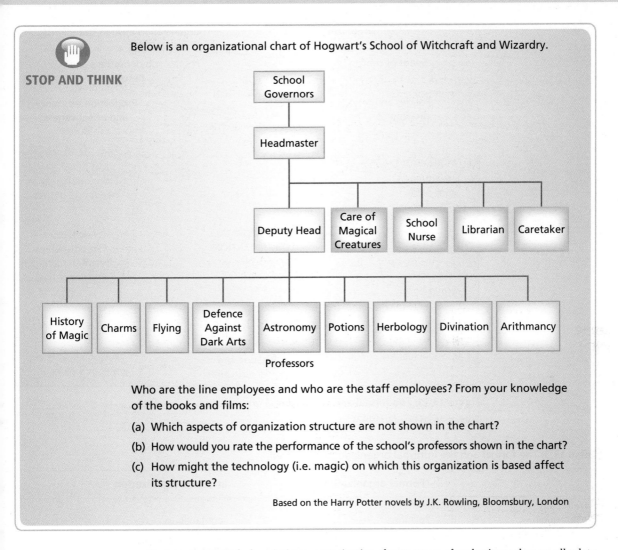

STOP AND THINK

Below is an organizational chart of Hogwart's School of Witchcraft and Wizardry.

Who are the line employees and who are the staff employees? From your knowledge of the books and films:

(a) Which aspects of organization structure are not shown in the chart?

(b) How would you rate the performance of the school's professors shown in the chart?

(c) How might the technology (i.e. magic) on which this organization is based affect its structure?

Based on the Harry Potter novels by J.K. Rowling, Bloomsbury, London

Formal organization
the documented, planned relationships established by management to coordinate the activities of different employees towards the achievement of the organizational goal.

Decisions about job descriptions, organization charts, types of authority and so on all relate to designing the **formal organization**. This refers to the documented, planned relationships established by management to coordinate the activities of different employees towards the achievement of a common goal, using the division of labour and the creation of a hierarchy of authority. These relationships between employees are all written down, and can be checked and modified, as required. However, to understand and explain the behaviour of people in organizations, it is also necessary to become familiar with the informal organization.

Informal organization
the undocumented relationships that arise spontaneously between employees as individuals interact with one another to meet their own psychological and physical needs.

The **informal organization** refers to the undocumented relationships that arise spontaneously between individuals in the workplace as they interact with one another, not only to do their jobs, but also to meet their psychological and physical needs. These interactions lead to the creation of relationships between individual employees (see below) and to the development of informal groups, each with their own values and norms of behaviour, which allow people to meet their social needs (see Chapter 10). These groups are separate from those specified by the formal organization.

Compared to the formal organization, the informal organization has a more transient membership, making it looser and more flexible, with interactions between individuals being more spontaneous and more emotional, resulting in their relationships being less clearly defined, and their involvement being more variable. The relationship between the formal and the informal organizations is shown in Figure 15.11. However, the informal organization created by employees can be in conflict with the formal organization established by management. Together, the two affect the human behaviours that occur within an organization. Some of the differences between the two are shown in Table 15.3.

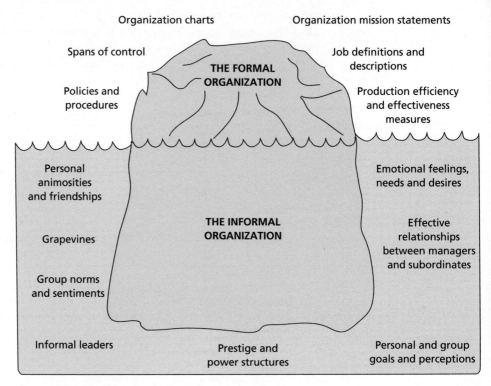

Figure 15.11: The formal and the informal organization
Source: from Lysons (1997).

Table 15.3: The formal and the informal organization compared

		Formal organization	Informal organization
A	structure		
	(a) origin	planned	spontaneous
	(b) rationale	rational	emotional
	(c) characteristics	stable	dynamic
B	position terminology	job	role
C	goals	profitability or service to society	member satisfaction
D	influence		
	(a) base	position	personality
	(b) type	authority	power
	(c) flow	top down	bottom up
E	control mechanism	threat of firing or demotion	physical or social sanction (norms)
F	communication		
	(a) channels	formal channels	grapevine
	(b) networks	well defined, follow formal lines	poorly defined, cut across regular channels
G	charting	organizational chart	sociogram
H	miscellaneous		
	(a) individuals included	• all individuals in work group	• only those 'acceptable'
	(b) interpersonal relations	• prescribed by job description	• arise spontaneously
	(c) leadership role	• assigned by organization	• result of membership
	(d) basis for interaction	• functional duties or position	• personal characteristics status
	(e) basis for attachment	• loyalty	• cohesiveness

Source: based on *Organizational Behaviour: Concepts and Applications*, by Gray/Starke, © 1997. Reprinted by permission of Prentice Hall, Inc., Upper Saddle River, NJ (Gray and Starke, 1984, p.412).

Division of labour increases productivity but specialization impedes communication and coordination between units. Employees cannot innovate, address new problems or advance knowledge frontiers on their own. Collaboration is essential to stimulate innovation and expand integration. The formal organization is the main way in which firms coordinate employee activities and core company functions. Some firms have tried to encourage innovation using their *formal organization*, by changing employees' departmental memberships, reporting relationships, job titles and role responsibilities. They have experimented with matrix structures, assigning employees simultaneously to both functional departments and cross-functional product teams, and having them report to two bosses at the same time.

Other firms have tried using the *informal organization*, by altering employees' personal relationships, social ties and groupings. As in informal groups, the informal organization structure is emergent and enacted. It comprises members' shared interests, emotional relations, activities and memberships outside the workplace, to generate employees' commitment to work and efficiency in the workplace. Companies have placed different individuals in the same office space and devised social events where employees from different departments can meet and interact.

Susan Biancani and her associates (2014) drew attention to the development of a third, new organizational form located between the formal and the informal organization which they label the semi-formal organization. It is an organization design intended to shape employees' relations by encouraging employee collaboration and increasing their innovation and productivity. It is particularly relevant to knowledge-intensive companies which rely on collaborations that span and integrate different departments, but is applicable to any firm wanting creativity and rapid problem solving. It can be used by any organization that is willing to delegate to employees the freedom to choose how to allocate some of their working time, and allow them to choose with whom to collaborate.

In a semi-formal organization structure employees can simultaneously hold their official position in a department and, at the same time, be members of other committees, task forces, advisory teams or interest groups. These additional relationships are allowed by the company but are not commanded by it. Individuals are not assigned or required to participate in them, as in a formal organization. They enter these secondary groupings voluntarily, as on secondment, on the basis of their interest. Additionally, and unlike with the informal organization, the company offers them support and coordination to do this.

To distinguish between the relationship between the formal, informal and semi-formal, Biancani at al. use the metaphor of the school curriculum. The formal organization is analogous to the prescribed, inflexible, assigned curriculum that schoolchildren must learn. The informal organization is equivalent to the social ties between pupils finding friends from different classes in the playground and forming friendship groups. The semi-formal corresponds to the extra-curricular – that is, the activities, projects and other opportunities available to pupils on a voluntary basis, in which only some pupils choose to participate. The authors give the following examples of semi-formal organizational arrangements:

- British Petroleum's (BP) Peer Assistant programme involves a specialized project team soliciting advice from those with similar experiences by inviting them to join it for several days. Invited peers attend voluntarily because they enjoy sharing knowledge they have gained from previous projects.

- Nokia's strategic roadmap for the coming year is shared with employees and strategic project teams are formed around specific goals and projects. Some team members are appointed by executives to these teams while other individuals join voluntarily. For the former employees, participation is part of their formal role in the organization, but for the latter it represents a semi-formal membership within the company.

- Johnson & Johnson's 'Stretch for Success' programme allows employees who want to learn about another department to spend a fifth of their time working in that department on a project, but continue to be responsible for all their normal duties in their own department. This represents semi-formal membership.

Semi-formal organization employees having voluntarily chosen secondary affiliations and memberships in addition to their official job, which they enter on the basis of their interest and which are supported and coordinated by their company.

Sexuality and the informal organization

Sexuality the way someone is sexually attracted to another person, whether it is to the opposite or the same sex.

Sex the basic physiological differences between men and women.

Gender culturally specific patterns of behaviour which may be attached to either of the sexes.

In contrast to the formal organization just described, the informal organization includes personal animosities and friendships, prestige and power structures, relationships between managers and subordinates, as well as emotional feelings, needs and desires. Sexuality is an important feature of the informal organization. It has been defined as the expression of our social relations to physical, bodily desires, real or imagined, by or for others, or for oneself, together with related bodily states and experience (Hearn et al., 1989). It is useful to contrast the concept of sex, which refers to the basic physiological differences between men and women, with gender, which refers to culturally specific patterns of behaviour which may be attached to either of the sexes (Oakley, 1972). For example, who should mow the lawn? Who should change the nappies? Most people say gender when they actually mean sex.

Many of the themes of this chapter – such as jobs, hierarchy, authority and roles – are significantly influenced by sexuality, an issue that is frequently ignored in management and organizational behaviour textbooks. However, Jeff Hearn and Pauline Parkin (2001) have provided a useful overview of sexuality at work. One reason for this neglect could be because organizations treat sexuality as something that should not occur within them. A distinction is made between the public and private spheres, and sexuality is seen as belonging to the latter. The sociologist Max Weber argued that bureaucracies were based on impersonality and strict rules, with a clear division between the public sphere (which was rational and efficient) and the private sphere (which consists of a person's emotional and personal life). The suppression of sexuality was one of bureaucracy's first tasks, as sexuality was considered irrational and emotional, caused distractions, and thus interfered with the goal of efficiency (Bilimoria and Pederit, 2006).

However, sexuality is an integral part of every employee's personality and identity, and affects their interactions with other workers (Riach and Wilson, 2007). It refers to the way that a person goes about expressing themselves as a sexual being. Sexuality surrounds people in every way and in many forms. Rosemary Pringle (1989, p.90) says that it is 'alluded to in dress and self-presentation, in jokes and gossip, looks and flirtations, secret affairs and dalliances, in fantasy'. Various other commentators have also written that organizations are a complex of work and play; that when you enter most organizations, you are entering a world of sexuality; and that since human beings are sexual, so too will be the places where they work (Hearn, 1993; Williams et al., 1999). Moreover, sexuality is closely related to power – the first reinforces the second. Both shape, control and maintain human interaction between employees, and therefore their behaviours. Power can be expressed through sexuality, and sexuality can be used to subordinate others to a lower status. Rosabeth Moss Kanter (1977) suggested that what may look like sex differences may, in reality, be power differences. Sexuality affects employees' work experiences, job performance, as well as the organizational balance of power (Fleming, 2007). Taking a historical perspective on men and women in the workplace, Julie Berebitsky (2012) argued that what actually goes on between men and women in the workplace has changed little, but what is acceptable has changed a great deal.

Fiona Wilson (2010) observes that at work, sexuality refers to sex roles, sexual preference, sexual attractiveness and notions of masculinity and femininity. According to Michel Foucault (1979), notions of masculinity and femininity are based on social meanings that have been socially and culturally constructed. These meanings therefore are not fixed, but are subject to a process of ongoing revision, through which sex is used to shape and control human relationships. Within organizations, sexuality manifests itself in issues such as sexual attractiveness; gender stereotyping; sex-typing of jobs; the glass ceiling; office romances; sexual harassment and emotional labour (Table 15.4). Nearly 20 years ago, Powell and Foley (1998) complained about the dearth of research on the topic of workplace romance. In the intervening period this gap has been rectified, and the most recent contributions are summarized by Malachowski et al. (2012).

Table 15.4: Issues of sexuality in organizations

Issue	Description
Sexual attractiveness	Men and women using their physical appearance to influence outcomes, e.g. decisions on appointments, promotions, pay
Gender stereotyping	Assumption that men and women possess different personality traits, e.g. men are strong, rational and firm; women are caring, emotional, passionate
Sex-typing of jobs	Stereotyped attitudes towards men's and women's abilities, so that jobs are sex-typed into 'male jobs' such as engineering or 'female jobs' such as nursing
Glass ceiling	Limitation of the seniority level to which women can rise – percentage of women occupying chief executive officer positions; on boards of directors; in top leadership positions
Office romances	Emotional, physical or sexual involvement with another employee affecting organizational behaviour: includes daydreaming; flirting; handholding; sexual intercourse in the office
Sexual harassment	Unwanted sexual attention that is perceived as threatening or offending; can be physical, verbal or non-verbal
Emotional labour	The management of feelings to create publicly observable facial and bodily displays

Since the 1960s, women have increasingly joined men in organizations. In Western societies, most people will spend more than a third of their adult life in the workplace, working in close proximity to one another. This, plus the social trends for later marriage and the long-hours culture, means that the boundaries between work and home have become blurred. Much courtship and mate selection now occurs at work. It is not surprising that about 30 per cent of workers will date a co-worker at some point in their careers (Nardi, 2008). Many relationships begin (and end) in the workplace even though some companies have policies banning office romances.

Sexuality and organizational image

Sexuality is also present in the way that a company may wish to be perceived by others. Virgin Atlantic Airlines' 2009 campaign for their 25th year anniversary had the slogan 'Still Red Hot'. Their television commercial featured a male pilot as well as female cabin crew wearing glamorous and sexy red suits walking through an airport. As they do so, mostly men ogle the group of gorgeous hostesses, and one inadvertently squirts hamburger filling over himself. The 90-second commercial caused an uproar (which perhaps it was designed to do), and complaints were sent to the Advertising Standards Authority. Search YouTube for 'Virgin Atlantic: 25 Years, Still Red Hot'. It was claimed that this advertisement was insulting to all women, especially those working in the aviation industry, as the all-female crew members were being promoted as the main reason for choosing the airline. The ASA responded by saying that even though some viewers might have found the representation of the women and men in the advertisement distasteful, it was unlikely to be seen as sexist towards men or women, or to reinforce those stereotypes (Sweney, 2009a, 2009b).

Robin Marchant/Getty Images

Virgin cabin crew

STOP AND THINK

Why might companies and business academics be reluctant to admit to the existence of sexuality within the workplace? What negative consequences might it have for them?

Workplace romances

Following the sackings and resignations of chief executives of several major organizations amid allegations of inappropriate sexual behaviour, many companies have revised their ethics codes to now stipulate that sexual advances, casual dating, fraternization or committed relationships between employees (particularly between managers and subordinates) are prohibited. Given that office romances are normal in working life, and that the Human Rights Act (1998) gives everyone the right to privacy, the question arises as to whether organizations have the right to enforce such a requirement. In 2014, CareerBuilder.co.uk surveyed 1,000 full-time workers in different UK industries and discovered that 39 per cent had had intimate relationships with a co-worker, and 16 per cent were doing so on an ongoing basis. Ten per cent of workers had left their employer because of their romantic relationship; 30 per cent of those office romances ended up with the couple marrying.

Today's organizations have facilitated mutual attraction and the formation of informal relationships between staff through their equal gender balance; amount of time employees are expected to spend at work; and the recruitment of like-minded employees with similar backgrounds, mindsets and educational levels. Commentators have noted that since human attraction is a natural process, the outright banning of workplace romances is impractical. They recommend that companies should not thwart relationships, but rather acknowledge their existence and find a way of protecting company interests while considering the human rights and the well-being of their employees. One option suggested is 'love contracts' (Gautier, 2015).

Sexuality through informal relationships between employees in organizations can have both negative and positive aspects. The negative consequences for individuals and their fellow employees include creating jealousies; distractions from work; decreased productivity; increased errors; reduced professionalism; and exposure to sexual harassment. For the organization, the dangers include having to fire an employee; losing valuable talent; staff replacement costs; law suits; as well as bad publicity. However, there are positive consequences. For example, a good work atmosphere can develop when informal relationships are encouraged. Rather than being a limitation on bureaucracy, sexuality can actually contribute to efficient operation. It can make work more fun and exciting for employees, thereby reducing their absenteeism and lateness, increasing their motivation and job satisfaction, and thus raising overall company performance. Some commentators have treated sexual behaviour as inappropriate, and as having nothing to do with work itself. However, they do acknowledge that sexuality is present within the workplace. Others say that informal relations are as important as formal relationships in order to motivate employees and make the organization function. An awareness of the effects of sexuality in the workplace provides a new perspective on organizational behaviour, and increases our ability to understand and manage it.

Home viewing

Erin Brockovich (2000, director Steven Soderbergh) is an unemployed single mother (played by Julia Roberts) with three children. After losing a car accident personal injury claim in court, she joins her attorney's law firm as a filing clerk. She discovers a systematic cover-up of the poisoning of a town's water supply by the Pacific Gas and Electric Company. The film demonstrates the sexualization of work. Brockovich makes her sexuality explicit in the way that she dresses and behaves. She wears her long blonde hair loosely, and dresses in tight, low-cut tops, short skirts, see-through blouses and high heels. Her sexuality and lack of self-control is shown as disrupting and threatening order in the office. Observe how she uses her sexual skills on a young male worker to obtain official documents. How does she persuade the working-class families of the town to agree to become plaintiffs in the lawsuit?

For further information about sexuality, feminine relational skills, gender stereotypes and power themes in this movie, see Bell (2008).

Roles in organizations

Role the pattern of behaviour expected by others from a person occupying a certain position in an organization's hierarchy.

Roles are a central feature of every organization structure, and are specified in the organization's hierarchy. All organizational structuring occurs through the specification of the roles that employees are expected to play. It follows that if individuals occupying different positions in the hierarchy have mutual and complementary expectations, then the patterning and predictability of their behaviour is increased. The formal positions identified on an organizational chart of a company imply the expectation of certain behaviours from any person occupying that office. This becomes the person's **role**. Roles are thus associated with positions in the organization and are involved in interactions. A single person plays many different and sometimes conflicting roles in life, both sequentially and simultaneously (e.g. mother, team leader, union official).

Subordinate swapping

The roles we play in organizations affect our behaviour. One company used role theory to resolve employee performance problems. Department managers met regularly to consider the possibility of exchanging their 'worst' performing subordinates. These discussions were based on the assumption that poor performance was the result of the role that a person was being asked to perform in the company. That is, that there were role expectations that the person could not meet. The company philosophy was that there were no 'bad' people (individuals with poor attitude, inadequate motivation or the wrong personality), but only individuals who were occupying roles that were unsuitable for them. The trading was a way of finding the poorly performing employee a different and more suitable role in the organization (Gray and Starke, 1984, p.124).

People's roles in organizations are ranked by status. Individuals occupying the role of manager are generally accorded more status that those occupying the role of cleaner. In other companies, the ranking of roles is less obvious. John van Maanen (1991) described the rank ordering of occupations at Disneyland:

1. Disneyland Ambassadors and Tour Guides. These were the upper-class, prestigious, bilingual women in charge of ushering tourists through the park.

2. Ride operators who either performed skilled work such as live narration, or who drove costly vehicles such as antique trains, horse-drawn carriages or the Monorail.

3. All the other ride operators.

4. Sweepers who kept the concrete grounds clean were designated as *proles*.

5. There was a still lower, fifth category of *sub-prole* or peasant status.

6. The 'lowest of the low' included food and concession workers, pancake ladies, peanut pushers, coke blokes, suds drivers and soda jerks.

Organizations are, to a degree, cooperative arrangements that are characterized by give-and-take, mutual adjustment and negotiation. Their members get on with one another, often without explicit guidance, instruction or direction. The concept of role aids our understanding of this aspect of organizational life by stressing that employees monitor and direct their own work behaviour in the light of what they know is expected of them.

It is common for people to refer to an organizational title or position (e.g. supervisor, scientist, manager) as the supervisor's role, scientist's role and manager's role, as though it were merely an established way of referring to these positions. What assumptions and problems does this use of the concept fail to appreciate?

Philip Zimbardo
(b.1933)

Gary Gershoff / WireImage

Many of the tasks involved in any job have been learned and assimilated so well by the employee that they become accepted as being part of the person. It raises the question of whether, in behaving in a certain way, we are ourselves or are just conforming to what the organization (and society) expects of us. Role relationships therefore are the field within which behaviour occurs. People's behaviour at any given moment, is the result of:

- their personalities;
- their perception and understanding of each other;
- their attitudes to the behavioural constraints imposed by the role relationship;
- the degree of their socialization with respect to constraints;
- their ability to inhibit and control their behaviours.

Prison experiment

Do our attitudes, values and self-image affect how we play roles in organizations (e.g. of a student, lecturer, doctor or doorman) or is it those organizational roles that determine our attitudes, values and self-image? In a classic experiment, Philip Zimbardo created his own prison at Stanford University to answer this question. He selected 21 young men who had responded to a newspaper advertisement, interviewing them to ensure they were mature, emotionally stable, normal, intelligent North American male students from middle-class homes with no criminal record. Each volunteer was paid $15 a day to participate in a two-week study of prison life. A toss of a coin arbitrarily designated these recruits as either prisoners or guards. Hence, at the start of the study, there were no measurable differences between the two groups assigned to play the two roles (10 prisoners and 11 guards).

Those taking the role of guards had their individuality reduced by being required to wear uniforms, including silver reflector glasses which prevented eye contact. They were to be referred to as Mr Correction Officer by the prisoners, and were given symbols of their power, which included clubs, whistles, handcuffs and keys. They were given minimal instructions by Zimbardo, being required only to 'maintain law and order'. While physical violence was forbidden, they were told to make up and improvise their own formal rules to achieve the stated objective during their 8-hour, 3-man shifts.

Those assigned the role of prisoners were unexpectedly picked up at their homes by a city policeman in a squad car. Each was searched, handcuffed, fingerprinted, booked in at the Palo Alto police station, blindfolded and then transferred to Zimbardo's 'Stanford County Prison' in the basement of the university's psychology building. Each prisoner's sense of uniqueness and prior identity was minimized. They were given smocks to wear and had nylon stocking caps on their heads to simulate baldness. Their personal effects were removed; they had to use their ID numbers; and were housed in stark cells. All this made them appear similar to each other and indistinguishable to observers. Six days into the planned 14-day study, the researchers had to abandon the experiment. Why?

In a matter of days, even hours, a strange relationship began to develop between the prisoners and their guards. Some of the boy guards began to treat the boy prisoners as if they were despicable animals, and began to take pleasure in psychological cruelty. The prisoners in turn became servile, dehumanized robots who thought only of their individual survival, escape and mounting hatred of the guards. About a third of the guards became tyrannical in their arbitrary use of power, and became quite inventive in developing techniques to break the spirit of the prisoners, and to make them feel worthless. Having crushed a prison rebellion, the guards escalated their aggression, and this increased the prisoners' sense of dependence, depression and helplessness. Within 36 hours, the first 'prisoner' had to be released because of uncontrolled crying, fits of rage, disorganized thinking and severe depression. Others begged to be paroled and

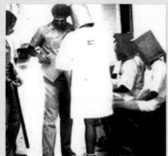

Archives for the History of American Psychology, The Drs. Nicholas and Dorothy Cummings Centre for the History of Psychology. The University of Akron

nearly all were willing to forfeit their money if the guards agreed to release them.

Zimbardo attributed these changes to a number of causes. First, to the creation of a new environment within which the two groups were separated from the outside world. New attitudes were developed about this new 'mini-world', as well as what constituted appropriate behaviour within it. Second, within this new prison world, the participants were unable to differentiate clearly between the role that they were asked to play (prisoner or guard) and their real self. A week's experience of (temporary) imprisonment appeared to undo a lifetime of learning. Human values and self-concepts were challenged, and the pathological side of human nature was allowed to surface. The prisoners became so programmed to think of themselves as prisoners

that when their requests for parole were refused, they returned docilely to their cells, instead of feeling capable of just withdrawing from an unpleasant university psychological research experiment.

Zimbardo concluded that individual behaviour is largely under the control of social and environmental forces, rather than being the result of personality traits, character or willpower. In an organizational context such as a prison, merely assigning labels to people and putting them in situations where such labels acquire validity and meaning appears sufficient to elicit a certain type of behaviour. The power of the prison environment was stronger than each individual's will to resist falling into his role. Zimbardo considered the relevance of the findings of his research, conducted in the 1970s, with the behaviour of US soldiers in Abu Ghraib prison in Baghdad in 2004 (Zimbardo, 2007).

Role conflict the simultaneous existence of two or more sets of role expectations on a focal person in such a way that compliance with one makes it difficult to comply with the others.

The roles that we play are part of our self-concept, and personality theory tells us that we come to know ourselves through our interactions with others. We play different roles throughout our lives, and these require us to use different abilities, thereby adding more aspects to our self-image. Which roles we play and how successfully we play them during our adulthood affects our level of self-esteem. Thus the roles that we play inside and outside the organization affect both our self-image and self-esteem. In his research, Philip Zimbardo showed that people possess mental concepts of different roles, and conform to them when asked or required to do so. The woman who is both a manager and a mother may experience **role conflict** when the expectations in these two important roles pull her in opposite directions.

STOP AND THINK Identify any two roles that you currently occupy simultaneously in different social contexts, e.g. work, home, leisure. Identify a role conflict that you regularly experience as a result of such multiple role occupancy.

Changing roles: master and servant?

Sharon Bolton and Carol Boyd (2003) studied the work of airline cabin crew. In an effort to gain a competitive advantage through superior customer service, international airlines have introduced highly selective recruitment programmes for cabin crew that identify those applicants who possess the particular qualities required for the job. However, contrary to popular belief, possessing the 'right' personality is not enough. Having been selected, successful candidates undergo intensive training and culture management programmes. The airline goes to great lengths to inculcate its values into its new hires. Interestingly, customer service training takes the same amount of time as safety and emergency training; while training in areas related to the health and well-being of crew (e.g. dealing with violence, manual handling) is minimal or may not take place at all. The resounding message received by cabin crews is that what is most important is how they present themselves to passengers. One respondent noted that over the years, the airline industry had taught its cabin crews to be very

subservient. Flight attendants, like theatre or film actors, are asked to assume a particular identity that helps them to perform their work role more efficiently. In their case, they are asked to assume the status of servant in relation to the customer, who is the master.

One respondent stated that crew encountered verbal abuse on a daily basis; and that many people had no respect for them, seeing them as servants who were expected to carry their bags and place them in the overhead lockers. Another flight attendant with 21 years of experience, who had had to suffer passenger rudeness, said that the 'passenger is always right' and they are fully aware of this and take advantage of the situation. They know that they can say anything they like to cabin staff, usually do, and get away with it. The airline requires the work routines to be predictable and to correspond continually to predetermined standards. Temporal and spatial constraints mean that there is little room for any variation in routine: the airline needs to be able to rely on employees to give a homogeneous role performance on every occasion.

Peter Jordan/Alamy

Formalization

Rules procedures or obligations explicitly stated and written down in organization manuals.

A defining characteristic of every bureaucratic organization's structure is its **rules**. From the 1930s, senior managements in large organizations increasingly adopted systems of bureaucratic (rule-governed) control. **Formalization** became widespread. This complemented the control exercised through machinery, and replaced that exercised through supervisory commands. Rules serve to regulate and control what individuals do and, if employees comply with them, the rules ensure the predictability of employee behaviour within organizations. For example, as part of the routine process of monitoring its restaurant managers, McDonald's requires 72 safety protocols to be performed daily in each of its restaurants (Robbins and Judge, 2013, p.221). Both parties can benefit. For employees, rational and fair rules avoid managers' personal biases. This is true despite the fact that the rules are devised and policed by management, who can relax or ignore them at their discretion. Unions use rules to restrict the arbitrary power of employers, and demarcation rules protect jobs. Although rules can cause frustration to employees, they also reduce role ambiguity.

Formalization the degree to which an organization has written rules, operating procedures, job descriptions, organizational charts and uses formal, written communication.

Management also benefits from rules. It uses formal rules and procedures to coordinate the activities of different employees, and to establish conformity. Bureaucratic structures create job hierarchies with numerous job titles, each with its own pay rate. Elaborate formal rules (based on apparently 'objective' criteria) provide a basis for evaluating employee performance and determining rewards. Government rules on equality seek to stop discrimination at work based on race, sex, age, religion or national origin. Rules are part of management's attempt to 'routinize' tasks so as to remove the uncertainties involved in dealing with the environment. Provided that the environment is stable and unchanging, it is likely to be an effective strategy.

STOP AND THINK Think of some of the rules that you have encountered in organizations to which you currently belong, or used to belong. How effective are they in directing the behaviour of individuals? What problems do they cause, and what advantages do they offer, and for whom?

Centralization versus decentralization

A fundamental question faced by every chief executive is what kinds of decisions are to be made and by whom. The answer determines both the distribution of power within an organization (see Chapter 22) and the allocation of company resources. Some senior executives prefer to retain decision-making power in their hands, and thus run highly centralized organizations. **Centralization** refers to the concentration of authority and responsibility for decision-making power in the hands of managers at the top of an organization's hierarchy. Others choose to delegate their power, giving junior managers more individual autonomy, self-directed teams greater freedom, and introducing job enrichment for shop floor workers. Thus, their organizations are much more decentralized in their structure. **Decentralization** refers to the downward dispersion of authority and responsibility for decision making to operating units, branches and lower-level managers.

Centralization the concentration of authority and responsibility for decision-making power in the hands of managers at the top of an organization's hierarchy.

New technology has facilitated this by making information easily available to all levels of employees, right down to the shop floor. The question of whether and how much to centralize or decentralize has been one of the major topics discussed in organizational structuring. Each approach has its own advantages:

Decentralization the dispersion of authority and responsibility for decision making to operating units, branches and lower-level managers.

Centralization advantages

- greater uniformity in decisions is possible;
- senior managers are more aware of an organization's future plans and are more likely to make decisions in its best interests;

- fewer skilled (and highly paid) mangers are required;
- greater control and cost effectiveness in company resources are possible;
- less extensive planning and reporting procedures are required.

Decentralization advantages

- lower-level decisions can be made faster;
- lower-level management problems can be dealt with quickly by junior staff;
- lower-level managers have an opportunity to develop their decision-making skills;
- increases creativity, innovation and flexibility;
- increased motivation of lower-level employees entrusted to make decisions rather than always following orders issued at higher level;
- an organization's workload is spread so as to allow top-level managers more time for strategic planning.

STOP AND THINK

As a shop floor employee, would you prefer your company to be centralized or decentralized? Why?

The balance between centralization and decentralization changes on an on-going basis. It does so, in their view, in response to changes in company size, market opportunities, developments in new technology and, not least, the quality of existing decision making. Some cynics argue that whichever of the two is currently fashionable, it will be superseded by the other in due course. This may occur for no other reason than the incoming chief executive wishing to make a highly visible impact on his or her managers, employees, shareholders and financial analysts. Table 15.5 contains John Child's (2015) summary of the basic choices that a company has to make concerning the various elements or components of its organization structure. Beginning with this chapter and continuing with the next two, we shall examine these choices.

Table 15.5: Basic organization structure choices

Component	Choice
Hierarchy Levels/layers Authority Reporting lines	Tall vs. flat Centralized vs. decentralized Single vs. multiple
Specialization	Which logic of specialization: function, process, product, region? Specialized roles vs. general roles Clear role definitions vs. fuzzy role definitions
Hierarchy and specialization	Specialized hierarchies vs. use of mixed teams High vs. low job autonomy and content
Rules and schedules	Mandatory vs. discretionary Rule-based orientation vs. relationship-based orientation
Systems	Oriented towards reducing uncertainty vs. emphasis on signalling the need to adapt
Control	Which strategy of control: personal bureaucratic, target-based, cultural or HRM-based?
Integration	Vertical vs. horizontal Degree of formalization: direct contact, liaison roles, task forces, coordinators, teams, matrix structures

Component	Choice
Reward	Criteria: hierarchical level, performance, market rate Individual vs. group-based Frequent vs. periodic
Boundary crossing and networking	Intensity of network Role of contract vs. trust Short-term vs. long-term links Dominated vs. equal-partner networks Virtual vs. non-virtual
Outsourcing	Outsourcing value-chain activities vs. peripheral support activities only
Alliances	Equity vs. contractual One-partner-dominated vs. integrated management
Organizing across borders	Global vs. local emphasis Bases of integration: business, function, region?

Source: from Child (2015, p.11). Used with permission.

 RECAP

1. **Explain how organization structure affects human behaviour in organizations.**

   - The procedures employees are required to follow, and the rules by which they are required to abide, all control and direct their behaviour in specified directions.

   - The roles that people play, and the expectations that others have of role holders, all direct the behaviour of employees. Indeed, in the long term, these may even lead to a change in the personality of the employee.

2. **List the main elements of organization structure.**

   - The main elements include: chain of command; hierarchical levels; line employees; rules; staff employees; role expectations; span of control; departmentalization; authority; and job description.

3. **Relate the concept of span of control to that of organization hierarchy.**

   - The narrower the span of control, the taller the organization hierarchy (and vice versa), and the greater the consequences for employees of having one or the other.

4. **Identify line and staff relationships on an organization chart.**

   - Line relationships are depicted vertically on an organization chart, indicating that those above possess the authority to direct the behaviours of those below.

   - The seniors have responsibility for the work of the juniors, while the juniors are accountable for their work to their seniors.

   - Staff relationships are depicted horizontally on an organization chart, indicating that those who possess specific expertise (e.g. in personnel, computing matters) advise those in line positions.

5. **Distinguish between the formal, informal and semi-formal organization of a company.**

   - The formal organization refers to the collection of work groups that have been consciously designed by senior management to maximize efficiency and achieve organizational goals. The informal organization refers to the unofficial network of relationships that spontaneously establish themselves between individuals in an organization on the basis of their common interests and friendships. The semi-formal organization refers to the voluntary, interest-based involvement of employees in secondary groups, in addition to their formal jobs, which has company support.

   - The three forms consist of the same people, albeit arranged in different ways.

6. **Understand the nature and impact of sexuality on organizational behaviour.**

   - Sexuality refers to sex roles, sexual preferences, sexual attractiveness and notions of masculinity and femininity in organizations.

   - Sexuality manifests itself in issues of sexual attractiveness, gender stereotyping, sex-typing of jobs, the glass ceiling, the gender pay gap, work–life balance, office romances, sexual harassment and sexual minorities.

Revision

1. Discuss the disadvantages of centralization and decentralization.

2. Why do organization structures differ? Which is the best organization structure?

3. Suggest how a managers' role might be affected by the seniority of his or her position in the hierarchy, the industry sector and organizational size.

4. What are the costs and benefits for those involved in romances at work? Should a company ignore or actively discourage romantic relationships between its employees? What can senior management do to minimize the problems associated with workplace romances?

Research assignment

Imagine that you are designing an organization structure for your new business – a café, bakery, travel agency or a similar, single shop on the high street.

1. What are the specific tasks to be accomplished by your shop's employees?

2. Draw an organization chart based on employee tasks. Each position on the chart will perform specific tasks or be responsible for particular outcomes.

3. Three years later, your business is successful, and you want to open a second shop three miles away. What challenges would you face running your business at two locations? Draw an organization chart that shows both business locations.

4. Five years later, your business has expanded to five locations in two cities in the same country. How do you keep in touch with them all? How do you coordinate and control what is going on in them? Draw an updated organization chart, and explain your rationale for it.

5. Twenty years later, you have 75 business locations in five European countries. What issues and problems do you have to deal with through organization structure? Draw an organization chart for your organization, indicating who is responsible for customer satisfaction, and explaining how information will flow through this enlarged organization.

Adapted from Daft et al. (2010, pp.129–30)

Springboard

Colleen Malachowski, Rebecca Chory and Christopher Claus (2012) 'Mixing pleasure with work: employee perceptions of and responses to workplace romance', *Western Journal of Communication*, 76 (4): 358–79. The paper begins by reviewing the most recent research on workplace romances thereby providing the basis for further reading.

Robert Duncan (1978–79) 'What's the right organization structure?', *Organizational Dynamics*, 7 (3): 59–73. This classic article provides a structured framework with which managers can determine which type of organization structure is most suitable for their particular company.

Bill McEvily, Giuseppe Soda and Marco Totoriello (2014) 'More formally: rediscovering the missing link between formal organization and informal social structure', *Academy of Management Annals*, 8 (1): 299–345. The authors attempt to bring together the studies into formal and informal structures which, in their view, have been considered separately.

Philip Zimbardo, (2007) *The Lucifer Effect: How Good People Turn Evil*. London: Rider. The author describes how the organizational context in which individuals work (including the structure) affects their behaviour, irrespective of their individual attributes such as personality, learning or motivation.

OB cinema

Aliens (1986, directed by James Cameron): DVD track 14, 1:00:47–1:08:08 (8 minutes). The second film in this science fiction series is set in the distant future on planet LV-426. The characters include Lieutenant Gorman, the senior officer of the space marines, Sergeant Apone, Corporal Hicks, Private Hudson and others. In addition to these military personnel, there is Burke, who represents the Weyland-Yutani Corporation which owns the facilities on the planet, and Ripley (played by Sigourney Weaver), who is employed by it. The scene begins with Ripley shouting at Gorman 'Get them out of there, do it now' and ends at the point at which Corporal Hicks says 'It's the only way to be sure. Let's do it!' Which elements of organizational structure are illustrated in this clip?

OB on the web

Search YouTube for Philip Zimbardo's famous study 'The Stanford Prison Experiment'. Then locate his TED talk 'Philip Zimbardo: the psychology of evil'. Zimbardo generalizes his findings into different organizational contexts. He talks about 'bad apples', 'bad barrels' and 'bad barrel-makers'. In other words, do not blame the individual, blame the organizational context (including the organization structure) in which the individual is operating. Does Zimbardo's argument mean that individuals (negligent bankers, brutal soldiers, lazy students) no longer have to feel responsible for their own actions?

Search for Yves Morieux's TED talk 'As work gets more complicated, six rules to simplify'. He argues that complexity of organizational functioning, reflected in its organization structure, is demotivating employees and draining them of their commitment to their work for their companies. He offers a number of solutions. How practical are his offered solutions? What are the problems in implementing them?

CHAPTER EXERCISES

1. Max Weber Engineering Limited

Put yourself in the role of an experienced, senior manager in this situation. Focus on the objective. Using your knowledge of the concepts, theories, authors, models and frameworks acquired so far from course lectures and reading, as well as your personal experience, evaluate the advantages and limitations of each of the four options, which are the only options proposed to you by the top management team. Assess the strengths and weaknesses of each.

Objective   To recommend a course of action that will improve the firm's competitiveness.

Your problem   You are the longest serving senior manager of a large company that has an organization structure with six levels of hierarchy and a top management team. In comparison to competitors of similar size, information flow through the levels of your company is slow. Also, when decisions for implementing change are made by top management, they take a long time to implement. A team of consultants has been hired to analyse your company's organization structure and to eliminate two levels of the hierarchy, and has recommended the removal of the divisional and departmental layers. The de-layered middle managers will be incorporated into the group leader and professionals levels, losing their power but not their salary. Once management's plan for de-layering became known to employees, protests ensued. Staff were afraid that the remaining four hierarchical levels – president and board, senior management, team leaders and shop floor employees – would offer few opportunities for promotion. The young, successful middle managers were concerned about their jobs and career prospects. There was a concern that an increase in the span of control of the few remaining senior managers would mean that they would be unable to cope with the number of individual employees and their problems. However, the top management team made it clear that they wanted to implement the flattened hierarchy, but that it was looking for ways of dealing with employees' concerns and problems. As an experienced manager you have been asked to make a recommendation.

Your options

1. Engage a team of human resource (personnel) specialists to advise all levels of staff on the different aspects of empowerment programmes, and especially managers on their new roles as coaches.

2. Improve information flow by hiring in-house consulting staff. These personal assistants to the top management can act as staff employees, and they can screen and filter information from the lower levels before presenting it directly to top management.

3. Create project teams after eliminating two levels of hierarchy. This will create an organic structure, with flexible teams reporting directly to the top management. Hierarchy is irrelevant in teams.

4. Introduce a new reward and incentive system to motivate employees. Salaries should in the future be based on individual achievement, not hierarchical position, and team performance encouraged through team bonuses.

2. Human button

Objectives

1. To list the elements of organization structure.
2. To identify examples of organization structure elements.
3. To assess how structure elements contribute to achieving organizational goals.

Briefing

1. Read the case study *Human button* below, and identify the main organization structure elements described. Can you define them?
2. What are this organization's goals? How does this organization structure operate to achieve them?

Human button

The responsibility for the British nuclear deterrent rests with the Royal Navy. Its fleet of four ballistic submarines – the SSBNs (Ship Submersible Ballistic Nuclear) - is based at Faslane in Scotland. One of the submarines – *HMS Vanguard*, *Victorious*, *Vigilant* or *Vengeance* – is always on patrol, undetectable, in the North Atlantic. They patrol for 90 days at a time; do not surface except in an emergency; and are not allowed any communication out of the boat. Every day, the captain is required to write a patrol report and a narration, explaining why certain things were done. Each SSBN is organized into departments, each headed by a senior officer who reports to the captain: Logistics (divided into Catering Services, Supply Chain and Personnel); Marine Engineering; Medical; Warfare; and Weapons Engineering. Only a few of the most senior officers are allowed to know its location. Each is armed with up to 16 Trident II, D5 submarine-launched, ballistic missiles whose destructive power is equivalent to all the explosives used in the Second World War. Even if Britain was utterly destroyed in a surprise attack, that one, lone submarine will always be ready and able to strike back with overwhelming force. That is the theory of nuclear deterrence.

There is a human button communication system that triggers the retaliation procedure and has many built-in redundancy factors to anticipate problems. At one end of the communication chain is the British Prime Minster who makes the final decision. The PM's directive, detailing the target and release time, is sent from the government emergency room, somewhere below Whitehall. It is conveyed through his Chief of Defence Staff to the bunker facility at Northwood, under the Chiltern Hills in the South of England, known as 'The Hole'. Located there is Task Force 345's operations room from where the command and control of Britain's nuclear deterrent is exercised. At Northwood, the prime ministerial directive is authenticated, first by one A-list and then by one-B-list officer. The National Firing Message, as it is known, is then put into the system and goes onto the broadcast, which is continuously transmitted to the SSBN at sea. On board the submarine, the firing order is scrutinized by two officers, and checked against codes in the submarine's safe. Three keys are engaged, and the captain gives the order to fire.

What happens if the Prime Minister is killed or the Hole is destroyed in a pre-emptive nuclear attack? In anticipation of this, the PM nominates an *alternate* – that is, a decision maker from the Cabinet, who will make a decision in their place, if required. In addition, early in each new Prime Minister's tenure, the Cabinet Secretary briefs the PM on the choices to be made from beyond the grave. Since the 1960s, each Prime Minister has written what is known as a *Letter of Last Resort*. It details what the PM's wishes are in the event of a nuclear attack on the United Kingdom. There are believed to be four options for the submarine commander: retaliate; do not retaliate; put yourself under the command of the United States or Australian Navy; or 'submarine captain to use his own judgement'. The Prime Minister makes his choice, writes the letter in longhand, signs it personally, and a copy of it is placed in the safe of each of the four nuclear submarines. Britain is the only nuclear power that uses this letter system. When the Prime Minister demits from office, his letter of last resort is destroyed unread.

In a deteriorating geopolitical situation, if the submarine captain loses contact with Northwood, he first assures himself that Britain is an irradiated ruin and much of its population is dead. His orders are then to go, with his Executive Officer, to the safe in the submarine floor, remove the PM's letter of last resort, and act on its contents. However, it is not the captain who pulls the nuclear trigger. The submarine is brought up to hover position, still submerged, before firing, and the launch order is communicated by the captain to his Weapons Engineering Officer (known as 'The Weo'), who has the rank of Lieutenant Commander. It is he who pulls the trigger on the Colt 45 pistol handle whose wire runs from its butt. This allows the Weo to check other data on his control panels while holding the nuclear trigger in his hand. The trigger can only be activated if the captain turns a key on a panel in the control room. Below is the verbatim transcript of the final section of the launch procedure, as used in the practice drill. It represents the end of the firing chain which began with the Prime Minister's order. Below is the oral exchange between the commanding officer (A) and his various subordinates (B), who respond by confirming orders and asking for permission. After the sound of a click, the Weo says 'One away'. The first missile will have gone, and the end of the world will have arrived:

A: Hover command, commence hovering

B: Commence hovering

A: Stop engine

B: Stop engine

A: Ship control in condition 1SQ

B: Condition 1SQ, Roger

A: Weo in the missile control centre – clocks

B: Check

A: Come IRT

B: Check

A: Slow ready handover

B: Semi-package has been shifted, we're on the active target package, in access to the safe, missile spinning up

A: I have the system. . .

A: We are fire control. Fire control in condition 1SQ for strategic launch

B: Fire control in condition 1SQ for strategic launch, Roger

A: Command Weo, weapons system in condition 1SQ for strategic launch

B: Weo requires permission to fire

A: Supervisor Weo, initiate fire 1

(click)

One away

Case based on 'The human button', BBC Radio 4 programme, 2 December 2008: Richard Knight, 'Whose hand is on the button?', 2 December 2008, BBC website, http://news.bbc.co.uk/1/hi/uk/7758314.stm; Royal Navy website: http://royalnavy.mod.uk

Employability assessment

With regard to your future employment prospects:

1. Identify up to three issues from this chapter that you found significant.

2. Relate these to the competencies in the employability matrix.

3. Decide what actions you need to take to maintain and/or develop those competencies under each of the four headings of the employability matrix.

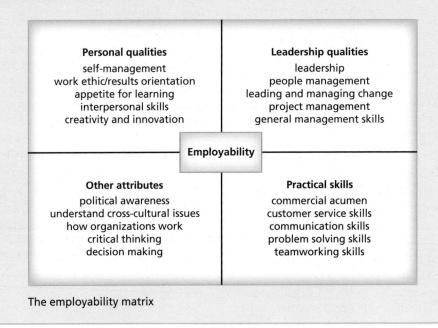

The employability matrix

References

Albers, S., Wohlgezogen, F. and Zajac, E.J. (2016) 'Strategic alliance structures: an organization design perspective', *Journal of Management*, 42 (3): 582–614.

Bell, E. (2008) *Reading Management and Organization in Film*. London: Palgrave Macmillan.

Berebitsky, J. (2012) *Sex and the Office: A History of Gender, Power and Desire*. New Haven, CT: Yale University Press.

Biancani, S., McFarland, D.A. and Dahlander, L. (2014) 'The semiformal organization', *Organization Science*, 25 (5): 1306–24.

Bilimoria, D. and Piderit, S.K. (2006) *Handbook on Women and Business in Management*. Northampton: Edward Elgar Publishing.

Bock, L. (2015) *Work Rules*. London: John Murray.

Boddy, D. (2011) *Management: An Introduction* (5th edn). Harlow, Essex: Financial Times Prentice Hall.

Bolton, S.C. and Boyd, C. (2003) 'Trolley dolly or skilled emotion manager: moving on from Hochschild's managed heart', *Work, Employment and Society*, 17 (2): 289–308.

Brazil, J.J. (2007) 'Mission impossible?', *Fast Company*, 114 (April): 92–109.

Chandler, A.D. (1988) 'Origins of the organization chart', *Harvard Business Review*, 66(2): 156–57.

Child, J. (2015) *Organization: Contemporary Principles and Practice* (2nd edn). Chichester: Wiley.

Cole, G.A. and Kelley, P. (2011) *Management: Theory and Practice* (7th edn). Andover, Hants: Cengage Learning EMEA.

Daft, R.L., Murphy, J. and Willmott, H. (2010) *Organization Theory and Design*. Andover, Hants: South-Western Cengage Learning.

Duncan, R.B. (1979) What is the right organization structure? Decision tree analysis provides the answer', *Organizational Dynamics*, 7 (3): 59–80.

Edwards, D. (2011) *I'm Feeling Lucky: The Confessions of Google Employee Number 59*. London: Allan Lane.

Fleming, P. (2007) 'Sexuality, power and resistance in the workplace', *Organization Studies*, 28 (2): 239–56.

Foucault, M. (1979) *Discipline and Punish*. Harmondsworth, Middlesex: Penguin Books.

Fox, A. (1966) *Industrial Sociology and Industrial Relations, Research Paper 3*. London: Royal Commission on Trade Unions and Employers' Associations

Gautier, C. (2015) *The Psychology of Work*. London: Kogan Page.

Gray, J.L., and Starke, F.A. (1984) *Organizational Behaviour: Concepts and Applications* (3rd edn). Columbus, OH: Merrill Publishing.

Hamel, G. (2011) *Reinventing the Technology of Human Accomplishment*, YouTube video.

Harvard Business Review (2014) 'The chart that organized the 20th century', pp.32–33.

Hearn, J. (1993) 'Emotive subjects: organizational men, organizational masculinities and the (de)construction of emotions', in S. Fineman (ed.), *Emotion in Organizations*. London: Sage Publications, pp.142–66.

Hearn, J. and Parkin, P.W. (2001) *Gender, Sexuality and Violence in Organizations: The Unspoken Forces of Organization Violations*. Thousand Oaks, CA: Sage

Hearn, J.R., Sheppard, D.L., Tancred, P. and Burrell, G. (eds) (1989) *The Sexuality of Organization*. London: Sage Publications.

Jervis, F.R. (1974) *Bosses in British Business*. London: Routledge and Kegan Paul.

Kanter, R.M. (1977) *Men and Women of the Corporation*. New York: Basic Books.

Koontz, H. (1966) 'Making theory operational: the span of management', *Journal of Management Studies*, 3(3): 229–43.

Kunisch, S., Müller-Stewens, G. and Campbell, A. (2014) 'Why corporate functions stumble', *Harvard Business Review*, 92 (12): 111–17.

Lawler, E.E. (1988) 'Substitutes for hierarchy', *Organizational Dynamics*, 17 (1): 5–15.

Leavitt, H.J. (1965) 'Applied organizational change in industry: structural, technological and humanistic approaches', in J.G. March (ed.), *Handbook of Organizations*. Stokie, IL: Rand McNally, pp.1144–70.

Levitt, S.D. and Dubner, S.J. (2005) *Freakonomics*. London: Penguin Books.

Levitt, S.D. and Venkatesh, S.A. (2000) 'An economic analysis of a drug-selling gang's finances', *Quarterly Journal of Economics*, 115 (3): 755–89.

Lorsch, J.W. (1977) 'Organizational design: a situational perspective', *Organizational Dynamics*, 6 (2): 2–14.

Lysons, K. (1997) 'Organizational analysis', *British Journal of Administrative Management, special supplement*, no. 18 (March/April).

Malachowski, C., Chory, R. and Claus, C. (2012) 'Mixing pleasure with work: employee perceptions of and responses to workplace romance', *Western Journal of Communication*, 76 (4): 358–79.

Nardi, H. (2008) *The Greenwood Encyclopedia of Love, Courtship and Sexuality Through History* (6th edn). Westport, CT: Greenwood Press.

Oakley, A. (1972) *Sex, Gender and Society*. London: Temple Smith.

Powell, G. and Foley, F. (1998) 'Something to talk about: romantic relationships in organizational settings', *Journal of Management*, 24 (3): 421–48.

Pringle, R. (1989) *Secretaries Talk: Sexuality, Power and Work*. London: Verso.

Riach, K. and Wilson, F. (2007) 'Don't screw the crew: exploring the rules of engagement in organizational romance', *British Journal of Management*, (18) 1: 79–92.

Robbins, S.P. and Judge, T.A. (2013) *Organizational Behaviour* (15th edn). Harlow, Essex, Pearson Education.

Simons, R. (2005) 'Designing high-performance jobs', *Harvard Business Review*, 83(7/8): 54–62.

Sweney, M. (2009a) 'Virgin ad prompts complaints of sexism', *Guardian*, 9 February, www.guardian.co.uk/media/2009/feb/09/virgin-atlantic-ad-sexistofcom

Sweney, M. (2009b) 'Virgin ad not sexist, rules ASA', *Guardian*, 9 February, www.guardian.co.uk/media/2009/feb/09/virgin-atlantic-ad-not-sexist-rules-asa

The Economist (2008) 'If looks could kill', 25 October, pp.97–98.

The Economist (2010) 'Schumpeter: too many chiefs', 26 June, p.74.

The Economist (2012) 'A pixelated portrait of labour', 10 March, p.74.

The Economist (2013) 'Schumpeter: Titans of innovation', 27 April, p.68.

Theobald, N.A. and Nicholson-Crotty, S. (2005) 'The many faces of span of control: organization structure across multiple goals', *Administration and Society*, 36 (6): 648–60.

Van Maanen, J. (1991) 'The smile factory: work at Disneyland', in E.H. Schein, P.J. Frost, L.F. Moore, M.R. Louis, C.C. Lundberg and J. Martin (eds), *Reframing Organizational Culture*. Newbury Park, CA: Sage Publications, pp.31–54.

Venkatesh, S.A. and Levitt, S.D. (2000) 'The financial activities of an urban street gang', *Quarterly Journal of Economics*, 115 (3): 755–89.

Williams, C.L., Giuffre, P.A. and Dellinger, K. (1999) 'Organizational control, sexual harassment and the pursuit of pleasure', in Annual Reviews Inc. (ed.), *Annual Review of Sociology: Volume 25*. Palo Alto, CA: Annual Reviews Inc., pp.73–93.

Wilson, F. (2010) *Organizational Behaviour and Work: A Critical Introduction* (3rd edn). Oxford: Oxford University Press.

Zimbardo, P.G. (2007) *The Lucifer Effect: How Good People Turn Evil*. London: Rider & Co.

Chapter 16 Organization design

Key terms

corporate strategy

organization design

traditional authority

charismatic authority

legitimate authority

bureaucracy

managerial activities

managerial roles

contingency approach to organization structure

technological determinism

technical complexity

technological interdependence

mediating technology

long-linked technology

intensive technology

task variety

task analysability

environmental determinism

environmental complexity

environmental dynamism

mechanistic organization structure

organic organization structure

differentiation

integration

strategic choice

Learning outcomes

When you have read this chapter, you should be able to define those key terms in your own words, and you should also be able to:

1. Distinguish between charismatic, traditional and legitimate forms of authority.

2. State the main characteristics of a bureaucratic organization structure as specified by Max Weber.

3. Distinguish Fayol's six managerial activities and the main ideas of the classical management school.

4. Distinguish Mintzberg's ten management roles.

5. Identify the writers who comprise the early contingency approach and state their main individual contributions.

6. Discuss the strengths and weaknesses of early ideas on the design of organization structure and the practice of management.

7. Identify the influence of early organization design ideas on contemporary organizations.

Why study organization design?

Corporate strategy
establishing the aims
of a company and the
means by which these
will be achieved.

A recent survey of global executives by the management consultancy McKinsey revealed that almost 60 per cent of them had experienced organizational redesign in the last two years, and a further 25 per cent had undergone it three or more years ago (Aronowitz et al., 2015). In contrast, past generations of employees could expect an organizational upheaval once or twice during their careers. It appears that companies are now in a state of near-permanent change. The design of an organization is the outcome of senior management's decision about its **corporate strategy** which refers to establishing the aims of a company and the means by which these will be achieved. Whenever a company changes its strategy, it alters the other variables, as depicted in Jay Galbraith's STAR model shown in Figure 16.1 (Galbraith, 2002; Kates and Galbraith, 2010).

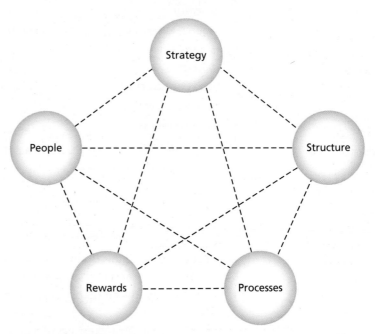

Figure 16.1: Galbraith's STAR model

Organization design
the integration of
structure, people,
rewards and processes
to support the
implantation of an
organization's corporate
strategy.

Organization design refers the integration of structure, people, rewards and processes to support the implantation of that corporate strategy. It is therefore not limited only to structural considerations, but also affects, and is affected by, the other variables. In this chapter, however, we shall focus on the structural choices that managers make.

As Patricia Cichocki and Christine Irwin (2014) explain, the choice of organization structure within an organizational design process involves more than just deciding about job titles, boxes and reporting relationships on an organizational chart. Good organization design will contribute to company effectiveness and success by allowing individuals, groups and departments to achieve their intended goals. Citing Charles Handy (1993), they remind designers that structures should be as simple as they can be, but as complex as they must.

Max Weber and bureaucracy

Max Weber, a German sociologist and philosopher writing at the start of the twentieth century, was the first to address the topic of the design of organization structures in his theory of bureaucracy. If Frederick Taylor was interested in the one best way to perform a job, Weber was concerned with the one best way to structure an organization. Literally, bureaucracy means 'rule by office or by officials'. An organization's structure determines where formal power and authority is located and this was what Weber was most interested in. Here, power is used to refer to the capacity of individuals to overcome resistance on the part of others, to exert their will, and to produce results consistent with their interests and objectives. Weber studied societies in history and distinguished three different types of authority – **traditional**, **charismatic** and **legitimate authority** (Weber, 1947).

It is legitimate authority that concerns us here, as it carries with it 'position power' (power deriving from the position occupied within the organization). Because of the process of rationalism in modern society (the belief that the human mind can discover innate laws which govern the workings of the universe), legitimate authority has predominated. **Bureaucracy** is the form of organization structure associated with legitimate authority. The six characteristics of bureaucracy are shown in Figure 16.2.

Traditional authority the belief that the ruler has a natural right to rule. This right was either God-given or by descent, as with the authority of kings and queens.

Charismatic authority the belief that the ruler has some special, unique virtue, either religious or heroic, as with the authority of religious prophets, charismatic politicians and film stars.

Legitimate authority based on formal, written rules that have the force of law, e.g. the authority of presidents, managers, lecturers.

Bureaucracy legal-rational type of authority underpinning a form of organization structure that is characterized by job specialization, authority hierarchy, formal selection, rules and procedures, impersonality and impartiality and recording.

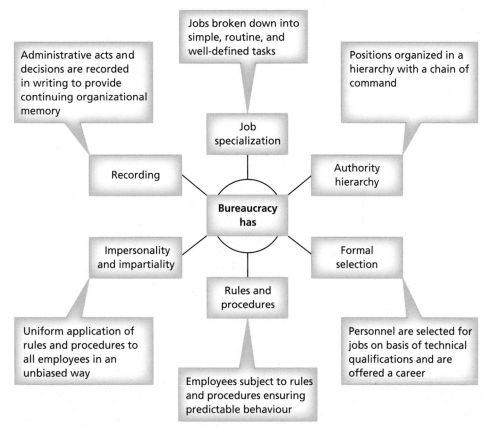

Figure 16.2: Characteristics of bureaucracy

Source: adapted from Robbins, Stephen P.; Coulter, Mary. *Management*, 10th ed., © 2009, p.45. Reprinted and electronically adapted by permission of Pearson Education, Inc., Upper Saddle River, New Jersey.

Within a bureaucracy, we do what managers, civil servants and university lecturers tell us, not because we think that they have a natural right to do so, or because they possess some divine power, but because we acknowledge that their exercise of power is legitimate and hence supported by two factors:

- The demonstrable logical relevance of their requests, directions and instructions to us. Their commands must seem rational by being justified through their relevance to the tasks of the bureaucracy and, ultimately, to its objectives.

- A shared belief in the norms and rules of the bureaucracy that have been arrived at rationally (not based on tradition or personal whim) and which possess a law-like character.

Weber believed that an organization based on *legitimate authority* would be more efficient than one based on either traditional or charismatic authority. This was because its continuity was related to the formal organization structure and the positions within it, rather than to a particular person who might leave or die. Not every bureaucratic organization will possess all the characteristics that Weber identified. However, the more of them that it is has, the more bureaucratic it will be.

Weber used the term bureaucracy to refer to a particular type of organization structure, in which work was divided, coordinated and controlled. Whereas in the past, authority had been based on nepotism or whim, in bureaucratic organizations it was based on rational principles. Bureaucracy for him was a form of organization that emphasized speed, precision, regulation, clarity, reliability and efficiency. This was achieved through a fixed division of tasks, imposing detailed rules, regulations and procedures and monitoring through hierarchical supervision.

Many aspects of Weber's model reflected the organizational circumstances of his time. In the early twentieth century, establishing employment relationships on the basis of professional selection, and creating continuity of employment and career structures, was unusual when the methods then most commonly used were amateur, personal and haphazard. Because these practices were adopted so widely, so long ago, it is difficult to believe that there was a time when organizations did not keep detailed written records (see Hall, 1963). Weber's model gave little consideration to people's behaviours or their attitudes.

Dress rules at UBS and Google

Employee work wear is a key aspect of every organization's corporate image and reflects its corporate culture. Companies are therefore keen to ensure that their employees wear appropriate clothing when working alongside colleagues and meeting clients. However, how detailed the rules concerning appropriate dress in the workplace are varies considerably between companies. At one extreme, there is UBS, a Swiss bank, which issued a 42-page employee dress code to its staff. It required female staff not to wear tight, revealing shirts, ankle chains, flashy jewellery, or to let their underwear show. Male bank employees were informed that they should not wear socks with cartoon motifs or a three-day beard on their faces. Moreover, their ties should match the bone structure of their face. Other useful advice included avoiding tight shoes, as they cause a strained smile.

The new UBS dress code is an attempt aimed at improving the bank's image, which suffered after it accepted Europe's biggest bailout – £37 billion – during the 2008 financial crisis. A UBS spokesperson said staff and clients had responded well to the rules which were being implemented in five offices in Switzerland. Staff appearance is important, said one financial PR consultant: 'If banks are spending money on plush carpeting and flowers in vases, then you don't want people romping around in jeans.' In contrast, there is Google, the search engine company, whose four-word, official office dress code is 'You must wear clothes' (Edwards, 2011; Jacobs, 2010; Kay, 2011; Sparkes and Salkeid, 2010).

The strength of bureaucracy lies in its standardization. Employee behaviour is controlled and made predictable. In Weber's conception, this was achieved not through time-and-motion study, but through the application of rules, regulations and procedures. This ensures that different people in the same organization carry out their work in a similar way. Bureaucratic organizations have a reasonably consistent set of goals and preferences. They devote few resources to time-consuming information searches or the analysis of current activities to check if these are meeting stated goals. Instead, they rely on rules, tradition, precedent and standard operating procedures. Little time is spent on decision making since decisions follow from the established routines, and few action alternatives are considered. The bureaucratic emphasis is on stability, fairness and predictability (Pfeffer, 1981).

Weber was struck by how the bureaucratic structure of a company routinized the processes of its administration, in a way similar to how a machine routinized production. His ideas developed independently, yet they neatly complement those of Frederick Taylor.

While Taylor focused on the worker on the shop floor, Weber's interest lay in administrative rules and an organization hierarchy that progressed down from the top of the organization. Nevertheless, Weber would have approved of the disciplining, rational conditioning and training of workers proposed by Taylor. Different organizations can be compared in terms of the degree of their bureaucratization using the previously defined dimensions of job specialization, authority hierarchy, formal selection, rules and procedures, impersonality and impartiality, and recording.

Table 16.1: Positive and negative consequences of a bureaucracy

Characteristic	Positive consequence	Negative consequences	
		For the individual	For the organization
1. Job specialization	Produces efficient, repetitive working	Overspecialization of employees' skills and knowledge prevents them recognizing or caring about problems not in their domain	Inhibits job rotation and hence flexible use of personnel, and thus can reduce overall productivity
2. Authority hierarchy	Clarifies who is in command	Prevents employees contributing to decisions	Allows errors to be hidden
3. Formal selection	Most appropriate person appointed to a position and promoted	Can restrict the psychological growth of the individual in their job	Individuals throughout the company are promoted to their level of incompetence
4. Rules and procedures	Employees know what is expected of them	Introduces delays; stifles initiative and creativity	Leads to individual and sub-unit goals replacing organization objectives; rules define *minimum* levels of acceptable performance
5. Impersonality and impartiality	Fosters efficiency, reduces bias	Dehumanizes those it purports to serve – officials are prevented from responding to unique features of clients who are treated as standard cases	Creates a climate of alienation through the firm as employees come to see themselves as small cogs in a wheel
6. Recording	Creates an organization history that is not dependent on individual memory	Employees come to see record-keeping as an end in itself rather than means to an end	Recorded precedents stifle attempts at company innovation. Inhibits flexibility, adaptability and responsiveness

In modern usage, the term bureaucracy has acquired a negative meaning amongst the public and the media. For example, when people come up against obstructiveness in any aspect of organizational life, they complain about there being 'too much bureaucracy' or 'too much red tape'. In response, governments and companies promise to remove or reduce it. Weber's view was in direct opposition to this. For him, bureaucracy was the most efficient form of social organization precisely because it was coldly logical and did not allow personal relations or feelings to get in the way of achieving goals.

Rules and bureaucratic procedures provide a standard way of dealing with employees that avoids favouritism and personal bias. Everyone knows what the rules are and receives equal treatment. However, there is often frustration at having to follow what appear to be seemingly illogical rules, and thereby experience delays. This change in meaning has occurred because the principles of bureaucracy, originally designed to maximize efficiency, also resulted in inefficiencies. These negative aspects, costs or 'dysfunctions' of bureaucracy were the focus of debates in organizational behaviour during the 1950s and 1960s (Merton, 1940; Gouldner, 1954; Blau, 1966). The positive and negative consequences of bureaucracy are summarized in Table 16.1.

Bureaucracy around the world

Every year the International Finance Corporation (part of the World Bank) compiles a report on bureaucracy (red tape) around the world. Its *Doing Business* report looks at government rules, and measures the duration and costs of standard business procedures – for example, how long it takes to register a company (one day in New Zealand, 65 days in the Congo); to register a property (one day in Portugal, 513 days in Kirbati); to obtain a construction permit (five steps in Denmark, 51 steps in Russia); to enforce a simple contract through the courts (150 days in Singapore, 1,420 days in India). In the 2012 *Ease of Doing Business* rankings, the top five countries were Singapore, Hong Kong, New Zealand, United States and Denmark, and the bottom three were Chad, Central African Republic and Congo-Brazzaville. The IFC shames world governments into cutting pointless rules and streamlining their processes. In the last six years 94 per cent of the 174 economies surveyed have either simplified their processes or implemented reforms (*The Economist*, 2011).

Thomas Diefenbach and Rune By (2012) argue that, historically, the design of organizations has been shaped by the dual ideas of the vertical organization of tasks (hierarchy) and the rule-bound execution of tasks (bureaucracy). Despite now being considered 'evil', as they put it, both continue to exist, albeit in modified forms. Bureaucratic firms can achieve an acceptable or even exceptional level of efficiency, while those companies which have not adopted bureaucratic features have failed. There is a prevailing view that organizations should be structured on the basis of rationality. This means that a hierarchical structure is more likely to produce rational decisions and better control within an organization than any other (for example, one based upon teams). Commentators agree that hierarchy and bureaucracy establish not only functional but also social relationships, i.e. they place employees in certain relationships to each other. Hierarchy and bureaucracy are also persistent – they exist through time and space and in almost all cultures. Indeed, Pfeffer (2015) recently claimed that organizations needed hierarchy if they were not to descend into anarchy, while Diefenbach and By (2012) argued that most organizations today continue to be based upon the hierarchical, bureaucratically administered social relationships of superiors and subordinates.

Home viewing

Gosford Park (2001, director Robert Altman) is the story of an English house party taking place in a manor house during the 1920s. The guests come from different social classes, and many bring their own servants with them. Assess which types of authority are demonstrated by the characters. Consider how the roles are played. How is the authority possessed by the servants 'below stairs' contingent on the status of their masters 'upstairs'? What other elements of bureaucratic organization structure can you spot?

Henri Fayol and managerial activities

Henri Fayol qualified as a mining engineer in 1860 after which he joined the Commentary-Fourchambault combine, a company in which he was to spend his entire working life. In 1866, he became manager of the Commentary collieries and, in 1888, at the age of 47, he was appointed to the general manager position at a time when the financial position of the company was critical. By the time he retired in 1918, he had established financial stability in the organization. Fayol is credited with 'inventing' management – that is, distinguishing it as a separate activity, and defining its constituent elements. Interestingly, the word *management* is not translatable into all languages, nor does the concept exist in all cultures. Managing of course occurs, but is not always treated as anything special or separate.

It was in 1916, the year after Frederick Taylor died, that Fayol's book *General and Industrial Administration* was published. In it, Fayol put down in a systematic form the experience that he had gained while managing a large organization. He stressed methods rather than personalities, seeking to present the former in a coherent and relevant fashion. This formed his theory of organization. While Taylor focused on the worker on the shop floor – a bottom-up approach – Fayol began from the top of the hierarchy and moved downwards. However, like Taylor, he too believed that a manager's work could be reviewed objectively, analysed and treated as a technical process which was subject to certain definite principles which could be taught. Fayol identified six managerial activities that supported the operation of every organization and needed to be performed to ensure its success. Although his list of management activities was originally developed over 80 years ago, it continues to be used to this day. It is shown in Table 16.2.

Managerial activities activities performed by managers that support the operation of every organization and need to be performed to ensure its success.

Table 16.2: Fayol's six managerial activities

Forecasting	Predicting what might happen in the future
Planning	Devising a course of action to meet that expected situation
Organizing	Allocating separate tasks to different departments, units and individuals
Commanding	Providing direction to employees, now more commonly referred to as *directing, motivating* or *leadership*
Coordinating	Making sure that previously separated, assigned tasks are integrated and people are working well together
Controlling	Monitoring progress to ensure that plans are being carried out properly

The six management activities are interrelated. For example, a company management team begins by *forecasting* the demand for its product (e.g. steel wire). It requires a sales forecast and will use market research to develop one. Once it is clear that there is a market for the product, the next activity, *planning*, will take place. For Fayol, planning involved 'making a programme of action to achieve an objective'. He collectively referred to forecasting and planning as *purveyance*. Because they are so closely related, many authors and books treat them as a single management activity.

Having made the plan, the third activity to be performed is *organizing*. This involves breaking down the main task into smaller pieces, and distributing them to different people. In a company structured along functional lines (accounting, production, marketing), the organizing of people may involve creating a special, temporary project team consisting of members from the different functions. This is the matrix structure to be discussed in a later chapter.

Fayol used the word *commanding* to describe his fourth management activity. It has been defined as 'influencing others towards the accomplishment of organizational goals'. Today, we would refer to it as *directing, motivating* or *leading*. Whichever term is chosen, performing this activity involves the manager ensuring that employees give of their best. To do this, managers must possess knowledge of the tasks to be done and of the people who are to do them. This management activity is mainly, although not exclusively, performed in a face-to-face situation. The fifth managerial activity, *coordinating*, involves ensuring that the various tasks previously distributed to different employees through organizing are being brought together and synchronized with one another. Coordination can be achieved through emails, meetings and personal contacts between the people carrying out their unique job tasks.

Forecasting, planning and organizing

With a heavy clunk, the steel outer doors of the Svalbard Global Seed Vault close, shutting out the howling Arctic gale and entombing a tonne of new arrivals: 25,000 seed samples from America, Columbia, Costa Rica, Tajikistan, Armenia and Syria. Opened in 2008, the Svalbard Vault is a backup for the world's 1,750 seed banks – the storehouses of agricultural biodiversity. The Afghani and Iraqi seed banks have already been destroyed by wars, and in 2012, the Philippines' national seed bank was destroyed by fire. Syria's bank at Aleppo is under threat. The

Svalbard Vault is protected by two airlocks at the end of a tunnel sunk 160 metres into the permafrost of Norway's Arctic archipelago outside the village of Longyearbyen, one of the world's most northerly habitations. It is maintained at a constant temperature of minus 18 degrees Celsius. This is serious disaster preparedness. If its electricity were cut, the vault would take two centuries to warm to freezing point. Its concave tunnel head is designed to deflect the force of a missile strike. The facility is nicknamed the Doomsday Vault (*The Economist*, 2012).

Mari Tefre/Global Crop Diversity Trust/Rex Shutterstock

The sixth and final managerial activity is *controlling*. This involves monitoring how the objectives set out in the plan are being achieved, with respect to the limitations of time and budget that were imposed. Any deviations are identified, and action taken to rectify them. It may be that the original plan will have to be amended. Although Fayol's six managerial activities have been presented as a sequence, in reality they occur simultaneously in a company. However, forecasting and planning tend to be primary. There are also loops when original plans have to be changed because certain resources are found to be unavailable (when organizing) or when cost overruns are discovered (through controlling).

Fayol's ideas are referred to as the *classical theory* of organizations or management. Many commentators feel that it mirrors, at the macro-organizational level, what scientific management offered at the micro-organizational level. Classical theory considered that there was one, best organization structure which would suit all organizations, irrespective of their size, technology, environment or employees. This structure was based on the application of certain key principles reflecting the 'logic of efficiency', which stressed:

- functional division of work;
- hierarchical relationships;
- bureaucratic forms of control;
- narrow supervisory span;
- closely prescribed roles.

Airbus 350: a challenge of coordination

The Airbus A350-XWB is a wide-bodied, long-range airliner. The plane is the first of its kind. It is built mainly from lightweight composite materials, and is an assemblage of millions of parts governed by a million lines of code. A decade ago, a simple design miscalculation on the company's A380 superjumbo airliner required miles of wiring to be removed and reinstalled. The immediate cause of that problem was a breakdown in the snap-together, final assembly process in Toulouse. The A380's rear fuselages are made in Hamburg, and were supposed to arrive in Toulouse with all their wiring ready to plug into the forward parts coming in from factories in north and west France. Each A380 contains 500 km of wiring, weighing 580 tonnes with 100,000 electrical connections, and this is woven through its walls and floor (see diagram). When the two halves of the aeroplane arrived, they did not match up. The wires were found to be too short to connect up with each other. Hamburg's failure to use the latest three-dimensional modelling software meant that nobody anticipated the effect of using lightweight aluminium wiring rather than copper. The aluminium made the bends in the wiring looms bulkier. Worse still, engineers who scrambled to fix the problem did so in different ways. So the early aircraft all have their own, one-of-a-kind wiring systems. This and engine supply problems set production schedules for the A380 back two years, leading to $6 billion of losses.

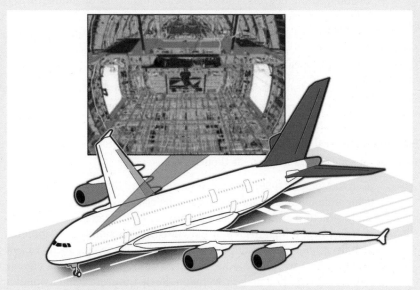

Source: www.popularmechanics.com

This failure in coordination led to a company restructuring. Its Chief Executive reported: 'We have changed our whole organization.' Airbus may look like an aircraft manufacturer but it is more of an integrator. It develops the overall plan of the plane, but then outsources the design and manufacture of the parts, which it then fits together. The company has its own facilities in Toulouse (France), Broughton (Wales), Filton (England) and Hamburg (Germany). Over 7,000 engineers work on the A350, but only half of them are Airbus employees. To meet this coordination challenge, Airbus adopted standardized design software throughout the company. It also created a single, electronic rendering system of the aeroplane, called 'digital mock-up' (DMU), that every engineer working on the plane can use at any time. This allows any changes to be seen by everyone (*The Economist*, 2006; *Fortune*, 2007; Wise, 2014).

STOP AND THINK   What are the advantages and disadvantages of having management principles based on the experience of successful managers?

Criticism of classical management

When considering classical management theory, it is important to locate it in its historical context. The managers of the period were dealing with larger, more complex organizations than had existed up to then. At the beginning of the twentieth century many new companies were established. They employed vast numbers of people, had numerous plants and employed new technologies. All of this needed coordinating. With no model or experience to fall back on, those who managed these organizations had no choice but to develop their own principles and theories as to what to do to run them well. Inevitably these principles were grounded in their day-to-day experience of managing, and owed much to the models offered by military, religious and governmental institutions. These were the only equivalent, large organizations at the time. Over the years, various writers have criticized Fayol's principles (March and Simon, 1958; Child, 1969; Peters and Waterman, 1982; Thomas, 2003). Their criticisms included that he:

- misleadingly proposed a single, standardized organizational model as the optimum one;
- promoted a militaristic, mechanistic organization, which stressed discipline, command, order, subordinates and esprit de corps;

- overlooked the negative consequences of tight control and narrow task specialization, which can demotivate employees and hinder efficiency;
- overemphasized an organization's formal structure, while neglecting processes such as conflict management, decision making and communication;
- underestimated the complexity of organizations;
- based his ideas on unreliable personal knowledge, rather than systematic research evidence;
- lacked a concern with the interaction between people;
- underestimated the effects of conflict;
- underrated the capacity of individual workers to process information;
- misunderstood how people thought.

Gareth Morgan (1989) presents a continuum of different organization structure designs ranging from a bureaucratic one possessing classical features at one extreme, to a flexible, organic structure at the other (see Figure 16.3). The latter possesses little task specialization, few rules, a high degree of individual responsibility and authority, and much delegated decision-making authority. Morgan stated that a bureaucracy could probably evolve from numbers 1 to 3, and perhaps even to number 4. But for an organization to move to 5 or 6 would require a major revolution. Such a transformation would involve not only a change in an organization's structure, but also in its culture (see Chapter 4). If achieved, it would mean a loss of its bureaucratic features.

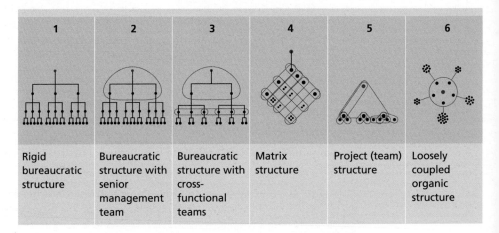

1	2	3	4	5	6
Rigid bureaucratic structure	Bureaucratic structure with senior management team	Bureaucratic structure with cross-functional teams	Matrix structure	Project (team) structure	Loosely coupled organic structure

Figure 16.3: Types of organization structure
Source: from Morgan (1989, p.66).

Rigid bureaucratic structure

This is Weber's classic bureaucratic organization structure. The company operates in a very stable environment. Its structure is pyramid-shaped, and under the control of a single chief executive. Because all important principles have been codified, and every contingency is understood and has been anticipated, it is unnecessary for the executive to hold meetings.

Bureaucratic structure with senior management team

The environment is generating novel problems which cannot be anticipated, and for which responses cannot be codified. The chief executive creates a management team of departmental heads who meet regularly to deal with non-routine problems. Department heads have authority over their area of responsibility.

Bureaucratic structure with cross-functional teams

For problems requiring an interdepartmental view, a team is assembled consisting of lower-level staff from different departments. Members attend discussions as departmental representatives. They give the 'departmental view'; report back on developments to their department head; convey problems and information to that person; and implement decisions made higher up. They operate as a less rigid bureaucracy.

Matrix structure

This is the matrix structure described in the next chapter. It attaches as much importance to projects or customer groups as to functional departments such as marketing and production. Employees report to two bosses – their departmental boss and their project boss.

Project team structure

In this design, the majority of the organization's core activities are tackled through project teams. If functional departments do exist, they play a background role. The task consists of completing a series of projects, and the vehicle for task achievement is the team. These teams are given the freedom to manage themselves within the strategic parameters defined by senior management. The organization possesses more the features of a network of interaction than of a bureaucratic structure.

Loosely coupled organic structure

A small core of staff represents the organization and sets its strategic direction. They form its 'inside' centre and sustain a network which is coupled to others, located 'outside'. They use contracting to get key operational activities performed. This network of firms is held together by its current product or service. The firm is really an open-ended system of firms, ideas and activities. It lacks a clear organization structure and a definable boundary, making it difficult to determine what or who is inside or outside.

Persistence of bureaucracy

Why do the bureaucratic structural features described in this chapter continue to persist in the majority of large companies to the present day? Writers such as Leavitt (2005), Du Gay (2005) and Robbins (1990) have suggested a number of reasons to account for their continued existence.

1. *Success*: For the most part, over the last 100 years bureaucracy has worked. It has done so, irrespective of technology, environment and people, and irrespective of whether the organization has been a manufacturing, medical, educational, commercial or military one.
2. *Large size*: Successful organizations survive and grow large, and the bureaucratic form is most efficient with large size.
3. *Natural selection favours bureaucracy*: Bureaucracy's natural features, the six identified at the start of this chapter, are inherently more efficient than any others, and thus allow the organization to compete more effectively.
4. *Static social values*: The argument is that Western values favour order and regimentation and bureaucracy is consistent with such values. People are goal-oriented and comfortable with authoritarian structures. For example, workers prefer clearly defined job responsibilities.
5. *Environmental turbulence is exaggerated*: The changes currently being experienced may be no more dynamic than those at other times in history. Management strategies can also reduce uncertainty in the environment.
6. *Emergence of professional bureaucracy*: Bureaucracy has shown its ability to adjust to the knowledge revolution by modifying itself. The goal of standardization has been achieved in a different way among professional employees.
7. *Bureaucracy maintains control*: Bureaucracy provides a high level of standardization, coupled with centralized power, which is desired by those in command. For this reason senior managers who control large organizations favour this organization design.

Harold Leavitt (2005) believed that the bureaucratic hierarchy in modern organizations was increasing rather than declining, and it was being helped by advances in technology. The authoritarian structures remain intact today, but are cloaked by a veil of humanism. According to Leavitt, organizational hierarchies are particularly resilient, managing to change, while retaining their basic nature. They can favour one management style over others (participative, analytical or 'hot groups'), and make that the basis of their organizational culture. They can also isolate some of their characteristics in separated subunits (e.g. Xerox's Palo Alto Research Centre) whose creation involved separating a 'hot group' from the rest of the company. They can break into smaller units; form into matrix structures; and even use technology to rid themselves of people. Despite these transmutations, the basic core of the bureaucratic organizational model remains intact.

In modern organizations, power and authority continue to lie with those at the top of the hierarchy. John Child argued that hierarchy pandered to some of the weaknesses in human nature. It 'offers some people better rewards than others, often on the basis of seniority rather than performance; it indulges people's need to feel more important than others; gives people a sense of personal progression through promotion up the ladder; legitimizes the exercises of power by some people over others' (Child, 2005, p.394). Bureaucratic structures appeal to senior management as they centralize power in their hands, and allow them to control those at the bottom of the hierarchy. Although classical theory and bureaucracy have similarities, a flavour of their differences on four important dimensions are highlighted by Child (2015), as shown in Table 16.3.

Table 16.3: Classical theory and bureaucracy

Dimension	Classical theory	Bureaucracy
Specialization	Division of labour according to specific functions	Designated roles and 'offices' Horizontal specialization) job positions and departments); vertical specialization (hierarchical levels)
Hierarchy	Vertical lines of authority; authority to correspond to the responsibilities of each position	Clearly defined formal hierarchy based on officially assigned responsibilities and authority
Control	Control by hierarchical superiors through unity of command	Insistence on following codes and rules – bureaucratic control through formalization
Coordination	Achieved primarily by managers with limited spans of control	Through adherence to rules and procedures; also through formal committees

Source: Child (2015, p.32). Used with permission.

Henry Mintzberg and managerial roles

Managerial roles
behaviours or tasks that a manager is expected to perform because of the position that he or she holds within a group or organization.

While Henri Fayol focused on managerial activities, Henry Mintzberg, a Canadian management academic, studied the different roles performed by managers. He researched how managers spent their time. His work led to a reassessment of the nature of managerial work within organizations, and a redefinition of the roles of the manager within organizational structures. Mintzberg (1973, 1975) studied chief executives in large and medium-sized companies, categorizing the different behaviours associated with each of their positions, and distinguished ten **managerial roles** which he classified under the three headings of *interpersonal*, *informational* and *decisional*, as shown in Table 16.4. Through their interpersonal roles managers acquired information; through their informational roles they determined the priority of information; and through their decisional roles they put it to use.

Mintzberg's research revealed a difference between what managers actually did, and what they said they did. He showed that a manager's job was characterized by pace, interruptions, brevity and fragmentation of tasks. In addition, managers preferred to communicate face to face; and spent a great deal of time in meetings or in making contacts with others. Mintzberg argued that the ten roles that he identified could describe the nature of managerial work more accurately than other frameworks.

Managers matter

David Garvin (2013) explained how, since its early days, both the founders and the engineers at Google questioned the value of managers. In 2002, the company eliminated all engineering managers and established a completely flat organization structure that recreated a college environment in an effort to encourage rapid idea development. The experiment only last a few months. Larry Page was swamped with staff questions on anything and everything. They realized that managers made non-engineering contributions in the form of communicating strategy, helping staff prioritize projects, facilitating collaboration, supporting career development and ensuring that company processes and systems were aligned with company goals. Google now has 5,000 managers, 1,000 directors and 100 vice presidents to manage 37,000 employees.

However, if your highly skilled, hand-picked, newly hired engineers do not value management, how can you run your company effectively? How do you turn doubters into believers? Garvin describes how Google set out to prove management's worth by using the same analytical rigour and tools that it used to hire the engineers in the first place. Its people analytics group launched Project Oxygen, which asked the question 'Do managers matter?' This research programme measured key management behaviours and cultivated them through communication and training. It collected data from staff exit interviews, Googlegeist ratings, performance reviews and employee surveys. From these, the Project Oxygen team concluded that managers did indeed matter. Moreover, it identified eight positive behaviours shared by its high-scoring managers who led small and medium-sized teams at the first and second level of management. A good manager:

- is a good coach;
- empowers the team and does not micromanage;
- expresses interest and concern for members' success and personal well-being;
- is productive and results oriented;
- is a good communicator – listens and shares information;
- helps with career development;
- has a clear vision and strategy for their team;
- has the technical skills that helps them advise their team.

The project used data-driven decision making to pinpoint specific, desirable, measureable management behaviours, and translated these into detailed, hands-on guidance for company managers. The company discovered that data-driven cultures responded well to data-driven change.

The concept of role was introduced earlier in this chapter. One aspect of it is that any role holder can choose how to carry it out. In the case of a manager, they can decide how they wish to blend the ten listed roles, taking into account organizational constraints and opportunities. For Mintzberg, management is an art, rather than, as Fayol would argue, a teachable science.

Mintzberg stated that all managerial work was encompassed by these ten roles, but that the prominence of each role depended on the managerial level in the company hierarchy and the type of business. His study has provided the modern focus for all the subsequent research into debates about the nature of management. His work is most often contrasted with that of Henri Fayol.

Mintzberg (2009) reviewed the research conducted into management roles over the past four decades, and developed what he calls a general model of managing (Figure 16.4). This model is more elaborate than his original list of ten management roles. It presents three planes of managerial operation – information, people and action; distinguishes between internally and externally focused roles; lists six major roles – communicating, controlling, leading, doing, linking and dealing; and within these six, enumerates 23 sub-roles (Mintzberg, 2009, p.90).

Table 16.4: Mintzberg's ten managerial roles

Role	Description	Examples
Interpersonal roles arise directly from a manager's formal authority and concern relations with others		
Figurehead	Performs symbolic, representative obligatory ceremonial, legal and social duties	Greets visitors, presents retirement gifts, signs contracts; takes clients to lunch, opens premises, attends annual dinners
Leader	Creates the necessary culture and structure to motivate employees to achieve organizational goals	Increases productivity through hiring, staffing, developing, coaching, training and directing employees Provides challenging assignments
Liaison	Maintains network of contacts with those inside and outside own unit or organization who provide information and favours	Attends staff and professional meetings, lunches with customers, meets departmental managers; also uses email and phone
Informational roles concern how information is used in the manager's job, where it comes from and to whom it is communicated		
Monitor	Scans environment for information to understand the working of own organization and its environment	Questions subordinates and contacts; receives information from network contacts; reads business magazines, talks to customers and attends conferences
Disseminator	Transmits information received from outsiders to the members of own organization (*internal* direction)	Makes phone calls; sends emails; writes reports, holds meetings with bosses, peers and subordinates
Spokesperson	Transmits information to outsiders on organization's views, policies, actions and results (*external* direction)	Gives press conferences, media interviews, speeches to external groups; prepares weekly status reports; conducts internal team briefings
Decisional roles: their requirements are determined by the manager's role, seniority and availability of information		
Entrepreneur	Searches the organization and its environment for new opportunities, and initiates planned, *voluntary* changes	Develops new products, processes and procedures; reorganizes departments; and implements innovative employee payment systems
Disturbance handler	Takes corrective action when organization has to react to important, *involuntary*, unexpected changes	Intervenes to avoid a strike; deals with customer complaints; resolves personal conflicts between staff
Resource allocator	Allocates resources to different departments by making approval decisions	Budgets, schedules, programmes, assigns personnel, plans strategically, determines manpower load, sets targets
Negotiator	Participates in sales or labour negotiations Resolves interdepartmental arguments	Negotiates merger details, supplier contracts, wage settlements and internal disputes

Source: based on Mintzberg (1973, 1975).

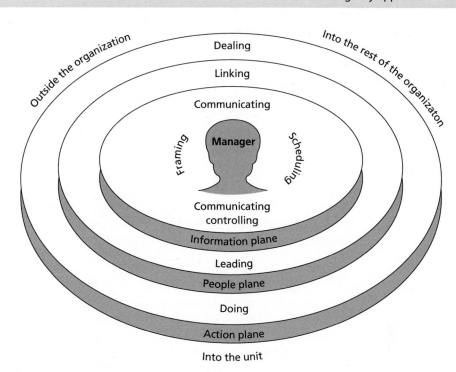

Figure 16.4: Henry Mintzberg's general model of managing

Source: Mintzberg (2009, p.48).

Home viewing

Watership Down (1978, director Martin Rosen) is based on the book by Richard Adams. The amorphous group of ten rabbits are united by having to flee their home warren. They encounter several difficult and dangerous situations before finally establishing a permanent warren on Watership Down. A major theme of the story is how a shrewd, buoyant, young rabbit, Hazel, becomes transformed into the great leader, Hazel-rah. As you watch the film, make a note of which of Mintzberg's ten management roles Hazel plays, and when in the story. Decide which roles he does not play himself and which he delegates to other rabbits. Which of his behaviours shows leadership?

Contingency approach

Contingency approach to organization structure a perspective which argues that to be effective, an organization must adjust its structure to take into account its technology, its environment, its size and similar contextual factors.

The contingency approach to organizational behaviour asserts that the appropriate solution in any specific organizational situation depends (is *contingent* upon) the circumstances prevailing at the time. This approach has been influential in topics such as work design, leadership and, not least, organization structuring. The contingency approach to organization structure argues that, to be effective, an organization must adjust its structure in a manner that takes into account the type of technology it uses, the environment within which it operates, its size and other contextual factors.

The contingency approach holds that:

- there is no one best way to design an organization;

- an organization's structure must 'fit' its environment;

- the better the fit between an organization's structure and its environment, the more effective it will be;

- employees' needs are best met when a company is properly structured and its management style is appropriate for the task in hand.

Managers need to analyse their own organization and its environment; decide and implement the most appropriate structure for the time; manage in an appropriate manner, continually monitor the situation as it changes; and revise the structure and their leadership style as required.

Thus organization design is an on-going management task. Weber's bureaucratic organization structure, described earlier in this chapter, is said to be appropriate for (matches) a stable environment, while a turbulent company environment requires a more flexible organization structure. The contingency approach was a reaction to management thinking in the first half of the twentieth century which was dominated by the search for the 'one best way'. Taylor, Weber and Fayol all recommended single, universal solutions to management problems, often in the form of laws or principles. Subsequent contributions to the contingency school came from many different researchers who studied wage payment systems, leadership styles and job design. They sought to identify the kinds of situations in which particular organizational arrangements and management practices appeared to be most effective.

Determinism versus strategic choice

The main debate within the contingency approach to organization structuring is between two of its sub-schools – the determinists and the strategic choice thinkers. The determinists assert that 'contextual' factors, like an organization's size, ownership, technology or environment, impose certain constraints on the choices that their managers can make about the type of structure to adopt. If the organization's structure was not adapted to its context, then opportunities would be lost, costs would rise, performance would be reduced, and the organization's existence could be threatened. They view the aforementioned variables as *determining* the organization's structure. Meanwhile, strategic writers contend that a company's structure is not predetermined in this way. Instead they say that it is always the outcome of a *choice* made by those in positions of power.

Contingency and technological determinism

Technological determinism
the argument that technology can explain the nature of jobs, skill and knowledge requirements, and organization structure.

Joan Woodward, James Thompson and Charles Perrow are the leading figures in the school of **technological determinism**. They all agree that technology requires that certain tasks be performed, and that this in turn determines jobs, organization structures and attitudes and behaviours. However, they differ both in the way in which they classify technologies, and in how they conceive of the relationship been technology and organization structure.

Joan Woodward and technological complexity

Joan Woodward was a British academic whose work from the 1950s continues to have an impact today for at least three reasons (Woodward, 1958). First, she created a typology for categorizing and describing different technologies, giving us a 'language' with which to discuss them. Second, by discovering that no single organization structure was appropriate for all circumstances, she ended the supremacy of classical management theory, and ushered in the modern, contingency approach to the design of organization structures. Third, by recognizing the impact of technology on organization design, she began a research tradition that has enhanced our understanding of the relation of new technologies to organizational forms.

Woodward studied 100 firms in south-east England. Having established their levels of performance, she correlated measures of company performance with different elements of organization structure which had been proposed by Weber, Fayol and other writers. These elements included the number of hierarchical levels, the span of control, the level of written communication, and so on. She had expected her analysis to reveal the relationship between some of these elements of organization structure and the level of company performance, but it failed to do so.

In her search for an alternative explanation, she noted that her firms used different technologies. She grouped their technologies into three main categories according to their systems of production – unit, mass and process. These were based on increasing **technical complexity** (1 = least complex; 10 = most complex) as shown in Figure 16.5. In unit production, one person works on a product from beginning to end – for example, a cabinetmaker producing a piece of hand-built furniture. In mass production, the technology requires each worker to make an individual contribution to a larger whole, such as fitting a windscreen on a car assembly line. In process production, workers do not touch the product, but monitor machinery and the automated production processes, such as in chemical plants and oil refineries. Technical complexity is usually related to the level of mechanization used in the production process.

Technical complexity
the degree of predictability about, and control over the final product permitted by the technology used.

STOP AND THINK

Woodward's classification of technologies is based on the manufacture of products. How well does it fit the provision of services? Consider services such as having your windows cleaned, buying a lottery ticket, insuring your car, or having a dental check-up, etc. What alternative classification system would you need for these?

Woodward (1965) discovered that a firm's organization structure was indeed related to its performance, but through an important, additional variable – technology. The 'best' or most appropriate organization structure – that is, the one associated with highest performance – depended (or was *contingent* upon) the type of technology employed by that firm. She introduced the concept of the 'technological imperative' – the view that technology determines an organization's structure. Specifically, she held that it was the complexity of the technology used that determined the structure.

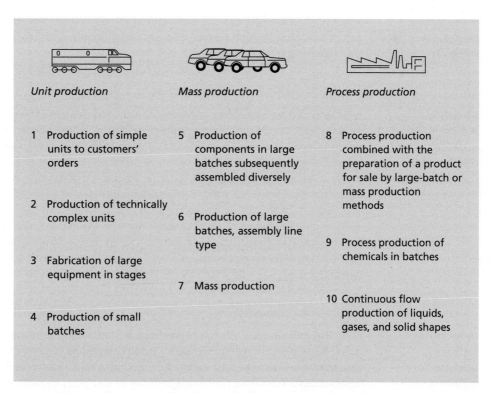

Figure 16.5: Woodward's classification of 100 British manufacturing firms according to their systems of production

Source: from Woodward (1958, p.11).

Woodward identified differences in the technical complexity of the process of production and examined the companies' organization structures. She found that as the technology became more complex (going from type 1 through to type 10) two main things occurred. First, the length of the chain of command increased, with the number of management levels rising from an average of three to six. The proportion of managers to the total employed workforce rose, as did the proportion of indirect to direct labour. Her second major finding was that the increasing complexity of technology meant that the chief executive's span of control increased, as did that of supervisors. The span of control of first-line supervisors was highest in mass production and lowest in process production. Span of control refers to the number of subordinates supervised by one manager and represents one of the ways of coordinating the activities of different employees.

Woodward argued that a relationship existed between a company's economic performance and its technology. Her conclusion was that 'there was a particular form of organization most appropriate to each technical situation' (Woodward, 1965, p.72). The reasoning underlying this conclusion is that the technology used to manufacture the product, or make available the service, places specific requirements on those who operate it. Such demands, for example in terms of the need for controlling work or motivating staff, are likely to be reflected in the organization structure. The technology–structure link is complemented by the notion of effective performance, which holds that each type of production system calls for its own characteristic organization structure.

> **Technological interdependence**
> the extent to which the work tasks performed in an organization by one department or team member affect the task performance of other departments or team members. Interdependence can be high or low.

James Thompson, technology and interdependence

The second contributor to the technological determinist perspective school was a sociologist, James Thompson (1967). He was not interested in the complexity of technologies (as was Woodward), but in the characteristic types of technological interdependence that each technology created. His argument was that different types of technology create different types of interdependence between individuals, teams, departments and firms. These specify the most appropriate type of coordination required, which, in turn, determines the structure needed (see Figure 16.6).

Mediating technology creates pooled interdependence

> **Mediating technology**
> technology that links independent but standardized tasks.

Mediating technology allows individuals, teams and departments to operate independently of each other. Pooled task interdependence results when each department or group member makes a separate and independent contribution to the company or team performance. The individual outputs are pooled. For example, lecturers running their own courses, secretaries in a firm, sales representatives on the road, insurance claims units, and supermarket checkout operators. Since each individual's performance can be easily identified and evaluated, the potential for conflict between departments or individuals is low.

Thus, predetermined rules, common forms and written procedures all act to coordinate the independent contributions of different units and separate employees, while clearly defined task and role relationships integrate the functions. This produces a bureaucratic organization form in which the costs of coordination are relatively low.

Long-linked technology creates sequential task interdependence

> **Long-linked technology**
> technology that is applied to a series of programmed tasks performed in a predetermined order.

Long-linked technology requires specific work tasks to be performed in a predetermined order. Sequential task interdependence results when one department, group or individual employee must perform their task before the next can complete theirs. For example, in an organizational behaviour course taught by three lecturers, sequential task interdependence means that the first one has to complete their sessions on individual psychology before the second can teach group psychology, followed by the third, who presents the material on organization structure. In a furniture factory, a cupboard has to be assembled before the handles can be attached. Sequential task interdependence means that a department's or

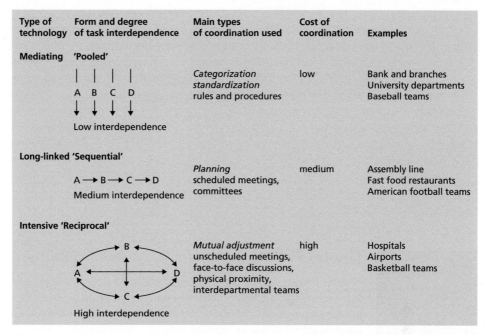

Figure 16.6: Thompson's typology of technology, interdependence and coordination

group member's performance cannot be easily identified or evaluated, as several individuals, groups or departments make a contribution to a single product or service.

At the company level, coordination is achieved through planning and scheduling which integrates the work of different departments. At the group level, coordination is achieved by close supervision of workers, forming work teams consisting of employees of similar levels of skills; and motivated by rewarding group rather than individual performance. The relative cost of coordination with this type of technology is medium.

Intensive technology creates reciprocal task interdependence

Intensive technology
technology that is applied to tasks that are performed in no predetermined order.

Intensive technology creates reciprocal interdependence, where all the activities of all the different company departments or all of the team members are fully dependent on one another. The work output of each serves as the input for another. For example, in an organizational behaviour course which uses the group project method, a group of students can call upon different lecturers to provide them with knowledge or skill inputs to enable them to solve the project problems. Each lecturer would notice what the other had done, and would contribute accordingly. For this reason, with reciprocal task interdependence, the sequence of required operations cannot be predetermined.

Thus, the mechanisms of coordination include unscheduled meetings, face-to-face contacts, project groups, task forces and cross-departmental teams. This in turns necessitates a close physical grouping of reciprocally interdependent units, so that mutual adjustment can be accomplished quickly. Where this is impossible, then mechanisms like daily meetings, email and teleconferencing are needed to facilitate communication. The degree of coordination required through mutual adjustment is much higher than what is necessary for the other technologies discussed, and is thus the most expensive of the three.

Team game metaphors

Robert Keidal (2014) argued that by using the games of baseball, American football and basketball as metaphors, and placing them within an integrated framework, it was possible to understand many organizations and their problems. Each game has its own structures, processes and player behaviours. With respect to *task interdependencies*, baseball exhibits pooled interdependence (each player makes a discrete contribution to the whole);

American football displays sequential interdependence (groups of players make serial, cumulative contributions); and basketball features reciprocal interdependence (in which all players interact in a back-and-forth manner). He gives examples of companies defined by each game: Salmon Brothers (ca. 1986), the late financial power-house, represents baseball; United Parcel Service (UPS) represents football; and Pixar Animation Studios repre-sents basketball.

Keidal goes on to argue that each sport represents its own key organizational variable. Baseball reflects the division of labour (autonomy); American football reflects hierarchy (control); and basketball reflects collaboration (cooperation). Nearly every complex organizational chal-lenge, he says, calls for a particular blend of these three variables. He recommends *triangular thinking*, which is the process of looking at organizational issues in terms of achieving a balance between these three variables. Together, these games, and the variables they represent, form a coherent, logical system or 'trade-off space' which managers can use to aid their critical thinking and assist their decision making.

Charles Perrow, technology and predictability

Charles Bryce Perrow (b.1925)

Task variety the number of new and different demands that a task places on an individual or a function.

Task analysability the degree to which standardized solutions are available to solve the problems that arise.

Charles Perrow (1970) is the third contributor to the technological determinist school. He saw technology's effect on organization structure as working through its impact on the predictability of providing the service or manufacturing a product. He considered two dimensions. The first he labelled **task variety**. This referred to the frequency with which unexpected events occurred in the transformation (inputs to outputs) process. Task variety would be high if many unexpected events occurred during a technological process. The second he termed **task analysability**. This refers to the degree to which the unexpected problems could be solved using readily available, off-the-shelf solutions. Task analysability would be low if individuals or departments had to search around for a solution and rely on experience, judgement, intuition and problem-solving skills, and high if they did not (see Figure 16.7).

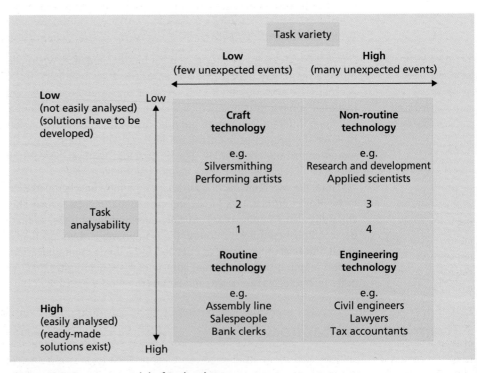

Figure 16.7: Perrow's model of technology

Source: from Perrow, Charles, *Organizational Analysis*, 1E. © 1970 Wadsworth, a part of Cengage Learning, Inc. Reproduced by permission. www.cengage.com/permissions.

Types of technology

On the basis of these two dimensions, Perrow categorized technologies into four types, and discussed the effects of each one upon an organization's structure. He was particularly interested in coordination mechanisms, discretion, the relative power of supervisors and the middle managers who supervised them.

1. *Routine technology*: In cell 1 are tasks which are simple and where variety is low (repetitive task). Task analysability is high (there are standard solutions available). Examples include supermarket checkout operations, and fast food restaurants.

2. *Craft technology*: In cell 2 is craft technology, characterized by low task variety and low task analysability. The number of new problems encountered is small, but each requires some effort to find a solution. Examples include a plumber fitting a bath or shower; an accountant preparing a tax return.

3. *Non-routine technology*: In cell 3 are complex and non-routine tasks, where task variability is high (with many new or different problems encountered), and task analysability is low (problem is difficult to solve). The tasks performed by research chemists, advertising agencies, high-tech product designers and top management teams are all examples of non-routine technology.

4. *Engineering technology*: In cell 4, engineering technology is characterized by high task variety and low task analysability. Many new problems crop up, but each is relatively simple to solve. Civil engineering companies which build roads and bridges exemplify this type of technology, as well as motor manufacturers producing customized cars.

When an organization's tasks and technology are routine, its structure is likely to resemble that proposed by Weber and Fayol. With a tall hierarchy, channels of authority and formal, standardized operating procedures are used to integrate the activities of individuals, groups, units and departments. In contrast, when a firm's tasks and technology become non-routine and complex, an organization will tend to use a flatter hierarchy, more cross-functional teamworking, greater face-to-face contact to allow individuals, groups units and departments to observe and mutually adjust to each other and to engage in decision making and problem solving. The differences between the two structures will be manifested in the number and types of formal rules and procedures used, the degree to which decision making is centralized, the skill levels of workers employed, the breadth of supervisors' span of control and the means used for communication and coordination.

Contingency and environmental determinism

Environmental determinism
the argument that internal organizational responses are primarily determined by external environmental factors.

Environmental complexity the range of external factors relevant to the activities of the organization; the more factors, the higher the complexity.

The second strand of determinism in organization structuring has been environmental. Several writers have had an interest in the relationship between a company's environment and its structure. Some of them argue that company success depends on securing a proper 'fit' or alignment between itself and its environment (see Chapter 2). For them, environmental determinism means that the environment determines organization structure. One prominent environmental determinist, Paul Lawrence, even said, 'Tell me what your environment is and I shall tell you what your organization ought to be' (Argyris, 1972, p.88).

The environmental determinists see the organization as being in constant interaction with its environment (see Figure 16.8). That environment consists of 'actors' or 'networks' (e.g. competitors, investors, customers). It includes the general economic situation, the market, the competitive scene and so on. Each organization has its own unique environment. The greater the number of actors or networks that are relevant to a given company, the more complex its environment is said to be. Organizations vary in the relative degree of their environmental complexity (Duncan, 1972, 1973, 1974, 1979).

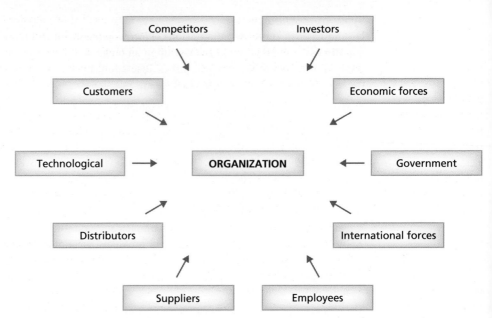

Figure 16.8: An organization depicted in its environment consisting of different actors, stakeholders and networks

Environmental dynamism the pace of change in relevant factors external to the organization; the greater the pace of change, the more dynamic the environment.

Those same actors and networks in an organization's environment can also change a great deal or remain the same. They thus differ in their degree of environmental dynamism. Different industries vary widely in their degree of dynamism. At one extreme of stability is the mainframe computer industry where new players must confront the barriers of an entrenched set of standards and the costs of switching are high. Here, the concepts of market segmentation, economies of scale and pre-emptive investment are all still important. Mainframe computers are not immune to change, as the PC revolution showed, but there are periods of considerable stability. In the middle of the range, one finds businesses like branded consumer goods. Substitution ranges from medium to high, and new entrants can replace established ones but not overnight. Survival and success depend upon capabilities and network relationships. Most industries are located in this middle ground. At the extreme of turbulence is a situation where customers can constantly and easily substitute. The environment consists of networks of players whose positions and prospects suddenly and unpredictably change. Many internet businesses are located at this end of the spectrum. For example, the popularity of the social networking website Facebook rapidly surpassed that of My Space, which had previously been dominant.

Environmental determinists argue that because a company is dependent on its environment for its sales, labour, raw materials and so on, that environment constrains the kind of choices an organization can make about how it structures itself. As the environmental situation changes, the organization–environment relationship also changes. Hence, to be effective, a company has to structure and restructure constantly to maintain alignment (or 'fit'). The environmental determinists use the key concepts of environmental uncertainty and complexity in their explanations.

Mechanistic and organic organization structures

In the late 1950s in Britain, Tom Burns (1914–2002) and George Stalker studied the behaviour of people working in a rayon mill. Rayon is a yarn or fibre produced by forcing and drawing cellulose through minute holes. They found that this economically successful company with contented staff was run with a management style which, according to contemporary wisdom about 'best' management practice, should have led to worker discontent and inefficiency. Some time later, the same authors studied an electronics company.

Mechanistic organization structure one that possesses a high degree of task specialization, many rules, tight specification of individual responsibility and authority, and centralized decision making.

Again it was highly successful, but used a management style completely different from that of the rayon mill studied earlier. This contradiction gave the authors the impetus to begin a large-scale investigation to examine the relationship between management systems and the organizational tasks. They were particularly interested in the way management systems changed in response to changes in the commercial and technical tasks of the firm (Burns and Stalker, 1961).

The rayon mill had a highly stable, highly structured character, which would have fitted well into Weber's bureaucratic organizational model. In contrast, the electronics firm violated many of the principles of classical management. It discouraged written communications, defined jobs as little as possible, and the interaction between employees was on a face-to-face basis. Indeed, staff even complained about this uncertainty. Burns and Stalker gave the label **mechanistic organization structure** to the former and **organic organization structure** to the latter (Table 16.5). These represented organization structures at opposite ends of a continuum. Most firms would be located somewhere in between.

Organic organization structure one that possesses little task specialization, few rules, a high degree of individual responsibility and authority, and one in which decision making is delegated.

Burns and Stalker argued that neither form of organization structure was intrinsically efficient or inefficient, but that rather that it all depended (was contingent) on the nature of the environment in which a firm operated. In their view, the key variables to be considered were the product market and the technology of the manufacturing process. These needed to be studied when the structure of a firm was being designed. Thus, a *mechanistic structure* may be appropriate for an organization which uses an unchanging technology and operates in relatively stable markets. An *organic structure* can be more suitable for a firm that has to cope with unpredictable new tasks. Later, Rosabeth Moss Kanter (1983) relabelled these two constructs *segmentalist* and *integrative*, and argued that segmentalist systems stifled creativity, while integrative ones were more innovative.

Table 16.5: Characteristics of mechanistic and organic organization structures

Characteristic	Rayon mill (mechanistic)	Electronics (organic)
Specialization	High – sharp differentiation	Low – no hard boundaries, relatively few different jobs
Standardization	High – methods spelled out	Low – individuals decide own methods
Orientation of members	Means	Goals
Conflict resolution	By superior	Interaction
Pattern of authority, control and communication	Hierarchical – based on implied contractual relation	Wide net based upon common commitment
Locus of superior competence	At top of organization	Wherever there is skill and competence
Interaction	Vertical	Lateral
Communication content	Directions, orders	Advice, information
Loyalty	To the organization	To project and group
Prestige	From the position	From personal contribution

Source: based on Litterer (1973, p.339).

Individual or structural problems?

In Britain, an enquiry into the conditions at the Mid Staffordshire NHS Foundation Trust Hospital between 2005 and 2009, which cost the lives of up to 1,200 patients, revealed a catalogue of hospital failures. Patients had been left unattended and food and water had often been unavailable. Robert Francis, the enquiry leader, condemned the 'appalling and unnecessary suffering'. He went on make 29 recommendations, which included persuading doctors to reveal their mistakes, teaching compassion to nurses and registering healthcare

→

assistants. Meanwhile, proposed government solutions included sending hospital board executives on training courses in error reduction and attracting 'elite managers'. Together, the message being sent was that the problem is 'bad' people, and that the solution has to be 'good' (or better) people.

Alan Fox criticized the 'psychologistic' approach, which explained behaviour in organizations in terms of individual's personalities and managerial leadership (which are clearly visible and easily understandable) while ignoring structural factors (which are hidden and less easy to grasp) (see the previous chapter). For example, the NHS faces the challenge of implementing structural reforms while protecting standards, and balancing local responsibility and central control. Simple sounding goals can be complicated by the scale and complexity of the NHS. Implementing Francis' proposals can create more organizational upheavals, known as 're-disorganizations' by staff who have experienced them in the past. Although not exposed to private competition, NHS hospitals do operate within a political climate which looks to assign blame for failure (*The Economist*, 2013).

Differentiated and integrated organization structures

Differentiation the degree to which the tasks and the work of individuals, groups and units are divided up within an organization.

During the 1960s, Paul Lawrence and Jay Lorsch (1967) built on the work of Burns and Stalker, using the concepts of *differentiation* and *integration*. First, consider differentiation. Differentiation refers to the process of a firm breaking itself up into subunits, each of which concentrates on a particular part of the firm's environment. A university differentiates itself in terms of different faculties and departments or colleges and schools. Such differentiation inevitably leads to the subunits developing their own goals, values, norms, structures, time frames and interpersonal relations that reflect the job that they have to do, and the uncertainties with which they have to cope.

Differentiation can take two forms. *Horizontal differentiation* is concerned with how work is divided up between the various company departments and who is responsible for which tasks. *Vertical differentiation* is concerned with who is given authority at the different levels of the company's hierarchy. High horizontal differentiation creates many different departments, producing a flat structure as shown on an organization chart. High vertical differentiation results in many hierarchical levels, creating a tall structure. Lawrence and Lorsch found that effective organizations increased their level of differentiation as their environment became more uncertain. These adjustments allowed staff to respond more effectively to their specific sub-environment for which they were responsible. On the other hand, the more differentiated the subunits became, the more their goals would diverge and this could lead to internal conflicts.

Integration the required level to which units in an organization are linked together, and their respective degree of independence.

Turning next to integration, this refers to coordinating the work performed in the previously divided (differentiated) departments, so as to ensure that it all contributes to accomplishing the organizational goal. Thus, having divided the university into faculties/departments or colleges/schools, there is the need to ensure that they all contribute to the goals of high-quality research, excellent teaching and income generation. Lawrence and Lorsch found that as environmental uncertainty increased, and thus the degree of differentiation increased, so organizations had to increase the level of their integration (coordination) between different departments and their staffs, if they were to work together effectively towards the common goal. Coordination is achieved through the use of rules, policies and procedures; goal clarification and communication; temporary task forces; permanent project teams; and liaison and integrator roles.

When environmental uncertainty is low, differentiation too is correspondingly low. Because the units share common goals and ways of achieving them, the hierarchy of authority in a company and its standard procedures are sufficient to integrate the activities of different units and individuals. However, as uncertainty increases, so too does the need for integration. While integration is expensive, using up the resources of time, money and effort, a failure to integrate can be equally problematic, leading to conflict between departments which has to be resolved. Lawrence and Lorsch argued that the level of uncertainty in the environment that a firm has to cope with, would determine the organization structure that was most appropriate for it.

How well are the activities performed by your educational institution differentiated and integrated? Identify the problems and recommend solutions that would improve organizational performance from the student perspective.

Strategic choice

The debate about contemporary organization design involves a consideration of the decisions that managers make about their organizations within their environments. Thus, strategic choice and environment are central concepts. Both Tom Burns and George Stalker (1961) and Paul Lawrence and Jay Lorsch (1967) stressed the importance of an organization's environment. Their original contributions were concerned primarily with the market conditions, and took a deterministic perspective. Their critics, however, pointed to the neglect of *choice* in decisions about organization structure. John Child (1972, 1997) rectified this omission, arguing that there was no one best organization structure, and that companies could have different structures. However, he disagreed with the contention that those structures were *determined* by 'external, operational contingencies'. Instead, he stressed the part played by powerful leaders and groups, who exerted their influence to create organization structures which suited their particular values and preferences.

Strategic choice
the view that an organization's environment, market and technology are the result of senior management decisions.

Strategic choice holds that managers who control an organization make a strategic choice about what kind of structure it will have. They also manipulate the context in which their company operates, and how its performance is measured. The decisions about the number of hierarchical levels, the span of control, division of labour and so on, are ultimately based on the personal beliefs and political manoeuvrings of the senior executives who make them. Strategic choice researchers continue to focus on companies' environments, but they have become interested in how senior managers make the choices that link their firms' strategies to their organization structures. Strategic choice researchers have criticized the deterministic writers on a number of issues:

1. *The idea that an organization should 'fit' its environment.* That is, while there are choices about organization structure design, these will be relatively limited. Thus, for two similar companies operating in a stable environment to succeed, each would make similar choices about the shape of their organization structures. However, there are examples of companies making very different structural choices in the same circumstances and both succeeding.

2. *The idea that cause and effect are linked in a simple (linear) manner.* This ignores the fact that organizations are part of a larger, complex environmental system consisting of other organizations with which they interact. Managers can influence and shape their own company environments. The idea that organizations merely adapt to their environment is too simple a view.

3. *The assumption that the choice of organization structure is an automatic reaction to the facts presented.* Studies show that decisions are made by managers on the basis of the interpretations that they have made about the nature of their environment. The same environment can be perceived in different ways, by various managers who might implement different structures, which can be equally effective.

4. *The view that choices of organization structure are not political.* Linked to the previous point, political factors will impinge on choices about structure as much as issues of perception and interpretation (see Chapter 22).

Child (1997) suggested that organization structuring was a political process in which power and influence were used to decide on the types of jobs, levels of hierarchy, spans of control, etc. that were to be adopted and, by implication, which markets to enter and which companies to link up with. His work stimulated discussion in three main areas:

- The human agents (individuals or groups) who exercise choice in the design of organizations.
- The nature of the environment within which an organization exists.
- The relationships between organizational agents (e.g. managers) and that environment.

Figure 16.9 summarizes the contrasting approaches to structuring organizations discussed in this chapter.

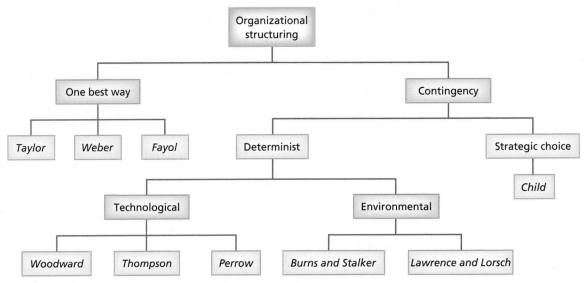

Figure 16.9: Contrasting theoretical approaches to organization structuring

Google restructures

In 2015, Google announced that it was changing the design of its organization. It created a new structure with a new, parent (holding) company called Alphabet Inc. which consists of a collection of different companies. Those companies which are not focused primarily on the internet, and which are unrelated to each other, have been separated out from Google, and set up on their own, as shown on the right-hand side of the organization chart. Not all of these will be familiar to consumers. Calico focuses on increasing human longevity; Fiber builds high-speed internet connections; Google Capital is its investment arm; Google Ventures is its venture-capital vehicle; X deals with moon shots, driverless cars, drone delivery, internet-delivering balloons and Google Glass; Life Sciences researches glucose-sensing contact lenses; Nest is a smart-home devices company; and Sidewalk Labs aims to improve cities.

Google remains the biggest company and a subsidiary within Alphabet. It contains most of the products that people are familiar with. At the time of writing the new structure has not yet been finalized. Its final organization structure is likely to resemble that shown in the organization chart. Job roles and titles were also changed. Larry Page, formerly Google's CEO, became CEO of Alphabet; Sergey Brin became President of Alphabet; and Eric Schmidt (previously Google chairman) became its executive chairman; while Sundar Pichai was appointed to be the CEO of a slimmed down Google.

In a blog post, Larry Page explained that Google had become a diverse group of businesses. Between 2001 and 2015 it had acquired over 180 other companies. The aim of the reorganization was to create a simpler organization structure that was 'cleaner and more accountable'. Internally the objective was to give these companies independence and the opportunity to develop their own brands. Externally, it was to give investors greater clarity about corporate strategy and a clearer idea of how much was being spent on new products (BBC Online News, 2015; Kleinman, 2015; Page, 2015).

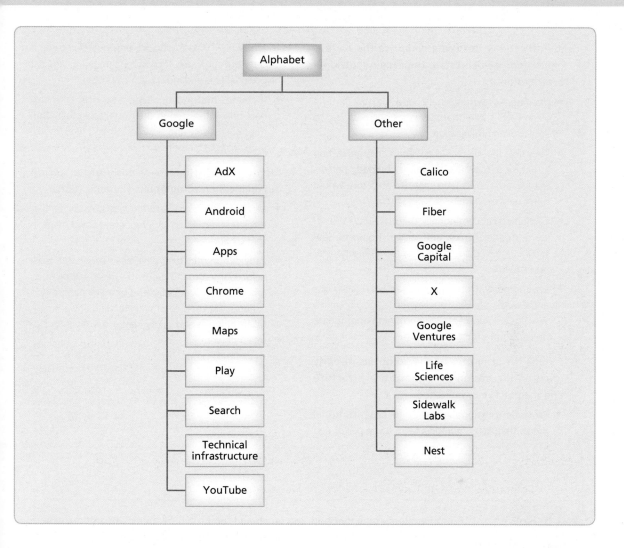

```
                        Alphabet

         Google                        Other

          AdX                           Calico

          Android                       Fiber

          Apps                          Google
                                        Capital

          Chrome                        X

          Maps                          Google
                                        Ventures

          Play                          Life
                                        Sciences

          Search                        Sidewalk
                                        Labs

          Technical                     Nest
          infrastructure

          YouTube
```

 RECAP

1. **Distinguish between charismatic, traditional and legitimate forms of authority.**

   - Traditional authority is based on the belief that the ruler has a natural right to rule.

   - Charismatic authority is based on the belief that the ruler has some special, unique virtue, either religious or heroic.

   - Legitimate authority is based on formal written rules which have the force of law.

2. **State the main characteristics of a bureaucratic organization structure as specified by Max Weber.**

   - Job specialization, authority hierarchy, formal selection, rules and procedures, impersonality and impartiality and recoding.

3. **Distinguish Fayol's six managerial activities and the main ideas of the classical management school.**

   - Fayol distinguished six managerial activities: forecasting, planning, organizing; commanding; coordinating and controlling.

   - The classical management school was based on the experience of managers and consultants rather than researchers.

4. **Distinguish Mintzberg's ten managerial roles.**

   - His ten managerial roles are figurehead, leader, liaison, monitor, disseminator, spokesperson, entrepreneur, disturbance handler, resource allocator and negotiator.

5. **Identify the writers who comprise the contingency approach and state their main individual contributions.**

   - Contingency writers challenged Max Weber and Henri Fayol's view that there was one best way to structure an organization.

   - They held that there was an optimum organization structure that would maximize company performance and profits, and that this structure would differ between firms.

   - Technological contingency theorists Joan Woodward, Charles Perrow and James Thompson saw technology as determining appropriate organization structure.

   - Environmental contingency theorists Tom Burns and Graham Stalker, Paul Lawrence and Jay Lorsch saw the environment as determining appropriate organization structure.

6. **Discuss the strengths and weaknesses of early ideas on the design of organization structure and the practice of management.**

   - Provides a rationally designed organizational model that allows complex tasks to be performed efficiently. Persons who are best qualified to do it carry out the work. It provides safeguards against personal bias and individual favouritism.

   - It creates dysfunctional consequences of members only interested in their own jobs, following rules obsessively and slow to respond to changes. Bureaucracies perpetuate themselves.

7. **Identify the influence of early organization design ideas on contemporary organizations.**

   - Modern organizations continue to possess the features first described by Weber and Fayol nearly a century ago.

   - Early design principles have been successful, have helped large organizations to survive and prosper, reflect the static social values of many nations and cultures, are capable of withstanding environmental turbulence and allow senior management to retain power.

Revision

1. Commentators argue that both too much and too little bureaucracy in an organization demotivates employees and causes them stress. How can this be?

2. How does uncertainty affect the successful operation of rationally designed organization structures such as those proposed by Weber and Fayol?

3. Define and distinguish differentiation from integration. Using an example from your experience or reading, illustrate these two processes in operation, and the highlight some of the problems that can be encountered.

4. Explain how technology and environment might influence the structure of an organization. Consider their effect on coordinating activities.

Research assignment

Interview a middle or senior manager about their organization's structure. This could be a relative, a family friend or a past employer. Ask them to assess the strengths and weaknesses of the current structure in terms of allowing them to do their job well or achieving company goals. What changes would they like to make if they could? Your analysis of their comments should be related back to the material in this and the previous chapter – e.g. type of structure possessed, hierarchy, span of control, etc.

Springboard

Thomas Diefenbach and Rune By (eds) (2012) *Reinventing Hierarchy and Bureaucracy: From the Bureau to Network Organizations*, Research in the Sociology of Organizations: Volume 35. Bingley, UK: Emerald Group Publishing. A contemporary assessment of the prevalence and impact of hierarchy and bureaucracy from the Stone Age period through to 'super flat' organizations of today and tomorrow.

Elliot Jaques (1990) 'In praise of hierarchy', *Harvard Business Review*, 68 (1): 127–33. The author makes the argument for a hierarchical organization structure and against a 'flat' organization.

Henry Mintzberg (2009) *Managing*. Harlow, Essex: Financial Times Prentice Hall. The author develops his original ideas on managerial roles incorporating the research of others over the past 30 years, and presents a general model of managing.

Jeffrey Pfeffer (2015) *Leadership BS*. London: Harper Collins. The author considers leadership within the context of organizations and the role of managers.

OB cinema

Crimson Tide (1995, director Tony Scott), DVD track 4, 0:25:00–0.31.33 (7 minutes). This is the story of how a global emergency provokes a power play on-board a US nuclear submarine, between the battle-hardened Captain Frank Ramsay (played by Gene Hackman) who 'goes by the book', and his Executive Officer, Lieutenant Commander Ron Hunter (Denzil Washington). The captain regularly runs a weapons systems readiness test in preparation for launching nuclear missiles. The clip begins with a loudspeaker announcement saying 'Attention all hands, the fire has been contained', and ends with Ramsey saying to Hunter 'We're here to defend democracy, not to practise it'.

As you watch this clip of the weapons test, identify an example of each of Weber's six principles of bureaucracy.

Bureaucratic principle	Examples
1. Work specialization	
2. Authority hierarchy	
3. Employment and career	
4. Recording	
5. Rules and regulations	
6. Impersonality and impartiality	

OB on the web

On YouTube, watch Gary Hamel's lectures 'Passion trumps intellect' (2:21), as he presents his hierarchy of human capabilities at work, and his 'Gary Hamel: reinventing the technology of human accomplishment' (16:32), where he considers the question of how to build organizations that are both fit for the future and fit for human beings. Give examples of how, in the past, the organizations have attempted to secure employee capabilities and suggest how managers might redesign their company structures for the future, to encourage and obtain the three employee capabilities located at the top of Hamel's hierarchy.

CHAPTER EXERCISES

1. Debra's diary

Objectives   1. To contrast managerial roles with managerial activities.

2. To identify examples of each.

Briefing   1. Remind yourself of Mintzberg's ten managerial roles and Fayol's six managerial activities.

2. Form groups and nominate a spokesperson.

3. Read the case *Debra's Day* and then:

   (a) Identify one example of each of the Mintzberg's ten roles (tasks 1–10).

   (b) Identify one example of each of the Fayol's six managerial activities engaged in by Debra (tasks 11–16).

Debra's diary   Debra is the chief executive of a large private hospital in London. In an effort to manage her time better, she kept a diary of the tasks she performed over a couple of days.

	Mintzberg	Fayol
1. Held a meeting with all staff to inform them about the government's new requirements for the feeding and management of elderly patients.		
2. Closed the ward with patient infection (MRSA) problem; instigated a 'deep clean' procedure to ensure that this outbreak within the hospital had been contained; and introduced a new hygiene management code of conduct.		
3. Had the opportunity to buy a CAT scanner at a huge discount price, if we acted immediately. I called each of the board members to get them to agree to the investment. Some were unsure, but I managed to persuade them.		
4. Went to the local radio station to represent the hospital, to be interviewed about our work and answer listeners' calls.		
5. Gave a presentation to a training course which clarified hospital goals, and stressed the importance of staff's role in achieving them.		
6. Had lunch with our local Member of Parliament and got advanced information about future trends in government healthcare policy and funding.		
7. Spent two hours surfing the web to discover how our hospital compares in terms of numbers of patients and staff as well as facilities, with our competitors here and abroad.		
8. Acted to resolve a dispute between a doctor in charge of the X-Ray department and the union representative, concerning technicians.		
9. Finalized the budgets for all the hospital departments in line with our income and organizational objectives.		
10. Gave a speech at the Effective Healthcare Conference describing our hospital's approach to waste management.		
11. Held a meeting with the different department heads to ensure nursing staff were being efficiently allocated to the different wards.		
12. Reviewed the food purchase data to ensure that all foodstuffs had been obtained in accordance with procedures laid down by the hospital, and that the quantities of food supplied by vendors had been specified.		

	Mintzberg	Fayol
13. Used internet to discover illness trends among the population so as to anticipate increases and decreases for our various medical services.		
14. Devised a new 'pay for performance' compensation system which ensured that those who had exceeded their targets were appropriately rewarded.		
15. In anticipation of the upcoming annual inspection, I compiled a list of tasks to be completed then assigned these to the various senior managers.		
16. Discussed with the board of directors how the expansion of our obesity care provision would be managed over the next five years.		

2. Simulating organizational design issues

Objectives

1. Understand how the organizational information processing requirements and uncertainty are affected by the characteristics of tasks, environment and people.

2. Consider different ways of structuring an organization to deal with uncertainty, either reducing information processing needs or by enhancing information processing capabilities.

Instructions

Read the following scenario, and respond to the questions as directed by your instructor.

Step 1 (30 minutes)

Imagine that you are a member of a group of 10–13 students who are competing with other teams to prepare an advertising poster for a local shop. Your client requires that your team's poster should contain at least three colours, some artwork, and an impactful phrase or caption that catches the attention of passers-by and is memorable. Your group has 30 minutes to decide how you will organize yourself to produce this poster. You have hired a management consultant to advise you. Your consultant recommends that:

- Your 'organization' should structure itself along functional lines. Dividing into three equal-sized subgroups, each will specialize in a different aspect of poster production The first will deal with poster layout (selection of poster size, shape, layout, colours, general arrangement); the second will focus on artwork (executing the drawings and lettering); while the third will decide on the choice of the written content.

- To avoid confusion about the different roles and responsibilities (and to avoid disruption) the three subgroups should be placed in separate but adjacent rooms.

- Each subgroup should appoint its own leader.

- Your 'organization' should also have an overall coordinator.

Which of your consultant's recommendations do you agree or disagree with? Give your reasons.

Step 2 (10 minutes)

After 20 minutes, each group submits a plan to the instructor describing how they have decided to organize themselves for their task. The plan can be in the form of an organization chart or a written statement. They indicate their areas or agreement and disagreement with the consultant's recommendations.

Step 3 (20 minutes):

The group(s) reform and discuss some of the following questions as directed by the instructor:

1. Consider the relationship between the nature of the task (poster production) and the consultant's proposed structure. Where does it match or mismatch? State its strengths and weaknesses.

→

2. Does the time pressure make the consultant's proposed structure more or less appropriate? Why?

3. Should the three sets of activities described be performed sequentially or concurrently? Give your reasons.

4. Is the hierarchical structure of the organization (three levels of coordination – workers, subgroup leaders, overall coordinator) and the physical separation of the three subgroups likely to help or hinder the achievement of the task? Explain.

5. What intergroup communication needs must be met for the task to be achieved?

6. What is likely to be the role of the three subgroup leaders?

7. What aspects of the task contribute to its uncertainty?

8. What are the implications of such task uncertainty for the coordination of activities?

9. What are the possible trade-offs between task specialization by subgroup, and the coordination of the activities between them?

These activities are adapted from J.W. French (1993) 'Simulating organizational design issues', *Journal of Management Education*, 17 (1): 110–13.

Employability assessment

With regard to your future employment prospects:

1. Identify up to three issues from this chapter that you found significant.

2. Relate these to the competencies in the employability matrix.

3. Decide what actions you need to take to maintain and/or develop those competencies under each of the four headings of the employability matrix.

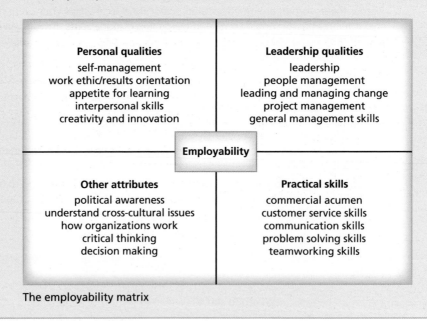

Personal qualities
self-management
work ethic/results orientation
appetite for learning
interpersonal skills
creativity and innovation

Leadership qualities
leadership
people management
leading and managing change
project management
general management skills

Employability

Other attributes
political awareness
understand cross-cultural issues
how organizations work
critical thinking
decision making

Practical skills
commercial acumen
customer service skills
communication skills
problem solving skills
teamworking skills

The employability matrix

References

Argyris, C. (1972) *The Applicability of Organizational Sociology*. London: Cambridge University Press.

Aronowitz, S., de Smet, A. and McGinty, D. (2015) 'Getting organizational redesign right', *McKinsey Quarterly*, June, pp.1–11.

BBC Online News website (2015) 'Google unveils surprise restructuring under Alphabet', 10 August.

Blau, P.M. (1966) *The Dynamics of Bureaucracy* (2nd edn). Chicago, IL: University of Chicago Press.

Burns, T. and Stalker, G.M. (1961) *The Management of Innovation*. London: Tavistock Publications.

Child, J. (1969) *British Management Thought*. London: George Allen and Unwin.

Child, J. (1972) 'Organizational structure, environment and performance: the role of strategic choice', *Sociology*, 6 (1): 1–22.

Child, J. (1997) 'Strategic choice in the analysis of action, structure, organizations and environments: retrospect and prospect', *Organization Studies*, 18 (1): 43–76.

Child, J. (2005) *Organization: Contemporary Principles and Practice* (1st edn). Oxford: Blackwell Publishing.

Child, J. (2015) *Organization: Contemporary Principles and Practice* (2nd edn). Chichester: Wiley.

Cichocki, P. and Irwin, C. (2014) *Organization Design: A Guide to Building Effective Organizations*. London: Kogan Page.

Diefenbach, T. and By, R.T. (2012) 'Bureaucracy and hierarchy – what else?', in Diefenbach, T. and By, R.T. (eds), *Reinventing Hierarchy and Bureaucracy: From the Bureau to Network Organizations*, Research in the Sociology of Organizations: Volume 35. Bingley, UK: Emerald Group Publishing.

Du Gay, P. (2005) *The Values of Bureaucracy*. Oxford: Oxford University Press.

Duncan, R.B. (1972) 'Characteristics of organizational environments and perceived environmental uncertainty', *Administrative Science Quarterly*, 17 (3): 313–27.

Duncan, R.B. (1973) 'Multiple decision making structures in adapting to environmental uncertainty: the impact on organizational effectiveness', *Human Relations*, 26 (3): 273–91.

Duncan, R.B. (1974) 'Modifications in decision making structures in adapting to the environment: some implications for organizational learning', *Decision Sciences*, 5 (4): 705–25.

Duncan, R.B. (1979) 'What is the right organization structure? Decision tree analysis provides the answer', *Organizational Dynamics*, 7 (3): 59–80.

Edwards, D. (2011) *I'm Feeling Lucky: The Confessions of Google Employee Number 59*. London: Allan Lane.

Fortune (2007) 'The big picture', 155 (4), 5 March, pp.57–64.

French, J.W. (1993) 'Simulating organizational design issues', *Journal of Management Education*, 17 (1): 110–13.

Galbraith, J. (2002) *Designing Organizations*. San Francisco: Jossey Bass.

Garvin, D.A. (2013) 'How Google sold its engineers on management', *Harvard Business Review*, 91 (12): 75–80.

Gouldner, A.W. (1954) *Patterns of Industrial Bureaucracy*. New York: Free Press.

Hall, R.H. (1963) 'The concept of bureaucracy: an empirical assessment', *American Journal of Sociology*, 69 (1): 32–40.

Handy, C. (1993) *Understanding Organizations* (4th edn). London: Penguin.

Jacobs, E. (2010) 'Sandy, sandy eggshell or eggy sand? What kind of khaki to wear to work?', *Financial Times*, 24 December, p.6.

Kanter, R.M. (1983) *The Change Masters: Corporate Entrepreneurs at Work*. London: George Allen & Unwin.

Kates, A. and Galbraith, J.R. (2010) *Designing Your Organization: Using the STAR Model to Solve 5 Critical Design Challenges*. San Francisco: Jossey Bass.

Kay, J. (2011) 'A smart business dressed in principles not rules', *Financial Times*, 12 January, p.11.

Keidel, R.W. (2014) 'Team sports metaphors in perspective', *Organizational Dynamics*, 43 (4): 294–302.

Kleinman, Z. (2015) 'What else does Google's Alphabet do?', *BBC News website*, 11 August.

Lawrence, P.R. and Lorsch, J.W. (1967) *Organization and Environment*. Boston, MA: Addison Wesley.

Leavitt, H.J. (2005) *Top Down: Why Hierarchies are Here to Stay and How to Manage Them More Effectively*. Boston, MA: Harvard Business School Press.

Litterer, J.A. (1973) *The Analysis of Organizations*. Chichester: John Wiley.

March, J. and Simon, H.A. (1958) *Organizations*. New York: Wiley.

Merton, R.K. (1939/1940) 'Bureaucratic structure and personality', *Social Forces*, 18 (1/4): 560–68.

Mintzberg, H. (1973) *The Nature of Managerial Work*. London: Harper Collins.

Mintzberg, H. (1975) 'The manager's job: folklore and fact', *Harvard Business Review*, 53 (4): 49–61.

Mintzberg, H. (2009) *Managing*. Harlow, Essex: Financial Times Prentice Hall.

Morgan, G. (1989) *Creative Organization Theory*. London: Sage Publications.

Page, L. (2015) 'Google announces plans for new operating structure', 10 August, https://investor.google.com/releases/2015/0810.html

Perrow, C. (1970) *Organizational Analysis: A Sociological View*. Belmont, CA: Wadsworth.

Peters, T.J. and Waterman, R.H. (1982) *In Search of Excellence: Lessons from America's Best Run Companies.* New York: Harper & Row.

Pfeffer, J. (1981) *Power in Organizations.* London: Harper Collins.

Pfeffer, J. (2015) *Leadership BS.* London: Harper Collins.

Robbins, S.P. (1990) *Organization Theory.* Englewood Cliffs, NJ: Prentice Hall.

Robbins, S.P. and Coulter, M. (2009) *Management.* Upper Saddle River, NJ: Pearson Education Inc.

Sparkes, I. and Salkeid, L. (2010) 'No sexiness in the city: female staff ordered to wear loose-fitting skirts and flesh-coloured underwear by UBS', *MailOnline*, 16 December, www.dailymail.co.uk/news/article-1338871/No-sexiness-city-Female-staff-ordered-wear-flesh-coloured-underwear-UBS.html

The Economist (2006) 'The airliner that fell to earth', 7 October.

The Economist (2011) 'It's jungle out there', 22 October, p.79.

The Economist (2012) 'Banking against Doomsday', 10 March, p.67.

The Economist (2013) 'After the fall', 9 February, p.28.

Thomas, A.B. (2003) *Controversies in Management* (2nd edn). London: Routledge.

Thompson, J.D. (1967) *Organizations in Action.* New York: McGraw Hill.

Weber, M. (1947) *The Theory of Social and Economic Organization* (A. M. Henderson & T. Parsons, Trans.). Oxford: Oxford University Press.

Wise, J. (2014) 'How to debug a jet', *Bloomberg Businessweek*, 17 February, pp.52–57.

Woodward, J. (1958) *Management and Technology.* London: HMSO.

Woodward, J. (1965) *Industrial Organization: Theory and Practice.* Oxford: Oxford University Press.

Chapter 17 **Organizational architecture**

Key terms

meta-organization

organizational architecture

departmentalization

functional structure

divisional structure

matrix structure

team-based structure

cross-functional team

boundaryless organization

collaborative relationship structure

outsourcing

offshoring

reshoring

hollow organization structure

modular organization structure

virtual organization structure

co-opetition

strategic alliance

joint venture

user contribution system

crowdsourcing

on-demand companies

Learning outcomes

When you have read this chapter, you should be able to define those key terms in your own words, and you should also be able to:

1. Appreciate the reason for chief executives' need to design and redesign their organization's structure.

2. Distinguish three eras of organizational design and what factors stimulated each.

3. Distinguish between functional, divisional, matrix and team-based organization structures.

4. Distinguish between an outsourcing relationship and hollow, modular and virtual organization structures.

5. Understand the trend towards companies' collaborative relationships with competitors and customers, and their involvement in virtual communities.

Why study organizational architecture?

Work has increasingly become 'net work', done in a self-organized way that relies on individual initiative and is performed in a collaborative, negotiated fashion, rather than through management fiat (Halgin et al., 2015). Dimitrina Dimitrova and Barry Wellman (2015, p.443) write that 'Changing social norms have resulted in new ways of organizing that in turn affect how people work with colleagues, use information technology, find information, advice and guidance, and where they set up shop'. Gulati et al. (2012) use the term **meta-organization** to refer to networks of firms or individuals not bound by authority-based employment relationships but characterized by a system-level goal.

Meta-organization networks of firms or individuals not bound by authority-based employment relationships but characterized by a system-level goal.

Many companies have become networked as a result of the 'triple revolution' – the impact of social networks, the internet and mobile platforms (Rainie and Wellman, 2012). Networked organizations are judged to be able to respond rapidly to uncertainty. They have been described as 'choardic' – able to generate order out of chaos (Child, 2015). They can reshape the way that employees work and how they themselves function because they are coordinated by social networks, and are better at exchanging information. All these changes have affected companies' organization structures, authority relations and information flows. They are challenging the traditional, hierarchical organizational structures of present-day companies.

This 'beyond the organization' trend is changing the relationships between different organizations, between organizations and their owners, between their employees and their consumers, and is creating new organizational forms (Miles et al., 2010). Traditional firms in sectors such as car manufacture, pharmaceuticals and media have begun collaborating with each other for mutual benefit. But what exactly constitutes a 'new' organizational form? Puranam et al. (2014) argue that an organization's structure can be conceptualized as offering solutions to four problems that all organizations face:

- *Novelty in task division* – new ways of converting company goals into individual and group tasks. How can one identify and arrange the performance of interrelated sub-tasks and their associated information transfers, to allow the achievement of organizational goals?

  In the warehouse, every task a worker performs is dispensed electronically and tracked. A central computer coordinates and individually tailors work for each employee. It assigns order-fillers their discrete tasks which come packaged as 'trips.' Each employee receives a wireless mini-computer and headset and a vehicle for moving the goods. The computer directs order-fillers to their collection points using voice-guided instructions. Operators deliver their loads to the dispatch dock and the computer then directs them to their next trip. It records how quickly each employee has completed their last trip and informs them of their cumulative shift performance. (Elliott and Long, 2016)

- *Novelty in task allocation* – new ways of assigning employees to tasks (e.g. contributors self-select themselves to perform the tasks that they prefer rather than being assigned them by someone in authority).

  At Oticon, a Danish manufacturer of hearing aids, project leaders with an idea compete to attract resources and recruit staff to deliver results. Employees themselves decide whether or not to join a project team and could be members of the 100 or so projects that exist at any one time. Project teams are formed and reformed on a regular basis (Foss, 2003). At Lync, a company producing audio visual conferencing and instant messaging systems, rather than have the four managers pick their team members, the 85 individual staff, acting as free agents, choose which of the four teams they want to join (Birkinshaw, 2013).

- *Novelty in reward distribution* – new ways of rewarding contributors (e.g. stress on intrinsic rewards based on the task itself; peer evaluation; reputation enhancement; financial rewards going beyond wages).

At Google, intrinsic rewards for employees come from 'building cool stuff for users'. As regards extrinsic rewards, every employee, at every level in every country, is eligible for share options, which are based on their contribution and performance. These are not distributed equally as exceptional performance can have a disproportionally great impact on the company. Hence, Google's compensation system allows an employee to receive between two and ten times more than a colleague in the form of bonuses and shares. The company uses the 'just allocation of extreme rewards based on distributive and procedural justice'. Employees can also reward each other for great work 'above-and-beyond' individual contribution using the *gThanks* programme (pounced 'gee thanks'). The company also rewards 'thoughtful failure' so as to support and encourage a culture of risk taking (Bock, 2015).

- *Novelty in information provision* – new ways of creating shared knowledge using IT to enable the coordination of activities of often geographically dispersed contributors, creating new modular architecture which allows different individuals to work independently but in parallel.

  Google's code base, the collection of source code that makes all its products work, which includes its algorithms, is made available to all employees, including new hires, on their first day at work. The company intranet shows what everyone else is working on. The company shares all this information and expects Googlers to keep it confidential. Weekly TGIF ('Thank Goodness It's Friday') meetings hosted by Page and Brin include Q&A sessions for the entire company where thousands attend in person, and others through online rebroadcast. Everyone in the company knows what is going on. This avoids groups doing redundant work without knowing it and wasting resources; it clarifies differences in the goals of different groups; and it avoids internal rivalry (Bock, 2015).

Organizational architecture the framework of linked internal and external elements that an organization creates and uses to achieve the goals specified in its mission statement.

The term **organizational architecture** refers to the framework of linked internal and external elements that an organization creates and uses to achieve the goals specified in its mission statement. It thus not only includes the internal arrangements that a firm makes to deploy its various business processes, but also includes linkages to outsiders (other individuals, groups and organizations) who come together to form a temporary system for mutual benefit. The first part of this chapter will focus on internal structural arrangements, while the second part will consider external linkages.

Organizational structures had been a way of institutionalizing and managing stability, but now they have had to become far more flexible and adaptive to accommodate uncertainty in the form of discontinuous, disruptive change. In the past, it was thought that an organizational arrangement whereby the company performed all its tasks internally was the best way to gain competitive advantage. Now, working with others has come to be seen as the best way to reduce costs and increase efficiency and productivity. Consequently, answers to the question of 'who does what' now extend beyond the organization's own boundary to encompass its partners, competitors, customers and other communities of interest. Meta-organizations address the question of how to organize relations between legally autonomous entities, whether firms in a network or individuals in a community, without recourse to the authority inherent in employment contracts (although other forms of contract may play a role).

Historically, the initial problem for management was building and maintaining large-scale production processes and the organizations that operated them. Then attention focused on coordinating and controlling these large, complex organizations and facilitating their orderly growth. Most recently, the focus has shifted onto inter-organizational relationships. Building on the work of Robert Duncan (1979), Narasimhan Anand and Richard Daft (2007) traced the changes in the design of organization structures. They distinguish three eras of organizational design, shown in Table 17.1, illustrating how management thinking about organization structure changed from vertical organization to horizontal organizing, and now to boundaryless hollow, modular, virtual and collaborative structures. In this chapter, we shall draw heavily on these authors' explanatory structure and use their framework to compare and contrast the changes that have occurred in the design of organizations.

Table 17.1: Eras of organizational design

Era 1	Era 2	Era 3			
Mid-1800s to late 1970s	1980s to mid-1990s	Mid-1990s to date			
Self-contained vertical organization structures	Self-contained horizontal organization structures	Boundaryless organization structure			
		Hollow	Modular	Virtual	Collaborative

Source: based on Anand and Daft (2007)

STOP AND THINK   Think of an example of a change to the structure of an organization with which you are familiar. How has this changed the way that you and others do your work?

Era of self-contained organization structures

The first era identified by Anand and Daft (2007) lasted over a century from the mid-1800s to the late 1970s. During that time, the ideal organization was held to possess the following characteristics:

- self-contained;
- having clear boundaries between itself and its suppliers, customers and competitors;
- transforming the inputs from suppliers into completed products or services;
- meeting its transformation process requirements internally;
- hierarchically based.

Fjeldstad et al. (2012) stressed that these self-contained organizations were based on hierarchy which was used for both control and coordination. It involved setting goals, monitoring their fulfilment, allocating resources and managing interdependencies.

Departmentalization the process of grouping together activities and employees who share a common supervisor and resources, who are jointly responsible for performance, and who tend to identify and collaborate with each other.

Their design emphasized the need to adapt to environmental conditions, and to maximize control through reporting relationships and a vertical chain of command (Galbraith, 1973). Anand and Daft (2007, p.335) list the underlying design principles of a self-contained organization structure as:

- group people into functions or departments;
- establish reporting relationships between people and departments;
- provide systems to coordinate and integrate activities both horizontally and vertically.

A department designates a distinct area or branch of an organization over which a manager has authority for the performance of specified activities. Thus job grouping or the **departmentalization** of jobs constitutes an important aspect of organizational design. During this era, the functional, divisional and matrix organization structures became popular. All three rely on vertical hierarchy and the chain of command.

Functional structure an organizational design that groups activities and people according to the similarities in their work, profession, expertise, goals or resources used.

Functional structure

A **functional structure** groups its activities and people, from the bottom to the top, according to the similarities in their work, profession, expertise, goals or resources used – e.g. production, marketing, sales and finance (Figure 17.1). Each functional activity is grouped into a specific department. A university business school may group its staff into the main subject fields (finance, human behaviour; strategy, marketing and operations management).

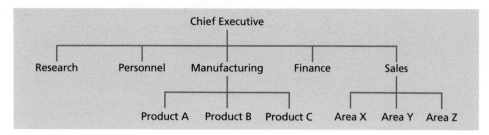

Figure 17.1: Functional organization structure

Divisional structure

Divisional structure
an organizational
design that groups
departments together
based on the product
sold, the geographical
area operated in, or the
type of customer served.

A **divisional structure** divides an organization up into self-contained entities based on their organizational outputs – products or services provided, the geographical region operated in or the customer groups served. Each division is likely to have its own functional structure replicated within it or receive functional support (e.g. marketing, human resources) from its headquarters. Each division operates as a stand-alone company, doing its own research, production, marketing, etc. (Chandler, 1962). British hospitals are increasingly divisionalized, with surgery and medical diagnostics receiving support from finance and estates.

Product-based: A single motor company can organize around its different automotive brands. For example, Daimler's divisions include Mercedes-Benz and Smart, while BMW's include BMW and Mini. Most university business schools offer undergraduate, postgraduate and non-graduating courses. A product or service-based organization structure is shown in Figure 17.2.

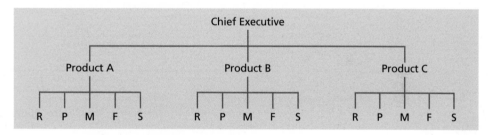

Figure 17.2: Product-based organization structure

Geography-based: Grouping on this basis is used where the product or service is provided within a limited distance. It meets customers' needs effectively and economically, and lets senior management check and control how these are provided. Hotels and supermarkets are organized in this way, so are ferry companies based on particular sea routes. A university business school may have a main campus, a city centre location and an out-of-town residential (hotel) facility. A geography-based organization structure is shown in Figure 17.3.

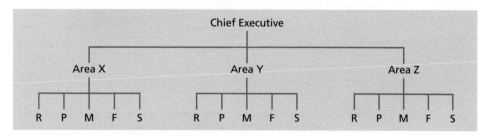

Figure 17.3: Geography-based organization structure

Customer-based: The company can be structured around its main customers or market segments. A large bank's departments may be personal, private, business and corporate.

A university business school's clients include students, companies and research-funders. BT was divided into BT Retail (business and residential customers) and BT Wholesale (corporate customers). A customer-based organization structure is shown in Figure 17.4.

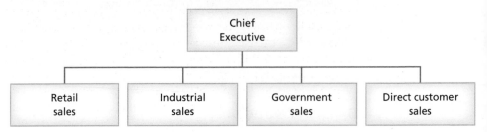

Figure 17.4: Customer-based organization structure

Matrix structure

Matrix structure
an organizational
design that combines
two different types of
structure resulting in an
employee having two
reporting relationships
simultaneously.

A **matrix structure** combines a vertical structure with a strong horizontal overlay. The former provides downward control over the functional departments, and the latter allows interdepartmental coordination This structure comprises employees working in temporary teams composed of employees from different functions (e.g. marketing, human resources, production) contributing to specific projects. This structure has two lines of authority. Each team member reports to two bosses – their project team manager and their functional (department) manager (e.g. the head of production). There is thus a dual, rather than a single, chain of command. A matrix organization structure is shown in Figure 17.5.

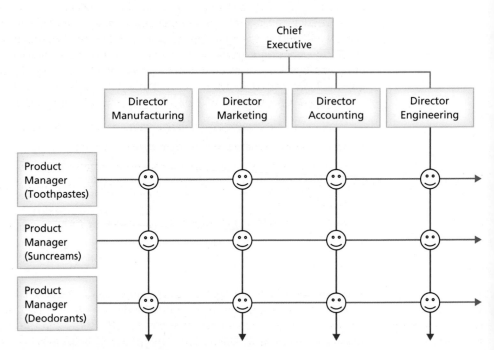

— The director of each functional department exercises line authority through the vertical chain of command.

— The product manager exercises authority through the horizontal chain of command, over those staff from the functional departments who have been assigned to work on the product.

☺ Employees at the intersections have two bosses. They report simultaneously to the director of their functional department (manufacturing, marketing, accounting, or engineering) as well as to their product manager (toothpastes, suncreams, or deodorants).

Figure 17.5: Matrix organization structure

As a student, the most likely place that you are likely to encounter a matrix structure is on your university course or module, if it is taught by lecturers from a number of different university departments. These contributing lecturers report to two different bosses. One of these is responsible for the function, in this case their university academic department (e.g. Accounting, Economics, Law or Management). Their other 'boss' is the course or module coordinator responsible for the teaching, tutoring and assessments for the module.

Matrix structures can cause problems (Davis and Lawrence, 1978). Jon Katzenbach and Adam Michaels (2013) argue that when matrix organizations fail, it is often the result of a focus on structure to the exclusion of culture (see Chapter 4). The formal elements of organization design are normally addressed – the organization chart is altered, who reports to whom is specified and decision-making responsibilities are assigned. However, the cultural changes needed to support the newly created matrix structure are typically ignored. Changing structure is comparatively easy – roles, job titles and departments are concrete and visible. In contrast, the cultural norms, values and beliefs that form the web that connects people together, and influences how they do their daily work, is intangible and difficult to define and map. They stress that in a matrix structure, collaboration between different departments requires a culture that encourages behaviours such as openness, a willingness to try new things and an acceptance of mistakes.

Era of horizontal organization structures

The second era identified by Anand and Daft (2007) lasted from the 1980s to the mid-1990s. It promoted horizontal organization structures with a team- and process-based emphasis. It developed in response to the limitations of the earlier organization structures. These included difficulties of interdepartmental coordination, the ineffectiveness of vertical authority-based reporting systems, and the new opportunities offered by computers and networks to increase organizational information processing capacity. During this time, emphasis was placed on reshaping (eliminating) organizations' internal boundaries to improve horizontal coordination and communication. Anand and Daft (2007, p.332) list the underlying design principles of a horizontal organization structure as:

- organize around complete workflow processes rather than tasks;
- flatten hierarchy and use teams to manage everything;
- appoint team leaders to manage internal team processes and coordinate work;
- permit team members to interact with suppliers and customers facilitating quick adaptation;
- provide required expertise from outside the team as required.

Team-based structure

Team-based structure an organizational design that consists entirely of project-type teams that focus on processes rather than individual jobs, coordinate their activities, and work directly with partners and customers to achieve their goals.

The above principles were predominantly implemented by means of a team-based structure, which treats teams as the organizing units of work. The company uses teams as the main way to coordinate the activities within it (Forrester and Drexler, 1999). Here, individual employees are assembled into teams in a way similar to being assigned to traditional, functional departments. In one version, the organization consists *entirely* of different teams, each of which coordinates their own activities, and works with their partners and customers, to achieve their goals. Each team member possesses a different expertise (e.g. marketing, manufacturing, finance, human resources), which contributes to the team's completion of its task or project. Team-based organizations have flattened hierarchies. This involves designing organizations around processes rather than tasks (Mohrman et al., 1997). The teams focus on processes that need to be done rather than on individual jobs. In order for the different members to coordinate their contributions successfully, they must share information effectively with each other (Cherns, 1976).

These teams are characterized by horizontal communication, shared or rotated leadership and delegated decision making that gives authority to junior staff to make decisions on their own. Once the goal has been achieved, the team moves onto a new project, perhaps reforming its membership before doing so. A true team-based structure is rarely found in organizations. Where it does exist, it tends to be in smaller organizations. A team structure is very flat, as shown in Figure 17.6. A university department may use a team structure. Academic staff may be members of a multidisciplinary research team contributing to a project funded by a research council; a teaching team responsible for delivering lectures and tutorials; and an administrative team, ensuring rooms are booked, student grades awarded and legal requirements complied with.

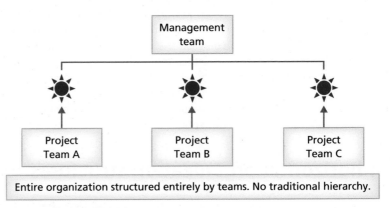

Figure 17.6: Team-based organization structure

An example of an organization with a team-based structure is Square D, a large US manufacturer of electrical equipment based in Lexington, Kentucky. In 1998, the company divided its 800 employees into 20–30 self-managed teams which were wholly responsible for their own products from start to finish. Another rare example is Whole Food Markets Inc., also in the United States, a retailer of natural foods. Each of its shops is an autonomous profit centre consisting of about ten teams. Each small, decentralized team (e.g. grocery, vegetables, bakery, prepared food) has its own team leader. It also has complete control over recruiting and selecting new employees. Using team-based hiring, after 90 days, potential hires need two-thirds of the team's support to join the staff permanently (Erickson and Gratton, 2007). The team leaders in each shop are a team; the shop leaders in each region are a team; and the company's six regional presidents are also a team (Fishman, 2007).

Self-management at Morning Star

Gary Hamel (2011) listed the problems with companies having a hierarchy of managers, saying that it:

- incurred a significant cost in managers' wages;
- skewed or killed decision making by creating numerous approval layers;
- increased the likelihood of calamitous decisions as top managers were furthest away from frontline realities;
- created centralized decision making that prevented poor decisions being challenged;
- disenfranchised low-level employees, reducing their scope of authority, creativity and contributions.

Organizations require coordination and control, but is there a way of securing the benefits of flexibility and the discipline of a tightly knit hierarchy, without the necessity to have a management superstructure? Hamel gives the example of Morning Star, a private company in California. It was started in 1970 as a one-truck owner-operator transporting tomatoes. Today the company is the world's largest tomato processor, a global market leader with double-digit growth for the past 20 years, with revenues of $700 million a year. It has no bosses or titles and no promotions; its employees negotiate responsibilities with their peers; everyone can spend the company's money; individuals are responsible for acquiring the tools needed to do their jobs; and compensation decisions are peer-based.

Morning Star's organizational vision is to create a company in which all team members (associates) will be self-managing professionals, initiating communications and coordinating their activities with their colleagues, customers, suppliers and fellow industry participants, without the need for direction from others. To achieve this, the company employs a management model built on the principle of self-management which contains six key elements:

- *Personal mission statements.* Employees prepare personal mission statements detailing how they will contribute to the company's goal. Each is responsible for achieving their own mission, and acquiring the necessary training, resources and cooperation to do so.

- *CLOU agreements.* Annually, all employees negotiate a Colleague Letter of Understanding with those who are most affected by their work. These form the operating plan that provides the coordination and structure necessary to achieve the mission. It covers 30 activity areas and details the performance metrics for each.

- *Empowerment of employees.* Decision-making authority is given to frontline employees. It allows them to hire staff when they feel overloaded or new roles need filling, and to purchase tools and equipment needed to do their jobs.

- *No role descriptions.* Roles are not centrally defined, thereby allowing employees to take on greater responsibilities as they gain experience and develop their skills. This encourages staff to drive change beyond their immediate areas of work responsibility, thereby creating innovation.

- *Competition for impact.* The lack of a hierarchy, job titles and a career ladder means that competition becomes focused on who can contribute most to the company. Career progression involves mastering new skills and discovering better ways of serving colleagues. It is reflected in differing compensation levels.

- *Freedom to succeed.* Giving employees freedom to do the things they like. This creates enthusiasm and better performance. However, to exercise their freedom wisely, employees have to assess the impact of decisions, and that is why all teams have their own profit-and-loss accounts.

How then is control exercised, when no one is in charge?

- *Targets and data.* Some 3,000 CLOUs cover Morning Star's full-time employees, provide a high degree of coordination. Their metrics allow employees to check if they are meeting associates' needs; people are held accountable for results; and they receive cross-company information allowing them to see how they influence other areas.

- *Calculation and consultation.* Before spending any company money, employees have to build a business case for doing so, detailing the expected return on investment. They have to consult colleagues, persuade them, and gain their agreement.

- *Conflict resolution.* How is underperformance or failure to meet CLOU commitments to others dealt with? Initially the two parties meet to resolve the matter. Unresolved issues are taken to a mutually acceptable mediator; then, if necessary, further to a panel of six colleagues; and if not resolved there; to the president who makes a binding decision.

- *Peer review and challenge.* At the end of each year, individuals receive feedback from their CLOU colleagues. Business units defend their previous year's performance, justifying their use of resources, acknowledging shortfalls, and presenting improvement plans.

- *Elected compensation committees.* At the end of each year, all employees assess how they performed in terms of their CLOU goals, return on investment targets and other metrics. Staff elect local compensation committees which check these self-assessments and uncover unreported contributions. It uses this data to set individual compensation levels to ensure that pay matches the value that the employee has added to the company.

There have been various other company attempts to collapse organizational hierarchies; establish managerless systems; and create boss-free, employee-empowered, self-organizing team work environments. These include firms such as Zappos, the US online shoe retailer owned by Amazon (*The Economist*, 2014); WL Gore & Associates (maker of Gore-Tex fabric); Valve, a Washington videogames maker (Kelion, 2013); and 6Wunderkinder, a Berlin management software development company (Vasagar, 2014). The newest manifestation of this old idea is labelled *holacracy* – 'a way of running an organization that removes power from a management hierarchy and distributes it across roles' (www.holacracy.org).

Rather than totally eliminate managers, it is far more common for a traditional, vertically structured company to add teams to the bottom of its hierarchy. Only lower-level employees, those who manufacture the product or provide the service, come to operate as teams rather than as individuals. When this type of work arrangement is used on a regular basis, the organization may claim to be using a team-based structure. In reality, however, all that has happened is that it has grafted a teamworking format onto the lower hierarchical levels of an existing functional or divisional structure. Its organizational chart will look like that shown in Figure 17.7.

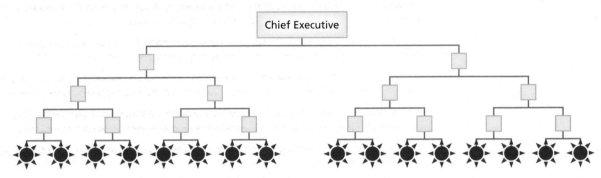

Figure 17.7: Traditional organization structure with teams at lowest level

Cross-functional team employees from different functional departments who meet as a team to complete a particular task.

This 'teams-at-the-bottom' structure may use a **cross-functional team** approach in which a number of teams consisting of employees from various functional departments, at about the same hierarchical level, are formed to complete particular tasks. As before, the benefits of this arrangement include access to the different expertise of members, improved horizontal communication and better inter-departmental coordination. Typical issues addressed by cross-functional teams are solving a problem, developing or launching a new product, or initiating a change programme. The development of the Ford Motor Company's Escape gas-electric hybrid sports utility vehicle involved cross-functional teamworking.

Boeing's production teams

The 787 Dreamliner is a medium-sized, wide-bodied, twin-engine jet capable of carrying 210 to 330 passengers. To produce it, the company created an organization structure consisting of Life Cycle Product Teams (LCPT) that have responsibility for the life-cycle cost of their product. Each LCPT has a team leader, an engineering leader, a manufacturing leader, finance and business leader and a global partner leader, and has responsibility for the design, production and delivery of their product on schedule and on cost to the 787 programme. The LCPTs operate like companies within the bigger programme. They are of two types – vertical and horizontal.

The horizontals are the departments, the functions which are also called the 'chimneys'. In the case of Boeing, these are Fuselage, Interior, Wing Empennage and Gear, and Propulsion. The verticals are the project trams which cut across these functional departments and are called Systems, Production Operations and Services. Thus, if you were a Boeing employee you would be both a member of the Fuselage department reporting to your Fuselage department boss and, simultaneously, a member of the Systems team reporting to your Systems project boss.

Final assembly of 787 aeroplane

Vertical LCPTs are responsible for the plane's structural components such as fuselage, interior, wings, propulsion, vertical tail, and the landing gear. Their task is to deliver their product into final assembly, where it all gets integrated with the others and built into the aeroplane. Horizontal LCPTs address matters relevant to all the different structural component teams. They are labelled systems, services and production operations. The Systems LCPT is responsible for the architecture, testing and the systems that go into the aeroplane. It ensures that the systems architecture for hydraulics, electrical and other systems on the airplane are all integrated. The Services LCPT is responsible for obtaining the input for the structural repair manual which comes from managers in the horizontal teams. The Production Operations LCPT is responsible for putting this aeroplane together and their work begins once final assembly is initiated (Dodge, 2007a; 2007b).

There are many different structural forms that era 1 and era 2 organizations can take. To help our understanding, Christopher Mabey (1998) and his colleagues offered a conceptual framework based on the juxtaposition of three dimensions. These distinguish firms with different internal structures, but all of them exist within conventional organizational boundaries. These authors' three dimensions are:

Decision making: Organizational structures differ in terms of where decisions are made. They range from centralized (decisions made at the top) through to decentralized (power delegated for people to make decisions lower in the hierarchy).

Rules prevalence: Companies differ in terms of how many written rules, operating procedures, job descriptions, organizational charts they have, and their use of formal, written communication. This dimension is called formalization, and ranges from few rules to many rules.

Size of organization: Firms differ in size. The size dimension is usually measured in terms of the number of employees and ranges from large to small.

As summarized in Table 17.2, organizations have structures based on the main organization functions, where employees sharing common skills are placed together. This reflects Weber's bureaucracy. Then we have various divisional structures (product/service, geography, customer), selected to be most suited to a company's activities. Next there is the matrix stricture, creating cross-functional teams consisting of individuals from different departments within the company. Finally, we have a structure based entirely on teams which are given limited autonomy to complete an entire production process.

Table 17.2: Era 1 and 2 organization structures

Structure	Decision making	Rules	Size
Functional	Highly centralized	Many	Large
Divisional	Centralized	Some	Medium
Matrix	Decentralized	Several	Intermediate
Team-based	Highly decentralized	Few	Small

Home viewing

The film *Other Peoples' Money* (1991, director Norman Jewison) shows a how a firm's failure to react to an external threat leaves it vulnerable to a hostile takeover. New England Wire and Cable (NEWC) is an old-fashioned manufacturing company, paternalistically led for 26 years by Andrew Jorgenson (played by Gregory Peck), who values stability and predictability. However, he is unaware of the developing problems in one of his company's divisions which requires urgent re-engineering and diversification. Meanwhile, Garfield Investment Corporation (GIC), headed by Lawrence Garfield (played by Danny DeVito) looks for firms that are ripe to be taken over, and expects to make a substantial profit by liquidating NEWC. As you watch the film, consider some of the reasons that corporate restructuring takes places? How does Jorgenson's leadership and decision-making style leave his company vulnerable to a takeover?

Era of boundaryless organizations

Boundaryless organization one possessing permeable internal and external boundaries which give it flexibility and thus the ability to respond to change rapidly.

The third era identified by Anand and Daft (2007) began in the mid-1990s and continues to this day. It is characterized by the development of an organization architecture called the boundaryless organization. This concept views firms as possessing permeable boundaries, both internally and externally. The firm behaves like an organism, encouraging better integration among its functional departments and closer partnerships with outsiders, so as to facilitate the free exchange of ideas and information, in order to maximize its flexibility and be able to respond rapidly to change. The term was coined by the former chief executive of General Electric (GE), Jack Welch, who wanted to eliminate barriers inside his company, not only horizontally, between GE's different departments, but also vertically, between the different levels of GE's management hierarchy. He also sought to break down barriers outside, between his company and its customers, suppliers and other stakeholders (Ashkenas et al., 2002).

Many organizations are adopting this approach in order to become more effective. Due to increasing costs and time pressures, companies now rarely innovate on their own. Instead, they increasingly seek partners with whom they can collaborate to share costs and speed up development. Adopting this type of organizational design involves establishing collaborative relationships with suppliers, competitors, customers, third parties and participants in online communities. Increasingly, we are seeing examples of loosely interconnected assemblages of companies operating different types of collaborative relationship structures (Schilling and Steensma, 2001).

Collaborative relationship structure a structure that involves a relationship between two or more organizations, sharing their ideas, knowledge, staff and technology for mutual benefit.

This approach has been facilitated by the opportunities created by improved communication technology (internet, mobile phones) and the rise of emerging economies (China, India), as well as by management's acceptance that an organization cannot efficiently perform alone all the tasks that are required to make a product or offer a service. Organizational structuring involves translating company policy into practices, duties and functions that are allocated as specific tasks to individuals and groups. However, increasingly these individuals and groups can be located outside the company. In the last 20 years, the focus has moved from hierarchy (single chain of command) to heterarchy (multiple chains of command); from bureaucracy to adhocracy; from structures to processes; from real to virtual; and from closed to open.

Outsourcing

Outsourcing contracting with external providers to supply the organization with the processes and products that were previously supplied internally.

Underpinning all the developments in organizational structure in this era has been outsourcing. This describes a situation in which an organization contracts with another firm to provide it with either a business process, such as paying its staff wages (payroll), or supplying it with a component for its final product (e.g. a computer hard drive, a steering wheel or a packaging box), which it would have previously made itself. Figure 17.8 illustrates this relationship, showing that outsourcers can supply both products and processes. Anand and Daft (2007) identified three types of organization structure used in boundaryless organizations, all of which used the outsourcing principle – hollow, modular and virtual. To these we can add a fourth type – collaborative.

When his River Rouge plant was completed in 1928, Henry Ford boasted that it had everything it needed to turn raw materials into finished cars – 100,000 workers, factory space, railway track, docks and furnaces. Today, 'The Rouge' remains Ford's largest plant, but most of the parts are made by subcontractors, and are merely fitted together by the plant's 6,000 employees. Even the local steel mill supplying Ford is run by Severstal – a Russian company (*The Economist*, 2011). In recent decades, outsourcing has transformed global business. Companies have contracted out everything from 'mopping the floors' (providing cleaning services) to 'spotting the flaws' (in internet security software code). Even war is

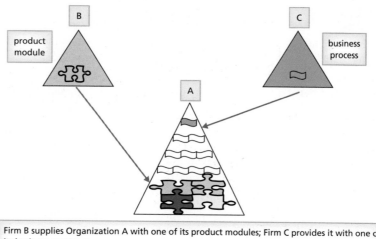

Firm B supplies Organization A with one of its product modules; Firm C provides it with one of its business processes.

Figure 17.8: Outsourcing relationship

Offshoring contracting with external providers in a different country to supply the organization with the processes and products that were previously supplied internally.

Reshoring Returning to the home country the production and provision of products and services which had previously been outsourced to overseas suppliers.

now outsourced. The United States military outsourced many tasks to private security contractors such as Blackwater Worldwide in Iraq (Scahill, 2007). In Afghanistan, it had more contract workers than regular troops.

Companies have outsourced to cut costs, slim operations and to concentrate on their core activities such as product development and marketing. When a business process or a product is acquired by an organization from a firm located in a different country, it is referred to as **offshoring** (Lampel and Bhaila, 2011). Nike's factory in Vietnam is an example of offshoring. It is estimated that the value of new outsourcing contracts every year in the world is $100 billion. Davis-Blake and Broschak (2009, p.322) argued that:

Because outsourcing changes what workers do, how they do it, with whom they do it, and what they are paid for, outsourcing is as significant a change in the nature of work and organization as the industrial revolution, scientific management or the emergence of the mature bureaucratic form, each of which fundamentally affected both work and workers

Outsourcing in retreat?

Outsourcing has become one of the most contentious inter-organizational arrangements. There are now signs that companies are rethinking their approach to outsourcing. American data shows a decline in outsourcing due to the economic situation, the maturity of the market (much of what can be outsourced already has been) and increasing problems. Outsourcing can go wrong in many different ways. There have been legal disputes about outsourcing. Large car companies can squeeze their smaller parts suppliers so much that the latter cut corners. Over-promising, sloppy contract writing and injudicious sub-(sub)contracting, have all caused problems. An outsourcing problem cannot be easily corrected. When companies outsource, they usually eliminate the department that used to do it. They become entwined with their contractors, handing over sensitive commercial information to them, and wanting them to work alongside their own staff. Extracting oneself from this relationship is difficult. It is easier to close a department than rebuild it. Sacking a contractor is no solution, as factories then grind to a halt through lack of parts. In 2011, the Japanese earthquake and tsunami in northern Japan had a major impact on the makers of cars, construction equipment and electronic products.

For all these reasons, companies are rethinking outsourcing and supply chain strategies and some are bringing more work back in-house (called **reshoring**). General Electric has added nearly half a million jobs in the US in recent years as rapid wage growth in emerging economies, coupled with sluggish pay in the country, has eroded the labour cost advantage of offshore suppliers. However, they are not jettisoning them. The business logic behind outsourcing remains compelling provided that it is done correctly. Those tasks which are peripheral to a firm's core business are better and more cheaply done by specialists. Outsourcing is growing in emerging markets, and in Europe (especially Germany and France), even if not in the United States. Large outsourcing deals are being replaced by smaller, less rigid ones; relationships are being established with several and not just one contractor; and shorter contracts are replacing longer ones (*The Economist*, 2013).

Hollow organization structure

Hollow organization structure an organizational design based on outsourcing an organization's non-core processes which are then supplied to it by specialist, external providers.

Outsourcing the majority of a company's non-core *processes* such as human relations, payroll, purchasing, logistics and security (as opposed to the production of parts) creates a hollow organization structure. John Child (2015) explained that the removal of previously internally provided processes or services 'hollows out' the organization, reducing its boundaries, size and workforce – hence the name. Specialist suppliers then provide these for the company, as illustrated in Figure 17.9.

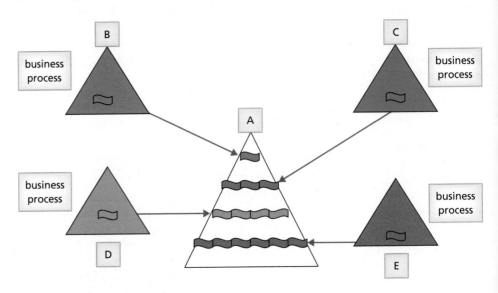

Firms B, C, D and E provide Organization A with all its business processes.

Figure 17.9: Hollow organization structure

Some automobile manufacturers have even outsourced the assembly of their entire vehicles (*The Economist*, 2002). This leaves the company free to concentrate on those things which represent the core of their activity, those that it does best, and those which lead to more value creation, such as research, design and marketing. Its remaining small number of core staff concentrate on strategic matters, including the integration of the contributions of the multiple external providers that it has created.

Anand and Daft (2007, p.335) list the underlying design principles of a hollow organization structure as:

- determine the non-core processes that are not critical to business performance, that do not create current or potential business advantage and that are unlikely to drive growth or rejuvenation;
- harness market forces to get non-core processes done efficiently;
- create an effective and flexible interface;
- align incentives between the organization and its outsourcing provider.

Nike, the sports goods company, considers its core competencies to be in marketing and distribution, rather than in manufacturing. In consequence, the company relies on contract manufacturers located in low-cost labour areas of the world which produce merchandise bearing Nike's well-known swoosh logo.

Modular organization structure

Modular organization structure an organizational design that involves assembling product chunks (modules) provided by internal divisions and external providers.

A **modular organization structure** is also based on outsourcing. However, unlike the hollow structure discussed earlier, in which outsourced processes such as logistics, payroll or warehousing are supplied by outsiders, a modular structure outsources the production of *parts* of the total product. Internal and external contractors supply component parts that the company then assembles itself. A company can break down its product's design into chunks that are then manufactured by both its internal divisions and external contractors. NASA's Space Shuttle, and computer hardware and software companies, aircraft manufacturers and household appliances firms, all organize themselves in this way. The analogy most often used is that of a Lego structure in which the different bricks are manufactured by a variety of different, external companies, and then fitted together (Schilling and Steensma, 2001). A modular organization structure is shown in Figure 17.10.

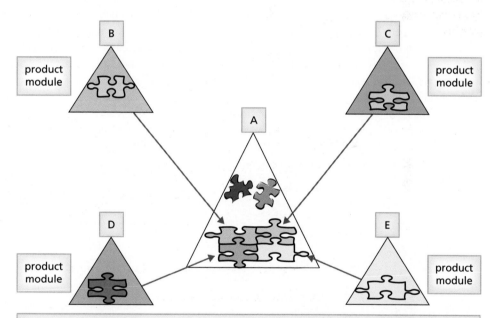

Firms B, C, D and E provide different product modules to Organization A, which produces its own as well, and assembles all of them.

Figure 17.10: Modular organization structure

Anand and Daft (2007, p.337) list the underlying design principles of a modular organization structure as:

- break products into self-contained modules or chunks, capable of standalone manufacture;
- design interfaces to ensure different chunks work together;
- outsource product chunks to external contractors who can make them more efficiently;
- ensure that the company can assemble the chunks that are produced internally and those supplied by external providers.

This involves a single large hub company located at the network's centre, that out-sources chunks of its production functions to external providers, except those it deems to be strategically vital and close to its core competence. Acer Computers is an example of an organization that has turned itself into a modular company. It broke itself up into modules that network together and with outside suppliers and marketers, to create multiple profit centres. It now concentrates on research, design and branded marketing, while spinning off its manufacturing facilities into a separate company, Wistron, which focuses on competitive outsourcing (Shih et al., 2006).

Modular partners

In order to develop and manufacture its 787 Dreamliner model, Boeing Commercial Airplanes dramatically altered its usual approach, in effect creating a network organization. Boeing's assembly plants are the final stage in a long and hugely complex global supply chain. This consists of about 1,300 'tier 1' suppliers, providing parts to Boeing from 5,400 factories in 40 countries. These in turn are fed by thousands of other 'tier 2' suppliers which, in turn, receive parts from countless others.

This form of organizational structure did not work for Boeing. Steve Denning (2013a, 2013b) detailed the many problems the company encountered. Unfinished Dreamliners had been scattered around its Everett plant due to a range of problems – a shortage of fasteners that hold the plane together; faulty horizontal stabilizers from an Italian supplier; parts not fitting together; suppliers failing to deliver their components on time; and Boeing

having to take over some of its subcontractors to stop them collapsing financially. Jim Albaugh, head of Boeing's commercial airliner division, admitted that too much of the Dreamliner's production had been contracted out. Some of that work has since been brought back in-house, so that the company could check it more carefully. It established a 'war room' that monitored the outside parts and raw materials, sending out 'examiners' to visit suppliers to ensure that their production met Boeing's needs. In October 2011, the first Dreamliner, operated by ANA Airlines, made its first commercial flight from Tokyo to Hong Kong. It was three years late and billions of dollars over budget. By 2015, the situation had recovered, and by mid-year, the company had delivered 64 planes. However, in future, companies like Boeing will need to think long and hard about how to employ outsourcing (*The Economist*, 2012a, 2012b; *All Things 787*, 2015).

Modular partners

The State/ABACA/Press Association Images

Virtual organization structure

Virtual organization structure an organizational design that uses technology to transcend the constraints of legal structures, physical conditions, place and time, and allows a network of separate participants to present themselves to customers as a single entity.

The **virtual organization structure** consists of a temporary network of nodes (entire organizations, parts of organizations, teams, specific individuals) linked by information technologies which flexibly coordinate their activities, and combine their skills and resources, in order to achieve common goals, without requiring traditional hierarchies of central direction or supervision. In this structure, the outsourcing company becomes primarily a 'network coordinator', and – when supported by sophisticated technology – a virtual organization.

A virtual organization is viewed as a single entity from the outside by its customers despite consisting of a network of separate companies. McKinsey, a management consultancy, reported that a new class of company was emerging which used collaborative Web 2.0 technologies intensively to connect the internal efforts of employees and to extend the organization's reach to customers, partners and suppliers (Bughin and Chui, 2011). A virtual organization structure is shown in Figure 17.11.

Anand and Daft (2007, p.339) list the underlying design principles of a virtual organization structure as:

- create boundaries around a temporary organization with external partners;
- use technology to link people, assets and ideas;
- each partner contributes their domain of excellence;
- disband or absorb after opportunity ends.

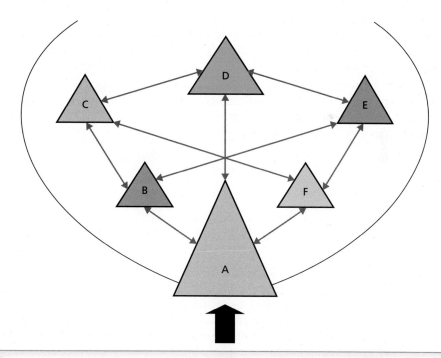

An organizational design that uses technology to allow a network of separate companies to present themselves as a single entity to customers

Figure 17.11: Virtual organization structure

Many observers see virtual organizations as a panacea for many of the current organizational problems. A virtual organization has the capacity to form and reform to deal with problems and (potentially) provide a flexible response to organizational needs and changing circumstances. The concept has generated considerable discussion and debate among managers, management consultants and business commentators, although they disagree about its nature. In the light of this, Warner and Witzel (2004) list the six features that nearly all virtual organizations possess (Table 17.3). These authors argue that organizations should not be classified into virtual or non-virtual categories. All firms can possess some degree of *virtuality* and this can take different forms. They say that every organization is a mixture of virtual and tangible elements and they identify six dimensions along which companies can choose to organize their activities on a virtual or a tangible basis:

- nature of product;
- nature of working;
- relationship with suppliers;
- relationship with customers;
- relationship between firm's elements;
- relationship with between managers and employees.

Table 17.3: Features of virtual organizations

Feature	Description
1. Lack of physical structure	Less physical presence than conventional organizations. Fewer tangible assets such as offices or warehouses, and those possessed are physically dispersed.
2. Reliance on communication technologies	Technology is used dynamically to link people, assets and ideas. Communication networks replace the physical structure of a conventional organization, to define it and give a shape to its activities.
3. Mobile work	Communication networks reduce the importance of where work is physically located, meaning that individuals and team members no longer have to be physically co-located to work together on a common task.
4. Hybrid forms	Short- or long-term collaboration between agencies can take various forms, called hybrids, including networks, consortia and webs, to achieve a mutual goal.
5. Boundaryless and inclusive	Not confined to legal entities, but can encompass suppliers and distributors, working with producers, and even involving customers in the production process.
6. Flexible and responsive	Can be rapidly assembled from a variety of disparate elements, to achieve a certain business goal and then, as required, be dismantled or reconfigured.

Source: based on Warner and Witzel, 2004, pp.3–5.

A supermarket's internal operations are traditionally physical and tangible, but its links with its suppliers are virtual through its automated product reordering system. Thus the question to ask of an organization is not whether it is virtual or non-virtual, but to what degree, and in what ways, does it possess virtuality. Additionally, whatever an organization's virtual–tangible 'asset mix' may be, it can be managed in a virtual or in tangible way.

Collaboration

In traditional organization structures, units were either within an organization – 'densely connected' – or outside the organization, and not attached at all. In both situations, relations with external suppliers were at arm's length. David Nadler of Mercer Delta Consulting, an organizational structure ('architecture') consultancy company, argues that many of today's companies 'co-habit', using joint ventures and strategic alliances. He says that what is inside and outside the company, which was previously clear, has now become blurred. However, when different businesses become connected to varying degrees, it causes them problems of dependency and uncertainty, which in turn creates risk. What happens when a partner in a joint venture goes bankrupt? How do banks ensure that employees of companies to which they have outsourced services do not steal their customers' PIN numbers? Commentators even suggest that companies now need an 'extended organizational form' – one shape for their external operations and another for their in-house activities.

David Nadler sees companies increasingly consisting of a number of strategically aligned businesses that are linked closely where there are opportunities to create value by leveraging shared capabilities, but only loosely where the greater value lies in the undifferentiated focus (Nadler and Tushman, 1997). This implies that close and loose relationships will coexist within and between organizations. Bob de Wit and Ron Meyer (2014) provide a taxonomy of inter-organizational, collaborative relationships (Table 17.4).

Table 17.4: Example of collaborative relationships

	Non-contractual arrangements	**Contractual arrangements**	**Equity-based arrangements**
Multilateral arrangements	• **Lobbying coalition** (e.g. European Roundtable of industrialists) • **Joint standard setting** (e.g. Linux coalition) • **Learning communities** (e.g. Strategic Management Society)	• **Research consortium** (e.g. Symbian in PDAs) • **International marketing alliance** (e.g. Star Alliance in airlines) • **Export partnership** (e.g. Netherlands Export Combination)	• **Shared payment system** (e.g. Visa) • **Construction consortium** (e.g. Eurotunnel) • **Joint reservation system** (e.g. Galileo)
Bilateral arrangements	• **Cross-selling deal** (e.g. between pharmaceutical firms) • **R&D staff exchange** (e.g. between IT firms) • **Market information sharing agreement** (e.g. between hardware and software makers)	• **Licensing agreement** (e.g Disney and Coca-Cola) • **Co-development contract** (e.g. Disney and Pixar in movies) • **Co-branding alliance** (e.g. Coca-Cola and McDonald's)	• **New product joint venture** (e.g. Sony and Ericsson in cell phones) • **Cross-border joint venture** (e.g. DaimlerChrysler and Beijing Automotive) • **Local joint venture** (e.g. CNN Turk in Turkey)

Source: from De Wit and Meyer (2014, p.144).

Currently, companies are seeking alliances for reasons which can be categorized under economic, social and technological (Gratton, 2007, Gratton et al., 2007; *The Economist*, 2015c):

Technology

- *Industry fusions:* New technology brings previously separate industries together. Insurers such as Allianz in Germany are collaborating with Google to establish a start-up centre in Munich that aims to use data analysis to improve the insurance market. Similarly, financial institutions have joined mobile telecoms operators to offer mobile payments.

- *Advances in collaborative technology:* Companies' collaborative experiences are supported by advanced technology (videoconferencing, Skype, email, voicemail, social networks, wikis and blogs). The current, wired-up generation of Facebook and Twitter users who are joining the commercial world prefer these ways of communicating, and this affects collaboration between businesses.

Economic

- *Knowledge economy:* The move towards a knowledge economy and a focus on the innovation of products and services.

- *Rise of partnership strategies:* A change in perception away from seeing companies as competing for a piece of a finite cake (*value appropriation*) and towards their making the cake bigger (*value creation*).

- *Cross-border links:* Reciprocal relations between Western companies and those in developing countries has allowed the former to cut costs and enter new markets, and the latter to go global. Dr Reddy's Laboratories of India and Merck of Germany are cooperating to produce cheaper cancer therapies that are going out of patent protection.

- *Costs:* In some industries, technology costs are now so large that companies cannot fund them on their own. Motor car manufacturers have had to invest in electric, hybrid, hydrogen fuel-cell and propulsion systems while struggling to meet ever stricter carbon dioxide emission targets. This has resulted in collaborations between Toyota and BMW (fuel cells), Ford and Daimler (gearboxes) and Renault-Nissan and Avtovaz of Russia.

Social

- *Working styles of Generation Y:* Unlike the competitive post-war baby-boomers, Generation Y (up to 30 years) is particularly adept at, and places value upon, collaborating with others.

- *Consumer pressure:* The increasing popularity of online shopping has forced physical shop owners to work with others. Hence, to entice customers in, the New York store of Uniqlo, a Japanese clothing retailer has struck a deal with Starbucks to have a coffee shop on its premises. H&M, another clothes retailer, works with I:Co, a logistics firm, to free up their customers' wardrobe space by returning old clothes which are then sold second-hand or recycled.

However, alliances can be dangerous and have negative consequences for their partners. Alliance companies have to learn to trust each other, while guarding against being exploited.

Video case: objectives of collaboration abroad

In this five-minute *Financial Times* video, Della Bradshaw talks to Andrea Sironi, rector of Bocconi University, who discusses the reasons why business schools have been actively collaborating with each other in recent years.

Collaboration with suppliers

Morgan Witzel (2007, p.4) noted that 'Whereas collaboration used to be a matter of integrating organizations, now it is increasingly seen as a matter of integrating activities. In other words, tasks are carried out by the person or organization that is most suited to the specific issuee.' While most inter-firm relationships in the early networks through the 1980s were managed by contracts, some manufacturers realized that both upstream suppliers and downstream distributors possessed technical and market knowledge that was of value to them. They thus created cross-firm relationships with their suppliers that allowed such knowledge to be used to the mutual advantage of all supply chain members. Hence, discussions of organization structure and the alternatives to bureaucracy now focus increasingly on collaborative, inter-organizational relationships (Miles et al., 2010).

McLaren and partnerships

However successful this year's McLaren Formula 1 racing car is, it will bear little relation to next year's. Such is the pace of change in F1 engineering that 95 per cent of it will be different. The planning and design take place in McLaren's Technology Centre in Woking, England, but the ideas generated are implemented in far-flung corners of the globe. A McLaren F1 racing car contains 15,000 –16,000 separate parts that are manufactured by 750 companies. Jonathan Neale is McLaren Racing's managing director. His job is to coordinate all this activity. 'I can just pick up the phone and say, "I can't solve this problem. I need some help. I can tell you what the problem is but I don't know how to solve it"', he says. Partnerships are the lifeblood of McLaren and its rival teams.

A lot of this is about management process and organization. I run a high speed organization, but it's a small-to-medium enterprise of 500 people. I can't possibly expect to have the world's leading know-how in fuel lubrication, bonding and adhesive material, yet I need that to compete. So how do we get that? We plug into our partners. I have access to global research and developments in fuel lubrication.

McLaren illustrates that technological developments, speed of change and globalization mean that a single organization, however successful, can no longer 'do it all themselves'. Even the largest companies have had to develop collaborative relationships with outsiders (Blitz, 2007, pp.22–3).

Collaboration with competitors

Co-opetition a form of cooperation between competing organizations which is limited to specified areas where both believe they can gain mutual benefit.

Collaboration with competitors can take the form of 'cooperative competition', which is called **co-opetition**. This occurs when two or more organizations decide that they do not possess an individual competitive advantage in a field, want to share common costs, or wish to innovative quickly but lack the necessary resources, knowledge or skill to do so (Brandenburger and Nalebuff, 2002). An example is the cooperation between Peugeot and Toyota on shared components for a new city car for Europe. In this case, companies will save money on shared costs, while remaining fiercely competitive in other areas. For co-opetition to work, companies need to define very clearly where they are working together, and where they are competing. Co-opetition can take the legal-structural form of a strategic alliance or a joint venture.

Martin Nowak and Roger Highfield (2011) argue that the fittest do not survive merely by outrunning their rivals. The winners find ways to work together, avoid escalating conflicts and build trust and cooperation which allow each party to flourish. The losers are those who punish others and perish as a result. Based on Charles Darwin's evolutionary principles, they argue that humans are 'super co-operators'. As a species, humans trust each other and work together, rather than beat each other. It is cooperation and not competition that underpins innovation. Without it there can be neither construction nor complexity. Some of the world's largest industries exhibit alternating patterns of competition and cooperation. Microsoft and Intel have dominated personal computing but that has not prevented them fighting about how to divide the profits. They cooperate to create value, but compete to appropriate it.

Strategic alliance

Strategic alliance an arrangement in which two or more firms agree to cooperate to achieve specific objectives while remaining independent organizations.

A **strategic alliance** is a tight, formalized, contractual relationship with a legal element, in which firms cooperate over the medium to long term to achieve certain commercial objectives for mutual advantage, while remaining independent entities. Each alliance partner provides their own resources, products, equipment, expertise, production facilities or funding. In a strategic alliance, companies merge a limited part of their domain with each other, and attempt to achieve the competitive advantage that might have individually eluded them. Alliances tend to be established over a single, specific initiative, although they may be later extended to cover other activities between the participating companies (Figure 17.12).

If you travelled by plane to come to university, your airline is likely to be a member of one of three mega-alliances in the international airline industry – SkyTeam, Star Alliance and Oneworld. These account for 69 per cent of the world's air revenue passenger miles. This provides convenience and connectivity for passengers and provides the airlines with marketing, branding and code sharing.

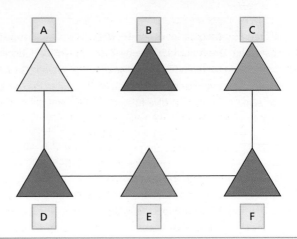

Organizations A, B, C, D, E, and F cooperate, providing resources, to achieve specific objectives while remaining independent entities.

Figure 17.2: Strategic alliance

To be successful, an alliance between firms requires strategic fit (complementary goals), cultural fit (complementary values) and organizational fit (complementary structures). The primary reason for alliance creation is to secure specific competencies and resources to survive and succeed in globalizing markets, particularly those in which technologies are rapidly changing. Alliances can bring about organizational learning. Rather than the partners being involved in skill substitution (one produces, while the other sells), they can learn from each other, thereby strengthening the areas in which each is weakest. However, research shows that alliances often end in disappointment for the organizations involved (Koza and Lewin, 1999).

Renault–Nissan–Daimler alliance

Rajesh Kumar (2014) explained that to the surprise of many, the Renault–Nissan alliance which had been established in 1999 was now the most successful one in the automotive industry. Nissan had experienced years of low profitability and had been under pressure to find a partner. Renault's merger with Volvo had failed, and it wished to expand its global presence. The assets possessed by the two companies were complementary. Nissan's presence in North America and its superior engineering capability would assist Renault's global ambitions, while Renault's cash would help Nissan reduce its debt, and its expertise in innovative design would benefit the Japanese firm. Despite the complementarity, scepticism remained about the future of the alliance. The two companies had very different organizational cultures (Chapter 4) and no experience of working together. Analysts at the time described it as a 'marriage of desperation' for both parties, but it may be a marriage of convenience.

Despite this, the alliance has prospered. In 2015 it reported record synergies of €3.80 billion which had come particularly from purchasing, engineering and manufacturing, and the launch of the alliance's first Common Module Family (CMF) vehicle. Later in the same year, the alliance announced that it had signed a contract with Daimler to start a manufacturing joint venture in Mexico called COMPAS (Cooperation Manufacturing Plant Aguascalientes) which would be led by an international management team from Nissan and Daimler (Blog Alliance, 2015). On the basis of his analysis of successful and unsuccessful alliances, Kumar offers managers a list of what they should do (e.g. invest in the negotiation process; foster an alliance mindset; be constructive and proactive) and should not do (e.g. be judgemental; demonstrate inflexibility; rush into an alliance) to create a successful one.

Joint venture

Joint venture an arrangement in which two or more companies remain independent, but establish a new organization that they jointly own and manage.

Another form of co-opetition is the **joint venture**. Competitors may wish to pool resources or collaborate to challenge other competitors. Here, two companies remain independent, but establish a new organization into which they both contribute equity and which they jointly own. They control the newly created firm, sharing its expenses and revenues. The relationships between them are formalized, either through shareholding arrangements or by agreements specifying asset-holding and profit distribution.

Airbus is a well-known company which is also a joint venture. Toyota has a number of joint venture plants with companies around the world (e.g. General Motors, Peugeot), all of which use the Toyota Production System. The joint venture is popular with Western companies operating in China, providing companies with low-cost entry into new markets. Sony Ericsson was established as a joint venture in 2001 to produce mobile phones. It combined Sony's consumer electronics expertise with Ericsson's know-how in technological communication. Both companies stopped making their own mobile phones (Figure 17.13).

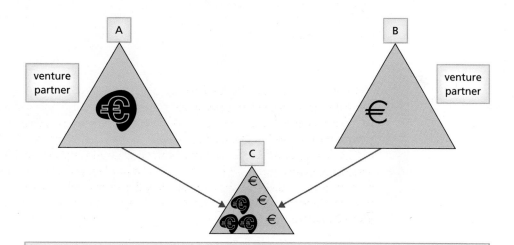

Organization A and Organization B invest equity in a newly created, jointly-owned, firm, C.

Figure 17.13: Joint venture

The odd couple

If you are on a short-haul flight, the chances are that your aircraft's engines were made by CFM International. CFM is an unusual yet durable joint venture between US-based General Electric (GE), the world's most successful conglomerate and standard bearer of raw Anglo-Saxon capitalism, and Snecma, a French firm owned by Safran. CFM's engines power 71 per cent of the world's fleet of single-aisle aircraft. They can be found in Boeing 737s, DC8s, Airbus A320s and the AWACS. It supplies 400 commercial and military customers worldwide. These are the workhorses of aviation, and constitute the largest market for engines, much bigger than that for wide-bodied jumbos. The joint venture began in 1974 when both companies wanted to expand beyond their mostly military customers into the growing civilian business. At the time,

this was dominated by Pratt & Whitney, which had the best-selling engine for single-aisle planes. As the technological leader, it saw no need to collaborate with anyone. Snecma decided against linking up with Rolls-Royce after a failed collaboration on Concorde engines. That left GE, which was anxious to get close to Airbus, which was founded in 1970 and was then Europe's nascent aircraft consortium.

The European home of this odd pairing is an old military airfield on the edge of the forest of Fontainebleau, outside Paris, while the American component is based within GE's aero-engine division in Cincinnati, Pennsylvania. Despite a huge disparity in size, the two firms operate their joint venture on a simple and equitable basis. In both factories, the core module of the CFM

→

engine (a GE design originally developed for fighter aircraft) is married to a French front fan and low-pressure turbine. Each partner is responsible for the research, design and production of its modules. Many companies set up joint ventures and other forms of collaboration, but few have one that is so central to their entire business. GE and Snecma share nothing but engine parts and sales, and they split the proceeds roughly 50–50. Jet engines may be awesomely complicated machines worth millions of dollars each, but the secret to making them successfully seems to be to keep it simple. The two companies have extended their partnership through to 2040 and are cooperating in the development of the new generation of LEAP engines (*The Economist*, 2007; www.cfmaeroengines.com, 2015).

Martin Hayhow/AFP/Getty Images

Collaboration with third parties

Back in 2008, T-Mobile, a mobile phone company operator owned by Germany's Deutsche Telecom, launched its new phone, the G1, made by HTC, a Taiwanese manufacturer. The device was the first to be based on Google's Android software (*The Economist*, 2008). Android is a fully 'open' operating system and Google hoped to attract third parties such as other telephone operators and handset makers to adopt Android for their smartphones. While today Google's smartphone platform is not yet seen by app developers as outpacing Apple's iOS, it now matches it in many respects. In 2013, it became the world's most popular app platform. Android has managed to win over many developers, creating a larger selection of apps than its main rival. Apple was planning to open up more of its iOS platform to developers (Bradshaw, 2013a, 2013b).

Collaborating with users

User contribution system a method of aggregating people's contributions or behaviours in ways that are useful to others.

At first glance, Amazon, eBay, Google, Wikipedia, You Tube, the Mozilla Foundation and Facebook appear to have little in common. Some charge users, others are free. Some are profit-making organizations, others are not. However, they all use what are called **user contribution systems**. These are methods of aggregating people's contributions or behaviours in ways that are useful to others, and these are responsible for much of their success. The idea is not new. Firms have always used customer satisfaction surveys and focus groups to provide them with feedback to improve their products. When Maxwell House wanted to develop a new brand of instant coffee, it avoided the usual market testing approach. Instead, it approached its customers directly, obtained data from them, created a model for the 'ideal' coffee, and used this as the basis for developing the new product (Witzel, 2007). Commercial companies are now developing ways in which unlimited numbers of people outside them can volunteer their time, energy and expertise, to improve things for themselves, and increase profits for the company. User contribution systems are underpinned by a range of new, consumer-based technologies collectively referred to as Web 2.0 (see Chapter 3).

User contribution systems can involve customers and sales prospects, as well as people with no previous connection with the company. One recent incarnation is called *unsourcing*. It involves companies setting up online communities to enable peer-to-peer support among users. Customers' problems are answered by unpaid individuals who have bought and used the same products. This is done in discussion forums set up on the company's own website or on social networks like Facebook and Twitter. It is being used by companies such as Tom Tom, Lenovo and Logitech. A user contribution structure is shown in Figure 17.14.

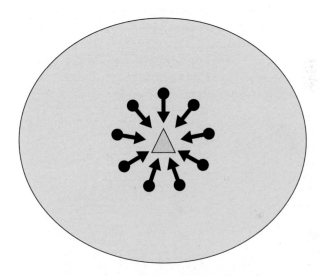

An organization uses the contributions of countless individual volunteers to help it achieve its goals.

Figure 17.14: User contribution system

The contribution of users can be active, as when they donate their work, expertise or information, or it can be passive (and even unknowing), as in the case of behavioural data gathered from them automatically when they participate in a transaction. Wikipedia, a non-profit organization, offers a free encyclopaedia, written and frequently updated by unpaid experts in their fields. eBay makes a profit without any inventory because its customers fill its shelves. Less obviously, Google's search engine relies on the algorithmic aggregation of links created by others on websites, while its advertisement placement system depends on data from people's click behaviour.

Assembling producers with users

Back in 1998, LEGO® released a new product – a 727-part set called *Mindstorms*®. It contained a microchip that made a variety of movements possible. The product was a great success, selling 80,000 sets. However, to the company's surprise, it was being bought by adults for their own use, and not for children. Quite quickly, its users hacked the toy's code and created a variety of new applications from soda machines to blackjack dealers. The new

→

programs spread quickly over the internet and were more sophisticated than Lego had itself developed. Over 40 guidebooks advised users on how to get the most out of this LEGO set. Initially, LEGO reacted negatively, feeling that customers were misusing their products. However, after a period of confusion and inaction, the company started to listen to their product's '(ab)users' in an effort to discover what they were doing with it. Following discussions, the company decided that they were doing something interesting and important, even though it differed from LEGO's own business plan. They discovered that the product's (re)creators formed a community around the LEGO brand and shared a passion for innovation.

These users had produced physical and aesthetic add-ons to products, such as clothes for figures, and batteries for trains and cars. They had developed new play themes such as LEGO *Harry Potter* and LEGO *Life on Mars*. Indeed, some product fans even devised new building techniques using existing bricks to produce new building styles, models and colour effects. While the majority of users' improvements were incremental, which left the basic product unchanged, just over 10 per cent were radical innovations involving new experiences and play processes. These included mosaic building – translating an image into pixels (LEGO bricks) and then assembling it digitally; strategy games such as BrickWars involving multiplayer role playing; LDraw, an open-source software program which allows users to create virtual LEGO models and scenes; and BrickFilms, which animators use to create short films using LEGO figures. The LEGO company now cooperates with its user community allowing them to interact and co-create for mutual benefit. Having such an active and innovative community keeps the company focused on new products, helps it to market product innovations and increases the chances of success as the product is devised by the consumers themselves. In the autumn of 2013, it released Mindstorms EV3. This version contains a programmable brick that controls all the other elements and can itself be controlled by an iPad or an iPhone (Kornberger, 2010; Hattersley, 2013).

Koichi Kamoshida/Getty Images

Most user contribution systems offer no financial incentives, so what motivates individuals to contribute? Cook (2008) suggests six reasons:

- *By-product:* involuntary involvement when they provide data as a by-product of a transaction (e.g. every Amazon shopper adds to its recommendation engine).
- *Practical solutions:* to obtain short-term, practical benefits (e.g. using the Del.icious.us site to organize their own website bookmarks which when aggregated, produces an index to the web useful to others).

- *Social rewards:* to gain interaction with others, to become a member of a community of common interests (e.g. Facebook).

- *Reputation:* to gain recognition (e.g. receiving Amazon's badge for being a 'Top 1,000 reviewer') or the admiration of peers.

- *Self-expression:* to have the opportunity to air their thoughts, opinions or creative expression, or to gain feedback from others (e.g. millions of YouTube videos).

- *Altruism:* to help others or to let the truth to be known.

Why have companies developed user contribution systems? The systems create value for businesses as a consequence of the value that they deliver to their users. User benefits include personalized purchase recommendations, obtaining hard-to-find items, reduced prices, establishing new personal and business relationships, as well as membership of a community. Company benefits include improved products, enhancement of customer loyalty, better served customers, more business, reduced costs and improvements in employee performance. Harhoff and Mayrhofer (2010) gave examples of organizations establishing user communities – BMW around its series of high-powered M cars; Sun Microsystems around its operating system Solaris; the Mozdev Group's development of its solutions-based web browser Firefox, which is coordinated by the Mozilla Foundation. Cook (2008) provides a user contribution taxonomy, which is shown in Figure 17.15.

User Contribution Systems

Active		Passive	
Aggregates content	Aggregates stuff for sale	Aggregates behavioural data	Aggregates resources
Opinion and ratings: Zagat guides	Goods: eBay online marketplace	Buying behaviours: Amazon's product recommendations	Computing capacity: Skype internet-based phone system
Expertise: Wikipedia encyclopedia	Advertising: Google's AdWords advertising placement system	Web-linking behaviour: Google's search engine algorithm	Computer sensing capabilities: Honda's InterNavi traffic information service
Software code: Firefox web browser	Services (and goods): Craigslist online marketplace	Company behaviour: Westlaw's PeerMonitor law firm database	
Creative expression: YouTube video-sharing site			
Social connections and personal information: Facebook social networking site			

Figure 17.15: User contribution taxonomy

Source: reprinted by permission of *Harvard Business Review*. From 'The contribution revolution: letting volunteers build your business' by Cook, S., 86(10) 2008. © 2008 by the Harvard Business School Publishing Corporation, all rights reserved.

Crowdsourcing the act of taking a task traditionally performed by a designated agent (employee or contractor), and outsourcing it to an undefined, generally large group of people, in the form of an open call for assistance.

Crowdsourcing is a term coined by Jeff Howe in *Wired* magazine (Howe, 2006, 2009). It refers to the act of taking a task traditionally performed by an employee or a contractor and outsourcing it to an undefined, generally large group of people, in the form of an open call for assistance. BBC Radio's Traffic Unit regularly asks motorists stuck in traffic jams to call in on their mobile phones and report holdups which it then broadcasts over the air.

This process invites constituencies of stakeholders to collectively solve problems and exploit opportunities (Gouillart and Billings, 2013). Large problems can present great opportunities but they require the collaboration of hundreds or thousands of people. Providing a platform allows individuals to connect and engage with one another to create value for their organization and for themselves. Creating a co-creation system begins with identifying a large problem whose solution requires the help of many people from different organizations to solve.

Operationally, crowdsourcing involves organizations asking crowds of internet users to provide creative ideas, analyse data, supply information, help develop a new technology, carry out a design task (also known as 'community-based design' or 'distributed participatory design'), or help capture, systematize and analyse large amounts of data. Kevin Boudreau and Karim Lakhani (2013) argue that the crowdsourcing is not being used as widely or effectively as it could be, because companies do not know which kinds of problems are best suited to it and how to manage the crowdsourcing process. On the basis of their research, they identified four forms that crowdsourcing could take. These they labelled contests, collaborative communities, complementors and labour markets.

- *Contests:* A company identifies a problem, offers a cash prize, and broadcasts an invitation to submit solutions. An example would be the British Parliament, in 1714, establishing the Longitude Prize to find a way of determining longitude at sea. Contests separate contributions and maximize different experiments.

- *Collaborative communities:* A company joins forces with an online community to create a product. For example, in 1998, IBM joined forces with Apache, an online community of webmasters, to develop its web server infrastructure. Collaborative communities marshal the outputs of multiple contributors and aggregate them into a coherent and value-creating whole.

- *Complementors:* Transforming your product into a platform that generates complementary innovations – e.g. iTunes was organized around Apple's core mobile products (iPod, iPad and iPhone) setting up a large numbers of geographically dispersed developers who created innovations such as software apps and user-generated podcasts, that complemented these products. Complementors provide a vast number of solutions to many different problems and not just one.

- *Labour markets:* Using conventional contracting, labour markets link buyers to sellers of services, matching the former's skills with the latter's needs. This is the on-demand organization model, exemplified by Uber, Handy and SpoonRocket providing chauffeurs, cleaners and restaurant meals. Labour markets work when you know what you are looking for, and what an appropriate problem solver looks like.

However, there are problems in using ideas or information supplied by community members. The firm has to check that these have not been sent to rivals, do not infringe patents, and have not been stolen. Second, volunteers become reluctant to contribute if they feel that someone is profiting from their hard work, hence the success of non-profit collaborations. Successful solvers in the InnoCreative network are paid between $10,000 and $100,000. Obviously, getting unpaid or cheaper members of the public to do your work for you is less expensive than hiring your own staff or paying consultants. Structurally, in the case of both non-profit and commercial organizations, the organizational boundary becomes perforated, as contributions to the organizational goals come from both internal, company staff and from volunteer outsiders.

STOP AND THINK

Are user-contribution systems a good way of providing the public with the opportunity to participate and share their expertise with companies whose products and services they use? Or have companies cynically managed to persuade gullible, emotionally challenged online users, to contribute their time, creativity and effort for free, in return for a spurious sense of participation in some sort of 'community' or a sense of 'ownership' of something?

What mode of collaboration should a firm adopt when linking with others? Gary Pisano and Roberto Verganti (2008) suggest that senior management should ask two questions about their company's network participation and governance. First, given its corporate strategy, how open or closed does it want its network of collaborators to be? Second, who should have the power to decide which problems the network will tackle and which solutions will be adopted?

- *Participation: open or closed?* Collaborative networks differ in terms of participation. Totally open collaboration means that anyone can join the network (suppliers, customers, hobbyists, institutions – even competitors). The sponsor announces a problem, and requests contributions from an unlimited number of problem-solvers. It is like a throwing an open house party – you set the date and location and hope that the right people will come. Open-source software projects like Linux, Apache and Mozilla all exemplify open collaboration networks, as does threadless.com, the T-shirt retailer. In contrast, in a closed network, a firm will tackle its problem with one or two parties, which it chooses on the basis of their possession of the required capabilities. This is like a private club which you are invited to join. Alessi, an Italian company famous for the postmodern design of its home products, invited 200 collaborators to submit designs.

- *Governance: hierarchical or flat?* Collaborative networks also differ in terms of governance. This relates to who gets to define the problem and choose the solution. In a hierarchical network, the 'kingpin' firm alone decides on the importance of problems, how they will be addressed, what represents an acceptable solution and which solutions will be implemented. This allows it to control and secure a larger part of the innovation's value. In contrast, in a flat network, the different parties are equal partners and share the power to decide key issues. Such decentralized decision making, say Pisano and Verganti, allows collaborators to share the costs, risk and technical challenges of innovating.

Using the dimensions of participation and governance, Pisano and Verganti propose four basic modes of collaboration (Figure 17.16). They label these *elite circle* (closed and hierarchical network), *innovation mall* (open and hierarchical), *innovation community* (open and

Innovation mall A place where a company can post a problem, anyone can propose solutions, and the company chooses the solutions it likes best. **Example:** *InnoCentive.com website where companies can post scientific problems.*	**Innovation community** A network where anybody can propose problems, offer solutions and decide which solutions to use. **Example:** *Linux open-source software.*		**Open**
Elite circle A select group of participants chosen by a company that also defines the problem and picks the solutions. **Example:** *Alessi's handpicked group of 200-plus design experts who develop new concepts for home products.*	**Consortium** A private group of participants that jointly select problems, decide how to conduct work, and choose solutions. **Example:** *IBM's partnerships with select companies to jointly develop semiconductor technology.*	**PARTICIPATION**	**Closed**
GOVERNANCE			
Hierarchical	**Flat**		

Figure 17.16: Four ways to collaborate

Source: reprinted by permission of *Harvard Business Review*. From 'Which kind of collaboration is right for you?' by Pisano, G. and Verganti, R., 86(12), 2008. Copyright © 2008 Harvard Business School Publishing Corporation, all rights reserved.

flat) and *consortium* (closed and flat). These authors state that each has its own particular advantages and challenges, offers a company access to different capabilities assets, and is suited to specific types of problems.

With respect to participation, by choosing an open network a firm gains access to an extremely large number of problem-solvers, and thus to the possibility of obtaining a vast quantity of ideas. Moreover, it does not need to specify its contributors beforehand. The disadvantages are that it does not attract the best contributors, and that its chance of finding the best solutions from among the mountain of submissions is low. Pisano and Verganti state that open networks are most effective when participating in them is easy, with the problem being divided into small, well-defined chunks that contributors can work on independently; when there is one or just a few solutions that can be clearly defined; when the proposed solutions can be evaluated at low cost; when the difference between an ideal solution and an average solution is not large; and when the chance of missing out on a greatly superior solution proposed by an elite participant is small.

With a closed network, a firm receives solutions from the best contributors in a selected knowledge domain (e.g. software); the best partners prefer to participate in closed networks, and the chance of receiving a few suitable ideas from a small number of collaborators is high. Closed networks are most effective when a firm knows the knowledge domain from which the best solution is likely to emerge, when it can pick the best experts itself, when the problem is large and cannot be broken up into parts, and when everyone's expertise is required.

With respect to governance, a hierarchical form is best when a firm possesses the capabilities and knowledge to define a problem and evaluate the submitted solutions, when it can choose the direction to take, understands users' needs, and can first divide and then integrate outsiders' contributions. Flat forms work best when no single company possesses total capability on its own, and when all collaborators have a vested interest in how a problem is solved and want a role in decision making.

The dark side of new organizational forms

In a prophetic article written nearly 20 years before the boundaryless organization received media or research interest, Bart Victor and Carroll Stephens (1994) discussed the 'dark side' of the brave new world of the twenty-first century, networked, information rich, de-layered, lean and hypercompetitive organizational structures. These authors discussed the 'new org form' language of empowerment, high commitment, downsizing, restructuring and re-engineering. They observed:

1. An increase in the numbers of workers who have only temporary, part-time or short-contract jobs; and noted the increases in income inequalities rather than in shared benefits.

2. The creation of jobs in virtual occupations with workers performing whatever tasks are required to achieve the work goal, instead of having a role anchored in the organization and codified in a job description.

3. New organizational forms offering roles defined by the task and the location of the worker. Time, space and shifting group membership can become the primary definers of responsibility and accountability for the virtual wage slave.

4. Traditional indicators of status becoming blurred as obligations become networked and diffused, and the rights of employees become increasingly ephemeral.

5. Employees being expected to exhibit a feverish commitment to their company, and many, fearing job loss, comply despite the one-sidedness of the deal.

6. That not everyone is at ease with the free-floating demands of the hyper-flexible workplace. Many people thrive on predictability and routine.

7. The periodic deskilling (based on technical progress) is replaced by the incessant demand for innovation and adaptation. The new 'learning organization' insists that everyone becomes a self-motivated, continuous learner. Those who do not are threatened with obsolescence.

8. The flat organizations force more demanding and intrusive interpersonal relations. Teams and networks call for new levels and kinds of cooperation. No one can escape the demand to interact or to be interactive.

9. Employees' values are offered up as fodder to be transformed by management for organizational ends. The high-velocity, high-commitment, 'flash-in-the-pan' collectivities offer no ongoing relationships, no safe havens and no personal space.

Victor and Stephens (1994) concluded that in the discussions of new organizational forms, there is much talk of empowering, challenging and equalizing, but there is also much fear and loathing. More recently, John Gapper (2015, p.13) reported: 'More and more people work for virtual platforms instead of companies; work is auctioned to pools of contractors; median wages stagnate while returns on capital rise; some duties of doctors and lawyers may soon be done by machines. Is this what we want?' These authors believe that twenty-first century new organizational architecture extracts a high price from everyone who is involved in it.

On-demand companies companies which use technology to fulfil consumers' demands in real-time by the immediate supply of goods and services which is driven by the efficient, intuitive digital mesh layered over existing infrastructure networks.

At the present time, on-demand companies provide a good example of a new organizational form. These are companies which use technology to fulfil consumers' demands in real-time by the immediate supply of goods and services which are driven by an efficient, intuitive digital mesh layered over existing infrastructure networks. Mike Jaconi (2014) observed that never before in the history of man could a consumer buy anything they wanted, at any time they wanted, simply by tapping a button on their smartphone.

Evgeny Morozov (2015) speculated that powerful tech organizations that were currently altering how we buy things could sweep away the existing entire economic organizational model. He referred to this as platform capitalism, which, in his view, would transform the way that goods and services are produced, shared and delivered. In this participatory model, customers use their smart phones to engage more directly with providers to do a range of things which previously required the intervention of an organization. Uber connects passengers with drivers; Airbnb connects guests with hosts; Amazon connects book buyers with booksellers. These intermediate 'platform organizations', which are facilitating transportation, accommodation and reading, represent a new and previously unknown organization form. How they relate to employment and disability legislation, payment processes, security and other company processes is still unclear.

On-demand companies – here today, gone tomorrow?

The bringing together of computing power and freelance workers has created the new phenomenon of on-demand companies. As individuals, we use them to supply us with chauffeurs (Uber), cleaners (Handy) and flowers (BloomThat). These on-demand companies act as middle men, matching our individual needs with people and monitoring quality. They also supply other firms. Elanc-oDesk offers companies the services of 10 million freelance programmers; Eden McCalum can supply 500 freelance consultants at a fraction of the price of McKinsey staff; Business Talent Group supplies bosses for companies wanting to address specific problems without hiring more senior executives; and Tongal has a network of 40,000 video-makers. At present, on-demand companies have little in the way of offices or full-time contract employees, but use computers to convert a customer-company's needs into a set of worker's tasks while accessing spare time and spare cognitive capacity around the globe.

However, these on-demand companies are not without their own problems. First, their attempt to minimize costs to clients creates problems in training, motivating, retaining and managing those who supply their services. Second, they claim they do not employ the workers that they supply, but courts are currently deciding if they must reclassify their contract workers as regular employees, thereby incurring retrospective labour bills. Third, they face the problem of size and scaling up. When barriers to the entry of competitors are low, and employee loyalty is non-existent, it is difficult for them to build up a network to suitable size. Some Uber drivers also work for its competitor, Lyft. 'On-demand companies may find themselves stuck in a world of low margins, high promotional costs and labour churn as they struggle to attain the sort of market dominance that locks in their network advantages' (*The Economist*, 2015a, 2015b).

STOP AND THINK How accurate have Victor and Stephens' predictions been? What evidence from your reading, or your experience of work organizations can you provide that either confirms or contradicts their nine fears?

 **RECAP**

1. **Appreciate the reason for chief executives' need to design and redesign their organization's structure.**
   - Organization structure is one of the ways of achieving organizational goals.
   - An organization's structure will be changed as a result of changes in its strategy, size, technology, environment, globalization and diversification.

2. **Distinguish three eras of organizational design and what factors stimulated each.**
   - Era 1: mid-1800s to late 1970s – self-contained organization structures.
   - Era 2: 1980s to mid-1990s – horizontal organization structures.
   - Era 3: mid-1990s to date – boundaryless organization structure (hollow, modular, virtual and collaborative).

3. **Distinguish between functional, divisional, matrix and team-based organization structures.**
   - A functional structure groups activities and people according to the similarities in their work, profession, expertise, goals or resources used.
   - A divisional structure splits an organization up into self-contained entities based on their organizational outputs, geographical region operated in, or the customer groups served.
   - A matrix structure combines two different types of structure (e.g. function and product).
   - A team-based structure consists entirely of project-type teams that coordinate their activities, and work directly with partners and customers to achieve their goals.

4. **Distinguish between an outsourcing relationship and hollow, modular and virtual organization structures.**
   - An outsourcing relationship involves contracting with external providers to supply the organization with the processes and products that were previously supplied internally.
   - A hollow organization structure is based on outsourcing an organization's non-core *processes* which are then supplied to it by specialist, external providers.
   - A modular organization structure involves assembling product chunks (modules) provided by internal divisions and external providers.
   - A virtual organization structure uses technology to transcend the constraints of legal structures, physical conditions, place and time, and allows a network of separate participants to present themselves to customers as a single entity.

5. **Understand the trend towards companies' collaborative relationships with competitors and customers, and their involvement in virtual communities.**
   - Collaboration has become a matter of integrating activities rather than integrating organizations.
   - Factors contributing to increased collaboration include the rise of partnership strategies, the knowledge economy, the working style of generation Y and advances in collaborative technology.
   - The increasing speed of change means that individual organizations lack the necessary resources, knowledge or skill to respond individually so have to collaborate with others.

Revision

1. Why might Max Weber and Henri Fayol be surprised by developments in contemporary organizational design arrangements?

2. Suggest how changes in organization structuring over the last 50 years have affected what workers and managers do, and how they do it.

3. In the literature, inter-organizational collaboration is presented as the way forward. Consider the potential negative consequences of this arrangement for the companies involved and their employees and managers.

4. Why are network and virtual structures preferred by managers seeking to encourage entrepreneurship and innovation?

Research assignment

This chapter reported Warner and Witzel's (2004) view that every organization possessed a mixture of virtual and tangible elements (p.572). They identified six dimensions along which organizations can choose to organize their activities on a virtual or a tangible basis:

- nature of product;
- nature of working;
- relationship with suppliers;
- relationship with customers;
- relationship between teams;
- relationship between managers and employees.

Review the discussion on virtuality and organizations in this chapter. Through personal contact, gain access to two different organizations. Using the six dimensions above as a basis for discussion, interview a manager from each organization to determine its virtual–tangible elements balance.

(1) Write a report on the strengths and weaknesses of the balance based on your interview findings.

(2) What effects does the balance have on employees' working patterns?

(3) Identify where your findings are consistent with, and where they contradict the textbook account of strengths and weaknesses of virtual forms of organization.

Springboard

Øystein Fjeldstad Charles Snow Raymond Miles and Christopher Lettl (2012) 'The architecture of collaboration', *Strategic Management Journal*, 33 (6): 734–50. The authors discuss how environmental challenges are leading to inter-organizational collaboration and consider the implications of this for organizational architectures.

Ranjay Gulati, Phanish Puranam and Michael Tushman (2012) 'Meta-organizational design: rethinking design in inter-organizational and community contexts', *Strategic Management Journal*, 33 (6): 571–86. The authors review the research on the growth of collaborative relationships between firms, the rise of outsourcing and the challenges of 'coordinating beyond the boundary'.

Liliana Pérez-Nordtvedt, Ross O'Brien and Abdul Rasheed (2013) 'What are temporary networks and when are they useful?', *Group and Organization Management*, 38 (3): 392–421. The authors distinguish different types of networks, based on the speed of their formation and time duration, which are increasing being formed to respond to unpredictable environmental changes.

Phanish Puranam, Oliver Alexy and Markus Reitzig (2014) 'What's "new" about new forms of organizing?', *Academy of Management Review*, 39 (20): 162–80. The authors consider the factors and processes which have created and shaped the organizational structures of the past, and those that are shaping them in the present.

OB cinema

Lord of the Rings; Fellowship of the Ring (2001, director Peter Jackson): DVD Chapter 27: 01:23:07–01:29:44 (4 minutes). The scene entitled 'The Council of Elrond' begins when Elrond says 'Strangers from distant lands, friends of old' and ends when Pippin asking 'Great! Where are we going?' Elrond, the leader of the elves, welcomes the various peoples of Middle Earth. Heated arguments break out among the elves, dwarves, hobbits and men who argue over who can be trusted to travel to Mount Doom with the ring in order to destroy it. The scene shows the different factions and their distrust of each other. Elrond persuades these factions to put aside their differences for the mutual benefit of all in Middle Earth. The Fellowship thus created, represents a strategic alliance. Consider the following questions:

- Under what circumstances would different factions (companies) unite to form a strategic alliance?
- What are the costs and benefits to the firms that form strategic alliances?
- Can you find some examples of recent strategic alliances in media? How successful have they been?

Based on Ambrosini et al. (2008)

 OB on the web

Search YouTube for 'The Matrix Pyramid – working in a matrix organization' (5.54), which provides a succinct summary of some of the key personal effectiveness skills needed by employees in order to work successfully within a matrix organization structure. Then search for 'Making the matrix work: the Campbell Soup story' (7:58), where Doug Conant discusses how he used team formation to introduce a matrix organization at the Campbell Soup Company. What problems did he encounter?

CHAPTER EXERCISES

1. University strategic alliances

Objectives
1. To consider the reasons for the creation of strategic alliances in higher education.
2. To evaluate the costs and benefits of this form of organizational design.

Briefing
1. Form into groups as directed by your instructor.
2. Read the exercise below.
3. Brainstorm the reasons why universities seek strategic alliances with each other around the world. Classify them under the main headings.
4. Answer the following questions:
    - What factors might have stimulated universities to seek strategic alliances with one another?
    - What benefits can universities obtain by joining such alliances?
    - What factors shape the ability of global university alliances to create collaborative advantage for their members?

Since the late 1990s, there has been an increase in inter-university alliances intended to achieve strategic goals. American, British and Australian universities in particular, have expanded into international markets (particularly in South East Asia) usually by establishing a strategic alliance with an existing local university or college. Some have opened branch campuses. Three major alliances have been established: Association of Pacific Rim Universities (APRU), Universitas 21 and the Worldwide Universities Network. Strategic alliances are designed to provide mutual benefits. These institutions have a variety of different reasons for seeking to establish such partnerships. Many such alliances often begin with courses and teaching.

Many international students go to these foreign countries to study, but there are also substantial opportunities for these foreign universities to directly offer their programmes to them in their home countries. Strategic alliances have become a popular entry strategy. Typically, a foreign university seeks an established higher education institution that is well located, has reasonably good facilities, an organized administration and management system, as well as access to suitable teaching staff. The university will then provide its course materials to local instructors to permit them to deliver the teaching course. Occasionally, the university will provide a 'home lecturer' to either run an educational programme or oversee the student assessments. At the end of their programme of study, the students will receive a degree from the recognized, foreign university, which is usually quite prestigious for the graduates. Fees are charged at a standard per subject basis and the foreign university and the local one divide the income on a predetermined basis. However, inter-university alliances are not limited to courses and teaching and may include other collaborations.

Based on Gunn and Mintrom (2013)

2. Designing your organization's structure

Objectives

1. To translate an organization idea into a structural form depicted on an organization chart.
2. To understand the issues involved in designing organizations.
3. To examine structural alternatives when redesigning a company to deal with growth.

Briefing

1. Form into groups as directed by your instructor.
2. Read the exercise below.
3. Work with your group members to complete the task at the end of each stage.

Exercise

You are eating a lunchtime sandwich and drinking a coffee. You are not impressed with either. You believe that you can do better, and decide to start your own, distinctive bakery here, in this town/city. You think of the range of bakery products that people eat; when, where and how they eat them; and what bakery products your various competitors sell (other bakeries, supermarkets, coffee shops).

Stage 1: Decide what products your start-up bakery will sell. What services will it provide? Will these be produced on-site, bought in from outside, or a combination of both? What tasks need to be performed? What jobs need to be filled? Draw the organization chart of your start-up bakery. Your group should be prepared to justify the choice of its organization design.

Stage 2: Your bakery is in its third year of operation and is very successful. You decide to open a second bakery. Decide whether it will be similar or different to the first, and where it will be located geographically. How do you intend to manage both bakeries at the same time? Draw an organization chart showing your two bakeries and justify your organization design choices.

Stage 3: Five years on and you are a successful entrepreneur. You now have five bakeries. Where have you opened these other bakeries? How do you keep in touch with what is going on in all of them? How do you deal with issues of human resources, control and information systems? What are your biggest problems? How have you dealt with them in terms of your structural design decisions? Draw an organization chart showing your five-bakery company and justify your organization design decisions.

Stage 4: Ten years further on and you have gone international. You have 80 bakeries spread around the five countries that are nearest to your own. What issues and problems do you have to deal with as a result of your decision to enter foreign markets in terms of organization structure? Draw an organization chart showing your international bakery company and justify your organization design decisions.

Debrief
- Groups share, compare and justify their organization design choice at each of the stages of their bakery company's growth.
- In turn, spokespersons display their own groups' organizational charts, highlighting the similarities and differences with other groups, and justifying their own group's choices.
- The class pays particular attention decisions about organization structure which relate to the systems and mechanisms that facilitate information flow, coordination and control.

Exercise adapted from Harvey and Morouney (1998)

Employability assessment

With regard to your future employment prospects:

1. Identify up to three issues from this chapter that you found significant.
2. Relate these to the competencies in the employability matrix.
3. Decide what actions you need to take to maintain and/or develop those competencies under each of the four headings of the employability matrix.

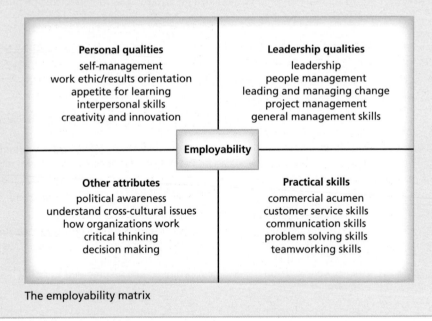

Personal qualities
self-management
work ethic/results orientation
appetite for learning
interpersonal skills
creativity and innovation

Leadership qualities
leadership
people management
leading and managing change
project management
general management skills

Employability

Other attributes
political awareness
understand cross-cultural issues
how organizations work
critical thinking
decision making

Practical skills
commercial acumen
customer service skills
communication skills
problem solving skills
teamworking skills

The employability matrix

References

All Things 787 (2015) '787 Dreamliner 2015 mid year report', http://nyc787.blogspot.co.uk

Ambrosini, V., Billsberry, J. and Collier, N. (2008) 'Teaching soft issues in strategic management with films: arguments and suggestions', *International Journal of Management Education*, 8 (1): 63–72.

Anand, N. and Daft, R.L. (2007) 'What is the right organization design?', *Organizational Dynamics*, 36 (4): 329–44.

Ashkenas, R., Ulrich, D., Jick, T. and Kerr, S. (2002) *The Boundaryless Organization: Breaking the Chains of Organization Structure* (2nd edn). San Francisco, CA: Jossey Bass.

Birkinshaw, J. (2013) 'Reorganizing from the bottom up: Microsoft Lync engineers chose teams', *Financial Times*, 24 January, p.12.

Blitz, R. (2007) 'Winning formula', *Financial Times Magazine*, 11 August, pp.22–23.

Blog Alliance (2015) 'Daimler and Renault-Nissan alliance start manufacturing joint venture in Mexico', 28 July, http://blog.alliance-renault-nissan.com/

Bock, L. (2015) *Work Rules: That Will Transform How you Live and Lead*. London: John Murray.

Boudreau, K.J. and Lakhani, K.R. (2013) 'Using the crowd as an innovation partner', *Harvard Business Review*, 9 1(4): 61–69.

Bradshaw, T. (2013a) 'Google set to download its way past Apple in app platform rivalry', *Financial Times*, 3 June, p.1.

Bradshaw, T. (2013b) 'Android's advance closes the gap on Apple', *Financial Times*, 3 June, p.19.

Brandenburger, A.M. and Nalebuff, B.J. (2002) *Co-opetition* (2nd edn). London: Profile Business Books.

Bughin, J. and Chui, M. (2011) 'The rise of the networked enterprise: Web 2.0 finds its payday', *McKinsey on Business Technology*, No. 22, Spring, pp.6–13.

Chandler, A.D. (1962) *Strategy and Structure: Chapters in the History of American Industrial Enterprise*. Cambridge, MA: MIT Press.

Cherns, A. (1976) 'The principles of socio-technical designs', *Human Relations*, 29 (8): 783–92.

Child J. (2015) *Organization: Contemporary Principles and Practice* (2nd edn). Chichester: Wiley.

Cook, S. (2008) 'The contribution revolution: letting volunteers build your business', *Harvard Business Review*, 86 (10): 60–69.

Davis, S.M. and Lawrence, P.R. (1978) 'Problems of matrix organizations', *Harvard Business Review*, 56 (3): 131–42.

Davis-Blake, A. and Broschak, J. (2009) 'Outsourcing and the changing nature of work', *Annual Review of Sociology*, 35: 321–40.

Denning, S. (2013a) 'Lessons every CEO must learn', *Forbes Magazine*, 17 January, www.forbes.com/sites/stevedenning/2013/01/17/lessons-every-ceo-must-learn /

Denning, S. (2013b) 'What went wrong at Boeing', *Forbes Magazine*, 21 January, www.forbes.com/sites/stevedenning/2013/01/21/what-went-wrong-at-boeing /

De Wit, B. and Ron Meyer, R. (2014) *Strategy Synthesis* (4th edn). Andover, Hants: Cengage Learning EMEA.

Dimitrova, D. and Wellman, B. (2015) 'Networked work and network research: new forms of teamwork in the triple revolution', *American Behavioural Scientist*, 59 (4): 443–56.

Dodge, J. (2007a) 'Designing around the clock, and the world', *Design News*, no.62, 4 June, pp.97–100.

Dodge, J. (2007b) 'Boeing 787 Dreamliner engineering chief describes partners organization', *Design News*, 15 May, 2007.

Duncan, R. B. (1979) 'What is the right organization structure? Decision tree analysis provides the answer', *Organizational Dynamics*, 7 (3): 59–80.

Elliott, C.S. and Long, G. (2016) 'Manufacturing rate busters: computer control and social relations in the labour process', *Work, Employment and Society*, 19 (1): 153–74.

Erickson, T.J. and Gratton, L. (2007) 'What it means to work here', *Harvard Business Review*, 85 (3): 104–12.

Fishman, C. (2007) 'Total teamwork: Imagination Ltd', *Fast Company*, 19 December.

Fjeldstad, Ø.D., Snow, C.C., Miles, R.E. and Lettl, C. (2012) 'The architecture of collaboration', *Strategic Management Journal*, 33 (6): 734–50.

Forrester, R. and Drexler, A.B. (1999) 'A model of team-based organization performance', *Academy of Management Executive*, 13 (3): 36–49.

Foss, N.J. (2003) 'Selective intervention and internal hybrids: interpreting and learning from the rise and decline of the Oticon spaghetti organization', *Organization Science*, 14 (3): 331–49.

Galbraith, J. (1973) *Designing Complex Organizations*. Boston, MA: Addison Wesley.

Gapper, J. (2015) 'Technology has to create more than disruption', *Financial Times*, 22 January, p.13.

Gouillart, F. and Billings, D. (2013) 'Community powered problem solving', *Harvard Business Review*, 91 (4): 70–77.

Gratton, L. (2007) 'Building bridges for success', Understanding the Culture of Collaboration supplement, *Financial Times*, 29 June, pp.2–3.

Gratton, L., Voigt, A. and Erickson, T. (2007) 'Bridging fault lines in diverse teams', *Sloan Management Review*, Summer, 48 (4): 22–29.

Gulati, R., Puranam, P. and Tushman, M. (2012) 'Meta-organizational design: rethinking design in inter-organizational and community contexts', *Strategic Management Journal*, 33 (6): 571–86.

Gunn, A. and Mintrom, M. (2013) 'Global university alliances and the creation of collaborative advantage', *Journal of Higher Education Policy and Management*, 35 (2): 179–92.

Halgin, D.S., Gopalakrishnan, G.M., and Borgetti, S.P. (2015) 'Structure and agency in networked distributed work: the role of work engagement', *American Behavioural Scientist*, 59 (4): 457–74.

Hamel, G. (2011) 'First, let's fire all the managers', *Harvard Business Review*, 89 (12): 48–60.

Harhoff, D. and Mayrhofer, P. (2010) 'Managing user communities and hybrid innovation processes: concepts and design implications', *Organizational Dynamics*, 39 (2): 137–44.

Harvey, C. and Morouney, K. (1998) 'Organization structure and design: the Club Ed exercise', *Journal of Management Education*, 22 (3): 425–28.

Hattersley, M. (2013) 'Hackable Lego Mindstorms EV3 robots can be controlled with an iPad', *Digital Arts*, 9 January, www.digitalartsonline.co.uk/news/ hacking-maker/hackable-lego-mindstorms-ev3-robots-can-be-controlled-with-ipad /

Howe, J. (2006) 'The rise of crowdsourcing', www. wired.com/wired/archive/14.06/crowds.html

Howe, J. (2009) *Crowdsourcing: Why the Power of the Crowd is Driving the Future of Business*. London: Crown Business.

Jaconi, M. (2014) 'The on-demand economy is revolutionizing consumer behaviour; here's how', *Business Insider*, 13 July, www.businessinsider.com/ the-on-demand-economy-2014-7?IR = T

Katzenbach, J.R. and Michaels. A. (2013) 'Life in the matrix', *Strategy + Business*, issue 72, 27 August, www.strategy-business.com/ article/00207?gko = 0f623.

Kelion, L. (2013) 'Valve: how going boss-free empowered the games maker', *BBC News Technology*, 23 September, www.bbc.co.uk/news/ technology-24205497

Koza, M.P. and Lewin, A.Y. (1999) 'Putting the S-word back in alliances', *Financial Times Mastering Strategy Supplement*, 1 November, pp.12–13.

Kornberger, M. (2010) *The Brand Society: How Brands Transform Management and Lifestyle*. Cambridge: Cambridge University Press.

Kumar, R. (2014) 'Managing ambiguity in strategic alliances', *California Management Review*, 56 (4): 82–102.

Lampel, J. and Bhaila, A. (2011) 'Living with offshoring: the impact of offshoring on the evolution of organizational configurations', *Journal of World Business*, 46 (3): 346–58.

Mabey, C., Salaman, G. and Storey, J. (1998) *Human Resource Management: A Strategic Introduction* (2nd edn). Oxford: Blackwell.

Miles, R.E., Snow, C.C., Fjeldstad, Ø.D., Miles, G. and Lettl, C. (2010) 'Designing organizations to meet 21st-century opportunities and challenges', *Organizational Dynamics*, 39 (2): 93–103.

Mohrman, S.A., Cohen, S.G. and Mohrman, A.M. (1997) *Designing Team-Based Organizations*. San Francisco, CA: Jossey-Bass.

Morozov, E. (2015) 'Where Uber and Amazin rule: welcome to the world of the platform', *The Guardian online*, 7 June.

Nadler, D. and Tushman, M. (1997), *Competing by Design, The Power of Organizational Architecture*, Oxford: Oxford University Press

Nowak, M. and Highfield, R. (2011) *Super Co-operators*. New York: Free Press.

Pisano, G. and Verganti, R. (2008) 'Which kind of collaboration Is right for you?', *Harvard Business Review*, 86 (12): 78–86.

Puranam, P., Alexy, O. and Reitzig, M. (2014) 'What's 'new' about new forms of organizing?', *Academy of Management Review*, 39 (20): 162–80.

Rainie, L. and Wellman, B. (2012) *Networked: The New Social Operating System*. Cambridge, MA: MIT Press.

Scahill, J. (2007) *Blackwater: The Rise of the World's Most Powerful Mercenary Army*. London: Serpent's Tail.

Schilling, M.A. and Steensma, H.K. (2001) 'The use of modular organizational forms: an industry level analysis', *Academy of Management Journal*, 44 (6), pp.1149–69.

Shih, S., Wang, J.T. and Yeung, A. (2006) 'Building global competiveness in a turbulent environment: Acer's journey of transformation', in W.H. Mobley and E. Weldon (eds), *Advances in Global Leadership*. Bradford: Emerald Group Publishing, pp.201–17.

The Economist (2002) 'Incredible shrinking plants', 23 February, pp.99–101.

The Economist (2007) 'Odd couple', 5 May, pp.71–72.

The Economist (2008) 'The un-iPhone', 27 September, p.84.

The Economist (2011) 'Schumpeter: The trouble with outsourcing', 30 July p.62.

The Economist (2012a) 'Faster, faster, faster', 28 January, p.59.

The Economist (2012b) 'Outsourcing is so passé', Technology Quarterly, 2 June, pp.7–8.

The Economist (2013) 'Coming home'', 19 January, pp.6–8.

The Economist (2014) 'Schumpeter: The holes in holacracy', 5 July, p.62.

The Economist (2015a) 'Workers on tap', 3 January, p.5.

The Economist (2015b) 'There's an app for that', 3 January, pp.13–15.

The Economist (2015c) 'Schumpeter: managing partners', 23 May, p.61.

Vasagar, J. (2014) 'Experiment with a bit of anarchy', *Financial Times*, 29 January, p.10.

Victor, B. and Stephens, C. (1994) 'The dark side of the new organizational forms: an editorial essay', *Organization Science*, 5 (4): 479–82.

Warner, M. and Witzel, M. (2004) *Managing in Virtual Organizations*. London: International Thomson Business Press.

Witzel, M. (2007) 'Types of collaboration: the right vehicle', Understanding the Culture of Collaboration supplement, *Financial Times*, 29 June, p.4.

Part 5 **Leadership processes**

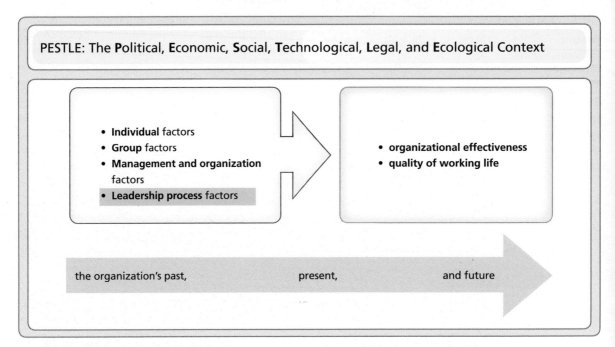

PESTLE: The **P**olitical, **E**conomic, **S**ocial, **T**echnological, **L**egal, and **E**cological Context

- **Individual** factors
- **Group** factors
- **Management and organization** factors
- **Leadership process** factors

- **organizational effectiveness**
- **quality of working life**

the organization's past,   present,   and future

A field map of the organizational behaviour terrain

Introduction

Part 5, Management processes, explores the following five topics:

- *Leadership*, in Chapter 18
- *Change*, in Chapter 19
- *Decision making*, in Chapter 20
- *Conflict*, in Chapter 21
- *Power and politics*, in Chapter 22.

Each of these topics has an enormous impact on how employees are managed, how they experience their work environment, and how successful their organization is in achieving its goals. Each topic concerns the process of managing, which involves both managers and non-managers. Thus, the most junior of employees may be called upon to exercise leadership skills, become involved in group decision making, and attempt to resolve a conflict between colleagues – while engaging in political behaviour in order to increase their power.

Most organizations in the twenty-first century are facing major changes in order to respond to turbulent economic, social, geopolitical and technological developments. Chapter 18 on leadership introduces this keynote topic by covering various current perspectives and their practical implications. Chapter 19 explores the nature of change, considering effective organization and management approaches along with the individual implications. This chapter concludes with an exploration of innovation processes in organizations, and what it takes to be an innovator. Chapter 20 on decision making considers different models of decision making, different types of decisions, different decision makers, and different problems in decision making. This chapter challenges the notion that most decisions are made logically for the benefit of the organization by managers who possess the necessary information and authority. Chapter 21 on conflict considers contrasting perspectives on this challenging topic, and stresses that how you perceive a situation influences what actions you will take. This chapter examines how the way in which a company is organized engenders conflicts which, in turn, have to be managed using conflict resolution devices. Finally, Chapter 22 addresses the abstract but critical concept of power in organizations, turning to the practice of organizational politics, the latter often being defined as 'power in action'. The political perspective provides an alternative to the rational standpoint found in many management-oriented textbooks. 'Playing politics' is often seen in negative terms. This chapter challenges this view, suggesting that the skilled use of organizational politics is necessary if leaders and managers are to make things happen, and get things done.

Invitation to see

Brendan McDermid/Reuters

Jack heads for the big league: Alibaba executives including Jack Ma, its founder, enjoy a stunning debut in New York. The share price soared immediately, valuing the Chinese online retailer at more than $220 billion. A similar photo marking this event appeared in *The Times*, 20 September 2014

1. **Decoding**:   Look at this image closely. Note in as much detail as possible what messages you feel that it is trying to convey. Does it tell a story, present a point of view, support an argument, perpetuate a myth, reinforce a stereotype, challenge a stereotype?

2. **Challenging**: To what extent do you agree with the messages, stories, points of view, arguments, myths, or stereotypes in this image? Is this image open to challenge, to criticism, or to interpretation and decoding in other ways, revealing other messages?

3. **Sharing**:   Compare with colleagues your interpretation of this image. Explore explanations for differences in your respective decodings.

You're the management consultant: what would you advise?

Our company is planning to merge with a competitor next year. The two organizations have complementary strengths, and although it will be challenging, this merger will create opportunities to grow our combined market share. However, the companies have their headquarters in different cities, and there is duplication of head office functions, so the merger is going to involve reorganization and redundancies. Our staff know this, of course, and they are feeling insecure. I know from the office gossip that many staff have already started looking for other jobs. The last thing we need, however, is a talent drain. We want to keep our brightest people to help develop the new organization, but we can't promise a future for everyone. Making this more complicated, we have a strong trade union that is demanding information and consultation. I want to keep morale high, and to treat people fairly, but I'm not sure how to achieve this. You're the management consultant. What would you advise?

Chapter 18 Leadership

Key terms

leadership

great man theory

consideration

initiating structure

contingency theory of leadership

structured task

unstructured task

situational leadership

new leader

superleader

transactional leader

transformational leader

distributed leadership

Learning outcomes

When you have read this chapter, you should be able to define those key terms in your own words, and you should also be able to:

1. Explain the apparent difference between the concepts of leadership and management.

2. Understand the relationships between personality traits and effective leadership.

3. Understand the challenges facing women who aspire to leadership roles, and the social and business cases for 'boardroom diversity'.

4. Understand why effective leaders either adapt their style to fit the organizational and cultural context in which they operate, or find contexts which fit their personal style.

5. Explain contemporary trends in this field concerning new leadership, distributed leadership, and the argument that leaders are unnecessary.

Why study leadership?

You do people, period, not my fault

Asked in 2014 about leading the twenty-first century organization, the American management consultant Tom Peters (then aged 71) said:

> If you're a leader, your whole reason for living is to help human beings develop – to really develop people and make work a place that's energetic and exciting and a growth opportunity, whether you're running a housekeeping department or Google. I mean, this is not rocket science.
>
> It's not even a shadow of rocket science. You're in the people-development business. If you take a leadership job, you do people. Period. It's what you do. It's what you're paid to do. People, period. Should you have a great strategy? Yes, you should. How do you get a great strategy? By finding the world's greatest strategist, not by being the world's greatest strategist. You do people. Not my fault. You chose it. And if you don't get off on it, do the world a favour and get the hell out before dawn, preferably without a gilded parachute. But if you want the gilded parachute, it's worth it to get rid of you.
>
> People say that fame is important, but in the end it really isn't. People say that wealth is important, but in the end it really isn't. My ex-wife had a father who was in the tombstone business. I've seen a lot of tombstones. None of 'em have net worth on 'em. It's the people you develop. That's what you remember when you get to be my age. (Heywood et al., 2014, pp.5–6)

Leadership the process of influencing the activities of an organized group in its efforts toward goal setting and goal achievement.

Leadership appears to be a key determinant of organizational effectiveness, whether we are discussing an army, an orchestra, a street gang, a political party, a mountaineering team, or a multinational corporation. It is not surprising to find, therefore, that leadership is a focus of intense interest. This focus is a recent phenomenon. In 1896, the United States Library of Congress had no books on leadership (Heller, 1997). The global literature on leadership is now vast.

Leadership is a controversial topic. We hear the complaint that 'we need more leadership'. However, the organizational hierarchy and formal authority that underpin leadership positions are now being challenged. We equate leadership with positions of power, influence and status, but leadership can be seen at all levels of an organization. Leaders have job titles and working conditions which symbolize their status. But flat structures, self-managing teams, knowledge work, and virtual and networked organizational forms all weaken traditional leadership positions based on hierarchy and symbolism.

Ralph Stogdill (1950), an influential early commentator, defined leadership as an influencing process aimed at goal achievement. That definition has three components. First, it defines leadership as an *interpersonal process* in which one individual seeks to influence the behaviour of others. Second, it sets leadership in a *social context*, in which the other members of the group to be influenced are subordinates or followers. Third, it identifies a criterion for effective leadership – *goal achievement* – which is one practical objective of leadership theory and research. Most definitions of leadership share these processual, contextual and evaluative components.

STOP AND THINK

Consider those who you would call leaders, in business, politics, sport, music, the arts. What characteristics – skills, abilities, personality traits – do they have in common?

Which of those leaders have had a positive impact, and which a negative impact? Do those whose impact was negative deserve the label of 'leader'?

Compare your list of leaders with that of colleagues. How can the term 'leader' be applied to such a range of different personalities, whose actions have led to different outcomes?

Traditionally, most leaders have been men; this may be reflected in your answers to our 'Stop and think'. Concern at the low numbers of women in senior organizational roles heightens importance of leadership today, and we will explore this problem shortly. We discussed in the introduction to this text how the portrayal of women in films and on television reflects wider social values and beliefs, and how movies help to maintain established stereotypes. Films rarely show women in positive or empowering ways (Ezzedeen, 2013).

Geena Davis (2015) argues that films reinforce unconscious bias against women. Analysing 120 successful movies, she found that, in family films, the ratio of male to female characters is 3:1, and this has not changed since the 1940s. Only 23 per cent of the films studied had a female leading character, and only 10 per cent had a gender-balanced cast. She also found that 'Female characters in G-rated animated movies wear the same amount of sexually revealing clothing as female characters in R-rated films. And even more baffling, women make up only 17 percent of characters in crowd scenes' (Davis, 2015, p.2). She concludes that:

> If women are continually depicted as one-dimensional, sidelined, stereotyped, hypersexualized, not given leadership roles or simply absent, it sends a very clear message: women and girls are not as important as men and boys. And that has an enormous impact on business and society. (Davis, 2015, pp.2–3)

Given the benefits of diversity at all levels of an organization – especially in the top team – male dominance is not just a problem for women seeking leadership careers. This raises wider social and organizational concerns. We need a better understanding of the forces that shape leadership stereotypes and biases in order to counter them, to achieve an appropriate gender balance.

Source: Cartoon Stock

This chapter explores six contrasting perspectives on leadership:

1. *Trait-spotting*: Identifies the personality traits and related attributes of the effective leader, in order to facilitate the selection of leaders.

2. *Style-counselling*: Characterizes different leadership behaviour patterns to identify effective and ineffective leadership styles, in order to improve the training and development of leaders.

3. *Context-fitting*: Contingency theories argue that leadership effectiveness depends on aspects of the organizational and cultural setting.

4. *New leadership*: 'Superleaders' and 'transformational leaders' are heroic, inspirational visionaries who give purpose and direction to others.

5. *Distributed leadership*: Leadership behaviour is not confined to those with formal senior roles, but can be observed across all organizational levels.

6. *Who needs leaders?* Transformational leaders can destabilize an organization by driving too much change too quickly, causing burnout and initiative fatigue; middle managers with change skills are more effective.

Trait-spotting was popular until the 1940s, when inconsistent research findings led to the approach being largely abandoned. Style-counselling was then popular until the late 1960s, when it was overtaken by contingency theories, which dominated thinking until the early 1980s. At that point, the 'new leadership' movement emerged. Towards the end of the twentieth century, the distributed nature of leadership attracted attention. In the twenty-first century, several commentators challenged the value of leadership, noting that 'celebrity bosses' often damaged organizational performance and reputation with rapid and radical changes. However, each shift in emphasis and approach has not replaced earlier thinking. All of those perspectives can be seen in today's research and practice.

Leadership versus management

What is the difference between leadership and management? Some commentators argue that leaders and managers make distinctly different contributions. Others argue, however, that leadership is simply one facet of a complex management role. Warren Bennis and Burt Nanus (1985) famously argued that 'managers do things right', while 'leaders do the right thing'. Leaders are thus often seen as visionaries who drive new initiatives. Managers simply seek to maintain order and stability. The leader is prophet, catalyst, mover–shaker, strategist. The manager is technician, administrator, problem-solver. The leader influences others to sign up to their vision, inspires them to overcome obstacles, and generates positive change. The manager establishes plans and budgets, designs and staffs the organization, monitors and controls performance, and delivers order and predictability.

This is a 'good guys, bad guys' caricature: leaders exciting, managers dull. Observing that this is inaccurate and insulting, Julian Birkinshaw (2010) argues that leadership and management must be seen as complementary, as roles that the same person plays at different times, as 'two horses pulling the same cart'. Another leading commentator in this field, Henry Mintzberg (2009, pp.8–9), also poses a fundamental challenge to the distinction between leaders and managers:

> Frankly, I don't understand what this distinction means in the everyday life of organizations. Sure, we can separate leading and managing conceptually. But can we separate them in practice? Or, more to the point, should we even try? We should be seeing managers *as* leaders, and leadership as management practised well.

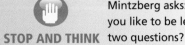

STOP AND THINK Mintzberg asks: Would you like to be managed by someone who can't lead? Would you like to be led by someone who can't manage? How would you respond to those two questions?

For Mintzberg (2009), a manager's roles include framing (deciding, focusing, establishing the context in which others work) and scheduling (slicing up concerns, deciding how to allocate time). The work involved in fulfilling those roles takes place on three planes: information, people and action (Table 18.1). Looking at this view of the 'people' plane, leadership is one facet of the management role.

Table 18.1: The three planes of managerial work

Plane of managerial work	Management roles
Information	Communicating, controlling
People	Leading, linking to others
Action	Getting things done, negotiating, building coalitions

Trait-spotting

For the first half of the twentieth century, researchers assumed that they could identify the personality traits and other qualities of effective leaders. It would then be possible to select individuals who possessed those characteristics, and to promote them to leadership positions.

The qualities of successful leaders

Summarizing conference presentations on the subject, and offering an up-to-date example of 'trait-spotting', Hayley Kirton (2015) argues that leaders need the following seven abilities, to:

- *make decisions in unpredictable circumstances*: deal with uncertainty, operate 'outside your comfort zone', provide a sense of direction;

- *grow from an unfortunate situation*: learn from failures how to deal with complexity;

- *listen*: recognize that leaders do not have all the answers in complex, diverse workplaces;

- *accept feedback*, especially constructive criticism, as a learning tool;

- *be self-aware*: get in tune with your feelings, make intuitive decisions when appropriate;

- *keep emotions in check*: manage them, do not let your emotions manage you;

- *read others' emotions*: be aware of how others are feeling, and adapt to engage them.

Great man theory
a historical perspective which argues that the fate of societies, and organizations, is in the hands of powerful, idiosyncratic (male) individuals.

This search for the qualities of good leaders was influenced by **great man theory**. Great man theory focused on political figures, arguing that leaders reach positions of influence from which they dominate and direct the lives of others by force of personality. There is no equivalent 'great woman theory'. Great men are born leaders, and emerge to take power, regardless of the social, organizational or historical context. Research thus focused on identifying the traits of these special people. Ralph Stogdill reviewed hundreds of trait studies (1948, 1974) and compiled this typical list:

- strong drive for responsibility;
- focus on completing the task;
- vigour and persistence in pursuit of goals;
- venturesomeness and originality in problem solving;
- drive to exercise initiative in social settings;
- self-confidence;
- sense of personal identity;
- willingness to accept consequences of decisions and actions;
- readiness to absorb interpersonal stress;
- willingness to tolerate frustration and delay;
- ability to influence the behaviour of others;
- capacity to structure social systems to the purpose in hand.

Advice for aspiring leaders

Richard Bracken, chairman and chief executive of Healthcare Corporation of America, was asked what advice he would give to aspiring leaders:

First, make sure you're working in an organization where there is a good fit between your core values and the organization's values – it will be difficult to be engaged and productive if there is a misalignment. Second, stay focused on delivering in your current position; many otherwise highly capable people are too quick to be thinking about the next promotion. No one likes a team member who is focused on the next opportunity. Also, don't be intimidated by the tough assignments, the ones others may not want. These are often the places where you can grow and prove yourself. And finally, never forget that taking calculated risks is the mark of a good leader. And once you commit, it's important never to go at it halfway. (Kirkland et al., 2013, p.4)

It is difficult to challenge these qualities. Can we say that leaders should lack drive, persistence, creativity and the ability to influence others? These are desirable qualities in many roles, however, and do not appear to be unique to leaders.

Research did not produce a consistent set of leadership traits, and as studies covered a wider range of settings, more qualities were identified. Almost 80 characteristics were reported from a review of 20 studies of leadership traits (Bird, 1940). More than half of these traits had been identified in only one study, very few appeared in four or more investigations, and only 'intelligence' was reported in at least half of the studies reviewed. In addition, many of these traits are vague. Willingness to tolerate delay? Capacity to structure social systems? Readiness to absorb stress? It is difficult to see how trait-spotting can be used in a leadership selection context, as originally intended.

Are you an alpha male or alpha female?

According to Kate Ludeman and Eddie Erlandson (2006), around 75 per cent of the world's testosterone-driven, high-achieving executives are 'alpha males'. They take charge, dominate, conquer and make things happen. Clever and effective, they can also cause damage, to themselves and to the companies they lead. Persistence can become stubbornness. Self-confidence leads to an unwillingness to listen to others. Those strengths, in other words, can be fatal weaknesses. There are fewer alpha women, and they do less damage because they empathize rather than confront, and are less angry and impatient. There are four types of alpha leader, each with good and bad characteristics:

Commanders: intense, magnetic, push others hard, but ignore rules and create fear.

Visionaries: creative, inspiring, but ignore reality, and are closed to input.

Strategists: quick, analytical, but opinionated, not team players, and don't admit mistakes.

Executors: problem-solvers, eye for detail, get things done, overcritical micromanagers.

Organizations run by dysfunctional alphas have higher rates of illness, staff turnover, absenteeism, burnout and early retirement (Rushe, 2006). To find out if you have what it takes to be an alpha, score each of these items from 'strongly agree' (0) to 'strongly agree' (10):

- No matter what, I don't give up until I reach my goal.
- When I play a game, I like to keep score.
- I sometimes rant and rave when I don't get my way.
- My opinions and ideas are usually the best ones.
- When others don't agree, I lose my temper.
- I am accustomed to being the centre of attention.
- People have described me as a 'natural born leader'.
- I believe the end usually justifies the means.
- I only collaborate with peers when I have to.
- There are a lot of people who are just plain stupid.

Scoring

0–25	Absolute wimp; keep tissues on your desk.
26–50	Bit of a pushover.
51–75	Ambitious but afraid to wield the knife.
76–100	Congratulations, you're an alpha.

By 1950 it appeared that there was little value in continuing to identify leadership traits, although some weak generalizations did emerge (Shaw, 1976; Fraser, 1978). Leaders tend, on average, to score higher on measures of:

- *ability*: intelligence, relevant knowledge, verbal facility;
- *sociability*: participation, cooperativeness, popularity;
- *motivation*: initiative and persistence.

The trait-spotting approach was abandoned by most researchers, who switched their attention, first to leadership *styles*, and then to characteristics of *context*. However, it has been difficult to overcome the belief that effective leaders must have *some* traits in common, and the search for those personality markers and other attributes continues. Paradoxically, therefore, although dating from the 1940s, trait-spotting is a contemporary perspective, which can be seen in leadership competency models, such as the 'transformational leadership behaviours' approach discussed later in this chapter.

Another contemporary example can be found in the work of Brian Hoffman et al. (2011), who distinguish between 'trait-like' and 'state-like' characteristics of leaders. Trait-like characteristics are those which are thought to be mainly inherited. State-like characteristics are those which can be learned and developed. The researchers combined evidence from 180 studies that explored links between leaders' characteristics and their effectiveness. They found 13 factors associated with leader effectiveness, including seven trait-like and six state-like characteristics (Table 18.2).

Table 18.2: Traits, states, and leader effectiveness

Effective leaders	
Trait-like characteristics	**State-like characteristics**
Achievement motivation	Interpersonal skills
Energy	Oral communication
Dominance	Written communication
Honesty/integrity	Administrative/management skills
Self-confidence	Problem-solving skills
Creativity	Decision making
Charisma	

In theory, because state-like characteristics involve behaviours, they should have a greater direct impact on leader effectiveness than trait-like characteristics, which affect performance indirectly. However, this study found that the effects of trait-like and state-like characteristics were much the same. Also, although the links between these characteristics and performance were positive, the effects were weak. This means that the differences between effective and ineffective leaders cannot be explained by traits and states alone. A leader's performance is affected by many other factors. Luck, according to the Nobel prizewinner Daniel Kahneman (2011, p.207), also contributes to the apparent success of individual leaders and their organizations:

> Because luck plays a large role, the quality of leadership and management practices cannot be inferred reliably from observations of success. And even if you had perfect foreknowledge that a CEO has a brilliant vision and extraordinary competence, you still would be unable to predict how the company will perform with much better accuracy than the flip of a coin.

Kahneman (2011) argues that we prefer simple messages of success and failure based on a clear understanding of cause and effect, and that we overlook the power of luck. The message that effective leaders must all have some traits and attributes in common is indeed clear and simple. In spite of evidence to the contrary, the search for those key traits looks likely to continue.

Do women have the wrong traits?

Male and female management styles

'I just walked into my office and asked my staff if any of them would rather work for a man. Two of the women said, "Yes. If you were a man, you would be easier to manipulate". The men said nothing.' (Daisy Goodwin, television producer, 2011)

For most of the twentieth century, it was widely assumed that leaders had to be *men*. Being female was not a desirable leadership trait. Leadership research was mostly done by men whose subjects were men. Women were largely ignored in leadership research until the 1990s, and are still poorly represented in senior management roles. Rachel Suff and Dianah Worman (2015) report that women account for only 23 per cent of board directors of FTSE 100 and 17 per cent of FTSE 250 companies (Financial Times Stock Exchange index of share prices). However, in 2011, when a voluntary target of 25 per cent was set in the UK, those proportions had been 12.5 per cent and 8 per cent respectively.

There has therefore been progress, but the pace of change has been faster in some countries than in others. Susan Vinnicombe et al. (2015, p.14) found that 'In Europe in 2014 the percentage of women on top boards varied from 5.2 percent in Portugal to 38.9 percent in Norway. The UK was the fifth highest country in Europe and the world.' That research found that 41 of the companies in the FTSE 100 had reached the 25 per cent target. Diageo and Intercontinental Hotels Group both had 45 per cent female representation on their boards. Other European countries are ahead of the UK:

> Seven of the top 10 countries for female representation among senior executives are in eastern Europe, headed by world leader Russia, where four out of every 10 business leaders are women, according to research by Grant Thornton, a professional services provider. The global average, according to the firm's latest report on women in business, is for 22 percent of senior jobs to be held by women. In eastern Europe, that figure is 35 percent.
>
> Poland is the best performer in the EU with 37 percent of senior management jobs held by women, followed by the Baltic states of Latvia, Lithuania and Estonia. The EU average is 26 percent, with the UK on 22 percent [at the time of writing], and Germany, at 14 percent, lagging behind. (Fox, 2015, p.14)

In 2005, Norway passed a law requiring public companies to allocate 40 per cent of board seats to women. Other countries have similar regulations: Belgium, France, Italy, the Netherlands and Spain. The national context is important. Norway has a tradition of using quotas to achieve social goals. In the UK, it is assumed that businesses and individuals should be free from government interference.

Diversity benefits, soft and hard

In many cultures, gender equality is seen as a goal worth pursuing in its own right. It is perhaps disappointing therefore, if not surprising, that debate has focused on 'the business case' for appointing more women to board positions. What are the commercial benefits?

Research shows that there are qualitative and financial outcomes. Suff and Worman (2015) surveyed 450 human resource professionals who identified the following benefits of having more women on boards of directors:

- bring different perspectives to decision making;
- reflect the wider diversity of society at large;
- serve as positive role models;
- are more innovative and creative;
- promote the organization's reputation;
- improve business performance.

Most commentators agree that bringing different perspectives is beneficial. But having just one or two women on a company board makes little difference. When there are three or more, they are less likely to be ignored. Anita Woolley and Thomas Malone (2011) studied the collective intelligence of teams. Subjects were given IQ tests, and then allocated randomly to problem-solving teams; the teams were given collective intelligence scores based on their team performance. The researchers found that collective intelligence was not related to the intelligence of the individual members. However, collective intelligence was higher in teams that had more women members. Why? Having smart individuals is important, but social sensitivity – a capability which women seem to display more strongly than men – also contributes to team performance:

> In theory, yes, the 10 smartest people could make the smartest group, but it wouldn't just be because they were the most intelligent individuals. What do you hear about great groups? Not that the members are all really smart but that they listen to each other. They share criticism constructively. They have open minds. They're not autocratic. And in our study we saw pretty clearly that groups that had smart people dominating the conversation were not very intelligent groups. (Woolley and Malone, 2011, p.32)

Diversity in the Gulf

In 2015, women held less than 1 per cent of board and executive positions in private and public organizations among the Gulf Cooperation Council (GCC) states of Bahrain, Kuwait, Oman, Qatar, Saudi Arabia and the United Arab Emirates. Over the past decade, a small number of women have been appointed to senior roles, but most are the only women near the top of their organizations. Women face the same barriers to promotion in the GCC as in other countries, but there are additional challenges, including cultural norms, traditions, biases and expectations. Women and men do not socialize outside professional contexts. This means that women cannot attend informal social gatherings where men exchange information and develop their networks. In Saudi Arabia, employers provide separate working areas for women, and sometimes separate entrances and lifts.

Tari Ellis et al. (2015) surveyed 550 male and female middle and senior managers in the GCC and interviewed 50 women in leadership roles. Two-thirds of all those surveyed said that the subject of women in leadership was part of their organization's strategic agenda. In the United Arab Emirates, 85 per cent said that this was on their agenda, but that proportion was less than half in Saudi Arabia. Women were more optimistic about change; 74 per cent said that women in leadership would become increasingly important, but only 51 per cent of the men agreed with that.

About 60 per cent of survey respondents said that women in leadership roles were a key driver of organizational effectiveness; 80 per cent of female respondents agreed with this, but only 53 per cent of the men. One of the benefits of gender diversity concerns the more balanced mix of leadership strengths. Women in the GCC scored more highly than men in the survey on four critical leadership behaviours: efficient communication, people development, inspiration, and participative decision making. The survey also revealed that:

> In the GCC the presence of women leaders prompts a greater sense of formality in company meetings – most likely because there are fewer occasions for

→

mixed-gender interactions there than in other regions and participants behave more formally when they do occur. Interestingly, the majority of leaders we talked to – men and women alike – felt that the added formality led to more task-focused and efficient discussions. (Ellis et al., 2015, p.5)

Interviewees also emphasized the benefits of involving more women in the development of products and services for which women were the main customers. One GCC executive said: 'We need to make women in leadership sound uneventful and normal'; it seems that this is starting to happen, slowly.

Several studies suggest that gender diversity on company boards improves financial performance. An analysis by the facilities management company Sodexo found that companies whose boards are at least one-third women perform better than rivals, generating 53 per cent higher returns for shareholders, and 42 per cent better profit margins (Cooper, 2013). Regina Reinert et al. (2015) studied the relationship between the proportion of women in senior roles in 264 Luxembourg banks, and the banks' performance from 1999 to 2013. A 10 per cent increase in the numbers of women in top roles improved a bank's future return on equity by over 3 per cent a year. This effect doubled during the global financial crisis of 2007 to 2009 compared with stable market conditions, 'which indicates that gender diversity seems to be of particular value during periods of economic downturn' (Reinert et al., 2015, p.14). In the most successful banks, women's share of top management positions was between 20 and 40 percent.

Thomas Barta et al. (2015) studied the executive board composition and returns on equity of 180 public companies in France, Germany, the United Kingdom and the United States from 2008 to 2010. Gender and cultural diversity were measured by the numbers of women and foreign nationals on each board. The companies ranked in the top 25 per cent for diversity had returns on investment over 50 per cent higher, on average, than those in the bottom 25 per cent. Another study focusing on senior women produced similar results. It is possible that companies that are performing well have more freedom to develop diversity programmes. The researchers argue, however, that organizations with more diverse top teams have a broader strategic perspective, and that they *should* perform better.

Tom Peters on women in management

Asked about making organizational change happen, the American management consultant Tom Peters said that, after his presentations on the subject, many managers would tell him that they enjoyed his speech, but that they could not implement his ideas because their boss would not let them:

Now one answer to that is to put more women in management. They know how to do a work-around. Men don't know how to do work-arounds, because

the only thing we understand is hierarchy. That's an exaggeration, of course, but then the neuroscientists tell us it's not that big an exaggeration. The male response is, 'I can't do anything about it 'cause my boss is really against it'. And the female response, by and large, would be, 'Well, I know Jane who knows Bob who knows Dick, and we can get this thing done'. They do it circuitously. (Heywood et al., 2014, p.8)

Barriers and solutions

There are obvious reasons for the small numbers of women in leadership roles, and there are more subtle explanations. Discrimination by male colleagues and family responsibilities are the traditional reasons. Research by the Chartered Institute for Personnel and Development (2015), based on the views of 2,000 working women, identified three other factors:

- *Self-confidence*: Women often lack the confidence to seek promotion, argue for a pay rise, or ask for development opportunities.

- *Working the room*: Many women say that they lack networking skills, which limits their ability to get help from appropriate advisers and mentors.

- *Embracing individuality*: Pressure to 'act like men' and to conform to the 'alpha female' stereotype holds many women back.

The Institute argues that 'Organizations need to foster an environment in which women don't feel the pressure to act like men – or in any other contrived way – in order to succeed. In fact, our contributors emphasized that women have unique and natural advantages in leadership that need to be celebrated' (CIPD, 2015, p.6).

There is evidence that women and men disagree on the nature of the problem. Boris Groysberg and Deborah Bell (2013) report the results of a survey of 294 women and 104 men, most of whom were US company directors. The aim was to develop understanding of the differences between men's and women's experiences as directors. Although gender diversity is generally welcomed, the researchers found that many boards did not know how to take advantage of this. The survey asked if women brought special attributes to their role: 90 per cent of female directors said that they did, but only 56 per cent of the males agreed. The survey also asked if female directors faced gender-related problems: 87 per cent of female directors agreed, but 56 per cent of the males said no. The problems that women said they faced were different from the problems that men said women faced (Table 18.3).

Table 18.3: The different perceptions of women and men

Problems that women say they face	Problems that men say women face
Not being heard and listened to	Limited access to and acceptance on boards due to weaker networks and the old boys' club
Not accepted as an equal or part of the 'in' group	Lack of experience and industry knowledge
Establishing credibility	Bias and prejudice
Stereotyped expectations of women's behaviour	Having to work harder to prove themselves

The main concerns for female directors were not being heard and not being treated as equals; men, however, did not recognize that their female colleagues faced these problems. These sharply different perceptions and experiences interfere with relationships, and with board functioning. To improve their effectiveness, boards thus need to become more inclusive, as well as more diverse.

Table 18.4: The gender diversity ecosystem

Top management commitment	Chief executive's priority Targets for women's representation in senior positions Company culture with consistent gender diversity goals
Women's development programmes	Networking events Mentors and external coaches Leadership skills development
Collective enablers (human resource policies and infrastructure)	Control of gender bias in recruitment, appraisal, promotion Flexible working patterns encouraged not penalized Facilitate remote working Action to increase number of women applicants Processes to retain top performing women Meetings scheduled only during business hours Childcare facilities, in house or external Job search programmes for partners and spouses

The problems do not lie exclusively with women's capabilities and perceptions. Research by McKinsey, a consulting firm, concludes that cultural and socioeconomic factors also discourage gender diversity (Devillard et al., 2012). Social support systems such as childcare facilities and parental leave influence diversity. Many women with initially high ambitions turn down promotion because of family and other commitments. The researchers argue that organizations need to develop a 'gender diversity ecosystem', combining senior management commitment, development programmes and 'collective enablers' such as supportive human resource policies (Table 18.4).

Glass slope, glass ceiling, glass cliff

Source: previously appeared in *Why Women Mean Business*, Wiley (Wittenberg-Cox, A. and Maitland, A., 2009) © Roger Beale

This discussion explains what is now called the 'glass ceiling', created by male-dominated boards, which stops women reaching senior roles. Suff and Worman (2015) note that women also have a 'glass slope' to climb before reaching that ceiling, while men are helped by a 'glass escalator' which carries them to the top. Michelle Ryan and Alexander Haslam (2005, 2007) argue that women promoted to senior roles face another set of problems. Their research found that companies are more likely to change the composition of their boards of directors when performance drops than when it is improving. Ryan and Haslam suggest that poor company performance can trigger the appointment of women to the board, because diversity leads to higher performance. They also observe that this means promoting women into positions that carry a high risk of failure. As women are a minority among senior managers, they are more visible, and their performance tends to be scrutinized more closely. The researchers conclude that women were being 'set up to fail', being placed on a 'glass cliff', in difficult organizational conditions which made their positions precarious. Women may then find that they are held responsible for poor performance caused by factors that were in place before they were promoted. Women may be underrepresented in senior management ranks, but they may be overrepresented in vulnerable senior positions.

Women who climb the glass slope and crack the glass ceiling may thus find themselves on a glass cliff. The traditional acronym TMTM (think management, think male) may have been replaced by TCTF (think crisis, think female). A number of factors may contribute to the appointment of female executives in times of trouble: a desire to protect male managers, perhaps, or to change the status quo. It may also be the case that the risky roles are the only ones available to women, who are more likely to accept the challenge when offered due to the barriers to promotion that they face elsewhere.

Evidence continues to support the concept of the glass cliff. Mark Mulcahy and Carol Linehan (2014) analysed 138 UK companies that had reported a loss in the period 2004 to 2006, after two consecutive years of reported profits. These companies were matched with those that had not made losses. The study found that where reported losses were severe, the gender composition of company boards was more likely to favour women than where losses were small: 'The crucial point is that increased female representation is significantly more likely to occur in precarious situations, particularly in severe, "big loss" scenarios as we have demonstrated here' (Mulcahy and Linehan, 2014, p.436).

As we have seen, the evidence shows that female representation on UK company boards has been increasing (Vinnicombe et al., 2015). However, Mulcahy and Linehan (2014) consider whether, as the global financial crisis recedes, fewer women will be appointed to board positions in future.

Bad but bold or wonderful but weak

In management roles, men are traditionally seen as 'bad but bold', and women are seen as 'wonderful but weak'. A series of studies by Jessica Kennedy and Laura Kray (2014) has produced support for these stereotypes, by exploring how men and women respond to ethical dilemmas at work.

"I took a course in ethics, but everything was contradicted by the course I took in *accounting*."

In their first study, 38 men and 65 women read 14 short stories involving ethical compromises, choosing between money and status, or honesty and the well-being of others. For example, would you use a cheap product that was known to cause lethal allergic reactions in some people, so that you could meet financial targets and win a performance bonus? Would you allocate a talented subordinate to a minor project and publicize their mistakes in order to damage their reputation? Participants in this study were asked to rate how morally outraged (or not) they were by these actions, and to indicate whether or not they thought such behaviours made business sense. Women reported more moral outrage at these ethical violations, in which they perceived less business sense than did men.

In a second study, 94 male and 84 female students read descriptions of three jobs, each involving an ethical issue. As a consultant, would you give honest advice to a client, or collect the fee? Would you invest in a company that used unethical business practices to generate profits? Some of these jobs were set in 'low ethical compromise' companies, where employees were expected to conform to ethical standards. Other jobs were in 'high ethical compromise' settings, in which the company norms emphasized profits. Once again, men were not affected by these ethical dilemmas, and women reported less interest in jobs that involved making ethical compromises. Finally, 54 male and 52 female students were given a word association test. This showed that women made stronger implicit links between business and immorality than did men.

This suggests that women are more reluctant than men to pursue business careers because they are less willing to behave in ways that compromise ethical values.

This conclusion, however, could have other beneficial outcomes:

> Retaining more women may have positive ethical consequences for business organizations. As women occupy positions with authority, they may improve the ethical standards of the organizations in which they work, if they can maintain these standards on the way up the hierarchy. (Kennedy and Kray, 2014, p.58)

Other research suggests that improving ethical standards can also improve financial results. Fred Kiel (2015) reports a study in which over 8,000 employees rated 100 chief executives on four character traits: integrity, responsibility, forgiveness and compassion. The average return on assets (ROA) of organizations whose leaders had the highest ratings was five times that of those with the lowest ratings – 9.35 per cent ROA, compared with 1.93 per cent.

STOP AND THINK

What other steps might women take in order to strengthen their organizational positions and achieve promotion to more senior managerial positions?

Style-counselling

The low numbers of women in senior leadership roles thus has little or nothing to do with 'female' traits and attributes. Going back to the 1950s, problems with the traits approach meant that the research focus switched to leadership, management and supervisory style. Instead of selecting leaders on the basis of personality traits, why not train and develop leaders to use appropriate behaviour patterns? This research tradition argues that a considerate, participative, democratic and involving leadership style is more effective than an impersonal, autocratic and directive style.

Two projects, known respectively as the Michigan and Ohio studies, underpinned the investigation of management style. Based mainly on a study of foremen at the International Harvester Company, the work of the Survey Research Center in Michigan in the 1940s and early 1950s (Katz et al., 1950) identified two dimensions of leadership behaviour:

1. **employee-centred behaviour**: focusing on relationships and employee needs;

2. **job-centred behaviour**: focusing on getting the job done.

Consideration
a pattern of leadership behaviour that demonstrates sensitivity to relationships and to the social needs of employees.

This work ran concurrently with the influential studies of Edwin Fleishman and Ralph Stogdill, at the Bureau of Business Research at Ohio State University (Fleishman, 1953a, 1953b; Fleishman and Harris, 1962; Stogdill, 1948; Stogdill and Coons, 1951). The Ohio results also identified two categories of leadership behaviour which they termed consideration and initiating structure. The considerate leader is relationships- and needs-oriented. The leader who structures work for subordinates is task- or job-centred.

The considerate leader is interested in and listens to subordinates, allows participation in decision making, is friendly and approachable, and supports subordinates with personal problems. The leader's behaviour indicates trust, respect, warmth and rapport. This enhances subordinates' feelings of self-esteem and encourages the development of communications and relationships in a work group. The researchers first called this dimension 'social sensitivity'.

Initiating structure
a pattern of leadership behaviour that emphasizes performance of the work in hand and the achievement of product and service goals.

The leader who initiates structure decides how things are going to get done, structures tasks and assigns work, makes expectations clear, emphasizes deadlines, and expects subordinates to follow instructions. The leader's behaviour stresses production and the achievement of goals. This is the kind of emphasis that the scientific management school (Chapter 14) encouraged, but task orientation in this perspective has a positive, motivating aspect. The researchers first called this leadership dimension 'production emphasis'.

Home viewing

Star Trek (2009, director J.J. Abrams) tells the story of how James T. Kirk (played by Chris Pine) became captain of the *USS Enterprise*. When the previous captain Christopher Pike is lost, the Vulcan crew member Mr Spock (Zachary Quinto) takes command, as the most senior officer on board. As you watch this movie, consider the following questions. What *leadership traits and behaviours* do Kirk and Spock each display? How would you describe the dominant *leadership style* of each of these two characters? Why do the other officers eventually accept Kirk as their commanding officer? To what extent does the *context* in which Kirk and Spock are operating influence who is more likely to be an effective leader?

Consideration and structure are independent behaviour patterns. A leader can emphasize one or both. Job satisfaction is likely to be higher, and grievances and staff turnover lower, when the leader emphasizes consideration. Task performance, on the other hand, is likely to be higher when the leader emphasizes the initiation of structure. Inconsiderate leaders typically have subordinates who complain and who are more likely to leave the organization, but can have comparatively productive work groups if they are high on initiating structure. This theory is summarized in Figure 18.1.

The work of another Michigan researcher, Rensis Likert (1961), reinforced the benefits of considerate, performance-oriented leadership. From interviews with supervisors and clerks in an American insurance company, he found that supervisors in highly productive sections were more likely to:

- receive general as opposed to close supervision from their superiors;
- give general as opposed to close supervision to their subordinates;
- enjoy their responsibility and authority, and spend more time on supervision;
- be employee- rather than production-oriented.

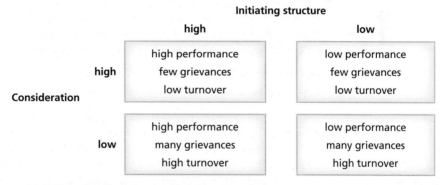

Figure 18.1: The Ohio State leadership theory predictions

Likert and his team identified four systems of leadership:

System 1: *Exploitative autocratic*, in which the leader

- has no confidence and trust in subordinates;
- imposes decisions; never delegates;
- motivates by threat;
- has little communication and teamwork.

System 2: *Benevolent authoritative*, in which the leader

- has superficial, condescending trust in subordinates;
- imposes decisions; never delegates;

- motivates by reward;
- sometimes involves subordinates in solving problems.

System 3: *Participative*, in which the leader

- has some incomplete confidence and trust in subordinates;
- listens to subordinates but controls decision making;
- motivates by reward and some involvement;
- uses ideas and opinions of subordinates constructively.

System 4: *Democratic*, in which the leader

- has complete confidence and trust in subordinates;
- allows subordinates to make decisions for themselves;
- motivates by reward for achieving goals set by participation;
- shares ideas and opinions.

Likert concluded that effective supervisors adopted either system 3 or system 4, which he called an 'alternative organizational life style'. However, recent research by Roderick Kramer (2006) suggests that, in certain contexts, what he describes as an intimidating leadership style can be effective, too.

Beverly Alimo-Metcalfe and Margaret Bradley (2008; Alimo-Metcalfe and Alban-Metcalfe, 2010) agree with Likert in arguing that a participative, engaging style improves performance. They studied 46 mental health teams involved in implementing organizational change, and found that engaging leadership increases employee motivation, job satisfaction and commitment while reducing stress. Each team had a designated leader, but as teams were on call around the clock, different members took the leadership role at different times. Engaging leadership had the following dimensions:

- involving stakeholders early: this helps to establish lasting relationships;
- building a collective vision: this means that the team 'owns' the work and the goals;
- no team hierarchy: leadership devolves as appropriate, even with an appointed leader;
- supportive culture: informal support from colleagues, formal support from supervision, so people can share problems, seek advice and take risks;
- successful change management: team members are consulted about change and their views are taken into account.

Engaging with others was one of three dimensions of leadership identified in this study. The second was *visionary leadership*, which involves having clear goals, being sensitive to stakeholder needs and interests, and inspiring them with passion and determination. The third, *leadership capabilities*, involves competencies such as understanding strategy, ensuring goal clarity, setting success criteria, commitment to high standards, and designing supportive systems and procedures. Of these three dimensions, engagement had the greatest impact on attitudes and performance, while leadership vision and capabilities had only limited effects. This study concludes that the development of leadership competencies should focus on encouraging a culture of engagement, at all levels of the organization.

The great intimidators

Roderick Kramer (2006) challenges the view that managers must be nice and not tough, and should be humble and self-effacing rather than intimidating. Kramer argues that intimidation is an appropriate style when an organization has become rigid or unruly, stagnant or drifting, or faces resistance or inertia. Abrasive leadership gets people moving. Intimidators are not bullies, but can use bullying tactics when time is short, and the stakes are high: 'They are not averse to causing a ruckus, nor are they above using a few public whippings and ceremonial hangings to get attention. They're rough, loud, and in your face' (Kramer, 2006, p.90).

"In his mysterious way, God has given each of us different talents, Ridgeway. It just so happens that mine is intimidating people."
Source: © Joseph Mirachi

Intimidators have 'political intelligence'. The socially intelligent manager focuses on using the strengths of others, through empathy and soft power, to achieve the outcomes they desire. The politically intelligent manager focuses on weaknesses and insecurities, using coercion, fear and anxiety. Working for an intimidating leader can be a positive experience. Their sense of purpose can be inspirational, their forcefulness is a role model, and intimidators challenge others to think clearly about their objectives. Kramer (2006, p.92) quotes a journalist who said, 'Don't have a reputation for being a nice guy – that won't do you any good'. Intimidation tactics include:

Get up close and personal.   Intimidators work through direct confrontation, invading your personal space, using taunts and slurs to provoke and throw you off-balance.

Get angry.   Called 'porcupine power', this involves the 'calculated loss of temper' (use it, don't lose it), using rage and anger to help the intimidator prevail.

Keep them guessing.   Intimidators preserve an air of mystery by maintaining deliberate distance. Transparency and trust are fashionable, but intimidators keep others guessing, which makes it easier to change direction without loss of credibility.

Know it all.   'Informational intimidators' can be very intimidating. It doesn't matter whether 'the facts' are correct, as long as they are presented with total confidence at the right time.

Context-fitting

The Michigan and Ohio perspectives offer leaders 'one best way' to handle followers, by adopting the 'high consideration, high structure' ideal. This advice is supported by the fact that most people *like* their leaders to be considerate, even when they are performance oriented as well. The problem, however, is that one leadership style may not be effective in all settings. Several commentators have developed frameworks showing how leadership effectiveness also depends on context.

Robert Tannenbaum and Warren Schmidt

Departing from 'one best way', Robert Tannenbaum and Warren Schmidt (1958) considered the autocratic–democratic choice of style as a continuum, from 'boss-centred leadership' at one extreme to 'subordinate-centred leadership' at the other. This is illustrated in Figure 18.2.

The steps in this continuum are presented as alternatives for the leader. Tannenbaum and Schmidt gave their article a subtitle: 'should a manager be democratic or autocratic – or something in between?' The answer, they suggest, depends on three sets of forces:

Forces in the manager: personality, values, preferences, beliefs about employee participation, confidence in subordinates;

Forces in the subordinates: need for independence, tolerance of ambiguity, knowledge of the problem, expectations of involvement;

Forces in the situation: organizational norms, size and location of work groups, effectiveness of teamworking, nature of the problem.

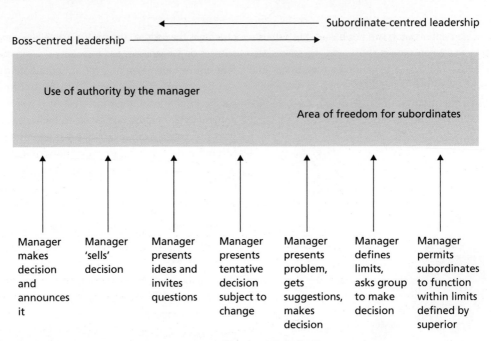

Figure 18.2: The Tannenbaum–Schmidt continuum of leadership behaviour

Source: reprinted by permission of Harvard Business Review. From 'How to choose a leadership pattern' by Tannenbaum, R. and Schmidt, W.H., Vol 37, March–April, reprinted in May–June, 1973. Copyright © 1958 by the Harvard Business School Publishing Corporation, all rights reserved.

Contingency theory of leadership a perspective which argues that leaders must adjust their style taking into account the properties of the context.

Having concentrated on 'forces in the manager', and challenged the notion of 'one best way' to lead, research now turned to consider the properties of the context in which the leader was operating. These properties included the people being led, the nature of the work they were doing, and the wider organizational setting. This perspective implies that leaders must be able to 'diagnose' the context, and then decide what behaviour will 'fit' best. As the best style is contingent (i.e. depends) on the situation, this approach is known as the **contingency theory of leadership**.

STOP AND THINK

Leadership theory seems to be consistent in arguing that a considerate, employee-centred, participative and democratic style is more effective.

In what context would an inconsiderate, goal-centred, impersonal and autocratic leadership style be effective? (See *OB cinema*, this chapter, for possible answers.)

Structured task a task with clear goals, few correct or satisfactory solutions and outcomes, few ways of performing it, and clear criteria of success.

Unstructured task a task with ambiguous goals, many good solutions, many ways of achieving acceptable outcomes, and vague criteria of success.

Fred Fiedler

Fred Fiedler developed one of the first contingency theories of leadership (Fiedler, 1967; Fiedler and Chemers, 1974, 1984). From studies of basketball teams and bomber crews, he found that leadership effectiveness is influenced by three sets of factors:

1. The extent to which the task in hand is structured.

2. The leader's position power.

3. The nature of the relationships between the leader and followers.

This argument distinguishes between a **structured task** and an **unstructured task**.

STOP AND THINK   Would you describe the task of writing an essay for your organizational behaviour instructor as a structured or as an unstructured task? Would you prefer this task to be more or less structured, and how would you advise your instructor to achieve this?

Fiedler identified three typical sets of conditions in which a leader might have to work:

Condition 1	Condition 2	Condition 3
Highly structured task	Unstructured task	Unstructured task
High position power	Low position power	Low position power
Good relationships	Moderately good relationships	Poor relationships

In condition 1, task-oriented leaders get better results, because they set targets and monitor progress. Relationships-oriented leaders get poor results because they want to maintain their relationships.

In condition 2, relationships-oriented leaders get better results, as relationships are key to exerting influence. In this case, the task-oriented leader who lacks position power gets poor results.

In condition 3, which is highly unfavourable, task-oriented leaders once again get better results, by structuring the situation, reducing uncertainty and ignoring resistance. The relationships-oriented leader is reluctant to pressure subordinates, avoids confrontations and pays less attention to the task.

Fiedler's theory confirms the importance of context in determining leader effectiveness, and supports the argument that there is no one best set of leadership traits or behaviours. But can leaders change style to fit the context? Fiedler felt that most managers and

When bossy is better

In a recent reworking of Fiedler's perspective, Stephen Sauer (2012) argues that you should base your choice of leadership style on your status. Newly appointed leaders in particular may be perceived as having low status because of their age, experience or education. Experiments with business students showed that low-status leaders got better ratings when they took charge and told their teams what to do. Low-status leaders who adopted a participative style and asked their teams for opinions got lower ratings. Why? If team members think that their new leader has low status, asking for their input may be seen as lack of confidence and competence.

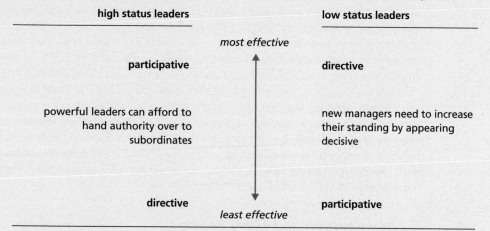

supervisors have problems in changing their styles. To be effective, he argued, *leaders have to change their context* (perhaps move to another organization), to find conditions in which their preferred style was most likely to be effective.

Paul Hersey and Ken Blanchard

Another influential contingency theory was developed by Paul Hersey and Ken Blanchard (1988). Like Fiedler, they argue that the effective leader 'must be a good diagnostician'. Unlike Fiedler, however, they believe that leaders can adapt their style to meet the demands of the situation in which they operate. Hersey and Blanchard call their approach **situational leadership**.

Situational leadership an approach to determining the most effective style of influencing, considering the direction and support a leader gives, and the readiness of followers to perform a particular task.

Their theory of describes leadership behaviour on two dimensions. The first concerns 'task behaviour', or the amount of direction a leader gives to subordinates. This can vary from specific instructions, at one extreme, to delegation, at the other. Hersey and Blanchard identify two intermediate positions, where leaders either facilitate subordinates' decisions, or take care to explain their own. The second dimension concerns 'supportive behaviour', or the social backup a leader gives to subordinates. This can vary from limited communication, to considerable listening, facilitating and supporting. The model thus described four basic leadership styles:

Telling: High amounts of task behaviour, telling subordinates what to do, when to do it and how to do it, but with little relationship behaviour.

Selling: High amounts of both task behaviour and relationship behaviour.

Participating: Lots of relationship behaviour and support, but little task behaviour.

Delegating: Not much task behaviour or relationship behaviour.

Hersey and Blanchard argue that the willingness of followers to perform a task is also a key factor. At one extreme, we have insecure subordinates, reluctant to act. At the other, we have confident and able followers. Superimpose the readiness continuum on the top half of the model and you have a basis for selecting an effective leadership style. The view that insecure subordinates need telling, while willing groups can be left to do the job, is consistent with other theories. The strengths of this perspective thus lie with its emphasis on contextual factors, and on the need for flexibility in leadership behaviour.

Daniel Goleman

Daniel Goleman (2000) reported research by the management consulting firm Hay McBer involving 4,000 executives from around the world. This identified six leadership styles which affect 'working atmosphere' and financial performance. The findings suggest that effective leaders use all of these styles, like an 'array of clubs in a golf pro's bag'. Each style relies on an aspect of *emotional intelligence* (see Chapter 6) which concerns skill in managing your emotions, and the emotions of others. Goleman's six styles are summarized in Table 18.5.

While coercion and pacesetting have their uses, the research showed that these styles can damage 'working atmosphere', reducing flexibility and employee commitment. The other four styles have a consistently positive impact on climate and performance. The most effective leaders, Goleman concludes, are those who have mastered four or more styles, particularly the positive styles, and who are able to switch styles to fit the situation. This is not a 'mechanical' matching of behaviour to context, as other contingency theories imply, but a flexible, sensitive and seamless adjustment.

David Snowden and Mary Boone

David Snowden and Mary Boone (2007) also argue that leaders have to adjust their style to suit the context. Contexts vary in terms of how simple or complex they are. The *Cynefin* framework (pronounced ku-*nev*-in) identifies four types of context: simple, complicated,

Table 18.5: Goleman's six leadership styles

Style	In practice	In a phrase	Competencies	When to use
Coercive	Demands compliance	'Do what I tell you'	Drive to achieve, self-control	In a crisis, with problem people
Authoritative	Mobilizes people	'Come with me'	Self-confidence, change catalyst	When new vision and direction is needed
Affiliative	Creates harmony	'People come first'	Empathy, communication	To heal wounds, to motivate people under stress
Democratic	Forges consensus	'What do you think?'	Collaboration, teambuilding	To build consensus, to get contributions
Pacesetting	Sets high standards	'Do as I do, now'	Initiative, drive to achieve	To get fast results from a motivated team
Coaching	Develops people	'Try this'	Empathy, self-awareness	To improve performance, to develop strengths

complex and chaotic. Leaders can use this approach to determine how best to operate. *Cynefin* is a Welsh term that refers to the many factors in our environment. Simple and complicated contexts are ordered and predictable, and correct choices can be based on evidence. Complex and chaotic contexts are untidy and unpredictable, and decisions have to be based on emerging patterns. Effective leaders can change their styles to match the changing environment. This approach is summarized in Table 18.6.

Being effective in one or two of these contexts is not good enough. Depending on the circumstances, a leader could be faced with all four contexts at the same time: a simple financial problem, a complicated product design issue, a complex threat from overseas competitors, and a serious accident. Snowden and Boone (2007, p.75) conclude that 'Good leadership requires openness to change on an individual level. Truly adept leaders will know not only how to identify the context they're working in at any given time, but also how to change their behaviour and their decisions to match that context.'

Table 18.6: Context and leadership

Context	Characteristics	The leader's job
Simple	Repeating patterns, consistent events Clear causal relationships; right answers Known knowns Fact-based management	Sense, categorize, respond Ensure processes are in place Delegate; use best practices Clear, direct communications; intensive interaction unnecessary
Complicated	Expert diagnosis required Causal relationships Discoverable, more than one right answer Known unknowns Fact-based management	Sense, analyse, respond Create panels of experts Listen to conflicting advice
Complex	Flux and unpredictability No right answers; emergent patterns Unknown unknowns Many competing ideas; need for creativity and innovation Pattern-based leadership	Probe, sense, respond Experiment, allow patterns to emerge Increase interaction and communication Use methods to generate ideas Encourage dissent and diversity

→

Table 18.6: Context and leadership (*continued*)

Context	Characteristics	The leader's job
Chaotic	High turbulence No clear causal relationships, no point looking for right answers Unknowables Many decisions, no time to think High tension Pattern-based leadership	Act first, sense, respond Look for what works, not for right answers Immediate action to re-establish order (command and control) Clear, direct communication

Assessing contingency theories

Contingency theories argue that the most effective leadership style depends on the context. Organization structures, management skills, employee characteristics and the nature of their tasks, are unique. No one style of leadership is universally best. There is, however, a large body of research which suggests that a considerate, participative or democratic style of leadership is generally more effective than a directive, autocratic style. There are two main reasons for this.

First, participative management is part of a long-term social and political trend in Western economies, which has raised expectations about personal freedom and quality of working life. These social and political values encourage resistance to manipulation by impersonal bureaucracies, and challenge the legitimacy of management decisions. Participation thus reflects democratic social and political values. Many commentators would note, however, that individual freedom, quality of working life and genuine participation are still lacking in many organizations in different parts of the world.

Second, participative management has been encouraged by studies which have shown that this style is generally more effective, although an autocratic style can be effective in some contexts. A participative style can improve organizational effectiveness by tapping the ideas of those who have 'frontline' knowledge and experience, and by involving them in a decision-making process to which they then become committed. This approach is encouraged by the growth in numbers of knowledge workers who expect to be involved in decisions affecting their work, and whose knowledge makes them potentially valuable contributors in this respect.

People who are involved in setting standards or establishing methods are thus more likely to experience 'ownership' of such decisions, and are therefore more likely to:

- accept the legitimacy of decisions reached with their help;
- accept change based on those decisions;
- trust managers who ultimately ratify and implement decisions;
- volunteer new and creative ideas and solutions.

Autocratic management stifles creativity, ignores available expertise, and smothers motivation and commitment. However, there is no doubt that autocratic management can be effective:

- when time is short;
- when the leader is the most knowledgeable person;
- where those who participate will never agree with each other – but a decision must be made.

There are advantages in consistency, and leaders who change their style from one situation to another may not inspire confidence or trust. Contingency perspectives, however, argue that leaders should be able to adapt to their context:

1. It is now broadly accepted that leaders and managers can learn from experience and adjust their behaviour according to the circumstances.

2. Organizations are not rigid arrangements with fixed tasks and structures. With the growth in demand for flexibility, adaptability, improved quality of working life and participation, leaders and managers who fail to respond will face problems.

3. The leader or manager who adapts in a flexible way to changes in circumstances may be seen as more competent than one who sticks rigidly to traditional routines.

Contingency theories have attracted criticisms. One criticism concerns the ability of leaders to diagnose the context in which they are operating, given the vague nature of the situational variables identified by different theories. In addition, contingency theories often overlook other key dimensions of context, such as the organization culture, degree of change and levels of stress, working conditions, external economic factors, organizational design and technology. All of these factors potentially influence the leadership process in ways not addressed by any of these theoretical accounts.

A second criticism concerns whether leaders can adapt their styles to fit the context in the ways the theories suggest. Personality may not be flexible enough. Inherent traits may inhibit managers from being participative in some circumstances and dictatorial in others. The manager who is motivated by affiliation, valuing friendship, may find it hard to treat others in an impersonal and autocratic way. The styles and expectations of other managers in an organization may also be influential.

Employee first, customer second: leadership lessons from India

Peter Cappelli and colleagues (2010) argue that Indian companies have developed a new model of leadership, different in style and emphasis from leadership models commonly found in the West. The development of this new model dates from the early 1990s when economic reforms in India simplified the regulatory environment and exposed Indian companies to international competition. So where do the senior leaders of Indian companies today focus their energies? Their top four priorities are to be:

1. chief input for business strategy;

2. keeper of organization culture;

3. guide, teacher, and role model for employees;

4. representative of owner and investor interests.

Executives in the US and the UK would have to put short-term shareholder interests first, and not fourth, but leaders in India are more concerned with long-term investment in people:

Far more than their Western counterparts, these leaders and their organizations take a long-term, internally focused view. They work to create a sense of social mission that is served when the business succeeds. They make aggressive investment in employee development, despite tight labour markets and widespread job-hopping. And they strive for a high level of employee engagement and openness. The higher priority these executives place on keeping the culture and guiding and teaching employees underscores their focus on human capital development. (Cappelli et al., 2010, p.92)

Cappelli and colleagues interviewed over 100 executives who explained the success of their companies in terms of employees' positive attitudes, which they sought to inspire in four main ways:

- *creating a sense of mission*: involvement in social issues, community services, infrastructure – employees feel their work has an impact;

- *engagement through openness and reciprocity*: caring for employees and their families – 'employee first, customer second' policy;

- *empowering through communication*: inviting challenge and criticism, allowing employees to contribute to problem-solving, questioning traditional deference to hierarchy;

- *investing in training*: heavier investment in employee development than in Western countries (25 per cent of new hires in the US receive no training during their first two years; new hires in India typically receive at least 60 days of formal training in their first year).

The researchers argue that, while these policies are not novel, they are emphasized consistently in a coherent package which Western leaders could adapt to their own circumstances, particularly with regard to investment in training, and strengthening their social mission.

New leadership

New leader an inspirational visionary, concerned with building a shared sense of purpose and mission, creating a culture in which everyone is aligned with the organization's goals and is skilled and empowered to achieve them.

In the search for new ideas in the late twentieth century, the key role of heroic, powerful, visionary, charismatic leaders was recognized. Several new terms were invented to describe this role. We had the **new leader**, an inspirational figure motivating followers to higher levels of achievement. However, we also had the **superleader**, who is able to 'lead others to lead themselves' (Sims and Lorenzi, 1992, p.295). These terms clearly overlap, and are closely related to the popular and influential concept of transformational leadership.

Transformational leadership

Superleader a leader who is able to develop leadership capacity in others, empowering them, reducing their dependence on formal leaders, stimulating their motivation, commitment and creativity.

The new leadership movement began with the work of James McGregor Burns (1978), whose study of political leaders distinguished between the **transactional leader** and the **transformational leader**. Transactional leaders see their relationships with followers in terms of trade, swaps or bargains. Transformational leaders are charismatic individuals who inspire and motivate others to perform 'beyond contract'.

Noel Tichy and Mary Anne Devanna (1986) argue that transformational leaders have three main roles: recognizing the need for revitalization, creating a new vision, and institutionalizing change. Bernard Bass and Bruce Avolio (Bass, 1985a, 1985b; Bass and Avolio, 1990, 1994) similarly claim that transformational leadership involves 'the Four Is':

Transactional leader a leader who treats relationships with followers in terms of an exchange, giving followers what they want in return for what the leader desires, following prescribed tasks to pursue established goals.

- Intellectual stimulation: encourage others to see what they are doing from new perspectives.
- Idealized influence: articulate the mission or vision of the organization.
- Individualized consideration: develop others to higher levels of ability.
- Inspirational motivation: motivate others to put organizational interests before self-interest.

The Transformational Leadership Questionnaire developed by Beverly Alimo-Metcalfe and John Alban-Metcalfe (2002, 2003) identifies 14 behaviours (or competencies) in three categories:

Transformational leader a leader who treats relationships with followers in terms of motivation and commitment, influencing and inspiring followers to give more than mere compliance to improve organizational performance.

Leading and developing others

- showing genuine concern
- empowering
- being accessible
- encouraging change

Personal qualities

- being transparent
- acting with integrity
- being decisive
- inspiring others
- resolving complex problems

Leading the organization

- networking and achieving
- focusing team effort
- building shared vision
- supporting a developmental culture
- facilitating change sensitively.

Research with public sector managers and employees suggests that these behaviours can increase job satisfaction and motivation, and reduce stress. Alimo-Metcalfe and

Alban-Metcalfe also found that women were seen as more transformational than men on most of these behaviours, and were rated as better than men on being decisive, focusing effort, mentoring, managing change, inspiring others and openness to ideas. Are these new labels a fresh development in leadership theory and practice? George Hollenbeck and colleagues (2006) argue that identifying the characteristics or competencies of transformational leaders takes us back to the 'great person' view of leadership and trait-spotting, overlooking what we know about the influence of context on leadership effectiveness.

STOP AND THINK

Considering business and political leaders – past or present – with whom you are familiar, directly or through the media, which come closest to these definitions of new leader, superleader and transformational leader?

The new, super, transformational leader looks like a 'one best way' approach. Does this vindicate trait-spotting and discredit contingency perspectives?

Distributed leadership

We need leadership to be distributed

'We observe that the need for leadership has changed following the global shifts in the ways we work today. While organizations are seen to be better at understanding leadership at the highest levels in the hierarchy, many are now seeking to devolve leadership down the line, expecting more junior managers and employees without managerial responsibility to treat the organisational agenda as their own. The need for leadership throughout the organization has only recently been acknowledged, mostly as front-line and middle managers have been asked to support continuous organizational change and generate discretionary effort by staff, as well as to apply informal leadership techniques in order to influence internal and external colleagues who do not report to them directly' (Zheltoukhova, 2014, pp.2–3).

Distributed leadership the collective exercise of leadership behaviours, often informal and spontaneous, by staff at all levels of an organization.

Do we need visionary superheroes? Recent studies show how changes can be implemented by people at all levels of an organization. This is known as distributed leadership.

Leadership theory traditionally assumes that others will not act without 'strong and effective' leadership. We need leaders to generate the ideas and to provide the directions, the 'orders from above', which inspire followers, don't we? Peter Gronn (2002, 2009) contrasts this traditional idea of focused leadership, emphasizing the individual, with distributed leadership. Distributed leadership involves many people acting in concert, in formal and informal, spontaneous and intuitive roles (Bryman, 1996; Caldwell, 2005). These roles may not be permanent. Leadership functions can be shared. The leadership role can move from one person or group to another, as circumstances change. Leadership can thus involve role-sharing and turn-taking, rather than belonging to one person.

Distributed leadership is encouraged by flatter structures, teamwork, knowledge work, developments in communication technology, and 'network' organization forms. In turbulent economic conditions, many organizations are unstable and are evolving in novel ways. This often means creating new types of inter-organizational collaboration (see Chapter 17). The scale and complexity of these changes involve more people, compared with change that only affects one part of an organization. These trends combine with the fashion for empowerment and engagement (Chapter 9). Debra Meyerson (2001) highlights the importance of behind-the-scenes, 'below the radar' change leadership of middle managers. Joseph Badaracco (2001, p.126) describes a 'quiet approach to change leadership', emphasizing 'small things, careful moves, controlled and measured efforts'. In appropriate conditions, staff with motivation and capabilities can lead and implement change covertly, quietly, by stealth, just as effectively as 'celebrity bosses', without destabilizing the organization and burning out colleagues.

One of the problems with distributed leadership is that the capabilities and contributions of those who are involved may not be recognized. Sylvia Ann Hewlett and colleagues (2005) observe that members of ethnic minority groups, while holding junior posts in their organizations, often have major community leadership roles, with capabilities and talent that are neither recognized nor used by their main employer. These are the 'unsung heroes' who take personal responsibility, and risk, for driving change without always waiting patiently for others, or simply following directions.

David Buchanan et al. (2007) describe how complex changes to improve cancer services in a British hospital were implemented by a large number of people acting together to meet the same goals and targets, without formal change management plans, structures and roles. Although four key people were involved at different stages, they were not senior managers, and the change process also involved 19 other individuals, and 26 managerial, administrative and clinical groups, patients' representatives and other organizations. Their contributions were informal and fluid, and complemented each other. The researchers note how responsibility for these changes 'migrated' around various groups and individuals. They conclude that implementing change with 'nobody in charge' can be just as effective as traditional methods. This approach is not dependent on individuals or small teams, and survives the departure of the lone change agent.

Shift your mindset to be seen as a leader

Do others see you as a leader, or not? Age, race, gender, appearance and personality all play a role in how others assess you; tall, good-looking, extravert white men over the age of 40 are often seen more positively than their opposites – but those properties are hard to change. Expertise, competence and commitment are also good indicators – but these are difficult for others to judge quickly. Your status seems to be determined by factors that you cannot control.

Adam Galinsky and Gavin Kilduff (2013) argue that it is possible to improve your status, dominance and influence at work. They recommend 'shifting your mindset', a factor which is under your control, because this can improve your chances of being seen as a leader. The aim is to use more proactive behaviours, such as speaking up and speaking earlier, acting more assertively, offering more ideas, taking the initiative, acting to solve problems and expressing confidence.

There are three psychological states that help us to behave proactively: a 'promotion' focus on aspirations and goals, happiness and feelings of power. These states have been shown to reduce levels of the stress hormone cortisol, and increase optimism and confidence. You can prepare yourself for your next meeting by simply writing a few short notes on your smartphone. To shift to a promotion focus, describe your ambitions and what you hope to achieve. To stimulate happiness, write about when you have felt excited and 'high'. To feel more powerful, write about a time when you had power over someone else.

In experiments with this technique, participants who had prepared to feel promotion-focused, happy and powerful behaved more proactively, and were granted higher status than those who were not prepared in this way. The former were more likely to be described by others as 'group leader'. Further experiments showed that this effect can be a lasting one. Those who are given high status are then treated in ways that reinforce that position – given more information and speaking opportunities.

The researchers claim that this proactive mindset, even if it is temporary, can also improve your interviewing, negotiation and presentation skills. They conclude (Galinsky and Kilduff, 2013, p.130):

> We now know that a small change in the thoughts and feelings you bring to your first encounter with a group – activated by something as quick and easy as a writing task – can have a significant impact on your status in it. Conventional wisdom says that success comes from having the right attributes, or from being in the right place at the right time. Our research suggests that it is also a matter of being in the right frame of mind at the right time.

Ksenia Zheltoukhova (2014) identifies four trends that are shaping leadership roles:

1. *Frequency and pace of change*: faster information sharing and aggressive competition means that decisions have to be taken faster, which means devolving responsibilities 'down the line'.

2. *Greater transparency and global consumer choice*: standards of business behaviour are now public and consumers can switch rapidly to competitors if they feel that an organization is breaching those standards.

3. *Collaborative working*: flat structures and external partnerships mean that people have to influence others over whom they have no line management authority.

4. *Workforce diversity*: need to address a wider range of different needs and motivations across the workforce – work has to appeal to a wider range of expectations than in the past.

Copyright 2009
Harvard Business Review
Magazine

These trends encourage a devolved, distributed approach to leadership, but hierarchy, bureaucracy, a focus on short-term goals, and individual reward systems undermine that approach. Distributed leadership does not imply a complete shift away from formal, senior figures with prestige titles who continue to exercise leadership functions. What is required is a 'twin track' approach in which visionary individual leaders, and a widely dispersed leadership decoupled from high office, work together.

Who needs leaders?

Throughout the twentieth century, it was unquestioningly accepted that leadership was indispensable. A novel perspective emerged in the opening years of the twenty-first century, challenging the enthusiasm for charismatic, visionary, transactional superleaders. Here is a perspective which argues that some leaders are *dangerous*.

Nick Morgan (2001, p.3) is critical of 'larger-than-life leaders and their grand strategies', arguing for 'a quieter, more evolutionary approach to change, one that relies on employee motivation instead of directives from on high'. He argues that organizations should reduce the amount of change, focus instead on incremental improvements, and 'above all lose the notion that you need heroic leaders in order to have meaningful, sustained change (p.2). This is consistent with views on organizational change (explored in Chapter 18), particularly Eric Abrahamson's (2004) approach to 'painless change' which is carefully staged and paced.

Quy Huy (2001) also dismisses the role of visionary leadership, arguing that it is middle managers who achieve the balance between change and continuity, and that radical change imposed from the top makes this difficult. Jim Collins (2001) argues that 'larger than life' leaders are not always effective, and that the most powerful senior executives display what he calls 'level 5 leadership', combining humility with persistence. We have already met Meyerson's (2001) 'tempered radicals' who operate 'below the radar', and Badaracco's (2002) 'unglamorous, not heroic, quiet approach to leadership'. It is important to pay attention to these 'non-leadership' contributions to organizational change.

Rakesh Khurana (2002, p.62) is scathing in his assessment of transformational leaders. The popular stereotype is the charismatic individual who wins the confidence of investors and the business press, inspires employees, defeats overwhelming competition and turns around dying companies. This is the white knight, the lone ranger, the heroic figure. Khurana has four criticisms of these characters:

1. They 'reject limits to their scope and authority [and] rebel against all checks on their power and dismiss the norms and rules that apply to others'. In other words, they can be beyond the influence and control of other senior colleagues.

2. They rely on 'the widespread quasi-religious belief in the powers of charismatic leaders'. This belief allows them to 'exploit the irrational desires of their followers'.

3. They encourage the attribution error of understanding success in terms of the actions of prominent leaders, while overlooking 'the interplay of social, economic, and other impersonal forces that shape and constrain even the most heroic individual efforts'.

4. New chief executives often deliberately destabilize their organizations, to foster revitalization. However, this can be harmful, if not disastrous, as a number of corporate scandals in the early twenty-first century illustrated.

As discussed earlier, visionary leaders are expected to drive radical change, while managers maintain order and stability. However, Khurana regards the transformational leader as a 'dangerous curse'. This backlash against 'new leaders' has two interesting dimensions.

- The combined views of Morgan, Huy, Collins, Myerson, Badaracco and Khurana take the debate back to the distinction between leadership and management. We discussed the perspective which argues, 'leadership is good – management is bad'. This argument is now reversed, with the claim that leaders can be dangerously destabilizing while managers drive change more effectively.

- In this approach, organizational effectiveness depends on competent managers with change agency skills, and not on heroic visionaries with charismatic personalities.

Video case: image of 'superhero' chief needs a rethink

This five-minute *Financial Times* video is presented by Andrew White from Oxford Saïd Business School. He challenges the need for charismatic leaders, arguing that this style is no longer appropriate. Senior leaders need to be able to work with a range of external stakeholders – regulators, activists, community groups – whose access to and use of social media make them more powerful. The ability to manage these diverse groups is a key leadership capability. He also introduces the concept of 'ripple intelligence' – understanding complexity and the 'knock on' effects of actions.

RECAP

1. **Explain the apparent difference between the concepts of leadership and management.**

   - Leaders are typically portrayed as inspiring, change-oriented visionaries.

   - Managers are typically portrayed as planners, organizers and controllers.

   - In practice, the roles overlap, are complementary, and can be difficult to distinguish.

2. **Understand the relationships between personality traits and effective leadership.**

   - Many factors, besides personality traits, influence leadership effectiveness.

   - It has proved difficult to establish a consensus on specific traits.

   - The characteristics of the leader's role also influence behaviour and effectiveness.

3. **Understand the challenges facing women who aspire to leadership roles, and the social and business cases for 'boardroom diversity'.**

   - Women are traditionally powerless due to discrimination and exclusion by male behaviour.

   - Women have social and interpersonal leadership qualities, improve performance by widening management discussions, and are now more likely to be promoted on merit.

   - Board gender-diversity is seen in many countries as socially desirable for equality reasons, and there is evidence suggesting that board diversity is positively linked to corporate performance.

   - Women who climb the glass slope eventually hit a glass ceiling, preventing their further progress into more senior management roles.

   - When organizations are in financial difficulty, they often appoint women to senior roles, where they are then vulnerable to failure; this has been described as a 'glass cliff'.

4. **Understand why effective leaders either adapt their style to fit the organizational and cultural context in which they operate, or else find contexts which fit their personal style.**

   - Considerate behaviour reduces labour turnover and improves job satisfaction.

   - Initiating structure improves performance but reduces job satisfaction.

   - Effective leaders combine consideration with initiating structure.

   - Contingency theory argues that leaders are more or less effective depending on how structured the task is, how powerful the leader is, and how good the relationships are.

   - Situational leadership advises the manager to use telling, selling, participating and delegating styles depending on the task, relationships and employee readiness.

   - Some commentators argue that leaders cannot change their behaviour, and that to be effective they have to find organizational contexts that are suitable for their leadership style.

   - Most commentators argue that leaders can and should adapt their behaviour to fit the context and the culture in which they are operating.

5. **Explain contemporary trends in this field concerning new leadership, the dispersal of leadership, and the argument that leaders are unnecessary.**

   - One trend emphasized charismatic, visionary, inspirational new leaders.

   - New leadership, superleader and transformational leadership are close synonyms.

   - Distributed leadership can be observed at all organizational levels.

   - The new visionary leader helps to develop leadership capability in others.

   - The new leader has the right traits, and the right style, for the contemporary context, thus combining notions of trait-spotting, style-counselling and context-fitting.

   - A more recent trend views charismatic, visionary leaders as dangerous because they can destabilize an organization; change management capabilities are more important.

Revision

1. What is the difference between leadership and management, and why is it difficult to separate these concepts in practice?

2. Why is trait-spotting such a popular theme in leadership research? What has trait-spotting told us about the personality markers of successful leaders? What are the problems with this perspective?

3. Traditionally, leaders have been men with special qualities. Why are women now more likely to be considered as effective leaders?

4. The concept of transformational leadership is popular. What advantages and drawbacks come with this leadership style?

Research assignment

The chief executives of private and public sector organizations are often in the news: online, blogs, Twitter, television. Sometimes they attract media interest because their organization has been innovative and successful. When an organization has contributed to an accident, failure or disaster, the media will report that, too. Find two chief executives who are in the news when you study this chapter. If possible, identify one male and one female chief executive. Note what the news reports say about their personalities and other attributes. Can you identify examples of male–female stereotyping in those reports? How do the media reports link the personalities and attributes of those chief executives to the successes and failures that stimulated interest in them in the first place? From the evidence in this chapter, what feedback can you give to the media reporters on the accuracy and validity of their assessments of those two leaders?

Springboard

Jeffrey Pfeffer (2015) *Leadership BS: Fixing Workplaces and Careers One Truth at a Time*. New York: Harper Business. Criticizes the 'leadership industry' for offering unhelpful advice based on wishful thinking that produces unrealistic images of leadership roles. Argues that leaders sometimes have to do bad things to achieve good results. See discussion of power in Chapter 22.

S. Alexander Haslam, Stephen D. Reicher and Michael J. Platow (2010) *The New Psychology of Leadership: Identity, Influence and Power*. Hove, East Sussex: Psychology Press. Argues that charisma is not an attribute of a leader, but an attribution made by followers. Successful leaders are those who can capture and champion the identity of the group to which they belong, and whose interests they advance.

Faaiza Rashid, Amy C. Edmondson, and Herman B. Leonard (2013) 'Leadership lessons from the Chilean mine rescue', *Harvard Business Review*, 91 (7–8), pp.113–19. Analyses the rescue of 33 miners who were trapped over 2,000 feet underground in 2010. This was a leadership challenge as well as a technical one. What leadership capabilities are required to deal with crises such as this?

Sheryl Sandberg (2013) *Lean In: Work and the Will to Lead*. New York: Knopf. A controversial corporate feminist manifesto from the chief operating officer of Facebook. Argues that women are largely to blame for derailing their own careers, by 'leaning back' in meetings, and not pushing for promotion. Offers advice to women from her experience on 'leaning in' to progress their careers.

Paul Vanderbroeck (2014) *Leadership Strategies for Women: Lessons From Four Queens on Leadership and Career Development*. New York and London: Springer. Examines four historical female leadership role models: Cleopatra of Egypt, Isabella of Spain, Elizabeth I of England and Catherine the Great of Russia. Identifies their leadership competencies and the key factors in their career success, offering practical guidance for contemporary career management and leadership.

 OB cinema

The Devil Wears Prada (2006, director David Frankel): DVD track 2: 0:03:20 to 0:09:47 (7 minutes). Track 2 begins with Andy coming out of the lift and heading for the office reception desk; clip ends when she is called back into the office as she is walking away. Based on the novel by Lauren Weisberger, this movie tells the story of a naive young aspiring journalist, Andrea (Andy) Sachs (played by Anne Hathaway) who gets a job as assistant to the famous editor-in-chief of the fashion magazine *Runway*. The magazine's powerful and ruthless editor Miranda Priestly (Meryl Streep) is a legend. In this clip, we see Andy arriving for her job interview as 'second assistant' with Miranda's 'first assistant' Emily Charlton (Emily Blunt). Miranda, however, decides to conduct the interview herself.

1. How would you describe Miranda Priestley's leadership style? Identify specific behaviours to support your conclusions.

2. What impact does Miranda's leadership style have on those around her? Identify specific employee behaviours to support your conclusions.

3. Good boss or bad boss: what is your assessment of this leadership style? Cite specific evidence of her impact on individual performance and organizational effectiveness to support your judgement.

4. To what extent does this leadership style apply in the real world, beyond Hollywood? Consider aspects of individual personality, organizational context and industry sector in making this judgement.

5. Why do you think Miranda Priestly gave Andy the job?

 OB on the web

Many individuals are described as leaders because they are *charismatic*. (We will explore referent power – the power of the charismatic personality – in Chapter 22.) We tend to think of charisma as something which some people just have, and others do not. However, can you learn how to be charismatic? Olivia Fox Cabane (2013) is an executive coach who specializes in 'high potential leadership', and who teaches charisma to executives. Search for her name on YouTube, and find her presentation on 'The science of first impressions'. Having watched her presentation, what is your assessment? Could you learn to be more charismatic? How would this contribute to your employability and to your career? For further suggestions on the tactics that you can use in order to develop your charisma, see Antonakis et al. (2012).

CHAPTER EXERCISES

1. Management and leadership

Objectives
1. To explore differences in the definition of the terms management and leadership.
2. To consider whether and how our understanding and use of these terms is changing.

Briefing
Are leadership and management different roles, or do they overlap? Look at this list of activities. Are these leadership activities, or management activities, or could they fall into both categories? Use the activities matrix to locate each of those activities depending on whether you feel they are management-oriented, leadership-oriented, or both (based on Gillen, 2004).

Activities list
1. Delegate tasks
2. Plan and prioritize steps to achieve task goals
3. Ensure predictability
4. Coordinate effort
5. Provide focus
6. Monitor feelings and morale
7. Follow systems and procedures
8. Provide development opportunities
9. Monitor progress
10. Appeal to rational thinking
11. Act as interface between team and others
12. Motivate staff
13. Inspire people
14. Coordinate resources
15. Give orders and instructions
16. Check task completion
17. Ensure effective induction
18. Unleash potential
19. Look 'over the horizon'
20. Be a good role model
21. Use analytical data to support recommendations
22. Explain goals, plans and roles
23. Appeal to people's emotions
24. Share a vision
25. Guide progress
26. Create a positive team feeling
27. Monitor budgets and tasks
28. Use analytical data to forecast trends
29. Take risks
30. Build teams

Activities matrix

Managerially oriented	Elements of management and leadership	Leadership oriented

Class discussion Consider why you placed each of those activities in those categories:

1. What makes an activity a management activity?

2. What is distinctive about leadership activities?

3. If you put some activities in the middle, why did you do that?

4. Are there any current trends and developments which encourage managers to monitor and control rather than to exercise leadership?

2. Leadership in practice

Objectives 1. To relate the theory and concepts of leadership to practice.

2. To assess critically how leaders are typically seen and portrayed.

Briefing 1. Identify two business, sports or political leaders, one male and one female, past or present, with whom you are familiar through the media, or through movies based on their lives.

2. What traits and other characteristics do they have? To what extent do they conform with traditional female and male leadership stereotypes?

3. How are their leadership styles portrayed: participative, considerate, task-oriented, autocratic, transformational, for example? How do their styles influence their effectiveness?

4. What conclusions can you draw about leadership effectiveness, and about the way in which society sees leaders?

Employability assessment

With regard to your future employment prospects:

1. Identify up to three issues from this chapter that you found significant.

2. Relate these to the competencies in the employability matrix.

3. Decide what actions you need to take to maintain and/or develop those competencies under each of the four headings of the employability matrix.

Personal qualities	**Leadership qualities**
self-management	leadership
work ethic/results orientation	people management
appetite for learning	leading and managing change
interpersonal skills	project management
creativity and innovation	general management skills

Employability

Other attributes	**Practical skills**
political awareness	commercial acumen
understand cross-cultural issues	customer service skills
how organizations work	communication skills
critical thinking	problem solving skills
decision making	teamworking skills

The employability matrix

References

Abrahamson, E. (2004) *Change Without Pain: How Managers Can Overcome Initiative Overload, Organizational Chaos, and Employee Burnout*. Boston, MA: Harvard Business School Press.

Alimo-Metcalfe, B. and Alban-Metcalfe, J. (2002) 'The great and the good', *People Management*, 8 (11): 32–34.

Alimo-Metcalfe, B. and Alban-Metcalfe, J. (2003) 'Under the influence', *People Management*, 9 (5): 32–35.

Alimo-Metcalfe, B. and Alban-Metcalfe, J. (2010) 'Leadership: commitment beats control', *Health Service Journal*, 22 February, p.7.

Alimo-Metcalfe, B. and Bradley, M. (2008) 'Cast in a new light', *People Management*, 14 (2): 38–41.

Antonakis, J., Fenley, M. and Liechti, S. (2012) 'Learning charisma', *Harvard Business Review*, 90 (6): 127–30.

Badaracco, J.L. (2001) 'We don't need another hero', *Harvard Business Review*, 79 (8): 121–26.

Balazs, K. (2002) 'Take one entrepreneur: the recipe for success of France's great chefs', *European Management Journal*, 20 (3): 247–59.

Barta, T., Kleiner, M. and Neumann, T. (2012) 'Is there a payoff from top-team diversity?', *McKinsey Quarterly*, April, pp.13–15.

Bass, B.M. (1985a) *Bass and Stogdill's Handbook of Leadership: Theory, Research and Managerial Applications* (3rd edn). New York: Free Press.

Bass, B.M. (1985b) *Leadership and Performance Beyond Expectations*. New York: Free Press.

Bass, B.M. and Avolio, B.J. (1990) 'The implications of transactional and transformational leadership for individual, team and organizational development', *Research and Organizational Change and Development*, 4: 321–72.

Bass, B.M. and Avolio, B.J. (1994) *Improving Organizational Effectiveness through Transformational Leadership*. Thousand Oaks, CA: Sage Publications.

Bennis, W.G. and Nanus, B. (1985) *Leaders: The Strategies for Taking Charge*. New York: Harper & Row.

Bird, C. (1940) *Social Psychology*. New York: Appleton-Century.

Birkinshaw, J. (2010) *Reinventing Management: Smarter Choices for Getting Work Done*. Chichester, West Sussex: Jossey-Bass.

Bryman, A. (1996) 'Leadership in organizations', in Stewart R. Clegg, Cynthia Hardy and Walter R. Nord (eds), *Handbook of Organization Studies*. London: Sage Publications, pp.276–92.

Buchanan, D.A., Addicott, R., Fitzgerald, L., Ferlie, E. and Baeza, J. (2007) 'Nobody in charge: distributed change agency in healthcare', *Human Relations*, 60 (7): 1065–90.

Burns, J.M. (1978) *Leadership*. New York: Harper & Row.

Cabane, O.F. (2013) *The Charisma Myth: How Anyone Can Master the Art and Science of Personal Magnetism*. New York: Portfolio/Penguin.

Caldwell, R. (2005) *Agency and Change: Rethinking Change Agency in Organizations*. Abingdon: Routledge.

Cappelli, P, Singh, H., Singh, J.V. and Useem, M. (2010) 'The India way: lessons for the US', *Academy of Management Perspectives*, 24 (2): 6–24.

Charter, D. (2012) 'A gentle touch in the boardroom? Don't bet on it', *The Times*, 28 March, p.37.

Chartered Institute for Personnel and Development (2015) *Breaking the Boardroom: A Guide for British Businesses on how to Support the Female Leaders of the Future*. London: Chartered Institute for Personnel and Development.

Collins, J. (2001) *Good to Great: Why Some companies Make the Leap and Others Don't*. New York: Harper Collins.

Cooper, K. (2013) 'Female bosses make firms more money', *The Sunday Times*, 29 September, p.14.

Davis, G. (2015) 'Addressing unconscious bias', *McKinsey Quarterly*, February, pp.1–4.

Devillard, S., Graven, W., Lawson, E., Paradise, R. and Sancier-Sultan, S. (2012) *Women Matter 2012: Making the Breakthrough*, McKinsey & Company, London.

Ellis, T., Marcati, C. and Sperling, J.M. (2015) 'Promoting gender diversity in the Gulf', *McKinsey Quarterly*, February, pp.1–8.

Ezzedeen, S.R. (2013) 'The portrayal of professional and managerial women in North American films: good news or bad news for your executive pipeline?', *Organizational Dynamics*, 42 (4): 248–56.

Fiedler, F.E. (1967) *A Theory of Leadership Effectiveness*. New York: McGraw-Hill.

Fiedler, F.E. and Chemers, M.M. (1974) *Leadership and Effective Management*. Glenview IL: Scott, Foresman.

Fiedler, F.E. and Chemers, M.M. (1984) *Improving Leadership Effectiveness: The Leaders Match Concept* (2nd edn). New York: John Wiley.

Fleishman, E.A. (1953a) 'The description of supervisory behaviour', *Journal of Applied Psychology*, 37 (1): 1–6.

Fleishman, E.A. (1953b) 'The measurement of leadership attitudes in industry', *Journal of Applied Psychology*, 37 (3): 153–58.

Fleishman, E.A. and Harris, E.F. (1962) 'Patterns of leadership behaviour related to employee grievances and turnover', *Personnel Psychology*, 15 (1): 43–56.

Fox, H. (2015) 'Women in eastern Europe lead the way to senior roles', *Financial Times*, 7 May, p.14.

Fraser, C. (1978) 'Small groups: structure and leadership', in Henri Tajfel and Colin Fraser (eds), *Introducing Social Psychology*. Harmondsworth: Penguin Books, pp.176–200.

Galinsky, A.D. and Kilduff, G.J. (2013) 'Be seen as a leader', *Harvard Business Review*, 91 (12): 127–30

Gillen, T. (2004) *Leadership or Management: The Differences*. London: CIPD.

Goleman, D. (2000) 'Leadership that gets results', *Harvard Business Review*, 78 (2): 78–90.

Goodwin, D. (2011) 'We're too harsh on the bitchy bosses', *The Sunday Times*, *News Review* section, 27 March, p.4.

Gronn, P. (2002) 'Distributed leadership as a unit of analysis', *Leadership Quarterly*, 13 (4): 423–51.

Gronn, P. (2009) 'Leadership configurations', *Leadership*, 5 (3): 381–94.

Groysberg, B. and Bell, D. (2013) 'Dysfunction in the boardroom', *Harvard Business Review*, 91 (6): 88–97.

Heller, F. (1997) 'Leadership', in Arndt Sorge and Malcolm Warner (eds), *The Handbook of Organizational Behaviour*. London: International Thomson, pp.340–49.

Hersey, P. and Blanchard, K.H. (1988) *Management of Organizational Behavior: Utilizing Human Resources*. Englewood Cliffs, NJ: Prentice-Hall International.

Hewlett, S.A., Luce, C.B. and West, C. (2005) 'Leadership in your midst: tapping the hidden strengths of minority executives', *Harvard Business Review*, 83 (11): 74–82.

Heywood, S., De Smet, A. and Webb, A. (2014) 'Tom Peters on leading the 21st century organization', *McKinsey Quarterly*, September, pp.1–9.

Hoffman, B.J., Woehr, D.J., Maldagen-Youngjohn, R. and Lyons, B.D. (2011) 'Great man or great myth? A quantitative review of the relationship between individual differences and leader effectiveness', *Journal of Occupational and Organizational Psychology*, 84 (2): 347–81.

Hollenbeck, G.P., McCall Jnr, M.W. and Silzer, R.F. (2006) 'Leadership competency models', *Leadership Quarterly*, 17 (4): 398–413.

Huy, Q.N. (2001) 'In praise of middle managers', *Harvard Business Review*, 79 (8): 72–79.

Katz, D., Maccoby, N. and Morse, N.C. (1950) *Productivity, Supervision, and Morale in an Office Situation*. Ann Arbor, MI: University of Michigan Institute for Social Research.

Kahneman, D. (2011) *Thinking, Fast and Slow*. London: Penguin Books.

Kennedy, J.A. and Kray, L.J. (2014) 'Who is willing to sacrifice ethical values for money and social status? Gender differences in reactions to ethical compromises', *Social Psychological and Personality Science*, 5 (1): 52–59.

Khurana, R. (2002) 'The curse of the superstar CEO', *Harvard Business Review*, 80 (9): 60–6.

Kiel, F. (2015) *Return on Character*. New York: Knopf.

Kirkland, R., Srinivasan, R. and Schlesinger, R. (2013) *Leading in the 21st Century: An Interview with HCA CEO Richard Bracken*. New York, McKinsey & Company.

Kirton, H. (2015) 'Seven key traits to develop for successful future leaders', *People Management*, 9 July, www.cipd.co.uk/pm/peoplemanagement/b/weblog/archive/2015/07/09/seven-traits-hr-should-be-teaching-future-leaders.aspx

Kramer, R.M. (2006) 'The great intimidators', *Harvard Business Review*, 84 (2): 88–96.

Likert, R. (1961) *New Patterns of Management*. New York: McGraw-Hill.

Ludeman, K. and Erlandson, E. (2006) *Alpha Male Syndrome: Curb the Belligerence, Channel the Brilliance*. Boston, MA: Harvard Business School Press.

Meyerson, D.E. (2001) *Tempered Radicals: How People Use Difference to Inspire Change at Work*. Boston, MA: Harvard Business School Press.

Mintzberg, H. (2009) *Managing*. Harlow, Essex: Financial Times Prentice Hall.

Morgan, N. (2001) 'How to overcome "change fatigue"', *Harvard Management Update*: 1–3.

Mulcahy, M. and Linehan, C. (2014) 'Females and precarious board positions: further evidence of the glass cliff', *British Journal of Management*, 25 (3): 425–38.

Reinert, R.M., Weigert, F. and Winnefeld, C.H. (2015) 'Does female management influence firm performance? Evidence from Luxembourg banks', University of St Gallen, Working Papers on Finance No.2015/1.

Rushe, D. (2006) 'Alpha males can make and break a business', *The Sunday Times*, Business Section, 3 September, p.11.

Ryan, M.K. and Haslam, S.A. (2005) 'The glass cliff: evidence that women are over-represented in precarious leadership positions', *British Journal of Management*, 16 (2): 81–90.

Ryan, M.K. and Haslam, S.A. (2007) 'The glass cliff: exploring the dynamics surrounding the appointment of women to precarious leadership positions', *Academy of Management Review*, 32 (2): 549–72.

Sauer, S.J. (2012) 'When bossy is better for rookie managers', *Harvard Business Review*, 90 (5), p.30.

Shaw, M.E. (1976) *Group Dynamics* (2nd edn). New York: McGraw Hill.

Sims, H.P. and Lorenzi, P. (1992) *The New Leadership Paradigm*. Newbury Park, CA: Sage Publications.

Snowden, D.J. and Boone, M.E. (2007) 'A leader's framework for decision making', *Harvard Business Review*, 85 (11): 69–76.

Stogdill, R.M. (1948) 'Personal factors associated with leadership', *Journal of Psychology*, 25: 35–71.

Stogdill, R.M. (1950) 'Leadership, membership and organization', *Psychological Bulletin*, 47 (1): 1–14.

Stogdill, R.M. (1974) *Handbook of Leadership: A Survey of Theory and Research*. New York: Free Press.

Stogdill, R.M. and Coons, A.E. (eds) (1951) *Leader Behaviour: Its Description and Measurement, Research Monograph No.88*. Columbus, OH: Ohio State University Bureau of Business Research.

Suff, R. and Worman, D. (2015) *Gender Diversity in the Boardroom: Reach for the Top*. London: Chartered Institute for Personnel and Development.

Tannenbaum, R. and Schmidt, W.H. (1958) 'How to choose a leadership pattern', *Harvard Business Review*, 36 (2): 95–102 (reprinted in May–June 1973).

Tichy, N.M. and Devanna, M.A. (1986) *The Transformational Leader*. New York: Wiley.

Vinnicombe, S., Doldor, E., Sealy, R., Pryce, P. and Turner, C. (2015) *The Female FTSE Board Report 2015: Putting the UK Progress Into a Global Perspective*. Cranfield: Cranfield University School of Management.

Woolley, A. and Malone, T. (2011) 'What makes a team smarter? More women', *Harvard Business Review*, 89 (6): 32–33.

Zheltoukhova, K. (2014) *Leadership: Easier Said Than Done*. London: Chartered Institute for Personnel and Development.

Chapter 19 **Change**

Key terms

triggers of change	resistance to change
transformational change	stakeholder
initiative decay	organization development
initiative fatigue	innovation
coping cycle	sustaining innovations
Yerkes–Dodson law	disruptive innovations
readiness for change	operational innovations

Learning outcomes

When you have read this chapter, you should be able to define those key terms in your own words, and you should also be able to:

1. Explain why effective change management is important, to organizations and to individuals.

2. Identify the main external and internal triggers of organizational change.

3. Explain the issues that management must take into account to ensure that change is successful.

4. Understand the typical characteristics of human responses to change.

5. Understand the nature of resistance to change and approaches to overcoming it.

6. Explain the advantages and limitations of participative methods of change management.

7. Understand the significance of innovation, and the distinction between sustaining, disruptive and operational innovations.

8. Explain the organizational properties that stimulate and stifle innovation respectively.

9. Recognize the challenges facing innovative change leaders.

Why study change?

Designed not to change

'The reality is that today's organizations were simply never designed to change proactively and deeply – they were built for discipline and efficiency, enforced through hierarchy and routinization. As a result, there's a mismatch between the pace of change in the external environment and the fastest possible pace of change at most organizations. If it were otherwise, we wouldn't see so many incumbents struggling to intercept the future' (Hamel and Zanini, 2014, p.1).

Organizations must change, to keep up with economic and geopolitical developments, competitor behaviour, changing customer demands and expectations, new legislation and regulations, new materials, new technologies – and many other surprises. Failure to change, and to change rapidly, can threaten an organization's survival. You as an individual must also be able and willing to change. In order to 'future proof' your career, Lynda Gratton (2011) argues that you will need to acquire new knowledge and skills every few years, allowing you to change from one job and organization to another. Failure to change as an individual will put your employability, and your career, at risk.

Managing change well, however, seems to be difficult. Most estimates put the failure rate of planned organizational changes at around 60 to 70 per cent (Burnes, 2011; Rafferty et al., 2013). In a global survey of 2,000 executives by the consulting company McKinsey, only 26 per cent of respondents said that their change initiatives had increased performance and enabled the organization to make further improvements (Jacquemont et al., 2015). The evidence behind these kinds of claims has been disputed (Hughes, 2011), but no studies have yet reported a 70 per cent success rate.

STOP AND THINK

How would you respond to these 'true or false' questions?

- People have a natural resistance to change.   true or false?
- People get bored with routine and seek out new experiences.   true or false?
- Older people are more resistant to change.   true or false?

Did you answer 'true' to all three statements? These positive responses are inconsistent with each other, and contradict the evidence. For example, many people when they retire from work take up radically new activities and hobbies: painting, acting, community involvement, learning a musical instrument. We cannot have natural resistance to change and seek new experiences at the same time.

Change is a constant, and it is a constant challenge, for organizations, and for us as individuals. The need for organizational and personal change is prompted by many different **triggers of change**.

Triggers of change disorganizing pressures that make current systems, procedures, rules, organization structures, processes, roles, and skills inappropriate and ineffective.

External triggers for organizational change include (see Chapters 2 and 3):

- economic and trading conditions, domestic and global;
- new technology and materials;
- demographic trends, silver tsunami, Gen Y, Gen C;
- changes in consumers' demands and expectations;
- activities and innovations of competitors, mergers and acquisitions;
- legislation, regulation, government policies, corporate social responsibility demands;

- shifts in local, national and international politics;
- changes in social and cultural values.

  Internal triggers for organizational change can include:

- design of new products and services;
- low performance and morale, high stress and staff turnover;
- appointment of a new senior manager or top team;
- inadequate skills and knowledge base, triggering training programmes;
- office and factory relocation, closer to suppliers and markets;
- recognition of problems triggering redistribution of responsibilities;
- innovations in the manufacturing process;
- new ideas about how to deliver services to customers.

Cloud control

External triggers for organizational change can have 'knock on' effects on internal support functions not directly involved in shifts in strategy. Adobe is a global software company, known for products such as Acrobat, Flash Player and Photoshop. Based in San Jose, California, Adobe has 11,000 employees in 43 countries, with annual revenues of US$4.5 billion, half of which are generated outside the US. New technologies, however, are opening up opportunities for small competitors.

In 2011, Adobe decided to stop selling its licensed products in shrink-wrap packages and became a cloud-based provider of digital services. Instead of receiving a CD in a box, customers either download the software they require or pay a monthly subscription. For employees, this meant new ways of working, and a new role for the human resource (HR) function.

Adobe had a traditional office-bound administrative HR function. That worked well when Adobe was selling software products, but was less appropriate to the cloud-based approach. HR had to work as 'business partners', located in employee resource centres. HR consulting teams worked on problems directly with senior managers and with staff on the ground. HR roles became more varied and, being less office-bound, more people-oriented. Rather than wait for calls, HR staff conducted 'walk-ins', visiting on their own initiative parts of the company to explore what support they could provide. Adobe employs large numbers of 'millennials' (Gen Ys) who are motivated by innovation, change and personal development. Keeping them engaged meant designing varied, challenging jobs.

Adobe also stopped conducting annual performance reviews, as they consumed a lot of management time, demotivated staff and contributed to high staff turnover. With the new 'check in' system, staff review and set their own development goals when they think this is appropriate, with immediate and ongoing feedback rather than an annual conversation. HR runs workshops for managers on providing effective, positive feedback. Staff turnover has fallen to its lowest level ever.

Why did HR at Adobe change the way in which it operated? Because the company strategy and culture had changed, and HR had to find new ways of working to support those developments

Based on Smedley (2014), and www.adobe.com/company/fast-facts.html

Change is not simply a matter of reacting to triggers. Organizations and individuals can anticipate trends and opportunities, and be proactive as well. Susan Mohrman and Edward Lawler (2012, p.42) argue that we need to focus on 'next practice' as well as 'best practice':

> The major challenge for organizations today is navigating high levels of turbulence. They operate in dynamic environments, in societies where the aspirations and purposes of various stakeholders change over time. They have access to ever-increasing technological capabilities and information. A key organizational capability is the ability to adapt as context, opportunities, and challenges change.

One of the best-known metaphors for change was developed by Kurt Lewin (1951), who argued for the need to *unfreeze* the current state of affairs, to *move* to a desired new state, then to *refreeze* and stabilize those changes. However, as Mohrman and Lawler suggest, refreezing is no longer an option. 'Repeat change' is the norm, and 'permanent thaw' is a better metaphor. The environment for most organizations seems likely to remain turbulent, and change will be on the management agenda for some time. Change is thus a core topic, for managers concerned with organizational performance, adaptability and survival, and for individuals concerned about employability and careers.

Making change happen

Robert Gascoyne-
Cecil, 3rd Marquess
of Salisbury, and
UK Prime Minister
to Queen Victoria,
1885–1892

'Change? Change? Why do we need change? Things are quite bad enough as they are.'

Organizational change takes many different forms, affecting structures, culture, working practices, information systems, and so on. Changes also vary in 'depth', from shallow to deep, as shown in Table 19.1. Minor changes may be surface or shallow, and have limited impact on people and performance. Penetrating and deep changes are more wide-ranging in their effects. Faced with the geopolitical, economic, demographic, sociocultural and technological trends and developments (explored in Chapters 2 and 3), most organizations today appear to need deep transformational change. This is more difficult to implement than shallow change, as it is more costly and time-consuming, requires greater management expertise, and affects larger numbers of people in more significant ways.

In most organizations, many changes are likely to be underway at the same time, at different depths. We cannot argue that 'all change must be deep change'. Deep change is appropriate when dealing with 'deep problems', while fine-tuning is an appropriate response to minor concerns. Surface and shallow changes can also provide critical support for deeper changes.

**Transformational
change** large-scale
change involving
radical, frame-breaking
and fundamentally
new ways of thinking,
solving problems and
doing business.

Table 19.1: Depth of organizational change

Surface	**Fine-tuning**: focus on efficiency
↓	**Restructure**: centralize, decentralize
Shallow	**Reallocate resources**: grow some departments, cut others
↓	**Improve business planning**: symbolize a shift in thinking
Penetrating	**Change the leadership**: new CEO with major change remit
↓	**Change the organization's definition of success**: create new goals, objectives, targets to change behaviour
Deep	**Change the mission, vision, values and philosophy**: symbolize a radical shift in thinking and behaviour
↓	
Transformational	**Paradigm shift**: change how we think, how we solve problems, how boundaries are defined, the way we do business: frame-breaking, mould-breaking, fundamental, strategic change

The advice for managers on implementing change – on how to make it happen – is straightforward, with different commentators offering similar guidance, usually in the form of a checklist. One of the best-known sets of guidelines comes from John Kotter (2007). His research into over 100 American companies identifies the following eight steps to successful transformational change:

1. Establish a sense of urgency for the proposed changes.
2. Create a powerful team to guide and drive the implementation.

3. Develop a vision to direct the change efforts, and a strategy to achieve the vision.

4. Communicate the new vision and strategy.

5. Empower others to help achieve the vision, removing obstacles, encouraging risk taking.

6. Plan for and create short-term wins, and recognize and reward those involved.

7. Consolidate improvements and develop new ideas and projects to support the vision.

8. Ensure that new approaches are embedded in the organization culture.

For successful change, Kotter suggested a careful planning process, working through these eight issues more or less in sequence, and not missing or rushing any of them. This takes time. Given the pace of change, perhaps many organizations try to take too many shortcuts to put change in place more quickly, and get it wrong as a consequence. Does this work in practice? Steven Appelbaum et al. (2012) reviewed the evidence relating to Kotter's model, and found support for most of the individual steps. However, despite Kotter's argument about integrating the eight stages, no studies have evaluated the framework as a whole. On the other hand, there was no evidence to challenge the practical value of the approach, which remains popular because it is easy to understand and to use.

Kotter (2012, p.52) subsequently revised his framework, arguing that the eight steps should be seen as 'change accelerators', to speed up change. His new argument has three aspects. First, Kotter argues that the accelerators must operate concurrently, rather than in sequence. Second, change must not rely on a small core group, but on many change agents from across the organization. Third, traditional hierarchy must be complemented by flexible and agile networks.

Although Kotter focused his work on transformational change, his guidelines have been applied to the management of change in general. Reducing the task to these eight steps suggests that change, which is usually complex and untidy, can be controlled and managed effectively in a more or less logical and predictable manner. Also, having to handle such a small number of issues appears to lessen the scale of the management challenge. Success seems to be pretty much guaranteed. Why, then, is the failure rate of change so high? Have Kotter, and other commentators who have adopted similar 'change checklist' approaches, oversimplified the change management task?

Why change fails

Reviewing the conclusions of studies of information technology project failures, Richard Bacon and Christopher Hope (2014, p.2) conclude that:

> They all say roughly the same thing: if what you want keeps changing; or you can't commit the required money; or you keep changing the person in charge; or the person at the top doesn't care about the project; or you have an unrealistic timetable; or you fail to test the system properly; or if you don't provide enough training; or you don't have a Plan B; or you don't realize that the bigger the project the greater the chance of its being overtaken by events or new technology; or you don't realize that the suppliers are quite capable of telling you that they can deliver when they can't; then don't be surprised if you end up with a mess that damages your organization, costs much more than it is supposed to, and doesn't work.

Boris Ewenstein et al. (2015) suggest that the failure rate of planned change efforts could be reduced by innovative applications of social media (see Chapter 3). These new digital tools can be used to:

- give employees immediate feedback on progress;
- tailor information to individual roles and needs;
- sidestep the hierarchy and establish direct contacts;

- build community and shared purpose among people who are physically distant from each other;
- demonstrate achievements in real time.

Initiative decay
an organizational phenomenon where the benefits from a change initiative 'evaporate', when attention shifts to other issues and priorities.

Initiative fatigue the personal exhaustion and apathy resulting from the experience of too much organizational change.

They argue that 'applying new digital tools can make change more meaningful – and durable – both for the individuals who are experiencing it and for those who are implementing it' (Ewenstein et al., 2015, p.1).

Despite the many pressures, there is a feeling that constant change can be damaging; that we need to slow things down, and perhaps keep some things the same. Rapid pace creates the problem of **initiative decay** (or 'improvement evaporation'), where the benefits of one change are lost because the organization moves on to deal with new priorities. There is now concern, therefore, with how to sustain changes that are already in place (Buchanan et al., 2007).

A further problem is **initiative fatigue**, as people become tired of constant demands to do things differently, work better, smarter, faster, harder. Initiative fatigue appears to be widespread, affecting all levels of an organization, and reducing enthusiasm for more change.

STOP AND THINK

If you want a high-flying, fast-track career, you are unlikely to get far if you focus your energies on shallow changes. Shallow changes do not contribute much to organizational performance, and will not improve your visibility or reputation. You would be advised to work on deep changes, as long as they are successful.

What happens if all ambitious managers try to drive deep changes in the interests of progressing their careers?

Management hackathons, digital hives, and social chains

Arne Gast and Raul Lansink (2015) describe how some companies are using the networking and collaboration possibilities of social media to accelerate change by widening employee engagement. At one company, social technologies allowed employees to contribute to corporate strategy through an 'open source' process that began with an organization-wide discussion about risks to the company's growth, and future opportunities.

A 'management hackathon' is an online platform through which participants can discuss ideas, express opinions and contribute their expertise. 'Digital hives' are online hubs that encourage collective problem solving and encourage organizational change. To work effectively, hives must be based on an explicit policy that allows unrestricted interactions with no fear of repercussions, and be

focused on a specific issue with milestones and deadlines. Hives are egalitarian and transparent, based on selected user groups, whose inputs are continuously tracked. Participants are rewarded with public praise, peer recognition, and by the implementation of their ideas.

The Dutch bank ABN AMRO has pioneered the use of 'social chains'. These are digital platforms that link people who contribute to a particular value chain, such as acquiring and issuing cards. At ABN AMRO, meetings and email are discouraged, and people in the value chain across the organizational 'silos' work 'out loud' online, to share how they do things, and to address problems that affect the whole value chain. As social technology develops, we are likely to see further experiments of this kind, and new models will be developed.

The acceleration trap

Is constant change 'the new normal'? Is rapid, 'accelerated' change necessary and desirable? From a study of 4,900 US companies in 18 industries, Yong-Yeon Ji et al. (2014) note that some organizations ('hares') respond rapidly and aggressively to changing conditions – hiring or laying off parts of the workforce, for example. Others ('tortoises') try to maintain consistency, and make smaller adjustments. The study showed that employment instability lowered organizational performance. However, although very high instability was damaging, so was very low instability. Highly stable organizations may be too rigid and inflexible.

The researchers advise, therefore, a 'slow and steady' approach, changing in response to external conditions, but retaining talented employees. Change too slowly, and the organization's survival may be at risk. Change too quickly, and staff may be overloaded and demotivated – which could also threaten performance and survival. If the competition is changing rapidly, however, then 'slow and steady' could be a high-risk strategy (see the box 'Up tempo in China').

Up tempo in China

Considering what Western organizations can learn from Chinese management methods, especially about the speed of change, Edward Steinfeld and Troels Beltoft (2014, p.50) argue that:

> For several reasons – policy uncertainty, the vast number of competitors populating most sectors in China, legacies of traditional Chinese approaches to business, etc. – commercial success in China is often intimately linked with tempo. Innovation in this sense involves not the development of brand new technology, but rather the introduction of incrementally upgraded products with unprecedented rapidity. The new product may provide slightly new functionality, or it may simply offer an existing product at a slightly lower price point. Either way, its introduction permits the producer, at least for a brief period of time, to realize a slightly higher margin. In virtually all cases, winners in this system develop enhanced capabilities for speed in design, speed to market and speed in debugging.

Thomas Hout and David Michael (2014, p.106) support that argument:

When Apple had to redesign the screen of its first iPhone at the last minute, its Shenzhen supplier roused its engineers out of bed, developed a better screen, and overhauled the production line – in just four days' time. Tencent, China's leading internet service portal, illustrates how companies gain an advantage by quickly rolling out new offerings in China. Tencent now has over 700 million users, but it is often criticized for innovating little and imitating a lot. It was launched in Shenzhen in 1998 by five founders as a free instant-messaging service named QQ, with a friendly-looking penguin wearing a red scarf as its mascot. Its key strengths are the rate at which it has added more features – such as games, search, an e-commerce marketplace, music, microblogs, and even a virtual currency called Q-coins – and the ease with which users can connect with one another. Visit a café anywhere in China, and almost everyone will be connected to QQ but doing different things. Yet, there's nothing completely new on the website, which earned profits of around $2.5 billion in 2013. Tencent just beats everyone else to it.

Heike Bruch and Jochen Menges (2010) also argue that constant change leads to corporate burnout. In many organizations, intense market pressures encourage management to increase the number and speed of activities, raise performance goals, shorten innovation cycles, and introduce new systems and technologies. When the chief executive insists on this furious pace, the achievements turn into chronic overloading. Working constantly under time pressure, with priorities frequently changing, focus is scattered, staff become tired and demotivated, and customers get confused.

IQconcepts/Shutterstock.com

Bruch and Menges call this 'the acceleration trap'. They found that in companies that were 'fully trapped', 60 per cent of employees felt that they lacked the resources to get their work done, compared with only 2 per cent who felt that way in companies that were not 'trapped'. They also found three typical patterns (Bruch and Menges, 2010, p.83):

- *Overloading*: staff have too many activities, but not enough time or resources.
- *Multiloading*: focus is reduced by asking employees to take on too many different activities.
- *Perpetual loading*: the organization operates close to capacity all the time, giving employees no chance to rest or retreat, but only to ask, 'When is the economizing going to come to an end?'

If you answer 'yes' to five or more of the following statements, then your organization may have an 'acceleration culture' (Bruch and Menges, 2010, p.85):

- Is it hard to get important things done because too many other activities diffuse focus?
- Is there a tendency to drive the organization to the limits of its capacity?
- Does the company value hard effort over tangible results?
- Are employees made to feel guilty if they leave work early?
- Do employees talk a lot about how big their workload is?
- Are mangers expected to act as role models by being involved in multiple projects?
- Is 'no' a taboo word, even for people who have already taken on too many projects?
- Is there an expectation that people must respond to emails within minutes?
- After work, do staff keep their mobile phones on because they feel they need to be reachable?

How can an organization escape from the acceleration trap? Be clear about strategy and goals. Stop less important work. Have a system that identifies more and less important initiatives. And 'declare an end to the current high-energy phase'. At one company studied by Bruch and Menges, the chief executive insisted that managers identify only three 'must-win battles', to concentrate attention and energy, instead of the 'ten top priority goals' with which they used to work.

Change and the individual

David Schneider and Charles Goldwasser (1998) introduced 'the classic change curve' (Figure 19.1). In the middle of the curve sits a 'valley of despair', suggesting that that change can mean loss and pain for those who are affected by it. Schneider and Goldwasser (1998, p.42) argue that this is probably inevitable in most cases of change, and that is useful to be aware of this and to weaken the impact if possible:

> A leader of change must anticipate employees' reactions, another key factor in the process. As shown [Figure 19.1], these reactions occur along a 'change curve'. The blue line represents what is, unfortunately, typical. Unrealistically high expectations at the outset of a programme lead to a relatively deep 'valley of despair' when change doesn't come as quickly or easily as anticipated. Over time, employees do see a 'light at the end of the tunnel' and the change eventually produces some positive results. The red line illustrates what is possible with effective change management: a less traumatic visit to the valley and greater results as the programme reaches completion.

Coping cycle the emotional response to trauma and loss, in which we experience first denial, then anger, bargaining, depression, and finally acceptance.

The classic change curve draws on research concerning how individuals cope with traumatic personal loss, such as the death of a close relative. Elizabeth Kübler-Ross (1969) argued that we deal with loss by moving through a series of stages, each characterized by a particular emotional response. The coping cycle has since been used to help understand responses to major organizational changes.

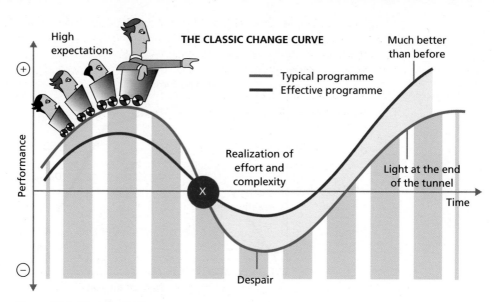

Figure 19.1: The classic change curve
Source: Schneider and Goldwasser (1998, p.42).

The five stages in the Kübler-Ross coping cycle are defined in Table 19.2. This is an 'ideal' model. We may not all experience the same sets of responses. We may omit stages, revisit some, or pass through them more or less quickly than others. This can be a useful diagnostic tool. If we know where in the response cycle a person is, we could offer helpful support.

Table 19.2: The coping cycle

Stage	Response
Denial	Unwillingness to confront the reality; 'this is not happening'; 'there is still hope that this will all go away'
Anger	Turn accusations on those apparently responsible; 'why is this happening to me?'; 'why are you doing this to me?'
Bargaining	Attempts to negotiate, to mitigate loss; 'what if I do it this way?'
Depression	The reality of loss or transition is appreciated; 'it's hopeless, there's nothing I can do now'; 'I don't know which way to turn'
Acceptance	Coming to terms with and accepting the situation and its full implications; 'what are we going to do about this?'; 'how am I going to move forward?'

Yerkes–Dodson law
a psychology hypothesis which states that performance increases with arousal, until we become overwhelmed, after which performance falls.

Just how much pressure can we take from organizational change? Psychology has long argued that the relationship between arousal, or sensory stimulation, on the one hand, and human performance, on the other, varies systematically, in the form of an 'inverted U' function. This is known as the **Yerkes–Dodson law** (Figure 19.2), named after Robert M. Yerkes and John D. Dodson (1908).

The Yerkes–Dodson law argues that task performance increases with arousal, stimulation and pressure. This explains why the time you spend revising for an examination seems to become more productive as the examination date draws closer. Here is the basis for the claim 'I work better under pressure'. However, this hypothesis also says that, if the pressure gets too high, the individual will become stressed and exhausted, and performance will fall. This explains why, when you delayed all of your revision until the night before, you did badly the following day.

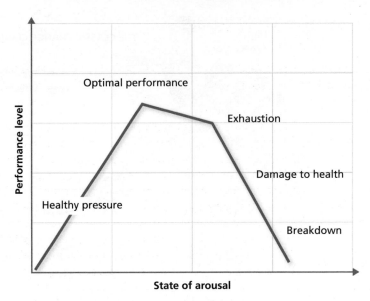

Figure 19.2: Pressure and performance – the inverted-U function

Performance may be low if a job is repetitive and boring, where arousal is low. Performance can sometimes be improved in such settings with background music, conversation and job rotation. Now suppose that the job is enriched and becomes more interesting, responsible and demanding, making more use of the individual's skills and knowledge. As the level of pressure increases, performance is likely to increase. However, a point will eventually be reached where the pressure becomes so great that it is overwhelming rather than stimulating. At this point fatigue and stress set in, and eventually ill-health and breakdown can occur if the pressure continues to escalate.

The Yerkes–Dodson law applied to work settings is summarized in Table 19.3, which plots changes in response, experience and performance for escalating pressure levels. Deciding the optimal level of pressure is difficult, because this depends on the individual. Also, appropriate levels of stimulation depend on the difficulty of the task. If the task is easy, more stimulation can be applied. Music destroys our concentration during a chess game, but is enjoyable while backing up computer files.

Table 19.3: The pressure–performance relationship explained

Pressure level	Response	Experience	Performance
Very low	Boredom	Low levels of interest, challenge and motivation	Low, acceptable
Low to moderate	Comfort	Interest aroused, abilities used, satisfaction, motivation	Moderate to high
Moderate to high	Stretch	Challenge, learning, development, pushing the limits	High, above expectations
High to unrealistic	Stress	Overload, failure, poor health, dysfunctional coping behaviour	Moderate to low
Extreme	Panic	Confusion, threat, loss of self-confidence, withdrawal	Low, unacceptable

As we have seen, organizational change can generate such pressure. How can we tell what levels of pressure people are experiencing, or when people are getting 'too close to the edge'? There are many proxy measures that show when people are suffering excess pressure: staff turnover, sickness rates, unexplained absences, accidents and mistakes, customer complaints, grievances. Physical appearance also changes as people become stressed, and interpersonal relationships can become strained.

Readiness and resistance

The American composer, John Cage, once said: 'I can't understand why people are frightened of new ideas. I'm frightened of the old ones' (www.quotationspage.com).

Readiness for change is a predisposition to welcome and embrace change.

From a practical change implementation perspective, it is usually useful to ask the question: are the conditions right, or do we have to do some preliminary work before we go ahead? One approach to preparing the ground is based on the concept of readiness for change.

Readiness for change is a predisposition, perhaps even impatience, to welcome and embrace change. Where readiness is high, change may be straightforward. Readiness depends on understanding the need for change, knowing the direction and the goal, having a clear plan, and enough resources and capable people to implement it. Where the ingredients are in place, and readiness is high, resistance may be localized and weak. If readiness is low, implementation will be more difficult, and some 'groundwork' may be required in order to increase levels of readiness among those who are going to be affected. Readiness factors can potentially be managed. Timing can also be important. Some readiness factors may strengthen naturally, on their own, as events unfold.

Alannah Rafferty et al. (2013) view change readiness as an individual attitude which has both cognitive and emotional (or 'affective') dimensions. 'Collective readiness' for change, of a group or organization, is based on the shared beliefs which develop through social interaction and shared experiences. Underpinning an individual's change readiness, they argue, are five beliefs:

1. *Discrepancy*: the belief that change is needed.
2. *Appropriate*: the belief that the proposed change is an appropriate response.
3. *Efficacy*: the individual's perceived capability to implement the change.
4. *Principal support*: the belief that the organization (management, peers) will provide resources and information.
5. *Valence*: the individual's evaluation of the personal costs and benefits; no benefits, no overall positive evaluation of readiness.

Individual change readiness is demonstrated through support for, openness towards, and commitment to change. These attitudes and behaviours can be influenced by three sets of factors. The first concerns external pressures, including industry and technology changes, new regulations, and professional group memberships. The second set of factors concerns 'internal context enablers', including change participation and communication processes, and leadership. The third set of factors concern personal characteristics and include needs, values and traits such as self-confidence, risk tolerance, dispositional resistance to change and self-efficacy.

From a management perspective, therefore, individuals' readiness for change can be assessed, and can also be influenced. The research evidence points in particular to the power of the internal enablers. Individual readiness for change can be influenced by processes that are designed to enhance participation in decisions, by high-quality change communications, and by perceptions of the organization's history of change (previous experience, support for change, congruence of values). Again, there are practical steps that can increase the probability that a change initiative will be welcome and successful – and most of those steps involve little or no cost.

The importance of high-quality communication

'Researchers have focused on the importance of effective communication with employees during change. Empirical research has demonstrated that high-quality change communication increases acceptance, openness, and commitment to change. Furthermore, the failure to provide sufficient information or providing poor-quality information can result in a number of problems, including cynicism about change and widespread rumours, which often exaggerate the negative aspects of change' (Rafferty et al., 2013, p.122).

Readiness for change may of course be low. Past experience, and the perceived nature and impact of the proposed changes, may make it difficult to influence readiness levels. Those who are responsible for progress may therefore have to address resistance to change.

Change has positive and negative aspects. On the one hand, change implies experiment and the creation of something new. On the other hand, it means discontinuity and the dismantling of traditional arrangements and relationships. Despite the positive attributes, change can be resisted because it involves confrontation with the unknown, and loss of the familiar. It is widely assumed that resistance to change is natural. Many people find change both painful and frustrating.

There are many sources of resistance to change, but the main ones seem to be:

- *Self-interest*: We want to protect a status quo with which we are content and regard as advantageous. Change may threaten to push us out of our 'comfort zone', and away from what we enjoy. We develop vested interests in organization structures and technologies. Change can mean loss of power, prestige, respect, approval, status and security. Change can also be personally inconvenient. It may disturb relationships and other arrangements that have taken time and effort to establish. It may force an unwelcome move in location, and alter social opportunities. Perceived as well as actual threats to interests and values are thus likely to generate resistance. We have a personal stake in our specialized knowledge and skills, and may not be willing to see these made redundant or obsolete.

Resistance to change an unwillingness, or an inability, to accept or to discuss changes that are perceived to be damaging or threatening to the individual.

When asked "would you rather work for change, or just complain?" 81% of the respondents replied, "Do i have to pick? This is hard."

Toothpaste For Dinner.com

Source: Drew Fairweather

- *Misunderstanding*: We are more likely to resist change if we do not understand the reasons behind it, or its nature and consequences. Resistance can thus be reduced by improved understanding. However, if managers have little trust in employees, information about change may be withheld, or distorted. If employees distrust managers, information may not be believed. Incomplete and incorrect information create uncertainty and rumour, which increases the perception of threat, and also raises defensiveness. The way in which change is introduced can thus be resisted, rather than the change itself.

- *Different assessments*: We each differ in how we see and evaluate the costs and benefits of change. A major threat for me can be a stimulating challenge for you. Contradictory assessments are more likely to arise when communication is poor. As we have seen, communication is a component of effective change implementation, and this can be key to creating a common understanding of what is going to happen.

- *Low tolerance for change*: We differ in our abilities to cope with change and uncertainty. Change that requires us to think and behave in different ways can challenge our self-concept. We each have ideas about our abilities and our strengths. One response to

Organization development

Organization development the systematic use of applied behavioural science principles and practices to increase individual and organizational effectiveness.

Organization development (OD) approaches begin with the assumption that organizational problems are due to conflict caused by poor communication and lack of understanding. OD has a toolkit, based on a set of core values concerning how organizations should treat their employees. This toolkit dates from the 1960s, but global economic conditions in the twenty-first century have made organizations acutely aware of the importance of employee motivation and engagement, where OD can make major contributions. OD aims to improve both organizational effectiveness and individual capabilities, through the systematic application of social and behavioural science knowledge and techniques.

Stephen Robbins and Timothy Judge (2008, p.654) outline the OD values:

- *Respect*. Individuals should be treated with dignity and respect.
- *Trust*. The healthy organization is characterized by trust, authenticity and openness.
- *Power equalization*. Effective organizations do not emphasize hierarchical control.
- *Confrontation*. Problems shouldn't be hidden; they should be openly confronted.
- *Participation*. Those who are affected by change will be more committed to its success when they are involved in the decisions.

OD argues that 'bureaucracy is bad' and that the caring, sharing, empowering organization is a better place to work, and is financially and materially more effective. The 'bureaucracy-busting' agenda relies on the diagnosis of problems and solutions summarized in Table 19.5.

Table 19.5: Bureaucratic diseases and OD cures

Bureaucratic disease	Symptoms	OD cures
Rigid functional boundaries	Conflict between sections, poor communications	Teambuilding, job rotation, change the structure
Fixed hierarchies	Frustration, boredom, narrow specialist thinking	Training, job enrichment, career development
Information only flows down	Lack of innovation, minor problems escalate	Process consultation, management development
Routine jobs, tight control	Boredom, absenteeism, conflict for supervisors	Job enrichment, job rotation, supervisory training

OD has an extensive toolkit of 'interventions', illustrated in Table 19.6.

Table 19.6: Common OD interventions

Intervention	Explanation	Application
Action research	Results from a study are used to design improvements which are the subject of further study	To solve known problems which have unclear solutions
Sensitivity training	Technique for improving self- and other-awareness through unstructured group discussions	To develop interpersonal skills and emotional intelligence
Structure change	Job rotation, job enlargement and enrichment, autonomous teams, organization restructuring	Various uses – empowerment, improve information flow, signal priorities, new directions
Force-field analysis	Method for assessing the driving and restraining forces with respect to change	To plan actions to manage the force-field in order to facilitate the change process

Table 19.6: Common OD interventions (*continued*)

Intervention	Explanation	Application
Process consultation	External consultant facilitates problem solving by helping clients to develop own insights	To solve problems while developing the organization's own diagnostic capabilities
Survey feedback	Employee opinion survey findings are fed back to help identify actions to improve performance	To generate evidence which can help to solve leadership, culture, communications, morale and other problems
Teambuilding	Various methods to identify team roles, and to rate factors influencing team effectiveness	To help team members understand their roles and improve collaboration
Intergroup development	Clarify the mutual expectations of groups that must work together to be effective	To improve understanding and resolve conflict between sections or functions
Role negotiation	Clarify the mutual expectations of individuals who must work together to be effective	To reconcile differences between two individuals and to improve collaboration and interaction

There are three criticisms of OD.

1. It ignores organizational power inequalities, claiming that conflict is due to poor communication, and not to a conflict of interests between management and employees.

2. It focuses on 'soft' attitudes and values, rather than on 'hard' operational and financial results.

3. OD interventions take time. Improved effectiveness, difficult to measure, based on intangible values, in the long run, after an expensive programme – this is not a compelling promise in a fast-moving competitive world.

OD: an anachronism?

Dating from the 1960s, OD values inclusion, communication, collaboration and empowerment. Do these values still apply in today's fiercely competitive markets where corporate survival may depend on rapid top-down change? Bernard Burnes and Bill Cooke (2012) suggest, however, that values are even more important now. Many economies are struggling with the impact of organizations which have used unethical, and financially or environmentally unsustainable practices. In these circumstances, they argue that OD, 'with its humanist, democratic and ethical values, wide range of participative tools and techniques, and experience in promoting behavior changes, is ideally placed to play a leading role in the movement to a more ethical and sustainable future' (Burnes and Cooke, 2012, p.1417).

Mike Beer (2014, p.61) from Harvard Business School makes a similar case:

With the corporate scandals of the past decade, clear evidence that we are doing damage to our planet, and the great recession of 2008, higher ambition CEOs are reframing the purpose of their firm from increasing shareholder value to contributing to all stakeholders. This trend is opening up new opportunities for the field of OD to help these higher ambition leaders to create a better world. Higher ambition companies integrate head, heart, and hands.

However, the benefits of OD can include:

- improved productivity, morale, commitment to success;
- better understanding of organizational strengths and weaknesses;
- improved communications, problem solving and conflict resolution;
- creativity, openness, personal development;
- decrease in politicking;
- better management and teamwork, increased adaptability;
- ability to attract and retain quality people.

Do current economic conditions encourage or discourage the use of OD, and why?

Why change, when you can innovate?

'Anyone who has never made a mistake has never tried anything new' (Albert Einstein)
'Trying is the first step towards failure' (Homer Simpson)

Is 'change' an appropriate response to a fast-paced unpredictable world? To keep ahead of the competition, organizations must be creative and innovative. In the public sector, innovation is necessary in order to meet rising public expectations with regard to service cost and quality.

Innovation is not limited to new products. Most organizations also want to create new ways to organize, to develop new working practices, and to provide customers, clients or patients with innovative services. As a result, the term **innovation** is usually defined in broad terms, to mean the adoption of any device, system, process, programme, product or service *new to that organization*. This definition means that an idea may have been developed and applied elsewhere, but if it is 'new in this setting', then it can be regarded as an innovation *here*.

Innovation the adoption of any device, system, process, programme, product or service new to a particular organization.

Innovation and creativity are often seen as individual attributes, and inventors are sometimes seen as mavericks. However, innovation and creativity also have *organizational* dimensions. Despite commercial pressures, some organizational norms, systems and practices are receptive to innovation, while others encourage risk avoidance. Creative people in the wrong organization are likely to be less creative. However, ordinary people in an organization that encourages innovation are more likely to become more creative in that environment.

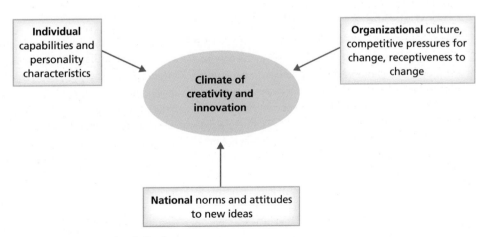

Figure 19.4: Innovation influences

The innovation process also has a *cultural* dimension. Some countries (e.g. United States, Germany) are considered to be more innovative than others (e.g. Britain, China). These differences are difficult to explain, and are influenced by social norms as well as by low investment in new technology, and weak training practices. The individual, organizational and national cultural influences on creativity and innovation are summarized in Figure 19.4.

Sustaining innovations
innovations which make improvements to existing processes, procedures, services and products.

Clayton Christensen, Richard Bohmer and J. Kenagy (2000) distinguish between sustaining innovations and disruptive innovations. Sustaining innovations improve existing products and processes: a more efficient motor car, a mobile phone with video capability. Disruptive innovations introduce wholly new processes and services: electric cars, social networking websites. Innovations that are disruptive do not necessarily mean chaos and upheaval, as what is disrupted is often traditional ways of thinking and acting. However, truly disruptive innovations may be harder to manage, because they are riskier, and because there are no established routines for handling them.

STOP AND THINK

Identify three to five sustaining innovations that have affected you over the past year.

Identify three to five disruptive innovations that have affected you. Did you welcome these innovations because they were beneficial, or did you have cause to complain?

Disruptive innovations
innovations which involve the development of wholly new processes, procedures, services and products.

Operational innovation inventing entirely new ways of working.

Commercial companies have always focused on innovations with new technology, products and services. Michael Hammer (2004) also advocates a focus on operational innovation finding new ways to lead, organize, work, motivate and manage.

Hammer (2004) describes a motor vehicle insurance company which introduced 'immediate response claims handling', operating 24 hours a day. This involved scheduling visits to customers by claims adjusters who worked from their vehicles, and would turn up within nine hours. Previously, when the adjusters were office-based, it could take over a week to inspect a damaged vehicle. Handling 10,000 claims a day, adjusters were empowered to estimate damage and write cheques on the spot. These operational innovations led to huge cost savings, with fewer staff involved in claims handling, better fraud detection, and reduction in payout costs. Customer satisfaction and loyalty also improved.

Not a good Kodak moment

Kodak invented the first digital camera in 1975, and the first megapixel camera in 1986. So why did the development of digital photography drive Kodak to bankruptcy in 2012? In 1975, the costs of this new technology were high, and the image quality was poor. Kodak believed that it could take at least another ten years before digital technology began to threaten its established camera, film, chemical and photo printing paper businesses. That forecast proved to be accurate, but rather than prepare, Kodak decided to improve the quality of film, with sustaining innovations. With hindsight, it is easy to spot that mistake. But the market information available to management from the 1970s to the 1990s, combined with the company's financial performance, made the switch to digital appear risky. In 1976, Kodak accounted for 90 per cent of film and 85 per cent of camera sales in America. Kodak's annual revenues peaked in 1996, at $16 billion; profits in 1999 were $2.5 billion. However, success encouraged

complacency, and reinforced confidence in the brand. Analysts noted that it might be unwise to switch from making 70 cents on the dollar with film, to 5 cents with digital. But by 2011, Kodak's revenues had fallen to $6.2 billion, and the company was reporting losses.

Kodak's competitor, Fuji, recognized the same threat, and decided to switch to digital while generating as much return as possible from film, and developing new lines of business, including cosmetics based on chemicals used for film processing. Both companies had the same information, but came to different assessments, and Kodak was too slow to respond. By the time Kodak began to develop digital cameras, mobile phones with built-in digital cameras had become popular.

Kodak invented the technology, but did not recognize just how disruptive an innovation digital would prove to be, making its traditional business obsolete (Barabba, 2011; *The Economist*, 2012).

Video case: automotive industry and technology

This two-minute *Financial Times* video is presented by Andy Sharman (FT motor industry correspondent) who describes the effects of disruptive innovation in the automotive industry. In future, traditional manufacturers may just build the shells that are then filled with the electronics and software developed and produced by others. The main competitors facing car makers do not even belong in the automotive sector. Which other industries are faced with 'out-of-sector' competition?

The best practices puzzle

Why do 'best practices' not spread more quickly? New ideas and methods that are developed and work well in one context are often not adopted elsewhere. This is known as 'the best practices puzzle' and it is not new. Don Berwick (2003) notes that the treatment for scurvy, first identified in 1601, did not become standard practice in the British navy until 1865, over 260 years later. Why the delay?

The stethoscope will never be popular

'That it [the stethoscope] will ever come into general use, not withstanding its value, I am extremely doubtful; because its beneficial application requires much time, and it gives a good deal of trouble both to the patient and practitioner, and because its whole hue and character is foreign, and opposed to all our habits and associations. It must be confessed that there is something ludicrous in the picture of a grave physician formally listening through a long tube applied to a patient's thorax, as if the disease within were a living being that could communicate its condition to the sense without' (John Forbes, in the preface to his translation of *De L'Auscultation Mediate ou Traite du Diagnostic des Maladies des Poumons et du Coeur* [A Treatise on Diseases of the Chest and on Mediate Auscultation], by R.T.H. Laennec, T &G Underwood, London, 1821).

Everett Rogers (1995) argues that the probability of an innovation being adopted is increased when it is seen to have the following six properties:

- advantageous when compared with existing practice;
- compatible with existing practices;
- easy to understand;
- observable in demonstration sites;
- testable;
- adaptable to fit local needs.

For innovations to diffuse effectively, Rogers argues that the perceptions of adopters, and properties of the organizational context, are as important as the innovation itself. Unless you believe that an innovation will help you to improve on current methods, you are unlikely to be persuaded. New ideas have to be adapted (sometimes significantly) to fit local conditions.

Rogers also argues that the adoption of innovations follows a pattern. First, small numbers adopt, followed by 'take-off', then achieving a critical mass of adopters. Finally, saturation is reached, typically short of 100 per cent (you never convince everyone). The pattern of diffusion depends on local circumstances, and is influenced by the five groups in Table 19.7.

Diffusion of a new idea relies initially on innovators and early adopters, and subsequently on the pace at which the early and late majority are swayed. These are not fixed categories. An individual may be an early adopter of one idea, but a late adopter of another. To be an innovator or a laggard depends as much on the context as on the individual. This perspective has two conclusions. First, diffusion is rarely a sudden event, but a protracted process, triggered and developed by contextual factors as well as individual perceptions and interpersonal communications. Second, there is no 'one best way' to influence people to change; interventions must consider individual needs and perceptions.

Table 19.7: From innovators to laggards

Innovators	Usually the first in their social grouping to adopt new approaches and behaviours, a small category of individuals who enjoy the excitement and risks of experimentation
Early adopters	Opinion leaders who evaluate ideas carefully, and are more sceptical and take more convincing, but take risks, help to adapt new ideas to local settings, and have effective networking skills
Early majority	Those who take longer to reach a decision to change, but who are still ahead of the average
Late majority	Even more sceptical and risk averse, wait for most of their colleagues to adopt new ideas first
Laggards	Viewed negatively by others, the last to adopt new ideas, even for reasons that they believe to be rational

To infinity and beyond

The animation studio Pixar gave us the movie *Toy Story*, and the cartoon character Buzz Lightyear (with his 'to infinity' catchphrase), in 1995. The company has produced two more instalments of *Toy Story* and other successful movies such as *Finding Nemo*, *Cars*, *The Incredibles* and *Ratatouille*. How can a company be creative, and then go on being creative, especially when its president and its 'chief creative officer' are in their 60s and 50s respectively (*The Economist*, 2010)?

The two senior managers are charismatic leaders. But Pixar is also *organized* to be creative. Hollywood studios usually start with good ideas and then hire creative people to turn those into movies. Pixar starts by recruiting creatives and then gets them to keep generating ideas. Pixar's 1,200 employees take collective responsibility for projects, sharing their work-in-progress in daily meetings to get feedback and inspiration. This is adapted from Toyota's 'lean production' method, getting feedback from production line workers to fix problems. Pixar's teams are also required to conduct 'post mortems' on finished films, identifying at least five things that did not go well, as well as five that did.

Creativity depends on organization and management as well as on creative individuals. For Pixar, this involves looking to other companies and sectors for inspiration. And it means getting people to work with organization structures and a strong culture (see Chapter 4), while giving them the freedom to come up with new ideas, and to keep being creative (Catmull, 2014). The documentary movie *The Pixar Story* (2007, director Lesley Iwerks) describes the company's first six years, attributing the company's success to a combination of creativity and hard work.

© Geoff Moore/Rex Features

Building a creative climate

Rosabeth Moss Kanter (1983, 1989) contrasts what she calls *segmentalist* organization cultures from *integrative* cultures. A segmentalist culture is preoccupied with hierarchy, compartmentalizes its decision making, and emphasizes rules and efficiency. An integrative culture is based on teams and collaboration, adopts a holistic approach to problem solving, has no time for history or precedent, and emphasizes results. It is not surprising to find Kanter arguing that bureaucratic, mechanistic, segmentalist cultures tend to be 'innovation smothering', and that adaptable, organic, integrative cultures are innovation stimulating.

How simple rules encourage innovation

'To illustrate how simple rules can foster innovation, consider the case of Zumba Fitness. That company's fitness routine was developed when Alberto Perez, a Columbian aerobics instructor, forgot to take his exercise tape to class and used what he had at hand – a tape of salsa music. Today, Zumba is a global business that offers classes at 200,000 locations in 180 countries to over 15 million customers drawn by the ethos, "Ditch the workout. Join the party".

'Zumba's executives actively seek out suggestions for new products and services from its army of over 100,000 licensed instructors. Other companies routinely approach Zumba with possible partnership and licensing agreements. In fact, it is deluged by ideas for new classes (Zumba Gold for baby boomers), music (the first *Zumba Fitness Dance Party* CD went platinum in France), clothing, fitness concerts, and video games, such as Zumba Fitness for Nintendo Wii. Zumba's founders rely on two simple rules that help them quickly identify the most promising innovations from the flood of proposals they receive. First, any new product or service must help the instructors – who not only lead the classes but carry Zumba's brand, and drive sales of products – to attract clients and keep them engaged. Second, the proposal must deliver FEJ (pronounced "fedge"), which stands for "freeing, electrifying joy" and distinguishes Zumba from the "no pain, no gain" philosophy of many fitness classes' (Sull, 2015, pp.2–3).

Exploring how organizations smother and stimulate innovation, Göran Ekvall (1996; Ekvall and Ryhammar, 1999) developed the concept of *creative organization climate*. Climate is a combination of attitudes, feelings and behaviours, which exists independently of the perceptions and understandings of individual members (see the box 'How simple rules encourage innovation'). The ten dimensions of the creative climate are summarized in Table 19.8.

Table 19.8: Dimensions of the creative organization climate

Dimension	Promoting innovation	Inhibiting innovation
Challenge	People experience challenge, joy and meaning and invest high energy	People are alienated, indifferent, unchallenged, and are apathetic
Freedom	People make contacts, give and receive information freely, discuss problems, make decisions, take initiative	People are passive, rule-bound, anxious to remain within their well-established boundaries
Idea support	People listen to each other, ideas and suggestions are welcomed	Suggestions are quickly rejected as faults and obstacles are found
Trust and openness	High trust climate, ideas can be expressed without fear of ridicule	Low trust climate, people are suspicious of each other, afraid to make mistakes
Dynamism and liveliness	New things happening all the time, new ways of thinking and problem solving	Slow jog with no surprises, no new projects or plans, everything as usual
Playfulness and humour	Relaxed atmosphere with jokes and laughter, spontaneity	Gravity and seriousness, stiff and gloomy, jokes improper

→

Table 19.8: Dimensions of the creative organization climate (*continued*)

Dimension	Promoting innovation	Inhibiting innovation
Debates	Many voices are heard, expressing different ideas and viewpoints	People follow an authoritarian pattern without questioning
Conflicts	Conflict of ideas not personal, people behave in a mature manner, based on psychological insight	Personal and emotional tensions, plots and traps, gossip and slander, climate of 'warfare'
Risk taking	Rapid decisions and actions, experimentation rather than detailed analysis	Cautious, hesitant mentality, work 'on the safe side', 'sleep on the matter', set up committees before deciding
Idea time	Opportunities to test fresh ideas that are not part of planned work activity, and these chances are exploited	Every minute booked and specified, pressures mean that thinking outside planned routines is difficult

STOP AND THINK

Think of an organization with which you are familiar, perhaps one where you are currently employed, or one where you have worked recently.

Assess that organization's climate on Ekvall's ten dimensions, in terms of how it promotes or inhibits innovation.

Where the organization inhibits innovation, what practical steps could management take to strengthen the creative climate, to promote innovation?

To be an innovator and lead change

Do you want to be a change leader, implementing new ideas? Being creative and driving change can be frustrating, as well as rewarding. The development of something new often involves such a high failure rate. (James Dyson's famous bagless vacuum cleaner went through over 5,000 prototypes to get to the winning design.) A lot of trial and error is necessary, to find out what works best. Despite corporate mission and value statements encouraging staff to be creative and to take risks in a 'no blame culture', management does not always look favourably on failure. In some cases, being innovative can jeopardize your job security and career.

Rosabeth Moss Kanter's (2002) rules for stifling innovation

1. Regard a new idea from below with suspicion, because it's new, and because it's from below.

2. Insist that people who need your approval to act first go through several other levels of management to get their signatures.

3. Ask departments or individuals to challenge and criticize each other's proposals. That saves you the job of deciding; you just pick the survivor.

4. Express criticism freely, and withhold praise. That keeps people on their toes. Let them know that they can be fired at any time.

5. Treat identification of problems as signs of failure, to discourage people from letting you know when something in their area isn't working.

6. Control everything carefully. Make sure people count anything that can be counted, frequently.

7. Make decisions to reorganize or change policies in secret, and spring them on people unexpectedly. That keeps people on their toes.

8. Make sure that requests for information are fully justified, and make sure that it is not given out to

managers freely. You don't want data to fall into the wrong hands.

9. Assign to lower level managers, in the name of delegation and participation, responsibility for figuring out how to cut back, lay off, move people around, or otherwise implement threatening decisions you have made. And get them to do it quickly.

10. And above all, never forget that you, the higher-ups, already know everything important about this business.

Amy Edmondson (2011) argues that not all change failures are bad. She explores the reasons for failure on a spectrum ranging from blameworthy to praiseworthy (Table 19.9). At one extreme, deviance, breaking the rules deliberately, is blameworthy. At the other end of the spectrum, experiments to discover whether something new will work or not are praiseworthy. Do managers recognize this spectrum, and treat employees accordingly?

> When I ask executives to consider this spectrum and then to estimate how many of the failures in their organization are truly blameworthy, their answers are usually in single digits – perhaps 2 percent to 5 percent. But when I ask how many are *treated* as blameworthy, they say (after a pause or a laugh) 70 percent to 90 percent. The unfortunate consequence is that many failures go unreported and their lessons are lost. (Edmondson, 2011, p.50)

Edmondson advises promoting experimentation, not blaming individuals when organizational circumstances have contributed to failure, and analysing carefully the reasons for failures, going beyond obvious and superficial reasons. In addition, the 'messengers' who speak out with bad news, awkward questions, concerns, or make mistakes, 'should be rewarded rather than shot'. Management should welcome the knowledge, and work out how to fix the problem. It is also necessary, she concludes, to be clear about which acts are blameworthy, and hold people accountable.

Table 19.9: Blameworthy and praiseworthy failures

Blameworthy	**Deviance**	Individual chooses to violate prescribed process or practice
	Inattention	Individual inadvertently deviates from specifications
	Lack of ability	Individual lacks skills, conditions, or training for the job
	Process inadequacy	Competent individual follows faulty or incomplete process
	Task challenge	Individual faces a task too difficult to be executed reliably
	Process complexity	A complex process breaks down under novel conditions
	Uncertainty	People take reasonable actions leading to undesired results
	Hypothesis testing	Failed experiment to see whether an idea will work
Praiseworthy	**Exploratory testing**	Experiment to expand knowledge leads to undesired result

Source: Reprinted by permission of Harvard Business Review. From 'Strategies for learning from failure' by Edmondson, A.C., 89(4) 2011. Copyright (c) 2011 by the Harvard Business School Publishing Corporation; all rights reserved.

The five habits of disruptive innovators

Why are some people more innovative than others, and make it look easy and effortless? It is often assumed that 'creatives' are special people with unique skills. However, Jeff Dyer, Hal Gregersen and Clayton Christensen (2011) argue that anyone can be innovative by using the right approach. Their research suggests that the best innovators have these five habits:

Associating	Innovators are good at seeing connections between things that do not appear to be related, drawing ideas together from unrelated fields
Questioning	Innovators are always challenging what others take for granted, asking 'why is this done this way – why don't we do it differently?'
Observing	Innovators watch the behaviour of customers, suppliers, competitors – looking for new ways of doing things
Experimenting	Innovators tinker with products and business models, sometimes accidentally, to see what happens, what insights emerge
Networking	Innovators attend conferences and other social events to pick up ideas from people with different ideas, who may face similar problems, in other fields

Individuals can become more innovative by following this advice, and by collaborating with 'delivery-driven' colleagues. Dyer and colleagues argue that organizations also need to encourage these habits, stimulating employees to connect ideas, to challenge accepted practices, to watch what others are doing, to take risks and try things out, and to get out of the company to meet others.

Who are your most capable strategic change leaders?

Research by the consulting company Pricewaterhouse Coopers (PwC) has found that only 8 per cent of senior managers have the strategic leadership capabilities required to drive organizational change (Lewis, 2015). From a survey of 6,000 managers in Europe, the highest proportion of strategic leaders were women over the age of 55 – a group which has traditionally been overlooked in the search for change leadership skills.

PwC defines a strategic leader as someone who has 'wide experience of settings, people, and also of failure, which engenders humility or perspective and resilience, so that they know what to do when things don't work'. Women over 55 were more likely to:

- see situations from multiple perspectives;
- think and work outside the existing system;
- identify what needs to change;
- be able to persuade or inspire others to follow them;
- use positive language;
- be open to frank and honest feedback;
- exercise power courageously.

One consultant (female) at PwC said: 'Historically women over the age of 55 would not have been an area of focus, but as the research suggests, this pool of talent might hold the key to transformation and in some cases, business survival' (Lewis, 2015).

The perceived need for rapid and continual adjustment to events and trends has made change management a key organizational issue. Change is no longer something which disturbs the stable fabric from time to time, but is an ever-present feature. However, some commentators argue that change is damaging when it is rapid and ongoing, and that the initiative stream should be carefully timed and paced. The significance of context, in shaping the opportunities for and directions of change, is now better understood and appreciated. Finally, the organizational capability to change rapidly and often is seen as contributing to competitive advantage and survival, and not just to performance improvement. These trends are summarized in Table 19.10.

Table 19.10: Trends in organizational change

Change in the twentieth century	Change in the twenty-first century
One theme among many	A management preoccupation
Importance of participation and involvement	Recognition of need for directive methods
Rational-linear model of change management	Messy, untidy change processes
Change driven by small elite groups	Change is everyone's responsibility
Focus on change agents	Focus on disruptive innovators
Implementation method is critical	Implementation must be tailored to context
Changes must be frequent and fast	Need to consider timing and pacing with care
Aimed at organizational effectiveness	Aimed at competitive advantage and survival

Home viewing

Inside Job (2010, director Charles Ferguson, narrated by Matt Damon) examines the global financial crisis of 2008. Over the previous decade, deregulation allowed the finance industry to take risks that older rules would have discouraged. As you watch this film, identify the various stakeholders (including academics), their competing interests, their relationships, and their efforts to conceal sensitive information. How did those competing interests, relationships and 'information games' contribute to the crisis? The film concludes that, despite this crisis, the underlying system has remained much the same. How has the sector been able to avoid fundamental changes to financial regulation? What does this account reveal about the nature of organizational change in general?

 RECAP

1. **Explain why effective change management is important, to organizations and to individuals.**

   - Organizations that do not adapt to changing circumstances may see their performance deteriorate, and may go out of business.

   - The pace of organizational change means that individuals need to 'future proof' their careers by constantly gaining new knowledge and skills.

2. **Identify the main external and internal triggers of organizational change.**

   - Change can be triggered by factors internal and external to the organization, and can also be proactive by anticipating trends and events.

   - Change varies in depth, from shallow fine-tuning, to deep transformational change.

   - The broad direction of change in most organizations is towards becoming less mechanistic and bureaucratic, and more adaptive, responsive and organic.

3. **Explain the issues that management must take into account to ensure that change is successful.**

   - The 'basics' of change implementation include clear benefits, strong leadership, powerful change agents, constant communication, employee engagement, short-term wins, and making sure that change is embedded in the culture.

   - The timing and pacing of change are also important: too slow, and organizational survival may be at risk, but too fast, and staff may be overloaded, and demotivated by initiative fatigue.

4. **Understand the typical characteristics of human responses to change.**

   - Emotional responses to traumatic changes differ, but the typical coping cycle passes through the stages of denial, anger, bargaining, depression and acceptance.

   - The Yerkes–Dodson Law states that the initial response to pressure is improved performance,

→

and that increasing pressure leads to fatigue, and ultimately breakdown.

- The evidence suggests that continuous organizational changes lead to work intensification, burn-out and initiative fatigue.

5. **Understand the nature of resistance to change and approaches to overcoming it.**

- Resistance to change has many sources, including self-interest, lack of trust and understanding, competing assessments of the outcomes, and low tolerance of change.

- One technique for addressing possible resistance to change, as well as identifying and strengthening support for change, is stakeholder analysis.

- The main prescribed approach for avoiding or dealing with resistance is participative management, in which those affected are involved in implementation.

- The use of manipulation and coercion to implement change are advocated by some commentators, but the 'political' role of management in change is controversial.

6. **Explain the advantages and limitations of participative methods of change management.**

- Participative methods can generate creative thinking and increase employee commitment to change, but this process is time-consuming.

- Some commentators argue that rapid and major corporate transformations are more successful when implemented using a dictatorial or coercive style.

7. **Understand the significance of innovation, and the distinction between sustaining, disruptive and operational innovations.**

- Innovation has become a strategic imperative in order to compete and to survive.

- Sustaining innovations are those which improve existing services and products.

- Disruptive innovations introduce completely new services and products.

- Operational innovations concern new ways of organizing, managing and working.

8. **Explain the organizational properties that stimulate and stifle innovation respectively.**

- A creative organizational climate is one which promotes lively and challenging debate, freedom of expression, trust and openness, humour, risk taking, giving people time to try out new ideas – and has a high level of receptiveness to new ideas.

- Organization properties that stifle innovation include rigid rules, suspicion of new ideas, low trust, criticism freely given, jokes seen as improper, aversion to risk and tight time pressures.

- Creative individuals outside creative organizational climates are likely to stop innovating; anyone in a creative climate is capable of being creative, and will be encouraged to innovate.

9. **Recognize the challenges facing innovative change leaders.**

- The successful development of something new is exciting and challenging, but can involve a high rate of failure before the winning design is found.

- Organizations vary in their tolerance for and treatment of failure; even 'praiseworthy' failures can attract blame and punishment.

- We can become more innovative by practising the five habits of associating, questioning, observing, experimenting and networking.

Revision

1. What are the basic rules of change implementation? Although these appear to be simple, the failure rate of organizational changes is high. How can that failure rate be explained?

2. What are the main sources of resistance to organizational change, and how should resistance be managed?

3. Organizations are advised to change rapidly in order to compete to survive. What dangers come with this advice?

4. What are the main types of innovation, and how can an organization develop a climate that encourages individuals to be more creative?

Research assignment

Choose an organization that has experienced major change. Arrange to interview two managers who were involved in implementing this change. Using John Kotter's guide to corporate transformation, find out how the changes were managed. For each step, find out what was involved, how it was done, and how well it worked:

1. Establish a sense of urgency.
2. Form a guiding coalition.
3. Create a vision.
4. Communicate the vision.
5. Empower people to act on the vision.
6. Create 'short-term wins'.
7. Consolidate improvements to produce further change.
8. Embed new approaches in the organization's culture.

Finally, ask your managers for their assessment of these changes. Once you have discovered how the changes were managed, rate the organization on a 1 to 10 scale for each heading (1 = very poor; 10 = very good). A score of 8 suggests disaster; a score of 80 implies success. To what extent is your assessment consistent with that of the managers you interviewed?

Now develop an assessment that answers the following questions:

- What should management have done differently in implementing these changes?
- What should management do differently the next time when implementing organizational change?

Springboard

Chatman, J. (2014) 'Culture change at Genentech: accelerating strategic and financial accomplishments', *California Management Review*, 56 (2): 113–29. This is a case study of successful culture change in a pharmaceuticals company, using a participative approach.

Clay, A. and Phillips, K.M. (2015) *The Misfit Economy: Lessons in Creativity from Pirates, Hackers, Gangsters and Other Informal Entrepreneurs*. New York: Simon & Schuster. Argues that idealistic 'misfits' make the best innovators because they are tired of the discipline and obedience encouraged by most organizations – and they want to change that.

Palmer, I., Dunford, R. and Buchanan, D.A. (2016) *Managing Change: A Multiple Perspectives Approach* (3rd edn). Chicago: McGraw-Hill. Comprehensive text exploring need for change, what changes, managing resistance, implementation methods, sustainability, and the capabilities of change agents, managers or leaders.

Hamel, G. and Zanini, M. (2014) *Build a Change Platform, Not a Change Program*. London: McKinsey & Company. Argues that the leader's role is not to design a change programme, but to build a change platform, by allowing anyone in the organization to set priorities, diagnose barriers, suggest solutions, recruit support and initiate change.

 ## OB cinema

Charlie's Angels (2000, director Joseph McGinty Nichols – 'McG' – 2000): DVD track 14, 0:35:57 to 0:38:10 (3 minutes). Clip begins outside the Red Star corporation headquarters; clip ends when Alex says 'Better yet, can anyone show me?'

→

Alex (played by Lucy Liu), masquerading as an 'efficiency expert', leads the Angels into the Red Star corporation headquarters building, in an attempt to penetrate their security systems. As you watch this three-minute clip, paying careful attention to details, consider the following questions:

1. Is this an organization that stimulates or smothers creativity and innovation?

2. How do you know? What are the clues, visual and spoken, that support your assessment of the organization culture?

 ## OB on the web

Go to YouTube and search for Clayton Christensen. You will find several clips where he is talking about innovation in general, and about disruptive innovation in particular. Watch two or three of these short clips. From listening to Christensen himself, what can you add to your understanding of the nature and importance of innovation – to an organization, and to you personally?

CHAPTER EXERCISES

1. Implementation planning

Objectives   1. To apply change implementation theory to a practical setting.

2. To assess the value of 'best practice' textbook advice on how to implement change effectively.

Briefing   Due to a combination of space constraints and financial issues, your department or school has been told by senior management to relocate to another building seven kilometres from your existing site within the next three months. Your management have in turn been asked to draw up a plan for managing the move, which will affect all staff (academic, technical, secretarial, administrative), all students (undergraduate, postgraduate), and all equipment (classroom aids, computing). The new building will provide more space and student facilities, but offices for academic staff are smaller, the building is on a different bus route, and car parking facilities are limited. Senior management have reassured staff that email will allow regular contact to be maintained with colleagues in other departments and schools which are not being moved.

You have been asked to help management with their planning. Your brief is as follows:

1. Conduct a stakeholder analysis, identifying how each stakeholder or stakeholder group should be approached to ensure that this move goes ahead smoothly.

2. Assess the readiness for change analysis, identifying any 'groundwork' that may have to be done to ensure the move goes ahead smoothly.

3. Determine your change implementation strategy. Is a participative approach appropriate, or is dictatorial transformation required? Justify your recommendation by pointing to the advantages and limitations of the various options you have explored.

4. With reference to the basic rules of change described in this chapter, draw up a creative and practical action plan for implementing this change effectively.

Prepare a presentation of your results to colleagues.

2. Force-field analysis

Objective   To demonstrate the technique of force-field analysis in planning change.

Briefing   Force-field analysis is a method for assessing the issues supporting and blocking movement towards a given set of desirable outcomes, called the 'target situation'. The forces can be scored, say from 1 (weak) to 10 (strong), to calculate (approximately) the balance of forces.

If the driving forces are overwhelming, then the change can go ahead without significant problems. If the resisting forces are overwhelming, then the change may have to be abandoned, or delayed until conditions have improved.

If the driving and resisting forces are more or less in balance, then the force-field analysis can be used to plan appropriate action. The extent to which the force-field is balanced is a matter of judgement. Used in a group setting, this method provides a valuable way to structure what can often be an untidy discussion covering a wide range of factors and differing perceptions.

For this analysis, your target situation is 'to double the time that I spend studying organizational behaviour'. In groups of three, complete the analysis using the following table as a guide. First identify as many driving and restraining forces as you can. Then, reach a group consensus on a score for each of those forces, from 1 (weak) to 10 (strong). Finally for this stage of the analysis, calculate the totals for each side of the force-field.

Target situation: to double the time that I spend studying organizational behaviour

Scores	Driving forces>>>>>	<<<<<Restraining forces	Scores
	= total driving forces score	total restraining forces score =	

When you have completed this analysis, and added the scores, estimate the probability (high, medium or low) of reaching your target situation *if the force-field stays the same*.

Now draw a practical action plan for managing the field of forces that you have identified in order to increase the probability of reaching the target situation. In devising your action plan, remember that:

1. Increasing the driving forces can often result in an increase in the resisting forces. This means that the current equilibrium does not change, but is maintained with increased tension.

2. Reducing the resisting forces is preferable as this allows movement towards the desired outcomes or target situation without increasing tension.

3. Group norms are an important force in shaping and resisting change.

Employability assessment

With regard to your future employment prospects:

1. Identify up to three issues from this chapter that you found significant.
2. Relate these to the competencies in the employability matrix.
3. Decide what actions you need to take to maintain and/or develop those competencies under each of the four headings of the employability matrix.

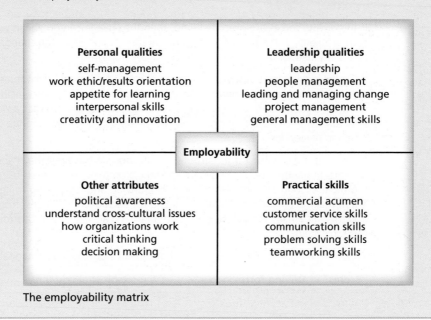

Personal qualities
self-management
work ethic/results orientation
appetite for learning
interpersonal skills
creativity and innovation

Leadership qualities
leadership
people management
leading and managing change
project management
general management skills

Employability

Other attributes
political awareness
understand cross-cultural issues
how organizations work
critical thinking
decision making

Practical skills
commercial acumen
customer service skills
communication skills
problem solving skills
teamworking skills

The employability matrix

References

Appelbaum, S.H., Habashy, S., Malo, J.-L. and Shafiq, H. (2012) 'Back to the future: revisiting Kotter's 1996 change model', *Journal of Management Development*, 31 (8): 764–82.

Bacon, R. and Hope, C. (2014) 'The billions we have spent on IT that doesn't work', *The Times*, 20 August, pp.2–3.

Barabba, V. (2011) *The Decision Loom: A Design for Interactive Decision-Making in Organizations.* Axminster, Devon: Triarchy Press.

Beer, M. (2014) 'Organization Development at a crossroads', *OD Practitioner*, 46 (4): 60–61.

Berwick, D.M. (2003) 'Disseminating innovations in health care', *Journal of the American Medical Association*, 289 (15): 1969–75.

Bruch, H. and Menges, J.I. (2010) 'The acceleration trap', *Harvard Business Review*, 88 (4): 80–86.

Buchanan, D.A., Fitzgerald, L. and Ketley, D. (eds) (2007) *The Sustainability and Spread of Organizational Change: Modernizing Healthcare.* London: Routledge.

Burnes, B. (2011) 'Why does change fail, and what can we do about it?', *Journal of Change Management*, 11 (4): 445–50.

Burnes, B. and Cooke, B (2012) 'Review article: The past, present and future of Organization Development: taking the long view', *Human Relations*, 65 (11): 1395–429.

Catmull, E. (2014) *Creativity, Inc: Overcoming the Unseen Forces That Stand in the Way of True Inspiration.* New York: Bantam Press.

Christensen, C.M., Bohmer, R. and Kenagy, J. (2000) 'Will disruptive innovations cure health care?', *Harvard Business Review*, 78 (5): 102–12.

Coch, L. and French, J.R.P. (1948) 'Overcoming resistance to change', *Human Relations*, 1: 512–32.

Dyer, J., Gregersen, H. and Christensen, C.M. (2011) *The Innovator's DNA: Mastering the Five Skills of Disruptive Innovators*. Boston, MA: Harvard Business School Press.

Edmondson, A. (2011) 'Strategies for learning from failure', *Harvard Business Review*, 89 (4): 48–55.

Ekvall, G. (1996) 'Organizational climate for creativity and innovation', *European Journal of Work and Organizational Psychology*, 5 (1): 105–23.

Ekvall, G. and Ryhammar, L. (1999) 'The creative climate: its determinants and effects at a Swedish university', *Creativity Research Journal*, 12 (4): 303–10.

Ewenstein, B., Smith, W. and Sologar, A. (2015) *Changing Change Management*. New York: McKinsey & Company.

Ford, J.D. and Ford, L.W. (2009) 'Decoding resistance to change', *Harvard Business Review*, 87 (4): 99–103.

Gast, A. and Lansink, R. (2015) 'Digital hives: creating a surge around change', *McKinsey Quarterly*, April, pp.1–9.

Gratton, L. (2011) *The Shift: The future of Work is Already Here*. London: Collins.

Hamel, G. and Zanini, M. (2014) *Build a Change Platform, Not a Change Program*. London: McKinsey & Company.

Hammer, M. (2004) 'Deep change: how operational innovation can transform your company', *Harvard Business Review*, 82 (4): 84–93.

Hout, T. and Michael, D. (2014) 'A Chinese approach to management', *Harvard Business Review*, 92 (9): 103–07.

Hughes, M. (2011) 'Do 70 per cent of all organizational change initiatives really fail?', *Journal of Change Management*, 11 (4): 451–64.

Jacquemont, D., Maor, D. and Reich, A. (2015) *How to Beat the Transformation Odds*. New York: McKinsey & Company.

Ji, Y.-Y., Gutherie, J.P. and Messersmith, J.G. (2014) 'The tortoise and the hare: the impact of employee instability on firm performance', *Human Resource Management Journal*, 24 (4): 355–73.

Jick, T.J. and Peiperl, M. (2010) *Managing Change: Cases and Concepts* (3rd edn). New York: McGraw-Hill.

Kanter, R.M. (1983) *The Change Masters: Corporate Entrepreneurs at Work*. London: George Allen & Unwin.

Kanter, R.M. (1989) *When Giants Learn to Dance: Mastering The Challenges of Strategy, Management, and Careers in the 1990s*. London: Unwin.

Kanter, R.M. (2002) 'Creating the culture for innovation', in F. Hesselbein, M. Goldsmith and I. Somerville (eds), *Leading for Innovation and Organizing for Results*. San Francisco: Jossey-Bass, pp.73–85.

Lewin, K. (ed.) (1951) *Field Theory in Social Science: Selected Theoretical Papers by Kurt Lewin*, London: Tavistock Publications (UK edition published 1952, edited by Dorwin Cartwright).

Lewis, G. (2015) 'Women over 55 best suited to lead transformational change, finds PwC', *People Management*, 18 May, www.cipd.co.uk/pm/peoplemanagement/b/weblog/archive/2015/05/18/women-over-55-best-suited-to-lead-transformational-change-finds-pwc.aspx

Kotter, J.P. (2007) 'Leading change: why transformation efforts fail', *Harvard Business Review*, 85 (1): 96–103 (first published 1995).

Kotter, J.P. (2012) 'Accelerate!', *Harvard Business Review*, 90 (11): 44–52.

Kotter, J.P. and Schlesinger, L.A. (2008) 'Choosing strategies for change', *Harvard Business Review*, 86 (7/8): 130–39 (first published 1979).

Kübler-Ross, E. (1969) *On Death and Dying*. Toronto: Macmillan.

McKinsey & Company (2014) *The Lean Management Enterprise: A System for Daily Progress, Meaningful Purpose, and Lasting Value*. New York: McKinsey Practice Publications.

MacLachlan, R. (2011) 'A switch in time', *People Management*, July, pp.36–9.

Maurer, R. (2010) *Beyond the Walls of Resistance* (2nd edn). Austin, TX: Bard Books.

Mohrman, S.A. and Lawler, E.E. (2012) 'Generating knowledge that drives change', *Academy of Management Perspectives*, 26 (1): 41–51.

Pascale, R.T. and Sternin, J. (2005) 'Your company's secret change agents', *Harvard Business Review*, 83 (5): 72–81.

Plsek, P. and Kilo, C.M. (1999) 'From resistance to attraction: a different approach to change', *Physician Exec*, 25 (6): 40–42.

Rafferty, A.E., Jimmieson, N.L. and Armenakis, A.A. (2013) 'Change readiness: a multilevel review', *Journal of Management*, 39 (1): 110–35.

Robbins, S.P. and Judge, T.A. (2008) *Organizational Behaviour* (12th edn). Upper Saddle River, NJ: Pearson Educational Inc.

Rogers, E. (1995) *The Diffusion of Innovation* (4th edn). New York: Free Press.

Schneider, D.M. and Goldwasser, C. (1998) 'Be a model leader of change', *Management Review*, 87 (3), 41–5.

Schön, D.A. (1963) 'Champions for radical new inventions', *Harvard Business Review*, 41 (2): 77–86.

Smedley, T. (2014) 'Send in the cloud', *People Management*, May, pp.43–44.

Stace, D. and Dunphy, D. (2001) *Beyond the Boundaries: Leading and Re-creating the Successful Enterprise.* Sydney: McGraw Hill.

Steinfeld, E.S. and Beltoft, T. (2014) 'Innovation lessons from China', *MIT Sloan Management Review*, 55 (4): 49–55.

Sull, D. (2015) 'The simple rules of disciplined innovation', *McKinsey Quarterly*, May, pp.1–10.

The Economist (2010) 'Planning for the sequel', 19 June, p.70.

The Economist (2012) 'The last Kodak moment?', 14 January, p.25.

Yerkes, R.M. and Dodson, J.D. (1908) 'The relationship of strength of stimulus to rapidity of habit-formation', *Journal of Comparative Neurology and Psychology*, 18 (5): 459–82.

Table 20.3: Rational decision making and bounded rationality contrasted

Rational decision makers …	Bounded rationality decision makers …
Recognize and define a problem or opportunity thoroughly	Reduce the problem to something that is easily understood
Search for a extensive set of alternative courses of action, gathering data on each	Develop a few, uncomplicated and recognizable solutions, comparable to those currently being used
Evaluate all the alternatives at the same time	Evaluate each alternative as it is thought of.
Select and implement the alternative with the most value *(maximize)*	Choose the first, acceptable alternative *(satisfice)*

Source: based on Simon (1979) and Kahneman (2003).

STOP AND THINK When you chose your current partner – girlfriend, boyfriend, wife or husband – did you maximize or satisfice? Is this distinction a useful way of explaining the decision-making process?

Bounded rationality, technology, information and decision making

Daan van Knippenberg and his colleagues (2015) consider that the idea that individuals, groups and organizations are bounded, both in terms of their rationality and in their ability to attend to information, is as true today as it was 50 years ago. What has changed, however, is the nature and volume of information and how managers locate and use it. We have seen major advances in electronics, computers, the internet, information technology, mobile communications, big data and cloud storage. More people and companies have easier access to more information than ever before in human history (see Chapter 3).

Yet the human ability to attend to and process information, and make decisions based upon it, has not radically changed. The basic decision-making process remains the same despite the transformative changes in the world. This growing volume of information, while it offers new opportunities, also competes for the attention of people, increasing their potential for information overload; fuelling biases in decision making, increasing the costs of information collection, storage, analysis and sharing, and distracting them from performing the job itself. Financial resources and management time have to be devoted to making best use of this information. How does one productively manage this wealth of information?

The world's capacity to store, communicate and compute information is fundamentally changing the way that individuals, groups, organizations and industries work. The ability to effectively and efficiently locate, pay attention to and process diverse information, is increasingly valued.

Back in 1957, Herbert Simon observed that the problem was not gaining access to information but rather that information consumed attention, which was a scarce resource. Information comes at us every minute through emails, the web, consumer data and social data. It arrives via our smart phones, tablets, television, radio and print media. The amount of information is increasing faster than the attention that decision makers can give it. Which information is most important? Which can be ignored?

Within organizations, this information tsunami is changing long-established decision-making practices. The challenge now is to make decisions under conditions of information overload rather than information scarcity. Companies are racing to capture their employees' expertise and experience, facilitate intra-organizational knowledge sharing, and connect with outsiders to gain ideas and innovate. Using databases, expertise directories and social technology platforms, emails, videoconferencing and collaborative software, companies are transferring best practice, learning to respond better to customers,

→

integrating their supply chains, and reducing knowledge losses when their employees leave.

However, it is the fundamental problem of bounded rationality that continues to loom large. People have always been limited in their attention and processing abilities as well as in their motivation to acquire and absorb information. Finding relevant and useful information for their tasks is becoming increasing

problematic. Employees must decide how much and which information to share or withhold; be able to transfer knowledge effectively and securely; and know how to react and respond to the information that they themselves receive. Thus, van Knippenberg et al. note, the information age continues to present us with long-standing challenges of information, attention and decision making.

Information

An information manager (Beske, 2013) reported that, on appointment to his job, he was told by his staff that:

The information you have is not what you want.

The information you want is not what you need.

The information that you need is not what you can obtain.

The information that you can obtain costs more than you want to pay.

What you are willing to pay will get you exactly the information you already have.

Prescriptive models

Prescriptive model of decision making an approach that recommends how individuals should make decisions in order to achieve a desired outcome.

A prescriptive model of decision making recommends how individuals *should* behave in order to achieve a desired outcome. This makes the rational model, described earlier, also a prescriptive one. Such models often also contain specific techniques, procedures and processes which their supporters claim will lead to more accurate and efficient decision making. They are often based on observations of poor decision-making processes, where key steps might have been omitted or inadequately considered. They are developed and marketed by management consultants as a way of improving organization performance through improved decision making.

One of the best known prescriptive models of decision making was developed by Victor Vroom and Philip Yetton (1973) and later expanded by Vroom and Arthur Jago (1988). The focus is on decision-making *situations* and on seven factors, to identify the decision-making style that is likely to be most effective in any given situation. It focuses on decision style, concerning *how* a leader decides in a given decision situation, rather than *what* a leader decides. It also concentrates on subordinate participation – the appropriate amount of involvement of the leader's subordinates in making a decision. The model consists of three main elements:

1. Decision participation styles.

2. Diagnostic questions with which to analyse decision situations.

3. Decision rules to determine the appropriate decision participation style.

The model is underpinned by two key concepts – quality and acceptability. The quality of the decision relates to it achieving the aim, the cost of its implementation, and the time taken to implement it. The acceptability of the decision relates to subordinates and anyone else either affected by the decision or who has to implement it. Leaders and managers generally select the highest-quality decision that is acceptable.

1. Decision participation styles

Five decision participation styles are identified: decide, consult individually, consult group, facilitate and delegate. These are shown ranging along a continuum (Table 20.4).

These reflect different amounts of subordinate participation in the leader's decision. Moving from left to right on the continuum:

- The leader discusses the problem or situation more with others.
- Others' input changes from merely providing information to recommending solutions.
- Ownership and commitment to the decision increases.
- The time needed to arrive at a decision increases.

Table 20.4: Participation in decision-making processes

	Leader-centred				Group-centred
	←――――――――――――――――――――――――――――――→				
Description	**(D)** **Decide** As leader, you feel you have the information and expertise to make the decision alone and then you either announce or 'sell' it to the group	**(CI)** **Consult Individually** As leader, you lack the required information or expertise. You therefore obtain this from your group members individually, either telling them the problem or not. You then make the decision alone	**(CG)** **Consult Group** As leader, you explain the situation and provide information to your group Together, solutions are generated and discussed. You then review these recommendations and make the decision alone	**(F)** **Facilitate** As leader, you explain the situation and provide information to your group. Acting as facilitator, you reconcile differences and negotiate a solution acceptable to everyone. The final decision is made by you and your group together	**(D)** **Delegate** As leader, you explain the situation, provide information, and set the boundaries for the decision to be made. You then delegate responsibility and authority for the final decision to the group, who make it themselves. You accept and implement it
Participants	Leader	Leader and others	Leader and others	Leader and others	Leader and others
Role of participants	Leader generates and evaluates solution alone	Individuals provide leader with skill or information	Group generates solutions or recommendations	Group negotiates a solution with leader	Group generates, evaluates and makes the decision
Who makes the decision?	Leader	Leader	Leader (perhaps reflecting group inputs)	Leader and group together	Group

Source: based on Vroom (2000, p.84).

2. Diagnostic questions with which to analyse situations

It was found that leaders used different decision participation styles in different situations; and all of these various styles could be equally effective, depending on the situation. To determine which style is most suitable in a given situation, Vroom asks seven diagnostic questions. The answers to these seven questions, in the form of 'high' (H) or 'low' (L), should determine the appropriate level of subordinate participation in the decision-making process.

1.	*Decision significance*	How significant is this decision to the success of the project or organization? If significance is high, then the leader needs to be closely involved.
2.	*Importance of commitment*	How important is subordinate commitment in implementing the decision? If importance is high, then leaders should involve subordinates.

3. *Leader expertise*

What is the level of the leader's information, knowledge or expertise in relation to the problem? If it is low, the leader should involve subordinates.

4. *Likelihood of commitment*

If the leader were to make the decision alone, would subordinates' commitment to it be high or low? If the answer is high, then subordinate involvement is less important.

5. *Group support for goals*

What is the level of subordinate support for the team's or organization's goals with respect to this situation? If it is low, the leader should not allow the group to make the decision alone.

6. *Group expertise*

What is the level of skill and commitment that group members have in working together as a team to solve the problem? If it is high, then more responsibility for the decision can be given to them.

7. *Team competence*

What is the level of subordinates' skills and commitment in working together as a team to solve the problem? If their skill and desire to work together cooperatively is high, then more responsibility for the decision can be given to them.

3. Decision rules

The Vroom–Yetton–Jago model provides a set of decision rules in the form of a decision tree to allow the selection of the most appropriate decision-making style, as shown in Figure 20.2.

Prescriptive decision-making models are hugely popular in the managerialist literature since they offer executives a step-by-step guide on how to make a decision. Modern ones combine vast amounts of data and increasingly sophisticated algorithms, and modelling has opened up new ways to improve company performance. These models can make very accurate predictions and guide difficult optimization choices while, simultaneously, helping firms to avoid the common biases that undermine judgments (Rosenzweig, 2014).

Explanatory models

Explanatory model of decision making an approach that accounts for how individuals, groups and organizations make decisions.

An **explanatory model of decision making** explains how a given decision was made. For example, there are studies of military fiascos which examine why generals took, or failed to take, certain actions. Often these explanations draw upon personality and leadership concepts and theories. The poor decisions made by teams have also been studied using concepts from the group level of analysis such as groupthink and group polarization. These will be examined later in this chapter. Finally, decisions such as whether to acquire or merge with another company have drawn upon the theories of conflict, power and politics, and offer explanations at the organizational level.

The studies have highlighted the limits to rationality and introduced the concept of bounded rationality. What else might affect the individual who makes a decision? Decision making involves choice, and choice requires both careful thought and much information. Excessive information can both overload and delay us. Many managers believe that making

---

Home viewing

The Martian (2015, director Ridley Scott) is a science fiction film about a NASA mission to Mars that goes wrong. Because of a storm, the space crew abort the mission leaving one of their members, Mark Watney (played by Matt Damon) marooned on the planet. The film shows numerous examples of problem solving and decision making, not only by Watney but also by his crew members and his employer. As you watch the film, make a note of each problem or decision to be solved or made, noting by whom, how is it done, and what the outcome is. Distinguish between the different types of decisions and the conditions under which each is made.

	1 Decision significance	2 Importance of commitment	3 Leader expertise	4 Likelihood of commitment	5 Group support for goals	6 Group expertise	7 Team competence	
	How significant is this decision to the success of the project or organization?	How important is subordinate commitment in implementing the decision?	What is the level of the leader's information, knowledge, or expertise in relation to the problem?	If the leader were to make the decision alone, would subordinates' commitment to it be high or low?	What is the level of subordinate support for the team's or organization's goals with respect to this situation?	What is the level of skill and commitment that group members have in working together as a team to solve the problem?	What is the level of subordinates' skills and commitment in working together as a team to solve the problem?	
P R O B L E M S T A T E M E N T	H	H	H	H	–	–	–	Decide
				L	H	H	H	Delegate
							L	Consult group
						L	–	Facilitate
					L	–	–	Consult individually
			L	–	H	H	–	Facilitate
					L	–	–	Consult group
		L	H	–	–	–	–	Decide
			L	–	H	H	–	Facilitate
					L	–	–	Consult individually
	L	H	–	H	–	–	–	Decide
				L	–	H	H	Delegate
						L	–	Facilitate
	L	L	–	–	–	–	–	Decide

Figure 20.2: Time-driven model of leadership

Source: adapted from *Organizational Dynamics*, 28(4), Vroom, V.H., Leadership and the decision making process, pp.82–94, Copyright 2000, with permission from Elsevier.

Heuristic a simple and approximate rule, guiding procedure, shortcut or strategy that is used to solve problems.

Bias a prejudice, predisposition or a systematic distortion caused by the application of a heuristic.

the right decision late is the same as making the wrong decision on time. Hence we speed up the process by relying on judgement shortcuts called heuristics.

The judgement **heuristics** and **biases** model represents current thinking in decision making and takes a further step away from the rational model. The leading authors in this field have been Daniel Kahneman and Amos Tversky (2000). Human beings have two ways of processing information and making decisions (Kahneman, 2011):

System 1 thinking: fast, automatic, instinctive and emotional; relies on mental shortcuts; generates intuitive answers to problems as they arise, effortlessly.

System 2 thinking: slow, logical and deliberate; requiring cognitive effort.

System 1 uses intuition and rules of thumb to take information and reach conclusions quickly. However, these shortcuts can cause errors, so System 2 thinking is needed to check whether our intuition is faulty or our judgement clouded by emotions. If our snap judgements are not corrected by analysis and deliberation, problems of bias will result, and poor decisions will be made. The biases in decision making operate at the subconscious level, are virtually undetectable, and have a powerful and immediate impact on individuals' judgement. Some of the most common decision-making biases are listed in Table 20.5.

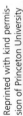

Daniel Kahneman
(b.1934)

Amos Tversky
(1937–1996)

Table 20.5: Common decision-making biases

Name of bias	Description
Anchor and adjustment	Judgement made by starting from an initial value or 'anchor', and then failing to adjust sufficiently from that point, before making the decision
Availability	Judgement of probability made on the basis of information that is readily available
Bandwagon	Believing in certain outcomes because others believe the same
Confirmation	Placing extra value on information that supports our favoured beliefs; ignoring that which does not; failing to search for impartial evidence
Controllability	Believing we can control outcomes more than is the case, leading us to misjudge the riskiness of our actions
Egocentrism	Focusing too narrowly on our own perspective, unable to imagine how others will be affected by our actions.
Loss aversion	Preferring to avoid losses to acquiring gains of the same amount, making us more risk averse than is rational
Optimism	Being excessively optimistic about the likelihood of positive outcomes from our planned actions and underestimating negative consequences
Overconfidence	Overestimating our skills and abilities; taking credit for past positive successes while ignoring the luck that might have been involved
Present	We value immediate rewards more highly than long-term gains
Representative	Basing judgements of probability on the basis of things with which we are familiar
Status quo	Preference for the status quo in the absence of pressure to change it
Sunk cost	Paying attention to unrecoverable, historic costs when considering future actions

Source: based on Kahneman (2011) and Beshears and Gino (2015).

To avoid decision-making biases, academics have offered managers various frameworks. For example, Jack Soll and his colleagues (2015) offer a solution to the problem of assigning too much or too little importance to the information that we have. They suggest three tactics as shown in Table 20.6.

Table 20.6: Tactics to avoid decision bias

Tactic	Effect	Example
Blinding	Anonymizing eliminates the influence of stereotypes, idiosyncratic associations and irrelevant factors	Orchestras audition players behind screens to prevent gender bias and students' exam papers have their names removed before grading
Checklists	Reduces errors by directing attention to most relevant information and avoiding forgetting	Selectors use structured interviews in which all candidates are asked the same questions, allowing inter-candidate comparisons
Algorithms	Ensure consistency by predetermining how much emphasis is placed on which information	Lenders use algorithms to assess applicants' creditworthiness and are now being used in employee hiring decisions

Source: adapted from Soll et al. (2015, p.68).

In a similar vein, Beshears and Gino (2015) offer a way to avoid poor decisions caused by cognitive biases by recommending a five-step approach based upon the differences between Kahneman's System 1 (thinking fast) and System 2 (thinking slow), as shown in Table 20.7.

Table 20.7: Decision steps to avoid cognitive biases

Step	Activity	Issue	Action
1	Understand how decisions are made	People process information and making decisions in two ways	System 1 way is automatic, instinctive and emotional System 2 way is slow, logical and deliberate
2	Define the problem	Ascertain if the problem is human behaviour that can be addressed using behavioural decision-making psychology	Examine if the problem can be narrowly defined Assess whether or not individuals are acting in their own best interest
3	Diagnose underlying causes	Decide if poor decision making is caused by insufficient motivation or cognitive biases	Is the problem the result of individuals' inaction? Is the problem the result of systematic errors affecting people's decisions?
4	Design solution	Select one of the behavioural psychology tools	Initiate changes that arouse emotions, exploit bias or simplify processes (activate fast System 1 thinking) Use group assessments, reflective reviews, planning meetings facilitate rational, considered judgements (activate slow System 2 thinking) Ignore both systems 1 and 2 by setting decision boundaries and building in automatic correction mechanisms

→

Table 20.7: Decision steps to avoid cognitive biases (*continued*)

Step	Activity	Issue	Action
5	Test solution	Thoroughly check proposed solution to avoid later mistakes	Specify a measurable target outcome Identify a range of possible solutions and then select one Introduce change in limited organizational areas and evaluate outcomes

Source: adapted from Beshears and Gino (2015, p.59).

Decision conditions: risk and programmability

Table 20.8 distinguishes different types of environmental conditions faced by organizations and labels these 'stable equilibrium', 'bounded instability' (or chaos) and 'explosive instability'. The condition under which a decision is made affects both how it is made and its outcome. Decisions differ in terms of their degree of risk involved and their programmability. Every decision is made under conditions of certainty, risk or uncertainty. We shall consider each in turn.

Table 20.8: Environmental and decision-making conditions

Environmental condition	Decision-making condition	Characteristics	Example
Stable equilibrium is a state in which the elements are always in, or quickly return to, a state of balance	Certainty	Alternatives and outcomes known and fully predictable	Fixed interest rate savings accounts
Bounded instability (or chaos) is a state in which there is a mixture of order and disorder, many unpredictable events and changes, and in which an organization's behaviour has an irregular pattern	Risk	Known alternatives with only probable outcomes predictable	Tomorrow's weather
Explosive instability is a state in which there is no order or pattern whatsoever	Uncertainty	Alternatives and outcomes poorly understood	Developing a new product

Certainty a condition in which managers possess full knowledge of alternatives; there is a high probability of these being available; being able to calculate the costs and benefits of each alternative; and having high predictability of outcomes.

In a situation of **certainty**, no element of chance comes between the alternative and its outcome, and all the outcomes are known in advance with 100 per cent certainty. In such circumstances, all that the individual has to do is to select the outcomes with the greatest benefit. A situation of total certainty is so rare as to be virtually non-existent. In the past, government bonds which guarantee a fixed rate of interest over a period of time, which will be paid barring the fall of the government, represented an example of certainty. However, as the financial instability of the Eurozone in the early 2010s showed, even government bonds carry an element of risk.

If decisions in organizations were constantly made in conditions of certainty, managers would not be needed, and junior, cheaper operatives, supplied with a rulebook, could replace them. Indeed, in conditions of certainty, a computer could quickly and accurately identify the consequences of the available options and select the outcomes with the greatest benefits. Managers are paid to make those tricky 'judgement calls' in uncertain conditions. In reality most organizational decisions are made under conditions of **risk**. Managers assess the likelihood of various outcomes occurring on the basis of their past experience, research or other information.

Risk a condition in which managers have a high knowledge of alternatives, know the probability of these being available, can calculate the costs and know the benefits of each alternative, and have a medium predictability of outcomes.

Uncertainty a condition in which managers possess low knowledge of alternatives, a low probability of having these available, can to some degree calculate the costs and benefits of each alternative, but have no predictability of outcomes.

Decisions made under **uncertainty** are the most difficult since the manager lacks the information with which to estimate the likelihood of various outcomes and their associated probabilities and payoffs (March and Simon, 1958, p.137). Conditions of uncertainty prevail in new markets, or those offering new technologies, or those aimed at new target customers. In all these cases there are no historical data from which to infer probabilities. In each case, the situation is so novel and complex that it is impossible to make comparative judgements.

Having related the various environmental conditions to their decision-making equivalents, let us summarize the characteristics of each with examples.

STOP AND THINK

Identify three separate events in your university career or work life involving certainty, risk and uncertainty. Consider each situation and think how it could change, or did actually change, from one condition to one of the other two.

Certainty

- From certainty to risk
- From certainty to uncertainty

Risk

- From risk to certainty
- From risk to uncertainty

Uncertainty

- From uncertainty to risk
- From uncertainty to certainty

From Samaras (1989, p.51)

The Eyjafjallajökull ash cloud: decision making in uncertainty

Jon Helgason/123RF.com

The icecap of the Eyjafjallajökull glacier in Iceland covers a volcano that is 1,666 metres in height. The volcano crater measures between 3 and 4 km in diameter. When the magma and the ice interact, they create an ash cloud. On Wednesday, 14 April 2010, a plume of ash rose 17,000 metres into the sky. Scotland's airports, amongst the closest to Iceland, began closing that evening, and the rolling airport shutdown continued southwards on the following days down to London Heathrow and London Stansted. For the next six days, the skies over the United Kingdom were quiet, as were most of those over continental Europe. When the final analysis was completed, it was found that the six-day airspace shutdown, the biggest since the Second World, War had cost the airlines £1.7 billion, and the airport operators €250 million. About 10 million people had been stranded or been unable to fly. A total of 10,000 flights had been cancelled, representing 75 per cent of European airline capacity and 30 per cent of worldwide capacity. Who made the decision to stop the planes flying and who made the decision to resume flying?

The National Air Traffic Services (NATS) took the decision to impose a zero flow rate – that is, it ceased

→

providing a service. Following discussion with the Civil Aviation Authority (CAA), the regulator of UK airspace, NATS made the decision by following guidelines that require zero volcanic ash in the atmosphere for safe flight. The International Civil Aviation Organization manual's chapter 3.4.8 dealing with volcanic ash states that there is no current agreement as to how much ash concentrations constitutes a hazard to jet aircraft engines. In view of this, it stated that 'regardless of ash concentration, AVOID, AVOID, AVOID'. The last word is repeated three times and written in capital letters. On that basis, UK airspace was shutdown.

Scandinavia had been affected first. The Finnish air force sent up five of its F-18 fighter planes over Lapland, and reported significant engine damage from volcanic particles. If large numbers of commercial aircraft began encountering ash clouds and required emergency procedures or re-routing, NATS would not be able to cope. The growing number of stranded passengers was creating political problems for governments, as well as financial problems for airlines and airport operators. The last two were unconvinced about the necessity for a blanket flying ban. By the following Monday, and while UK airspace was closed, Eurocontrol (responsible for all air traffic within the European Union) announced that 55–60 per cent of flights in their airspace would go ahead.

The underlying area of uncertainty was the lack of any indication as to what was a safe level of ash contamination in the air. The airlines had not set a safety limit, nor had aircraft manufacturers or aero engine manufacturers. On the following day, BA (British Airways) announced that 28 of its flights were heading into UK airspace and that it planned to land them, despite the ban. First Rolls-Royce, then Airbus and Pratt & Witney, and then the rest, all announced new, safe limits for the operation of their engines in ash cloud conditions. So what had changed? It was the rules – the criteria of safety. If the engine manufacturers had announced their safety limits years earlier or at the beginning of the crisis and not at the end, the decisions made would have been very different. Faced with evidence and under pressure, they finally stated explicitly that there was indeed a safe level of ash contamination that did not constitute a hazard to flying. Commentators attribute their previous reluctance to a combination of commercial and safety pressures. There are levels of contamination that impact upon the useful life of an engine but which do not impair its safe operation. In the case of the Eyjafjallajökull ash cloud, the absence of any available, accepted safety standard interfered with speedy and effective decision making (BBC Radio 4, 2010; *The Telegraph Online*, 2011).

Programmability of decisions

Routine decisions
decisions made according to established procedures and rules.

Adaptive decisions
decisions that require human judgement based on clarified criteria and are made using basic quantitative decision tools.

Innovative decisions
decisions which address novel problems, lack pre-specified courses of action, and are made by senior managers.

Organization members make many different decisions every day. Some decisions are routine while others are not. Routine decisions are those which involve the use of pre-established organizational procedures or rules. Routine decision makers are given considerable guidance as to what to do and how to do it through a well-established process, clearly defined goals, and the provision of information sources and decision rules. Examples of routine decisions include the re-ordering of stock items which have fallen to a certain level, the efficient routing of delivery vans, and the scheduling of equipment use. All these decisions tend to be repetitive and programmed, and are made by low-level employees on their own who rely on predetermined courses of action.

Adaptive decisions typically require a form of judgement that no computer program, however complex, can produce. They involve a range of variables which have to be weighted and compared. Quantitative decision tools such as break-even analysis, a pay-off matrix, can help to assist the manager's decision.

Finally, innovative decisions are made when a unique situation is confronted that has no precedent; when there are no off-the-shelf solutions; and when a novel answer has to be found. Innovative decisions are an outcome of problem solving; they frequently deal with areas of the unknown; and company professionals or top managers typically make them. Within the organizational context, such decisions tend to be rare. Examples would include the decision whether or not to acquire another company; to invest in a new technology; or to adopt a new marketing approach. The differences between these types of decisions are summarized in Table 20.9.

Table 20.9: Routine, adaptive and innovative decisions

	Decision type	
	Routine ⟵ **Adaptive** ⟶	**Innovative**
Goals	Clear, specific	Vague
Level	Lower level employees	Upper management
Problem	Well structured	Poorly structured
Process	Computational	Heuristic
Information	Readily available	Unavailable
Level of risk	Low	High
Involvement	Single decision maker	Group decision
Consequences	Minor	Major
Solution basis	Decision rule and procedures	Judgement, creativity
Decision speed	Fast	Slow
Time for solution	Short	Relatively long

STOP AND THINK Think of three different decisions that you have recently made. How well did they fit into this routine, adaptive, innovative decision framework? What additional decision-type categories would you add?

Group decision making

One of the main reasons why organizational activities are arranged around groups and teams is management's assumption that group decisions are better than individual decisions. The common-sense belief is that with many members contributing their diverse skills, knowledge and experiences, they will make better decisions than individuals (Hill, 1982). However, experimental research data show that while the average quality of a decision made by a *group* is higher than the average quality of a decision made by an individual, the quality of work group decisions is consistently below that made by their *most capable individual* member (Rogelberg et al., 1992).

STOP AND THINK Do you think that group decision making is superior to individual decision making? Why?

On the positive side, multiple individuals in a group can supply a greater range of knowledge and information to deal with more complex questions. Groups can generate more alternatives; can have a better comprehension of the problem using multiple perspectives; and permit the specialization of labour with individuals doing those tasks for which they are best suited. The effect of this can be to improve the quality of group effort, and facilitate wider decision acceptance since more members will understand the decision better and have a feeling of ownership of it through participation. On the negative side, there are concerns that groups work more slowly; that disagreements within them can create group conflict; and that group members may be intimidated by their group leader, creating only pseudo involvement in decision making. The pros and cons of group decision making are summarized in Table 20.10.

Table 20.10: Advantages and disadvantages of group decision making

Advantages	Disadvantages
Greater pool of knowledge: A group can bring much more information and experience to bear on a decision or problem than an individual alone.	*Personality factors*: Traits such as shyness can prevent some members offering their opinions and knowledge to the group.
Different perspectives: Individuals with varied experience and interests help the group see decision situations and problems from different angles.	*Social conformity*: Unwillingness to 'rock the boat' and pressure to conform may combine to stifle the creativity of individual contributors.
Greater comprehension: Those who personally experience the give-and-take of group discussion about alternative courses of action tend to understand the rationale behind the final decision.	*Diffusion of responsibility*: Members feel able to avoid responsibility for their actions believing it can be shouldered by the others present.
Increased acceptance: Those who play an active role in group decision making and problem solving tend to view the outcomes as 'ours' rather than 'theirs'.	*Minority domination*: Sometimes the quality of group action is reduced when the group gives in to those who talk the loudest and longest.
Training ground: Less experienced members learn to cope with group dynamics by actually being involved.	*Logrolling*: Political wheeling and dealing can displace sound thinking when an individual's pet project or vested interest is at stake.
	Goal displacement: Sometimes secondary considerations such as winning an argument, making a point, or getting back at a rival displace the primary task of making a sound decision or solving a problem.
	Group brainstorming: Reduces rather than increases the quantity and quality of ideas compared to individual performance.
	Groupthink: Sometimes cohesive 'in-groups' let the desire for unanimity override sound judgement when generating and evaluating alternative courses of action.
	Satisficing: Making decisions which are immediately acceptable to the group rather than the best ones.

Source: based on West et al. (1998) and Kreitner (1989).

Research has revealed that two main factors determine whether groups should be preferred to individuals. These are, first, how structured the task is, and, second, who the individuals are (Table 20.11). If the task to be performed is structured (has a clear, correct solution) then groups are better, although they take longer (Weber, 1984). In the case of unstructured tasks (no single correct answer and creativity required), individuals are better. Hence the counter-intuitive finding that performance of brainstorming groups is inferior to that of individuals.

Table 20.11: Individual and group performance compared

Factor	Individuals when	Groups when
Type of problem task	Creativity or efficiency is desired	Diverse skills and knowledge are required
Acceptance of decision	Acceptance is not important	Acceptance by group members is valued
Quality of the solution	'Best member' can be identified	Several group members can improve the solution
Characteristics of the individuals	Individuals cannot collaborate	Members have experience of working together
Decision-making climate	Climate is competitive	Climate is supportive of group problem-solving
Time available	Relatively little time is available	Relatively more time is available

Source: from *Diagnostic Approach to Organization Behaviour*, 4th ed., Allyn & Bacon (Gordon, J.R. 1993), p.253.

Problems with group decision making

Group polarization a situation in which individuals in a group begin by taking a moderate stance on an issue related to a common value and, after having discussed it, end up taking a more extreme decision than the average of members' decisions. The extremes could be more risky or more cautious.

Risky shift phenomenon the tendency of a group to make decisions that are riskier than those which individual members would have recommended.

Caution shift phenomenon the tendency of a group to make decisions that are more risk averse than those that individual members of the group would have recommended.

It is the very strengths of a group that are also its weaknesses. The cost of bringing individuals together in one place counters the benefits of getting contributions from supposedly independent minds. Four problems of group decision making will be examined here: group polarization, groupthink, brainstorming and escalation of commitment.

Group polarization

Group polarization refers to the phenomenon that occurs when a position that is held on an issue by the majority of group members is intensified (in a given direction) as a result of discussion (Lamm, 1988). This tendency can lead to irrational and hence to ineffective group performance. Social psychologists have documented the situation in which individuals in a group begin by taking a moderate stance on an issue related to a common value and then, after having discussed it, end up taking a more extreme stance. James Stoner conducted one of the earliest of these studies in the 1950s. He found that groups of management students were willing to make decisions involving greater risks than their individual preferences (Stoner, 1961). This phenomenon was referred to as the risky shift. However, the opposite can also occur, and is called the caution shift. Here a group can become more risk averse than the initial, average risk-averse tendencies of its individuals members (Lamm and Myers, 1978; Isenberg, 1986).

Patricia Wallace (2001) believed that group polarization may be partly responsible for the extremism often found on the internet, and the apparent absence of a temperate voice. An individual might hold a relatively moderate view about an issue initially. However, after talking with others about it over the internet, they are likely to move away from the middle view towards one of the extremes. Factors that contribute to group polarization are present on the internet in abundance. First, people talk and talk endlessly. Second, members are selective about what they share with others. As talk progresses, members become increasing reluctant to bring up items that might contradict the emerging group consensus. This creates a biased discussion where alternatives are insufficiently considered.

Groupthink

Groupthink is a mode of thinking that occurs when the members' strivings for unanimity override their motivation to appraise realistically the alternative courses of action. One

Groupthink a mode of thinking in a cohesive in-group, in which members' strivings for unanimity override their motivation to appraise realistically the alternative courses of action.

of the reasons why groups perform badly on complex, unstructured tasks is the dynamics of group interaction. Groups and teams can develop a high level of cohesiveness. This is generally a positive thing, but it also has negative consequences (Mullen et al., 1991). Specifically, the desire not to disrupt the consensus can lead to a reluctance to challenge the group's thinking which, in turn, results in bad decisions. Irving Janis (1982) studied a number of American foreign policy 'disasters' such as the failure to anticipate the Japanese attack on Pearl Harbor in 1941; the Bay of Pigs fiasco in 1961 when President John F. Kennedy and his administration sought to overthrow the government of Fidel Castro; and the prosecution of the Vietnam war between 1964–1967 by President Lyndon Johnson. Janis concluded that it was the cohesive nature of these important committees which made these decisions, and which prevented contradictory views being expressed (Moorhead et al., 1991). He named this process groupthink. He listed its symptoms and how it could be prevented. These are outlined in Table 20.12.

Table 20.12: Groupthink: symptoms and prevention steps

When groups become very cohesive, there is a danger that they will become victims of their own closeness.

Symptoms	Prevention steps
1. *Illusion of invulnerability*: members display excessive optimism that past successes will continue and will shield them, and hence they tend to take extreme risks	(A) Leader encourages open expression of doubt by members
2. *Collective rationalization*: members collectively rationalize away data that disconfirm their assumptions and the beliefs upon which they base their decisions	(B) Leader accepts criticism of his/her opinions
3. *Illusion of morality*: members believe that they, as moral individuals, are unlikely to make bad decisions	(C) Higher-status members offer opinions last
4. *Shared stereotypes*: members dismiss disconfirming evidence by discrediting its source (e.g. stereotyping other groups and their leaders as evil or weak)	(D) Get recommendations from a duplicate group
5. *Direct pressure*: imposition of verbal, non-verbal or other sanctions on individuals who explore deviant positions, express doubts or question the validity of group beliefs	(E) Periodically divide into subgroups
6. *Self-censorship*: members keep silent about misgivings about the apparent group consensus and try to minimize their doubts	(F) Members obtain the reactions of trusted outsiders
7. *Illusion of unanimity*: members conclude that the group has reached a consensus because its most vocal members are in agreement	(G) Invite trusted outsiders to join the discussion periodically
8. *Mindguards*: members take it upon themselves to screen out adverse, disconfirming information supplied by 'outsiders' which might endanger the group's complacency	(H) Assign someone to the role of devil's advocate
	(I) Develop scenarios of rivals' possible actions

Source: based on Janis (1982).

aspect of all organizations. However, if properly conducted, he believed it provided better ways of working by combining the energies of different team members who used their experience and knowledge to generate new ideas. In his view, conflict was essential to successful teamwork and organizational effectiveness. In consequence, conflict should be welcomed and managed appropriately. In contrast, Carsten De Dreu (2008) stated that conflict was always detrimental, and that the research that supported the beneficial aspects of workplace conflict was weak. He felt that organizations had to make efforts to manage conflict, not because it had positive effects but in order to minimize its negative consequences.

STOP AND THINK

Can you provide examples from your own work experience where conflict has led either to positive or negative outcomes?

Contrasting conflict frames of reference

Frame of reference a person's perceptions and interpretations of events, which involve assumptions about reality, attitudes towards what is possible, and conventions regarding correct behaviour.

A **frame of reference** refers to the influences which structure a person's perceptions and interpretations of events. These involve assumptions about reality, attitudes towards what is possible, and conventions regarding what is correct behaviour for those involved. The adoption of differing frames of references by opposing sides can impair the effective resolution of conflicts.

For example, in a labour dispute, the unions and management will look at the industrial relations bargaining situation from different points of view. Management may assume that the natural state of affairs is one in which there is no inherent conflict of interest between the different individuals, groups or collectivities that constitute the organization. It believes that managers and employees possess shared goals. From this frame of reference, cooperation is the norm, and all dissent is seen as unreasonable. Senior management cannot conceive how or why their authority might be challenged or why employees might engage in disruptive behaviour. In contrast, the union takes a different viewpoint. It sees profits as something to be fought over with senior management and company shareholders. From the union's frame of reference, each party seeks legitimately to maximize its own rewards. Industrial action aims to maximize the revenues going to labour, and is explainable in these terms.

The literature distinguishes four different frames of reference on conflict, based on the distinctions made by Alan Fox. They are labelled *unitarist*, *pluralist*, *interactionist* and *radical* (Fox, 1966). In this section, the first three will be introduced and contrasted, while the fourth, the radical, will be subjected to a more detailed analysis in its own section later. These frames are neither 'right' nor 'wrong', only different.

- The *unitarist* frame sees organizations as essentially harmonious and any conflict as bad.

- The *pluralist* frame sees organizations as a collection of groups, each with their own interests.

- The *interactionist* frame sees conflict as a positive, necessary force for effective performance.

- The *radical* frame sees conflict sees as an inevitable outcome of capitalism.

Moreover, academics will also adopt one of these frames when they teach the topic to their students or research it. Neither organization employees nor academics will necessarily make their chosen frame explicit, and thus students need to ask or deduce which conflict frame of reference is being used.

Pronoun test

Robert Reich described the 'pronoun test' that he used to evaluate the nature of the employment relationship in the companies that he visited as US Secretary of Labor during the first Clinton Administration, in the following way:

I'd say, 'Tell me about the company'. If the person said 'we' or 'us', I knew people were strongly attached to the organization. If they said 'they' or 'them', I knew there was less of a sense of linkage. (Rousseau, 1998, p.217)

Most of us are capable of bringing different frames of reference to bear on the situations that we face. If we analyse it this way, we reach these conclusions, but it we analyse it another way, we reach different conclusions. Some people (students, academics, managers) *may* be wedded to a particular perspective. This becomes obvious in their conversations, actions or writings. Their chosen frame of reference on conflict will determine:

- what they will notice in their environment;
- how they will interpret those noticed events;
- how they expect others to behave;
- how they will behave themselves.

However, there is value in being able to view conflicts from a number of different standpoints, to 'switch between frames', in part so that we can understand the viewpoints of others.

Unitarist frame of reference on conflict

Unitarist frame of reference on conflict a perspective that regards management and employee interests as coinciding and which thus regards organizational conflict as harmful and to be avoided.

The unitarist frame of reference on conflict views organizations as fundamentally harmonious, cooperative structures, consisting of committed, loyal, worker–management teams that promote harmony of purpose.

Stephen Ackroyd and Paul Thompson (1999) and Johnston (2000) identified the key features of the unitarist frame of reference:

1. Assumes a commonality of interests between an organization's workers and managers and, by implication, the company's owners (shareholders).

2. Accepts unquestioningly the political, economic and social framework within which management is performed, and adopts the language, assumptions and goals of management itself, which it supposedly seeks to study and understand.

3. Depoliticizes the relationships between individuals, groups and classes within the workplace, treating conflicts and contradictions as peripheral.

4. Explains actual, observed instances of workplace conflict in terms of either a failure of coordination or in psychological terms (personality clash or abnormal behaviour of deviant individuals).

5. Applies a liberal-humanistic, individually focused approach to conflict resolution, which is rooted in the human relations movement.

6. Holds that managers are capable of permanently changing the behaviour of employees in a conflict situation through the application of conflict resolution techniques.

7. Claims that economic, technological and political developments of the past have now virtually eliminated non-sanctioned employee behaviour within the organization.

8. Moves rapidly over the consideration of causes of conflict within the workplace, in order to focus on conflict resolution techniques.

9. Uses communication failures between management and employees (and the interference of 'third party agitators', normally unions) to explain workplace conflict.

Pluralist frame of reference on conflict

Pluralist frame of reference on conflict a perspective that views organizations as consisting of different, natural interest groups, each with their own potentially constructive, legitimate interests, which makes conflict between them inevitable.

The pluralist frame of reference on conflict views organizations as a collection of many separate groups, each of which have their own legitimate interests, thereby making conflict between them inevitable as each attempts to pursue its own objectives. This frame of reference therefore rejects the view that individual employees have the same interests as the management, or that an organization is one big happy family.

The pluralist frame takes a political orientation in that it sees that, some of the time, the interests of the different groups will coincide, while at other times they will clash and so cause conflict between them. The outbreak of conflict provides a 'relationship regulation' mechanism between the different groups. That is, it provides a clear sign to both parties as to which issues they disagree fundamentally about, and thus provides a sort of 'early warning system' of possible impending breakdown which would be to the disadvantage of all concerned. The most common clashes may be between unions and management, but will also include differences between management functions (production versus marketing); levels of management (senior management versus middle management) and between individual managers.

These differences do not prevent an organization from functioning since all groups recognize that compromise and negotiation are essential if they are to achieve their goals even partially. Hence, from this perspective, the job of management becomes that of keeping a balance between potentially conflicting goals, and managing the differences between these different interest groups. This involves seeking a compromise between the different constituents such as the employees, managers, shareholders and others, so that all these stakeholders, to varying degrees, can continue to pursue their aspirations. Underlying the pluralist view is the belief that conflict can be resolved through compromise to the benefit of all. However, it requires all parties to limit their claims to a level which is at least tolerable to the others, and which allows further collaboration to continue. A mutual survival strategy is typically agreed.

Acceptance of the pluralist frame implies that conflict is inevitable, and indeed endemic. However, it does not see conflict as harmful and to be eliminated, but believes that it must be evaluated in terms of its functions and dysfunctions. While a conflict may reinforce the status quo, it can also assist evolutionary rather than revolutionary change, acting as a safety valve. This keeps the organization responsive to internal and external changes while retaining intact its essential elements such as the organizational hierarchy and the power distribution. The inevitable conflict which results has to be managed so that organizational goals are reconciled with group interests for the benefit of mutual survival and prosperity. This on-going internal struggle acts to maintain the vitality, responsiveness and efficiency of the organization.

Interactionist frame of reference on conflict

Interactionist frame of reference on conflict a perspective that views conflict as a positive and necessary force within organizations that is essential for their effective performance.

The interactionist frame of reference on conflict views conflict as a positive force within organizations that is necessary for effective performance. It accepts the inevitability of conflict and argues that, to be dealt with constructively, conflict has to be institutionalized within the organization through systems of collective bargaining. The interactionist frame not only accepts the inevitability of conflict, but also contains the notion that there is an optimum level of it (neither too little nor too much), and that the way to achieve that level is through the intervention of the manager.

The interactionist frame believes that conflict should be encouraged whenever it emerges, and stimulated if it is absent. It sees a group or a department that is too peaceful, harmonious and cooperative as potentially apathetic and unresponsive to changing needs. It fears that extreme group cohesion can lead to groupthink (see Chapter 20), as identified by Irving Janis (1982) and Cosier and Schwenk (1990). This frame therefore encourages managers to maintain a minimum level of conflict within their organizations so to as to

Functional conflict a form of conflict which supports organization goals and improves performance.

Dysfunctional conflict a form of conflict which does not support organization goals and hinders organizational performance.

encourage self-criticism, change and innovation and thereby counter apathy. However, that conflict has to be of the appropriate type. Thus, functional conflict supports organization goals and improves performance, but dysfunctional conflict hinders organizational performance.

The relationship between the two is depicted on a bell-shaped curve shown in Figure 21.1. If there is insufficient conflict the unit or group may not perform at its best. However, too much conflict, and its performance deteriorates. Performance improvements occur through conflict exposing weaknesses in organizational decision making and design which prompts changes in the company.

Figure 21.1 is also sometimes referred to as the contingency model of conflict because it recommends that managers should increase or decrease the amount of conflict in their organizations depending (contingent) on the situation (Hatch, 1997; Hatch and Cunliffe, 2006). Thus, for example, in condition 1 there is too little conflict, and so managers need to stimulate more. In contrast, in condition 3, there is too much conflict and they need to reduce it. In both cases they seek to achieve an optimum level of conflict depicted in condition 2. Taffinder (1998) felt that at optimal intensity, conflict produced organizational benefits which managers rarely exploited and even suppressed by applying conflict resolution approaches too rapidly. Amongst the benefits of functional conflict that he listed were:

- motivating energy to deal with underlying problems;
- making underlying issues explicit;

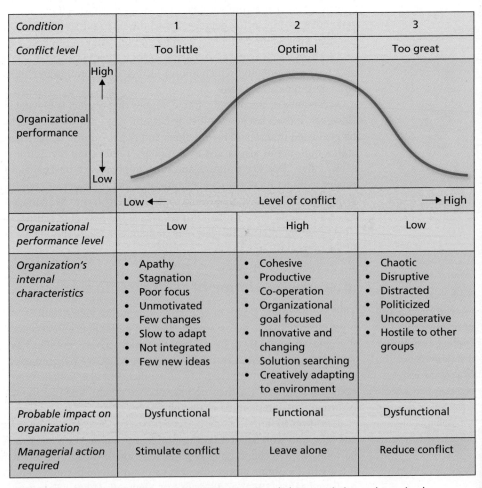

Condition	1	2	3
Conflict level	Too little	Optimal	Too great
Organizational performance			
Organizational performance level	Low	High	Low
Organization's internal characteristics	• Apathy • Stagnation • Poor focus • Unmotivated • Few changes • Slow to adapt • Not integrated • Few new ideas	• Cohesive • Productive • Co-operation • Organizational goal focused • Innovative and changing • Solution searching • Creatively adapting to environment	• Chaotic • Disruptive • Distracted • Politicized • Uncooperative • Hostile to other groups
Probable impact on organization	Dysfunctional	Functional	Dysfunctional
Managerial action required	Stimulate conflict	Leave alone	Reduce conflict

Figure 21.1: Types of conflict, internal organizational characteristics and required management actions

Source: based on Hatch (1997, p.305) and Robbins and Judge (2013, p.504).

- sharpening employees' understanding of real goals and interests;
- enhancing mutual understanding between different groups of employees;
- stimulating a sense of urgency;
- discouraging engagement in avoidance behaviour;
- preventing premature and often dangerous resolution problems.

Coordination failure and conflict

The process of organizing by senior managers acts to divide up work activities, and a conflict can thus be seen as a symptom of management's failure to adequately coordinate these same activities later on. The coordination–conflict four-stage model organizes the diverse theoretical discussions and research findings into a framework that explains how conflict in organizations arises and how it might be managed (Figure 21.2). Such management may involve either the use of conflict resolution approaches (to reduce or eradicate conflict) or conflict stimulation approaches (to encourage and increase conflict).

Organizing

The first stage of the model consists of organizing, defined as the process of breaking up a single task, and dividing it among different departments, groups or individuals. For example, a car company allocates the work involved in building a new vehicle to its different subdivisions (departments, groups and individuals) – human resources, accounting, production, sales and research. Such functional specialization is one of many bases on which to divide the total work involved. Specialization is rational because it concentrates specialists in proper departments, avoids duplication, allows performance goals to be established, and specifies practices.

All forms of such horizontal specialization (divisions between departments) result in each subunit becoming concerned with its own particular part of the total objective and work process. The degree of such separation of tasks can vary, but it creates the conditions in which conflict can potentially arise. It does so because, by definition, each department, group or individual receives a different part of the whole task to perform. This differentiates it from the other departments in six areas:

1. Goals orientation and evaluation
2. Self-image and stereotypes
3. Task interdependencies
4. Time perspective
5. Overlapping authority
6. Scarce resources.

1. Goals orientation and evaluation

Each department is given its own goal, and its members are evaluated in terms of how well they achieve it. Ideally, the goals of different departments, groups and individuals, although different, should be complementary, but in practice this may not be so. Moreover, the measurement process can reinforce differences. Each department's unique goals and evaluation methods lead it to have its own view about priorities, and how these are best achieved.

2. Self-image and stereotypes

Employees in each department become socialized into a particular perception of themselves and of the other departments in the company. A group may come to see itself as more vital

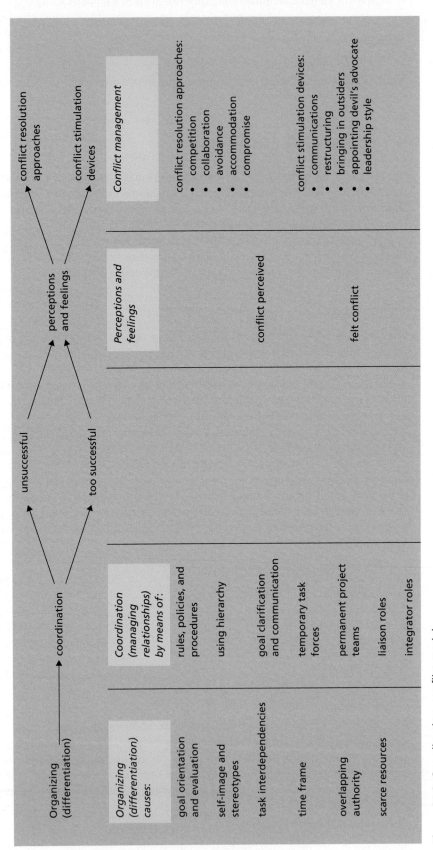

Figure 21.2: Coordination–conflict model

Perceptions and emotions

Unsuccessful coordination need not necessarily ignite a conflict. Perception plays an important part. It is only if one of the parties – individual, group or department – becomes aware of, or is adversely affected by the situation and cares about it, that potential conflict turns into perceived conflict. It occurs only when one party realizes that another is thwarting its goals. It is only at this stage that the conflict issue becomes defined and 'what it is all about' gets decided. Specifically, each party considers the origins of the conflict, why it emerged, and how the problem is being experienced with the other party. The way that the conflict is defined at this stage will determine the type of outcomes that the parties are willing to settle for in the later stages.

Not only must a party perceive a conflict, but it must also feel it. That is, it must become emotionally involved in experiencing feelings of anxiety, tension, frustration and hostility towards the other party. The emotional dimension of conflict shapes perceptions. For example, negative emotions result in an oversimplification of issues, reductions in trust, and negative interpretations of the other party's behaviour. Positive emotions, in contrast, increase the chances of the parties taking a broader view, seeing the issue as a problem to be solved, and developing more creative solutions.

Conflict management

Within an organization, management may judge that there is too much or too little conflict.

In the case of the former, the existing coordination devices may be inadequate, thereby causing too much conflict. In such a case, the company will manage the situation by implementing conflict resolution approaches to reduce or eliminate the immediate conflict, before adjusting the coordination mechanism to prevent it occurring in the future. Alternatively, they may consider that the coordination devices are working too well, thereby causing complacency and apathy. In this case, they may introduce conflict stimulation approaches to increase conflict. Thus, within organizations, conflict can be managed through a combination of conflict resolution and conflict stimulation approaches.

Conflict resolution approaches

Conflict resolution a process which has as its objective the ending of the conflict between the disagreeing parties.

Kenneth Thomas (1976) distinguished five conflict resolution approaches based upon the two dimensions of:

- how assertive or unassertive each party is in pursuing its own concerns;
- how cooperative or uncooperative each is in satisfying the concerns of the other.

He labelled these approaches *competing* (assertive and uncooperative); *avoiding* (unassertive and uncooperative); *compromising* (mid-range on both dimensions); *accommodating* (unassertive and cooperative); and *collaborating* (assertive and cooperative). They are summarized in Figure 21.4 and defined in Table 21.3.

Unless managers are flexible and capable of switching between conflict resolution approaches, their ability to resolve conflicts effectively will be limited. In practice, all individuals, whether managers or not, habitually use only a limited number of approaches (perhaps just one) to resolve all the conflicts in which they are involved. It is not surprising that their success is limited.

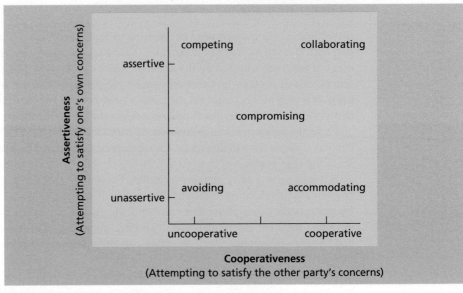

Figure 21.4: Conflict resolution approaches compared

Source: reprinted from *Organizational Behaviour and Human Performance*, Vol.16, No.1, T.H. Ruble and K.Thomas, Support for a two-dimensional model of conflict behaviour, p.145, Copyright 1976 with permission from Elsevier.

Table 21.3: Conflict resolution approaches compared

Approach	Objective	Your posture	Supporting rationale	Likely outcome
1. Completing	Get your way	'I know what's right. Don't question my judgement or authority.'	It is better to risk causing a few hard feelings than to abandon the issue.	You feel vindicated, but the other party feels defeated and possibly humiliated.
2. Avoiding	Avoid having to deal with conflict	'I'm neutral on that issue. Let me think about it. That's someone else's problem.'	Disagreements are inherently bad because they create tension.	Interpersonal problems don't get resolved, causing long-term frustration manifested in a variety of ways.
3. Compromising	Reach an agreement quickly	'Let's search for a solution we can both live with so we can get on with our work.'	Prolonged conflicts distract people from their work and cause bitter feelings.	Participants go for the expedient rather than effective solutions.
4. Accommodating	Don't upset the other person	'How can I help you feel good about this? My position isn't so important that it is worth risking bad feelings between us.'	Maintaining harmonious relationships should be our top priority.	The other person is likely to take advantage.
5. Collaborating	Solve the problem together	'This is my position, what's yours? I'm committed to finding the best possible solution. What do the facts suggest?'	Each position is important though not necessarily equally valid. Emphasis should be placed on the quality of the outcome and the fairness of the decision-making process.	The problem is most likely to be resolved. Both parties are committed to the solution and satisfied that they have been treated fairly.

Source: adapted from *Developing Management Skills for Europe*, Whetton, D., Cameron, K. and Woods, M., Pearson Education Ltd © 2000, p.345.

Dean Tjosvold and colleagues (2014) reviewed 40 years of conflict research in order to help managers and employees to deal with increasingly complex conflicts. These writers concluded that mutual benefit relationships and open-minded discussion represented the best foundations for constructive conflict resolution (see Figure 21.5)

MUTUAL BENEFIT RELATIONSHIPS	OPEN-MINDED DISCUSSION	CONSTRUCTIVE CONFLICT
Dual concerns Social value Cooperative goals	Intergrative style Problem solving Motivated information processing Constructive controversy	Quality resolutions Strong relationships Individual development

Figure 21.5: Relationships, discussion and conflict
Source: Tjosvold et al. (2014, p.547).

With respect to mutual benefits relationships, they recommend that protagonists should be aware of how the conflict could be resolved in ways that promoted their own interests, the interests of the other party and, most critically, both sets of interests simultaneously. Protagonists' commitment to promoting each other's outcomes was therefore the basis for open-minded discussion. Open-mindedness involves freely expressing one's own views; listening to and understanding opposing ones; considering the others' reasoning for their positions; willingness to actively search for evidence against one's own favoured beliefs and ideas; and a preparedness to weigh such evidence impartially and fully, so as to integrate the various ideas into mutually acceptable solutions.

STOP AND THINK   Think about a specific domestic, friendship or work context that involved conflict. How did you deal with it? Did you compete, avoid, compromise, accommodate or collaborate?

Organizational conflict cultures

Thomas showed that individuals had distinct ways of resolving workplace conflicts, but do entire companies? Does the organizational context in which employees work define the expected and acceptable ways in which conflict should be resolved? In short, do companies possess distinct *conflict culture preferences* (see Chapter 4)? This was the question asked by Michele Gelfand and her colleagues (2012). They obtained information from 862 employees who worked in 159 branches of the same American bank. They found that the different branches had their own, distinct, socially shared norms as to how conflict within them should be resolved. The researchers found three conflict cultures:

- *Collaborative*: Conflict norms stress active, cooperative discussion of conflict. The assumption is that cooperative behaviours and open conflict resolution is appropriate.

- *Dominating*: Conflict norms encourage active confrontation in order to publicly win disputes. The assumption is that disagreeable or competitive behaviours are acceptable.

- *Avoidant*: Conflict norms stress passive withdrawal in cases of disagreement. The assumption is that conflict is dangerous and should be suppressed, and that harmonious relationships are essential.

Thus Gelfand et al.'s research discovered that three of Thomas' individual conflict resolution approaches were reflected at the organizational level in the form of distinct company conflict cultures in the various bank branches. But how did these different unit-level cultures develop?

The researchers ascribed the causes to leaders' behaviours and employees' personality traits (see Chapter 6) in the different branches. Thus leaders' cooperative conflict

→

resolution approaches were positively related to collaborative conflict cultures and negatively related to dominating cultures. Branch leaders with avoiding conflict resolution approaches contributed to avoidant cultures. Branches with members high on the personality trait of agreeableness contributed to collaborative cultures, while those who were disagreeable and extraverted helped to develop dominating cultures.

Conflict resolution and negotiation

Richard Walton and Robert McKersie's (1965) classic research into negotiation behaviour distinguished distributive bargaining strategies from integrative bargaining strategies (Table 21.4).

Table 21.4: Bargaining strategies

Integrative bargaining Win–win strategy	Distributive bargaining Win–lose strategy
1. Define the conflict as a mutual problem.	1. Define the conflict as a win–lose situation.
2. Pursue joint outcomes.	2. Pursue own group's outcomes.
3. Find creative agreements that satisfy both groups.	3. Force the other group into submission.
4. Use open, honest, and accurate communication of group's needs, goals, and proposals.	4. Use deceitful, inaccurate, and misleading communication of group's needs, goals, and proposals.
5. Avoid threats (to reduce the other's defensiveness).	5. Use threats (to force submission).
6. Communicate flexibility of position.	6. Communicate high commitment (rigidity) regarding one's position.

Source: Johnson and Johnson, *Joining Together: Group Theory and Group Skills*, 1st edn, © 1975, pp.182–3. Reprinted and electronically adapted by permission of Pearson Education, Inc., Upper Saddle River, New Jersey.

Distributive bargaining a negotiation strategy in which a fixed sum of resources is divided up, leading to a win–lose situation between the parties.

Integrative bargaining a negotiation strategy that seeks to increase the total amount of resources, creating a win–win situation between the parties.

Distributive bargaining operates under zero-sum conditions. It seeks to divide up a fixed amount of resources, creating a win–lose situation. Purchasing a new car exemplifies this. The more the buyer pays, the more profit the seller makes and vice versa. Here the pie is fixed, and the parties bargain about the share each receives. Within an organization, distributive bargaining takes place between the trade (labour) unions and management. Issues involving wages, benefits, working conditions and related matters are seen as a conflict over limited resources. **Integrative bargaining** is the type of bargaining which seeks settlements that can create a win–win solution. A union–management agreement which increases productivity and profits, and wages in line with both, would be an example of integrated bargaining because the size of the total pie is increased. Integrative bargaining is preferable to distributive bargaining because the latter makes one party a loser. It can create animosities and deepens divisions between people who have to work together on an ongoing basis.

Studies have revealed similarities between conflict resolution approaches and negotiation strategies (Savage et al., 1989; Smith, 1987). Of the five conflict resolution approaches described earlier, four of them (competing; avoiding, compromising and accommodating) involve one or more of the parties sacrificing something, and would therefore be classified as distributive. David Whetton and colleagues (1996) suggested that these distributive strategies matched the natural inclination of those individuals who approached conflicts with a 'macho man', 'easy touch' or 'split the difference' style, and they thus engendered competition, exploitation or irresponsibility. Roger Fisher and William Ury (1981) from the Harvard Negotiating Project developed a scheme of 'principled negotiation' which sets out guiding principles to apply when preparing and engaging in face-to-face negotiations, and what to do if the other side does not 'play the game' (Ury, 1991: Ury and Patton, 1997).

Conflict stimulation approaches

Conflict stimulation
the process of
engendering conflict
between parties where
none existed before, or
escalating the current
conflict level if it is too
low.

Management may judge that there is too little conflict. Interactionists argue that there are conditions in organizations when what is needed is more and not less conflict – **conflict stimulation** (Sternberg and Soriano, 1984, Robbins, 1974). John Kotter (1996) discussed the dangers of complacency, and the need to drive employees out of their comfort zones. Amongst the complacency-smashing and potentially conflict-stimulating techniques used by senior management were the following:

- Create a crisis by allowing a financial loss to occur or an error to blow up.
- Eliminate obvious examples of excess like corporate jet fleets and gourmet dining rooms.
- Set targets like income, productivity and cycle times so high that they can't be reached by doing business as usual.
- Share more information about customer satisfaction and financial performance with employees.
- Insist that people speak regularly to dissatisfied customers, unhappy suppliers and disgruntled shareholders.
- Put more honest discussions of the firm's problems in company newspapers and management speeches. Stop senior management's 'happy talk'.

Various techniques can be used to stimulate conflict where none existed before, in order to encourage different opinions and engender new thinking and problem solving:

1. *Communications*: Managers can withhold information 'to keep them guessing' or send large amounts of inconsistent information ('we're expanding' 'we're going bust') to get people arguing. They might send ambiguous or anxiety-provoking messages.

2. *Restructuring a company*: Realigning working groups and altering rules and regulations, so as to increase or create interdependence between previously independent units. This can easily stimulate conflict, particularly if the goals of the newly interdependent departments are made incompatible (e.g. one department's objective being to minimize costs, the other's being to maximize market share).

3. *Bringing in outsiders*: Adding individuals to a group whose backgrounds, values, attitudes or management styles differ from those of existing members. For example, by recruiting senior executives with a career experience in automobile manufacture to manage health care organizations.

4. *Devil's advocate method*: Within an organization, a person is assigned the role of critic, to stimulate critical thinking and reality testing. For example, in deciding whether to embark on an e-commerce strategy, one team member might be assigned the devil's advocate role to focus on its pitfalls and dangers.

5. *Dialectic method*: This method explores opposite positions called 'thesis' and' antithesis'. The outcome of the debate between the two is the 'synthesis' which, in turn, becomes the new thesis to be opened up for debate. Before deciding on a takeover, a company may establish two or more teams, give them access to the same information, and give them the task to argue for and against the acquisition decision. The conflict of ideas throws up alternatives, which can be synthesized into a superior, final decision.

6. *Leadership style:* Organizations can appoint managers who encourage non-traditional viewpoints, rather than authoritarian ones who might be inclined to suppress opposing viewpoints. Leadership style has been found to be a key element in organization change programmes and in particular those involving changes in organization culture.

Conflict expression

Conflict expression
the verbal and non-verbal communication of opposition between people in a conflict situation.

Laura Weingart and her colleagues (2015) observed that individuals fought over the same things in different ways. They studied conflict expression, defined as the verbal and non-verbal ways in which individuals express their opposition to others in conflict situations. Different conflict expression styles elicit different kinds of emotions, perceptions and reactions. These will affect how the conflict process unfolds, the impact it has on the parties concerned, and the outcomes that occur, such as conflict escalation or de-escalation. Past research into how couples fight with each other has led to accurate predictions of whether or not they would split up. Weingart argued that every type of conflict was expressed with different degrees of directness and intensity. They used these two dimensions to 'map' different conflict situations.

Directness

The vertical dimension of the framework is labelled *directness* and refers to whether the sender conveys their opposition message explicitly or implicitly to the receiver. With high-directness conflict expression the sender explains to the other party that there is a problem, what the problem is, and what position they are taking with regard to it. The message is clearly and explicitly stated, leaving little need for receiver interpretation. Verbally, high directness involves oral statements of disagreement and, non-verbally, shaking one's head from side to side. In contrast, with low-directness conflict expression, the opposition message is ambiguous. The problem is hinted at but left to the receiver to work out, thereby leaving them with room to infer the position that the sender is taking. Verbally, low directness involves storytelling, asking reflective questions, poking fun at the other party or expressing the conflict to a third party. The source of the conflict is not explicitly identified and the receiver has to work hard to notice and make inferences.

Intensity

The horizontal dimension is labelled intensity and refers to the strength, force or energy with which the sender conveys their opposition message to the receiver. Fights involve greater message intensity than debates. The degree of intensity is determined by how entrenched the sender is in their position, and by their willingness to undermine the other's position. Verbally, high intensity involves personal attacks, threats, defending one's position, rebutting others' beliefs and perspectives. Such forceful expressions result in a response to the threat by the receiver, who fears a loss of personal goals or status. In contrast, low intensity is evidenced by people conveying a position with conviction, but having a willingness to discuss opposing opinions and viewpoints. The two parties are also able to assess the merits of each other's actions and views, and demonstrate a willingness to integrate these into their own response.

Since people everywhere use different degrees of directness and intensity in conflict situations, one can use these two dimensions to categorize and compare their different styles of conflict expression (Geller, 2015). These are shown in Figure 21.6.

- *Arguing* (high directness–high intensity): These conflicts are characterized by an absence of problem solving. Individuals would be shouting, making threats, storming out of the room or rolling their eyes. Deaf to others' viewpoints, they defend their own position, unwilling to understand the others'. Emotions generated include anger, frustration and tension.

- *Undermining* (low directness–high intensity): Involves dismissive or passive-aggressive behaviour. Teasing, back-stabbing or mobilizing coalitions are used to signal that some sort of a problem exists. However, the receiver is unclear why the sender is doing this since the problem is not stated. Despite the absence of overt hostility or open fighting,

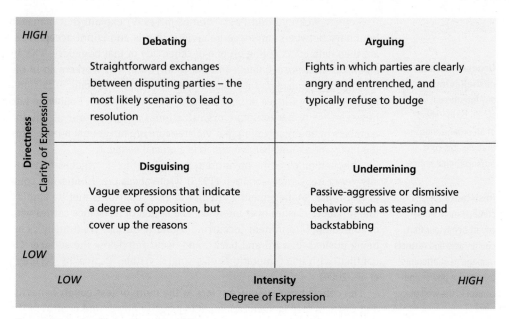

Figure 21.6: Conflict expression styles
Source: Geller (2015, p.2).

these conflicts generate feelings of anxiety, contempt and humiliation, and are likely to escalate.

- *Disguising* (low directness–low intensity): Entails parties withholding critical information and not saying what they really mean. Behaviourally, individuals engage in impoliteness or passive-aggressive behaviour such as intentionally missing a deadline so as to avoid a proposal being progressed. This generates feelings of irritation, hurt and confusion.

- *Debating* (high directness–low intensity): Here people are communicating their position clearly to the other party and are neither entrenched nor subversive. They deliberate and discuss their positions, and respond rationally and calmly. Feelings of frustration ('the person is opposing me') are coupled with excitement ('I see an opportunity to learn').

Weingart et al. (2015) argue that focusing on conflict expression rather than on conflict type helps us understand the conflict process better, shows us how conflict processes differ from one another, and helps us understand why people react to conflict differently.

Radical frame of reference

Radical frame of reference on conflict
a perspective that views organizational conflict as an inevitable consequence of exploitative employment relations in a capitalist economy.

Newspapers and human resource management magazines regularly carry accounts of company problems such as sexual harassment, racial harassment, theft and pilferage, bulling, organizational romance, sabotage and strikes. These are all examples of human behaviour in organizations, yet the previous unitarist, pluralist and interactionist frames of reference on conflict have difficulty in explaining such actions. Indeed, it is only the radical frame of reference on conflict that draws attention to such behaviour in organizations. The other conflict perspectives may recognize them but then ignore them. In contrast, the radical frame sees the workplace as an arena of conflict between managers (in their role as agents of the owners and controllers of the means of production) and the exploited employees. It holds that the logic of profit maximization involves managers relentlessly driving down the costs of production and controlling the production process. The radical frame of reference on conflict holds that as conflict is an endemic property of capitalist employment relations, it cannot be resolved by any management techniques.

Stephen Ackroyd and Paul Thompson (1999) explain that management establishes a boundary between employee behaviour that is and is not acceptable. Employee actions are then defined as falling on one or other side of that boundary. The authors use the term *organizational misbehaviour* to refer to anything that workers do in the workplace which management considers they should not do (with the specific exclusion of managerial misbehaviour, grey fringes of business and whistle-blowing). Following Linstead et al. (2014), however, we prefer to define **organizational misbehaviour** as any intentional action by members of an organization that violates core organizational norms. This definition stresses the motivation to misbehave which is a crucial element.

Although much of the literature refers to 'conflict' in organizations, overt conflict is actually very rare. Carter Goodrich (1975) wrote about the 'frontiers of control' and the notion of *resistance*. Management's attempt to exert control is met by employee resistance, and that produces clashes over interests. The notion of resistance carries with it the connotation of something intermittent (occurring regularly but not continually), changing (the frontier being pushed forward and back), and occurring below the surface. This is in contrast to conflict, with its connotations of a single, visible, explosion (Jermier et al., 1994; Sagie et al., 2004).

The concept of **resistance** refers to the more or less covert behaviour that counteracts and restricts management attempts to exercise power and control in the workplace. It has an application at all levels of the organizational hierarchy, from shop-floor employees developing ways of combating **alienation** through informal processes and actions, through professionals like engineers, academics or hospital doctors resisting management directions, right up to senior management resisting the control exercised by the board of directors. It also allows a consideration of how that resistance moves into different areas within the organization, and how the parties acquire and relinquish different types of power, and gain and lose ascendancy over each other.

Organizational misbehaviour any intentional action by members of an organization that violates core organizational norms.

Resistance (in conflict) more or less covert behaviour that counteracts and restricts management attempts to exercise power and control in the workplace.

Alienation feelings of powerlessness, meaninglessness, isolation and self-estrangement engendered by work and organization design.

Organizational misbehaviour

While employees can be an organization's greatest asset, they can also be its greatest liability. Organizational misbehaviour comes in many forms:

- *The fraudsters* – The Economist Intelligence Unit's 2013 survey of senior executives revealed that 70 per cent of companies had experienced at least one instance of employee fraud. Fraud can be petty (e.g. inflating expenses claims) or serious (e.g. former employees setting up rival companies using stolen company technology and purloining client lists).

- *The vandals* – Unlike thieves, who have a rational motive, vandals are driven by a desire for revenge. For example, an IT employee who discovered that he would be made redundant arranged access to his company's IT system from home and began inflicting damage by deleting files, publishing the chief executive's emails, and circulating pornographic photographs.

- *The boss-pleasers* – These are the star employees who bend and then break company rules in order to please their bosses. In recent years, the media have reported

instances of investment bank staff taking outsized, unauthorized risks which ended unhappily both for themselves and for their companies.

- *The saboteurs* – These are low-level employees who use the internet to blacken their employer's reputation. Examples include fast food employees posting videos or photographs of themselves 'abusing take away food'. This scares away customers and damages the reputation of the company.

- *The collaborators* – This involves employees within the company who collaborate with outsider hackers to steal company email, personal and credit card information. Cleaners can be bribed to swop a USB stick for a virus-laden lookalike. Some major cyberattacks on companies in recent years are suspected to have involved company staff.

How can companies deal with organizational misbehaviour? Suggestions include the following:

- *Information power* – Focus on those employees who have the greatest capacity to do them most harm; typically it is those who control money and information.

The more dependent firms become on information, the greater the power that accrues to IT departments and their staff.

- *Employee surveillance* – Companies already use software to monitor staff emails and phone calls. They may go further and employ 'spies' to listen to company gossip or monitor conversations in the smoking areas or at after-work drinks sessions.

- *Employee respect* – Many firms treat their employees with contempt. A survey by the consultants Accenture found that nearly a third of workers disliked their boss; the same number were looking for a new job; and 43 per cent felt they had received no recognition for their work. Treating one's employees with respect might offer a simple and cost-effective solution to organizational misbehaviour.

Based on *The Economist* (2015)

Noon et al. (2013) list five survival strategies that workers use to counter alienation (Table 21.5). They explain that each can be interpreted either as a form of employee consent or employee resistance by an outside observer, and that these strategies may be condoned and tolerated by management or judged to be unacceptable and punished. The authors also highlight the problem of interpreting the meaning of those engaging in these behaviours and their motivations. All this affects the nature and degree of conflict that may ensue between the workers and management.

Resistance and dissent on the internet

Abigail Schoneboom (2007, 2011a, 2011b) reviewed developments in work blogs. These are defined as internet-based employee work diaries that provide accounts of working or customer relationships. In these, organization members reflect critically upon their workplace experiences. These blogs offer employees the opportunity to find their voice, to form collective identities, and to express self-organized resistance in a climate where the channels for expressing disapproval are being continually closed down. Anonymous blogs sprang up in 2002 and included many from call centres with names like *Call Center Confidential* where their authors, low-level call centre employees, broadcast irreverent opinions about their work. Some of them contextualized call centre work in terms of Marx's theory of alienation, while others satirized their company's culture,

poking fun at management's attempt to build a family atmosphere. Some blogs like *Non-Working Monkey* ('Je suis un singe non-travaillant') incorporated audio-visual material to communicate their message better. Schoneboom argued that work blogs make the process of employees' creative resistance much more visible. James Richards (2008, 2012, 2015) noted that the popular management press had branded work blogs as a form of employee deviance or anti-business behaviour. However, others argue that blogs allow employees to act as vocal and resourceful critics of their own work circumstances. By critically distancing themselves from the corporate cultures in which they are immersed, work blogs provide employees with a community in which their oppositional identity can be sustained (Richards and Kosmala, 2013).

Edwards (1979) noted that the perpetual struggle for control in organizations is not always constant, obvious or visible. Because employees' tactics of resistance are often covert, some knowledge of a particular organizational context is required for researchers (and indeed for managers) to become fully aware of what is going on. Resistance, as opposed to conflict, in the workplace is reflected in 'soldiering' (output restriction), pilferage, absenteeism, sabotage, vandalism, practical joking and sexual misconduct. Ackroyd and Thompson (1999) reviewed the managerial and academic literature on the presence and absence of such misbehaviour at work, and concluded that typically such writings:

- provided sanitized accounts of employee behaviour that depicted employees as invariably constructive, conforming and dutiful;

Table 21.5: Employee survival strategies

Survival Strategy	Definition	Objectives	Examples	Interpreted as a form of consent	Interpreted as a form of resistance
Making out	Elaborate system of informal employee behaviour that regulates work processes and ensures targets are met, yet allows workers to reassert some control of their working day	Economic gain Fatigue reduction Time passing Boredom relief Social and psychological rewards Avoiding social stigma	Refuse collection staff 'totting' – searching through rubbish bins for valuables to keep or sell. Shop floor workers manipulating their piece-rate payment schemes	Acts of 'game playing' within the organization's rules which result in mutual benefit for employees and managers	Acts that undermine management control by bending the rules to satisfy the self-interest of employees
Fiddling	Illegitimately acquiring company products, services or time for personal use	Economic gain Proving interest and excitement Expressing frustration or resentment	Stealing office supplies, inflating expense claims, personal phone calls from work, 'cyber-loafing'; Supermarket staff 'grazing' – consuming crisps, sweets	'Deserved' perks that help subsidize wages and confer status on employees	Theft that affects profitability and undermines the integrity of everyone in the organization.
Joking	A permitted or required interaction in which one party makes fun of the other, who in turn, is required to take no offence	Maintaining social order Releasing frustration and tension Challenging authority Forging group identities Alleviating work monotony	Joke telling Banter Playful insults Teasing (permitted disrespect) Practical jokes, initiation rituals	Forms of group regulation that preserve the status quo and provide a way of letting off steam	Challenges to management authority that undermine the status and policies of managers and make them appear foolish
Sabotage	An intentional, malicious attempt to disrupt or destroy a work process or a product	Way of expressing temporary frustration with work process, rules, managers or any other aspect of the organization Way of asserting control over the work process	Spreading computer viruses Reporting company malpractices to the press Being intentionally rude to customers Disabling a photocopier	(a) Expressions of frustration or irresponsible behaviour (letting off steam) (b) Well-meaning actions that have unintended negative consequences	(a) Malicious acts against property and people, intended to 'get even' with the organization (b) Well-meaning actions intended to 'expose' the organization (whistleblowing)
Escaping	Removing oneself temporarily or permanently from one's work tasks	Coping with boredom	Physical withdrawal through late-coming, absenteeism or resignation; mental withdrawal through dreaming, 'going robotic', cynical distancing from company values	Acts of withdrawal that result in employees accepting the status quo, even though they disagree with management policy or objectives	Acts that result in withdrawal of goodwill or mental and physical effort, thereby reducing organizational performance and undermining management objectives

Source: based on Noon et al. (2013, p.260).

- saw employees' behaviour as being orderly, purposeful and directed towards the attainment of organizational (managerial) goals;

- defined 'normal' employee behaviour as that which was programmed by management (labelled 'pro-social') and which complied with managerial norms and values, and treated employees' deviations from those (management) expected standards of behaviour in organizations as *mis*behaviour (also labelled 'counterproductive work behaviour');

- assumed that when there was a lack of correspondence between management direction and the employees' response (i.e. occurrence of misbehaviour), what needed to change was the latter.

Resistance at McTells

Marek Korczynski (2014) conducted an ethnographic study of an English Midlands firm that manufactured and fitted window blinds that he called McTells. He showed how workers in the factory used music and humour to create a 'Stayin' Alive' culture to survive their alienating work. He quoted one worker as saying 'You'd commit suicide if there wasn't something in the background to sing along to'. The sense of community that workers developed also represented a form of resistance against their employer and the Taylorist work system employed. The workers had no union but engaged in acts of informal collective resistance on the shop floor which took six forms:

- *Output restriction*: Each job had a management-assigned production target which many workers could comfortably exceed. However, they did not do so, and 'held back' if they were in danger of exceeding it. They feared that overproduction would result in the target being raised.

- *Reduced effort*: In addition to restricted output, there was also a lack of concern with the quality of what they had produced. It was sufficient that their blind just passed the quality check.

- *Early stopping*: Workers extended their work breaks whenever possible and stopped work before the specified time. A collectively enacted pattern was established where individuals stopped work early and formed a queue at the time clock five minutes before finishing time.

- *Absenteeism*: There was a collective norm within the factory that workers had a right to take a day off whenever they felt they needed to, either for personal reasons or to avoid another alienating workday. In consequence, there was widespread absenteeism in the factory.

- *Non-participation*: There was reluctance by individuals to engage in workplace participation schemes like quality circles that management had instituted. AIM (Action and Ideas at McTells) and works council meetings were dismissed by workers as only giving the impression of engagement without actually offering it.

- *Fighting back*: The practice of standing up to supervisors' imposition of discipline was collectively underpinned. Workers made fun of supervisors, told jokes about them, challenged and defied their actions.

Korczynski was surprised by the continued existence of such extensive forms of informal job control by workers in an era of increased managerial proactivity and their prerogative in employment relations.

Table 21.6: Conflict frames of reference

Frame of reference	Beliefs	Assumptions	How to deal with conflict
Unitarist	Organizations are fundamentally harmonious, cooperative structures.	Accepts the internal management structure. Thinks of conflict as negative.	Humanistic approach to conflict resolution. Not interested in cause of conflict. Concentrates on resolution through communication. Managers able to change behaviour.

→

Table 21.6: Conflict frames of reference (*continued*)

Frame of reference	Beliefs	Assumptions	How to deal with conflict
Pluralist	Organizations are made up of diverse groups with varying needs and interests.	Conflict is inevitable. Conflict serves as a regulation mechanism between the different groups. Acts as an early warning system to provide signs that system will break down if conflict not dealt with.	Conflict does not prevent organizations from functioning. Groups recognize that compromise and negotiation are necessary if they are to achieve common goals. Manager's job is to balance conflict between various groups.
Interactionist	Conflict is a positive and necessary force and essential for effective organizational performance.	Conflict should be institutionalized through systems of collective bargaining. Optimum level of conflict; too much or too little is dysfunctional and impairs performance.	Seen as beneficial in motivating energy to deal with underlying problems. Enhancing mutual understanding of goals and interests.
Radical	Organizational conflict is an inevitable consequence of exploitative employment relations, in a capitalist economy, based on Marxist critique.	Fundamental aim of capitalist enterprise is to expand capital and generate profit which is divided between managers and shareholders. Competition forces low production costs, forcing employees to earn less, which creates conflict.	Management deals with conflict by limited effects of worker resistance, walkouts, strikes, or conflict.

Source: from *The Psychology of People in Organizations*, Ashleigh, M. and Mansi, A., Pearson Education Limited © Pearson Education Limited 2012.

Emotional labour

Emotional labour
the act of displaying organizationally required emotions during interactions with others at work.

As a student, have you ever worked in a bar, operated a checkout in a supermarket, or waited on tables in a restaurant, dealing with people face to face? What emotions did you experience when dealing with your customers – anger, fear, joy, love, sadness, surprise? Did you express those feelings to your customers at the time; did you bite your tongue and say nothing; or did you suppress your emotions and act in the opposite way to which you felt? If you did either of the last two, then you performed **emotional labour**, which is the act of displaying organizationally required emotions during interactions with others at work. While organizations cannot regulate their employees' unobservable inner emotional states, they can specify which emotions they want them to display to customers in the form of **display rules**. The company can then monitor their employees' outer observable behaviour to ensure that they conform to these emotional display rules.

Display rules
organizationally specified emotions that should be appropriately displayed in a given work setting.

Emotions are intense, short-lived reactions that are linked to a specific cause and which interrupt thought processes and behaviours. Since an emotion cannot be directly seen, it is communicated verbally and non-verbally. Thus one's 'display' of an emotion consists of 'a complex combination of facial expression, body language, spoken words and tone of voice' (Rafaeli and Sutton, 1987, p.33). Most work tasks involve two elements – physical labour and mental labour. The physical refers to walking, carrying, lifting, talking and similar behaviours. The mental involves knowing, understanding, analysing, applying and evaluating people, things and situations. However, there are many jobs that now require a third kind of labour – emotional. Thus, for those around the person,

Emotions intense, short-lived reactions that are linked to a specific cause and which interrupt thought processes and behaviours.

'what you see is not necessarily how they feel'. Individuals at all levels of the organizations disguise their true feelings, amplify other feelings and manufacture false ones, either because it helps them to do their jobs or because a failure to do so would endanger their continued employment.

Arlie Hochschild (1983) originated the term 'emotional labour' when she discussed employees' management of their emotions to create publicly observable facial and bodily displays. Her research focused on how flight attendants were required to put on fake smiles even when interacting with rude and often aggressive passengers. Emotional labour involves expending psychological effort to keep in check both your internal emotions and external behaviours. She argued that companies commercialize employees' feelings by requiring them to display their emotions as part of their job duties. Different jobs require different emotional displays (Humphrey et al., 2008).

Job	Emotion to be displayed
Undertaker	Solemnity, sadness
Supermarket checkout assistant	Friendliness
Nightclub bouncer	Irritation
Flight attendant	Happiness, reassurance
Nurse	Compassion
Waiter/waitress	Interest in customer

STOP AND THINK

What display rule do you think is appropriate for your university lecturer to have?

Surface acting
Displaying to others emotions that you do not actually feel.

Deep acting
Engaging in thoughts and activities so as to experience the actual emotions that you wish to portray when interacting with others.

Naturally felt emotion expression
when your natural and spontaneous emotions comply with organizationally required display rules.

Emotional dissonance the disparity between an individuals' felt and displayed emotions.

Emotional labour can be performed in three different ways, as shown below (Ashforth and Humphrey, 1993, 1995; Diefendorff at al., 2005):

- **Surface acting**: Suppressing your own genuinely felt emotions so as to match organizationally required display rules. When surface acting, employees do not actually feel the emotions that they display to others (e.g. an irritated lecturer smiling at a student asking a foolish question).

- **Deep acting**: Summoning up within yourself the emotion you want to portray and then letting those elicited emotions animate your outward emotional expressions when interacting with others (e.g. sales staff recalling past pleasant experiences to put themselves in a happy, friendly mood when dealing with customers).

- **Naturally felt emotion expression**: Employees spontaneously expressing a genuine emotion in a workplace situation (e.g. a volunteer worker responding with authentic feelings of sympathy and concern when seeing an injured refugee).

A well-known high street coffee shop chain requires its staff to greet customers within 30 seconds of their entering the shop; chat with customers before taking their orders; call out the coffee order, specifying the drink name, size and any modifications, in that order; make eye contact with the customer and say to them, 'Have a nice day'. Both surface acting and deep acting involve employees manipulating and 'acting out' their emotions in a way that an actor might do in the theatre. Employees come to give 'displays' or 'performances' during their work in front of an audience of customers. The gap between the emotions that you feel and those that you actually display is called emotional dissonance.

Fly and smile

Paul Doyle/Alamy

In the photograph, an experienced flight attendant demonstrates the facial expression that she uses at work. Is she performing genuine warmth or is it concealed irritation?

Flight attendants are under strong pressure from the airlines to show only 'positive' expressions of emotion. This is sometimes a challenge, since not all passengers are pleasant or cooperative. She and the other attendants have learned that you can say anything to a passenger as long as you smile. In the photograph, she performs the smile that she uses while dealing with unruly or inebriated passengers. The verbal content of what she says is quite negative, but as long as the attendant smiles while saying it, the passenger accepts the information without complaint. Were you correct?

The earliest studies into emotional labour were conducted on flight attendants (Hochschild, 1983). On a flight, cabin crew will always display reassurance, even if they are afraid: 'Even though I'm an honest person, I have learned not to allow my face to mirror my alarm or my fright', said one respondent. Airline management sees the nature of the interaction between flight attendants and passengers as central to the latter's perceptions of service quality. Competitive pressures have stimulated managerial initiatives to manage 'natural' delivery of quality customer service during customer–attendant interactions. Taylor and Tyler (2000) found that three particular uses of body language were fundamental in establishing rapport – walking softly, making eye contact and always smiling. Emotional labour was required when dealing with sick and nervous passengers, applying 'tender loving care' (TLC), and confronting emergency situations. Being friendly, cheerful and helpful involves an emotional display.

In organizations with a 'customer is always right' philosophy, service workers are taught to diffuse customer hostility and, in consequence, end up absorbing a raft of verbal abuse during the course of a normal working day. They come to accept such verbalized customer dissatisfaction, no matter how upsetting, as 'just part of the job'. The growing incidence of both verbal and physical customer violence is likely to increase both the volume and intensity of emotional labour in service industries. The drive for competitive advantage through enhanced customer service means that an integral part of every service worker's job is to transform customer dissatisfaction into satisfaction. If management fails to invest in violence reduction strategies, exposing service workers to increasing levels of customer violence, it increasingly exploits the emotional labour of its staff.

Richard Layard (2005) provides an example of emotional dissonance during an Olympic medal awards ceremony. He says that all three medallists on the rostrum can be seen to be smiling and waving, displaying feelings of happiness and joy in front of the cameras and the crowd. However, in this particular 'work situation' the displayed emotions of the gold medallist and the bronze medallist are likely to be naturally felt emotional expressions – the former because she won and the latter because she expected no medal at all. In contrast, the silver medallist's felt emotion may actually be disappointment due to a failure to win the gold (Medvec et al., 1995). Next time you watch an Olympic medal ceremony, look carefully at the faces of the three medal winners.

Mike Powell/Getty Images

Emotional labour consists of five key elements which can be illustrated with the example of fast food restaurant waitress (Taylor, 1998):

1. Employees consciously manage their emotions (either inducing or suppressing them) as part of their paid work requirement – 'I'll pretend to be enjoying my job'/'I'm really interested in and enjoy my job'.

2. They do this when interacting with others (customers, clients, other staff) within the workplace – the waitress smiles, greets the customer, shares a joke with them, asks them for their order.

3. They do so with the objective of creating in the customer a particular state of mind – the customer notes their behaviour ('I am being well treated'); experiences a particular emotion ('I'm satisfied with the product and service here'); and elicits a particular response ('I'll come here again to buy my next cheeseburger').

4. Emotional labour should boost the self-esteem of its receiver – 'I'm flattered by the attentions of the waitress. She thinks that I'm a great person'.

5. All this is done to serve the interests of the employer who prescribes, supervises and monitors the performance of the emotional labour ensuring that the organizationally required display rules are followed by staff.

As a result of the increasing similarity of the offerings provided to customers by different companies in the airline, fast food, financial services, tourism, hotel and call centre industries, organizations have attempted to differentiate themselves from their competitors by the way that their employees deal with customers. Hochschild drew attention to the importance of social interaction in service provision. The emotional style of offering a service is now often more important than the service itself. The interactions between service providers and their customers have become the determining element in the latter's evaluation of satisfaction. In this way, the emotional aspect of service provision has now taken precedence over the physical one. While Hochschild (2003) was concerned that emotion was being commodified through the 'commercialization of intimate life', other writers consider the harnessing of employees' emotional energy to improve customer service as a good thing (Kinnie et al., 2000).

Home viewing

In the film *Office Space* (1998, director Mike Judge) the boss of the waitress Joanna (played by Jennifer Aniston) explains to her that people can get a cheeseburger anywhere, but they choose to come to his restaurant because of its 'atmosphere and the attitude'. He complains about her 'lack of flair', referring to the low number of badges on her uniform. These signify her unwillingness to express herself (her identity) and to engage in 'deep acting'. Aniston becomes angry and quits her job (Bell, 2008).

Historically, service employees have always been encouraged, in a general way, to provide 'service with a smile' or to 'put on a good show'. However in recent years, emotional labour has become a specific part of the employment contract and the employee's discretion concerning which feelings to show and how to show them is reduced or completely eliminated. Emotional labour occurs when employees, as part of the wage-effort bargain, are required by their bosses to display emotions which cause customers to feel and respond in particular ways. The employer thus buys not only an employee's physical and mental labour, but also their emotional labour, in return for a wage. Bolton (2000, 2005) argued that employees' private emotional systems had been appropriated by management as a renewable resource. To ensure that employees perform as required, companies use a combination of three elements:

1. **Careful applicant selection**: Choosing the appropriate employee is the first step. Disney World interviews 50,000 aspiring employees annually, and is most interested in their personality, wanting people who are enthusiastic, and who exhibit a clean and honest appearance (Henkoff, 1994; Van Maanen and Kunda, 1989).

2. **Employee training**: Companies run training courses for new starts whose jobs involve face-to-face or voice-to-voice interaction with customers, to develop their abilities to display appropriate emotions. Disney's new hires orientation courses emphasize emotions rather than policies and procedures (Henkoff, 1994).

3. **Employee monitoring**: Organizations monitor staff interactions with customers to ensure that they conform to the required emotional display rules. Ghost travellers on airlines and mystery shoppers in stores act as customers, to check staff performance. In telesales and call centres, supervisors randomly record conversations for review purposes (Taylor, 1998). Companies also use feedback questionnaires to assess whether staff are eliciting the desired customer responses.

Following Hochschild's original study, early research into emotional labour first supported her conclusion that it was detrimental to employees. However, later research into how employees regulated their emotional displays painted a more complex picture. Some forms of emotional labour did indeed have negative effects on workers' health and wellbeing, other forms had no effects, and still others had positive effects. Thus it appears that emotional labour possesses both a dark side and a bright side. Researchers have reviewed the empirical evidence into the positive and negative effects of different types of emotional labour, on different classes of employees, in different industries and occupations, in order to understand its effects better (Grandey et al., 2015; Humphrey et al., 2015; Spector, 2015).

Leading with emotional labour

Nearly all empirical research on emotional labour has been conducted on service workers to the neglect of its use by leaders. Ronald Humphrey (2012) noted that leaders are exposed to many emotionally challenging events in their work, including accidents, interpersonal conflict, product defects and staff boredom. Studies show that managers perform emotional labour as often as service workers, and that it represents an important part of what they do. Emotional labour tactics can help managers gain control of the emotions that they display to others, including their followers.

In difficult times, maintaining a positive mood and improving morale is important. Employees want to have confidence in their leaders, which is impossible if the latter display emotions of fear, anxiety or uncertainty. In good times, leaders will want to motivate and encourage staff towards continued greater achievements. Using emotional labour can help improve the moods, job attitudes and the performance of their staff. Leaders use 'emotional contagion' to pass on appropriate emotions to others within the company and to their customers. Thus, the skilled use of emotional labour by leaders can help them establish better leader–follower relations and enable them to exhibit charismatic and transformational leadership. Given the difficulties of performing emotional labour, Humphrey recommends that it should be done in a way that promotes positive well-being rather than stress. Leaders who use the naturally felt emotional expression and deep-acting forms of emotional labour are more likely to establish trusting relationships with subordinates than those using surface acting (Brotheridge and Grandey; 2002; Humphrey et al., 2008).

 RECAP

1. **Distinguish between the four major frames of reference on conflict.**

   - The unitarist frame sees organizations as essentially harmonious and any conflict as bad.

   - The pluralist frame sees organizations as a collection of groups, each with their own interests.

   - The interactionist frame sees conflict as a positive, necessary force for effective performance.

   - The radical frame sees conflict sees as an inevitable outcome of capitalism.

2. **Distinguish between functional and dysfunctional conflict.**

   - Functional conflict is considered by management to support organizational goals, and it improves organizational performance.

   - Dysfunctional conflict is considered to impede the achievement of organizational goals and reduces company performance.

3. **Explain the relationship between organizing, coordinating and conflict.**

   - Organizing concerns dividing up a large task into sub-tasks, and assigning them to groups. Coordination brings those previously divided sub-tasks together to ensure that all activities are directed towards organizational goals. In the process of subdivision, departments acquire their own, subordinate goals and interests, which differ from organizational ones. Conflict ensues when these divergent interests and goals clash.

4. **List the causes of conflict in organizations.**

   - Individuals, groups, units and departments may be in conflict with each other due to the differences in their goal orientation and evaluations; self-image and stereotypes; task interdependencies; time perspectives; as well as overlapping authority and scarce resources.

5. **Distinguish the different organizational coordination devices.**

   - Coordination devices include rules, policies and procedures; using hierarchy; goal clarification and communication; temporary task force; permanent project teams; liaison roles and integrator roles.

6. **Explain the conditions under which conflict is resolved and stimulated in organizations.**

   - Some writers contend that conflict that is dysfunctional – it does not achieve organizational goals, wastes time, demotivates staff, wastes resources and generally lowers individual and hence organizational performance. In such cases it needs to be eliminated.

   - Other commentators argue that conflict stimulation is necessary if employees enter 'comfort zones'; are reluctant to think in new ways of doing things; and find it easier to maintain the status quo. In rapidly changing organizational environments such behaviour not only reduces organizational success, but may endanger its very existence.

7. List Thomas' five conflict resolution approaches.

- Thomas' five conflict resolution approaches are avoidance, accommodation, compromise, collaboration and competition.

8. Distinguish between distributive and integrative bargaining.

- Distributive bargaining refers to a negotiation situation in which a fixed sum of resources is divided up. It leads to a win–lose situation between the parties.

- Integrative bargaining seeks to increase the total amount of resources, and it creates a win–win situation between the parties.

9. Contrast the different conflict expression styles.

- The four conflict expression styles are arguing, undermining, distinguishing and debating.

10. Understand the different forms that emotional labour can take.

- The three forms that emotional labour can take are surface acting, deep acting and naturally felt emotional expression.

Revision

1. Briefly describe each of Thomas' five conflict resolution approaches and give an example of an organizational situation in which each would be most appropriate.

2. 'Since every unit and department in an organization has its own goals and interests, conflict will always be a feature of organizational life.' Consider the costs and benefits of conflict for the various organization stakeholders. Give your reasons and illustrate your points with examples.

3. Discuss some of the ways in which employees can resist management actions and deal with an unsatisfying work environment.

4. Is emotional labour as great a problem as some of the literature suggests? What defensive mechanisms can employees use to cope with the emotional labour demands of their jobs?

Research assignment

The skill of negotiating is an important one not only to resolve conflicts but also to obtain what you want in life. Go to a restaurant where you are not well known to the waiting staff or manager. Order something that is not on the menu and negotiate with the staff to get what you want. Before doing so, you should plan how you are going to go about this. Draw upon the textbook material, not only from this chapter, but also the other parts of this textbook (individual, group, structure). Your assignment report should:

(a) Give a description of what happened, detailing the reason the restaurant was chosen; what you ordered; how you began your encounter with the waiting staff; how the negotiation proceeded; what the outcome was; and what you would do differently next time.

(b) Explain which textbook theories, models and framework featured in your plan and how they might explain what happened to you.

Based on Volkema and Kapoutsis (2016)

Robbins, S.P. (1974) *Managing Organizational Conflict: A Non-traditional Approach*. Englewood Cliffs, NJ: Prentice Hall.

Robbins, S.P. and Judge, T.A. (2013) *Organizational Behaviour* (15th edn). Harlow, Essex: Pearson Education.

Rousseau, D. M. (1998) 'Why workers still identify with organizations', *Journal of Organizational Behaviour*, 19 (3): 217–33.

Ruble, T.T. and Thomas, K. (1976) 'Support for a two-dimensional model of conflict behaviour', *Organizational Behaviour and Human Performance*, 16(1): 143–155

Sagie, A., Stahevsky, S. and Koslowsky, M. (2004) *Misbehaviour and Dysfunctional Attitudes in Organizations*, Basingstoke: Palgrave.

Shapiro, B.P. (1977) 'Can marketing and manufacturing coexist?', *Harvard Business Review*, 55 (5): 104–14.

Savage, G.T., Blair, J.D. and Soreson, R.L. (1989) 'Consider both relationships and substance when negotiating strategy', *Academy of Management Executive*, 3 (1): 37–48.

Schoneboom, A. (2007) 'Diary of a working boy: creative resistance among anonymous workbloggers', *Ethnography*, 8 (4): 403–23.

Schoneboom, A. (2011a) 'Sleeping giants: fired work bloggers and labour organization', *New Technology, Work and Employment*, 26 (1): 17–28.

Schoneboom, A. (2011b) 'Workblogging in a Facebook age', *Work, Employment and Society*, 25 (1): 132–40.

Smith, W.P. (1987) 'Conflict and negotiation: trends and emerging issues', *Journal of Applied Social Psychology*, 17 (7): 631–77.

Spector, P.E. (2015) 'Introduction: the bright and dark sides of emotional labour', *Journal of Organizational Behaviour*, 36 (6): 747–48.

Sternberg, R.J. and Soriano, L.J. (1984) 'Styles of conflict resolution', *Journal of Personality and Social Psychology*, 47 (1): 115–26.

Taffinder, P. (1998) 'Conflict is not always a bad thing', *Personnel Today*, 10 September.

Taylor, S. (1998) 'Emotional labour and the new workplace', in P. Thompson and C. Warhurst (eds), *Workplaces of the Future*. Basingstoke: Macmillan, pp.84–103.

Taylor, S. and Tyler, M. (2000) 'Emotional labour and sexual difference in the airline industry', *Work, Employment and Society*, 14 (1): 77–95.

The Economist (2015) 'Schumpeter: The enemy within', 25 July, p.59.

Thomas, K.W. (1976) 'Conflict and conflict management', in M.D. Dunette (ed.), *Handbook of Industrial and Organizational Psychology*. Chicago, IL: Rand McNally, pp.889–935.

Thompson, J.D. (1967) *Organizations in Action*. New York: McGraw Hill

Tjosvold, D. (2008) 'The conflict-positive organization: it depends on us', *Journal of Organizational Behaviour*, 29 (1): 19–28.

Tjosvold, D., Wong, A.S.H. and Chen, N.Y.F. (2014) 'Constructively managing conflicts in organizations', *Annual Review of Organizational Psychology and Organizational Behaviour 2014*, pp.545–68.

Ury, W. (1991) *Getting Past No: Negotiating With Difficult People*. New York: Bantam Books.

Ury, W. and Patton, B. (1997) *Getting to Yes: Negotiating An Agreement Without Giving In* (2nd edn). London: Arrow Books.

Van Maanen, J. and Kunda, G. (1989) 'Real feelings: emotional expression and organization culture', in L.L. Cummings and B.M. Staw (eds), *Research in Organizational Behaviour*. Greenwich, CT: JAI Press, pp.43–103.

Volkema, R.J. and Kapoutsis, I. (2016) 'From restaurants to board rooms: how initiating negotiations teaches management principles and theory', *Journal of Management Education*, 40 (1): 76–101.

Walton, R.E. and McKersie, R.B. (1965) *A Behavioural Theory of Labour Relations*. New York: McGraw Hill.

Weingart, L.R., Behfar, K.J., Bendersky, C., Todorova, G. and Jehn, K.A. (2015) 'The directness and oppositional intensity of conflict expression', *Academy of Management Review*, 40 (2): 235–62.

Whetton, D., Camerson, K. and Woods, M. (1996) *Effective Conflict Management*. London: Harper Collins.

Whetton, D., Camerson, K. and Woods, M. (2000) *Developing Management Skills for Europe* (2nd edn). Harlow, Essex: Financial Times Prentice Hall.

Chapter 22 **Power and politics**

Key terms

power	acceptance
power priming	compliance
reward power	resistance (in influencing)
coercive power	organization politics
referent power	political skill
legitimate power	need for power
expert power	Machiavellianism
strategic contingencies theory	locus of control
influence	risk-seeking propensity

Learning outcomes

When you have read this chapter, you should be able to define those key terms in your own words, and you should also be able to:

1. Appreciate the importance of power and politics in organizations.
2. Compare and contrast different perspectives on power.
3. Distinguish different bases of power.
4. Identify organizational factors which enhance the power of departments.
5. Differentiate between influencing techniques and the tactics of organization politics.
6. Identify the characteristics of individuals most likely to engage in political behaviour.
7. Explain how women use and are affected by organization politics.

Why study power and politics?

Take a moment and think about a leader

'Take a moment and think about a leader in your organization whom you would consider to be political. How would you describe that leader? Some common descriptions that may immediately come to mind are self-serving, manipulative, phony, or untrustworthy. You may conjure up images of secret pacts made behind closed doors or on the golf course. Or, perhaps, you came up with descriptions such as influential, well-connected, trustworthy, or concerned for others. Often, the idea of a leader being political is associated with negative perceptions and behaviors. In reality, though, political skill is a necessity and can be a positive skill for leaders to possess when used appropriately. Indeed, when we view political skill through this lens, it is difficult to envision any leader being effective without it' (Braddy and Campbell, 2014, p.1).

The popular view is that power corrupts, and that organization politics means underhand, cunning, manipulative 'dirty tricks' and backstabbing. While there may be some truth in these images, the problem is that leaders and managers who do not have power, and who are either unwilling or unable to 'play the politics' of their organizations, have difficulty in getting anything done. Inescapable features of organizational life, power and politics can be damaging, but can be also used in positive and constructive ways, to solve problems, generate consensus, and drive change.

"Do I really want all this power? I think I do."

Source: © 3/4/1967, www.cartoonbank.com

We like to think of our organizations as rational and orderly, with decisions based on evidence and reason, focusing on efficiency and effectiveness. However, organizations are also political systems, where decisions are shaped by influence tactics designed to promote the interests of individuals or coalitions. Jeffrey Pfeffer (2010) argues that, as organizations become less hierarchical, and rely more on networks and teams, the effective use of power and influence becomes more important. Current trends thus put a premium on political skill. Power and politics are entwined. Power can be seen as the ability to get other people to do what you want them to do, and it is often necessary to use political tactics to achieve those ends. Politics is thus called 'power in action'. Pfeffer (2010) argues that management failures can often be attributed to lack of political skill.

An organization's members do not always share the same values and goals. Disagreements over the definitions of problems, and how best to solve them, can be expected. Disputes of this kind are often healthy, exposing different perspectives and issues. What happens, however, when that open sharing of views fails to produce a consensus? Sometimes, those with the best ideas win. Often, the winners are those who are better able to exercise influence 'behind the scenes', by 'playing politics'. Good ideas do not always sell themselves, and rational arguments may not be effective on their own. As the American diplomat Henry Kissinger once said:

> Before I served as a consultant to [President John F.] Kennedy, I had believed, like most academics, that the process of decision-making was largely intellectual and all one had to do was to walk into the President's office and convince him of the correctness of one's view. This perspective, I soon realized is as dangerously immature as it is widely held. (Pfeffer, 1992, p.31)

Securing the city

Sean Adair/Reuters

Christopher Dickey (2009) describes how, following the terrorist attacks on the World Trade Center on 11 September 2001, the New York Police Department (NYPD) created a Counter-Terrorism Bureau (CTB). To be successful, the CTB had to be invisible to the public, who were paying for this service through taxation, and the Bureau's intelligence gathering took place elsewhere on the planet, which meant taking New York cops off the city streets. The new Real Time Crime Center at One Police Plaza in Manhattan cost US$11 million. Three years after the attacks, however, people had started to forget.

To counteract the apathy, the Bureau organized impressive shows of force, deliberately turning up without warning at high-profile targets like the Empire State Building, in order to remind the public that the bad guys were still out there.

The CTB also had to work effectively with other agencies, particularly 'the three letter-guys': FBI, CIA, ATF, DEA. Relations between the FBI and the CTB were managed through a Joint Terrorism Task Force. The head of the NYPD intelligence Division was David Cohen:

> Cohen's years at Langley and in the New York office of the CIA had taught him 'there's no such thing as information sharing, there is only information trading', as he told his colleagues at the NYPD. You go to the FBI and say, 'Tell me what you're doing', they're going to say, 'Go f*** yourself', is the way another senior official with the NYPD put it.
>
> Back channels to the CIA or other parts of the intelligence community could only take you so far. To get the stuff you needed, you had to be able to pull your weight. You had to be giving as well as getting. Otherwise you were going to be like the puny kid having sand kicked in his face by bullies. (Dickey, 2009, p.140)

This led to an 'overseas program', with NYPD operatives working abroad in liaison positions with forces which had their own counter-terrorist units, to exchange and gather intelligence. This meant that Cohen was able to establish a power base through his own intelligence operation, and the three-letter guys had to come and ask him for information. Information sharing then became possible. The ability to understand and to use power and organization politics effectively are therefore fundamental to the success of the NYPD CTB in its efforts to detect and prevent future attacks.

Management decisions are often the result of influence, bargaining, negotiation and jockeying for position. Leaders and managers who lack power, and who are not skilled in working with the politics of an organization, struggle to make things happen and to get things done. These capabilities make you more employable. After the job interviews, someone on the panel might say, 'this candidate is very well qualified ... but'. They are referring to lack of political skill: do not get caught by 'the but problem'.

An understanding of power and politics also allows us to assess the power of others, and to respond accordingly, regardless of whether or not we ourselves are power hungry. Psychologists use the term 'power tells' to describe the various signs and clues that indicate how powerful someone is – or how powerful they want to be (Collett, 2004). The power tells of dominant individuals include:

- sitting and standing with legs far apart (men);
- appropriating the territory around them by placing their hands on their hips;
- using open postures;
- using invasive hand gestures;
- smiling less, because a smile is an appeasement gesture;
- establishing visual dominance by looking away from the other person while speaking, implying that they do not need to be attentive;
- speaking first, and dominating the conversation thereafter;
- using a lower vocal register, and speaking more slowly;
- more likely to interrupt others; more likely to resist interruption by others.

The power tells of submissive individuals include:

- modifying speech style to sound more like the person they are talking to;
- more frequent hesitations, using lots of 'ums' and 'ers';
- adopting closed postures;
- clasping hands, touching face and hair (self-comfort gestures);
- blushing, coughing, dry mouth, heavy breathing, heavy swallowing, increased heart rate, lip biting, rapid blinking and sweating are 'leakage tells' which reveal stress and anxiety.

Knowledge of these tells means that we can 'read' the power signals of others. This also means that we can control our own tells so that we appear to be more (or less) powerful.

Power in organizations

Power the capacity of individuals to overcome resistance on the part of others, to exert their will, and to produce results consistent with their own interests and objectives.

Power is a 'contested concept' because a number of competing perspectives have been developed. It is therefore useful to be able to view this concept from different angles, and to be aware of their respective strengths and limitations.

Power is also a difficult topic to conceptualize. The following three contrasting perspectives share some similarities. The first views power as something you possess, an attribute or characteristic of the individual. The second views power as a property of the relationship between one individual (or group) and another. The third perspective sees power as embedded in social and organization structures.

Power as property of the individual

This perspective sees power as something that you possess, a set of resources that you accumulate. How much power do you have? Where did it come from? How can you acquire more power? Some of the main sources of power in an organization are shown in Table 22.1. Notice that some of these sources of power relate to the position that a manager holds in the organization (structural sources; see Chapter 15), while others relate to their personal attributes (individual sources).

Table 22.1: Power as property

Structural sources	Individual sources
Formal position, authority, allies, supporters	Energy, endurance, stamina
Access to and control over resources including information	Ability to focus energy, avoid wasteful effort
	Sensitivity to and ability to read others
Physical and social position in the organization's communication network	Flexibility in choice of means to achieve goals
Centrality of section to the business	Personal toughness, willingness to engage in conflict and confrontation
Role in resolving business-critical problems	Able to 'play the subordinate' or 'team member' in order to enlist the support of others
Degree of department unity, lack of dissent	
Being irreplaceable, pervasiveness of the role	

Source: Pfeffer (1992).

Power priming the process of making yourself feel more powerful, which in turn allows you to feel less stressed, and to behave as a more confident, persuasive and powerful person.

From this perspective, as power is something you can accumulate, you can take deliberate action to strengthen both your structural and individual sources of power. Look for jobs in key departments, make friends with influential power brokers, join important networks and projects, develop your interpersonal skills, impression management techniques, and emotional intelligence (Chapter 7). Be aware, however, that others in the organization are also trying to accumulate power. You can win more power, but if you are not careful, you can lose it.

Waiter power

A prominent American politician and ex-basketball superstar, Bill Bradley, was invited to make a speech at a political banquet (Jackson and Carter, 2000). During the meal, the waiter came round and served Bradley with a pat of butter. Bradley asked if he could have two pats of butter.

'Sorry', the waiter replied, 'Just one pat each.' 'I don't think you know who I am', Bradley responded.

'I'm Bill Bradley, Rhodes Scholar, professional basketball player, world champion, United States senator.' 'Well', the waiter said, 'Maybe you don't know who I am.' 'As a matter of fact I don't', Bradley replied. 'Who are you?'

'I'm the guy', said the waiter, 'who's in charge of the butter.'

STOP AND THINK   Given what you know about structural sources of power, can you explain why accountants tend to be more powerful and influential than human resource managers?

Power priming

Adam Galinsky's research shows that we can feel and behave like a more powerful person by using a technique called **power priming**. The method is simple: to become power-primed, think of a time in which you had power over others, and remember how that felt. You can also be powerless-primed, by thinking of a time when you lacked power. Power priming can be reinforced by adopting a power posture (see the discussion of power tells), and by listening to power anthems (a technique used by Serena Williams, who can often be seen wearing headphones when walking onto the tennis court).

In one experiment, students were first asked to write about a time when they either had power or lacked power. They were then asked to write an application

Table 22.7: Political tactics

Image building	We all know people who didn't get the job because they didn't look the part – appearance is a credibility issue: support for the right causes; adherence to group norms; self-confident manner
Information games	Withholding information; bending the truth; white lies; timed release of information; overwhelming others with complex technical details
Structure games	Creating new roles, teams and departments, abolishing old ones, in order to promote supporters and sideline adversaries, and to signal new priorities
Scapegoating	Ensure that someone else is blamed, that this is the fault of another department, or external factors, or my predecessor, or trading conditions, or a particular individual; avoid personal blame
Alliances	Doing secret deals with influential others to form a critical mass, a coalition, to win support for and to progress your proposals
Networking	Friends in high places; 'wine and dine' them to get your initiatives onto the senior management agenda; improve your visibility; gather information
Compromise	Give in, all right, you win this time, I won't put up a fight and embarrass you in public – if you will back me next time
Rule games	Refuse requests because they have not followed correct procedures or are contrary to company policy; accept similar requests from allies on the grounds of 'special circumstances'
Positioning	Choose and move to roles that make you visible and appear successful; withdraw from failing projects; locate yourself appropriately in the building; sit in the 'right' place at meetings
Issue selling	Package, present and promote your plans and ideas in ways that make them more appealing to your target audiences
Dirty tricks	Keep dirt files for blackmail; spy on others; discredit and undermine competitors; spreading false rumours; corridor whispers

The main categories of political tactics are summarized in Table 22.7 (Buchanan and Badham, 2008). But why does political behaviour arise in the first place? Jean-Francois Chanlat (1977) identified four sets of factors driving political behaviour: personal, decisional, structural and organizational change.

STOP AND THINK What is your attitude towards organization politics and political skill? Are these behaviours unethical, and to be avoided? Is a degree of political skill a requirement for success in your chosen career?

Personal drivers

Organizations hire people who have ambition, drive, creativity and ideas of their own. Thus recruitment, appraisal, training and promotion policies all directly encourage political behaviour. For example, staff selection methods seek to identify candidates who possess the personality traits related to a willingness to use power and engage in political behaviour. These traits include the *need for power*, *Machiavellianism*, *internal locus of control* and *risk-seeking propensity*.

Need for power

Need for power
(*n*Pow) the desire to
make an impact on
others, change people
or events, and make a
difference in life.

David McClelland (1961) developed the theory that three types of need in particular are culturally acquired, or learned. These are the **need for power** (*n*Pow), the need for achievement (*n*Ach), and the need for affiliation (*n*Aff). Some of us have a strong need to influence and lead others, and are thus more likely to engage in political behaviour. Since a desire to control others and events, and to have an impact on what is going on, is often associated with effective management, it is not surprising that selectors look for this trait in candidates for managerial jobs (McClelland and Boyatzis, 1982).

McClelland et al. (1976) distinguish between 'institutional managers' and 'personal power managers'. The latter seek personal gain at the expense of others and 'are not disciplined enough to be good institution builders' (McClelland and Burnham, 1995, p.130):

> [They] exercise their power impulsively. They are more often rude to other people, they drink too much, they try to exploit others sexually, and they collect symbols of personal prestige such as fancy cars or big offices.

Institutional managers, in contrast, combine power motivation with self-control, and represent 'the socialized face of power' (McClelland and Burnham, 1995, p.129):

> [T]he good manager's power motivation is not oriented towards personal aggrandizement but toward the institution that he or she serves. [They] are more institution minded; they tend to get elected to more offices, to control their drinking, and have a desire to serve others'

Good 'institutional' managers have the following profile:

- they feel responsible for developing the organizations to which they belong;
- they believe in the importance of centralized authority;
- they enjoy the discipline of work, and getting things done in an orderly way;
- they are willing to sacrifice self-interest for organizational welfare;
- they have a keen sense of justice, concerning reward for hard effort.

In other words, good managers use power in the interests of the organization, rather than in pursuit of self-interest. The use of power can therefore be acceptable, as long as it is subject to discipline, control and inhibition. However, this viewpoint argues that institution building and personal career enhancement can be pursued at the same time.

Machiavellianism

Machiavellianism
a personality trait or
style of behaviour
towards others which
is characterized by (1)
the use of guile and
deceit in interpersonal
relations; (2) a cynical
view of the nature of
other people; and (3)
a lack of concern with
conventional morality.

Niccolò Machiavelli
(1469–1527)

Machiavellianism is another trait which those who tend to engage in organization politics are likely to possess. Niccolo Machiavelli was a sixteenth century Florentine philosopher and statesman who wrote a set of guidelines for rulers (princes in particular) to use in order to secure and hold on to power. These were published in *The Prince*, and suggested that the primary method for achieving power was the manipulation of others (Machiavelli, 1514). Since then, Machiavelli's name has come to be associated with opportunism and deceit in interpersonal relations.

Richard Christie and Florence Geis (1970) produced a famous study of Machiavellian personality characteristics. Those who score highly on their Machiavellian test – 'High Machs' – tend to agree with statements such as:

- The best way to handle people is to tell them what they want to hear.
- Anyone who completely trusts anyone else is asking for trouble.
- Never tell anyone the real reason you did something unless it is useful to do so.

'Low Machs' tend to disagree with those statements. High Machs prefer to be feared than to be liked. They manipulate others using their persuasive skills. They initiate and control interactions, are prepared to use deceit, engage in ethically questionable behaviour, and believe that the means justifies the desired end.

Internal locus of control

Locus of control an individual's generalized belief about internal (self-control) versus external control (control by the situation or by others).

A third trait that encourages political behaviour is an individual's locus of control. Some people believe that what happens to them in life is under their own control; they have an *internal* locus of control. Others believe that their life situation is under the control of fate or other people; they are described as having an *external* locus of control (Rotter, 1966). It is the 'internals', who believe that they control what happens to them, who tend to use more political behaviour than 'externals'. Internals are more likely to expect that their political tactics will be effective, and are also less likely to be influenced by others.

Political blunders

As suggested earlier, to develop a career, you need political skill, or 'savvy and street smarts'. Andrew DuBrin (2016) identifies the serious political blunders which can damage your reputation and career, and the mistakes which cause embarrassment:

Career-damaging blunders

1. Humiliating others in public (praise in public, criticize in private)
2. Violating the organization's code of ethics and standards of conduct
3. Uncontrolled greed, even if large sums of money are obtained legally
4. Sending negative messages through corporate emails, websites, and social media
5. Bypassing the boss
6. Showing hostility and seeking revenge in an exit interview
7. Being indiscreet in one's private life
8. Conducting an improper office romance

Embarrassing blunders

1. Being politically incorrect
2. Displaying impatience for promotion
3. Gossiping about taboo subjects and sharing too much personal information
4. Attacking the organization's values and cherished customs – its 'sacred cows'
5. Refusing to take holidays
6. Showing insensitivity to cross-cultural differences
7. Rejecting business social invitations
8. Wearing sexually provocative clothes
9. Inappropriately consuming alcohol
10. Being insensitive to public opinion

DuBrin argues that you should avoid these political blunders. What do you think?

Risk-seeking propensity

Risk-seeking propensity an individual's willingness to choose options that involve risk.

A final personality trait that can determine whether a person engages in political behaviour is their risk-seeking propensity. Engaging in political behaviour is risky, and there are negative as well as positive outcomes for those who do it. They could be demoted, passed over for promotion, or given low performance assessments. Some people are naturally risk averse, while others are risk seekers (Madison et al., 1980; Sitkin and Pablo, 1992). Risk seekers are more willing to engage in political behaviour. For those who are risk averse, the negative consequences of a failed influencing attempt outweigh the possible benefits of a successful outcome.

The need for power, Machiavellianism, internal locus of control and risk-seeking propensity – these personality characteristics are associated with a strong desire for career advancement. All organizations have a proportion of ambitious individuals who compete with each other, arguing and lobbying for their ideas, innovations and projects. However, traditional organizational structures are hierarchical, and there are fewer positions available at each higher level. Those who are ambitious, therefore, are in constant competition to secure those scarce senior posts.

Decisional drivers

The extent to which politics enters the decision-making process depends on the type of decisions. Decisions vary; some are structured, and others are unstructured. Structured decisions are programmable, and can be resolved using clear decision rules. Routine decisions, such as how much stock to order, are structured. Normally, if a decision is structured or programmed, and if there is no opposition to what a manager wants to do, then it will be less necessary to use politics.

The problem is, the number of management decisions that can be based simply on information, calculation and logic is small. Unstructured decisions also depend on judgement, experience, intuition, preference, values and 'gut feel'. Unstructured or unprogrammable decisions are more common, and virtually all senior management decisions are unstructured to some degree. Examples include:

- Should we maximize short-term profitability, or develop our medium-term market share instead?

- Should we develop our human resource management function, or outsource this to a specialist management services organization?

- Should we develop our technical expertise in that sector, or buy another company that already possesses this capability?

Home viewing

The film *Contact* (1997, director Robert Zemeckis) is about Dr Eleanor (Ellie) Arroway (played by Jodie Foster). It recounts humankind's first contact with aliens. The task of searching for extraterrestrial life is fraught with personal, scientific, economic, political and ethical uncertainties. While she may be an excellent scientist, Ellie is not a good organizational politician. As you watch the film, answer the following questions. What organizational political mistakes does Ellie make? What political skills does Dr David Drumlin display? What mistakes does Ellie make in the President's advisory committee meeting? What tactics does Drumlin use to maintain his controlling position? What advice would you give Ellie if she wanted to become a more effective organizational politician?

With unstructured decisions, one can expect different managers with their own experiences, opinions, values and preferences, to disagree. This debate is natural and valuable. Put another way, 'When two people always agree, one of them is unnecessary' (Pfeffer and Sutton, 2006, p.31). Since information, calculation and logic cannot help to reach an unstructured decision, what strategies are left? In these kinds of situations, those involved are more likely to use political tactics to gain the support of others, and to deflect resistance when necessary, in order to ensure that their preferred course of action is endorsed.

In other words, political behaviour is a direct consequence of the fact that there are more unstructured decisions around than structured ones, particularly at higher levels of an organization, where such decisions tend to be made most often.

Structural drivers

Organization structures tend to be based on departments or functions, which compete with each other: purchasing, production, marketing, sales, finance, human resources. These different functions have their own goals, priorities and perspectives: sales wants to maximize

Advertising expert (m)	Charted accountant (m)
Chief financial offer (f)	General manager (m)
Operations manager (f)	Marketing manager (f)
Industrial engineer (m)	Computer programmer (f)
Product designer (m)	Industrial chemist (m)
Public relations expert (m)	In-house legal advisor (m)
Company trainer (m)	Human resource manager (f)

Employees (m) = male; (f) = female

Five environmental change scenarios

1. The existing small batch production of generators will be replaced by a state-of-the-art, automated assembly line.

2. New laws about engine and factory emissions are being passed by the European Parliament.

3. Sales are greatly reduced, and the industrial sector seems to be shrinking.

4. The company is planning to go international in the next year or two.

5. The Equality Commission is pressing companies to establish better male–female balance in senior posts and is threatening to 'name-and-shame' companies.

Adapted from J.E. Barbuto (2000) 'Power and the changing environment', *Journal of Management Education*, 24 (2): 288–96.

2. Politics in decision making

Objectives

1. To contrast perceptions about the use of politics in decision making.

2. To predict when and where politics will be used in organizations.

3. To contrast political with rational decision making processes.

Briefing

1. Individually, using the worksheet, rank each of the 11 organizational decisions (a to k) in terms of the extent to which you think politics play a part. Rank the most political decision as '1' and the least political as '11'. Enter your ranking in the first column on your worksheet – 'Individual Ranking'.

2. Form groups of four to seven members. Rank the 11 items again, this time as a group. Use consensus to reach agreement (that is, listen to each person's ideas and rationale before deciding). Do not vote, bargain, average or toss a coin. Base your decision on the logical arguments made by group members rather than your personal preference. Enter your rankings in the second column on the scoresheet – 'Team Ranking'.

3. After all teams have finished, your instructor will read out the rankings produced by a survey of managers which indicates the frequency with which they believe that politics plays a part in each type of decision. As these are read out, enter them in column three on the scoresheet – 'Manager Ranking'.

4. Still in your groups:

    (a) Compare the individual rankings (column 1) of group members. On which decisions did group members' perceptions differ significantly? Why might that be?

    (b) Compare your group ranking (column 2) with the manager ranking (column 3). On which decisions did group and managers' perceptions differ significantly? Why might that be?

→

Scoresheet

To what extent do you believe politics plays a part in the decision?

1 = most political   11 = least political

Decision	1	2	3
	Individual ranking	Team ranking	Manager ranking
a. Management promotions and transfers			
b. Entry-level hiring			
c. Amount of pay			
d. Annual budgets			
e. Allocation of facilities, equipment, offices			
f. Delegation of authority among managers			
g. Interdepartmental coordination			
h. Specification of personnel policies			
i. Penalties for disciplinary infractions			
j. Performance appraisals			
k. Grievances and complaints			

5. In plenary, answer the questions as directed by your instructor:

   (a) What distinguishes the most political decision items (ranked 1–4 in column 3) from the least political (ranked 8–11)?

   (b) In what circumstances might a rational decision process be used in making a decision, and when would a political process be used?

   (c) Research suggests that that political behaviour occurs more frequently at higher rather than lower levels in organizations. Why should this be so?

   (d) How would you:

   • apply rationality to those decisions currently possessing a large political element?

   • politicize decisions currently made using rational processes?

   (e) How would you advise a manager who felt that politics was bad for the organization and should be avoided at all costs?

   Based on Gandz and Murray (1980)

Employability assessment

With regard to your future employment prospects:

1. Identify up to three issues from this chapter that you found significant.

2. Relate these to the competencies in the employability matrix.

3. Decide what actions you need to take to maintain and/or develop those competencies under each of the four headings of the employability matrix.

Bureaucracy: legal-rational type of authority underpinning a form of organization structure that is characterized by job specialization, authority hierarchy, formal selection, rules and procedures, impersonality and impartiality and recoding.

Caution shift phenomenon: the tendency of a group to make decisions that are more risk averse than those that individual members of the group would have recommended.

Centralization: the concentration of authority and responsibility for decision-making power in the hands of managers at the top of an organization's hierarchy.

Certainty: a condition in which managers possess full knowledge of alternatives; a high probability of having these available; being able to calculate the costs and benefits of each alternative; and having high predictability of outcomes.

Chain of command: the unbroken line of authority that extends from the top of the organization to the bottom and clarifies who reports to whom.

Charismatic authority: the belief that the ruler has some special, unique virtue, either religious or heroic, e.g. the authority of religious prophets, charismatic politicians and film stars.

Choking: Performing worse under pressure than expected in situations with a high degree of perceived importance.

Chronotype: a cluster of personality traits that can affect whether someone is more active and performs better in the morning or in the evening.

Classical decision theory: assumes that decision makers are objective, have complete information and consider all possible alternatives and their consequences before selecting the optimal solution.

Coding: the stage in the interpersonal communication process in which the transmitter chooses how to express a message for transmission to someone else.

Coercive power: the ability to exert influence based on the other's belief that the influencer can administer unwelcome penalties or sanctions.

Cognitive psychology: a perspective which argues that what we learn are mental structures; mental processes can be studied by inference, although they cannot be observed directly.

Collaborative relationship structure: a structure that involves a relationship between two or more organizations, sharing their ideas, knowledge, staff and technology for mutual benefit.

Collective fit: team members' shared assessments of their compatibility with each other and with the requirements of their group task.

Communication climate: the prevailing atmosphere in an organization – *open* or *closed* – in which ideas and information are exchanged.

Communication network analysis: a technique that uses direct observation to determine the source, direction and quantity of oral communication between co-located members of a group.

Communication pattern analysis: a technique that uses analysis of documents, data and voice mail transmission, to determine the source, direction and quantity of oral and written communication between the dispersed members of a group.

Communication pattern chart: indicates the source, direction and quantity of oral and written communication between the dispersed members of a group.

Communication process: the transmission of information, and the exchange of meaning, between at least two people.

Communigram: a chart that indicates the source, direction and quantity of oral communication between the members during a group meeting.

Compensatory mechanisms: processes that delay or reduce employment replacement effects, and which lead to the creation of new products and services, and new jobs.

Compliance (in the context of a group): a majority's influence over a minority.

Compliance: reluctant, superficial, public and transitory change in behaviour in response to an influencing request, which is not accompanied by attitudinal change.

Computerization: job automation by means of computer-controlled equipment.

Concurrent feedback: information which arrives during our behaviour and which can be used to control behaviour as it unfolds.

Conflict: a process that begins when one party perceives that another party has negatively affected, or is about to negatively affect, something that the first party cares about.

Conflict expression: the verbal and non-verbal communication of opposition between people in a conflict situation.

Conflict resolution: a process which has as its objective the ending of the conflict between the disagreeing parties.

Conflict stimulation: the process of engendering conflict between parties where none existed before, or escalating the current conflict level if it is too low.

Conformity: a change in an individual's belief or behaviour in response to real or imagined group pressure.

Conjunctive task: a task whose accomplishment depends on the performance of the group's least talented member.

Consideration: a pattern of leadership behaviour that demonstrates sensitivity to relationships and to the social needs of employees.

Constructivism: a perspective which argues that our social and organizational worlds have no ultimate objective truth or reality, but are instead determined by our shared experiences, meanings and interpretations.

Contingency approach to organization structure: a perspective which argues that, to be effective, an organization must adjust its structure to take into account its technology, its environment, its size and similar contextual factors.

Contingency theory of leadership: a perspective which argues that leaders must adjust their style taking into account the properties of the context.

Controlled performance: setting standards, measuring performance, comparing actual with standard, and taking corrective action if necessary.

Conversion: a minority's influence over a majority.

Co-opetition: a form of cooperation between competing organizations which is limited to specified areas where both believe they can gain mutual benefit.

Coping cycle: the emotional response to trauma and loss, in which we experience first denial, then anger, bargaining, depression and finally acceptance.

Corporate social responsibility: the view that organizations should act ethically, in ways that contribute to economic development, the environment, quality of working life, local communities and the wider society.

Corporate strategy: establishing the aims of a company and the means by which these will be achieved.

Cross-functional team: employees from different functional departments who meet as a team to complete a particular task.

Crowdsourcing: the act of taking a task traditionally performed by a designated agent (employee or contractor), and outsourcing it to an undefined, generally large group of people, in the form of an open call for assistance.

Cybernetic analogy: an explanation of the learning process based on the components and operation of a feedback control system.

Data analytics: the use of powerful computational methods to reveal and to visualize patterns and trends in very large sets of data.

Decentralization: the dispersion of authority and responsibility for decision-making to operating units, branches and lower level managers.

Decision-based evidence-making: marshalling facts and analysis to support a decision that has already been made elsewhere in the organization.

Decision making: the process of making choices from among a number of alternatives.

Decoding: the stage in the interpersonal communication process in which the recipient interprets a message transmitted to them by someone else.

Deep acting: engaging in thoughts and activities so as to experience the actual emotions that you wish to portray when interacting with others.

Deindividuation: an increased state of anonymity that loosens normal constraints on individuals' behaviour, reducing their sense of responsibility, and leading to an increase in impulsive and antisocial acts.

Delayed feedback: information which is received after a task is completed, and which can be used to influence future performance.

Delegation: managers granting decision-making authority to employees at lower hierarchical levels.

Departmentalization: the process of grouping together activities and employees who share a common supervisor and resources, who are jointly responsible for performance, and who tend to identify and collaborate with each other.

Descriptive model of decision making: a model which seeks to portray how individuals actually make decisions.

Differentiation: the degree to which the tasks and the work of individuals, groups and units are divided up within an organization.

Differentiation perspective on culture: sees organizations as consisting of sub-cultures, each with its own characteristics, which differ from those of its neighbours.

Discretionary behaviour: freedom to decide how work is going to be performed; discretionary behaviour can be positive, such as putting in extra time and effort, or it can be negative, such as withholding information and cooperation.

Disjunctive task: a task whose accomplishment depends on the performance of the group's most talented member.

Display rules: organizationally specified emotions that should be appropriately displayed in a given work setting.

Disruptive innovations: innovations which involve the development of wholly new processes, procedures, services and products.

Distributed leadership: the collective exercise of leadership behaviours, often informal and spontaneous, by staff at all levels of an organization.

Distributive bargaining: a negotiation strategy in which a fixed sum of resources is divided up, leading to a win–lose situation between the parties.

Divisional structure: an organizational design that groups departments together based on the product sold, the geographical operated in, or type of customer served.

Double-loop learning: the ability to challenge and to redefine the assumptions underlying performance standards and to improve performance.

Drive: an innate, biological determinant of behaviour, activated by deprivation.

Dysfunctional conflict: a form of conflict which does not support organization goals and hinders organizational performance.

Emotional dissonance: the disparity between an individuals' felt and displayed emotions.

Emotional intelligence: the ability to identify, integrate, understand and reflectively manage one's own and other people's feelings.

Emotional labour: the act of displaying organizationally required emotions during interactions with others at work.

Emotions: intense, short-lived reactions that are linked to a specific cause and which interrupt thought processes and behaviours.

Employee engagement: being positively present during the performance of work by willingly contributing intellectual effort, experiencing positive emotions and meaningful connections to others.

Employment cycle: the sequence of stages through which all employees pass in each working position they hold, from recruitment and selection, to termination.

Empowerment: organizational arrangements that give employees more autonomy, discretion and decision-making responsibility.

Encounter stage of socialization: the period of learning in the process during which the new recruit learns about organizational expectations.

Environment: issues, trends and events outside the boundaries of the organization, which influence internal decisions and behaviours.

Environmental complexity: the range of external factors relevant to the activities of the organization; the more factors, the higher the complexity.

Environmental determinism: the argument that internal organizational responses are primarily determined by external environmental factors.

Environmental dynamism: the pace of change in relevant factors external to the organization; the greater the pace of change, the more dynamic the environment.

Environmental scanning: techniques for identifying and predicting the impact of external trends and developments on the internal functioning of an organization.

Environmental uncertainty: the degree of unpredictable turbulence and change in the political, economic, social, technological, legal and ecological context in which an organization operates.

Equity theory: a process theory of motivation which argues that perception of unfairness leads to tension, which motivates the individual to resolve that unfairness.

Escalation of commitment: an increased commitment to a previously made decision, despite negative information suggesting one should do otherwise.

Ethical stance: the extent to which an organization exceeds its legal minimum obligations to its stakeholders and to society at large.

Ethics: the moral principles, values and rules that govern our decisions and actions with respect to what is right and wrong, good and bad.

Evidence-based decision making: a situation in which a decision is made that follows directly from the evidence.

Evidence-based management: systematically using the best available research evidence to inform decisions about how to manage people and organizations.

Expectancy: the perceived probability that effort will result in good performance, and is measured on a scale from 0 (no chance) to 1 (certainty).

Expectancy theory: a process theory which argues that individual motivation depends on the *valence* of outcomes, the *expectancy* that effort will lead to good performance, and the *instrumentality* of performance in producing valued outcomes.

Expert power: the ability to exert influence based on the other's belief that the influencer has superior knowledge relevant to the situation and the task.

Explanatory model of decision making: an approach that accounts for how individuals, groups and organizations make decisions.

Explicit knowledge: knowledge and understanding which is codified, clearly articulated and available to anyone.

External adaptation: the process through which employees adjust to changing environmental circumstances to attain organizational goals.

External work team differentiation: the degree to which a work team stands out from its organizational context, in terms of its membership, temporal scope and territory.

External work team integration: the degree to which a work team is linked with the larger organization of which it is a part.

Extinction: the attempt to eliminate undesirable behaviours by attaching no consequences, positive or negative, such as indifference and silence.

Extreme job: a job that involves a working week of 60 hours or more, with high earnings, combined with additional performance pressures.

Extrinsic feedback: information which comes from our environment, such as the visual and aural information needed to drive a car.

Extrinsic rewards: valued outcomes or benefits provided by others, such as promotion, pay increases, a bigger office desk, praise and recognition.

Feedback (communication): processes through which the transmitter of a message detects whether and how that message has been received and decoded.

Feedback (learning): information about the outcomes of our behaviour.

Feedforward interview: a method for improving employee performance by focusing on recent success and attempting to create the same conditions in the future.

Fordism: a form of work design that applies scientific management principles to workers' jobs; the installation of single purpose machine tools to manufacture standardized parts; and the introduction of the mechanized assembly line.

Formal group: one that has been consciously created by management to accomplish a defined task that contributes to the organization's goal.

Formal organization: the documented, planned relationships, established by management to coordinate the activities of different employees towards the achievement of the organizational goal.

Formal status: the collection of rights and obligations associated with a position, as distinct from the person who may occupy that position.

Formalization: the degree to which an organization has written rules, operating procedures, job descriptions, organizational charts and uses formal, written communication.

Fragmentation (or conflict) perspective on culture: regards it as consisting of an incompletely shared set of elements that are loosely structured, constantly changing and which are generally in conflict.

Frame of reference: a person's perceptions and interpretations of events, which involve assumptions about reality, attitudes towards what is possible and conventions regarding correct behaviour.

Free rider: a member who obtains benefits from team membership without bearing a proportional share of the costs for generating that benefit.

Functional conflict: a form of conflict which supports organization goals and improves performance.

Functional relationship: one in which staff department specialists have the authority to insist that line managers implement their instructions concerning a particular issue.

Functional structure: an organizational design that groups activities and people according to the similarities in their work, profession, expertise, goals or resources used.

Fundamental attribution error: the tendency to emphasize explanations of the behaviour of others based on their personality or disposition, and to overlook the influence of wider contextual influences.

Gender: culturally specific patterns of behaviour which may be attached to either of the sexes.

Generalized other: what we think other people expect of us, in terms of our attitudes, values, beliefs and behaviour.

Gig economy: a system of employment in which freelance workers sell their skills and services, through online marketplaces, to employers on a project – or task basis.

Global virtual team: one that is nationally, geographically and culturally diverse and which communicates almost exclusively through electronic media.

Globalization: the intensification of worldwide social and business relationships which link localities in such a way that local conditions are shaped by distant events.

Goal orientation: the motivation to achieve goals – *aggressive masculinity versus passive femininity.*

Goal-setting theory: a process theory of motivation which argues that work motivation is influenced by goal difficulty, goal specificity and knowledge of results.

Great man theory: a historical perspective which argues that the fate of societies, and organizations, is in the hands of powerful, idiosyncratic (male) individuals.

Group: two or more people, in face-to-face interaction, each aware of their group membership and interdependence, as they strive to achieve their goals.

Group cohesion: the number and strength of mutual positive attitudes between individual group members.

Group dynamics: the forces operating within groups that affect their performance and their members' satisfaction.

Group norm: an expected mode of behaviour or belief that is established either formally or informally by a group.

Group polarization: a situation in which individuals in a group begin by taking a moderate stance on an issue related to a common value and, after having discussed it, end up taking a more extreme decision than the average of members' decisions. The extremes could be more risky or more cautious.

Group process: the patterns of interactions between the members of a group.

Group sanction: a punishment or a reward given by members to others in the group in the process of enforcing group norms.

Group self-organization: the tendency of groups to form interests, develop autonomy and establish identities.

Group socialization: the process whereby members learn the values, symbols and expected behaviours of the group to which they belong.

Group structure: the relatively stable pattern of relationships among different group members.

Groupthink: a mode of thinking in a cohesive in-group, in which members' strivings for unanimity override their motivation to appraise realistically the alternative courses of action.

Growth need strength: a measure of the readiness and capability of an individual to respond positively to job enrichment.

Habituation: the decrease in our perceptual response to stimuli once they have become familiar.

Halo effect: an overall assessment of a person which influences our judgement of their other specific characteristics.

Hawthorne Effect: the tendency of people being observed to behave differently than they otherwise would.

Heuristic: a simple and approximate rule, guiding procedure, shortcut or strategy that is used to solve problems.

Hierarchy: the number of levels of authority to be found in an organization.

High context culture: a culture whose members rely heavily on a range of social and non-verbal clues when communicating with others and interpreting their messages.

High performance work system: a form of organization that operates at levels of excellence far beyond those of comparable systems.

Hollow organization structure: an organizational design based on outsourcing an organization's non-core processes which are then supplied to it by specialist, external providers.

Huddle: a type of short-term, focused social interaction occurring between two or more individuals in an organization which discusses work issues and which enhances learning.

Human Relations approach: a school of management thought which emphasizes the importance of social processes at work.

Human resource management: the function responsible for establishing integrated personnel policies to support organization strategy.

Hygiene factors: aspects of work which remove dissatisfaction, but do not contribute to motivation and performance, including pay, company policy, supervision, status, security and physical working conditions.

Idiographic: an approach to the study of personality emphasizing the uniqueness of the individual, rejecting the assumption that we can all be measured on the same dimensions.

Impression management: the processes through which we control the image or impression that others have of us.

Influence: the process of affecting someone else's attitudes, beliefs or behaviours, without using coercion or formal position, such that the other person believes that they are acting in their own best interests.

Informal group: a collection of individuals who become a group when they develop interdependencies, influence one another's behaviour, and contribute to mutual need satisfaction.

Informal organization: the undocumented relationships that arise spontaneously between employees as individuals interact with one another to meet their own psychological and physical needs.

Initiating structure: a pattern of leadership behaviour that emphasizes performance of the work in hand and the achievement of product and service goals.

Initiative and incentive system: a form of job design in which management gives workers a task to perform; provides them with the financial incentive to complete it, but then leaves them to use their own initiative as to how they will perform it.

Initiative decay: an organizational phenomenon where the benefits from a change initiative 'evaporate' when attention shifts to other issues and priorities.

Initiative fatigue: the personal exhaustion and apathy resulting from the experience of too much organizational change.

Inner work life theory: a process theory of motivation which argues that our behaviour and performance at work are influenced by the interplay of our perceptions, emotions and motives.

Innovation: the adoption of any device, system, process, programme, product, or service new to a particular organization.

Innovative decisions: decisions which address novel problems, lack pre-specified courses of action, and are made by senior managers.

Instrumentality: the perceived probability that good performance will lead to valued rewards, and is measured on a scale from 0 (no chance) to 1 (certainty).

Integration: the required level to which units in an organization are linked together, and their respective degree of independence.

Integration (or unitary) perspective on culture: regards culture as monolithic, characterized by consistency, organization-wide consensus and clarity.

Integrative bargaining: a negotiation strategy that seeks to increase the total amount of resources, creating a win–win situation between the parties.

Intensive technology: technology that is applied to tasks that are performed in no predetermined order.

Interaction Process Analysis: a technique used to categorize the content of speech.

Interactionist frame of reference on conflict: a perspective that views conflict as a positive and necessary force within organizations that is essential for their effective performance.

Interactions: in Homans' theory, the two-way communications between group members.

Intermittent reinforcement: a procedure in which a reward is provided only occasionally following correct responses, and not for every correct response.

Internal integration: the process through which employees adjust to each other, work together and perceive themselves as a collective entity.

Internal work team differentiation: the degree to which a team's members possess different skills and knowledge that contributes towards the achievement of the team's objective.

Intrinsic feedback: information which comes from within, from the muscles, joints, skin and other mechanisms such as that which controls balance.

Intrinsic rewards: valued outcomes or benefits which come from the individual, such as *feelings of satisfaction, competence, self-esteem and accomplishment.*

Japanese teamworking: use of scientific management principles of minimum manning, multi-tasking, multi-machine operation, pre-defined work operations, repetitive short-cycle work, powerful first-line supervisors, and a conventional managerial hierarchy.

Job definition: determining the task requirements of each job in an organization. It is the first decision in the process of organizing.

Job description: a summary statement of what an individual should do on the job.

Job diagnostic survey: a questionnaire which assesses the degree of skill variety, task identity, task significance, autonomy and feedback in jobs.

Job enrichment: a technique for broadening the experience of work to enhance employee need satisfaction and to improve motivation and performance.

Joint venture: an arrangement in which two or more companies remain independent, but establish a new organization that they jointly own and manage.

Just-in-time system: managing inventory (stock) in which items are delivered when they are needed in the production process, instead of being stored by the manufacturer.

Knowledge management: the conversion of individual tacit knowledge into explicit knowledge so that it can be shared with others in the organization.

Leadership: the process of influencing the activities of an organized group in its efforts toward goal setting and goal achievement.

Learning: the process of acquiring knowledge through experience which leads to a lasting change in behaviour.

Learning organization: an organizational form that enables individual learning to create valued organizational outcomes, such as innovation, efficiency, environmental alignment and competitive advantage.

Legitimate authority: based on formal, written rules that have the force of law, e.g. the authority of presidents, managers, lecturers.

Legitimate power: the ability to exert influence based on the other's belief that the influencer has authority to issue orders which they in turn have an obligation to accept.

Line employees: workers who are directly responsible for manufacturing goods or providing a service.

Line relationship: one in which a manager has the authority to direct the activities of those in positions below them on the same line.

Locus of control: an individual's generalized belief about internal (self-control) versus external control (control by the situation or by others).

Long-linked technology: technology that is applied to a series of programmed tasks performed in a predetermined order.

Low context culture: a culture whose members focus on the written and spoken word when communicating with others and interpreting their messages.

McDonaldization: a form of work design aimed at achieving efficiency, calculability, predictability and control through non-human technology, to enhance organizational objectives by limiting employee discretion and creativity.

Machiavellianism: a personality trait or style of behaviour towards others which is characterized by (1) the use of guile and deceit in interpersonal relations; (2) a cynical view of the nature of other people; and (3) a lack of concern with conventional morality.

Maintenance activity: an oral input, made by a group member that reduces conflict, maximizes cohesion and maintains relationships within a group.

Managerial activities: activities performed by managers that support the operation of every organization and need to be performed to ensure its success.

Managerial roles: behaviours or tasks that a manager is expected to perform because of the position that he or she holds within a group or organization.

Mass production: a form of work design that includes mechanical pacing of work, no choice of tools or methods, repetitiveness, minute subdivision of product, minimum skill requirements and surface mental attention.

Matrix structure: an organizational design that combines two different types of structure resulting in an employee having two reporting relationships simultaneously.

Maximizing: a decision-making approach where all alternatives are compared and evaluated in order to find the best solution to a problem.

Mechanistic organization structure: one that possesses a high degree of task specialization, many rules, tight specification of individual responsibility and authority, and centralized decision making.

Subject index